# Comfort Women

## A Movement for Justice and Women's Rights in the United States

Edited by Jung-Sil Lee and Dennis P. Halpin

HOLLYM
Carlsbad, CA

Comfort Women: A Movement for Justice and Women's Rights in the United States
edited by Jung-Sil Lee and Dennis P. Halpin

Published by
Hollym International Corporation
2647 Gateway Rd. #105-223
Carlsbad, CA 92009
www.Hollym.com
contact@hollym.com

ISBN: 978-1-56591-385-1

Library of Congress Control Number: 2020937682

Printed in the United Stated of America

Cover art: Hung Liu, *Comfort Women*, 2006
oil on canvas, 80 x 160 in.
Private collection. Used with permission from the artist.

Cover design by Jino Lee

*Dedicated to the brave grandmothers who suffered and endured*

*inhumanity in the war and left us their legacies*

# CONTENTS

# Part II: The "Comfort Women" Movement becomes Transnational

# List of Illustrations

Most images from WCCW Visual Resource Center (WCCWVRC) unless otherwise specified

## Appendices

## Resources

## Index

# EDITORS AND CONTRIBUTORS

## Editors

**Jung-Sil (Julie) Lee** is an art historian, curator, and adjunct Professor at the George Washington University and Maryland Institute College of Art. Her Ph.D. in Art History from the University of Maryland explored the significance of public memorials in the Nineteenth Century French public sphere and their roles in reconciliation. Her minor area is Modern and Contemporary art focused on feminist theory and ritual practice. She curated extensive art exhibitions locally and internationally including the "comfort women" themed exhibition in 2017 sponsored by the Korean Ministry of Gender Equality and Family which travelled to four different cities. For a decade, she has served as the vice president and president of the non-profit organization, the Washington Coalition for Comfort Women Issues, Inc. (WCCW) where she educates and promotes public awareness on "comfort women." She has organized numerous academic conferences, art exhibitions, webinar lectures, internship programs, film screenings, the international film festival, and played a central role in the building of the "Comfort Women Memorial Peace Garden" in Fairfax County, Virginia (2014), and the "Statue of Peace" in Annandale, Virginia (2019) to reclaim the dignity of victims and prevent human trafficking. While she published book chapters and articles on "comfort women," she has devoted her time to archive primary and secondary sources and to document visual resources of 28 years of the "comfort women" redress movement in the U.S.
WCCW: www.comfort-women.org


**Dennis P. Halpin**, while serving as senior professional staff for Foreign Affairs Committee Chairman Henry Hyde in 2006, prepared materials for consideration of H.Res. 759. This was the first "comfort women" Resolution to be marked up by a Congressional Committee in September 2006. Lane Evans was the chief Congressional sponsor of H.Res. 759 as well as previous resolutions. Resolution 759 was used as background for H.Res. 121, sponsored by Representative Honda, which passed the House unanimously on July 30, 2007. Halpin also assisted Asia and Pacific Subcommittee staff director Lisa Williams in preparations for the first-ever hearing, convened by Chairman Eni Faleomavaega, with "comfort women" survivors as witnesses in February 2007. Dennis Halpin has long experience on the "comfort women" issue, having first met a "comfort woman" survivor while serving in the Peace Corps in South Korea in the early 1970s. He obtained the declassified "MacArthur Report" from the George W. Bush Administration in 2006 as background material for Chairman Hyde. In June 2014 he drafted an article for *America* magazine which advocated that Pope Francis meet with the "comfort women" survivors during a planned visit to Seoul—which the Pope subsequently did. In December 2016, he was a member of the American delegation which attended the opening of the first "comfort women" museum in Taiwan.

# Contributors

**Mike Honda** is a Japanese American, former congressman, and educator. As a member of the Democratic Party, he represented the 15th Congressional District of California from 2001 to 2017. He spent his early childhood in an internment camp in Colorado during World War II. Initially involved in education in California, he first became active in politics in 1971, when San Jose Mayor Norman Mineta appointed Honda to the city's Planning Commission. After holding other positions, Honda was elected to the Santa Clara County Board of Supervisors in 1990 and to the California State Assembly in 1996, where he served until 2001. In November 2003, Chairman of the Democratic National Committee Terry McAuliffe appointed Honda as Deputy Chair of the DNC. In February 2005, Honda was elected a Vice Chair of the Democratic National Committee under the chairmanship of Howard Dean. He championed for 2007 passage of House Resolution 121, "comfort women" Resolution, and has demanded an official apology, exposure archives, and public education by the Japanese government.

**Mindy L. Kotler** is founder and director of Asia Policy Point (APP), a membership nonprofit research center in Washington, D.C. studying the U.S. policy relationship with Japan and Northeast Asia. Its members include the leading American scholars, policy officials, analysts, journalists, and institutions that follow the region. APP has over 25 years of experience introducing new research, analysis, and information to the American Asia policy community. APP is known for its original work on the relationship between history and Asian regional security. Mindy Kotler is editor-in-chief of two weekly email newsletters, the *Asia Policy Calendar* and the *Japan Brief*. She received her MA from Yale University and her BA from Smith College. She was among the first class of girls to attend The Phillips Exeter Academy. She volunteers with the American Defenders of Bataan and Corregidor Memorial Society where she helps them tell the history of the American POWs of Japan in Washington.
Asia Policy Point: http://newasiapolicypoint.blogspot.com
American POWs of Japan: http://Americanpowsofjapan.blogspot.com

**Bonnie B.C. Oh, Ph.D**. is retired Distinguished Professor of Korean Studies of Georgetown University. She started college at Seoul National University, received her B.A. from Barnard College, Columbia University, M.A. from Georgetown University, and Ph.D. from the University of Chicago. A 38-year veteran in American higher education, she published widely on the Northeast Asia region in books, reference journals, and in encyclopedias, including *Legacies of the Comfort Women of WWII, American Military Government in Korea, 1945-1948, Korean Embassy in America*. She serves on the boards of the Washington Coalition for Comfort Women Issues Inc., Council on Korean Americans, Seoul National University Alumni Association, and the Korean Cultural Center of Chicago. Two consecutive years, she has organized and chaired panels at the AAS-in-Asia. Last year, at the 5th AAS-in-Asia in New Delhi, she tackled the issue of "Domestic Politics of Comfort Women Issues in China, South Korea, Japan, and the Philippines." This year, July 1-4, at the 6th AAS-in-Asia in Bangkok, Thailand, she dealt with "The Politics of Comfort Women Statues and Memorials."

**Margaret D. Stetz** is the Mae and Robert Carter Professor of Women's Studies and Professor of Humanities at the University of Delaware. In 2015, she was named by *Diverse: Issues in Higher Education* magazine to its list of the top 25 women in higher education. As well as being author of books such as *British Women's Comic Fiction, 1890-1990* and *Facing the Late Victorians*—and co-editor (with Bonnie B. C. Oh) of *Legacies of the Comfort Women of WWII* (2001) and (with Cheryl A. Wilson) of *Michael Field and Their World*—she has published more than 120 essays, which have appeared in various journals including *Victorian Studies*, the *Journal of Human Rights Practice*, *Literature/Film Quarterly*, and the *National Women's Studies Association Journal*. She has also lectured on the subject of "comfort women" at universities around the globe, from Japan to Spain. In 2017, she was chosen by the Republic of Korea's Ministry of Foreign Affairs as sole representative from the U.S. for the Korea Foundation's "Invitation Program for Distinguished Guests in Academia." She traveled to Seoul and met with academics and government officials for discussions of "comfort women" issues.

**Frank Joseph Shulman**, a professional bibliographer of Western-language writings about East, Southeast and South Asia since 1969, a graduate of Harvard University and the University of Michigan with degrees in East Asian History and Library Science, the editor of the journal Doctoral Dissertations on Asia (1975-1996), a university librarian and curator at the University of Maryland, College Park (1976-2001), and an independent researcher, is the author of many annotated books and article-length bibliographies and scholarly guides as well as a longstanding associate editor and contributor to both past printed volumes and the current online version of the Bibliography of Asian Studies of the Association for Asian Studies.

**Yangmo Ku** is Associate Professor of Political Science and Associate Director of the Peace and War Center at Norwich University. Dr. Ku's research focuses on the politics of memory and reconciliation in East Asia and Europe, North/South Korean politics, East Asian security, and the U.S. foreign policy. His co-authored book, titled *Politics in North and South Korea: Political Development, Economy, and Foreign Relations*, was published by Routledge in 2018. His previous research has also appeared in numerous journals, including: *the Journal of East Asian Studies, Asian Perspective, Journal of Peace and War Studies, Pacific Focus, Korea Journal, Asian Journal of Peacebuilding*, and *the Yale Journal of International Affairs*, as well as in two edited volumes on memory and reconciliation and North Korean nuclear issues. He received his Ph.D. in political science from the George Washington University and previously taught at the School of International Service at American University. He also serves as editor of a new academic journal titled *Journal of Peace and War Studies* and is often invited to teach intensive courses on the politics of the Korean Peninsula to U.S. federal agency workers.

# ACKNOWLEDGMENTS

The editors would like to express their appreciation for the scholars, activists, artists, and organizations whose main mission is to be a voice for the "comfort women." All parts of this book are based on or inspired by the testimonies given by "comfort women" in diverse forms. Victims and survivors of the "comfort women" system turned to leading activists of women's rights and courageously paved the way for the global "comfort women" movement. We are truly grateful for their bravery and endurance. They flew from South Korea and Australia to appear before the U.S. Congress to share the "comfort women" history, open the eyes of the public, and encouraged the nascent stage of the Washington Coalition for Comfort Women Issues (WCCW) in 1992. Starting with Hwang Keum-ju, the first to visit the U.S. and become the direct motivation for the founding of the WCCW, these brave women have presented stories which inspired all authors of this book and ignited the movement of "comfort women" redress activism for peace and women's rights.

We appreciate those innumerable people who gave their time, funds, wisdom, and energy to support the issue of "comfort women" in the U.S. whether from individual interest or at the organizational level. We can't even list all of the names from 28 years of "comfort women" movement history, but to name a few: U.S. House Representatives Mike Honda, the late Lane Evans, the late Chairman Eni Faleomavaega, the late Foreign Affairs Committee Chairmen Henry Hyde and Tom Lantos, the Foreign Affairs Committee Ranking Member at the time of passage of H.Res. 121, Ileana Ros-Lehtinen, Representative Jan Schakowsky, Representative Ed Royce, Representative William Lipinski, Speaker of the House Nancy Pelosi, former Speaker Newt Gingrich, all 167 cosponsoring Representatives for House Resolution 121 in 2007, Eli Rosenbaum from the U.S. Department of Justice, and Retired Bishop Young Jin Cho of the United Methodist Church. The movement started with a few initiators from the United Methodist Church, the founding president of WCCW, Dongwoo Lee Hahm, and her church colleague, Soon Im Kang, who compiled the first booklet of the issue with the members of the Women's Mission Association. The succeeding presidents of WCCW, Dr. Ok Cha Soh, Steve Choi, and Christine Choi have devoted enormous time to raise public awareness of the issue and made contributions in many areas.

We acknowledge all authors of this book who are extremely busy either with teaching at institutions or hectic work schedules, yet, completed their chapters with a passion and mission for the "comfort women" cause. They share their direct experiences with the issue either as pioneers of the movement or compilers of useful content for researchers, activists, and other inquisitive readers. There was immeasurable support and dedication by WCCW board members, officers, and WCCW fellows financially and practically, including Dr. Jaeheup Kim and Edward Jang who are photographers and compiled valuable resources.

Special thanks to two assistants for organizing the materials and designing them: Taeyi Kim, secretary and fellow of WCCW, and Jaeyop Kang, WCCW fellow. For proofreading manuscripts, the first and foremost WCCW intern, who edited the intern research book titled *Comfort Women: New Perspectives*, and is currently a medical student, Jonathan D. Kim, who made great efforts. We also wish to thank the compilers of resources and appendices. They are mainly students from George Washington University: Jaeyop Kang, Kyong Sik Kang, Ju Han Kim, Nancy Welch, Kyungchae Jang, Sungjun Kim, Seunghyun Min, Taeeun Uhm, Sumi Lee, Yujin Jeong, Yun Seong Ji, and Hanseul Choi, who compiled the resolutions and a list of diverse resources. Also, we wish to thank Kareem Sharaf of the Berlin Office of the UN International Organization of Migration (IOM) for conducting research on the Congressional and other U.S. government historic documents, including the 1945 declassified "MacArthur" report. We also thank Fletcher Calcagno and Lydia Yi who conducted the interviews with Representative Mike Honda.

This book has been supported by research grants from the Overseas Koreans Foundation. Further financial contributions came from WCCW board members; the founding president, Dongwoo Lee Hahm, former president Christine Choi, Jason H. Yoon, William Wonkyun Hwang, Raymond Naewon Lee, Joey Lee Gebhard Myungho (Lucy) Nam, and Jieun Chung. Jae Soo Lee, Jun Hyeong Park, and Hyunsook Cho, the executive committee for the Statue of Peace contributed to the publication as well. We also extend special thanks to Grace Presa from Hollym International Corp. publisher for recognizing the value of this book project and for facilitating its publication.

For the use of illustrations, photos, primary document, and maps, we wish to express appreciation to NARA II (National Archives and Records Administration), Maryland, USA; the Women's Active Museum on War and Peace, Tokyo, Japan; the House of Sharing, Kwangju, Korea; The Korean Council for the Women Drafted for Military Sexual Slavery by Japan (renamed The Korean Council for Justice and Remembrance for the Issues of Military Sexual Slavery by Japan), Seoul, Korea. We would like to thank to all of the U.S. organizations who have been dedicated to the "comfort women" issue and let us record their achievements, as well as all visual artists who generously gave permission to reproduce their works, filmmakers, activists, community leaders, and supporters of the U.S. "comfort women" memorials. We also give special thanks for the generous donation of artwork image use for the cover of this book by Hung Liu, one of the most renowned and important contemporary Chinese American artists.

More than anything, this book is for the younger generations who aspire for justice and a peaceful world through learning about the history of "comfort women," with the hope of enlightening the world. We do this in memory of the women who have left us their legacy of women's rights and their arduous paths that we will never forget and will always follow. With the hope of enlightening the world, this book is dedicated to the now activist grandmothers who were transformed from once innocent girls.

# EDITORS' NOTE

For translating Korean words into English, we mostly use the Revised Romanization of Korean, the official romanization system endorsed by the Ministry of Culture and Tourism in South Korea since 2000. The only exception is for chapter eight, "Western-Language Doctoral Dissertations on the Korean 'Comfort Women,' 1995–2004: An Annotated Bibliography with Brief Information about the Educational Backgrounds of the Dissertation Authors" authored by Frank Joseph Shulman. He mentions in his chapter introduction, "The McCune-Reischauer Romanization system is used throughout, but in all of the annotations, Korean names and terms are also provided according to the Revised Romanization system for Korean."

All names of people are notated as they are used by their own conventions. In Asian countries, especially in Korea and Japan, surnames precede given names. For example, Lee is the last name of Lee Yong-soo, a former "comfort women" victim. The naming convention of each of the Korean victims follows the way they were officially registered in the documents in Korean non-profit organizations (NPOs). However, we acknowledge the variation in the romanization of Korean names in other printed materials and documents such as in books, journals, dissertations. [e.g., Hwang Keum-ju may also be spelled Hwang Kum-ju or Kum-ju Hwang as seen in Kum-ju Hwang, "To Live Without Shame," *Muae: A Journal of Transcultural Production* 1 (1995), 199]. For people who do not live in Korea, Japan, China, and Taiwan, we keep the convention of given names followed by surnames. We also use the term "comfort women" only for the archival purpose as all past documents recorded them with such a term, but the grandmothers never meant to "comfort" anybody. They wanted to be called "grandmothers (*halmoni* in Korean)," a source of wisdom in the family.

# INTRODUCTION: WHY DO WE DEAL WITH THE COMFORT WOMEN ISSUE IN THE U.S.?

*Jung-Sil Lee & Dennis P. Halpin*

That which defines us as individuals also connects us to others, our stories resonating with people around the world, interwoven in an empathic network that makes us human; where the Personal becomes the Universal. Such is felt in the story and the history of the "comfort women," expressed through testimonies, written texts, musicals, films, artworks, and other accounts. Not only are these accounts made for the "comfort women" to begin to navigate the trauma that they had experienced, but they also serve to teach others and allow for many Americans and Asian Americans to become aware of and sympathize with the "comfort women." As the atrocities committed seven decades ago in the Indo-Pacific region continue to gain attention in the Western World, many have felt the conviction to act to ensure this history is remembered and taught to the next generation so that they may learn from the mistakes of the past. The legacies of these "comfort women" are revealed by grassroots campaigns and activism that has expanded into diverse dimensions and fields: social, juridical, humanistic, academic, educational, and artistic.[1]

During the Second World War, the Japanese Imperial Army began a practice of forcing women and girls in occupied Asian territories into sexual slavery. As the leading Japanese historian on "comfort women" issues, Yoshimi Yoshiaki provided solid and tangible evidence of the state-sanctioned crime of sexual slavery during wartime. The purpose of the Japanese military was to "comfort and relieve" the fear and stress of the soldiers through sexual servitude, and gave rise to their euphemistic label of "comfort women."[2] There are estimated to have been from 50,000 to as many as 400,000 "comfort women" throughout more than ten occupied countries.[3] This dark period of Asian history and the nature of the recruitment are still hotly debated and contested between the Japanese right-wing government, on the one hand, and sympathetic groups of activists and feminists, on the other, globally to this day. This is mostly between the victimized countries and the Japanese government. Interestingly, this battle has found a new and unexpected battlefield on American soil, where it has become one of the most intense human rights issues of the country. In part, the American interest in "comfort women" issues may be due to the increased awareness and conversations about sexual abuse, assault, and rape in recent years. This has included the contemporary feminist movement, making evident that the dark history and pain of the "comfort women" is not simply an isolated issue of the past. Instead, the "comfort women" served as a reflection of the atrocities that continue to plague modern society: rape, violations of human rights, sexual assault, sex trafficking, and broadly any war-time trauma.

The individual histories of the "comfort women" live on and resonate strongly with the American public and on the world stage not because the Japanese Imperial Army is continuing its practice. "Comfort women" represent something more universal and more troubling: the endemic assault on the rights and ownership of a woman's body and the patriarchal systems in place that leave such transgressions of basic human decency and the dignity of women unpunished. What has made many sympathetic to this cause is not just the horrific experiences of these women, but also the despondency when realizing that our present is not much better in terms of women's rights and justice than back in World War II. This book is dedicated to compiling and recording the tremendous efforts of diverse groups of people for the cause of the "comfort women" in the United States in hopes that readers can use and learn from these archived materials to prevent such atrocities in the future and to fight those battles today, where the voices of women in the past could not.

This book mainly focuses on the people and activities in the Washington metropolitan area along with the Washington Coalition for Comfort Women Issues (WCCW),[4] a non-profit organization founded in 1992 in Virginia. WCCW was the first organization of its kind in the U.S.; its mission has been to be a voice for "comfort women" since its founding twenty-eight years ago. WCCW has since fought for justice and the rights of the wartime victims known as "comfort women," who had not been able to speak up about their legal rights nor to reclaim their dignity. After the groundbreaking testimony of one former victim, Hwang Keum-ju at the Korean United Methodist Church of Greater Washington located in Vienna, Virginia, Korean American leaders gathered to organize WCCW and elected as its founding president Dongwoo Lee Hahm. WCCW has collaborated with other human rights organizations, federal, state, and local governments, elected officers, political activists, scholars, feminist activists, and artists throughout the years since 1992. We recognize their names in this book, their contributions, and their significance.

Some would see these wartime atrocities that happened sixty to seventy years ago in distant Asian countries as unrelated to the current U.S. political climate. Yet, this book provides perspective on how these issues are becoming more relevant day by day as feminist movements gain traction in the U.S. political arena. Indeed, in a time when groups are standing up against the commodification of women, the issue of "comfort women" rings particularly true to the issues tackled today. We now even call this new wave a "comfort women redress movement." We normally call something a "movement" if there is a group of people who share the same beliefs and ideas, and act toward a gradual development or change of an attitude, opinion, or policy in any given society. Why and what is the basis, foundation, and demands of the "comfort women movement?" This is the fundamental question that the authors and the compilers in this book try to determine in this "comfort women" discourse about what led to a pervasive and significant "movement."

One of the most valuable legacies of this issue is its educational and edifying purpose. Scholars, activists, and students from many regions in different disciplines who are eager to examine the issue have interpreted these histories, applying them to their respective fields to see what they can learn. WCCW recognized the needs of the persons who joined the "comfort women movement" to encourage these types of discussions. Many requests for historical documents made to the WCCW prompted the publication of this archiving book whose basic objectives are to collect, compile, and archive the last 28 years of the "comfort women movement" along with the victims and WCCW. We offer one reservoir of resources from which people can find insights whether it is political, social, academic, or artistic, and for those who would contribute to making the issue educational and inspirational for future generations.

One of the major obstacles the "comfort women" movement and, subsequently, this book faces, is the scarcity of primary sources. Much of the current understanding of the history and existence of these atrocities stems from first-hand testimonies from these wartime victims. However, deniers of the atrocity, particularly among far-right wing conservatives in Japan, have challenged these accounts due to the orally transmitted nature of the testimony and the alleged possibility of confusion or distortion of the testimony of victims. Even though WCCW works extensively with "comfort women" survivors who have made numerous visits to the U.S., many of the supporters of the movement have had to use a diverse array of secondary sources ranging from recordings, films, videos, social media, photos, prints, and other intermediate tools. Such obstacles have not dampened the conviction of these activists. Instead, this has led to the emergence of artists and activists expanding upon the movement through the re-contextualization of "comfort women" history in novel ways and through new media, thereby allowing them to revisit and better understand the war atrocities these women had experienced. By doing so, they look not just at the events that unfolded as a particular and tragic event in history, but from it, glean a more fundamental truth about human nature, history, and beyond. This book shows how the new narratives and interpretations of the issue allow for productive adaptations of the core message to reach and edify a larger audience in addition to continuing the documentation and legitimization of historical evidence.

As Marianne Hirsch[5] wrote, "postmemory" is the relationship of the personal, collective, and cultural trauma that one generation bears from the previous generation in experiences they can "remember" through stories and images without a direct encounter.

> Postmemory's connection to the past is thus actually mediated not by *recall* but by *imaginative investment, projection, and creation.* It is to be shaped—indirectly, by traumatic fragments of events that still defy narrative reconstruction and exceed comprehension. These events happened in the past, but their effects continue into the present. Activists reframe the archival images so as to grant them multiple afterlives in which they continue to develop, making past injustices and atrocities newly visible in future presents.[6]

This "postmemory" of "comfort women" history is represented and re-contextualized differently by the Asian diasporas in the U.S. compared to their counterparts in Asian nations, both in their approach and understanding. While American activists continue to support the seven demands proposed by the Korean NGO, The Korean Council (Jungdaehyup),[7] and share a common heritage with their Asian counterparts, activists in America have developed and diversified these memories by instilling within them a connection with the American political and societal mainstream. This book highlights cases and efforts where American regional organizations have restated the past atrocities in Asia while also trying to understand these events considering modern issues in America. At its inception, WCCW aimed to balance the norms of the East Asian diaspora on one hand while on the other hand, expand its discourses to other perspectives and dimensions. Especially recently, the issue of women's rights has once again entered the forefront all over the world under the new wave of the "#MeToo" movement.[8]

American activists, scholars, and artists used mediating tools to try to engage with the "comfort women" history in their own ways and to look for new perspectives with empathy.[9] Additionally, they compiled firsthand accounts of "comfort women" along with other sources to synthesize them as new memories from their existing corpus of experience and tools of understanding narratives. These "post-memories" have been circulated, expanded, and revisited through the effort of WCCW and others' activism and have contributed to the formation of the "comfort women movement" in the dimensions of public relations, legislation, education, exhibition, publication, and memorial building in the U.S. This archiving book covers these areas of the movement starting with the outlines of the WCCW history that showcase the scope of the "comfort women movement" in the U.S. The movement, unbeknownst to WCCW, had quickly spread to many other cities of the nation at the time and, we, through interviews with supporters in other regions, realized that similar activities were occurring all around the country. Although we would like to recognize their activism here, we have limited knowledge of this yet unexplored area of contemporary history that remains beyond the scope of this publication at the present time. We look forward to the impact that a united coalition could have in the future. As such, the proposal for solidarity among activists is another objective of this book.

The authors of each chapter deal with their specialized fields and perspectives that will provide diverse lenses to approach the issue. Also, the authors will include detailed documents and illustrations of "comfort women" related projects and activities. The first chapter of this book, the history and activities of WCCW, was based on a paper presented at the conference of *The Redress Movement for the Victims of Japanese Military Sexual Slavery: Looking back at the 27 year Movement* that was organized by Professor Pyong Gap Min of the Research Center for the Korean Community at Queens College, New York in October 2017. The founding president of WCCW, Dongwoo Lee Hahm, and the fifth president, Jung-Sil Lee, were invited to present the paper "Tracing the Twenty-Seven Years of the Comfort Women Movement in the U.S." The first chapter on the history of WCCW unavoidably overlaps with that 2017 paper, yet, it is rewritten and reassessed by the current book editor Jung-Sil Lee to re-evaluate the now 28 years of WCCW and other "comfort women" related history or activism in the U.S. This chapter will examine the "comfort women redress movement" both chronologically and thematically from its inception throughout the years although certain years are emphasized over others.

From its inception, WCCW has grown tremendously in terms of its membership and its scale of activities, while still maintaining its core mission to transmit a message of justice. Given that, many projects continue concurrently, making a clear chronological timeline not always easy. From its foundation to the present, these dimensions have only continued to expand. At its core, however, WCCW contributed grassroots campaigning that eventually led to legislation on federal and state levels and brought it forth for global discussions at the UN and UNESCO; education through organizing conferences, publication of teaching material, and internships; representation of the issue in the public sphere through exhibition of archival material and art works, film screenings, a film festival, two dedications of "comfort women" memorials; and current archiving projects. For a full description, Jung-Sil Lee records in the first chapter, the history of the WCCW and its work from 1992 up to 2019 detailing activities from grassroots advocacy which sprang from other developments.

The efforts of 15 years of grassroots "comfort women" movement activities in the U.S. without a doubt culminated in the passage of the 2007 House Resolution 121 (hereafter the Resolution or H.Res. 121) in the U.S. House of Representatives. A few of the contributors of this book played crucial roles in the process of achieving passage of the Resolution and will expand on the process and meaning in respect to their perspectives. Former Representative Mike Honda (D-CA) gave his support for the Resolution and, by his advocacy, significantly encouraged "comfort women" activism efforts. The second chapter of the book chronicles the experiences and context relevant to this monumental milestone offered by former Rep. Mike Honda.

We invited two other important figures whose contributions were enormous in passing the Resolution. They worked arduously at drafting the Resolution either as congressional staff or as the director of the nonprofit organization: Dennis Halpin (co-editor of this book) and Mindy Kotler. Mindy Kotler, director of Asia Policy Point scrutinizes the context of the U.S. political scene at the time and the broader discourse on women's issues including feminists' perception on 'rape' or 'sexual assault.' Further, she examines all details and context of six resolutions that were introduced into the U.S. House of Representatives from 1996 to 2006.

Dennis Halpin traces the history of the "comfort women" issue as a focus of policy and legislative concern for the U.S. House of Representatives. His is an insider's perspective, specifically from the point of view of a Congressional staff member charged with responsibility for Asian policy issues in the years prior to, and including, the 2007 Resolution when the House formally acted via its unanimous adoption of H.Res. 121. This chapter records the particular efforts of key Members of the House in moving forward the "comfort women" issue, both as a matter of clarification of the war crimes committed in the Pacific theater during the Second World War and as a more universal issue of human and women's rights.

The steady, unflinching efforts of House Member Lane Evans (D-IL) in introducing "comfort women" resolutions in a series of Congressional sessions before final adoption are noted as indispensable to the final success. Other key House actors include Henry Hyde (R-IL) who, in cooperation with Lane Evans, became the first House Chairman to hold a Committee markup of a "comfort women" Resolution (H.Res. 759) in September 2006, as well as conducting the first Congressional hearing on the specific issue of Imperial Japan's war crimes. Rep. Mike Honda stepped forward as the chief sponsor of H.Res. 121 after Evans and Hyde retired in January 2007; Asian Subcommittee Chairman Eni Faleomavaega (D-American Samoa), who conducted the first hearing in history with direct testimony of "comfort women" survivors, in February 2007; and Foreign Affairs Committee Chairman Tom Lantos (D-CA) and Ranking Member Ileana Ros-Lehtinen (R-FL) for moving H.Res. 121 forward through a Committee markup session, with a recorded vote (39-2) in June 2007, and sending it to the House Floor for final consideration in July 2007.

Finally, passage of H.Res. 121 would not have been possible without the leadership and steadfast support of then newly elected House Speaker Nancy Pelosi. Speaker Pelosi acted in sharp contrast to her immediate predecessor in the 109th Congress, Speaker Dennis Hastert (Hastert succumbed to the pressure of paid lobbyists for the Japanese government, including former Republican House leader Bob Michel, and refused to bring H.Res. 759 before the full House for consideration in 2006). In the 110th Congress, by contrast, Speaker Pelosi, a strong advocate for human and women's rights, moved H.Res. 121 swiftly forward on the House calendar after its markup by the Foreign Affairs Committee, leading to its unanimous adoption by the House on July 30, 2007.

Passage of H.Res. 121 was a historic and rather unprecedented action taken by the U.S. House of Representatives. Members went on record in support of victims of a long-festering human rights issue, with implications for current violence against women in armed conflicts. This action was taken despite other concerns, including the complication of relations with a major U.S. ally, Japan. It's noteworthy, too, that after more than two decades, notwithstanding vigorous lobbying efforts by the Ankara government coupled with serious national security considerations, the Armenian-American community was able to finally secure passage of a House Resolution in 2019 recognizing the Armenian Genocide under the Ottoman Turks. Thus, H.Res. 121's adoption stands out clearly as a major triumph for human and women's rights, for the grassroots advocacy of the Korean American community and its NGOs, and for the largely unsung Congressional leaders, mentioned above, who refused to forget what Rep. Faleomavaega referred fondly to as "our *halmonies*" (meaning "grandmothers" in Korean).

The second part of the book provides an overview of the ways in which the "comfort women" movement extends into diverse disciplines in the Humanities; Women's Studies, Asian History, Korean Studies, Art History, and Political Science, noting diverse research and approaches to the issue from their different academic perspectives. Professor Bonnie Oh at the Korean Studies program of Georgetown University wrote about the first academic conference on "comfort women," which was entitled "Legacies of Comfort Women of World War II" and held on September 30, 1996 at Georgetown University. Having taken place in the infancy of the "comfort women movement," now in its 28th year, the conference itself, the experiences of the planners, and its impact are considered as legitimate primary sources for this volume. Prof. Oh recalled the first academic conference on "comfort women" with every detail as organizer and convener; motivation, process, attempts at sabotage, its effect on college campuses, museums, and the U.S. Department of Justice's decision to include "comfort women" related war criminals among Japanese prohibited from entry to the United States. She comments on enduring legacies that have emerged since the conference: in the publication of the books and doctoral dissertations on the subject. The first was the book of the proceedings of the Georgetown symposium, *Legacies of Comfort Women of World War II*. The second was Frank Joseph Shulman's "chapter on annotated bibliography of the forty-six doctoral dissertations (1995–2004) on "comfort women" and biographies of their authors."

Margaret Stetz, professor of Women's Studies at the University of Delaware, writes the chapter "Girls and Military Sexual Slavery through a Feminist Intersectional Lens," to examine how and why the testimonies of Asian survivors of military sexual slavery within the "comfort system" achieved a sympathetic reception in the U.S. during the 1990s and the means by which these narratives circulated, especially throughout feminist communities. She also explores some ways in which the feminist understanding of these stories has changed, as American feminism itself has shifted toward intersectional perspectives that highlight oppression based on social categories such as ethnicity and age, rather than gender alone.

Jung-Sil Lee, art historian and independent curator, writes a chapter that analyzes the diverse genres and styles of artists who appropriated archived photographs and established documents regarding wartime crimes against "comfort women." In her chapter "Can the Arts Heal the Wartime Trauma of Sex Slaves? Case Study of Visual Art, Film, and Performing Arts," Lee shares her experience of curating art exhibitions with themes of "comfort women" and organizing film screenings, film festivals, and other artistic projects surrounding the "comfort women" movement such as documentary film making. In this chapter, she shows how artists re-contextualized historical documents for their own statements and played the role of historians or reporters studying violent atrocities against women; focusing on visual artists, Hung Liu, Tomiyama Taeko, Chang-Jin Lee, and others. Through their acts of appropriating, reporting, and re-contextualizing, the artists reclaim their lost subjects' dignity and pay homage to them through the interpretation of their experience and healing through artistic expression. Lee presented related papers at the CAA (College Art Association) titled "Artistic and Archival Presentation and Representation of Comfort Women History" in 2019 and "Unforeseen Controversy: Reconciliation and Re-contextualization through Comfort Women Memorials in the U.S." in 2018. Through summarizing the former paper, Lee analyzes how visual artists effectively appropriate and re-contextualize historical and archival documents to express their sympathy towards the victims known as "comfort women."

Frank Joseph Shulman, professional bibliographer and a university librarian and curator at the University of Maryland, College Park, contributes in his chapter a bibliography that is especially significant for future research on the "comfort women" issue. He compiled annotated doctoral dissertations about "comfort women" dating from 1995 with brief introductions about each dissertation author in his chapter "Western-Language Doctoral Dissertations on the Korean 'Comfort Women' 1995-2004: An Annotated Bibliography with Brief Information about the Educational Backgrounds of the Dissertation Authors." This chronologically arranged bibliography is a small portion of a larger body of 15,000 Western-language dissertations that will be published by the University of Michigan Press in his forthcoming reference work, "The First Century of Doctoral Dissertations on Korea, 1903-2004." His intention is that these annotated dissertations written about the "comfort women" will stimulate further studies on the issue and enable readers to gauge the scope of "comfort women" studies.

Yangmo Ku, professor of Political Science at Norwich University, provides and overview in his chapter: "Assessing the Transnational Comfort Women Movement, 1992-2019." He examines the way in which self-organized advocacy groups in South Korea, Japan, and other nations in the early 1990s have undertaken extensive transnational work in order to fight for the rights of "comfort women" that prompted the Japanese government to change its indifferent stance on the issue to a somewhat apologetic attitude. Given these facts, this chapter first explores how the transnational "comfort women" movement was initiated and has evolved over the last three decades. The chapter then analyzes to what extent and how such a movement has affected the Japanese government and society's reception of the issue. He completes his chapter with evaluations for both the achievements and limitations that the transnational "comfort women" movement has revealed. His chapter provides suggestions and directions for the future movement.

Jung-Sil Lee contributes the final chapter: "The Roles of 'Comfort Women' Memorials in the U.S.: Continued Activation of the Spirit of House Resolution 121." She observes the importance of the "comfort women" memorials as a premier indication of the memorialization of the issue. There have been 16 memorials built in the U.S. ranging from commemorative stone slabs to the Statue of Peace (Girl). Through research and interviews with leading figures of the committee, she uncovers context, meaning, and logistical aspects of these memorials. These memorials are not only to immortalize past atrocities, but to educate the public, and to become a focal point of activists producing related resolutions in certain cases.

What we aim to accomplish, or at least initiate, in this volume is to compile and archive not only a "comfort women" history – such written works having already been compiled extensively - but also the history of the "comfort women" redress movement in the U.S., specifically with regard to its setting in the nation's capital. We must say, however, that we are unable to include all the marvelous efforts and projects of the entire the U.S. in this volume. Such an effort would require future works and succeeding publications from other advocates. There are a few registered non-profit organizations in the U.S.: Washington Coalition for Comfort Women Issues (D.C.), Comfort Women Action for Redress and Education (CARE, formerly KAFC, Los Angeles, CA), Comfort Women Justice Coalition (CWJC, San Francisco, CA), Education for Social Justice Foundation (ESJF, San Francisco, CA), Youth Council of Fort Lee (YCFL, Fort Lee, NJ), and WeHope: Comfort Women Statue Project (Boston, MA). Many activists have been forming or developing coalitions and committees to build memorials, and coalescing their own formal organizations in their regions: Atlanta Comfort Women Memorial Task Force, Brookhaven, GA; Unforgotten Butterflies in Dallas, TX; The Committee for Statue of Peace in Chicago, IL; Butterfly for Hope in Washington, D.C. and Butterfly for Hope in Los Angeles, CA; George Washington University student groups such as Shout Out Unspoken Truth (SOUT); and Stand with Comfort Women at Yale and Connecticut Committee for Installing Statue of Peace in Hamden, CT. Beyond these active groups, there are far more clusters of students, scholars, politicians, and artists who have either exclusively dedicated their works or have been occasionally involved in the "comfort women" issue throughout the last 28 years in the U.S.[10]

We want this book to serve as a stimulus for further studies on the "comfort women" movement in the U.S. and to encourage these diverse advocates of the cause to continue their productive cultural and recontextualized works to deepen and expand on the discourse. We anticipate and expect positive and prolific outcomes of this movement in the future and hope to see the expansion or creation of new paradigms of "comfort women" discourses. More than anything, we hope this work can help in the fight for justice and rights for these "comfort women" survivors. They became examples of how much humans can survive under dehumanized conditions, and, after all the odds, they rose as activist leaders for reclaiming their dignities and for the global women's rights movement.

[1] The legacies of "comfort women" were examined from various perspectives in *Legacies of the Comfort Women of World War II,* ed. by Margaret Stetz and Bonnie B.C. Oh (Armonk, New York; London, England: An East Gate Book, M.E. Sharpe, Inc., 2001).

[2] The original purpose of establishment of comfort stations along the front lines of the Japanese military was to prevent rapes by the troops, to prevent sexually transmitted diseases, leakage of confidential information, and to promote and encourage militant spirits of soldiers. Yoshimi Yoshiaki, *Comfort Women: Sexual Slavery in the Japanese Military During World War II,* trans. by Suzanne O'Brien (New York: Columbia University Press, 1995), 42-75.

[3] Peipei Qui, Su Zhiliang, Chen Lifei, *Chinese Comfort Women* (New York: Oxford University Press, 2013), 37-42.

[4] Washington Coalition for Comfort Women Issues Inc. (WCCW) is a non-profit organization whose original mission statement in 1992 read: "The Washington Coalition for Comfort Women Issues (WCCW) was founded in December 1992 to promote research and education pertaining to crimes against 'comfort women' during World War II. It is an independent, non-profit, non-partisan educational organization that welcomes persons of every nationality. The WCCW believes that the Japanese government must clearly acknowledge its responsibility for crimes against 'comfort women.'" This original mission statement was revised to expand and broaden the perspective of global women's rights in 2000, 2015 and 2018 (A.1-1).

[5] Marianne Hirsch, *The Generation of Postmemory: Writing and Visual Culture after the Holocaust* (New York: Columbia UP, 2012), 1-25; "Connective Histories in Vulnerable Times," *PMLA* 129.3 (2014): 330-348.

[6] Hirsch, *The Generation of Postmemory*, 107.

[7] 'Jungdaehyup' has a new name: 'The Korean Council for Justice and Remembrance for the Issues of Military Sexual Slavery by Japan (The Korean Council)' and works for just resolution of the issue and prevention of wartime sexual violence. It was founded in Nov. 1990 as the first organization of its kind and encouraged Kim Hak-soon's courageous first testimony on August 14, 1991: http://womenandwar.net/kr/about-us/.

[8] Me Too Movement (or #MeToo) is a movement against sexual harassment and sexual assault against women and girls, initially used on social media Myspace in 2006 by sexual harassment survivor Tarana Burke. In 2017 #MeToo went viral as a hashtag after women began using it to tweet about the Harvey Weinstein sexual abuse allegations. The purpose of "Me Too" is to empower women through empathy and strength in numbers, especially young and vulnerable women, by visibly demonstrating how many women have survived sexual assault and harassment, especially in the workplace. The phrase and hashtag quickly developed into a broad-based, and eventually international movement: https://metoomvmt.org/.

[9] Dai-Sil Kim Gibson, *Silence Broken: Korean Comfort Women* (Iowa: Mid-Prairie Books Parkersburg, 1999) *see* Introduction 1-11.

[10] For a list of other organizations who work on "comfort women issues," *see* Resources 9.

# Part I

The U.S. Grassroots Movement
toward Legislative Advocacy

# 1. 28 YEARS OF WCCW ADVOCACY AGAINST INJUSTICE TO COMFORT WOMEN

*Jung-Sil Lee*

**Abstract**: This chapter introduces how the grassroots movement on "comfort women" in the United States came together through the support of many individuals and the Washington Coalition for Comfort Women Issues, Inc. (hereafter referred to as WCCW), a non-profit organization based in the Washington, D.C. metropolitan area. It explores the organizations and groups of people who have collaborated and supported the mission of WCCW. This chapter is based on the book chapter "Tracing 27 Years of the Redress Movement Led by the Washington Coalition for Comfort Women Issues" co-authored by Jung-Sil Lee and Dongwoo Lee Hahm in *Japanese Military Sexual Slavery* co-edited by Pyong Gap Min, Thomas R. Chung, and Sejung Sage Yim, and published by De Gruyter in 2020. The chapter was an outcome of a conference presentation by Jung-Sil Lee and Dongwoo Lee Hahm at *The Redress Movement for the Victims of Japanese Military Sexual Slavery: Looking Back at the 27-year Movement*, at Queens College, New York on October 14, 2017. Under the permission of the co-editors and the publisher De Gruyter, a substantial part is reused in this chapter but for archiving purposes, many additional details of events are revised and included along with appendices and illustrations. In many respects, this chapter consists of documents, memories, and interviews of former WCCW presidents, Dongwoo Lee Hahm, Ok Cha Soh, Christine Choi, and other contributing individuals.

## Introduction

Twenty-eight years ago, I first saw the horrific stories and scenes of young girls forced into Japanese sexual slavery through a historical Korean drama based on true stories called *Years of Upheaval* (1991–1992). It was very hard for me to deal with and accept that as part of my own history, although I only remember a few of the violent scenes. Almost fifteen years later and on the other side of the globe, I re-encountered this story that set me on a path to tear down the suppressed shame, pain, anger, and sorrow of this unforgettable past. The next 10 years as a part of WCCW helped shape my perceptions of history, during which I slowly built a stronger conviction to address the plight of "comfort women." I stand now deeply compelled by this journey of advocacy and self-discovery to cry out for their vindication. Resolving the unjust past and reclaiming their dignities and rights are going to be one of my goals for the rest of my life. Michel Foucault said that knowledge is power. However, sometimes the powerful aren't just, nor do they tell the true story. In my opinion, to pursue justice is to pursue truth, for which knowledge is essential. (From the presentation by Jung-Sil Lee at the conference in Queens College, NY, 2017).

What is most personal is most universal; although I live in an era long removed from the wartime sexual trauma of "comfort women"[1] history, I can still fiercely sense their pain. The wartime victims are euphemistically called "comfort women," a term used to encompass the women in Asia who were conscripted to be used in sexual slavery by Japanese soldiers during World War II as a way to encourage the soldiers in the field. This is regarded as an unlawful violation against human rights.[2] The issues are yet to be resolved; they have been hotly debated since 1991 when the first victim, Kim Hak-soon shared her experience with the world in her testimony, a watershed moment for this issue. Many people in all corners of the globe learned the history of "comfort women" of Asian countries that happened seventy years ago and were galvanized by this important and horrifying moment in history to educate the public so that such atrocities would not be repeated. Importantly, yet unfortunately, in its function to facilitate public discourse, the "comfort women" history has also served to provide a grim foil to the issues that still plague women today: sexual assault, human trafficking, mistreatment of women, unfair trial results of sex crimes, and war related trauma. This history's significance and power lies in the fact that a personal problem becomes "a public and universal issue" when it comes to be a repeated structural characteristic of the society and the current society is not making much advancement in terms of women's rights and justice.

This book is mainly dedicated to a recording of the activists, politicians, scholars, and artists in the U.S. from 1992 to 2019 who have strived to be a voice of "comfort women" along with WCCW, a non-profit organization founded in 1992, that was the first such organization in the U.S. For 28 years in the United States, a group of people from diverse backgrounds have worked for the same cause of humanity and the rights of victims ceaselessly: they have fought for justice and the dignity of "comfort women," who due to cultural and societal pressure, had not previously been able to have their voices heard nor fight for their legal rights and humanistic dignity. After the groundbreaking first testimony in the U.S. by one Korean woman named Hwang Keum-ju at the Korean Methodist Church of Greater Washington in Virginia, WCCW was founded and has worked with other organizations, elected officials, scholars, and ethnically diverse civic groups throughout these years. I will mention those names in this chapter and highlight their achievements (Fig. 1-1).

I tried to include detailed descriptions of "comfort women" related projects accompanied with primary resources and photos within and outside of WCCW. It describes the actions of major U.S. officials who contributed to this issue, such as the Director of the Department of Justice, the U.S. Congress with numerous congressmen and congresswomen, and local governments, and other elected officials. This chapter also summarizes several dimensions of WCCW activities: 1. The grassroots redress movement that eventually led to federal and local legislation; 2. A focus on public education and propagation of research through conferences, college tours, internships, and publications; 3. The artistic representations such as memorial building, film making, and organizing exhibitions of archival materials and art works; 4. The ongoing archiving projects of textual and visual resources. Because artistic representations of the issue are discussed in separate chapters of this volume, I limit myself to examine only other dimensions here. Also, I must say that I am not able to include all the marvelous efforts and projects performed by other organizations in America in this volume. That will require future work and succeeding publications.[3]

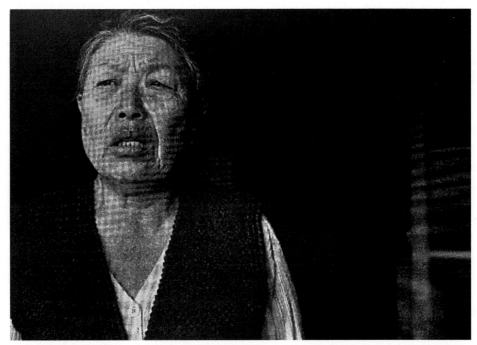

Fig. 1-1. Photo of Hwang Keum-ju, former "comfort woman" victim and survivor who visited the U.S. for the first time. New York and the Korean Methodist Church of Greater Washington, VA, November 1992.

## Founding of the Washington Coalition for Comfort Women Issues, Inc.

Before WCCW, a group of activists had come together to invite Hwang Keum-ju, a "comfort women" survivor to Washington, D.C. The initiating leader was Soon Im Kang, one of the members of the Association of Women's Mission at the Korean United Methodist Church of Greater Washington, Virginia. Kang recalled how she was involved initially in this issue. She was a student of Professor Lee Hyo-jae, one of the initiating representatives of The Korean Council for the Women Drafted for Military Sexual Slavery by Japan (The Korean Council) in Korea and a leading scholar of "comfort women" studies in Korea. Professor Lee informed Kang that The Korean Council team would visit the United Nations in New York with a "comfort women" victim in February 1992, as the first visit of the victims to the U.S. With a conviction to help The Korean Council, Kang manually produced the first "comfort women resource book" from her home and raised $3,500 by selling copies with the Association of Women's Mission and sent the funds to help the activism of The Korean Council in May 1992 (Fig. 1-2). Through her actions, Kang planted the seed for the foundation of WCCW and handed the reins to the founding President Hahm. Yet, she continued her contribution to its development for a decade until she stepped down from her position on the WCCW Board. Kang recently returned to the Board and recognized the other initiating contributors in New York and Toronto, Canada through interviews.[4]

Simultaneous protests against the injustice of "comfort women" happened in Canada and another region of the U.S. In 1991, a year before WCCW's founding, "The U.S. Eastern Korean Council" in New York was formed as a coalition that consisted of twenty-four Korean groups including New York and New Jersey Korean American Associations, YWCA, The Council of Korean Churches, Korean American Senior Citizens Society in New York, Church for UN, etc.[5] New York-based pastor Young-ho Kim was the core figure who had worked with Lee Hyojae and Yoon Jeongok, Ewha Woman's University professors and co-founders of The Korean Council. Pastor Kim attributes his motivation and inspiration for creating his resource book and activism to Sidong Dae and Hyegi Min from Toronto, Canada who compiled resources on "comfort women" from Korea and compiled a "comfort women" resource work around the same time as Kang's efforts. Kim recalled that Hyegi Min visited the victims in Korea in 1991 and compiled the resources with the help of pastor Sang-cheol Lee in the United Church of Canada to organize the invitation of Hwang Keum-ju, former "comfort woman," to the U.S.[6] It is notable that the role of Korean churches was phenomenal in the early stage of "comfort women" activism, yet, now most Korean churches consider the issue "taboo" defining it as too "political."

Kim, along with other supporters, organized a rally of 1200 participants in Dag Hammarskjold Plaza in front of the Japan Society near the United Nations Headquarters in New York in 1992.[7] Kim was devoted to getting the petition to report the case of "comfort women" at the Human Rights Council (former UN Commission on Human Rights) in Vienna and submitted the resources that he had compiled along with the resource submission to the ICJ (International Commission of Jurists) which also published a volume on "comfort women," that is believed to be the first book written in English on the victims[8] (Fig. 1-3). The report's findings conclude:

> Based on documents reviewed and interviews held, the mission concludes that it is clear that the Japanese Impérial Army initiated the setting up of a vast network of comfort stations for the exclusive use of the Japanese Impérial Army, before and during the Second World War. Chinese, Dutch, Filipino, Indonesian, Korean, Malaysian, and Taiwanese women and girls were targeted, put into these comfort stations and sexual services were extracted from them under duress. The Japanese military was responsible for the setting up, use, opération and control of the comfort stations. Detailed régulations were framed by the Japanese military in this regard. The mission also found that life in the comfort stations was a living hell for the women. They were beaten and tortured in addition to being repeatedly raped day after day by officers and soldiers. Living conditions were cramped and shabby, food was usually of a poor quality and in short supply. . . . When they were brought to the comfort stations, they were healthy in body and spirit. They left the comfort stations, diseased in body and crippled in spirit. The report also shows that the suffering of these women did not end after the war. After being abandoned by fleeing

Japanese soldiers, some of them reached home, only to live lives of isolation. The pain they have endured has continued throughout their lifetime.

Fig. 1-2. The cover of the first comfort women resource book made in the U.S. compiled and edited by Soon Im Kang. The complete 84 pages can be found at www.comfort-women.org.

Fig. 1-3. The cover of Ustinia Dolgopol Snehal Paranjape, "Comfort Women": an Unfinished Ordeal - Report of Mission (Geneva, Switzerland: International Commission of Jurists, 1994).

When Hwang Keum-ju visited Virginia and D.C. after the New York rally, she testified to her experience as a 17-year old sex slave during World War II and detailed life in the Japanese military "comfort station." She exclaimed, "I was raped by several tens of Japanese soldiers a day and the Japanese government now calls me a liar!"[9] All attendees were shocked and became sympathetic. Three days later, her story was aired by Fox News Channel 5 in the Greater Washington area and the public reaction was as though a bomb had exploded. The WCCW was established two weeks later, on December 12, 1992, and Dongwoo Lee Hahm was elected as the founding president.

Although there might have been more who had been initiated and involved in the New York rally and burgeoning activism, due to the lack of documents or contacts, the brief summary centers around the activities of the "comfort women" movement around WCCW since 1992 up to the present day (R.1). As indicated in the introduction, WCCW rapidly grew in size and in its scope of activities, yet from the beginning, the organizational activities have always touched upon almost all possible dimensions explained above to transmit the message on behalf of "comfort women," with emphasis on certain dimensions changing with time. That being said, these dimensions are not necessarily chronological, but most have been ongoing, simultaneous, or overlapping. As authors in this book are professional in their specific disciplines, they describe and analyze the issue through their perspectives and disciplines such as legislation, feminism, education, memorials and arts, this chapter is more focused on what and how these dimensions became a focus and the way in which WCCW has been involved and explored these areas.

## Grassroots Advocacy by WCCW

"Grassroots" movements are defined as "The basic level of society or of an organization especially as viewed in relation to higher or more centralized positions of power. In basic terms, a grassroots movement starts from nothing like actual grass roots, they start from the ground and grow up. Grassroots run by common people generally started by individuals and small groups with a focused idea, and always have a specific mission."[10] Although WCCW's Mission statement had three revisions since the initial statement (2000, 2015, and 2018)[11] (A.1-1), the ultimate and prime mission has always been constant: "founded to advocate for the rights of the 'comfort women' and their lawful reparation." WCCW was almost the first Korean American advocacy group registered as a non-profit organization (NPO) in the federal government demanding a specific request to the U.S. government.[12]

1992 saw the L.A. riots and marked a turning point in the Korean American population's understanding of its group identity and its subsequent shift towards an active engagement in politics.[13] Coincidently, around the same time, WCCW began to reach out to politicians and Members of Congress using the various tools typifying a grassroots movement: organizing public meetings and forums, marches, demonstrations, letter writing campaigns to elected officials, press conferences, media exposure, publications, and exhibits. The first effort of WCCW to fulfill its mission was to appeal to the U.S. House of Representatives to give an ultimatum to the Japanese government. For ten years, President Hahm intensely advocated for the "comfort women" issue to educate U.S. political leaders and the UN as recommended by Ms. Doi Takako, the keynote speaker at the Japanese International Symposium.[14] WCCW's successive presidents followed this mission, and mobilized to evangelize and to find strategic plans for the American public.

As a result, WCCW's first activity was a rally titled "Asians and Americans United to Redress Japanese War Crimes" in front of the Embassy of Japan located on Massachusetts Avenue in D.C. on March 1, 1993, a year after its founding and in commemoration of Korean Independence Movement Day. As remembered by the founding President Hahm, the first WCCW rally marching from the Embassy of Japan in D.C. was "to protest the Japanese government's rejection of its responsibility for crimes against 'comfort women,'" and second, "to promote the founding of WCCW." Approximately 150 WCCW members and Chinese Americans participated (A.1-2).

The following month, WCCW visited the Embassy of Japan and delivered the letter demanding an official apology from the Japanese government. Since then, WCCW organized rallies not on a regular basis, but upon the recurrence of certain issues related to "comfort women," or to express the global solidarity of the "comfort women" movement walking with other activists. The non-profit organization, The Korean Council for the Women Drafted for

Military Sexual Slavery by Japan (The Korean Council, in Korean *Jungdaehyup*) was founded in 1990 in Seoul, Korea, and started the Wednesday Demonstration vigil beginning in January 1992 with the surviving victims. Every Wednesday at noon they gathered in front of the Embassy of Japan in Seoul to demand an official apology and legal reparations. These gatherings continued for 28 years, recorded as the longest demonstration in the world.[15] WCCW recited The Korean Council's demands whenever the former "comfort women" victims visited D.C. and whenever the Japanese Prime Minister visited the U.S. Congress.

Fig. 1-4. WCCW organized the demonstration "Asians and Americans United to Redress Japanese War Crimes" in front of the White House, June 1994.

It has been a formidable and important task to carefully phrase and deliver WCCW's stance as a public statement for a large audience. WCCW had a vision of collecting 10,000 petitions to submit to the UN on December 11, 1992, even before the organization was formally established. In the next year, September 1993, WCCW delivered the official letter with the victims' demands to the Embassy of Japan in the U.S., along with the signatures of 8,000 others.[16] In September 24, 1993, Japanese Prime Minister Hosokawa Morihiro visited the United States to speak at the UN in New York. Thus, WCCW wrote an open letter addressed to Hosokawa, requesting an official apology and legal reparation to "comfort women" (A.1-3). The letter was published in *The Washington Post* on the same day as Hosokawa's speech at the UN General Conference.[17] The letter brought about further action, as 17 members of the U.S. Congress sent their own letters dated November 3, 1993, to Hosokawa, requesting the Japanese government to investigate the sexual slavery of "comfort women" during the Asia-Pacific War. This was the first major Congressional support of WCCW's redress movement (A.1-4).

In June 1994, when the Japanese Emperor revisited Washington, D.C. to meet with President Bill Clinton, WCCW organized another demonstration demanding full redress for Japan's war crimes (Fig. 1-4). WCCW invited Hwang Keum-ju and Prof. Lee Hyo-jae, a former representative and a founder of The Korean Council, to participate in the two sessions that were held in front of the White House: "Asians and

Fig. 1-5. WCCW demonstration during visit of Emperor Akihito to President Clinton, June 1994.

Americans United to Redress Japanese War Crimes" and "United against Japan for Justice and True History." (A.1-5) WCCW delivered a letter addressed to President Clinton and Emperor Akihito along with the petitions containing 8,000 signatures, demanding an official apology and legal reparation from the Japanese government (Fig. 1-5) (A.1-6).

Although diverse ethnic groups joined in the rally, the Korean women dressed in white traditional Korean costume, "hanbok," led the rally. The rally was conducted peacefully but with an emphatic demand for an official apology and legal reparation to be offered by the Japanese government.[18] The haunting scene of this demonstration with women wearing white Korean traditional costume had a dramatic effect. White Korean traditional costumes are used for shamanic dances (guk) by Korean "mudang" (Korean shaman) with long white silk scarves. It denotes a "mudang's" role as a medium to resolve all subjects' experience of "*han*." "*Han*" is a term frequently used to describe the hardship and emotion of "comfort women," and it is hard to translate in English.[19] It describes sustained pain, sadness, anger, remorse, and resentment deeply imprinted in someone's life and heart, and traditionally a "mudang's" role is to liberate the people from this emotion. These demonstrations in D.C. emulate the "mudang" and reiterate "*han*" embedded in the victims, while at the same time resembling aspects in the *salpuri dance*, part of a shaman's cleansing rite *ssitkimgut*. *Salpuri dance* became more of an artistic performance within the sphere of Korean traditional dance and has been included in many "comfort women" related projects and events afterwards[20] (Fig. 1-6). The fourth president Christine Choi mentioned that they also wore these traditional costumes to conjure up images of funeral clothing that mourning families in Korea wear during funerals, normally white or black hanbok.[21] The traditional Korean white "hanbok" conveyed a multi-layered meaning: mourning, consoling, and solemn healing for the victims' pain (A.1-7).

Fig. 1-6. WCCW demonstration in front of the White House led by women wearing Korean traditional dress, June 1994. *Photo by Doochan Hahm.*

There were countless demonstrations, press releases, and statements afterwards organized and proclaimed by WCCW as seen in the history of the organization. They became core elements of activism. In May 1997, WCCW organized the first press conference at the U.S. Capitol in collaboration with Chinese and Filipino communities, which led House Representative William O. Lipinski (D-IL, 1983–2005) to submit a resolution (House Concurrent Resolution 126) urging the Japanese government to make an official apology and pay legal reparations to reconcile with the "comfort women." It paved the way for further resolutions on the "comfort women" issue, including H.Res. 121, which finally passed in 2007.

During my presidency, WCCW published a full-page statement in *The Washington Post* on April 27, 2015, titled "Open Letters of Peoples of the United States and Japan." This statement coincided with Japanese Prime Minister Shinzo Abe's visit to the U.S. to deliver a speech to the joint session of Congress where he consistently denied the wartime atrocity toward "comfort women." WCCW also organized a press conference at the Rayburn House Office Building (A.1-8)[22] and a rally of 700 people on the 27th and 28th of April 2015, in front of the Capitol Building while Abe was speaking to Congress on April 28th (Fig. 1-7). WCCW collaborated with more than 30 organizations throughout the nation. Special guests who spoke at the event included Lee Yong-soo, a surviving "comfort woman," and Congressman Mike Honda, as well as other political leaders who supported the issue. Abe's visit prompted many journalists to report the issue and to interview WCCW officers, including correspondents from *The Washington Post, The Washington Times, BBC, CCTV,* and *Al Jazeera*[23] (A.1-9) (A.1-10). The speech of Abe also prompted WCCW to send the letter to the Japanese Emperor on July 2015 to ask his support to resolve the issue (A.1-11).

Fig. 1-7. WCCW organized a rally to demand an official apology from the Japanese government when Prime Minister Shinzo Abe visited the U.S. Congress to give a speech at the joint session, April 2015. *Photo by Jaeheup Kim.*

Fig. 1-8. UN press conference, Lee Yong-soo and Jung-Sil Lee, WCCW President, for WCCW official statement on the 2015 Korea-Japan agreement, March 8, 2016.

Disappointed by the Korea-Japan Bilateral Agreement on December 28, 2015, the WCCW made an official statement and presented it at the UN press conference on March 8, 2016, with the Coalition of Trafficking Against Women, KACE, and KAFC in support of the statement of The Convention on the Elimination of all Forms of Discrimination against Women (CEDAW) (Fig. 1-8). WCCW's statement criticized the agreement as insincere and disingenuous. WCCW regarded the bilateral agreement as a significant step backwards in the fight for the rights of "comfort women" since the agreement was largely done for political appearances with little underlying substance and posited without the consultation of the victims or at least non-government organizations (NGO) who had worked on the victims' behalf (A.1-12).

**The Passage of House Resolution 121**

Passage of House Resolution 121 in 2007 by Congress was the culmination of WCCW's 15 years of grassroots "comfort women" movement efforts in the United States. Advocates, legislators, and victims deliberated for a long time before coming up with this resolution. Among them, WCCW and its two presidents, Dongwoo Lee Hahm and Ok Cha Soh, played a pioneering role in the passage of the resolution by dedicating their time and passion in organizing demonstrations, lecture tours, press conferences, hearings, campaigns, archival exhibitions, conferences, and inviting former "comfort women" to the Hill. A significant first step for the recognition of the issue on the Hill, with sole focus on the "comfort women" issue, was achieved by Rep. Lane Evans (D-IL, 1983–2007), who became a dear friend of Ok Cha Soh.

The late Rep. Lane Evans, working with WCCW, looked deeply into this issue and saw it as a crime against humanity. He brought up "comfort women" history in the Congressional Record in 1999 and continued to put forth several resolutions regarding the issue.[24]

> We (as members of Congress), have a duty to help those who need our help. We have a duty to stand up for those who cannot stand up on their own. We have a duty to speak up for those who have no voice and to do what is just and what is right. . . . Let us lend them our strength. We must act and we must speak out, because in the end, people will remember not the words of enemies, but the silence of their friends. We must not remain silent.[25]

Prior to passage of the final resolution, Evans submitted House Concurrent Resolution 357 in 2000, H.Con.Res. 195 in 2001, H.Con.Res. 226 in 2003, H.Con.Res. 68 in 2005, and H.Res. 759 in 2006. The last resolution was passed unanimously by the House Committee on International Relations on September 13, 2006, but not brought to the House floor. Mindy Kotler and Ok Cha Soh recall that a stumbling block to bringing the resolution to the floor was due to vigorous lobbying by Japan which persuaded then-House Speaker Dennis Hastert (R-IL). The Japanese government hired lobbyist Bob Michel from Hogan Lovells, a lobbying company. He had worked as House Minority Leader of the Republican Party for fourteen years. Michel pressured Henry Hyde, Chair of the Committee on House International

Relations, asserting that it would deteriorate relations between Japan and the United States. Nevertheless, Lane Evans was able to persuade Hyde to be sympathetic to "comfort women" atrocities[26] (A.1-13). Ok Cha Soh points out the importance of the previous resolutions that energized the supporting groups that eventually helped to pass the final resolution in 2007. Its passage is the fruit of 15 years of tireless effort by WCCW members, Rep. Lane Evans, and many other supporters including Chinese NGOs, and earlier resolutions. Honda gave credit to his former colleague, now the late Evans, for the passage of H.Res. 121"[27] (A.1-14).

Due to Rep. Lane Evans' illness, Rep. Mike Honda (D-CA, 2001–2017), a third-generation Japanese American, submitted H.Res. 121 on January 31, 2007 after he took the torch from his friend Evans in December 2006. His Japanese American identity and speech carried symbolic importance as he clarified that the nature of the resolution would not harm the relations between Japan and the U.S. and did not attack the Japanese government but reconciled and strengthened relations among countries. Because he had experienced the Japanese internment camps when he was a child, Honda had a memory of what it meant to have one's human rights stripped away and a strong sense of what an "official apology" should be, as any American did, by erecting the memorial and paying the legal reparation.[28] Honda explained the difference between the American apology to Japanese Americans who suffered in internment camps and the Japanese apology to "comfort women" in Asian countries:

> . . . 1988, after the Congress had passed H.R. 442 and President Reagan signed it into law, did we feel that there was an unambiguous apology and setting the record straight. Japan has not done that officially. And they continue to double talk and whitewash the history of their activities and constantly attempt to change their history books in the junior high school and high school level. That in itself indicates that there is no sincere and historical responsibility being taken by the government of Japan. This is what we are seeking.[29]

Unfortunately, the Japanese government did not think that way and denounced the resolution's passage.[30] When the U.S. House Representatives unanimously passed the resolution on July 2007, under Chairman Tom Lantos, there was a deep consensus of ethical responsibility for justice and human rights among House Representatives.

> H.Res. 121—A resolution expressing the sense of the House of Representatives that the Government of Japan should formally acknowledge, *apologize*, and accept historical *responsibility* in a clear and *unequivocal* manner for its Imperial Armed Forces' coercion of young women into *sexual slavery*, known to the world as "comfort women," during its colonial and wartime occupation of Asia and the Pacific Islands from the 1930s through the duration of World War II (Summary of H.Res. 121, 110th Congress, 2007–2008).

As found in the full text of H.Con.Res. 226, Rep. Lane Evans wrote about the enormity of the issue, its graphic historical detail with statements from international authorities, such as the International Commission of Jurists (ICJ) and the United Nations Special Rapporteur on Violence against Women. Each version differs slightly from the other, but a few keywords remained in each version and were finally brought together in the final resolution. Among the keywords were *apology, responsibility, unequivocal, and sexual slavery;* words that highlight the stance and spirit of H.Res. 121.[31]

This issue was brought up after a shift in the American political timbre in the 20th century towards issues regarding slavery, forced labor, systematic rape, and crimes against humanity. In terms of slavery, the charters of international military tribunals provide a list of crimes against humanity. According to Article 6(c) of the Nuremberg Charter, "enslavement, deportation, and other inhumane acts committed against any civilian population [are to be known] as crimes against humanity."[32] The United States has played a crucial role in the development and support of the ideas and practices of human rights. The U.S. State Department periodically reports on human rights worldwide. Beyond investigating and maintaining extensive records[33] on slavery in the U.S., Congress was also ready to hear the voices of victims of foreign countries. Kinue Tokudome summarized in her article how the "comfort women" issues were revisited and interpreted as "human rights and current issues of humanity."[34]

Fig. 1-9. WCCW President Ok Cha Soh helped Rep. Mike Honda to organize the Congressional Hearing in preparation of the Passage of House Resolution 121. February 2007. *Photo by Christine Choi.*

Right before H.Res. 121 was passed, there was the House Hearing on "comfort women" issues on February 15, 2007 in the Asian Pacific subcommittee under the House Foreign Affairs Committee chaired by Eni Faleomavaega. WCCW invited three former "comfort women," Lee Yong-soo, Kim Kun-ja, and Dutch Australian, Jan Ruff O'Herne, who testified along with remarks by Ok Cha Soh, the president of WCCW, and Mindy Kotler, director of Asia Policy Point. During the hearing, Ok Cha Soh confirmed the stance of WCCW in terms of the apology and legal reparation from the Japanese government (Fig. 1-9).

> The statement challenged the issues of the Asian Women's Fund, which was privately funded, therefore, arguing that it cannot be regarded as an 'official' reparation for "comfort women." It addresses the apology issues, which should have been endorsed by the Japanese Diet, thus far only a few Japanese government officials have made near-apology statements on "comfort women" issues.[35]

Soh's statements further explored the logical context of the legal issues upon which lawsuits on "comfort women" had been filed in the D.C. Circuit Court in previous years (A.1-15). Mindy Kotler, director of Asia Policy Point and one of the drafters of H.Res. 121, identified "Japan's wartime military rape camps as the precedent of the modern issues of sexual slavery, sexual violence in war, and human trafficking that dominate today's discussion of war and civil conflict—Bosnia, Rwanda, Nicaragua, Sierra Leone, Darfur, Burma."[36] With the stories of "comfort women," Kotler as a feminist and faithful archivist of human rights history could engage in creating an expanded discourse of human trafficking that continues to be relevant to our current issues.[37]

The efforts of Lane Evans, Mike Honda, and Ok Cha Soh, former president of WCCW, played pivotal roles in contributing to passage of the 2007 resolution, but a year prior, in 2006, there were multiple organizations and individuals who contributed to the resolution and groundbreaking victory of the grassroots movement on the issue at large. It surely can be viewed as the first successful instance of Korean American grassroots movements reaching the federal level. Some of the contributors included: Washington Coalition for Comfort Women Issues (WCCW), Coalition 121 (co-chaired by Moon Hyung Rhee and William Ilsong Hong), National Korean American Associations, Korean American Civic Empowerment (KACE, formerly New York Voters' Registration Council),[38] Korean American Forum of California (KAFC—founded in the year 2012, now known as CARE), Global Alliance for Preserving the Truth of WWII, Asia Pacific WWII Atrocities Memorial Inc., Mindy Kotler, Dennis Halpin, Thomas Kim, and Annabel Park. These groups helped launch a nationwide campaign to petition for the passage of the resolution in addition to many others. The success of the passage of the Resolution was the outcome of a group effort from diverse people.

Passage of H.Res. 121 gave ongoing energy for "comfort women" activists, specifically to succeeding WCCW members. I was elected fifth WCCW president in 2015 and followed the steps of former presidents with grassroots activities, organizing seminars, exhibitions, media exposure, traveling lectures, and film screenings. Eight years after H.Res. 121 passage, in March 2015, Maryland Senator Susan Lee introduced the Resolution of Comfort Women, Maryland Senate Joint Resolution 3, and I was invited to give the testimony of what happened on behalf of former "comfort women" and to support the Resolution (Fig. 1-10) (A.1-16).

> WHEREAS, The people of Maryland honor the surviving victims who are now at the end of their lives, but were victimized at the beginning of their lives when they were too young to consent to prostitution and were ostracized even though they were clearly victims;
>
> WHEREAS, The Maryland General Assembly is determined to combat human trafficking in modern times through all appropriate legislative action, education initiatives, and commemorations to the victims of this horrible injustice and crime that has been perpetrated against so many people throughout history; now, therefore, be it
>
> RESOLVED BY THE GENERAL ASSEMBLY OF MARYLAND, That the General Assembly of Maryland hereby extends its profound hope that the historical record of the crimes against the "ianfu" or "comfort women" of World War II will serve as a lasting reminder to the world that crimes against humanity will not be condoned or tolerated; and be it further...[39] (A.1-17)

Susan Lee stated: "The war crime… happened in the past and we don't want it to happen anymore and certainly will fight against any modern-day human slavery and human trafficking." Stan Tsai, chairman of the Chinese Culture and Community Service Center and other human rights representatives, testified to support the Resolution at the Hearing on the

Fig. 1-10. Maryland Comfort Women Resolution sponsored by Maryland Senator Susan Lee, supporting statement presented by WCCW President Jung-Sil Lee, March 6, 2015.

Maryland Comfort Women Resolution on March 6, 2015. The Maryland Senate Joint Resolution affirmed that human trafficking was also an issue relevant to the legacy of "comfort women," and they added that to the issues of education, apology, responsibility, and sexual slavery of H.Res. 121. It was among many "comfort women" resolutions of state or city legislatures throughout the U.S. (R.3).

**Educational Initiatives**

The first WCCW involved academic forum on "comfort women" was cosponsored with Georgetown University and the Korea Society in 1996 as is discussed by Professor Bonnie Oh in detail in Chapter 5 of this volume. Even prior to when the academic conferences were held, WCCW had spearheaded various activities to educate the public along with congressmen and congresswomen with press conferences, testimonial events, and exhibitions. Yet, as the first academic event, WCCW organized an international conference on "comfort women" titled *The Comfort Women of World War II: Legacy and Lessons*, from September 30 to October 2, 1996, co-chaired by Georgetown University Prof. Bonnie Oh and Prof. Margaret Stetz. It was meaningful that the organizers invited Mutsuko Miki, the widow of the late Japanese Prime Minister Takeo Miki as the keynote speaker. She championed the "comfort women" issue during her husband's administration.[40] The conference also featured testimony by Kim Yoon-shim, a former "comfort woman" taken at the age of 13, which brought the audience to tears. Two months later, on December 4, 1996, the U.S. Department of Justice made an announcement of "16 Japanese War Criminals Barred from Entering the U.S.," which made the front page of *The Washington Post* (A.1-18). *The Washington Post* editorial on December 6, 1996 stated, "The Department of Justice's decision with considerable fanfare—has angered many Japanese but the United States has a right to say the war criminals are not wanted here[41] (Fig. 1-11).

Fig. 1-11. Lee Yong-soo with Eli Rosenbaum, Director of the Department of Justice at the WCCW event, April 26, 2007.

March 25–28, 1999, WCCW participated in KASCON XIII (Korean American Students Conference) presenting the documentary film *Comfort Women* at Stanford University. The theme of the conference was "Empowering the *Han*" and was co-hosted by WCCW, Stanford University, and the University of California, Berkeley. The keynote speaker was a "comfort woman" survivor. President Bill Clinton delivered an encouraging message about the importance of pursuing the history of immigrants and making it a shared lesson.[42]

In June 2001, founding President Dongwoo Lee Hahm resigned from her role after nine years of presidency. Ok Cha Soh, who was the executive secretary at the time, was elected as the next president of WCCW. Once she became the leader of WCCW, she received a letter from the Embassy of Japan, stating that there was no need for an apology and compensation since they had already been carried out in the past.[43] Yet, WCCW regards this apology as an unofficial statement that does not hold authority on a national level passed by the National Diet (Congress in Japan), and that the money from The Asian Women's Fund was not a legal nor official reparation. WCCW continued to argue that the apology and legal compensation were not made, and demanded official statements from the Japanese government[44] (Fig. 1-12).

Fig. 1-12. WCCW rally at D.C. Court House, March 23, 2005.

During the inauguration press conference, President Soh highlighted the mission of WCCW as educating the next generation in order to prevent future horrors that stem from the lack of education and censorship of history. She proclaimed that WCCW would devote resources to organizing seminars, forums, and exhibitions on U.S. major college campuses. Since the very first academic conference on "comfort women" cosponsored by Georgetown University and the Korea Society, WCCW has been involved in a tremendous amount of college lecture tours presenting the survivors, along with archival exhibits. This goal was amplified by the resolution of the Korean Student Associations (KSA) at several universities that decided to promote "comfort women" issues as well. The project set off from Harvard and travelled to Yale, Cornell, New York University, Princeton, and Georgetown. The touring seminar and testimony "Lessons of Courage; Restoring Honor" accompanied by survivor Hwang Keum-ju, left an indelible mark on the minds of these young people and garnered support from participating students who later became ardent advocates of the cause.

Many other activities, such as symposiums, forums, and talks, were cosponsored with other institutions such as University of Maryland in October 2002 and Brown University in November 2002. In the same year, the Midwest college tour continued to the University of Wisconsin, Northwestern University, Ohio State University, and the University of Michigan. A former "comfort woman," Choi Kapsun, accompanied the tour for testimonies. In 2003, WCCW continued to visit institutions in Boston: Boston College, Northeastern University, MIT, Wellesley College, and Tufts University. Kim Hwa Sun, a former "comfort woman," joined the tour. In 2003, WCCW participated in a panel at the KASCON at Cornell University. Vigorous evangelism of "comfort women" of WCCW to these academic institutions became seeds and aroused human rights activists who joined in the "comfort women" resolution grassroots movement a couple of years later (Fig. 1-13).

Fig. 1-13. WCCW College Tour Photo in KASCON21, *Jungang Ilbo*, April 4, 2007.

Succeeding WCCW presidents maintain the mission of educating both Congress and the public at large through educational gatherings accompanied by testimonial events or exhibitions. The targeted audience has extended to the younger generation such as middle school and high school students as emphasized by Prof. Margaret Stetz in her presentation of 2012 at the George Mason University Symposium organized by WCCW.[45]

Christine Choi was elected president of WCCW for the period 2009–2014. As with previous presidents, she sent out letters to leaders, including then U.S. President Barack Obama and the Emperor and Empress of Japan (A.1-19), and also held a demonstration on "Global Solidarity Action Day" in commemoration of the 1,000th Wednesday Demonstration

Fig. 1-14. George Mason Conference *Korean/Asian Comfort Women Issues Then and Now,* at George Mason University, December 1, 2012, chaired by Jung-Sil Lee in commemoration of WCCW's 20th anniversary.

in front of the Japanese Embassy in Seoul. When WCCW reached its 20th anniversary, WCCW turned to more subtle but more accessible and powerful ways of educating the public, through conferences and art exhibitions (Fig. 1-14). WCCW organized a 20th anniversary ceremony, symposium, and exhibition at George Mason University. It was the first fine arts exhibition organized by WCCW beyond the showcase of archival materials. Detailed information about artistic representation and WCCW sponsored exhibitions are described in chapter seven. To commemorate WCCW's 20th anniversary, Christine Choi organized a conference, film screening of *Silence Broken* by Dai Sil Kim-Gibson, and art exhibition on December 1, 2012. The conference theme was "Korean/Asian Comfort Women Issues Then and Now: Tracing its Historical, Political, and Cultural Aspects of the Comfort Women Movement in the U.S. and Korea" (A.1-20). Held at George Mason University, the events drew many students and occurred in conjunction with the first artistic exhibition on the subject of "comfort women."

One of the largest contributions of her presidency was to build the "Comfort Women Memorial Peace Garden" in Fairfax County, Virginia that is explained in chapter 10 (Fig. 1-15).

Fig. 1-15. Comfort Women Memorial Peace Garden, Fairfax, Virginia, Unveiling Ceremony on May 30, 2014. *Photo by Jung-Sil Lee*

When I became the fifth president of WCCW, I strived to organize academic events and work with institutions in terms of their specific missions. In 2015, during the Annual Kowinner International Convention, WCCW hosted a panel titled "Wartime Atrocity against Women: Comfort Women Case." In April 2016, WCCW was asked to invite former "comfort women" through the Department of Human Rights at Southern Methodist University in Dallas, Texas and they organized the testimonial event with WCCW.[46] I contacted the House of Sharing and mediated to invite grandmother Lee Ok-sun and the director Ahn Shin-kwon from the House of Sharing. The event turned out to be a huge success as it was the first visit of a "comfort woman" victim in the area and inspired a lot of people which led to the emergence of a new "comfort women" activism organization "Unforgotten Butterfly" led by Sinmin Park in 2019[47] (Fig. 1-16).

Fig. 1-16. Testimony by Lee Ok-sun at Southern Methodist University in Dallas, Texas, April 2016.

Each seminar and conference were geared towards the institution's mission, with close attention given to the needs of our collaborators in addition to contemporary emerging issues. For example, when WCCW organized the seminar and exhibition *The Sorrow and Hope of Comfort Women* in 2014 at Catholic University with the Center for International Social Development (CISD), its main goal was to promote international humanity in the interests of peace and justice. Reconciliation and healing were the key concepts of the seminar and exhibition, whereas the conference at the George Washington University collaborating with its History Department focused on "accurate history writing and history war" as termed by the Japanese right-wing in the midst of their history revisions.[48]

On May 2, 2016, WCCW organized the conference *History Writing: for Justice and Reconciliation of Comfort Women* cosponsored by the Sigur Center for Asian Studies at the George Washington University, as McGraw-Hill's history textbook included "comfort women" history. Prime Minister Shinzo Abe's administration requested the removal of the allegedly false information of it. McGraw-Hill responded, "Scholars are aligned behind the historical fact of 'comfort women,' and we unequivocally stand behind the writing, research, and presentation of our authors."[49] The conference was appropriately cosponsored with the Sigur Center for Asian Studies at George Washington University and its History department[50] (Fig. 1-17).

Fig. 1-17. "History Writing for Justice and Reconciliation of Comfort Women" conference, WCCW co-organized with the Sigur Center for Asian Studies and History Department at the George Washington University, May 2, 2016.

Later that year, on October 17th, the WCCW held another academic conference titled *Collateral Damage: Wartime Atrocity and Trauma* at John Jay College of Criminal Justice, City University of New York. The conference was held in conjunction with an art exhibition in the same building and many students visited both events as college professors gave an assignment about the "comfort women" issue. The college is one of the few nests of Human Rights Centers in the U.S. and its director was invited to speak. The "comfort women" issues were discussed and reflected on by diverse disciplines. Organizing the conference and exhibition simultaneously were huge tasks but mutually beneficial as the attendees received intellectual information while concurrently responding to it emotionally and visually[51] (Fig. 1-18).

Fig. 1-18. "Collateral Damage: Wartime Atrocity and Trauma," Conference at John Jay College of Criminal Justice, City University of New York, October 17, 2016.

In 2017, WCCW participated in a panel at the conference "Difficult Conversations: Thinking and Talking about Women, Genders, and Sexualities Inside and Outside of the Academy" at the 17th *Berkshire Conference on the History of Women, Genders, and Sexualities* held at Hofstra University, Hempstead, NY. It is the largest women's conference begun in 1973 born out of the women's movement and intended to celebrate "women's history." I was gladly surprised to learn there were two other panels on "comfort women" history in addition to ours. WCCW's panel title was "Narrative, Appropriation, and Styles of Objectivity when Confronting Crimes Against Humanity" where I, as an organizer and moderator, invited Prof. Chris Simson, Prof. Bonnie Oh, and Prof. Laura Barberán Reinares. The other panel titled "Comfort Women: Two Systems of Sexual Slavery and Historical Revisionism" chaired by Yukiko Hanawa consisted of presentations by Booja Kim, Akane Onozawa, and Tomomi Yamaguchi. Yuki Terazawa also chaired the panel "Exploring Issues of documenting and Preserving Survivors' Testimonies of Wartime Sexual Violence." I sensed the passion of the Japanese feminists and their dedication to justice for "comfort women" (A.1-21).

Another comprehensive two day-long conference "The Redress Movement for the Victims of Japanese Military Sexual Slavery: Looking back at the 27-year Movement" was held in Queens, NY on October 2017.[52] The organizer, Prof. Pyung Gap Min, invited most active and prominent "comfort women" scholars and activists in Asia and the U.S. I was co-presenter with the founding President Dongwoo Lee Hahm on behalf of WCCW. Since then, WCCW has been devoted to two educational objectives: the intern training program and the archiving project, one of which was realized through the high school intern book publication in 2019 and the other outcome is this volume.[53]

Fig. 1-19. "Year 2000 Remembrance: Women of Dignity and Honor" at the Rayburn House Office Building, Capitol Hill. Washington, D.C., September 20, 2000.

## Artistic Representation

Artistic representations are hard to be separated from any type of verbal presentations such as conferences, forums, or talks to intensify their impact and educational effect. In September 1994, President Hahm went to South Korea with Doochan Hahm, retired editor from *The Korea Times,* to interview victims and to record testimonies from 15 surviving victims. The interviews focused on their suffering in captivity and the belated campaign for justice; it turned into the first WCCW sponsored documentary *Comfort Women.* The film was screened in many locations along with the archival exhibition: the George Washington University, Wesley Seminary in Washington, D.C.; Falls Church, VA; the Fourth UN World Conference on Women, Beijing, China; Old Dominion University, Norfolk, VA; Chinese Community Center, Virginia Beach, VA; Atlantic Exhibition "The Forgotten Holocaust," Atlanta, GA; "The Asian Holocaust," St. Paul, MN; the UN, New York, NY; Free Library, Philadelphia, PA; the Church of Christ, Charlotte, NC; the University of Michigan, Ann Arbor, MI; and Cornell University, Ithaca, NY.[54]

WCCW organized a very unique event at the Rayburn House Office Building, Capitol Hill on September 20, 2000. It was a solemn commemoration to honor "comfort women." Nine surviving "comfort women" from across Asia were invited to attend the ceremony and to give testimonies to American audiences[55] (Fig. 1-19). The next day, WCCW organized a testimonial event at the U.S. Holocaust Museum, in Washington, D.C. In memory of those lost lives without names, WCCW placed a large empty white chair with a bouquet of yellow roses on it and wished honor and peace on their behalf. It could be called a "performance" or "installation" to mourn the victims. In conjunction

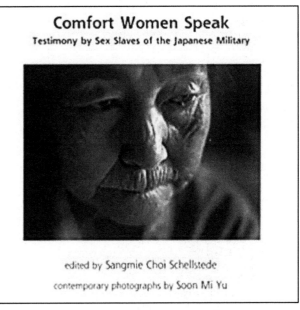

Fig. 1-20. Cover of WCCW first book, Comfort Women Speak: Testimony by Sex Slaves of the Japanese Military, 2000.

with "the Year 2000 Remembrance project," WCCW published its first book, *Comfort Women Speak: Testimony by Sex Slaves of the Japanese Military* (Fig. 1-20). The book includes testimonies of 19 "comfort women" survivors, photos of them, and excerpts of important documents of the UN and the International Commission of Jurists (ICJ).[56]

WCCW has been aware of the empowerment of the arts to convey "comfort women" history and has organized exhibitions, featuring primary sources and artistic reinterpretations. The artistic response to the theme of "comfort women" started to emerge in the arts world in various genres, including literature, film, visual art, and theater as discussed in detail in Chapter seven. After the first play, *Comfort Women* (1999 and 2004)[57] by Chungmi Kim, Dai Sil Kim-Gibson directed the film *Silence Broken* (2000), based on her book of the same title.[58] WCCW screened the film *Silence Broken* at the George Washington University in 2002 and then at Georgetown University in May, 2004, along with an exhibition of the art installation *Line of Violence* by Andrew Ward.[59] The most recent screening of *Silence Broken* was in 2014 at George Mason University in commemoration of the 20th anniversary of WCCW.

WCCW organized an archival exhibition titled "Comfort Women of World War II: An Indisputable Tragedy" at the Cannon House Office Building Rotunda, Capitol Hill, June 1–12, 1998. The exhibition was cosponsored by 30 community organizations, including the Congressional Human Rights Caucus, the Congressional Caucus on Women's Issues, the Congressional Asian Pacific American Caucus, and the Korea Society. For the opening ceremony, WCCW held a press conference with Korean and Filipino "comfort women" survivors, Kim Bok-dong and Losita Nacino, and Representatives Lane Evans and Robert A. Underwood. The Capitol Hill garden was packed with Congressional staff, students on field trips, tourists from around the world, and American, Korean, and Japanese journalists. The exhibition continued through from March 9–May 3, 1999, and later, the exhibition "Comfort Women of World War II" was held at the Free Library of Philadelphia[60] (Fig. 1-21).

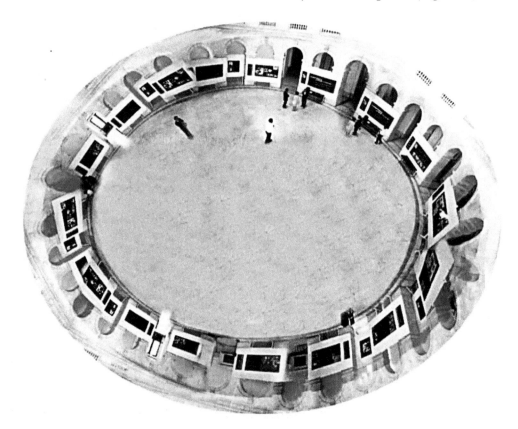

Fig. 1-21. WCCW organized exhibition "Comfort Women of World War II: An Indisputable Tragedy" at the Cannon House Office Building Rotunda, Capitol Hill, June 1–12, 1998.

## Archiving Project

Because surviving victims have aged and reached their nineties, once I became the fifth president, I have been dedicated to the mission of recording and archiving the history and activities of former "comfort women" and "supporters" to be accessible and teachable in the future. Ever since I became involved in the "comfort women" issue, I felt the urgency of education about the issue, both because of public ignorance of this history after all of WCCW's endeavors, and at the same time, the need and urgency of its educational materials by so-called "comfort women studies." The target audiences of education have been expanded from members of Congress (as well as other elected officers and lawmakers) and the general public to the younger generations such as college and high or middle school students, from Asian communities and scholars to non-Asian and pan-Asian communities. I was overwhelmed by various reasons for requests and by the diversity of requesters for primary or secondary documents to WCCW; politicians, activists, scholars, teachers, artists, filmmakers, students, NPOs, etc. all made requests. It compels me to explore all possible ways of education and strive to compile and archive materials related to "comfort women" history and activism.

As a result, the effort to archive diverse materials became one of the major missions of my presidency. WCCW launched a high school internship program and recruited college fellows since 2015. One of the challenging but rewarding experiments was a "webinar" project, first proposed by WCCW fellow, Hyewon Lee. The "History Writing" conference at the George Washington University was a capstone conference of the webinar project where students and WCCW interns met and learned through an online setting from activists and professors who are experts on the issue. [61] The pilot program went well. Webinar courses and seminars should be further explored in order to appeal to our media-oriented society along with other web-based "comfort women" material such as cell phone applications. Since 2016, WCCW launched the "WCCW Webinar and Archiving Project" to collect, archive, compile, and study primary and secondary sources regarding "comfort women" in order to bring to light the historical evidence in an organized way. [62] WCCW believes that a repository of documents and artifacts related to "comfort women" for posterity will bring many outcomes. Furthermore, this repository will be one of many sources that future historians who wish to document this painful era will be able to refer to. The mission of WCCW is to inform future generations of the women's movements and to rectify recorded history. To this end, it has been an immensely useful and ongoing project although we have a long way to go (Fig. 1-22).

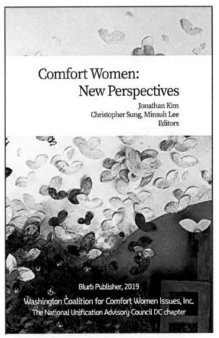

Fig. 1-22. WCCW intern book, *Comfort Women: New Perspectives*, edited by Jonathan Kim, Christopher Sung and Min Suh Lee, Blurb Publisher, November 2019.

WCCW has taken a leading role in teaching others and working toward a just and equitable final requiem for the survivors. At the same time, WCCW strives to view the issue holistically rather than as a single-issue coalition.[63] Our urgent mission is to archive the 28 years of WCCW activities and the "comfort women" movement at large through its primary and secondary sources and make it available to the next generation in order for them to remember the past and to understand that our issues transcend time and place. The vision of WCCW is to reach out to a larger audience through media and to keep this issue of "comfort women" alive long after its last victim has passed on. Our ultimate goal is to shine a light on the past, present, and future of the "comfort women" movement in its entirety, and to historicize and to commemorate stories of grandmothers in the right place (A.1-22 and A.1-23) (Fig. 1-23 and Fig. 1-24).

Fig. 1-23. H.Res. 121 10th Anniversary Ceremony group photo. Rayburn House Office Building, Washington D.C. July 27, 2017.

Fig. 1-24. Cake cutting ceremony by WCCW presidents during the WCCW 25th Anniversary Ceremony and the Banquet. The USG Conference Center, UMGC, MD, December 16, 2017.

[1] Japanese military "comfort women" is a controversial term in itself as victims never meant to comfort anybody and hate the term. The term and concept of "comfort women" originated from Japan's brothels industry. As a result, the UN has preferred to use the term "enforced sex slaves," while survivors have generally preferred to be called "grandmother," a respectful position and affectionate term in Asian countries. For Japan's "comfort women" system, *see* Caroline Norma, *The Japanese Comfort Women and Sexual Slavery During the China and Pacific Wars* (London: Bloomsbury, 2016).

[2] There were three reasons for the Japanese military to run comfort stations: to prevent the chronic problem of rapes outside of military camps, to prevent sexually transmitted diseases, and to cheer up Japanese soldiers. "Comfort stations" were under the direction of Japanese Army Central Command. Yoshimi Yoshiaki, *Comfort Women: Sexual Slavery in the Japanese Military During World War II* (New York: Columbia University Press, 1995), 84–85.

[3] *See* the list of other organizations who are working for the "comfort women" issue in Resource #9.

[4] Soon Im Kang, interviews by Jung-Sil Lee, April 28, May 4, 2018, and December 31, 2019.

[5] The remark by Chairman Yoon Mee-hyang that The Korean Council planted the "comfort women" issue in the United States referred to this coalition with New York activists. Yoon Mee-hyang, interview by Jung-Sil Lee, October 13, 2017 and Pastor Yong-ho Kim, interview by Jung-Sil Lee, May 12, 2018.

[6] Pastor Yong-ho Kim, interview by Jung-Sil Lee, May 12, 2018.

[7] Ibid.

[8] Ustinia Dolgopol Snehal Paranjape, *Comfort Women: an Unfinished Ordeal - Report of Mission* (Geneva, Switzerland: International Commission of Jurists, 1994), 7–8.

[9] For the whole content of Hwang's testimony *see* Dai Sil Kim-Gibson, *Silence Broken: Korean Comfort Women* (Iowa: Mid-Prairie Books Parkersburg, 1999), 12–31. Kim Gibson as a translator recorded the whole testimony.

[10] JoJo Swords, "Grassroots Activism: Make that Change," *ThoughtWorks,* November 16, 2017, https://www.thoughtworks.com/insights/blog/grassroots-activism-make-change.

[11] The mission statement of WCCW has expanded its concern toward the current day's sex trafficking issue and women's rights to collaborate with other organizations who share common interests.

[12] In 1904, Ahn Chang Ho (pen name Dosan) moved to California and established the first Korean American community in the U.S. called "Pachappa Camp." Dosan helped to found a local employment agency and negotiated labor agreements to form a "Gongnip Hyeophoe," or Cooperative Association, to foster a sense of community. The Gongnip Hyeophoe eventually developed into the Korean National Association. They participated in Korean Independence. Edward T. Chang and Hannah Brown "Pachappa Camp: the First Koreatown in the United States," *California History*, 95, no. 3 (Fall 2018): 46–56, accessed March 18, 2019, https://ch.ucpress.edu/content/95/3/46.

[13] Ethan Pak, "Los Angeles Riots: A Transition in Identity for Korean Americans," *Pacific Ties* (April 29, 2017), https://pacificties.org/los-angeles-riots-a-transition-in-identity-for-korean-americans/ "Many 1.5- and 2nd-generation Korean Americans established new organizations immediately following the riots. Organizations such as "the Koreatown Youth" and "Community Center and Koreatown Immigrant Workers Alliance" attempted to address post-riot needs and build connections to acquire resources. Others began establishing partisan organizations such as "the Korean American Democratic Committee."

[14] Dongwoo Lee Hahm recalls that her attendance at the Japanese International Symposium, *Asian Women for Peace* in April 1993 and meeting with Ms. Doy Takako, the keynote speaker who offered the key mission of WCCW, that was to garner action through the influence of the U.S. government; to urge the U.S. Congress Members to place political pressure on the Japanese government with a belief that "Only American Government pressure works for the Japanese government." Doy Takako was the Chairwoman of *Japan's Social Party.*

[15] Yoon Mee-hyang, *Wednesday for Twenty Years* (Seoul: Woongjin Junior, 2010), 21–28; she explains its origin, content, and purpose. It officially names "Wednesday Demonstration" demanding Japan to redress the "comfort women" issue. The Korean Council summarizes the seven demands of the demonstration as: 1. Acknowledge and admit responsibility for the drafting of sex slaves; 2. Make an official apology; 3. Reveal the truth of the past in its entirety about the crimes of military sexual slavery; 4. Erect memorials and a museum for

Comfort Women

the victims; 5. Make legal reparations to the victims; 6. Punish those responsible for the war crime; 7. Accurately record the crime in history textbooks.

[16] Moon Hyung Rhee (former co-chair of WCCW) was one of the leading figures for collecting signatures, Lecture on archival material of WCCW, at the Annual Forum of WCCW at KUSCO, Virginia, February 21, 2015.

[17] WCCW had no such fund. Founding President Dongwoo Lee Hahm recalls "I made the decision to take early retirement from the international organization where I had worked for 25 years. Fortunately, I became eligible to retire at the end of May 1993 and was able to avail the retirement fund for the publication in September of 1993. It was not an easy decision then. Now, I look back upon the past twenty-seven years of the "comfort women" movement, I consider it was the best decision I have made of which I am proud." Interview by Jung-Sil Lee, October 14, 2017.

[18] Dongwoo Lee Hahm, in her presentation in 2017, New York conference.

[19] C. Sarah Soh, *The Comfort Women: Sexual Violence and Postcolonial Memory in Korea and Japan* (Chicago and London: The University of Chicago Press, 2008), 80-81; the author explains "testimonial narratives" of victims in terms of their life stories filled with *han* narratives, but Soh focuses more on their formative years before their recruitment to show how the intersection of gender, class, and labor in the colonial capitalist system so exploited and victimized young women.

[20] During the unveiling ceremony of the *Comfort Women Memorial Peace Garden* (2014) and its anniversaries (2015, 2016) organized by WCCW, *salpuri* dancers were invited to perform in front of the victims and the audience.

[21] Christine Choi, interview by Jung-Sil Lee, May 2018.

[22] "South Korean Wartime Sex Slave Demands Apology from Abe," *CCTV*, April 24, 2015, https://www.youtube.com/watch?v=asymWeFO8pQ.

[23] Pamela Constable, "70 Years later, a Korean 'Comfort Women' demands apology from Japan" *The Washington Post,* April 22, 2015, https://www.washingtonpost.com/local/70-years-later-a-korean-comfort-woman-demands-apology-from-japan/2015/04/22/d1cf8794-e7ab-11e4-9767-6276fc9b0ada_story.html; "Comfort Women" during World War II demand an apology from Japan," *Al Jazeera America News,* April 29, 2015, http://america.aljazeera.com/watch/shows/live-news/2015/4/comfort-women-during-world-war-ii-demand-an-apology-from-japan.html; Eni Faleomavaega, "Time for Japan to apologize," *The Hill* , March 2015, https://thehill.com/blogs/congress-blog/foreign-policy/235134-time-for-japan-to-apologize; Jung-Sil Lee "China's Role in WWII, *The Heat, CCTV,* September 3, 2015, https://america.cgtn.com/2015/09/03/the-heat-chinas-role-in-wwii.

[24] Far before the first submission of the "comfort women" Resolution in 2000, Congressman William O. Lipinski introduced House Concurrent Resolution 126 in 1997 which expressed that the Japanese government should formally apologize for the war crimes committed by the Japanese military in World War II and pay reparations to the victims. By the end of 1998, in the 105th Congress, nearly 80 additional Members of Congress put their support behind the resolution by formally cosponsoring it; Jason Tai, "Let us Never Forget," *WCCW Newsletter* 5, 2002, 1–2.; For the complete steps and details regarding "comfort women" related resolutions *see Chapter* 3 contributed by Mindy Kotler who also summarized the history of the "comfort women" Resolution on her archiving website. "Comfort Women Legislative History in the U.S. Congress" August 15, 2007, http://www.jiaponline.org/resources/documents/ComfortWomenResolutionLegislativeHistory.pdf.

[25] Ok Cha Soh and Lane Evans, "Legislation on 'Comfort Women' in the U.S. Congress," in *Forced Prostitution in Times of War and Peace: Sexual Violence against Women and Girls*, eds. Barbara Drinck and Chung-noh Gross (Bielefeld: Kleine Verlag, 2007), 288.

[26] Ok Cha Soh, *Becoming Your Voice: Ok Cha Soh, Lane Evans, and "Japanese Comfort Women"* (Seoul: Sechang Media, 2015), 119–120.

[27] Mike Honda's remarks to the Korean National Assembly, "Peace and Prosperity in Northeast Asia," December 19, 2014.

28

[28] Inscription of the Japanese American memorial as "On February 19, 1942, 73 days after the U.S. entered WWII, President F. D. Roosevelt issued Executive Order 9066 which resulted in the removal of 120,000 Japanese American men, women, and children from their homes in the western states and Hawaii. . . . In 1983, almost forty years after the war ended, the federal Commission on Wartime Relocation and Internment of Civilians found that there had been no military necessity for the mass imprisonment of Japanese Americans and that a grave injustice had been done. In 1988, President Ronald W. Reagan signed the Civil Liberties Act which made an apology for the injustice, provided minimal compensation, and reaffirmed the nation's commitment to equal justice under the law for all Americans."

[29] Mike Honda, "The U.S. Demands Apology for Comfort Women," interview by Cheryl Corley, *Tell Me More, NPR*, July 31, 2007.

[30] In June, the Japanese Ambassador Ryozo Kato warned the United States that passage of the resolution would "almost certainly have lasting and harmful effects on the deep friendship, close trust and wide-ranging cooperation our two nations now enjoy." Justin McCurry, "Japan Rejects the U.S. Calls for Apology Over 'Comfort Women,'" *The Guardian*, July 31, 2007.

[31] The word "responsibility" was added to Resolution 759 and the word "unequivocal" added for the final Resolution of 121, along with the acknowledgment of the Kono Statement. *See* the changes and differences among "comfort women" memorials. "The Positive Interaction between Comfort Women Memorials and House Resolutions in the U.S.," by Joey D. Kim, *Comfort Women New Perspectives*, eds. by Jonathan D. Kim, Christopher Sung, and Min Suh Lee (San Francisco: Blurb Publisher, 2019), 44-58.

[32] Jinyang Koh, "Comfort Women: Human Rights of Women from Then to Present," *University of Georgia School of Law, LLM Theses and Essays*, 79, 2007: McDougall Report I, supra note 87, Karen Parker and Jennifer F. Chew, "Compensation for Japan's World War II War-Rape Victims," 17; Hastings Int'l & Comp. L. Rev. 497, 516 (1994), https://digitalcommons.law.uga.edu/stu_llm/79.

[33] "Confronting Historical Injustice: Comparative Perspectives, Slavery and Justice." Report of the Brown University, Steering Committee on Slavery and Justice, Brown University, 2003-2006, accessed August 2018, https://www.brown.edu/Research/Slavery_Justice/documents/SlaveryAndJustice.pdf.

[34] Kinue Tokudome, "Passage of H.Res. 121 on 'comfort women,' the U.S. Congress and Historical Memory in Japan," *The Asia-Pacific Journal*, Japan Focus 5, no. 8 (2007): 8.

[35] Ok Cha Soh, from the note of summary of the U.S. House Hearing, Subcommittee on Asia, the Pacific, and the Global Environment Committee on Foreign Affairs, February 15, 2007.

[36] Tokudome, "Passage," 4.

[37] The impact of the Hearing was great enough to publish the full-page advertisement "The Facts" in *The Washington Post* by Japanese revisionists and denialists on June 14, 2007 to disturb the sympathetic mood toward the "comfort women" issue in the D.C. area, https://www.jiaponline.org/documents/Jun14AdALLSignatoriesLIST.pdf.

[38] Director Dongsuk Kim from KACE joined around "the February Hearing" and started the grassroots campaign in California, New York, and Seattle while Ok Cha Soh, president of WCCW reached out to most Congress Members nationwide thanks to her long-time friendship with Rep. Lane Evans. Ok Cha Soh, interview by Jung-Sil Lee, August 20, 2018.

[39] Maryland Senate Joint Resolution 3, Senators Lee, Bates, Montgomery, Nathan–Pulliam, Ready, Conway, Pinsky, Kagan, Rosapepe, Salling, Simonaire, Waugh, and Young, introduced and read for the first time: February 6, 2015, Assigned to: Education, Health, and Environmental Affairs. Read second time March 13, 2015; they proposed "Honoring the Surviving Human Trafficking Victims of Asia and the Pacific Islands During World War II," http://mgaleg.maryland.gov/2015rs/bills_noln/sj/tsj0003.pdf.

[40] Mutsuko Miki advocated for the official compensation of "comfort women" in 1995 but joined the Asian Women's Fund, a charity established by the Tomiichi Murayama administration to compensate former "comfort women" that was not regarded as an "official and legal" reparation demanded by victims. Inviting her to the U.S. conference was criticized only because of her linkage to the Asian Women's Fund by some activists, yet, it is hard to devaluate her passion, conviction, and activism on the "comfort women" issue and victims.

[41] Pierre Thomas, "War Crimes List Bars 16 Japanese from the U.S.," *The Washington Post*, December 4, 1996, accessed February 25, 2019, https://www.washingtonpost.com/archive/politics/1996/12/04/war-crimes-list-bars-16-japanese-from-us/2dc9a6a0-a607-42b8-8f44-83d9c31a65cb/.

[42] President Bill Clinton speech excerpt: "The life of our nation has been continually renewed and enriched by the generations of people who have chosen to come here and become our fellow citizens. Each has brought a part of his or her own heritage, which over time becomes part of our common heritage—you can be proud of your roots and of the outstanding contributions [that] the Korean American people have made to our national life. You can be proud as well of your efforts to encourage the full participation of Korean Americans in the political, social, and economic life of our nation. As you gather as KASCON XIII to reflect on your shared history and to prepare for the challenges of the future, you have my best wishes for a productive and enjoyable conference," February 24, 1999.

[43] *See* the cited statement by George Hicks on report of The Korean Council regarding their and the victims' resolution not to accept the Treaty on Basic Relations between Japan and the Republic of Korea of 1965 regarding "comfort women" issues that had not emerged to the surface, nor mentioned. The author also includes the report of 1992 from the Japanese government and South and North Korean governments on "comfort women" issues. George Hicks, *The Comfort Women: Japan's Brutal Regime of Enforced Prostitution in the Second World War* (New York, London: W.W. Norton & Company), 220–236.

[44] Most WCCW statements throughout the years include these two demands: "official apology" and "legal reparation."

[45] Margaret Stetz, "Teaching about the 'Comfort System' of World War II: The Hidden Stories of Girls," in *War and Sexual Violence: New Perspectives in a New Era*, ed. Sarah K. Danielsson (Verlag Ferdinand Schoningh, 2019), 35–50.

[46] Due to more than 20 years of grassroots activities, many people search for resources and ask WCCW to share what we advocate; we are inundated with countless requests for lectures, talks, and materials.

[47] Unforgotten Butterflies, 2019, https://www.facebook.com/unforgottenbutterflies/.

[48] Japanese right-wing supporters denied that the Japanese government had committed any war crimes, claiming the women were not forcefully conscripted but were "well-paid and voluntary prostitutes." Onozawa Akane, "The Comfort Women and State Prostitution," *The Asia-Pacific Journal*, Japan Focus 10, no. 1 (2018): 16.

[49] Martin Fackler, "The U.S. Textbook Skews History, Prime Minister of Japan Says," *The New York Times*, January 29, 2015, accessed November 17, 2019, https://www.nytimes.com/2015/01/30/world/asia/japans-premier-disputes-us-textbooks-portrayal-of-comfort-women.html.

[50] The conference was held to celebrate the 2nd anniversary of the Comfort Women Memorial Peace Garden and as a Capstone Conference of the WCCW Webinar Project and co-chaired by Jung-Sil Lee and Jisoo Kim, Professor of History at GWU. The presentation topics were: Tomomi Yamaguchi "The History War and the Comfort Women Issue: Revisionism and the Right-Wing in contemporary Japan"; Bonnie Oh "Comfort Women Testimonies as Oral History"; Elizabeth Son "Performing Comfort Women Histories in Redressive Theatre."

[51] The conference *Collateral Damage: Wartime Atrocity and Trauma* was cosponsored by WCCW and Northeast Asian History Foundation and panel participants were Jung-Sil Lee (chair and organizer), Thalia Vrachopoulos (co-chair), George Andreopoulos ("The Moral and Legal Vocabulary of 'Collateral Damage'"), Bonnie Oh ("Collateral Damage Again"), Laura Barberán Reinares ("The Ethics of Representing Sexual Violence"), Tomomi Emoto ("Remembering, Performing, and Historicizing the Past in Postcolonial Japan and Korea").

[52] The Research Center for Korean Community at Queens College, *The Redress Movement for the Victims of Japanese Military Sexual Slavery: Looking Back at the 27 Year Movement*, Flushing, New York, October 13–14, 2017: participants were Alexis Dudden, Margaret Stetz, Bonnie Oh, Peipei Qiu, Na-Young Lee, Puja Kim, Mee-hyang Yoon, Shin-kwon Ahn, Angella Son, Tomomi Yamaguchi, Emi Koyama, Jung-Sil Lee, Dongwoo Lee Hahm, Mary McCarthy, Phyllis Kim, Judith Mirkinson, and Mina Watanabe.

[53] Jonathan D. Kim, Christopher Sung, and Min Suh Lee, eds. *Comfort Women: New Perspectives* (San Francisco: Blurb Publisher, 2019): eight students contributed either essays or research papers as a result of their intern training and year-long learning with the WCCW intern program. Their names are Jonathan D. Kim, Yuni Choi, Joey D. Kim, Jeanie Chang, Jehoon Seo, Yena Sossou, Ha Yan Lee (Triple A Project), and Min Suh Lee.

[54] Many reporters covered the issues of "comfort women" during the travelling exhibitions and WCCW was able to provide archival photos to *Time* magazine and the *U.S. News & World Report*. The "comfort women" issue was featured in; *Time* Magazine, June 17, 1996 and *U.S. News & World Report*, December 16, 1996. Dongwoo Lee Hahm, interview by Jung-Sil Lee.

[55] WCCW invited 10 former "comfort women" but only nine could attend: Kim Sang-hi, Kim Sook-duck, Kim Eun-ry, Lee Yong-soo, Moon Pil-gi, Hwang Keum-ju, Lola Ammonita, Lola Prescila, Liu Hauangar-tau. Presentation by Dongwoo Lee Hahm, 2017 New York conference.

[56] Sangmie Choi Schellstede, ed. *Comfort Women Speak: Testimony by Sex Slaves of the Japanese Military* (New York/London: Holmes & Meier, 2001).

[57] Chungmi Kim, *Comfort Women* [formerly called Hanako] (1999, 2004).

[58] Dai Sil Kim-Gibson, *Silence Broken: Korean Comfort Women* (Parkersburg, IA: Mid-Prairie Books, 1999).

[59] Dai Sil Kim-Gibson and I were invited to give the lecture when *Line of Violence* was exhibited by Penn Asian Senior Services (PASSI) on May 26, 2015 at International House Philadelphia. The work was originally created in 1998 by Andrew Ward, a Scottish artist, in collaboration with Jonathan Sisson (International Fellowship of Reconciliation). It reveals hand silhouettes of 53 former comfort women in two half circle installations measuring 7 1/2' high and 24' in total length. It was purchased by the Kyungnam museum in Korea on August 2015.

[60] The exhibition showcased archival photography of "comfort women" collected and duplicated from the National Archives and Records Administration II in Maryland; photos included black-and-white photography of "comfort women" when they were young at "comfort stations" in different locations.

[61] "In order to make its historical truth apparent and visible, and to ascertain diverse historical evidence, WCCW believes a web-based seminar (webinar) format that encompasses global participants is an appropriate and effective tool to collect the untapped and undiscovered sources and documents scattered all over the world. In addition, this project will bring tremendous value to our plan for creating a repository for documents and artifacts related to the history and current issues of 'comfort women.' From this, many types of soft-powered material or content will be created, such as book, paper, theses, articles film, artwork, educational material, journal, and other media. The Comfort Women Webinar Project will consist of a combination of lectures, presentations, workshops, and discussions that is broadcast over the web using specific video conferencing software. A key feature of a webinar is its interactive elements and collaborative nature—the ability to give, receive, discuss, and archive information." From "Objectives of the Project," part of the Syllabus of Webinar Pilot Program session, November 1, 2015.

[62] Full Syllabus for the Webinar Pilot Program in the spring 2016, see *Comfort Women: New Perspectives*, 131-135.

[63] Jung-Sil Lee, "The Future of the 'Comfort Women' Movement in Korea," *Washington Times*, October 14, 2015, C20. Accessed February 25, 2019, https://www.washingtontimes.com/news/2015/oct/14/jungsil-lee-the-future-of-the-comfort-women-movement/.

# 2. HOUSE RESOLUTION 121 (110TH CONGRESS) INTERVIEW WITH REPRESENTATIVE MIKE HONDA (D-CA)

*Mike Honda and edited by Mindy L. Kotler*

August 5, 2019:       Lydia Yi and Fletcher Calcagno
                      Asia Policy Point, Research Assistants

December 4, 2019:    Fletcher Calcagno, Asia Policy Point, Research Assistant
                      Edited by Mindy L. Kotler, Asia Policy Point, Director

---

*The following transcript has been edited for clarity.*

## REP. HONDA'S INTRODUCTION TO THE COMFORT WOMEN ISSUE

*Yi:* **How did you first get involved in the *"comfort women"* issue? Did you know about it beforehand or when did you really learn about it?**

*Rep. Honda*: The reason we're talking about "comfort women" is because I got involved in the late 1970s with some guys to move the Japanese American community and make a movement where President [Ronald] Reagan apologized to our community and he cited the Constitution and offered restitution.[1] But the big thing was that he recognized that the incarceration of Japanese Americans was based upon racial prejudice, war hysteria, and the failure, not the lack of, but the failure of political leadership.

So, I first discussed with you a mindset, you know, when I look at something and how I look at it. I got to know about this issue back in 1994. I sent my Chief of Staff Keith Honda [a cousin of Rep. Honda] back when I was on the Board of Supervisors[2] down in the County of Santa Clara to a photo exhibit at Stanford University that was hosted by the Alliance for Preserving the Truth of the Sino-Japanese War.[3] [This is] a Chinese American group funded by David and Cathy Tsang and they had that exhibit of POWs in the Philippines and they had photos and discussions around Unit 731, then they had photos and discussions around the sexual slavery issue in the areas where the Japanese had occupied Asia. And my Chief of Staff came back and said he felt ill after seeing all that. So, we decided that over time we were going to try and figure out how to do something about it, so we started to learn about the issue.

Once I got into the [California] State Assembly in 1996,[4] I started to pull information and people together [on Pacific War history]. This meant POWs who survived camps, Bataan, and being slaves in the Japanese mines. And I kept in touch with the Global Alliance folks. I [learned] more about [Unit] 731, and finally in 1999 I started to put together a Resolution called Assembly Joint Resolution 27,[5] which essentially asked[6] [the U.S.] Congress to urge Japan to recognize their actions between the years of 1932-1945, and recognize its historical responsibility.

Because of that, I started to get engaged with the Japanese Consulate in San Francisco. They met with me in my office a few times privately and they asked why I'm doing this. They were very confused and upset, and I told them it's the right thing to do, and then I explained the rationale that governments aren't individuals, they're an organ of a society, and they're responsible for the actions of the past, and they should move forward and recognize their mistakes and apologize.

And they were very confused because I looked Japanese and they asked "why are you doing this to us?" and I said "I'm asking you as a nation to apologize to the victims because I think it's an appropriate thing to do." And they said "well your State Assembly has nothing to do with the national stuff, so it's improper and you're out of place." So, I said "Okay just watch me." So, I got a pass, but I got a pass not without some difficulties.

I did not know there was a letter written by a woman named Irene Hirano[7] who was head of the National Japanese Museum [*sic*] in LA [Los Angeles] and she circulated a letter among the members of the Assembly saying this was an unnecessary, ill-conceived bill, and they should not support it. So, it was circulated, but I never saw it until later when I got a hold of that letter and I asked her if she was authorized by her Board to do this, and she said no. And I said, "Well, you should get authorization because you're acting as an individual, but you appear to have the authority of an organization, and if you're not, then you need to leave out the organization and just say this as an individual."

So, we had our battles and she had a cohort who was an assemblyman, George Nakano,[8] who represented Torrance and he circulated a [draft] resolution supposedly to neutralize mine and give the Assembly people a choice between mine and his. His essentially said that it's a resolution to study man's inhumanity to man [with no reference to Japan] and he was getting signatures so I just asked him "Are you doing this?" And finally, he admitted he was doing it, but he didn't ever admit as to why he was doing it.

Then he wanted a meeting with me and the Speaker of the Assembly,[9] which we did, and the Speaker supported my Resolution and his, and I said, "I'll sign yours because I think it's a broad thing, but it's got good intentions." And I asked if he [Nakano] wanted to sign mine and he said "Oh no, no." And the Speaker said George [Nakano] wanted two more weeks to work on his Resolution and I said, "Hell, I'll give him a month." And I got my Resolution through, and then the Consul General[10] [San Francisco] lost his job, and this resolution went to Congress,[11] and that's where I think [Congressman] Lane Evans [D-IL] comes into the picture along with [Congressman William] Lipinski [D-IL].

So that's how it started, and then I go to Congress in 2001,[12] and I said to myself "Oh we're at a national level now, let's do this again." And that's when I found out that Lane Evans and Lipinski had attempted to get a [similar] bill through, I'm not sure what the numbers were.

So, going through your questions, I didn't realize that Evans had done that until I was there working on this issue for a while. I got to be friends with Lane Evans, unbeknownst to me that he had been the author of a resolution on "comfort women." We became great friends and we hung out together, and later on I found out he had written this and that endeared him to me even more.

He had to retire because of his health [Parkinson's Disease as a result of exposure to Agent Orange], and before he left, I said I'd like to pick up and continue the issue, and so I started working on it.

The point here is that since I sent it [my Assembly resolution AJR 27] to Congress in 1999 to the time I got to Congress, Lane Evans and those guys were working on the issue as I was, the point is we got nowhere in our committees mainly because the Republican Party was in charge, right? After [House] Resolution 121 was passed, it became really popular among different folks, and so we started to take advantage of its passage politically and personally. I think that after reflecting on it, why didn't those folks who were chairmen of the Foreign Relations Committee and the Judiciary Committee, take the leadership in their own party to push this? Because after it got passed, they said they were very supportive, [but] you didn't see them actively doing anything. It was the [Asian American] community and our office that kept pushing it as an issue.

When [House] Resolution 121 passed they said "Congratulations, this is a wonderful thing that happened." And I said "This is just the first step. We have to follow through." Because I knew this Resolution didn't have any teeth. It just had public exposure and the public exposure has the power of the press and the only press that took it seriously was the Korean press. It became more popular in South Korea, and it had a [negative] reputation in Japan because the government was fighting it tooth and nail, suppressing newspapers that were reporting it, encouraging right-wing newspapers to defame it, and they started to pressure professors and activists.

So, the Japanese government got really active in it, while the U.S. government was just doing what it usually does. It didn't pay attention to it that much. But, when [Resolution] 121 was passed nine countries did follow suit. Thus, the impact of passing 121 was it brought it to the public eye, at a higher level, the issue of "comfort women" internationally. But none of that stuff wouldn't have happened if the women in South Korea didn't have the courage to speak up and break their silence. Breaking their silence was the major thing that happened, and in terms of paying homage, it is to those women that said they want to fight back and regain their own dignity and their own spirit and their own self-worth that was stripped of them as victims when they were young girls.

But they also had to fight cultural norms and finally the Korean community has gotten past the issue of them being shameful victims of the War to being courageous speakers for social justice and women's rights. I think we aided in that, but it was they who initiated in it, and them that we need to be cognizant of.

## CONGRESSMAN HONDA'S JAPANESE AMERICAN IDENTITY

*Yi*: **Thank you for that. Do you think that when you were going through this process, and you brought up that you talked to the Japanese Consulate, do you think you were more harshly judged because of your Japanese American identity?**

*Rep. Honda:* I don't think at that time they were being harsh. They were being diplomatic, and they acted confused and frustrated and one of them said "I spent this whole summer without a vacation because of you." What started to happen once it was passed at the state level and I was in Congress, newspapers would write, and right-wing media programs would interview me through satellite and ask questions like "Why are you doing this? Your face is..."

I don't think he [the Japanese diplomat] had the right words to say it because his English wasn't as broad as he needed, but what he meant was "You have a Japanese face?" I told them that I'm an American of Japanese descent, and it doesn't matter about being Japanese or not. The issue is that these women were violated and victimized by a systematic military process that put them into servitude. And that means they should be apologized to, and it should be an unambiguous apology.

You [Japan] should accept historical responsibility and offer reparations and put this episode into the textbooks of the children of Japan, so that they would not repeat the same mistakes because they were whitewashing Japan's military activities in Asia. I learned through this process how adept Japanese diplomats were, including Abe, in how they can say "We acknowledge, but it didn't really happen. Oh yes, we're upset for the suffering that they went through" rather than accepting that they were the ones that imposed that suffering.

[The Japanese diplomats and Abe say] that they [the "comfort women"] were not coerced. But if you're kidnapped or lied to, if you're tricked into something, I'm not sure you can get away with saying something isn't coercion.

## USAGE OF THE TERM "COERCION"

*Calcagno:* **Speaking about coercion, we know that coerce at the time was a buzzword so to speak of the Japanese right, do you think that the usage of the word "coerce" in**

Resolution was intentional? Was it symbolic for you? Or did it just happen to be the right word?

*Rep. Honda*: It was descriptive. They [the "comfort women"] were kidnapped and coerced into sexual slavery; they were coerced and held against their will, they were lied to; they were beaten; they were raped. So, they [the Japanese Right] try to mince words and the more they try to mince words the more pissed off I get. After a few years you get tired of being diplomatic towards the government, not so much the people. And this has to be clear, it's [the Resolution] not against the Japanese people, it's putting the Japanese leadership as responsible.

There were Japanese politicians that were trying to introduce appropriate bills [to the Diet]. The Democratic Party of Japan had power for about two years, but because of 70 years of LDP [rule] in a growing democracy, you get bureaucrats put into the system that disdain the [new] dominant party's position, practices, and policies. The bureaucracy continues to maintain a certain position.

## FOLLOW UP DECEMBER 4, 2019: USAGE OF THE WORD COERCION

*Calcagno*: **I understand that the word "coercion" was not in the original draft of the resolution. Do you recall how it ended up in the final text?**

*Rep. Honda*: Well, it was coercion. Kidnapping, coercion, lying. There were a variety of techniques that the Japanese military, and the people used to capture these girls. They would say that you have a job waiting for you in Japan, or China, things like that. Or they would outright capture them. There were two sisters who were French in what is now Vietnam, they were captured by Japanese officers, and they were used for sexual slavery, and both of those girls ended up dead.[13] But that's all recorded. So coercion is an accurate term.

*Calcagno*: **Of course, we just wondered if you knew who decided to include it in the resolution.**

*Rep. Honda*: Our staff, me. Yes, that's the word that the Japanese government didn't want to see there.

## PRIME MINISTER SHINZO ABE'S MARCH 1, 2007[14] STATEMENT

*Calcagno*:  **Abe specifically has said that Korean women were not "coerced" so to speak, is this surprising in any way? Is this an evolution or change from the way that you talked to Japanese diplomats when you were in the process of trying to pass the resolution? Or is it just the same rhetoric?**

*Rep. Honda:* No, when this [the "comfort women" issue] first came out in I think it was '92 [1993], the Secretary of the Cabinet Kono had done the research and came up with a comment that actually recognizes the act and the facts, he based his comment on research done by primary information and scholars. When he came out [with the Kono Statement], they were going to move forward on the issue, but it didn't get past the Chief Secretary of the Cabinet, and it didn't get through the Diet, so it didn't become law like we [in the U.S. Congress] made H.R. 442 into law [Civil Liberties Act of 1988: Restitution for World War II internment of Japanese-Americans and Aleuts].[15]

The signing by President [Ronald] Reagan that put it into the record that it was a mistake and it was based upon three things and they apologized unambiguously. That's why when we talk about internment of Muslims or travel bans, or putting illegal immigrants in camps, people understand that we had a precedent in doing so, and we learned that that was a mistake and we shouldn't do it again. That was the lesson learned, and that was the lesson that needs to be taken on in the Japanese government and the Japanese public-school system, and it needs to be nailed down as such so that it's not a fleeting action that will soon be forgotten but has to be embedded in their books.

## FOLLOW UP DECEMBER 4, 2019: HENRY HYDE'S COMFORT WOMEN LEGISLATION

*Calcagno:* **Please talk a little bit about Congressman Henry Hyde's attempts to get "comfort women" legislation passed in the House International Relations Committee in 2006.**

*Rep. Honda:* Congressman Henry Hyde [R-IL] did not have a resolution at the time. In 2006 [109th Congress] Lane Evans had a resolution. It was similar to earlier ones he had introduced in previous Congresses, but it never got anywhere because the Republicans were in charge. Usually, the resolution floundered in the International Relations Committee, which Hyde chaired.

*Calcagno:* **Lane's resolution [H.Con.Res. 68 (House Concurrent Resolution)] was rewritten by Hyde's staff and reintroduced as H.Res. 759. It had 58 cosponsors and Hyde made sure that it was approved by the International Relations Committee. Can you tell us how the transfer of responsibility went from the 2006 work on the "comfort women" to your hands?**

*Rep. Honda:* It never came from Hyde. I worked on it in 1999 in the State of California and sent that resolution over to the Congress, and I suspect that Lane Evans had picked up on it and tried to get it passed through the [International Relations] Committee. I suspect that was because of lobbying by people like Ray[mond] Calamaro and Bob [Robert] Michel, who was a former congressman from Illinois and House Minority Leader. Those two were lobbyists for the Government of Japan from Hogan & Hartson. I suspect that Bob Michel kept [Speaker of the House, Dennis] Hastert from ever having it come to the floor.

***Calcagno*: And Congressman Lantos and Evans?**

***Rep. Honda:*** Well [House Foreign Affairs[16] Chairman Tom] Lantos [D-CA] got it because we got it out of the [Asia, the Pacific, and the Global Environment] subcommittee. Lantos was reluctant enough getting it out of Committee, so Eni Faleomavaega [D-AS] on his own, as subcommittee chairman put it up for discussion and put it on his agenda in 2007 because in 2007 [November 2006 elections] we took over control of Congress and so Lantos became chair. It's my understanding that he didn't have the initiative, but Eni Faleomavaega did, and he put it on the agenda first thing in February of 2007.

## THE HOUSE RESOLUTION 121 PROCESS

***Calcagno*: Let's talk a little bit about the process of passing H.Res. 121 and a little less on why you got into the issue or why it's important. Did you have suspicions that maybe this resolution was going to be more successful given that there were recent failures to pass similar resolutions like H.Res. 759 which we talked about earlier?**

***Rep. Honda*:** Like I said when I first got there [to Congress] in 2001 I hadn't realized what progress, if any, was made until later when I got to know Lane [Evans], and the person that introduced me to Lane in service [sic] of the "comfort women" issue who was Dr. Ok Cha [Soh].[17] Through her I realized Lane had initiated action [on the "comfort women"] at the congressional level. But just taking it by the numbers I realized that we didn't have the power [to get it passed under a Republican Congress].

But we just kept going. [In 2007] Eni Faleomavaega[18] became Chairman of the Subcommittee on Asia [the Pacific, and the Global Environment on the House] Foreign Affairs [Committee]. Eni put that as one of his first agenda items, so I owe it to Eni, it was through his leadership and his support that we got it to a Subcommittee hearing [February 15, 2007],[19] and that's where the first hearing was.

I don't think a lot of Members of Congress realized that this was going on because the chamber [hearing room] was filled with cameras, more cameras than a lot of congressmen have ever seen in the room. We had three former "comfort women" testify before the subcommittee. Some Members of Congress did show up, and about 16 members had signed on [to the Resolution by then], and those who were notified about the hearing showed up.

After the hearing it was pretty emotional, a powerful hearing that Eni had facilitated and it was successful. [Thus, the resolution] passed the subcommittee and went on to the full committee.

I'd have to read the transcripts, not everyone voted for it, but a sufficient number voted to bring it onto the floor.[20]

There were a lot of dynamics that went along in the [Asian American] community, and many wanted to be counted for their efforts. I told people we got the votes, you don't have to spend money, just call people and encourage them to vote for it. But some of these folks said "Oh we have to raise money." So they raised money to put an ad in the *Washington Post*, which was unnecessary. The Japanese right-wing had put a large advertisement in the [*Washington*] *Post* [June 14], [thus] they felt it was necessary [to counter it].

## FOLLOW UP DECEMBER 4, 2019: ORGANIZING THE COMFORT WOMEN HEARING

*Calcagno:* **Speaking of Congressman Faleomavaega, please talk about the process of holding the hearing for the "comfort women." Especially because you only had a short amount of time to organize the hearing. Talk about how you decided who would speak.**

**Rep. Honda:** It's true that he only had a short amount of time to organize it, but the diaspora, was working on this for a while, and they were keeping tabs on what we were doing. President of WCCW, Dr. Ok Cha Soh and Dong Suk Kim was able to coordinate with the Korean "comfort women" and the other groups to bring Jan [Ruff] O'Herne, and *Halmoni* [Grandmothers], Lee Yong-soo and Kim Kun-ja to testify. And once that was done and they brought them over, Jan was from Australia and the other two were from South Korea. I believe that WCCW, KACE, and other Korean American groups probably footed the bill to get them over.[21]

My staffer [Ms.] Ayame Nagatani was the one coordinating with all those folks, and making sure that the hearing was fully vetted, and everyone was there, and that the media was ready. There were over 20 cameras there! In fact, Jim Costa [D-CA] came in to say something and he said that he'd never seen so many cameras present for one issue in all the years that he's been in Congress.

Lantos had to be pushed by Eni. A lot of the people who wanted to see this happen did a fundraiser for Lantos in California. I told them that this wasn't necessary, that this could just stand on its own. Once it came out of subcommittee with Eni, it went to the full committee in June so from February it took four months to get out. But there's a lot of lobbying going on and a lot of pressure going on from the Japanese government.

## FOLLOW UP DECEMBER 4, 2019: ADDITIONAL DETAILS ON THE HEARING

*Calcagno:* **In the last interview you mentioned that one of the "comfort women" Lee Yong-soo testified, could you talk about who else testified?**

***Rep. Honda:*** Mindy [Kotler], Ok Cha Soh, Jan [Ruff] O'Herne, and Kim Kun-ja.

***Calcagno:*** **Is there anything that you remember about Halmoni Kim's testimony?**

***Rep. Honda:*** Well, she, of course, told of her experience and told how difficult it was to talk about it. She was ashamed that this happened as were many other women that were victimized, and she married but didn't tell her children nor her husband, and she was living with that guilt as she was living her life. She talked about the impact that it had on her post-war. There was a documentary that came out about her post-war too.

***Calcagno:*** **In the Committee print of the hearing, Mindy Kotler, who testified, mentioned that she had requested for a number of documents to be put on the record. These included former Prime Minister Yasuhiro Nakasone's memoir of setting up a comfort station and acquiring four "comfort women" while a Naval officer in Indonesia. Unfortunately, none were. Do you know of any reason these documents may have been left out?**

***Rep. Honda:*** If she did, and the Chairman said "Without objection," then they should be in there. [Former Speaker of the House Dennis] Hastert may have had an interest in keeping them out, but he wasn't speaker by then. He was a lobbyist. The Japanese government and their two lobbyists seemed pretty effective. They are also possible influences. But if you give me that information, I can look for it. We can move forward on a technicality to include that in the record and amend the Congressional Record. That's important when somebody says something will be included. Especially Mindy, because Mindy is a Washington expert on the subject.[22]

## FOLLOW UP DECEMBER 4, 2019: CONGRESSMAN LANTOS ON RESOLUTION 121

***Calcagno:*** **I understand that Congressman Lantos was very hesitant about passing House Resolution 121. You said in our previous interview:**

***Rep. Honda:*** [The Resolution] finally came before the House floor for a vote and we went through the [procedural] motions, and I asked for a recorded vote, and the Chairman [Lantos] got up and said "He asked for a voice vote." I went to him and said "I wanted a roll call." And he said "No, you're getting a voice." And that upset me, I wanted to know who was gonna be for it and who was gonna be against it, but politically, you get that resolution through on a voice vote, and it gets the appearance that it was unanimous. I don't think it was unanimous.

***Calcagno:*** **Do you know why he did this?**

41

*Rep. Honda*: Well, that all happened in a matter of a minute or so, so I didn't have a chance to think on it, I just knew how I reacted.

**Calcagno: Do you know of what convinced Lantos that the resolution was a good idea?**

*Rep. Honda*: The fact was that we had the vote, and that a man of his reputation and background couldn't publicly say he was against it, after all he was a survivor of the Holocaust. Given all that and understanding the political process, he did his balancing act, but we got it through. If he were to say that he isn't for it, it would've been more difficult, but we would've been able to get it done because we had the votes and it got out of subcommittee. We also got it out of the full committee, but I don't think we had 100 percent support on that either. There were two negative votes in committee.

## H.RES. 121 AND JAPANESE GROUPS

*Yi:* **You spoke about how different groups opposed you, Japanese groups, obviously, so were there any prominent Japanese, governmental or non-governmental, groups that actually did support your resolution?**

*Rep. Honda*: The Japanese government didn't support it. Individuals supported it, [but] there were more, high-level individuals of the Japanese American community that did not support it. There were corporations that did not support it. The Japanese government had paid—I found out later, after the issue was voted on, a couple of weeks later—two lobbyists to work against our resolution. And one of them was an older guy, and I saw him at the Democratic Club, and he said, "Oh you're the son of a bitch that made me work and walk the Halls of Congress, against the resolution." I said, "Were you paid well?" They were paid well. But I didn't realize—a lot of things I didn't realize—that they had lobbyists working against us.

What I did realize, prior to the vote was there were many Asians walking the halls, in small groups, or couples. I had stopped and asked some who they were and what they were doing here, and they said, "Oh, we're here to support the resolution." "Oh, where are you from?" They'd be from California, you know, so there were, there was an activity that was going on that I didn't fully realize. So there was activity going on, so I believe, it could've been, the various Korean communities that organized, if not nationally, then regionally. And each one of them has to tell their own stories because I can't tell their stories.

I can't tell why they got involved, because there will be efforts by a lot of individuals and groups, that will want to make public, their part of how they brought it to the attention of their own communities. After the passage, it became even more important to the South Koreans, because they talked about this issue. And I did not know that the grandmothers [Korean reference to former "comfort women," *halmoni*], were going to be in front of the Japanese Embassy [in Seoul] with the [Peace] statue protesting and petitioning to Japanese diplomats to apologize. Which I think really speaks to the independent activism of the grandmothers, the "halmonies."

I think the great outcome, in my mind, of [H.Res.] 121, was that, they started to "live" together [cooperate]. All the different activists pulled together, and as a result, different venues started to become activated, to screen documentaries, documenting individual victims, by country, by individuals. Now there's a musical out there, called "Comfort Women!" More and more people are bringing it [the "comfort women"] to the public's attention.

People in California now got it into the social studies history textbooks.[23] This is a good step forward even though there may be some political innuendos in some of these textbooks that speaks to the Japanese government's position. And that's okay, because people will start talking about it, and ask the question: what really happened? The Japanese government tried to change the [high school textbooks published by] McGraw-Hill.[24] I met with the publishers, and they said, don't worry, we're not changing our story. So, it became a higher level of activity, which is what [Japanese Prime Minister Shinzo] Abe hates.

The Japanese mentality of Abe to defend his ancestors honor compels him to deny whatever it is that is said [about Japan's war crimes and atrocities]. He denies historical data and changes the narrative to his comfort level. And I was trying to understand, how can a leader of a country be so damn stupid? And I realized, it's not stupidity, it's his effort to shift the dialogue and the dynamics of it towards his comfort level, so he doesn't lose face, because his maternal grandfather was a government minister and also a pardoned [unindicted Class A] war criminal, and that plays into it. And I'm not sure that Abe's a Christian, because if he was a Christian, the concept of reconciliation might be easier to understand.

So, the focus now should not be on Abe, it should be on asking the Crown Prince, who is now the Emperor, to make a public comment that will guide his people in the right direction for the future. He doesn't have to say to Abe, and tell him, "apologize." but it would be sufficient for him to say something like, "Let's look at our past accurately, and humbly." He said something like that in the past, but I want him to say it as Emperor, because the Emperor does have *gravitas*. And he doesn't need to get involved in the politics, he can just get involved in the moral path that the Japanese need to go down. If he could do that, then I think there will be a greater expectation of the public, to have politicians make those changes. Like in this country, politics will not change unless the people pressure them. And so, it is, I think in Japan.

## FOLLOW UP DECEMBER 4, 2019: "THE FACTS" *WASHINGTON POST* ADVERTISEMENT

*Calcagno*: On June 14, 2007, "The Facts" ad was placed in *The Washington Post* by a Japanese right-wing group.[25] Do you know of any Members of Congress, or even non-congressional groups that had strong positive or negative reactions to the ad?

***Rep. Honda:*** No, I don't think it had any overriding positive reaction. I heard some folks in the coat room saying: "Wow they really took a full-page ad on this Mike." But my sense was that it was more of the same and was just another way of the Japanese Government spending the money and putting on whatever pressure it can. After that Prime Minister Abe put $600 million dollars into his budget in 2013/14 for "public diplomacy." Last year, I haven't verified this, but I think he got a billion dollars to fight contradictions to his view of history globally. He's got about 10-12 countries now globally where he wants to get rid of their "comfort women" monuments.

***Calcagno:*** **Yes, that [the elimination of the statues] is a very big diplomatic commitment.**

***Rep. Honda:*** Well the [Japanese] ambassador [Shinsuke Sugiyama, 2018] said his job in the United States is to persuade all the city officials to rescind their placement or to discourage them from doing this. They even sued us in Glendale, California and it even went up to the State Supreme Court, which did not accept to hear it. But since then, they've gotten sophisticated. The monument at Glendale got defaced. Someone spread dog feces on it. And they did it again, but this time we had a camera zoomed in on it. They weren't able to identify the guy, because he was in a hoodie, but he kicked over all the plants and defaced the statue again. Now it is considered a hate crime, so whenever this person gets caught, that person will be subject to criminal prosecution under the Hate Crime Act.

## HOW THE RESOLUTION SUCCEEDED AND FELL SHORT

***Yi:*** **In what ways do you think the "comfort women" Resolution was successful, and in what way could there still be more that could be done?**

***Rep. Honda:*** Success is in that it got passed.[26] Success is in the reaction that we got from the Japanese diplomats and Prime Minister, in that they don't want [sic] talked about. It was also successful, I think, in that it pushed the Japanese government and the South Korean government to come to some effort, or some conclusion [agreement], on December 28, 2015. So that meant the two governments, and probably the U.S. State Department was probably trying to push that also. But the outcome of that agreement, in my mind, is null and void, because it didn't take into account any of the aspects of the victims. And President Moon Jae In had declared that resolution as void. And now there is a national recognition of "comfort women" on August 14th.[27] In 1991, is when "Halmoni" Kim Hak-soon, had first spoken up. So now they have a national day that recognizes them. Monuments across this country, are being erected, as well as monuments in other countries.

It's successful because Abe had put into his budget, I can't remember, $600 million dollars maybe, to fight this. He selected Ambassador Shinsuke Sugiyama to make as part of his work to speak to the local governments and prevent more monuments and get rid of as many monuments as possible. It's successful because the Mayor of Osaka [Yoshimura Hirofumi] said he would [and did] withdraw their sister city relationship with San Francisco.[28]

But I really didn't care, because sister city relationships are not governmental; it is city to city, not nation to nation. So, if he wants to do that, then he is also impacting the local cities in Japan, and I think that brings to light how inane some of these mayors are, who support Abe. So general public opinion will start to grow that way.

The Prime Minister is pushing tariffs and trade barriers with South Korea, mainly because of South Korea's government's position on restitution to Koreans who were used as slave laborers in Japan during World War II, and the issue of sexual slavery. The desire of the South Korean government is that the Japanese government recognizes and apologizes appropriately. So, it's gotten to the point where international relationships are being impacted. I would've never thought that would happen.

I was a simple person. Just say sorry, that's all, and it would all be over. But I knew that the passage of 121 was not the final step, it was the beginning of the first step. We have to team up with other groups that are fighting human slavery, violence against women, different types of conflicts, and natural disasters. The UN has resolutions. So, we need to keep pushing that. And I think it was a success because the current [Japanese] ambassador used to be representing Japan in Geneva, and then the UN, improving the political rights, and pushing for social justice, for women globally.

My position is, really, get out of the way, stop doing this until you really accept full responsibility of the "comfort women" issue. Otherwise, all your words and your actions are nothing but loud jangling instruments that disturb people. That's why we have to return back to that issue, every time they pretend to be leaders in women's rights.

## CONGRESS' CONTINUING ROLE

*Calcagno*: **Do you think there is a continuing role for Congress, or in the United States, in this?**

*Rep. Honda*: Certainly. I believe, in 2014, I was on the Appropriations Committee, and we put Resolution 121 into the language of an Appropriations bill,[29] and President Obama signed it, which gave the Resolution a little bit more teeth, to require them to do something more active. And so, to Obama, I believe I had to say something, a little bit more consciously. I think Caroline Kennedy, the Ambassador to Japan, had to say something, and Hillary Clinton, the Secretary of State, certainly did say something publicly, saying that the term "comfort women" is euphemistic, and calls it what it is, its "sexual slavery." She said that about it.[30]

I think that Congress still has a role in it. They might start by stepping up on the issue by asking the question [to Japan], "is your behavior based upon your dissatisfaction of the popularity of [House] Resolution 121 that asks Japan to issue an apology?" When our Congress invited Abe to speak to the joint meeting, I had Halmoni Lee Yong-soo, up in the audience, as my guest.

## ABE'S ADDRESS TO CONGRESS APRIL 29, 2015 AND VISIT TO THE WHITE HOUSE

***Rep. Honda***: I think the Speaker of the House should invite President Moon Jae In to speak to a Joint Meeting of Congress, where he will have the podium as Abe did, to say something publicly on these issues [of reconciliation]. He could say then diplomatically, but he should say something. I think he's getting more international attention, in his effort to unify North and South Korea, and denuclearize North Korea, and bring an end to this split on the Korean Peninsula. And he also supports the issue of the apology, so I think Congress can provide opportunities for the South Korean leader to say something.

I mean, the Speaker [Paul Ryan R-WI] brought in Abe, which pissed off [President Barack] Obama, and me. They brought in Abe, which elevated Abe, so now Abe has credibility, I guess, in Japan. He's still not all that popular in Japan, but he still manages to win. So, we need to impact public opinion of Japan, by doing things outside of Japan. Then the social media, the public opinion, put more pressure on Abe, make him crazy. Yeah, there's a lot more we can do.

## FOLLOW UP INTERVIEW DECEMBER 4, 2019

*Calcagno*: **Previously, you have noted that Abe was brought to Congress. Are you referring to the April 2015 meeting?**

***Rep. Honda***: Yes, the 2015 address on Hirohito's birthday [April 29].[31]

*Calcagno*: **Was there anything you remember about that address?**

***Rep. Honda***: There wasn't anything striking. He did what he did best and skirted the issue of "comfort women." I invited Halmoni Lee Yong-soo to sit on the balcony and observe. [Dr. Lester Tenney, the former POW was also there by Mr. Honda's invitation. Tenney also attended the banquet for Abe that evening and met the Prime Minister] She wanted to yell at him but I told her we don't do that. I wanted her to be present.

## WHAT COULD HAVE BEEN DONE DIFFERENTLY

*Yi*: **If you were to do this [go through the process of passing legislation] again, is there anything you would do differently?**

*Rep. Honda*: Well something you could check out, too, when we got the Resolution, before the subcommittee and committee, after it passed the subcommittee, I caught a word, that I should've seen. The word was "prostitute." I asked my staff to change that word. Other than that, no, I don't think I could change anything. We took out the word "reparations" and just stuck to the apology. Politically, I just figured that once we get the apology, the politics between the two countries and reparations can become an issue. Japan has shown consistently, that they were willing to help with the money, but they always put the money in the funds in a way that makes it looks like, it's not restitution. It looks more like charity than restitution.

## HOW SHOULD JAPAN APOLOGIZE

*Calcagno*: **What do you think a complete apology would look like from Japan? Obviously, they could do the Cabinet Decisions, which is more binding. Is there anything beyond that, which they need to do?**

*Rep. Honda:* Well, a Cabinet Statement [Decision] is a good start. I don't speak Japanese, but the wording has to be unambiguous, or as written in the Resolution, "unequivocal." It has to be clear, because Japanese politicians are really good at not saying yes or no. You just have to say, use words like, "shall," and make sure the syntax of the terminologies is clear, without any equivocation. It has to be an unambiguous, unequivocal written apology. And then followed by actions to put the history, the factual history, of what happened in Asia, what happened in terms of "comfort women" into the textbooks, to teach youngsters, what had happened overseas during the war, what the government did to the kids to prepare them to be soldiers. That's all important.

## WHAT H.RES. 121 CAN TEACH THE U.S. ABOUT TRANSNATIONAL JUSTICE

*Calcagno*: **What lessons does this resolution teach us for future instances of wartime sexual violence and transnational justice in general?**

*Rep. Honda:* Like any great movement, from Christianity to Judaism to Islam, there is always a great teacher that speaks the truth. Despite persecution, "Halmoni" Kim Hak-soon is the one who broke the silence and said "I'm through with being ashamed. I'm angrier about being victimized and I understand now what happened to me, and I demand not only an apology but restitution." She broke the silence. She spoke first on behalf of thousands and thousands of victims, on behalf of those living and dead.

She started a whole movement that made people realize that we've been lied to, the truth had been concealed. One person can make a difference, they just need to have convictions of their beliefs, and then that will help make things happen. A lot of times it has to come from the grassroots, and that's the basis of this country where individual rights are protected. Free speech is protected; freedom of religion is protected; freedom of assembly is protected.

What we don't do well is support public education, in ways that textbooks should be written about appropriately. History is only determined by those who write the book, right? So, without it we start to understand that, hopefully, we need to change some of our myths, in this country like, Columbus did not discover America, how the word "discover" needs to be reviewed because there were people here already, and there were navigators that came to this continent.

So, the lesson is that you need to have the conviction of your beliefs and then speak them. For me, it's the Constitution that provides that blanket of security that guarantees. But it doesn't mean the government's going to always honor it. You really have to keep fighting to perfect our understanding, our implementation of the Constitution.

## ABE'S VISIT TO WASHINGTON APRIL 2007[32]

*Rep. Honda:* Prime Minister Abe spoke with President [George] Bush and [his National Security Advisor] Dr. Stephen Hadley, the two leaders of the Senate, Senate Majority Leader [Harry] Reid and [Senator] Inouye, and [Speaker of the House] Nancy Pelosi, and explained why he was frustrated about the Resolution. He said, "We already apologized." So Bush and Inouye say, "We accept your apology."[33] I asked what Reid and Pelosi said and was told he said nothing, and that he knew "Pelosi needed to be quiet." So, I was asked by the press, what I thought. I didn't know they had a meeting. They went on to tell me that Abe was explaining why this was such an issue for them, and that he apologized and wanted people to understand that Japan apologized. It still has to be checked out to see if it really did happen because the press had asked me what I thought, and my response to them was, "This is America. We have a right to say what we believe, and they have the right to make a decision." Call that an issue. But, I thought Bush and Inouye were out of line because those who accepted Abe's explanation and apology had no business doing it, because they were not victims. Period.

## FOLLOW UP DECEMBER 4, 2019: ROLE OF AYAME NAGATANI AND OTHER IMPORTANT STAFF

*Calcagno*: **Speaking of your staff, you recently mentioned your assistant Ayame Nagatani, were there other things that she did for the resolution other than helping out with the hearing?**

*Rep. Honda*: Yeah, if I recall correctly, our original wording came from my resolution that I did in California, except my resolution in California also included POWs and the Rape of Nanjing. For the purposes of House Resolution 121, it was narrowed down to "comfort women." That was the focus because I was doing another resolution on POWs on behalf of Dr. Lester Tenney, a Bataan Death March survivor. He was the lead person on the apology to the POWs.

*Calcagno:* So was Ms. Nagatani one of your staff while in California as well?

*Rep. Honda:* No, she was in D.C. The one in California was my Chief of Staff. And I mostly did a lot of the work in the Capitol there, a lot of the battles, myself.

*Calcagno:* Do you remember the name of your Chief of Staff when you were in the State Assembly?

*Rep. Honda:* Yeah, it was Keith Honda. He was my first cousin. He's an attorney from South Central LA. He went to UCLA, went to Hastings, Peace Corps after that, and after Peace Corps, he came back and I kept him on my campaign to work on my Board of Supervisors and kept him on my staff, so he trained my next Chief of Staff Jennifer Van der Heide. Another person who greatly contributed to the passage of the resolution was Eni's Chief of Staff, Dr. Lisa Williams. She could be difficult, but a very dedicated person. She knew that Eni wanted to make this a top priority and she fought for him. Eni himself bugged everyone on his committee who were reluctant because many people were pulling all the strings to keep us from doing this. You do have that letter from Senator Daniel Inouye [D-HI] to [Speaker of the House Nancy] Pelosi?

*Calcagno:* I'll have to check. [We do.][34]

*Rep. Honda:* Inouye said that in all his decades in the Senate, he had never once interfered with the workings of the House of Representatives. But he was making an exception with the "comfort women" Resolution by asking Pelosi not to do this. Frankly, that is pretty cheeky. Senators never comment on House legislation. It was all very odd. I think he got a lot of pressure from the Japanese government and the Bush Administration.

## CLOSING REMARKS

*Calcagno:* Any final comments?

*Rep. Honda:* I think in this effort it is important to recognize appropriate groups, give appropriate credit, in terms of what they did when they did it, why they did it. This resolution needs to be understood in terms of its human dynamics, political process, and the lessons learned in the evolution of this resolution. The success of the Resolution was only a beginning; we're still struggling for the end.

The people who should be apologizing, unfortunately, are fighting like hell to keep us from success. They continue denying history and undermine all the positive progress. We cannot let that happen, not because House Resolution 121 was successful, but because we owe an obligation to the victims, and it's not finished until the unambiguous, unequivocal apology and a follow-through with teaching the kids the truth about what happened, is accomplished. And that's the bottom line.

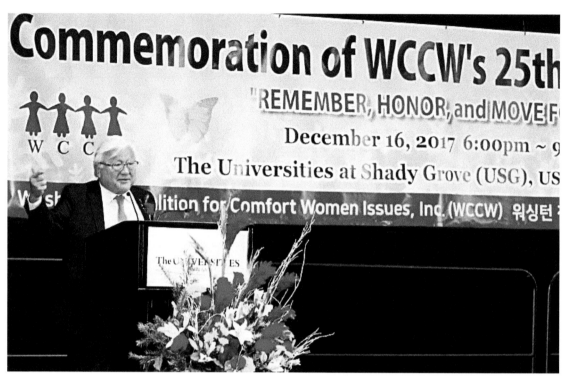

Fig. 2-1. Rep. Mike Honda's keynote speech at WCCW's 25th anniversary ceremony, December 16, 2017.

---

[1] H.R.442 (100th Congress) the Civil Liberties Act passed on 8/10/1988. Civil Liberties Act of 1988 (Pub.L.100–383, title I, August 10, 1988, 102 Stat. 904, 50a the U.S.C. § 1989b et seq.) *The Civil Liberties Act of 1988, Restitution for World War II internment of Japanese-Americans and Aleuts.*

[2] Mr. Honda was a Supervisor on the Santa Clara Board of Supervisors for one term from 1991–1996.

[3] http://aptsjw.global-alliance.net/; founded on May 2, 1992; name changed to Global Alliance for Preserving the History of WWII in Asia, https://www.global-alliance.net/home.html.

[4] Mr. Honda was an Assemblyman on the California State Assembly for two terms from 1996–2000.

[5] AJR 27 was approved by the Assembly on August 19, 1999. *See:* http://leginfo.legislature.ca.gov/faces/billTextClient.xhtml?bill_id=199920000AJR27.

[6] AJR 27 asked the government of Japan to apologize unambiguously and formally for crimes committed during WWII; AJR 27 also called upon the U.S. Congress to adopt a resolution calling on Japan to apologize.

[7] Irene Hirano became the founding president of the U.S. Japan Council, https://www.usjapancouncil.org/ in 2008. She married Senator Daniel Inouye in May 2008 and was widowed in December 2012. She formerly served as the president and founding (1988) CEO of the Japanese American National Museum in Los Angeles.

[8] George Nakano served from 1980-1984 as a City Council member for Torrance, California; starting in 1998 he served as a California State Assembly member for California's 53rd District.

[9] Antonio Ramón Villaraigosa (D), Speaker of the California State Assembly (1998–2000).

[10] Japanese Consul General Japan in San Francisco Hitoshi Tanaka (1998-2000), https://www.sf.us.emb-japan.go.jp/itpr_en/e_m01_06.html.

11 Joint Resolutions http://www.leginfo.ca.gov/pub/99-00/bill/asm/ab_0001-0050/ajr_27_bill_19990826_chaptered.html in the California State Assembly are passed onto Congress as a petition for their information. [106th] 1st Session. POM–362. A joint resolution adopted by the Legislature of the State of California relative to war crimes committed by the Japanese military during World War II; to the Senate Committee on Foreign Relations. October 6, 1999, Congressional Record Issue: Vol. 145, No. 134 — Daily Edition, [Pages S12099-S12100] https://www.congress.gov/crec/1999/10/06/modified/CREC-1999-10-06-pt1-PgS12099-4.htm.

12 Mr. Honda served as a representative from California's 15th Congressional District from 2001-2013; following a redistricting after the 2010 census, Mr. Honda represented California's 17th Congressional District with the start of the 113th Congress in 2013. He served on the Appropriations, Science, Space and Technology, Transportation and Infrastructure, and Budget committees. In 2003, he was appointed the Deputy Chair of the DNC, and served two terms from 2005-2013 as DNC Vice Chair. *See:* https://history.house.gov/People/Detail/15564.

13 *See:* Kayoko Kimura, "Stance on 'comfort women' undermines fight to end wartime sexual violence," *Japan Times*, March 4, 2015, https://www.japantimes.co.jp/community/2015/03/04/voices/stance-comfort-women-undermines-fight-end-wartime-sexual-violence.

14 Norimitsu Onishi, "Abe Rejects Japan's Files on War Sex," *The New York Times,* March 2, 2007, https://www.nytimes.com/2007/03/02/world/asia/02japan.html.

15 Chief Cabinet Secretary Yohei Kono announced on August 4, 1993 the results of a Japanese government study on the "comfort women." Kono was the Chief Cabinet Secretary of the Miyazawa government, which fell on June 18, 1993. Prime Minister Kiichi Miyazawa oversaw a caretaker government through August 5, in which, by law he could not enact any new policies. Without the approval of the Cabinet through a Cabinet Decision, the Kono Statement entered an equivocal and problematic political space between a personal expression of empathy and a governmental concern.

16 From 1975 to 1978 and from 1995 to 2007, the House Committee on Foreign Affairs was renamed the Committee on International Relations. In January 2007 (and January 1979), it changed back to its original name. Its jurisdiction is and was the same under both names.

17 Dr. Ok Cha Soh is a professor of Psychology at Columbia College; she also served as president of the Washington Coalition for Comfort Women Issues (WCCW) from 2001 to 2008.

18 Eni Faleomavaega was the second ever Congressional Delegate from American Samoa from 1989–2015, and at the time of his retirement was the longest-serving Delegate in House history.

19 *See:* https://www.govinfo.gov/content/pkg/CHRG-110hhrg33317/pdf/CHRG-110hhrg33317.pdf

20 Full Committee mark up and vote June 26, 2007, Yeas and Nays: 39 - 2. The "no" votes were Ron Paul (R-TX) and Tom Tancredo (R-CO) Congressional Record, [Daily Digest], [Pages D907-D910], June 26, 2007: https://www.congress.gov/congressional-record/2007/6/26/daily-digest/article/d907-1?q=%7B%22search%22%3A%22comfort+women%22%7D&s=2&r=1: https://drive.google.com/file/d/0B0RpBnvSNewfZUxYS05Dckh0cFk5aXBTbl9seDBYWkxERGZn/view.

21 Kim Dong-suk who was the executive director of KACE (Korean Americans for Civic Engagement) in New York was involved and able to coordinate for the collection of signatures from other States along with Coalition 121 Korean American National group: https://us.kace.org/.

22 Ms. KOTLER. "Thank you, Mr. Chairman. Thank you for the opportunity to testify today on Japan's contemporary responsibilities for its war crimes of Imperial Japan from 1932 to 1945. I am honored and humbled to be here with Ms. Ruff O' Herne, Grandma Kim and Grandma Lee. Before I proceed, I would like to submit for the record five supporting documents on Japan's involvement in establishing the Imperial military's comfort women system. Mr. FALEOMAVAEGA. Without objection." On page 41. https://www.govinfo.gov/content/pkg/CHRG-110hhrg33317/pdf/CHRG-110hhrg33317.pdf.

23 California's State Board of Education approved a new History-Social Science Framework for California Public Schools on July 18, 2016. *See:* https://www.nbcnews.com/news/asian-america/california-passes-textbook-standards-including-comfort-women-sikhs-n611501.

[24] In January 2015, Prime Minister Abe was quoted as saying "I just looked at a document, McGraw-Hill's textbook, and I was shocked," in reference to a California High School History textbook that included depictions of "comfort women" that portrayed the Japanese Imperial Army's actions in a negative light. *See:* https://www.nbcnews.com/news/asian-america/california-passes-textbook-standards-including-comfort-women-sikhs-n611501.

[25] For text *see*: http://www.sdh-fact.com/CL02_1/33_S4.pdf.

[26] Rubén Eloy Hinojosa (D-TX) was SPEAKER pro tempore. The resolution was agreed to under suspension of the rules. *See*: Congressional Record, July 30, 2007, Pages H8870-H8876, https://www.congress.gov/congressional-record/2007/7/30/house-section/article/h8870-1?q=%7B%22search%22%3A%22comfort+women%22%7D&s=1&r=1.

[27] On May 30, 2018 the Korean Ministry of Government Legislation announced that August 14 would be the International Memorial Day for "comfort women." August 14 marks the anniversary of Kim Hak-soon's 1991 testimony exposing Japanese Imperial Army war crimes against "comfort women."

[28] October 2018, *see*: https://www.sfchronicle.com/bayarea/heatherknight/article/Japanese-mayor-cuts-ties-between-SF-and-Osaka-13279584.php.

[29] The 113th Congress Committee on Appropriations issued a report on the 2014 fiscal year. It noted that "The Committee notes the passage of H.Res. 121 in the House of Representatives on July 30, 2007 and urges the Secretary of State to encourage the Government of Japan to address the issues raised in the resolution."

[30] "Clinton says 'comfort women' should be referred to as 'enforced sex slaves,'" *Japan Today*, July 11, 2012, https://japantoday.com/category/politics/clinton-says-comfort-women-should-be-referred-to-as-enforced-sex-slaves.

[31] "Toward an Alliance of Hope" – Address to a Joint Meeting of the U.S. Congress by Prime Minister Shinzo Abe, April 29, 2015, https://japan.kantei.go.jp/97_abe/statement/201504/uscongress.html.

[32] Abe's first the U.S. trip as prime minister, April 26-27, 2007. Met with Congressional leaders in Speaker Pelosi's office on April 26, 2007, http://www.nbcnews.com/id/18326048/ns/politics/t/japanese-prime-minister-abe-visits-us/#.Xg_Q_VVKgdU.

[33] PRESIDENT BUSH: The comfort women issue is a regrettable chapter in the history of the world, and I accept the Prime Minister's apology. I thought it was very—I thought his statements—Kono's statement, as well as statements here in the United States were very straightforward and from his heart. And I'm looking forward to working with this man to lead our nations forward. And that's what we spent time discussing today. https://georgewbush-whitehouse.archives.gov/news/releases/2007/04/20070427-6.html.

[34] While Rep. Honda mentioned that Senator Daniel Inouye wrote specifically to Speaker Pelosi, Senator Inouye sent a letter to the chairman of the committee of jurisdiction, the House Foreign Affairs Committee, Tom Lantos, March 5, 2007 (this letter mirrors the ones sent to all members of the House of Representatives and uses many of the same phrases in Japanese Embassy lobbying documents; Speaker Pelosi would, doubtless, have also received an identical or similar letter), accessed: https://drive.google.com/open?id=1JRBPs294_KkqtnQStS7tIIYjYx5paC_I.

# 3. "COMFORT WOMEN": THE MAKING OF U.S. HOUSE OF REPRESENTATIVES RESOLUTION 121, 110TH CONGRESS, 2007

*Mindy L. Kotler*

**Abstract:** House Resolution 121 of the 110th Congress advocating justice for Imperial Japan's wartime sex slaves—the "comfort women"—was a thoroughly American invention. From its conception to its passage in July 2007, the Resolution reflected a domestic political calculus rather than an international one. It was successful, where other similar resolutions were not, because it appealed to its American constituencies rather than responding to foreign interests. H.Res. 121 was part of a greater attitudinal change in the United States regarding violence against women.

## Introduction

In the 1990s, both the American public and the criminal justice system began to recognize sexual violence as a crime of power rather than a private family matter or something that only happens to "bad girls." CNN brought the rape victims of the Yugoslav and Rwanda civil wars into American living rooms. During the decade, rape became a topic of public discussion and a political issue.

Across the Pacific, former "comfort women" began to come forward. Their testimonies resonated within this greater awareness of sexual violence. Their stories of abuse and coercion were viewed outside both their Pacific War context and the view that rape was a "natural" consequence of war. Their trauma was now understood as a violation of universal human rights.

Members of the U.S. Congress echoed these concerns in their advocacy for the "comfort women." Unlike the other victims of wartime Imperial Japan, the "comfort women" had a story that transcended history. It folded neatly into the contemporary politics of advancing women's rights. The eight resolutions submitted to the House of Representatives from 1996 to 2007 reflect this evolution in thinking.

In addition, Japan's public struggles with apologies to the "comfort women" as well as for World War II helped focus congressional attention. The George W. Bush administration in 2001, redefined the U.S.-Japan Security Treaty as an alliance based on "shared values." The failure of Japan to take state responsibility for past war crimes, especially toward noncombatants, undermined this premise. The resolutions tried to correct this problem.

It is within this larger dialogue about rape, warfare, women's rights, history, and apology that I became involved in the 2006-2007 "comfort women" resolutions introduced in the U.S. House of Representatives. Prior to this time, I was an observer. My contribution to the "comfort women" story was to bring it into the American political discourse by reframing its history within the 21st century understanding of conflict-related sexual violence.

## A "Comfort Women" Resolution?

I did not thoroughly study the history of the "comfort women" until 2006. Prior to then, I was focused on Japanese industrial policy and war history. Involvement in a number of study groups to examine Asian regional security, convinced me that Japan's unsettled war history was the impediment to security cooperation and peace in the region. My interest was never as an activist, but as a historian hoping to solve a modern alliance problem. How the U.S. could reasonably and successfully help Japan resolve its many history issues with its occupied peoples and adversaries was an underlying question. The U.S. government did not have a policy for East Asian regional reconciliation. This was partly the fault of the lack of congressional oversight. Thus, understanding what Congress had done regarding Japanese war crimes and the "comfort women" was an important starting point for me.

## The First "Comfort Women" Resolution 1996 (104th Congress)

From 1996 to 2006, there were six unsuccessful resolutions asking the Japanese government to recognize and apologize for the trauma suffered by the "comfort women." A resolution is not a bill or a law. It is a legislative vehicle "used merely for expressing facts, principles, opinions, and purposes of the two Houses."[1] All the resolutions mentioning the "comfort women" were introduced only into the U.S. House of Representatives, the lower chamber of the U.S. Congress. All were also written as "House Concurrent Resolutions,"[2] needing approval in both the House and Senate. Each Resolution stalled in the House Committee on International Relations and was never presented for a vote.

The first formal mention of the "comfort women" in the U.S. Congress was in the 104th Congress (1995–1996). On May 25, 1995, California Republican Representative Robert K. Dornan spoke on the floor of the House about the book *Prisoners of the Japanese* by Gavan Daws.[3] He used the book as a vehicle to highlight the upcoming Memorial Day.[4] He also wanted to pressure Japan to apologize not only to the prisoners of war (POWs), but also for WWII at the upcoming 50th anniversary of its end. Among the many atrocities the Congressman listed, he specifically noted:

> Thousands of Korean women, teenagers, kidnaped [sic] and used as prostitutes for the Japanese Army, all the way down to Java and Sumatra, all over into Burma, into Thailand, young Korean teenagers used as prostitutes, called "comfort women," no official apology, Mr. Speaker, from the Japanese Diet, their congress, to Korea.[5]

On May 10, 1996, in the Second Session of the 104th Congress, Dornan introduced into the House of Representatives the first congressional resolution mentioning the "comfort women." This was H.Con.Res. 176[6] that had 13 cosponsors and was entitled: "Expressing the sense of the Congress concerning the maltreatment of United States military and civilian prisoners by the Japanese during World War II."

The Resolution's focus was on prisoners of war. Only one clause out of the 18 noted the "comfort women." This clause was also the only one that mentioned women, with the exception of the first clause that identifies, generally, military and civilian women prisoners of Japan. The Resolution, otherwise, focused on Japan's wartime atrocities that largely affected male victims. The relevant clause identifies the "comfort women" as "sex slaves of the Japanese military during World War II." It adds that they "deserve compensation of at least $40,000 for each individual" for "extreme pain and suffering." The call for compensation for Japan's victims in this Resolution, and others, guaranteed that the U.S. State Department would oppose the bill as it was viewed as violating the 1951 San Francisco Peace Treaty with Japan.

## The 105th and 106th Congresses (1997-2000)

Dornan's resolution, unamended, was reintroduced in the 105th Congress (1997–1998) as H.Con.Res. 126—"Expressing the sense of Congress concerning the war crimes committed by the Japanese military during World War II" by Illinois Democratic Congressman William O. Lipinski with 78 cosponsors.[7] Lipinski's Chief of Staff was Chinese-American Jason Tai who was active in a number Asian American affinity organizations. He brought Dornan's resolution to Lipinski's attention. Tai was able to explain to the congressman the deeply emotional and painful history of Japan's war crimes in Asia. He was also intent on building support for the resolution from a broad coalition of Imperial Japan's wartime victims.[8]

In the first session of the 106th Congress (1999–2000), the subject of "comfort women" received more attention, albeit remaining within the context of other Japanese war crimes. On October 6, 1999, a petition from the California Assembly was sent to the Senate's Committee on Foreign Relations. It was recorded as POM—36: "A joint resolution adopted by the Legislature of State of California relative to war crimes committed by the Japanese military during World War II." In general, the California State resolution, Assembly Joint Resolution No. 27,[9] mirrored in many of its clauses the past two House of Representatives resolutions.

The petition in multiple entries made clear that the "comfort women" were sex slaves from across the Indo-Pacific. People from the Andaman Islands, India were said to have been "tortured to death or forced into sexual slavery at 'comfort stations.'" The Japanese military was identified as having "enslaved millions of Koreans, Chinese, Filipinos, and citizens from other occupied or colonized territories during World War II, and forced hundreds of thousands of women into sexual slavery for Japanese troops." Again, the Government of Japan was asked to "pay reparations of at least $40,000 for the 'extreme pain and suffering' caused to each woman who was forced into sexual slavery by the Japanese military (referred by the Japanese military as 'comfort women')."[10]

One month later, on November 8, 1999, Illinois Congressman Lane Evans entered into the *Congressional Record* an extension of remarks devoted to "Japanese Comfort Women." He was the first to address the subject as a stand-alone issue to Congress.[11] He said:

I believe the Japanese government must do whatever can be done to restore some dignity for these women. The German government has formally apologized to the victims of the Holocaust as well as other war crimes victims and has gone to great lengths to provide for their needs and recovery, but the Japanese government has yet to do so. That is why, in the strongest possible terms, I call upon Japan to formally issue a clear and unambiguous apology for the atrocious war crimes committed by the Japanese military during World War II and offer reparations no less than $40,000 for each of the "comfort women."' The surviving women are advanced in age, and time is of the essence. They have waited so long. They should wait no longer. . . .[12]

The following year, on June 19, 2000, however, Evans took the lead to reintroduce the same text of the two prior Concurrent Resolutions on Japanese war crimes. As ranking member of the House Veterans Affairs Committee, many felt Evans should be the champion of this veterans-focused legislation. The result was H.Con.Res. 357—"Expressing the sense of Congress concerning the war crimes committed by the Japanese military during World War II."[13] Surprisingly, the resolution garnered only 46 cosponsors of which 17 were Republican. It too languished in the House Committee on International Relations.

Thus, for three Congresses from 1995–2000, the same Concurrent Resolution demanding an apology for Imperial Japan's war victims was repeatedly introduced in the House of Representatives. There was never a companion resolution in the Senate. All the Resolutions ended in the House Committee on International Relations[14] chaired by New York Republican Ben Gilman. Although these Resolutions represented a broad American constituency, especially WWII veterans, none succeeded.

## The First Stand-Alone "Comfort Women" Resolutions: 107th and 108th Congresses

In the 107th Congress (2001–2002), Congressman Lane Evans introduced the first congressional resolution focused solely on the "comfort women." Through his involvement with the past Japanese war crime resolutions, he became familiar with a number of advocates for both women's rights and "comfort women" justice. He developed a close friendship with a Korean American social psychology professor Dr. Ok Cha Soh who was able to explain the injustice felt by the Korean community from Japan's colonialization and use of Korean sex slaves.

The result was H.Con.Res. 195 [107th] "Expressing the sense of Congress that the Government of Japan should formally issue a clear and unambiguous apology for the sexual enslavement of young women during colonial occupation of Asia and World War II, known to the world as "comfort women."[15] This Resolution listed ten clauses outlining how Imperial Japan had abused women and girls in sexual servitude and denied them compensation. It also laid out suggestions for remedies by the current Government of Japan:

That it is the sense of Congress that the Government of Japan—
    (1)  should formally issue a clear and unambiguous apology for

the sexual enslavement of young women during the colonial occupation of Asia and the Pacific Islands during World War II, known to the world as "comfort women";

(2) should immediately pay reparations to the victims of these crimes;

(3) should educate future generations about this horrible crime against humanity; and

(4) should publicly refute claims that the subjugation and enslavement of "comfort women" never occurred.

Ms. Kim Soon-duk, a former "comfort woman," visited with Evans on July 24, 2001, the day he submitted the Resolution to Congress. In the *Congressional Record*, Evans said:

> It has been almost 56 years since Japan surrendered to the allied powers. Very few "comfort women" are still alive and time is running out for Japan to properly account for its actions. We must act soon and remember that there is no statute of limitations on crimes against humanity. When human rights are violated, the international community must act because we have a moral responsibility to do so. So, let us do what is just and what is right for the "comfort women" and other victims. Let us speak out for them. Let us stand up for them. Let us lend them our strength. We must act, and we must speak out because in the end, people will remember not the words of their enemies, but the silence of their friends.[16]

With only 27 cosponsors (just two Republican cosponsors),[17] the Evans' Resolution was not considered by the House Committee on International Relations and never reached a vote. In the 108th Congress (2003-2004), Representative Evans reintroduced the same Resolution on June 23, 2003 as H.Con.Res. 226 - Expressing the sense of Congress that the Government of Japan should formally issue a clear and unambiguous apology for the sexual enslavement of young women during colonial occupation of Asia, and for other purposes.[18] He had 32 cosponsors of which only one, Frank Wolf (R-VA-10) was a Republican. This Resolution was also never reviewed by the House Committee on International Relations and failed.

## The 109th Congress (2005-2006) and Getting to H.Res. 759

In the following Congress, the 109th (2005-2006), Congressman Evans made his fourth attempt to have Congress seek justice for Imperial Japan's "comfort women." On February 16, 2005, he again reintroduced the text of two past Resolutions. This was H.Con.Res. 68-- Expressing the sense of Congress that the Government of Japan should formally issue a clear and unambiguous apology for the sexual enslavement of young women during colonial occupation of Asia and World War II, known to the world as "comfort women." [19]

This Resolution had only 15 cosponsors. They included Mike Honda (D-CA) and Bernie Sanders (I-VT). There were *no* Republican cosponsors. The "Concurrent Resolution" was sent for review again to the Republican-controlled House Committee on International Relations. Although the prose in this Resolution had not changed from past ones, the circumstances surrounding its introduction had. Congressman Evans, a well-liked, Vietnam War veteran, was dying from Parkinson's Disease, thought to be caused by his exposure to Agent Orange. He was close to his fellow Illinois veteran Henry Hyde who was Chair of the Committee on International Relations and a Republican.[20]

Hyde, a Pacific War Navy veteran, was sympathetic to his ailing colleague's quest to achieve congressional recognition for the "comfort women." The Chairman was alarmed by Japanese Prime Minister Junichiro Koizumi's nationalist rhetoric and objected to his repeated visits to the war-venerating Yasukuni Shrine. Hyde was not convinced that Japan had made satisfactory atonement for its wartime behavior. Further, as a well-known anti-abortion advocate, Hyde was disgusted to learn of the forced abortions and physical abuse endured by the "comfort women."

As a 16-term, retiring congressman, Hyde also had the "luxury" of promoting legislation that he believed in, but would have been reluctant to support knowing that the Republican White House opposed. The Bush Administration had obstructed any legislation regarding Imperial Japan's Pacific War. Hyde was annoyed that the White House had undermined his 2005 resolution, H.Con.Res. 191—commemorating the 60th anniversary of the conclusion of the War in the Pacific and honoring veterans of both the Pacific and Atlantic theaters of the Second World War.[21] After his bill passed the House, it was received in the Senate on July 14, 2005 and referred to the Committee on Foreign Relations. Yet, no further action was taken.

The Bush Administration asked Senator Richard Lugar (R-IN), Chairman of the Senate Foreign Relations Committee to remove the third "resolved" clause that "reaffirms the judgment in Tokyo rendered by the International Military Tribunal for the Far East of 1946-1948 and the conviction of certain individuals as war criminals for their crimes against humanity." Senator Lugar refused, as did the Chairman of the Senate Veterans Affairs Committee Senator Larry Craig (R-ID). Thus, for the 109th Congress and the anniversary of the 60th anniversary of the end of WWII there was no full Congressional remembrance.[22]

The slight Hyde felt by the Administration's interference in his last effort to memorialize the end of "his" war, was compounded when he learned that Japan's nationalist Prime Minister Junichiro Koizumi might be asked to address a joint meeting of Congress during an official visit to the U.S. June 30 to July 1, 2006. To Hyde's further annoyance, Koizumi had watered down the famous Murayama Statement of Japanese government war apology. Chairman Hyde, thus, sent a letter on April 26 to the Speaker of the House Dennis Hastert objecting to Koizumi, who paid homage to Japanese war criminals at the Yasukuni Shrine, standing at the same podium as Franklin D. Roosevelt.[23] He then scheduled a hearing on "Japan's Relationship with Its Neighbors: Back to the Future?"[24] for June with some of Washington's leading Japan analysts. He wanted an airing of the political and security obstacles caused by Japan's still-unaddressed war crimes.

Hyde did not call the hearing simply to highlight his grievances with the Administration and Japan. He understood that the hearing would prepare the ground for his Committee's consideration of Evans' re-engineered "comfort women" Resolution. Under Hyde's guidance,

Evans introduced a new version of the Resolution on April 4, 2006 as H.Res. 759 - "Expressing the sense of the House of Representatives that the Government of Japan should formally acknowledge and accept responsibility for its sexual enslavement of young women, known to the world as "comfort women," during its colonial occupation of Asia and the Pacific Islands from the 1930s through the duration of World War II, and for other purposes."[25]

## Chairman Hyde's Guidance

As Chairman Hyde was determined to have his colleague Evans' "comfort women" Resolution approved by his Committee on International Relations, he wanted to have the text of H.Con.Res. 68 reexamined. He also understood the pitfalls of a Concurrent Resolution and not having a Republican cosponsor in a Republican-controlled Congress. Process and prose were to be adjusted.

New Jersey Republican Chris Smith was persuaded to be a cosponsor. Hyde insisted on a simple resolution needing only passage in the House. This reduced the resolution's legislative journey by confining it to the House of Representatives. As a senior member of the House, Hyde also had more control over the bill if it stayed in the House. Advocates and lobbyists could now concentrate their efforts on one Chamber. Getting the number of cosponsors needed for Committee consideration—60—would be easier.

Hyde was also concerned about both the tone and accuracy of the Resolution. To address these concerns, he instructed his Committee's Asia staffer Dennis Halpin to find a historian familiar with Pacific War history and contemporary East Asian politics to review the proposed Resolution before it was introduced. That person was me. Mr. Halpin emailed me the Resolution in early February 2006 to review and suggest revisions. Although I had written testimony and insertions for the record, I had never written legislation. I was not sure how much I could or should change, nor was I familiar, at the time, with legislative jargon.

When I first read the Resolution, I found out that the prose was too strident, angry, and unforgiving. There were unsubstantiated accusations, unrealistic goals, and, most important, a lack of relevance to Americans. The war history was sloppy. To me the obvious omission was that the text did not draw upon the growing awareness of violence against women or sexual violence in warfare.

My first task was to learn more. As noted above, I studied its legislative history. I then read widely and quickly books, journal essays, UN reports, NGO statements, and newspaper accounts about the "comfort women." I tried to understand why past resolutions failed. I recognized quickly which words and authors were controversial. I also discovered Western women as victims. As a result, I avoided the word "coercion" as it was misinterpreted by the Japanese as meaning only kidnapping. I also avoided: George Hicks' book as too journalistic; Seiji Yoshida's account of abducting girls on Jeju Island as discredited; and UN reports as too political. I was most influenced by the writings of Sarah Soh, Yoshimi Yoshiaki, and Yuki Tanaka, as well as, Andrew Horvat, Alexis Dudden, Tessa Morris-Suzuki, and Lily Gardner Feldman.

As a result of my research, I made minor changes to tone down the rhetoric, tighten the prose, shorten the clauses, and correct some of the historical facts. Among my additions were:

- the use of "comfort women" is considered "a current as well as past human rights issue"
- identify Japanese Government officials who have denied the "comfort women" as, both "elected and career"; and
- have the Government of Japan "accept responsibility" for its sexual enslavement of young women.

I also wanted to bring the bill closer to U.S. foreign policy objectives and the calls for the unique human rights of women. In addition, I wanted to align the resolution to the long-standing American goal of persuading Japan to be a "responsible" security partner and global stakeholder. The Bush Administration emphasized the U.S.-Japan relationship as one of shared values. Japan's unresolved war history with its Asian neighbors disrupted this narrative.

Most important, I removed the direct demands for compensation. I knew from prisoner of war legislative history that reference to reparations was certain to compel the U.S. State Department to object to the legislation and thus kill it. The State Department uses Article 14 (V)b in the 1952 San Francisco Peace Treaty that says "the Allied Powers waive all reparations claims of the Allied Powers" to stop any Japanese war crimes legislation that requests restitution.

To avoid State Department objections while maintaining the original intent, I felt a more effective strategy was to make a vague mention to the reports of international organizations, which had all concluded that compensation was necessary. Japan was asked "simply" to follow the recommendations of these world bodies. Japan was a member and signatory of all the noted UN institutions. Again, this was an effort to encourage Japan to be "responsible" among liberal democracies.

The much-debated number of 200,000 "comfort women" for the Imperial Japanese Armed Forces, colonial officials, and businessmen did not seem large to me. Nonetheless, I knew it was contentious and did my own calculations, albeit informally. The problem was one of definitions. Do you count only the women conscripted and trafficked or do you include the opportunities, the local hires, the orphanages, and the brothels purchased? I decided to include everyone and set the dates from 1937 to 1945. And I assumed a very high death rate from abuse, disease, and warfare.

My baseline was Japanese conservative nationalist military historian Ikuhiko Hata's estimate of 90,000 where he calculated three million soldiers and sailors where each woman was assigned 50 men with a 1.5 replacement rate.[26] To me, this seemed too low considering the actual number of men in arms (with the majority not in combat) when the war ended was over six million[27] and the number of military dead was 2.5 million.[28] In addition, the usual ratio cited in the literature was *ni-ku-ichi*: one woman for every 29, not 50, men.[29] None of the previous calculations included the untold number of Japanese colonial officials and businessmen who, according to fee schedules, could access the "comfort women" system.

These observations suggested a 100% replacement rate and a much larger demand than believed. I also assumed that most of the "comfort women" were not trafficked to specific battle zones, but extended rapes of captive local women, girls and boys throughout the Asia Pacific. Regional histories (backed by war crimes trial testimonies) suggest this as well. The effective destruction of Japan's shipping by Allied bombing further inhibited trafficking of the "comfort women." With these assumptions my calculations easily topped 200,000.

## Japan's Relationship with Its Neighbors: Back to the Future?

After I submitted my suggestions, I did not hear any more about the Resolution until June. I was unaware that my revisions were incorporated into the new "comfort women" Resolution, H.Res. 759. In May, I was asked to testify in June before the full House Committee on International Relations hearing on "Japan's Relationship with Its Neighbors: Back to the Future?" The result was that congressional affairs officials from both the Korean and Japanese embassies discovered me. I had visits from both. The hearing was, however, canceled twice, in both June and July, and rescheduled for September.

As I assumed that the Korean Embassy was aware of my work on the "comfort women" Resolution, I spoke to them about the rationale behind my edits. The Korean officials were taken aback and surprised to learn of my involvement in the redrafting of the legislation. Prior to this, only one member of the Korean Embassy was aware of my organization and then only as a subscriber to my calendar of Asia policy events newsletter. As a result, I was introduced to the Embassy's trade lobbyist Thomas Kim, who volunteered as a lobbyist for WCCW. He worked hard to garner congressional support for H.Res. 759. Kim repeatedly pointed out that he was doing "*this* for the women."

Thomas Kim was different from most lobbyists. Young and energetic, he was committed to his cause. He found that he had to activate a coalition that had never before come together for a political cause—the Asian American community. This was a new constituency for members of Congress. What I added to Kim's formidable lobbying talents, was a reliable resource on history and academic writing. Throughout the summer and fall, both members of Congress and the Congressional Research Service (CRS) occasionally called upon me for advice regarding the "comfort women." I would also answer historical questions from Kim and reporters that he directed my way. I assisted Kim in drafting fact sheets and talking points. I became his "scholar on call" to substantiate, edit, and temper his more political arguments.

I also developed a relationship with Rep. Evans' staff. His office asked me to participate as the scholarly expert along with Dr. Ok Cha Soh of WCCW at a September 21, 2006 press conference on Capitol Hill in support of the "comfort women" Resolution.[30] Filmmaker Dai Sil Kim-Gibson screened part of her documentary *Silence Broken* at the press conference. Several members of Congress [Chris Smith (R-NJ), Mike Honda (D-CA), Ed Royce (R-CA), and Diane Watson (D-CA)] all joined a very disabled Lane Evans in making statements.

Throughout the summer, Korean and Asian American activists and lobbyists, supported by international human rights organizations such as Amnesty International, secured nearly 60 congressional cosponsors including 16 Republicans for H.Res. 759. Their strategy built upon the new wording of the Resolution, which focused the issue away from a Korean national cause to one of the universal issues of human dignity and women's rights.

On September 24, 2006, the Resolution passed unanimously through the House Committee on International Relations. Chairman Hyde recommended that the Resolution be considered swiftly by the full House under the suspension of the rules (no debate and unanimous consent). The Resolution, however, never made it to the floor for a vote.

Japan's lobbyists, specifically former Minority Leader Bob Michel of Hogan & Hartson, convinced then-Speaker of the House Dennis Hastert, over a drink at the Capitol Hill Club, not to "report out" the Resolution for a floor vote. Michel reportedly argued that it was unnecessary to dredge up this past that would embarrass Japan's new, young Prime Minister Shinzo Abe. With the end of the 109th Congress in December 2006, so ended H.Res. 759.

## The Genesis of House Resolution 121

I learned a great deal about the legislative process and Japanese lobbying by defending H.Res. 759. I also learned that I needed a broader coalition of scholars and experts to help if there was ever another attempt at a resolution. There was strength in the neutral, matter-of-fact accounting of history. There is no need for hearsay or hyperbole in supporting arguments for the "comfort women" legislation. As noted, Holocaust scholar Deborah Lipstadt told me, "Just fight with the facts."

Advocates for the "comfort women" were emboldened by H.Res. 759's limited success. Properly worded and substantially supported by the Asian American and women's rights communities, a new resolution would be politically viable. Most significant, the resolution had energized the Korean American community—a nascent political group in the U.S. This was a critical development, as congressional interest in issues is based on constituencies. Lawmakers focus on who votes and who donates. The emergence of a new interest group was exciting.

Thus, supporters of the "comfort women," especially Thomas Kim, saw another opportunity to press for a new resolution after the November 2006 midterm congressional elections. To prepare, he contacted journalists to tell them the story of multi-million-dollar Japanese government lobbying on the "comfort women" and history. One result was the October 5, 2006 *Harper's Magazine* article by investigative journalist Ken Silverstein, "Cold Comfort: the Japan Lobby Blocks Resolution on WWII Sex Slaves."[31]

H.Res. 759 had capped a year of heightened awareness of the damaging effects of conflict-related violence against women. And the article highlighted the deep resistance of men in power to women's rights. The UN was studying sexual violence as a modern day peace and security challenge. Rape in warfare was becoming recognized as one of history's greatest silences. Research appeared showing that women were absent from ceasefire agreements, dismissed from disarmament programs, and rarely mentioned in peace negotiations. In 2006, the "comfort women" were a signature issue for both Amnesty International and V-Day.[32]

As a result, the "comfort women" issue moved beyond a grievance between Korea and Japan. It was no longer a "historical" war crime. The "comfort women" embodied a timeless problem faced by women and girls everywhere. At stake was the accountability of contemporary Japan in an era of new global norms for women, human rights, security, and violence.

## Writing of the "Comfort Women" Resolution

In November 2006, Democrats regained control of both the House and the Senate. The House of Representatives electing Nancy Pelosi (D-CA) as its first woman Speaker. Ms. Pelosi had been a "comfort women" cosponsor and her district is San Francisco, California, with strong Asian American and human rights constituencies. Mike Honda (D-CA) was named the new head of the Congressional Asian Pacific American Caucus. It was clear that the Asian American community was going to have a larger voice in this Congress than in the past.

By working with Representatives Hyde's and Evans' staff on the "comfort women" issue, I became known to a few within Congress as a serious expert on "comfort women" and Japanese war history. In December 2006, Mr. Kim, who worked closely with Honda's staff providing them information on the Evans "comfort women" Resolution, asked me to draft a new one. Kim was the "intermediary" between me and congressional staff, filtering congressional information requests.

In redrafting the Resolution, I felt that an important objective was to remove the "comfort women" issue as an impediment to regional relations and to create a roadmap to attain a satisfactory Japanese apology. Another task was to respond to and block Japan's many objections to the previous Resolutions. Informed by copies of their lobbying documents, I wanted to make it difficult for Japan's lobbyists to kill the Resolution.

I also knew I needed help from experts of Japanese history, politics, reconciliation, and translation. Thus, I began to put together a team.[33] This group first included then Connecticut College Japanese and Korean historian Professor Alexis Dudden, Dr. Mike Mochizuki of George Washington University, and Mr. Andrew Horvat, a Canadian journalist and scholar of Japanese reconciliation issues based in Tokyo. One limitation of past resolutions, I believed, was that they seemed too focused on one historical wrong and one ethnic group without any connection to the U.S. or contemporary foreign policy concerns. They also did not appeal to members on both sides of the aisle. I felt it was important to reframe the Resolution to make it relevant to the greater international human rights struggles.

In 2007, two issues were important to the United States and the Bush Administration: the U.S.-Japan alliance and combating human trafficking. Although separate, there was a link. Both were major, successful policy initiatives for the Bush Administration and both were associated with improving the American presence and image in Asia. Another link was that Japan came up short in both.[34] Internationally, the issues of the national reconciliation and sexual violence in conflict were prominent. Bosnia, Kosovo, Rwanda, Burma, Darfur, and many other national tragedies in which women were the primary victims dominated the world headlines. In June 2007, the UN created the UN Action Against Sexual Violence in Conflict (UN Action) that united the work of 13 UN entities with the goal of ending sexual violence in conflict and its accompanying culture of impunity.[35] Sexual violence was now viewed as a violation of fundamental human rights.

Regarding the U.S.-Japan alliance, I drew upon the language of the security dialogue in drafting the resolution. The focus of American efforts was to establish a working, reciprocal alliance with Japan. Washington wanted Japan to take responsibility and to commit adly to resolving international conflicts and participating in regional defense.

Thus, the draft included two important words from the security discussions: "unequivocal" and "responsibility." These words are ones that are sought by American negotiators in all agreements with Japan, whether it is trade or security. Horvat first suggested the use of the word "unequivocal" as opposed to "unambiguous" in referring to the apology. His decades of experience in Japan gave him a thorough understanding of what happens when something is unambiguous, but allowed to be equivocal.

Doubt, along with presenting one face to foreigners and another to domestic audiences, are constant features in Japanese diplomacy. Horvat was instrumental in ensuring that there were positive references to Japan's efforts toward the "comfort women." He counseled that praise was necessary for those who tried so hard to make things right for the victims. Horvat composed the first drafts of the paragraphs complimenting the now-defunct Asian Women's Fund.

The weakness in the draft, and one that continued to haunt the Resolution, was my sloppy wording of what Congress wanted the Government of Japan to do to ensure that an appropriate apology was offered to the "comfort women." I did not fully understand at the time the Japanese legislative process. The result is that I left the draft vague on what steps the Japanese government should take for the "comfort women." Past resolutions simply asked for an "official" governmental apology. Unfortunately, "official" could be interpreted a number of ways in Japanese. Here was a classic case of "unambiguous" vs. "unequivocal."

My final draft was submitted in early January 2007 to Mr. Kim, who then forwarded it to Mr. Honda's staff. Along the line, a number of changes were made. For example, I carefully avoided the word "coerce," knowing that this word was a hot button for Japan's right-wing who interpreted it narrowly as kidnapping. The "comfort women" system, however, fit the modern legal definition of sexual slavery, which is centered on coercion as defined as having no ability to leave or affect one's situation.

Mr. Kim, however, wanted to include it and likely reinserted it. Ironically, it was this word "coercion" that Japan's Prime Minister Shinzo Abe disputed during questioning in the Diet, resulting in his being criticized internationally for his insensitivity. Thus, this insertion proved to be a major boon for the Resolution.

More changes were made to the draft by Mr. Honda and the House Legislative Counsel. On a number of occasions, I had to defend my choice of the word "unequivocal" and told Honda's staff that they could change anything else, but "unequivocal" was foundational and should not be removed. On January 30, Mr. Honda "dropped the bill in the hopper" and it was assigned the bill number H.Res. 121.

## "Comfort Women" Hearing

Congressman Eni Faleomavaega (D-AS), Chairman of the House Foreign Affairs Subcommittee on Asia, the Pacific, and the Global Environment, in talking with his friend

Congressman Honda, decided that the best way to get the message out regarding the new Resolution would be a hearing with "comfort women." It would be a first and a very dramatic move—a good way for a new Committee Chairman to start his term. Thus, Faleomavaega's staff hurriedly arranged for a hearing on February 15, 2007.

I had only a few days to suggest possible surviving "comfort women" to testify at the hearing. At first, the organizers wanted all the witnesses to be Korean. I objected and felt that the hearing would be more powerful if it showed the diversity of the women swept up in the "comfort women" system. I suggested Mrs. Jan Ruff O'Herne, a Dutch, English-speaking survivor living in Australia. I had watched a 2001 TV interview with Mrs. O'Herne on the internet and was quite moved.[36] And frankly, I knew the power of having an elderly, white, Catholic woman testify to a predominantly white, conservative, male House of Representatives.

I was also asked to testify. Unfortunately, I was scheduled to go on a long-scheduled research trip on "comfort women" to Japan and Korea with my return the day before the hearing. Although I could not contribute much to the hearing planning, my trip to Japan and Korea was fortuitous. During my ten days in Japan and South Korea, I was able to meet with important "comfort women" scholars and activists. In Japan, I met with professors Hayashi Hirofumi, Yoshimi Yoshiaki, and Wada Haruki. Most important, I established a working relationship with the Women's Active Museum on War and Peace (WAM)[37] in Tokyo and their executive director Ms. Mina Watanabe.[38]

During the trip, I strengthened my ties with a number of scholars and translators in Japan who I had only known remotely. A significant meeting was with Michael Cucek, a political analyst who worked for a powerful Japanese businessman close to former Prime Minister Koizumi. He was personally familiar with the politics and language surrounding the Kono Statement and how the Japanese politicians finesse apology.

He pointed out the missing component in my conceptualization of what the Government of Japan needed to do to give an official statement. He explained the Japanese legislative process and the importance of a Cabinet Decision (*kakugi kettei*) to making an apology or any government statement *official*. His explanation, however, came minutes before I was to leave Japan for Korea, thus I asked him to write out what he had said and email it to me.

I spent the next few days preparing my congressional testimony in Seoul, on the KAL flight back to the U.S., on the floor of LaGuardia Airport in New York, at the Yale Club in New York City, and on the train to Washington mere hours before the hearing. The KAL flight had landed in New York during a snowstorm the day before the hearing. All flights out of New York were cancelled. By afternoon, my husband decided that I should stay in New York overnight and take the first train back, and hopefully make it to the hearing with about three hours to spare.

Throughout the process, I received answers to my questions from WAM and Cucek. WAM provided critical fact-checking, proofreading, and all the primary source documents that I tried to put[39] in the *Congressional Record*. Cucek provided the prose for all the more political sections of the testimony. I wrote the historical and impassioned sections. As I emailed Cucek after the testimony, "*You* spoke in the U.S. Congress today."

The highlight of the Congressional hearing, "Protecting the Human Rights of Comfort Women,"[40] were the testimonies of the three former "comfort women." Two came from South Korea accompanied by a baldheaded Buddhist nun and Mrs. O'Herne who traveled from Adelaide, Australia accompanied by Anna Song, co-founder and national director of the Friends of "Comfort Women" in Australia (FCWA).

As I predicted, there was not a dry eye in the packed hearing room after Mrs. O'Herne told of her being a convent-educated, virgin grasping her rosary as a drunken Japanese Army officer ripped off her clothes and raped her. The press did not report my testimony or that of Dr. Ok Cha Soh, president of WCCW. Also not reported was a visit to the hearing by Korea's Grand National Party member Ms. Park Geun-hye (who would later become South Korea's President).

During this time, Mr. Kim had to manage relations with the Embassy of Korea. He worked hard to keep the Embassy on the sidelines and to focus their efforts on getting agreement from Seoul that if Japan did give an apology that it would be warmly received (an opportunity missed). He also worked with the Embassy to keep Korean activists and legislators from hyping the issue in Korea. An overwrought South Korea would undermine the international and domestic efforts of the Resolution's supporters. There was no need for parallel legislation or demonstrations. While in Korea, I had an impassioned talk with women activists of The Korean Council for the Women Drafted for Military Sexual Slavery by Japan (The Korean Council) that they should not involve themselves in the U.S. initiative nor be critical of the U.S. during this time.[41]

After the hearing, I was told that the head of the Japanese Embassy congressional affairs section visited his Korean counterpart to ask/accuse him of manipulating the entire "comfort women" effort. Although the Korean Embassy was supportive, the issue had long gone beyond the control of the Embassy. It had become an American and liberal internationalist issue. The Embassy's job was merely to ensure that Korea was *not* involved. This, the Japanese did not understand (nor could). The Japanese diplomat was interested in stopping the "comfort women" Resolution and not in resolving the "comfort women" problem. It might have been interesting if the Korean diplomat had asked the Japanese official as to what Japan planned to do to resolve the apology issue as that was the most certain way to end congressional action. Japan was given an opportunity, but instead Tokyo simply saw it as a threat.

## Korean Community Activism

After the landmark February 15th "Comfort Women" Hearing, attendee Annabel Sohyun Park, a filmmaker was inspired to take up the cause. She became the national coordinator of the 121 Coalition, a network of second generation Korean Americans, and one of the most instrumental members of the greater team pushing for passage of the Resolution. Ms. Park, a Marshall Scholar and political activist, organized the Asian American communities to collect the 160 cosponsors of the resolution. This was unprecedented support for any issue by the Asian American community. Ms. Park noted that before attending the hearing, she had no strong attachment to the issue, but described hearing the testimony of the survivors as being akin to a "religious experience." She immediately set to work building a movement that would push for the passage of the Resolution. She felt that it had to be a national movement, so as to ensure that the resolution had a broad array of cosponsors in the House.

Connected with this was the problem of how to awaken the politically apathetic Korean Americans. She credits Japanese Prime Minister Abe for helping her mobilize the community. His March 1st remarks on the resolution in the Diet coincided with Korea's Independence Movement Day. Intended or not, his denial of the coercion of the "comfort women" was taken by Koreans worldwide as a targeted insult.[42] On March 2nd, Ms. Park emailed her contacts in the Asian American activist community, and got a larger-than-expected response thanks to Mr. Abe's remarks. Her initial effort yielded 60 Asian American organizations to sign on to the "comfort women" campaign. Ultimately, there were 200 pan-Asian groups involved, making "comfort women" a truly Asian American movement.

Prime Minister Abe's denial that women and girls were coerced or forced into becoming "comfort women" galvanized the "comfort women" movement. Ms. Park noted it generated incredible indignation and triggered the realization within the Asian American community of the need to be involved in the political process.

The rigorous academic work done to provide factual "comfort women" history and to show the more contemporary histories of rape in war, Ms. Park said, was important in connecting the disparate nodes of the nascent movement, as it helped reframe the issue from a Korean-Japanese disagreement to "a universal problem." The "comfort women" were not just another tragic episode of contested Korean history. Thanks to this new approach, Ms. Park said that the activists were better able to stand up to criticism, unlike before when activists would "crumble when attacked." Even more important, the reframing of the "comfort women" issue provided an understandable, brief "sound bite" to congressional supporters: "The "comfort women" are a fight for international women's rights. It is a fight against rape and human trafficking. It is a fight to protect today's and tomorrow's women." It is simply about human dignity.

The role played by the lobbyist Thomas Kim in doing behind-the-scenes work on behalf of the Resolution was equally critical to the Resolution's success. He helped the activists prepare a roadmap for their activities, but he did not micromanage the campaign. The activist network was able to tap his knowledge about Capitol Hill, learn who to approach, and get tips on how to frame the "comfort women" argument with members. He communicated to the activists how the members were reacting to the campaign and kept track of the shifting requirement imposed by House Foreign Affairs Committee Chairman Tom Lantos as to how many cosponsors were needed for the Resolution before he felt comfortable enough that there was enough of an American constituency supporting the Resolution and to successfully bring it to the full Committee for a vote.

The "comfort women" campaign, Ms. Park observed, was like a "guerrilla" insurgency. Various "cells" were working on behalf of the Resolution without knowing about the existence of other "cells." No one knew everything. Due to the fact that no single activist was aware of the full extent of activities being undertaken, Ms. Park had to manage egos, ensuring that each was receiving sufficient credit for their work. In particular, Ms. Park struggled daily to control

Ignatius Ding's Global Alliance (of Chinese Americans), who felt others were too soft on the Japanese. They had a good network, but there was always the risk that they would say something inappropriate or anti-Japanese that would jeopardize the whole process.

In contrast to the efforts of the Resolution's American supporters, the Japanese government's methods were top-down and less public. Japan's Washington Embassy used the old connections it had with lobbyists—especially Bob Michel, an influential former Republican congressman and House Minority Leader—to approach the White House and House GOP leaders about H.Res. 121. In many respects the Japanese and their advisers ignored the democratic process in the U.S. and appeared to assume that American foreign policy was an oligarchy. This strategy had succeeded in the past and no one thought it that this case would be any different.

I felt it was strange that the Japanese did not change their lobbying strategy to fit the fact that Congress was now under Democratic control. The Embassy greatly underestimated the influence of civil society and grass roots organizations on Congress. Neither the Prime Minister's office nor the Foreign Ministry appeared to understand that an unpopular Republican president would have little control over a newly empowered Democratic Congress. And finally, the Embassy did not realize the importance of combating human trafficking in the Bush Administration's foreign policy. This problem was always mentioned on U.S. Embassy websites as among the top five "hot issues." No one wanted to be identified as "for" the slave trade.

The activist network worked tirelessly to solidify congressional support. One member who had to be won over was Ileana Ros-Lehtinen (R-FL-18), the ranking member of the House Foreign Affairs Committee. She was strongly anti-communist, anti-China, and an advocate of the U.S.-Japan alliance. Her support was secured by her Filipino constituents and with amendments to the Resolution, suggested by the Japanese Embassy's lobbyists. Added were two clauses that complimented Japan as an important ally of the United States.

Another challenge was Tom Lantos, the Committee's chairman. The activists worked with the Filipino community in Lantos' district in the San Francisco Bay area to hand-deliver letters to Lantos' office. And in the end, his raw experience as a Holocaust survivor won him over.

Throughout the process, I continued to brief Mr. Honda, his office point person Ms. Ayame Nagatani, CRS, and Mr. Kim. I initiated briefing papers that were critical for better understanding Japanese responses and the historical facts. My scholars also had spirited discussions over translations and governmental procedure to ensure that the papers were accurate.[43]

## Japanese Government Hubris

The "best advocate" for the "comfort women" was then-Prime Minister of Japan, Shinzo Abe. An outspoken conservative nationalist, he entered office in the fall of 2006 with a stated goal of rescinding what little official status the 1993 Kono Statement had for setting an apology for Imperial Japan's establishment and management of the "comfort women" system. Abe established a committee to dispute the Kono Statement and his government did issue a Cabinet Decision in March 2007 stating that the Kono Statement was *not* a Cabinet Decision.

Wada Haruki, the Executive Director of the Asian Women's Fund (AWF) told me in 2007 that the work toward a U.S. congressional "comfort women" resolution saved the Kono Statement. If there had not been international, especially American, attention focused on Japan's apology, there would have been no resistance in Japan to modifying or eliminating the Kono Statement. That was a significant achievement, Dr. Wada believed. Interestingly, Wada did not see the need to pass the "comfort women" Resolution nor to confirm the Kono Statement with a Cabinet Decision.

Prime Minister Abe made two other public attempts to stop the "comfort women" Resolution and defuse the arising tensions. Both were unqualified disasters. As noted above, on March 1, 2007, an important historic Korean national holiday, Abe said in the Diet that he did not believe that there was evidence that the "comfort women" were "coerced." This view is a popular among Japanese conservative nationalists.

What Abe said is subject to interpretation. *The New York Times* Tokyo Bureau Chief Norimitsu Onishi, however, set the marker for its interpretation. He reported that Abe denied that "comfort women" were coerced and thus had no legitimate grievance against Japan. The "comfort women" were merely willing prostitutes. Onishi's translation shot around the world and generated a spate of editorials condemning the Japanese Prime Minister in all the world's major newspapers. *The New York Times* editorial, "No Comfort" most likely written by one of the members of my scholars committee, was the most influential.[44]

The next month, April, Mr. Abe made his first official visit to Washington. He went directly from his plane to Capitol Hill to meet with a select group of congressional leaders organized by Senator Daniel Inouye (D-HI) in the chambers of the Speaker of the House Pelosi. Prior to the meeting, Inouye, who opposed the "comfort women" Resolution, wrote a letter to the House leadership outlining his concerns. The letter noted the list of apologies provided by the Japanese Embassy (most of which made no direct mention of "comfort women") and added that the Senator thought that the Resolution would harm U.S.-Japan relations. It is highly unusual for a Senator to contact members of the House on legislation over which the Senate has no jurisdiction. Much of the letter, moreover, was cut and pasted from the Embassy of Japan lobbying documents (awkward punctuation and all).[45]

Without being asked, Abe told[46] those assembled that "I heartily sympathize, as a person and as the Prime Minister, with the former 'comfort women' who underwent hardships/privations; I am filled with the feeling of being sorry for [the fact] that they were put into extremely severe conditions/situation." Abe's interpreter actually used the expression "sense of being sorry." No one in the room understood what that meant other than it was not the apology they were waiting to hear. Senator Inouye ran damage control and added that Japan had apologized enough and that he was embarrassed that this issue had come up so many times in the House.

After the meeting I received calls from staffers present at the meeting asking what "feeling of being sorry" meant. I said that it was a literal translation from the Japanese of a very weak sense of empathy. The scholars in my group who were professional translators prepared a memo explaining the sentence's nuances to members of congress. Interestingly, after leaving Washington, Abe stated publicly on May 1st that he had *not* apologized to the "comfort women" in Washington (a memo was prepared on this as well). Thus, he confirmed what those present in the Speaker's office already knew. The meeting sealed the fate of the "comfort women" Resolution; it was to go forward unhindered.

If Abe's statement did not confirm to those present of the importance of the "comfort women" Resolution, then his joint press conference with the U.S. President did. Here, Abe gave another "apology" for the "comfort women." President George W. Bush responded that he *accepted* the Prime Minister's apology. The problem was that the apology was not his to accept. The President of the United States does not represent the "comfort women" (although there were some Americans). Here, Abe neatly and unwittingly set up a confrontation between the Democratic Congress and a Republican White House. The "comfort women" Resolution turned into an easy form of defiance to the President and a reminder that Congress matters.

The activist community used Abe's visit to publicize his retrogressive views. They paid for a quarter-page ad in the April 26, 2007 *Washington Post* discussing "The Truth About the 'comfort women,'" Amnesty International organized a protest near the White House complete with an aged "comfort woman" from South Korea. Every word Abe said seemed to energize the Korean American community. Ms. Park organized dynamic teams of elderly non-English speaking Korean Americans with articulate Korean American college students to visit congressional offices. These teams were aggressive in seeking out congressmen and encouraging them to cosponsor the "comfort women" Resolution. More importantly, they were a dramatic presentation of the new Asian American political power. These teams, the petitions, the fundraisers, the letters, and private meetings made an incredible impression upon members of Congress. The Asian American vote became meaningful.

In response to the Korean community's April advertisement, Japan's conservative nationalists paid over $100,000 for their own advocacy ad in *The Washington Post*. The June 14, 2007 full-page "The Facts" advertorial was a surprise. Although it did help galvanize support for the Resolution, it was not essential. The ad merely confirmed the unrepentant image of the current Japanese administration on the Hill. My team prepared for Congress an 18-page, detailed analysis of the statements and the backgrounds of all the signatories.[47]

Maddeningly, the ad also noted that American occupying forces in Japan had maintained comfort stations. This prompted Congressman Honda to ask the Congressional Research Service (CRS) to prepare a report on the issue. Yes, there were "comfort stations" during the first six months of American occupation of Japan. Called the Recreation and Amusement Association (RAA), they were set up by the interim Japanese government to meet the occupying forces. These brothels mirrored what Imperial Japan had established for its military. They were not an American invention. Allied Supreme Commander General Douglas MacArthur had them all shut down in February 1946.

The Japanese Embassy was reportedly appalled by the ad and did what it could to distance itself from its authors. They even issued a press statement denying involvement. The Japanese diplomats now understood that they could no longer defend Japan on the "comfort women" issue. Japan's conservative nationalists had seized the debate in the U.S. away from the diplomats' reasoned ambiguity. Some Japanese journalists even suggested that the ad's sponsors knew that the advertorial would be negatively perceived in the U.S. Their objective was for the "comfort women" Resolution to pass in order to spark a crisis in the U.S.-Japan relationship and sabotage Mr. Abe's efforts to improve Japan's relations with its Asian neighbors. There has been no concrete evidence supporting this view, however.

## Moving the Resolution to a Vote

The irony of the advertorial was that it appeared the same morning that Mr. Honda went to see House Speaker Nancy Pelosi to make "the ask" for her support of the Resolution going forward (a three-minute meeting). Basically, the ad solidified a decision that had already been made. And the strident language, so reminiscent of Holocaust deniers, allowed the lone Holocaust survivor in Congress and House Foreign Affairs Chairman Tom Lantos to feel comfortable with the Speaker's decision to move forward.

Behind the scenes, Mr. Kim worked closely with members of Congress to determine the timing of the House Foreign Affairs Committee vote (delayed to allow for Prime Minister Abe's April visit) and the subsequent floor vote. He also advised Ms. Park and others as to who, when, and how to approach members of Congress. My interns and I worked on translations, talking points, floor speeches, and answering questions. By the time there was a floor vote on the Resolution, the Asian American community activists had obtained 167 cosponsors, which was a historic high for a non-binding resolution.

Whereas there was only loose coordination between the three of us, and I was generally unaware of the political work being done, each component was incomplete without the other. On the night before the House Foreign Affairs Committee's vote on the Resolution, there was a flurry of emails and phone calls among me, Mr. Kim, and Mr. Cucek. We had only hours to respond to the Embassy of Japan's demands to the Republican Committee members to amend the Resolution. The Republican staff, however, appalled by the extensive Japanese revisions and prevarications pared them down.

The Japanese Embassy had persuaded Republicans Ileana Ros-Lehtinen and Dana Rohrabacher to submit revised resolutions. The requested changes focused on Japan as a reformed adversary that had become "the cornerstone of United States security interests in Asia and the Pacific and is fundamental to regional stability and prosperity." Rohrabacher wanted to scratch the entire Resolution in favor of one simply praising the U.S.-Japan alliance in combatting terrorism. In the end, two of Ros-Lehtinen's clauses on the alliance were added as well as an odd change to how a Japanese prime minister should deliver the apology.[48]

Reluctantly, I agreed to the changes and prepared a memo as to why they, in the end, were self-defeating for Japan. The essential words "responsibility" and "unequivocal" were retained. In fact, it was not until much later after the Resolution was passed, that the Japanese realized the importance of these words. Here it is interesting to note, I was never once contacted by a Japanese journalist. They seemed content to speculate about the Resolution and its origins.

On July 30, 2007, H.Res. 121, amended, passed unanimously. The Chair of the House Foreign Affairs Committee, Tom Lantos and its Ranking Member Ros-Lehtinen spoke on the floor in support of the Resolution. Mr. Lantos did the unusual and introduced the Resolution himself.

## In Retrospect

Passage in the House of Representatives of H.Res. 121 was a grand success. It depended upon a lot of work from unpaid dedicated activists, community leaders, and scholars. And it awakened the Korean American community across generations to value involvement in the political process.

Unfortunately, passage of this simple Resolution also energized Japan's right. Discrediting the people and facts of the Resolution roused those in Japan who felt the body politic needed to free itself from the "masochistic" postwar era. Shinzo Abe's return to power in late 2012 marked a revival of the assault on Japan's war history in general and the "comfort women" specifically. Right-wing groups found access to the Abe administration by advocating against the "comfort women" history. Sadly, by 2014 Abe was largely successful in stripping the Kono Statement of meaning and replacing it with doubt.

In 2006, Abe wanted Japan to follow the path of "value-oriented diplomacy." Japan was to be a solid supporter of the universal values of democracy, freedom, human rights, rule of law, and market economies. These are, however, political and economic systems not values in themselves. Undeterred, the second Abe administration reinvented this policy as defending the "liberal international order" and its values. Neither goal, however, can be accomplished without Tokyo gaining trust by coming to terms with its wartime past, especially the "comfort women." Central to this effort, Japan must convert its culture of impunity into one of justice and accountability. Prime Minister Abe still needs to define his country's values of compassion and contrition.

---

[1] https://www.congress.gov/resources/display/content/How+Our+Laws+Are+Made+-+Learn+About+the+Legislative+Process#HowOurLawsAreMade-LearnAbouttheLegislativeProcess-FORMSOFCONGRESSIONALACTION.

[2] https://www.house.gov/the-house-explained/the-legislative-process/bills-resolutions.

[3] Gavan Daws, *Prisoners of the Japanese: POWs of World War II in the Pacific* (New York: William Morrow & Co., 1994).

[4] Dornan also wanted to embarrass then-President Bill Clinton who had deceptively received a draft deferment from Bataan Death March survivor and head of the University of Arkansas ROTC Col. Eugene B. Holmes. *See*: https://www.congress.gov/congressional-record/1996/2/5/extensions-of-remarks-section/article/E168-2.

[5] https://www.congress.gov/congressional-record/1995/5/25/house-section/article/h5593-3?q=%7B%22search%22%3A%22%5C%22comfort+women%5C%22%22%7D&s=3&r=1.

[6] https://www.congress.gov/bill/104th-congress/house-concurrent-resolution/176/text.

[7] https://www.congress.gov/bill/105th-congress/house-concurrent-resolution/126.

[8] Author's telephone interview with Jason Tai on December 24, 2019.

[9] Assembly Joint Resolution No. 27. *Relative to the war crimes committed by the Japanese military during World War II*, http://leginfo.legislature.ca.gov/faces/billTextClient.xhtml?bill_id=199920000AJR27.

[10] https://www.congress.gov/crec/1999/10/06/modified/CREC-1999-10-06-pt1-PgS12099-4.htm.

---

[11] There was one prior stand-alone mention, but not for a legislative purpose. On July 18, 1995, Congresswoman Patricia Schroeder (D-CO) entered an extension of remarks into the Congressional Record commending Japan for its apology to the "comfort women." *See*: https://www.congress.gov/congressional-record/1995/7/18/extensions-of-remarks-section/article/e1453-2?q=%7B%22search%22%3A%22comfort+women%22%7D&s=1&r=1. Here it should also be noted, that Congresswoman Schroeder hosted as an intern in her Washington office Ms. Sanae Takaichi from mid-1987 to 1989. Takaichi went on to have a successful political career as an alt-right, "comfort women" denier in the LDP holding several positions in the Shinzo Abe I and II Cabinets.

[12] https://www.congress.gov/congressional-record/1999/11/8/extensions-of-remarks-section/article/e2307-2?q=%7B%22search%22%3A%5B%22%5C%22comfort+women%5C%22%22%5D%7D&s=9&r=1.

[13] https://www.congress.gov/bill/106th-congress/house-concurrent-resolution/195.

[14] From 1975 to 1978 and from 1995 to 2007, The House Committee on Foreign Affairs was renamed the Committee on International Relations. In January 2007 (and January 1979), it changed back to its original name. Its jurisdiction is and was the same under both names.

[15] https://www.congress.gov/bill/107th-congress/house-concurrent-resolution/195.

[16] https://www.congress.gov/congressional-record/2001/7/24/extensions-of-remarks-section/article/e1412-1?q=%7B%22search%22%3A%22%5C%22comfort+women%5C%22%22%7D&s=3&r=7.

[17] Frank Wolf (R-VA-10) and Chris Smith (R-NJ-4). It is unusual for any type of successful legislation not to be cosponsored by the party in power or not being the lead sponsor.

[18] https://www.congress.gov/bill/108th-congress/house-concurrent-resolution/226.

[19] https://www.congress.gov/bill/109th-congress/house-concurrent-resolution/68.

[20] Adam Clymer, "Former Rep. Henry Hyde Is Dead at 83," *The New York Times*, November 30, 2007, https://www.nytimes.com/2007/11/30/washington/29cnd-hyde.html.

[21] https://www.congress.gov/bill/109th-congress/house-concurrent-resolution/191?s=10&r=2.

[22] Conversations in 2007 and 2019 by the author with former House International Relations Asia staffer Dennis Halpin who worked closely with Chairman Hyde.

[23] https://www.japantimes.co.jp/news/2006/05/17/national/bid-to-address-congress-has-yasukuni-proviso/.

[24] https://www.govinfo.gov/app/details/CHRG-109hhrg29883/CHRG-109hhrg29883. This hearing was not held until September 14, 2006.

[25] https://www.congress.gov/bill/109th-congress/house-resolution/759.

[26] http://www.awf.or.jp/e1/facts-07.html.

[27] https://history.army.mil/books/wwii/MacArthur%20Reports/MacArthur%20V1%20Sup/ch5.htm#b6.

[28] https://www.mhlw.go.jp/stf/seisakunitsuite/bunya/hokabunya/senbotsusha/seido01/index.html.

[29] https://tinyurl.com/whymm79.

[30] This date is also Shinzo Abe's birthday, which was unknown to the meeting organizers.

[31] https://apjjf.org/-Ken-Silverstein/2253/article.html.

[32] https://www.vday.org/about.html#.XgFBN1VKgdU.

[33] The research "team" eventually included, but not limited to: William Brooks (former head of the Office of Translation, U.S. Embassy Japan), Tessa Morris-Suzuki (Australian National University); Tobias Harris (*Observing Japan*); Daniel Sturgeon (Rotary Peace Fellow); William Underwood (Independent Scholar); Daqing Yang (George Washington University); James Gibney (*Foreign Policy*); Lily Gardner Feldman (American Institute for Contemporary German Studies).

[34] Japan did not have anti-human trafficking laws until 2005.

[35] https://www.un.org/sexualviolenceinconflict/. The Office of the Special Representative of the Secretary-General on Sexual Violence in Conflict was established in 2009.

[36] https://www.youtube.com/watch?v=Mard9WrYn2I.

[37] https://wam-peace.org/.

[38] WAM is a research center, museum, library, and archive on the "comfort women." The Japanese women at WAM provided incredible research, translation, and support for my testimony and congressional briefings. They were prepared for quick, factual answers, retrieving documents, and committed to late nights of research

and translation. In many respects, the women at WAM are the true heroes of the "comfort women" Resolution.

[39] Although all the documents I requested to be placed in the Congressional Record, including former Prime Minister Nakasone's war memoir of setting up a comfort station in Indonesia, were approved by the Chairman in the record, none were printed in the official Committee hearing report. This is very unusual.

[40] https://www.govinfo.gov/content/pkg/CHRG-110hhrg33317/pdf/CHRG-110hhrg33317.pdf.

[41] http://womenandwar.net/kr/.

[42] https://nyti.ms/2Q9NDkU.

[43] Among these many memos were: *What Constitutes an "Official" Government Statement in Japan: With Special Reference to Apologies for "comfort women"* (April 2007); *Did Abe Apologize to the "comfort women" in his meeting on Capitol Hill?* (April 27, 2007); *Prime Minister Abe and his Government Disavow Notion of an "Apology" in Washington* (June 1, 2007); *Understanding the Embassy of Japan's Assertions on "comfort women": Liberties Taken with Facts and Language* (June 6, 2007); *Who They Are: Signatories to The Washington Post June 14th Open Letter to Congress on the "comfort women" Issue* (June 19, 2007).

[44] https://nyti.ms/2GsVdCA.

[45] https://drive.google.com/file/d/1JRBPs294_KkqtnQStS7tIIYjYx5paC_I/view?usp=sharing.

[46] I was told by various staffers who attended the meeting.

[47] I had to direct this research from California. On the same day as the advertorial, June 14, 2007, my husband had the first of a series of epileptic seizures brought on by a pulmonary embolism from deep vein thrombosis (DVT) while on a business trip to California.

[48] *See* June 26, 2007 "House Foreign Affairs Committee" markup transcript, 155-189, https://permanent.access.gpo.gov/websites/archives.republicans.foreignaffairs.house.gov/110/36421.pdf.

# 4. THE "COMFORT WOMEN" ISSUE BROUGHT TO THE FOREFRONT OF THE U.S. CONGRESS

*Dennis P. Halpin*

**Abstract:** This chapter addresses the involvement of key Members of Congress, including Lane Evans, Henry Hyde, Tom Lantos, Eni Faleomavaega and Ileana Ros-Lehtinen to raise the issue of the sexual servitude of the "comfort women," of Korean and a number of other nationalities, under the military of Imperial Japan in the Pacific Theater during the Second World War. This research will also be conducted from a perspective of how the "comfort women" issue has assumed a larger global meaning in the context of more recent examples of violence against women in armed conflicts and of the Me Too movement in the United States. The paper also examines how the long dormant Korean American community, assisted by other Asian victim ethnic communities, organized to ultimately successfully lobby to push forward an examination of the "comfort women" issue and sponsored House Resolution 121 by the U.S. House of Representatives.

## Introduction

The history of the "comfort women" issue as a focus of policy and legislative concern for the U.S. Congress (specifically the U.S. House of Representatives) began with the active involvement of Congressman Lane Evans, Democrat of Illinois. He reportedly gained some knowledge of the issue of sexual violence against women while stationed as a U.S. Marine in Okinawa during the Vietnam War. There have been a number of incidents of nonconsensual sex involving the U.S. service members and Okinawan women during the stationing of the U.S. military personnel on the island in the decades following the Second World War. The abduction and sexual assault of a twelve-year-old Okinawan girl by three U.S. servicemen on September 4, 1995, was of particular concern. This assault occurred just before former First Lady Hillary Rodham Clinton arrived in Beijing for the UN Fourth World Conference on Women. While in Beijing, on September 5th, Mrs. Clinton delivered her famous remarks that "women's rights are human rights." One of the first international demonstrations regarding the "comfort women" issue also occurred during this conference, organized by South Korean and Philippine NGOs in Huairou, China.

In this chapter, specific examples of Congressional action on the issue of "comfort women" will be discussed including the repeated resolutions introduced by Congressman Lane Evans of Illinois, starting in 2000 after the first "comfort women" survivors had emerged to give public testimony. The research goes into the key relationship between Representative Evans and Chairman Henry Hyde of the House Foreign Affairs Committee in the summer of 2006 which led to the first Committee markup in Congressional history of H.Res. 759 in the fall of 2006 as well as a Committee hearing at the same time on the damage done to Japan's relations with her neighbors due to unresolved human rights issues from the Pacific War, including most notably the "comfort women" issue. It will further examine the successful lobbying efforts of the Japanese Embassy and Government to convince then Speaker Dennis Hastert to block bringing H.Res. 759 to a vote on the Floor of the House in the closing days of the 109th Congress.

The research will demonstrate that the U.S. Congressional elections of November 2006, in which control of the House of Representatives flipped from Republican to Democratic control, was instrumental in the movement of the "comfort women" issue forward. (The new Speaker Nancy Pelosi and the Democratic leadership were far more sympathetic to a vetting of this major human rights and women's rights issue than the previous Republican leadership.)

This chapter will examine the subsequent successful actions of the 110th Congress, which convened in January 2007. These included the introduction of a new "comfort women" Resolution, H.Res. 121, by Congressman Mike Honda of California and the convening of the first-ever Congressional hearing including the testimony of "comfort women" survivors (two from Korea and one Dutch-Australian) by the new Chairman of the Asia Subcommittee Eni Faleomavaega. The research will indicate how extreme lobbying actions by the Japanese right-wing, including an offensive advertisement in *The Washington Post* newspaper which compared the U.S. soldiers' sexual activities in Occupied Japan to the "comfort women" system of sexual slavery, backfired with several influential Members of the House, including Ranking Republican Member on the House Foreign Affairs Committee Ileana Ros-Lehtinen. The research will record how, under the guidance of Foreign Affairs Committee Chairman Tom Lantos, H.Res. 121 was successfully marked up in Committee in June 2007. This was followed by the new Democratic leadership bringing H.Res. 121 to the Floor for a historic vote on July 30, 2007, where it was adopted on a motion to suspend the rules and a voice vote was taken. This action by the U.S. House of Representatives greatly raised the international profile of the "comfort women" issue and led to a subsequent adoption of similar resolutions by other law-making bodies.

The long-term impact, however, has seen renewed Japanese official and private efforts to remove Comfort Women memorials and statues in Palisades Park, New Jersey and Glendale, California as well as in Busan, Republic of Korea and the severing of Sister City ties between San Francisco and Osaka. At the same time the key American legislative figures in the U.S. House of Representatives who championed the "comfort women" issue have either passed away or retired from the House. The question is then: who will carry the legacy of "comfort women" forward, in the broader context of women's rights and sexual violence in conflict, now that Evans, Hyde, Honda, Faleomavaega, Ros-Lehtinen, and Lantos are all departed from the legislative stage?

## Lane Evans and Henry Hyde, Two Illinoisans

As with many international advocates for justice on the "comfort women" issue, Representative Evans, who was first elected to the U.S. House in 1982, reportedly became fully aware of the tragic circumstances of "comfort women" victims after Korean victim Kim Hak-soon came forward in Seoul in the summer of 1991 and demanded that Japan take responsibility for its war-time crimes of sexual servitude. Korean American human rights activist and current Columbia College professor Ok Cha Soh, former President of the Washington Coalition for Comfort Women Issues (WCCW), also actively engaged Representative Evans on the "comfort women" issue and advocated that concrete action be taken by the American Congress. As a result, beginning in 2001, Representative Evans repeatedly introduced resolutions in each Congress stating that "the Government of Japan should formally acknowledge and accept responsibility for its sexual enslavement of young women, known to the world as "comfort women," during its colonial occupation of Asia and the Pacific Islands from the 1930s through the duration of World War II." However, due to both vigorous lobbying efforts by the Japanese Embassy and Government, as well as concerns expressed by Members of Congress over a potential adverse impact on the U.S.-Japan alliance, none of these resolutions sponsored by Congressman Evans moved forward in the House.

That stalemate dramatically changed in 2006 when a number of factors came together to break the long-standing Congressional impasse on the "comfort women" issue. The Chairman of the then-named House Committee on International Affairs, Henry Hyde of Illinois, was a veteran of the Pacific Theater in World War II, having served as a U.S. Navy Captain in the invasion of Lingayen Gulf and the subsequent liberation of the Philippines from Imperial Japan's occupation. As such, Chairman Hyde became quite concerned when he learned that Japanese revisionists, including then Japanese Prime Minister Koizumi Junichiro, were paying regular visits to Tokyo's Yasukuni War Shrine to pay tribute to the spirit tablet of Prime Minister Hideki Tojo, the architect of the Pearl Harbor attack, as well as to the tablets of other convicted war criminals. Chairman Hyde, as a representative of WWII's "Greatest Generation," which still clearly remembered the surprising Imperial Japanese attack on Pearl Harbor, was so concerned over historic revisionism in Japan that he sent a letter as a House Committee Chairman to then Japanese Ambassador Ryozo Kato on October 20, 2005 (A.4-1):

> In this regard, I feel some regret over the continued visits of Japanese Government officials to the Yasukuni Shrine in Tokyo. As a World War II veteran of the Pacific, I deeply sympathize with the desire to honor the memory of the soldiers and civilians of all nations who died in the greatest conflagration of the Twentieth Century. I also understand the pain felt by those who lost loved ones in that horrific war. The Yasukuni Shrine, however, honors more than these persons. It pays tribute to the memory of Hideki Tojo and other convicted war criminals who gave the orders for the unprovoked attack on the U.S. Pacific Fleet at Pearl Harbor on December 7, 1941. This attack then plunged the nations of the Asia-Pacific region into four years of total warfare. The Shrine, thus, has become a symbol throughout Asia and the rest of the world of unresolved history from the Second World War and of those militaristic attitudes which spawned the War in the Pacific.[1]

Chairman Hyde was further concerned in the spring of 2006 when he learned of the suggestion that Japanese Prime Minister Koizumi, during an upcoming official visit to

Washington, D.C., address the Congress while at the same time continuing his annual visits to Yasukuni Shrine. Hyde, therefore, sent a letter to then Speaker of the House Dennis Hastert, a fellow Illinois Republican, on April 26, 2006 (A.4-2). In that letter Hyde stated that "There has been some press speculation that the expected visit by Prime Minister Koizumi might include the suggestion that he address a Joint Session of the Congress. That would also be most welcome with one important qualification: Prime Minister Koizumi, who will retire in September, has made a public pledge that he will visit the Yasukuni Shrine in Tokyo during every year of his Prime Ministership. He has not yet made such a visit in 2006. There is some suggestion that he will do so on or around August 15, the sixty-first anniversary of the end of hostilities in the Pacific War."[2] Hyde's letter noted further:

> This visit could give rise to potential embarrassment for the Congress, since President Franklin Roosevelt addressed his "date which will live in infamy" speech to this very same body on December 8, 1941. It would be an awkward juxtaposition of events if the Japanese Prime Minister were to visit a shrine that pays homage to Hideki Tojo and other leaders of Imperial Japan, who gave the orders for the unprovoked attack on the U.S. Pacific Fleet at Pearl Harbor, a mere few weeks after his appearance before the United States Congress. I am concerned that the dwindling number of living World War II veterans, who still remember Pearl Harbor as a younger generation of Americans remembers September 11th, would be concerned and even offended by such an occurrence.

Chairman Hyde fully intended that his letter to Speaker Hastert be kept private and confidential. However, a copy of the letter subsequently was leaked by an unknown source to the press, as reported by UPI.[3] The resulting uproar led to the cancellation of any potential plans for Prime Minister Koizumi to address the American Congress. As a result of that cancellation, President George W. Bush, as a consolation prize to his close friend, the Japanese Prime Minister, flew Koizumi after his Washington visit on Air Force One to Memphis for a visit to the Elvis Presley mansion and gravesite at Graceland. Koizumi is known as an unabashed Presley fan. The public address system on Air Force One reportedly played "Love Me Tender" and "Don't Be Cruel" inflight.[4] Priscilla and Lisa Marie Presley greeted the two leaders upon their arrival at Graceland. The Hyde letter to Hastert raised grave concern in Japanese lobbying circles. There was a fear that Hyde, as Chairman of the House Committee which oversees foreign relations, would take concrete action to further address the unresolved issue of Pacific War history before he surrendered his gavel as Chairman at the end of the 109th Congress in January 2007. Tokyo called upon one of its chief Washington lobbyists, the law firm of Hogan & Hartson (now Hogan Lovells) to seek to ensure that Chairman Hyde did not take any precipitous action. An article in *The Hill*, published on February 6, 2014, reported that "The Japanese government paid Hogan Lovells more than $523,000 from September 2012 to August 2013, according to Justice records."[5]

The firm had already sent one of its attorneys, Ray Calamaro, on repeated occasions in 2005 and 2006 to meet with Committee staff in charge of Asian issues in order to emphasize the importance of the U.S.-Japan alliance (once described as "the most important bilateral relationship in the world, bar none" by former U.S. Ambassador to Tokyo and Senate Majority Leader Mike Mansfield). Calamaro also warned of the irreparable damage that would be done to that alliance if the International Relations Committee undertook formal consideration of H.Res. 759, the latest House resolution introduced by Rep. Lane Evans, "Expressing the sense of the House of Representatives that the Government of Japan should formally acknowledge and accept responsibility for its sexual enslavement of young women, known to the world as "comfort women," during its colonial occupation of Asia and the Pacific Islands from the 1930s through the duration of World War II, and for other purposes."[6]

Calamaro, however, was not considered a prominent enough figure to directly approach Henry Hyde. For that mission, the law firm called upon its biggest gun, former House Minority Leader Bob Michel who had joined Hogan & Hartson as an adviser after his retirement from the House in 1995. Michel, an Illinois Republican like Hyde, has been the longest-serving Republican leader in the history of the House of Representatives and had known Hyde for decades. Soon after the letter from Chairman Hyde to Speaker Hastert had been leaked to the press, Bob Michel sought a meeting with his old colleague. There Michel explained the importance of the U.S.-Japan alliance and the need to leave past issues in the past—"to let bygones be bygones." At that meeting, which I attended, Michel drew a verbal pledge from Henry Hyde not to take any formal Committee action on H.Res. 759.

That Hyde decision, however, was to suddenly change during the summer of 2006 due to contact from yet another Illinois Congressman—Lane Evans. Mr. Evans was suffering from the debilitating effects of Parkinson's disease which had led to his decision not to seek re-election in the 2006 elections after having served twelve House terms. He and Henry Hyde had thus served over two decades together on the Illinois Congressional delegation. During the August recess, Evans, back in Illinois for medical treatment, placed a telephone call to Hyde in his office in the House Rayburn Office Building. Evans made a heart-felt appeal to Hyde in that memorable phone call. "Henry," he said, "even though we served on opposite sides of the aisle, we are both colleagues from Illinois—the Land of Lincoln. We are both retiring at the end of the current Congress. I am asking you, as a fellow Illinoisan, to do me a final favor and to address an issue of slavery just as Lincoln once addressed." Hyde, who was a bit surprised, asked what that favor was. "Henry, as Chairman of the International Relations Committee, could you bring my resolution, H.Res. 759, on the 'comfort women' issue, up for consideration by the Committee in a markup session this fall?" Evans asked. Hyde took a long pause as he considered the request. Then he said, "Okay, Lane, I can do that for you."

Thus, H.Res. 759 became the first "comfort women" Resolution ever to be formally considered and passed out of Committee for potential consideration in the entire history of the U.S. House of Representatives. Hyde, however, wished to have confirmation of the facts of the sexual slavery of the "comfort women" before formally undertaking such a major policy reversal. "Trust but verify," he said, quoting his political idol President Ronald Reagan. He tasked his staff to obtain documentation that would provide irrefutable evidence from the Congressional Research Service (CRS) on the "comfort women" issue. The Committee already had in its possession an extensive memorandum documenting the "comfort women" issue and explaining the continuing political controversy that surrounded it in a memorandum provided by veteran Specialist in Asian Affairs at the Congressional Research Service (CRS) Larry Niksch. Prepared on April 10, 2006, the report was presented as "responding to a number of inquiries, this memorandum provides background concerning the system of "comfort women" organized by the Japanese military during the 1930s and 1940s."[7]

**The State Department Report provides the irrefutable evidence**

Hyde, however, wanted further U.S. government documentation, preferably from the period when the reported crimes against "comfort women" victims were carried out. The Congressional Research Service (CRS), on behalf of Chairman Hyde and his Committee, made an inquiry to the State Department. The George W. Bush administration responded by providing a declassified report prepared under the name of Supreme Commander Douglas MacArthur, shortly after the end of the Pacific War. This report, titled "Amenities in the Japanese Armed Forces," was published on November 15, 1945 (A.4-4). It was published by "General Headquarters, Supreme Commander for the Allied Powers, by command of General MacArthur." It was prepared by the Allied Translator and Interpreter Section (ATIS), a joint Australian/U.S. World War II intelligence agency which was a centralized allied intelligence unit for the translation of intercepted Japanese communications, interrogations, and negotiations in the Pacific Theater, as well as for the investigation of Japanese war crimes. Australian and U.S. intelligence officers directly interrogated "comfort women" station managers and "comfort women" victims in the Burma Theater of operations.[8] Their findings included the following:

> A prisoner of war, a civilian brothel owner, captured with his wife and twenty army prostitutes near WAINGMAW on August 10, 1944, stated: prisoner of war, his wife and sister-in-law had made some money as restaurant keepers in KEIJO (Seoul) KOREA, but their trade declining, they looked for an opportunity to make more money and applied to Army Headquarters in KEIJO for permission to take "comfort girls" from KEIJO to BURMA. According to prisoner of war, the suggestion originated from Army Headquarters and was passed to a number of similar "Japanese businessmen" in Korea.

> Prisoner of war purchased 22 Korean girls, paying their families from 300 to 1000 yen according to the personality, looks, and age of the girl. These 22 girls were of ages 19 to 31. They became the sole property of prisoner of war and the Army made no profits from them. Headquarters, Korean Army gave him a letter addressed to all military headquarters of the Japanese Army, requesting them to furnish any assistance he might require, transport, rations, medical attention, etc. Leaving his sister-in-law to carry on the restaurant, prisoner of war and his wife, with their 22 girls, embarked at FUSAN on 10 July 1942 in a group of 703 girls, all Korean, and some 90 Japanese men and women, all of them of the same base sort as himself. They sailed on a 4000 ton passenger ship in a convoy of seven ships.

Free passage tickets were provided by Army headquarters, but prisoner of war paid for all meals during the voyage.

The report continued, "They called at FORMOSA where 22 other girls bound for SINGAPORE were taken on board and at SINGAPORE they transferred to another ship, arriving at RANGOON on 20 August 1942." Hyde, reading this detailed account of human trafficking, stated that the "MacArthur Report" represented "the smoking gun" that was needed to verify the officially organized "comfort women" system of human trafficking. He then ordered staff to prepare for a Committee markup session on Lane Evans' resolution H.Res. 759 when Congress reconvened from its summer recess in the fall of 2006. A markup session to consider this, as well as other pertinent legislation, was held on September 13, 2006. At the markup, the Committee, in a historic first for concrete action on the "comfort women" issue, agreed to seek consideration under Suspension of the Rules, (Amended) by Unanimous Consent, and sent H.Res. 759 to the Republican leadership (then in control of the House) for consideration for further Floor action by the entire House of Representatives.

## The Markup of House Resolution 759

Chairmen of Congressional Committees, when they have pending pieces of legislation under consideration, often convene a Committee hearing in order to obtain further relevant information from experts on the subject to be considered. Accordingly, Chairman Henry Hyde convened a hearing before the full International Relations Committee the next day, on September 14, 2006, titled "Japan's Relationship with Its Neighbors: Back to the Future?"[9]

Hyde's opening remarks gave a clear indication of the purpose for convening such a hearing in relation to the markup of H.Res. 759: "I recently returned from a two week fact-finding mission in the Asia-Pacific region, and the area I first encountered more than six decades ago as a young naval officer. Our delegation made a stop most poignantly in the Solomon Islands on August 16, the 61st anniversary of the end of World War II. It was in the Solomons at Guadalcanal that a horrific 6-month battle raged in 1942 and 1943." "We laid a wreath there on August 15th to honor those who fell. Abraham Lincoln of Illinois stated in his Gettysburg Address, 'The world will little note nor long remember what we say here, but it can never forget what they did here.' So the world took little note of our modest wreath laying in Guadalcanal." Hyde continued:

What is more significant, however, is that there were few other events to mark this important anniversary. Americans should ponder whether over a half century since the September 11th anniversary we just commemorated it will also draw only passing attention from a few historians. In Japan, by contrast, the prime minister visited a shrine to honor his nation's war dead on August 15th. This caused some disquietude among Japan's neighbors because that shrine also honors some convicted war criminals. . . . All of these sources of tension in the Asia-Pacific region require that we and our allies forge a united front; however, sadly, our history keeps getting in the way. Our two major allies in East Asia, Japan, and the Republic of

Korea, have never joined in a common alliance. At a time when the increasing North Korean nuclear threat casts a long shadow over the entire region, it is not in the national interest of the United States to have our key allies at odds with each other. . . . Thus, the question we wish to address today is, why has Europe been able to bury a contentious past while East Asia has not? Why has Europe risen from the ashes of war to form NATO, establish a European Union, even introduce a common currency, while East Asia lacks even fundamental regional security and economic institutions?. . . It is troubling to those of my generation to learn that Yushukan Museum in Tokyo is teaching younger generations of Japanese that the Second World War in Asia was launched by Tokyo to free the peoples of Asia and the Pacific from the yolk of western imperialism. I just visited Korea, the Philippines, Singapore, the Solomon Islands, and I can tell you that while some spoke frankly of bitter experiences remembered during the Japanese occupation, not one person in any of these countries told any member of our delegation that they fondly remembered the Imperial Japanese Army as liberators. The history being taught at this museum is not based on the facts, and it should be corrected.

The Committee's Ranking Member, Tom Lantos of California, a Holocaust survivor, expressed similar sentiments in his opening statement:

The most egregious example of Japan's historical amnesia is the practice of Japanese prime ministers visiting the Yasukuni shrine. As a survivor of World War II, I fully understand why Japanese leaders wish to pay homage to Japanese who die in service of their nation, any leader of a free and democratic nation would do so. But for the survivors of World War II in Asia and America, visits to the Yasukuni Shrine where 14 class A war criminals are interred would be the equivalent of laying a wreath at the graves of Himmler, Rudolph Hess and Hermann Göring in Germany. . . .[10]

My message to the incoming Japanese prime minister is very simple; paying one's respects to war criminals is morally bankrupt and unworthy of a great nation such as Japan. This practice must end. The Japanese Government has also approved textbooks which deny the Rape of Nanking, and imply that Japan was simply trying to protect other Asian nations from imperialism by launching World War II. I understand that only a few schools actually use these revisionist textbooks, but the fact that the Japanese Government approves them for use speaks loudly to the countries of Northeast Asia. Those who deny history are surely bound to repeat it, and this practice must also end.[11]

The hearing then heard from a panel of expert witnesses including: Michael J. Green, Ph.D., Associate Professor, Edmund A. Walsh School of Foreign Service, Georgetown University; Ms. Mindy Kotler Director, Asia Policy Point; Kurt Campbell, Ph.D., Senior Vice President, Henry A. Kissinger Chair in National Security, and Director of International Security Program, Center for Strategic and International Studies; and Ms. Yuki Tatsumi,

Research Fellow, The Henry L. Stimson Center. They discussed at length Japan's at times contentious post-World War II relations with its neighbors, brought about by what Representative Lantos had referred to pointedly as "historical amnesia" on such unresolved war crimes as the "comfort women" issue and the Rape of Nanking.

Immediately upon learning of the International Relations Committee actions—the favorable markup of H.Res. 759 followed immediately by a Committee hearing on the subject, Japan's Washington lobbyists sprang into action. Hogan & Hartson reportedly sent retired House Minority leader Bob Michel in great haste to see his fellow Illinois Republican, then Speaker of the House, Dennis Hastert. Michel reportedly used similar arguments to those he had made to Hyde—that House passage of H.Res. 759 would do irreparable damage to the U.S.-Japan alliance and that Japan had already sufficiently apologized so all sides should "let bygones be bygones." Hastert, who would go on to become an honorary co-chair of the Congressional Study Group on Japan (CSGJ) upon his retirement from the House in 2007, proved far more receptive to Bob Michel's arguments than Chairman Hyde utlimately had been. Hastert, in control through his leadership position of the House's legislative calendar, assured that H.Res. 759 would not be scheduled for consideration on the Floor of the House for the remainder of the 109th Congress—which ran until January 3, 2007.

## Michael Honda took the Torch for House Resolution 121

Then, however, something unforeseen by the Japan Lobby happened. The Democratic Party secured a majority in the House of Representatives in the November 2006 mid-term elections and Nancy Pelosi of California, a vocal advocate of human and women's rights, replaced Hastert as Speaker. Prospects for the passage in the near future of a House resolution addressing the long-smouldering 'comfort women' issue suddenly became quite promising.

The Democratic Party leadership had observed how the Republicans had dropped the ball on a key human rights and women rights issue of vital importance to the growing and influential Korean American community (according to the 2010 census, there are 1.7 million people of Korean ancestry living in the United States, with large communities in such key states as California, New York, New Jersey, Virginia, and Georgia). But with both Lane Evans and Henry Hyde now retired, the "comfort women" issue would need new advocates in the House to spearhead the adoption of a new, re-drafted resolution. Those advocates would include California Representative Mike Honda, the new incoming Chairman of the House Subcommittee on Asia, the Pacific and the Global Environment, Eni Faleomavaega, the incoming Chairman of the newly renamed House Committee on Foreign Affairs, Tom Lantos, and his spouse, Annette Lantos, and the incoming Ranking Republican Member on the Foreign Affairs Committee Ileana Ros-Lehtinen.

The first order of business, since the former H.Res. 759 had expired with the final adjournment of the 109th Congress, was to introduce in the new 110th Congress a similar "comfort women" Resolution. Representative Mike Honda, Chairman of the Congressional Asian Pacific American Caucus and a human rights advocate, wasted no time in taking up the torch left by the departed Lane Evans. He introduced the new House Resolution 121 during the first month of the new Congress on January 31st.[12]

Honda, a Japanese American Member of Congress, had personal experience with some of the racial and gender injustice which arose during the Second World War.  When he was one year old, he and his family were sent to  Camp Amache, a Japanese American internment camp in southeastern Colorado.  Yet, given his ethnic background, Representative Honda was also the subject of a particular vindicativeness on the part of the Japan Lobby, which considered him a "traitor" to his ancestral homeland.  One Japanese diplomat even referred to him disparagingly, in a private converation, as "a Hyundai (Korean made automobile) and not a Honda (Japanese made automobile)."  He was even marked for political defeat by certain lobbying groups through campaign financing.  This goal was finally achieved in 2016 when Mr. Honda was defeated for re-election after serving eight terms in the U.S. House of Representatives.

Honda, however, never hestitated in his efforts to achieve justice for "comfort women" victims, stating that rejection of the resolution that he sponsored would be the equivalent of stating that "women's issues are unimportant."  Drawing upon the language that had been previously developed by Representative Evans and his staff and subsequently in the Hyde Committee markup the previous year, Honda updated the resolution and made it more relevant to the universal issue of sexual violence in armed conflicts as continued in the modern world in such locations as Bosnia, Rwanda, Democratic Congo, and Burma.  These considerations are described in detail in the August 4, 2017 article for *The Diplomat*, titled "How the Japan-Korea 'Comfort Women' Debate Plays out in the U.S.," as written by Drake University international relations professor Mary M. McCarthy.[13]

Honda reportedly requested that Asia Policy Point Director Mindy Kotler assemble a team of scholars that, according to Kinue Tokudome, founder and executive director of the bilingual website *U.S.-Japan Dialogue on POWs*, would "ensure that Congress would fully understand the politics and the history surrounding the 'comfort women' issue. They were historians, political scientists, policy specialists, and security analysts from Japan, the U.S., and Australia. Congressman Honda received valuable input from this team including the contributions of skilled translators who read and analyzed the past statements that had been issued by the Japanese government." Key sections of H.Res. 121 are as follows:

> That it is the sense of the House of Representatives that the Government of Japan: (1) should formally acknowledge, apologize, and accept historical responsibility in a clear and unequivocal manner for its Imperial Armed Forces' coercion of young women into sexual slavery, known to the world as "comfort women," during its colonial and wartime occupation of Asia and the Pacific Islands from the 1930s through the duration of World War II;  (2) would help to resolve recurring questions about the sincerity and status of prior statements if the Prime Minister of Japan were to make such an apology as a public statement in his official capacity; (3) should clearly and publicly refute any claims that the sexual enslavement and trafficking of the "comfort women" for the Japanese Imperial Armed Forces never occurred; and (4) should educate current and future generations about this horrible

crime while following the recommendations of the international community with respect to the "comfort women."[14]

## The Hearing for the Passage of H.Res. 121

A second significant action in the new 110th Congress was the convening of the first Congressional hearing in history that included the direct testimony of "comfort women" survivors. Eni Faleomavaega, the first Asian Pacific Islander in history to head the House's Subcommittee on Asia, the Pacific and the Global Environment, chose the "comfort women" issue as the subject of his very first hearing as the new Chairman. On February 15, 2007, a hearing titled "Protecting the Human Rights of Comfort Women" was convened by the Subcommittee.[15] The Committee heard the direct, eye-witness testimony of three "comfort women" survivors: Lee Yong-soo of Korea, Kim Kun-ja of Korea, and Jan Ruff O'Herne of the Dutch East Indies/Australia. In addition, Representative Mike Honda presented testimony regarding his pending resolution on the "comfort women" issue. Mindy Kotler and Dr. Ok Cha Soh, the president of WCCW at the time, were also expert witnesses. Future President of the Republic of Korea Park Geun-hye was also in attendance at the hearing.

In his opening statement, Chairman Faleomavaega declared:

Civilized society cannot allow history to be revised or denied under any circumstances. Regardless of what bearing this, or any other issue, may have on bilateral relations or the U.S. foreign policy, civilized society has a moral obligation to remember, to give voice to those who have suffered, to pay living tribute to victims past and present, to defend human rights and human dignity. Otherwise we run the risk of another Holocaust or, in this case, young women being forced into sexual slavery.[16]

Mr. Honda's testimony included the basis for his introduction of House Resolution 121 on the "comfort women":

As members of the subcommittee know, I recently introduced H.Res. 121, a resolution calling on the Government of Japan to formally acknowledge, apologize, and accept historical responsibility in a clear and unequivocal manner for its Imperial Armed Force's coercion of young women and girls into sexual slavery during World War II, euphemistically known as comfort women. These violated women—mostly Korean, Chinese and Filipino, but include Dutch women as well—have too long been denied their dignity and their honor. My interest in seeking justice for the "comfort women" began during my career as a school teacher in San Jose. A couple of decades ago, I learned that Japan's ministry of education sought to omit or downplay the comfort women tragedy in its approved textbooks. As a teacher interested in historical accuracy and reconciliation, I knew the importance of teaching and talking about tragedy and injustice without flinching from the details. Without honesty and candor, there can be no foundation for reconciliation.[17]

The Congressional testimony of "comfort women" victim Lee Yong-soo on her abduction as a fourteen-year-old child included the following:

I live in Taegu, South Korea. My name is Lee Yong Soo. Sometimes I am a 14-year-old girl, and I look outside my window, and there is a girl, and there is a Japanese man, and they are saying something to each other, and they are gesturing me to come out. I did not know anything. I did not know what was going on but they gestured me to come out so I came out, and the girl and the Japanese soldier put their hand on my shoulder, and covered my mouth, and the soldier put something against my back, and like that in the middle of the night I was taken away.

When I was taken away, I was taken to a bridge. Underneath the bridge there were cars going by, and when I arrived there, I saw three other girls and they gave me a parcel, a ripped parcel, and I had a feel of what that parcel had inside it, and there were some clothes and some shoes. And then we were taken to a train station. We were taken on a train. It was my very first time in my entire life to board a train, and my head hurt a lot. I can even remember now I told them my head hurts, my head hurt, and they called me something like Chosenjin or something like that, and they started hitting me with their fists and kicking me with their feet. And they kicked me and punched me so much that I lost consciousness.[18]

Part of the Congressional testimony of "comfort women" victim Jan Ruff O'Herne:

They selected 10 pretty girls. I was one of the 10. We were told to come forward and pack a small bag. The first things I put in my bag were my prayer book, my rosary beads, and my Bible. I thought somehow these would keep me strong, and then we were taken away. The whole camp protested, and our mothers started to pull us back. I embraced my mother and two young sisters, not knowing if I was ever going to see them again. We were hurled into an army truck like sheep for the slaughter. We were terrified, and we clung to our bags and to each other. The truck stopped in the city of Semarang in front of a large Dutch colonial house. We were told to get out. Entering the house, we soon realized what sort of a house it was. A Japanese military told us that we were here for the sexual pleasure of the Japanese. The house indeed was a brothel.[19]

The hearing testimony was riveting and it had a dramatic impact on House Members who were considering whether or not to support the Honda resolution given the adverse impact it would likely have on U.S.-Japan relations at a critical juncture in the Pacific with a rising China and a nuclear armed North Korea.

## The Passage of House Resolution 121

The Japan lobby, realizing that with a new Democratic majority in the House it would be even more difficult to block passage of a "comfort women" resolution, reportedly called upon its most significant advocates—Senator Daniel Inouye and Japanese Ambassador Kato Ryozo. Both reportedly personally intervened with Foreign Affairs Committee Chairman Tom Lantos, asking him not to take formal Committee action—a markup—on H.Res. 121. Ambassador Kato also requested a personal meeting with Committee Republican Ranking Member Ileana Ros-Lehtinen, advising her of the possible adverse effects for the U.S. security and diplomatic concerns in the Pacific that the passage of H.Res. 121 might cause. Ambassador Kato also sent letters to Speaker Pelosi, Chairman Lantos, and other Congressional leaders, warning that "Congress's decision to move H.Res. 121 will only serve the purposes of those who wish to undermine the Japan-U.S. relationship."[20]

But the lobbying efforts did not finish there. There was the matter of a controversial advertisement placed in *The Washington Post* on June 14, 2007 by right-wing political leaders and academics in Japan that drew a parallel between the sexual behavior of the U.S. military forces during the occupation of Japan and the Imperial Japanese military-sanctioned "comfort women" system of sexual slavery.[21] That comparison naturally did not sit well with many Members of the House and actually backfired by increasing the number of House cosponsors for H.Res. 121—an additional 32 Members cosponsored H.Res. 121 after the publication of the controversial advertisement (out of a total of 167 House cosponsors). These included Ileana Ros-Lehtinen, the Foreign Affairs Committee Ranking Republican Member. (A private meeting with a Florida constituent, a Filipina-American professor from the University of Miami and a "comfort women" researcher, Evelina Galang, also led Representative Ros-Lehtinen to re-consider and sign on as a cosponsor for H.Res. 121.)

The Foreign Affairs Committee, under the leadership of Chairman Tom Lantos, convened on June 26, 2007. The Committee considered and debated H.Res. 121, in addition to other pending legislation under Committee jurisdiction. The Committee ordered that H.Res. 121 be reported out, as amended, and sent to the full House for consideration on the Floor. The only recorded vote on H.Res. 121 took place at this Committee markup, with 39 Yeas and 2 Nays. The two negative votes were cast by Republican Committee Members—Mr. Tancredo of Colorado and Mr. Ron Paul of Texas, the father of Senator Rand Paul. Vice President Mike Pence, who was a Committee Member at the time of the markup, did not cast a recorded vote on consideration of the "comfort women" Resolution.

Recorded statements by House Members at the markup indicate the gravity with which the U.S. House of Representatives viewed the issue of sexual slavery imposed by the military forces of Imperial Japan during the Pacific War. Chairman Lantos, a Holocaust survivor, made an opening statement included the following:

Yet, Japan's refusal to make an official government apology to the women who suffered as so-called "comfort women" is disturbing to all of us who value this relationship. The true strength of a nation is tested when it is forced to confront the darkest chapters in its history. Will it have the courage to face up to the truth of its past or will it hide from those truths in the desperate and foolish hope that they will fade with time? Post-war Germany made the right choice. Japan, on the other hand, has actively promoted historical amnesia. The facts are plain. There can be no denying that the Japanese Imperial Military coerced thousands upon thousands of women, primarily Chinese and Koreans, into sexual slavery during the war. The continued efforts by some in Japan to distort history and play a game of blame-the-victim are also highly disturbing.

Most recently, on June 14, members of the Japanese Government took out an advertisement in *The Washington Post* that smears the survivors of the "comfort women" system, including those who testified before our Subcommittee on Asia, the Pacific and the Global Environment. That advertisement suggests that these women, who were forcibly and repeatedly raped by soldiers, were engaged, and I quote, in 'licensed prostitution, that was commonplace around the world at the time.' This is a ludicrous assertion, totally counter to the facts.[22]

Mr. Faleomavaega, the Chairman of the Subcommittee on Asia, the Pacific and the Global Environment which convened the hearing earlier in 2007 as mentioned by Chairman Lantos, stated the following:

Thank you, Mr. Chairman. I first want to thank you and commend you and our distinguished senior ranking member Ms. Ros-Lehtinen for your leadership and efforts to support and to bring this proposed legislation in the form of a substitute for markup this morning in our committee. I also want thank our colleague and gentleman from California, Mr. Honda, for his sponsorship of this bill, as it also has the bipartisan support of some 140 members of the House. I also want to note that this resolution was previously passed by this committee in the past Congress under the able leadership of our previous chairman, and a gentleman and a good friend, the gentleman from Illinois, Mr. Hyde. I would be remiss if I did not also mention the name of our former colleague and friend, also the gentleman from Illinois, Mr. Lane Evans, who championed this bill, this legislation, for the past several years.[23]

Mr. Faleomavaega continued by noting the vital importance of the hearing that preceded the consideration of the resolution by the Full Committee. Mr. Faleomavaega stated:

. . . our Subcommittee on Asia, the Pacific and the Global Environment held a hearing in February of this year concerning the proposed legislation and for the first time ever in the history of the Congress, three women who previously served as sexual slaves to the Japanese Army soldiers during World War II personally came to this chamber, testified before our subcommittee: Ms. Lee Yong-soo, Ms. Kim Kun-ja, both from Korea, and the lady from Australia Ms. Jan Ruff O'Herne. Mr. Chairman, these women were raped and forced into sexual slavery, human trafficking by the soldiers of the Imperial Army of Japan during World War II. These women were among some 200,000 women from Korea, China, the Philippines, Indonesia, and other islands in the Pacific who were forced into prostitution, severely abused and tortured, and even killed by Japanese soldiers as a sport during the war.

In his statement at the markup, Committee Member Gary Ackerman of New York drew a direct comparison between the War Crimes committed by the Nazis in Europe against the Jewish community and the crimes committed by the Imperial Japanese military against "comfort women" victims:

The Japanese "comfort women" were no more willing participants in legalized prostitution at the hands of the Imperialist Japanese soldiers that committed these atrocities than were the Jews who went to the concentration camps, but being the society that we were at the time, we were so Europe-centric that we didn't concentrate and view as assiduously as we did (in) the West the atrocities that were conducted in the East by the Japanese. Mr. Speaker, these women who were victimized by the Japanese were very much like the Jews who were victimized by the Nazis.

They are now courageously, as so many of them have perished from the earth, the ones who are left, so many of them are so courageously finding their voice so that the world would know and recognize the horrors that went on in that part of the world by people who have not yet acknowledged, as the Japanese did. Forgive and forget, some people say. Forget, never. Forgive, it is not for the world to forgive. It is only for victims who can forgive. You can't forgive an atrocity perpetuated on somebody else. For that, the Nazis have to speak for the dead Jews, and the Japanese have to speak to the "comfort women." And it is time that the Japanese Government acknowledges on behalf of their predecessor government and soldiers who have participated in this horrible nightmare that pretty soon there will be no victims left of the "comfort women" who can even consider whether or not they want to forgive. It is not too late for the Japanese to do that, to make peace with themselves, and to restore the honor and integrity to that great society, and to apologize and to acknowledge so that history can move on and take away at least part of the stain that falls upon that country.[24]

Mr. Chris Smith of New Jersey pointed out in his remarks that "former Chairman Hyde and I co-authored an op-ed that was published in *The Washington Times* on April 25 urging Japan to come to grips with the history of Imperial Japan." He further noted:

> In early March, Japanese Prime Minister Shinzo Abe denied the coercion of young girls and women by the Japanese military, challenging both the legitimacy and sincerity of a 1993 government statement by then Chief Cabinet Secretary Kono, which was alluded to by Mr. Faleomavaega. In recent years, Japan has also sought to challenge the historical accuracy of "comfort women" through the revision of school textbooks. . . . I would also point out that this resolution comes up in the modern day context of human trafficking. We know that militaries around the world are magnets for traffickers.[25]

Mr. Dan Burton of Indiana made a comparison of the dark chapter of slavery in American history to Japan's past official involvement in sexual servitude:

> Japan is one of our great allies. They are a very stabilizing force in that part of the world and we really appreciate that, but I would like to bring to the attention, as my colleagues have, some of the things that happened in the world before that have been owned up to. The United States was involved in a horrible practice of slavery for a long time. We acknowledge that. We stopped that. England, under William Wilberforce, admitted and stopped slave trading after a big, big fight in the British Parliament. Germany, as has been mentioned a number of times, admitted genocide and the sexual slavery of women. So, in my opinion, if I were talking to members of the Japanese administration, I would just say, there is precedent for admitting wrongdoings. And I would urge you, to admit this terrible practice so the world can get it behind us.[26]

Ms. Diane Watson of California drew attention to House Resolution 121's chief sponsor, also of California, in her remarks:

> It is in the spirit of emancipation from the past as well as reconciliation and justice for the so-called 'comfort women' that I am certain Mr. Honda has introduced H.Res. 121. And the purpose is not to bash the Government of Japan, but rather to speak to truth, to speak to the fact that the historical and current plight of the "comfort women" has not been properly witnessed, nor has compensation to the victims been sufficiently provided. Mr. Honda's heritage as a Japanese American and the fact that he lived in a Japanese American internment camp in California during World War II are also pertinent and instructive. Approximately 40 years after the imprisonment of Japanese Americans, the United States Government formally apologized for its role and offered reparations. No nation's hands are clean when it comes to human rights violations.[27]

Mr. Joseph Crowley of New York, an Irish-American, raised the statement (in the form of apology) by then British Prime Minister Tony Blair on the subject of the Great Hunger (famine) in Ireland as a point of comparison:

> Only to have Prime Minister Tony Blair make a statement about the Great Hunger, and the culpability and responsibility of the British people to owe up to their responsibility in that. I believe, quite frankly, that that statement helped to lead the peace process in Northern Ireland forward. A recognition 150 years after the fact of that event helped to move the peace process forward. Without that acknowledgment, it would not have happened.[28]

Mr. Ted Poe of Texas raised the Rape of Nanking as pertinent to a discussion of Imperial Japanese War Crimes:

> Some of the true crimes of Japan have made it to the worldwide stage in such books as *Rape of Nankin* (sic), the forgotten holocaust of WWII, where 300,000 civilians in Nankin (sic) China were systematically tortured, raped, and murdered by the Japanese military. More people—civilians—killed in China in this one event than in both the atomic bombs of Hiroshima and Nagasaki.[29]

Others raised objections on international legal grounds or alliance concerns, including Mr. Donald Manzullo and Mr. Dana Rohrabacher, even though they both later voted with the "ayes" to report H.Res. 121 favorably out of Committee and send it to the full House for consideration. Mr. Manzullo said:

> What purpose is served by this body becoming involved in the dispute? Why are members of the House of Representatives going to be impaneled as a jury to determine whether or not the ostensible apologies offered by the Japanese are acceptable to the Koreans? How much more of the time of this committee, and how many other issues will we become involved in, when this is just a resolution? This is not the United Nations. This is not a court.[30]

Mr. Rohrabacher offered an amendment (later withdrawn) emphasizing the importance of the U.S.-Japan alliance. Mr. Rohrabacher stated:

> My amendment underscores many contributions made by Japan in the five decades since the end of World War II, and especially since 9/11. Japan's solidarity with us, its generosity, its courage has been vital to the success of numerous international efforts. Furthermore, Japan is a shining example of democracy. While repression and gross violation of human rights are still commonplace in China, in North Korea, and many other Asian countries, Japan stands as a proud contrast to that tyranny and injustice. My amendment is designed to balance off the criticism that is inherent in this legislation.[31]

Mr. Tom Tancredo of Colorado and Mr. Ron Paul of Texas, who were the only two Committee Members to vote against the favorable reporting of H.Res. 121, expressed displeasure. Mr. Tancredo said: "[A]sking the Japanese Government to take historical responsibility for atrocities by the defunct Imperial Era Government is somewhat, I think, counterproductive and unfair to the people of Japan."[32] Mr. Paul stated:

> But, quite frankly, I do also get confused about this whole issue of the perpetual need to apologize. If one does harm to another individual and they immediately recognize it, they can very easily apologize. But two or three generations later, compelling a generation that did not have direct responsibility to make apologies, that is another thing. . . . Our goal should not be to pick sides. . . .[33]

The new Democratic House leadership, under Speaker Pelosi, brought the measure quickly to the floor of the full House for consideration. On July 30, 2007 the title of the measure (H.Res. 121) was amended and the resolution was agreed to without objection. There was no recorded vote. In an article "Passage of H.Res. 121 on 'Comfort Women,' the U.S. Congress and Historical Memory in Japan," author Kinue Tokudome pointed out that: "On June 22, 2007, Ambassador Kato Ryozo wrote to House Speaker Nancy Pelosi and other key members of Congress that the adoption of this measure (H.Res. 121) 'will almost certainly have lasting and harmful effects on the deep friendship, close trust, and wide-ranging cooperation our two nations now enjoy.'[34] He also suggested that Japan might reconsider its role as one of the few loyal supporters of the U.S. policy in Iraq. Four days later the House Foreign Affairs Committee passed the resolution with an overwhelming majority, 39 to 2. Speaker Pelosi immediately issued a statement saying, "I look forward to the House of Representatives passing this resolution and sending a strong message that we will not forget the horrors endured by the 'comfort women.'" The Tokudome article further noted:

> H.Res. 121 was passed by the full House on July 30, 2007, after the Japanese Upper House elections were held in order to avoid affecting the outcome of the elections. There were some changes in the final version of the resolution. It was added that 'the United States-Japan alliance continues to be based on shared vital interests and values in the Asia-Pacific region, including the preservation and promotion of political and economic freedoms, support for human rights and democratic institutions, and the securing of prosperity for the people of both countries and the international community.'

"The sentence seeking a Japanese apology was also somewhat softened from the original version, 'Japan should have this official apology given as a public statement presented by the Prime Minister of Japan in his official capacity' to the versions appearing at the beginning of this article,"[35] as described by Annette Lantos, Foreign Affairs Committee Chairman Tom Lantos's spouse, who provided background information on the passage of the resolution to Kinue Tokudome.

Upon hearing the news from his retirement home in Illinois, where he was recovering from heart surgery, former House Committee Chairman Henry Hyde issued a statement:

> As a veteran of the Pacific War and former Chairman whose Committee favorably reported out this resolution last September, I welcome passage of H.Res. 121, the "comfort women" resolution. Protection of women and children from exploitation on the battlefield is not just an issue from the long-ago Second World War. It has relevancy for situations today, such as the tragedy unfolding in Darfur. The "comfort women" have come to symbolize all women suffering in these wartime situations.[36]

## H.Res. 121: An Unprecedented Congressional Resolution

The passage of H.Res. 121 overcame a number of historic obstacles, including geopolitical alliance issues and a reticence in the days before the "Me Too" movement to openly and candidly address issues involving sexual coercion in a public setting—in this case on the Floor of the U.S. House of Representatives. The Armenian-American community, which has long sought passage of a House resolution addressing the genocide carried out a century ago against the Armenian community by the Ottoman Turks, was amazed by the success of the Korean American community and women's rights organizations in procuring passage of H.Res. 121. The first Foreign Affairs Committee meeting I attended as a new staff member in the fall of 2000 concerned this Armenian Genocide issue. Then Chairman Ben Gilman met with former Representative Stephen Solarz who was lobbying on behalf of the Turkish government to block passage of the resolution. The argument was presented that consideration of such a resolution would adversely influence relations with a key NATO ally and that Ankara might even reconsider the stationing of the U.S. forces in Turkey. The House Subcommittee on International Operations and Human Rights had forwarded H.Res. 398, which commemorated the Armenian Genocide, to the full Committee for consideration earlier in the year. Chairman Gilman determined to take no further action on the resolution. This was despite the fact that then Representative James Rogan, who represented a district in California with a large Armenian American population, was seeking further action as he was in a tough re-election contest. He was facing Democrat Adam Schiff current Chairman of the House Intelligence Committee, in what was the most expensive Congressional race of that year.

Almost two decades later, the issue was not resolved. Public Radio of Armenia announced on March 12, 2019 that Congressman Schiff (D-CA) and Gus Bilirakis (R-FL) have sent out a "Dear Colleague" letter to other Members of the House which asked them to:

> . . . join us as a cosponsor of a resolution affirming the United States record on the Armenian Genocide, which recognizes and memorializes the historical fact of the Ottoman Empire's genocidal campaign against the Armenian people, as well as the Greeks, Assyrians, Chaldeans, Syriacs, and other religious minorities, from 1915 to 1923. . . . For decades, Turkey has deployed threats and an intense campaign of

lobbying to intimidate the Congress from recognizing the genocide carried out by the Ottoman Empire.[37]

This was followed by the formal introduction by the two Members of Congress of a new Armenian Genocide Resolution on April 8, 2019 with over 70 cosponsors. After two decades of lobbying, the Armenian Genocide Resolution (H.Res. 296) finally passed the House of Representatives on October 29, 2019 by a vote of 405-11.

The example of this onetime failed resolution demonstrates clearly the remarkable and historic achievement that passage of H.Res. 121 represented for the U.S. House of Representatives. When I arrived at the House as a staff member in 2000, the Korean American community had a low profile on Capitol Hill and very little expertise on how to effectively advocate for issues of concern for the community. Between 2001 and 2007, however, grassroots Korean American organizations and determined individuals like Annabel Park, studied the advocacy efforts of other ethnic communities which had produced noticeable success on the Hill, including the Taiwanese American, Jewish American and Irish American communities. They implemented an effective campaign of drop-by visits to Congressional offices, outdoor rallies and advocacy from constituents back in the Members' home districts. The result was a stellar record of achievement, not only on the "comfort women" Resolution but on such other issues as passage of the North Korean Human Rights Act in 2004 and the Congressional approval of KORUS FTA in 2011. Grassroots Korean American organizations such as the Washington Coalition for Comfort Women Issues (WCCW) and Korean American Civic Empowerment (KACE) played pivotal roles in advocating for the enactment of H.Res. 121 by the U.S. House of Representatives. Thus, the passage of H.Res. 121 would have been impossible without the effective mobilization of the Korean American community.

H.Res. 121 also would not have been possible without a dedicated group of Members of Congress. These Members include Speaker Pelosi, Representative Honda, Representative Evans, Chairman Hyde, Chairman Lantos, Chairman Faleomavaega, Representative Ros-Lehtinen, and Representative Schakowsky among others. They made a particular commitment to the passage of H.Res. 121 because of their own personal careers and biographies. Some had experienced the Second World War, some served in the Pacific, in either World War II or Vietnam; others had a particular commitment to human and women's rights. They all came together, however, in a bipartisan fashion to assure that the voices of the "comfort women" victims would not be snuffed out and that their suffering would not be forgotten. They also used the resolution to raise broader concerns about sexual violence in armed conflicts, which has continued into the twenty-first century in such varied places as the Democratic Republic of Congo, Burma and Iraq. In this regard, H.Res. 121 has proved to be a resolution of universal applicability and value and as the vocal grandmother of the current "Me Too" movement. H.Res. 121 set off a chain reaction of resolutions in foreign capitals, state legislatures and city councils and the construction of a number of "comfort women" memorials. Tokyo, like Ankara, has reacted with a well-financed and rather vindictive public lobbying campaign. In the case of Tokyo, however, there has been a failure to turn back the tide of history. The "comfort women" victims have prevailed.

Fig. 4-1. Chairman Eni Faleomavaega's follow-up visit, to meet with "my grandmothers" as he called them, at the House of Sharing in Gwangju City, Gyeonggi-do, Korea, September 4, 2009. © *Photo by Lisa Williams, Chief of Staff, House Subcommittee on Asia, the Pacific and the Global Environment.*

Fig. 4-2. Chairman Eni Faleomavaega visiting The House of Sharing, September 4, 2009 © *Photo by Lisa Williams.*

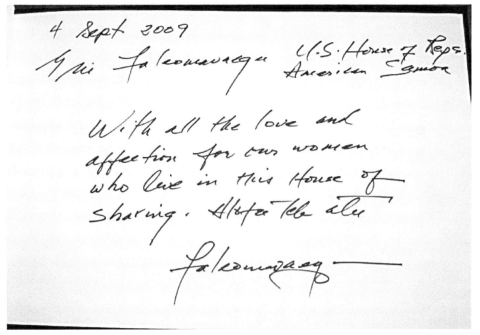

Fig. 4-3. Chairman Eni Faleomavaega's message to the ladies residing in the House of Sharing, South Korea, September 4, 2009.

Fig. 4-4. Rep. Mike Honda and Chairman Eni Faleomavaega's Visit to the House of Sharing, 2012 © *Photo by Lisa Williams.*

## Research of Dennis Halpin after Leaving Congress

"Japan and the Comfort Women: Not a 'Beautiful Country.'" *Washington Examiner,* July 1, 2014. https://www.washingtonexaminer.com/weekly-standard/japan-and-the-comfort-women-not-a-beautiful-country (accessed February 13, 2020).

"The U.S. Should Be Appalled by Japan's Historical Revisionism." *The National Interest,* March 9, 2015.

On the Yasukuni Shrine as a symbol of historic denial. http://nationalinterest.org/feature/us-should-be-appalled-by-japans-historical-revisionism-12381 (accessed March 13, 2020).

On the equivocation expressed in PM Abe's statement on the 70th anniversary of the end of WWII: "The Abe War Anniversary Statement: More Equivocation than Eloquence." *Washington Examiner*, April 17, 2015. http://www.weeklystandard.com/the-abe-war-anniversary-statement-more-equivocation-than-eloquence/article/1013141 (accessed February 13, 2020).

On how PM Abe should have used his U.S. Congressional address to apologize:
"Shinzo Abe should use Congress address to apologize." *The Hill,* April 21, 2015. http://thehill.com/blogs/congress-blog/foreign-policy/239482-shinzo-abe-should-use-congress-address-to-apologize (accessed March 13, 2020).

"The Sins of the Fathers: Japan's Unresolved Historic Legacy Sixty Years After the War in the Pacific." The ICAS Spring Symposium. http://www.icasinc.org/2005/2005s/2005sdph.html (accessed May 19, 2005).

On the apology issue and President Obama's upcoming summit trip to Japan:
"So Long, Harry: Will Obama's Apology Tour End in Hiroshima?" *Washington Examiner*, September 2, 2015. http://www.weeklystandard.com/so-long-harry-will-obamas-apology-tour-end-in-hiroshima/article/1023903 (accessed February 13, 2020).

---

[1] Hyde, Henry J. Henry J. Hyde to Ryozo Kato, Washington, D.C., October 20, 2005.
[2] Hyde, Henry J. Henry J. Hyde to Dennis Hastert, Washington, D.C., April 26, 2006.
[3] "Hyde Asks Koizumi to Stop Shrine Visits," *UPI.* May 15, 2006, https://www.upi.com/Top_News/2006/05/15/Hyde-asks-Koizumi-to-stop-shrine-visits/77981147692129/?ur3=1.
[4] "Bush, Koizumi Visit Graceland," *NBC News,* July 01, 2006, http://www.nbcnews.com/id/13626840/ns/politics/t/bush-koizumi-visit-graceland/#.XIp7yCJKgdU.
[5] Kevin Bogardus "Japan Turns to K Street amid Calls for Apology on WWII-era 'Comfort Women,'" *The Hill.* February 6, 2014, https://thehill.com/business-a-lobbying/business-a-lobbying/197599-japan-turns-to-k-street-amid-calls-for-apology-on.
[6] The U.S. House of Representatives—expressing the sense of the House of Representatives that the Government of Japan should formally acknowledge and accept responsibility for its sexual enslavement of young women, known to the world as "comfort women," during its colonial occupation of Asia and the Pacific Islands from the 1930s through the duration of World War II, and for other purposes. H. Res. 759. 109th Cong., 2d Session, April 04, 2006, https://www.congress.gov/109/bills/hres759/BILLS-109hres759ih.pdf.
[7] The U.S. Library of Congress. Congressional Research Service. Memorandum on the System of "Comfort Women" Organized by the Japanese Military during the 1930s and 1940s, by Larry Niksch. M-041006. 2006.
[8] General Headquarters Supreme Commander for the Allied Powers, *Amenities in the Japanese Armed Forces*, R. K. Sutherland, November 15, 1945.

[9] What follows are excerpts of the Committee markup of H. Res. 759. The U.S. House of Representatives. Committee on International Relations. *Japan's Relationship with Its Neighbors: Back to the Future?* 109th Cong., 2d Session, September 14, 2006, pp. 1-4. This complete transcript of the markup hearing can be accessed at: https://www.govinfo.gov/content/pkg/CHRG-109hhrg29883/pdf/CHRG-109hhrg29883.pdf.

[10] Ibid., 4.

[11] Loc. cit.

[12] The U.S. House of Representatives. 110th Congress, 1st Session, January 31, 2007. The text of the resolution can be accessed at: https://www.congress.gov/110/bills/hres121/BILLS-110hres121eh.pdf.
The transcript of the markup hearing of H.Res. 121 before the Committee on Foreign Affairs on June 26, 2007 can be accessed at: https://www.govinfo.gov/content/pkg/CHRG-110hhrg36421/pdf/CHRG-110hhrg36421.pdf. *See* especially pp. 156-190.

[13] Mary M. McCarthy, "How the Japan-Korea 'Comfort Women' Debate Plays out in the U.S." *The Diplomat*, August 7, 2017, https://thediplomat.com/2017/08/how-the-japan-korea-comfort-women-debate-plays-out-in-the-us/.

[14] The U.S. House of Representatives. H.Res. 121. 110th Congress, 1st Session, January 31, 2007, https://www.congress.gov/110/bills/hres121/BILLS-110hres121eh.pdf.

[15] The U.S. House of Representatives. Committee on Foreign Affairs. *Protecting the Human Rights of Comfort Women.* 110th Congress, 1st Session, February 15, 2007. The complete transcript of the hearing can be accessed at: https://www.govinfo.gov/content/pkg/CHRG-110hhrg33317/pdf/CHRG-110hhrg33317.pdf

[16] Ibid., 3.

[17] Ibid., 12.

[18] The complete testimony of Lee Yong-soo is at the complete transcript of the hearing, 17-23.

[19] The complete testimony of Jan Ruff O'Herne is at the complete transcript of the hearing, 23-28.

[20] Richard Cowan, "House Seeks Japan's Apology on 'comfort women,'" *Reuters,* July 30, 2007, https://www.reuters.com/article/us-japan-usa-sexslaves/house-seeks-japans-apology-on-comfort-women-idUSN3041972020070730.

[21] "Signatories to the June 14th *Washington Post* 'The Facts' Advertisement: Politicians, Professors, and Journalists," *Asia Policy Point,* July 25, 2007, accessed March 13, 2020, http://www.jiaponline.org/documents/Jun14AdALLSignatoriesLIST.pdf.

[22] Committee on Foreign Affairs on June 26, 2007, *op. cit.,* 156.

[23] Ibid., 167.

[24] Ibid., 170.

[25] Chris Smith & Henry Hyde, "The Truth about Japan's Comfort Women," *The Washington Times,* April 25, 2007, https://www.washingtontimes.com/news/2007/apr/25/20070425-092608-3474r/.

[26] Committee on Foreign Affairs on June 26, 2007, *op. cit.,* 156, 170-171.

[27] Loc. cit., 171.

[28] Ibid., 180.

[29] Ibid., 177. Editor's note: The correct book title that Rep. Poe referred to in the printed record is *The Rape of Nanking: The Forgotten Holocaust of World War II.*

[30] Ibid., 172.

[31] Ibid., 185.

[32] Ibid., 174.

[33] Ibid., 175-176.

[34] Kinue Tokudome, "Passage of H.Res. 121 on 'comfort women,' The U.S. Congress and Historical Memory in Japan," *The Asia-Pacific Journal* 5, no. 8 (August 1, 2007): 1-12.

[35] Ibid., 5-6.

[36] Ibid., 8.

[37] The full letter can be viewed at http://dearcolleague.us/2019/07/cosponsor-resolution-recognizing-and-memorializing-the-armenian-genocide-4/.

# Part II

The "Comfort Women" Movement
becomes Transnational

# 5. THE FIRST ACADEMIC CONFERENCE ON "COMFORT WOMEN": ITS IMPACT AND LEGACIES

*Bonnie B.C. Oh*

**Abstract:** For the archival book collection, I chose to write about the first academic conference on "comfort women" issues at Georgetown University, located in Washington, D.C. The conference was called, "The Comfort Women of WWII, Lessons and Legacies" and was held on September 30, 1996. I will examine the background and detailed efforts for this event and the impact of it.

## Background

There are several reasons to write about the first conference on "comfort women." First, it was held barely five years after Ms. Kim Hak-soon, the first person who "came out" in South Korea; second, the topic was hardly known at the time and yet the symposium was an unexpectedly big success and became the catalyst for the "comfort women" movement, opening the floodgate for countless large and small gatherings on "comfort women"; third, it became the basis for the decision of the U.S. Department of Justice to include three "comfort-station" perpetrators among the sixteen Japanese war criminals, who were to be prohibited from entry to the United States. Finally, at the risk of being criticized for being self-indulgent, I believe that my personal experience as one of the three co-conveners can be a legitimate primary source worthy of inclusion in the Archival Book Collection—in the tradition of oral history. On this last point, I would like to add that it is not just I, but the founder and co-founders of the Washington Coalition for Comfort Women Issues, Inc. (WCCW), who can be considered "living witnesses and primary sources." This is especially true of Mrs. Dongwoo Lee Hahm, an early retiree of the World Bank. Since its founding in 1992, we steadfastly remained engaged and active in the "comfort women" support and advocacy campaigns and movements. We are an aging group in our 80s and 90s but are "breathing" primary sources for the "comfort women" undertaking.

At the end of the text, I shared related photos, the conference poster, the banner, testimony scene, and a portrait of Mme Mutsuko Miki, keynote speaker. I introduce the text of Mrs. Miki's speech as an appendix, which was published in the winter 1996 Issue (No. 35) of the *Mid Atlantic Bulletin of Korean Studies* (pp. 11–13), which I edited. As stated in the text, Mme Miki fully acknowledged Japan's responsibility for the "comfort women" tragedy and urged her government and the people of Japan to take steps to amend Japan's past wrongdoing for the dwindling number of surviving "comfort women." It should be a required reading for the current Japanese political power holders to see if they still have the temerity to continue to deny the whole situation and rewrite history.

## Georgetown Conference on "Comfort Women" September 30, 1996

On the afternoon of September 30, 1996, an unprecedented event took place at the Bunn Intercultural Center auditorium of Georgetown University–an academic symposium on "comfort women," a topic that had hardly been heard of. The half-day conference, the very first academic meeting on the subject of "comfort women," opened on a sunny, early fall day on the hilltop at the southwestern part of Washington, D.C. It was a topic that had been hidden for half a century. The symposium was entitled "Comfort Women of World War II: Legacy and Lessons." The planners, including myself, did not anticipate it at the time, but we cracked a dam for future similar gatherings of the controversial issue across the United States and the world—to be held at numerous college campuses, museums, and non-governmental organizations. It was also speculated that the conference might have impacted the U.S. Department of Justice action to apply the Holtzman Amendment (1978) to Japanese war criminals. The amendment, named after Elizabeth Holtzman, a New York Congresswoman (1973–1981), had hitherto affected only the Germans. But on December 3, a little over two months after our assembly, the Justice Department issued a "Watch List" of sixteen Japanese individuals ineligible to enter the United States. Three among them had committed "comfort women"-related crimes. The Justice Department's decision was published on the editorial page of *The Washington Post* of December 4, 1996, under the heading, "War Criminals, Then and Now."[1]

I was one of the three primary co-conveners with Margaret Stetz, then from Georgetown, now Mae and Robert Carter Professor of Women's Studies and Professor of Humanities at the University of Delaware. There were others who assisted and supported us on behalf of the conference: Chris Simpson, professor of communications at American University in Washington, D.C., David Kim of the Washington office of the Korea Society (now closed), and Mrs. Dongwoo Lee Hahm from the Washington Coalition for Comfort Women Issues, Inc. (WCCW), which was established in 1992.

I want to share with the readers the difficulties and even hostilities we faced when we began exploring the idea of holding the conference: the humiliation of being turned away, the condescension of being ignored, and even an attempt to sabotage our meeting during the last stage of its preparation by the Japanese Embassy, and jubilation and elation at the conclusion of our endeavor met with unexpected enthusiastic encouragement and success.

The support for funding came from a few external sources ranging from the Maryknoll Fathers to the Korean Taekwondo Foundation. Within Georgetown, nineteen departments, programs, centers, and student organizations made donations ranging from $25–$50, an average of $100–$200 came from academic programs, and $3,000 was donated by the provost's office and a dean's office. Other individuals, within and outside of Georgetown, contributed small sums from their own pockets as well. This meant that Margaret Stetz and I walked, knocked, bowed, and pleaded almost up to the moment of the conference opening. Even as the conference was opening, we did not know if we could pay for the airfare and accommodations for three speakers from Korea, Australia, and Japan, including the first-class airfare for the keynote speaker, Mrs. Mutsuko Miki, the widow of former Japanese Prime Minister Takeo Miki (1974–1976).

Not only did we wear our soles thin, but we also had to overcome a lot of unsolicited advice and comments bordering on malice and threats from our some well-meaning and other not-so-friendly colleagues of all levels. Margaret Stetz was a tenured professor in the Department of English, but I was a special appointee with a glorified title on a yearly contract. Besides, I had just arrived at Georgetown a semester earlier. I was really putting myself in a precarious position. I could be dismissed at my superior's whim. Some of the counsel, such as "it would be a kiss of death for your academic career," sounded like intimidation to me. But my supportive husband, the late John Kie-chiang Oh, Ph.D., a highly esteemed scholar of Korean and Asian politics, urged me to "let things pass—'in one ear and out the other.'" Hard as it was not to be bothered, I tried to not allow disturbing remarks to settle in my head.

Despite the shortage of funding and the hostile environment in which we were operating, we did not want to compromise on the quality of the conference. We planned a half-day symposium, from 1 to 5 p.m. on the last day of September 1996, followed by a general reception and a small group dinner. That was all we could plan because that was the most we could afford. But we encountered amazing happenings. To borrow a sports stadium analogy, "Build, and they will come." And indeed, they came. We had dared tackle a taboo subject and were fearful of few showing up, but people came, in overwhelming numbers, "out of the woodwork." Those who had been working on the subject or related issues, sought us out and offered to present and display their work out of love and dedication to the cause—without honoraria, or even expenses. We only needed to provide the venue. A half-day conference expanded to on-going programs, which extended to two weeks: three consecutive evenings of film screenings; enlarged photo exhibits on ten 6x4 foot panels in the Galleria (atrium) of the Intercultural Center (ICC) conference building for five days; and an exhibit of books, catalogues, and art work in large glass cases for two weeks. This was nothing short of a miracle.

For the symposium itself, we lined up distinguished academic panelists, including Dr. Yuki Tanaka, then from Australia, a Japanese-born scholar, now of the Hiroshima Peace Institute. We also wanted to invite two central speakers: a high-profile keynoter, preferably a sympathetic Japanese, and a surviving "comfort woman." To find a former "comfort woman" was relatively simple. Mrs. Dongwoo Lee Hahm had a list of them on hand; and she contacted Ms. Kim Yoon-shim, who, as it turned out, was both healthy enough to travel from Korea and willing to give testimonials of her ordeal.

Finding a keynote speaker was another story. We had no one as late as 12 months into our planning and four months before the meeting. Then, in the May 13th edition of *The New York Times,* we noticed a short account about the resignation of Mrs. Mutsuko Miki (d. July 2012) from the Asian Women's Fund, a quasi-official fund that the Japanese government established in 1995 with "some acclaim and self-acclaim" to make payments to "comfort women" and help raise funds.[2] She was prominent not just because she was the widow of Takeo Miki but an internationally admired women's leader as a humanist and artist. She had agreed to lead the fund with the promise from the Japanese government that the latter would assist her and contribute to it. The Japanese government reneged on both promises of assisting to raise money and making compensation. According to the *Times* story, indignant Mrs. Miki resigned in protest. As soon as we noticed the *Times'* write-up, Margaret Stetz and I did not hesitate to decide that she would be our central speaker. It was reassuring that Mrs. Hahm had mentioned her name earlier.

I still do not know where we got such audacity and daring to invite a former Japanese prime minister's widow to a conference, where Japan would undoubtedly be a major topic but not necessarily in a flattering light. With the assistance of a first-year Japanese-born graduate student who was enrolled in my East Asian history class, we obtained Mrs. Miki's mailing address. In our letter of invitation, crafted elegantly and passionately by Stetz, we mentioned that the main purpose of our conference was to let the world know the existence of the "comfort women" system so that similar events would not recur. We also asked if she could send us the draft of her speech two weeks prior to the conference date. After an anxious month's waiting, we received a positive response for both: she would indeed present a keynote address and send us the draft in advance. Mrs. Miki's consent to be the central speaker was a huge boost to our confidence and energized us.

A month before our opening date, I received a call from my dean. I was then holding the title of "Distinguished Professor of Korean Studies" in the Asian Studies Program of the School of Foreign Service (SFS) at Georgetown University. The dean then was Robert L. Gallucci, Ph.D., a former diplomat and scholar.

"How's the conference planning going?" he asked as I was sitting across from his desk.

"Very well, very well indeed—beyond our expectations," I responded, "and the program is ready to go to a printer in a day or two."

"That's great. Congratulations." he commented.

"That's it? Bob, you wanted me to come down so that you could congratulate me? You worried me. When the dean calls, faculty members wonder. You know that, don't you?"

"No, there's something else I wanted to talk to you about."

"Oh, yes?" I was curious.

"Do you know who just visited me?"

"Who? I wouldn't know. You have many visitors." I responded.

"The Japanese DCM (Deputy Chief of Mission at the Embassy of Japan)."

"What did he want," I asked, "and why are you telling me this?" A flash of anxiety and foreboding passed through my mind, reddening my face.

"You don't mean . . .?" I whispered but the dean either didn't hear or pretended that he didn't. He didn't make any comments. Instead, he continued his conversation.

"He wanted me to prevent you from holding the 'comfort women' conference." Dean Gallucci looked at me and told me. My heart sank. My face got even more flushed and my heart beat faster. The prospect of canceling a nearly completed conference was maddening. But I tried to be calm and asked in as normal-sounding voice as I could.

"Are you going to?" I asked.

"What do you think? Do you think I am going to let the Japanese Embassy interfere with academic freedom at Georgetown?" I shrugged my shoulders. I truly didn't know what to think. *Was it possible there was something bigger at stake—not just between the University and the Embassy but also between the U.S. and Japan?*

A few moments passed, which seemed like an eternity, and I was nervous. Finally, the dean resumed the conversation.

"I told him that he was in the United States, and he could not meddle with academic freedom of an American institution of higher learning."

"Whew," I sighed, "I almost fainted."

"I hope not." The dean continued, "I fully support your project, and I will be happy to make the opening comment. One more thing, do you know what else I told the Japanese DCM?"

" . . ." I was without a clue.

"I told him. . ." I detected a look of pride pass through the dean's face. He continued, "I told him that if he or the Embassy in any way harassed our conference, I would call the media and inform them that Japan was interfering with American higher education. When I said that, the Japanese diplomat scurried out without even saying a proper goodbye." I noticed the dean referred to the conference as "our" conference. As I was leaving the dean's office, he added, "Just in case I won't have a chance to say it before the opening, I am telling you now that I am proud that Georgetown is holding the first academic conference on 'comfort women.'"

Thus, our conference planning went on uninterrupted. And the dean made an impassioned, supportive greeting statement at the opening of our conference. One could only imagine the number of big and small events happening in the life of a dean of the prominent School of Foreign Service at Georgetown University in the heart of the U.S. capital. And this, a half-day conference, could have not been a high-priority affair. It was on a topic, then hardly heard of, and brought by a foreign-born, older, specially appointed woman, not on a tenure-track or tenured professor. But in my estimate, Robert Gallucci rendered one of the most significant decisions he had made as a dean, upholding academic freedom and demonstrating personal commitment to integrity and justice. One could only wish that the Japanese would have learned the lesson and would not repeat a similar attempt, but sadly, this was only the beginning of Japanese meddling in "comfort women" affairs in years to come.

Mrs. Miki arrived at Dulles International Airport three days before the conference date. We went to meet her and hoped that she would give us her summary, which was promised to us two weeks before her arrival. We wanted to know the content of her speech. We were concerned about the possibility that she might have had a change of heart and had a 180-degree turn around of her position. She was a Japanese national, after all, and a former prime minister's widow to boot. The Japanese in general were, and still are, known to be staunchly nationalistic and she might be no exception. She had not sent us her speech draft. We wondered, "Were there any hidden meanings for her not to send us the draft?" We were terribly troubled with what she might say, but, out of politeness, we did not ask for a summary either at the airport or during the ride into town from Dulles International Airport.

There was no one from the Japanese Embassy to greet the eighty-year-old widow of a former prime minister. She did not act bothered, and no one mentioned that there were no Japanese Embassy personnel to welcome such a prominent Japanese. Mrs. Miki stayed at the university's conference center hotel and remained in the U.S. for a week. The principal organizers of the conference and student volunteers shared responsibilities for taking care of her. We showed her around the D.C. area, including an excursion to the Shenandoah and Luray Caverns in northern Virginia. During that time the Japanese Embassy did not invite her even for an afternoon tea.

The 350-capacity Intercultural Center (ICC) auditorium was filled to standing room only, which shocked the planners. While Mrs. Miki and Ms. Kim Yoon-shim, a former "comfort woman" spoke, the audience was so captivated that one could "hear a pin drop." When Ms. Kim talked about how her joyride, as a fourteen-year old, in a military truck turned into abduction to a military brothel, we could hear sniffles. But the crowd broke into standing applause when Mrs. Miki said, "Given the Imperial Army's involvement in these outrages, the Japanese government should play a direct role in compensating women."

That's all we wanted to hear—for now: the acknowledgment of the Japanese government's *direct* involvement in the "comfort women" system, the need for *governmental* compensation, and the apology. With such recognition from a former

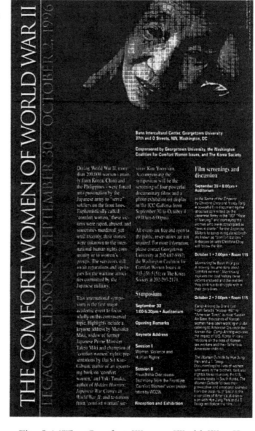

Fig. 5-1. "The Comfort Women World War II: Legacies and Lessons," Georgetown University Conference program poster, September 30, 1996 – October 2, 1996.

prime minister's widow, there could hardly be any further dispute about the Japanese government's direct participation in the "comfort women" establishments. Our conference was only the beginning, but we opened the door for debate. We were relieved and elated (A.5-1).

Fig. 5-2. Mrs. Mutsuko Miki, keynoter at Georgetown University conference, September 30, 1996.

Fig. 5-3. Ms. Kim Yoon-shim testifying and Sangmi Choi Schelstede, vice president of WCCW and interpreter, Georgetown University: September 30, 1996.

Fig. 5-4. Mrs. Dongwoo Lee Hahm, president of WCCW, viewing the photography exhibit at Georgetown University ICC Galleria, September 30, 1996

## Impact of the Conference

The reaction to the symposium was uniformly positive. Several of the planners, Mrs. Dongwoo Lee Hahm of WCCW, Chris Simpson of American University, David Kim of the Korea Society, Margaret Stetz, and I, spread out across America to college and university campuses, civic societies, women's groups, and non-government organizations to talk about our forum and the subject of "comfort women." The Free Library of Philadelphia and the U.S. Holocaust Memorial Museum were just two of the prominent organizations that hosted "comfort women" discussions. We also joined forces with the Chinese groups on WWII Japanese War Crimes. We invited the late Iris Chang, the author of *The Rape of Nanking*,[3] to our subsequent meetings. We became preachers for the cause.

"The Undying Spirits" was the title of the Free Library of Philadelphia public forum, held on May 13, 1999, which was followed by the two-week long photo exhibit. The Women's Development Institute International, headed by Ms. Imja Choi, a Korean-born businesswoman, feminist, and activist, organized them both. I was one of the three panelists with Eli Rosenbaum and Christopher Simpson. Rosenbaum was the director of the Office of Special Investigations of the U.S. Department of Justice (A.5-2).

A little over a year later, on September 18, 2000, we had a symposium at the U.S. Holocaust Memorial Museum in Washington, D.C. Ordinarily, the museum tended not to host events not directly related to the Nazi Holocaust. So, I was surprised when I was invited to be a panelist on the "comfort women" topic. The Helena Rubinstein auditorium in the museum was full and people were standing along the wall. I was one of the four panelists along with Susan Stamberg of National Public Radio (NPR), who happened to be my classmate at Barnard College in New York, Eli Rosenbaum, director of Special Investigations at the U.S. Department of Justice, and Grandma Kim Sang-hi, a former "comfort woman" with an interpreter.

## The Conference Volume, the First Academic Book on "Comfort Women"

I would be remiss if I neglected to mention this book that came about as the lasting impact and legacy of the Georgetown conference. After the conference, we received numerous requests for the information on the conference and on "comfort women." We were compelled to respond to them. Stetz and I co-edited/authored a volume, consisting of the conference proceedings and additional material, not just on the "comfort women" subject but also on related issues, such as the tradition of public brothels in Japan and violence against women in peace and war. Our book, *Legacies of the Comfort Women of World War II*, was published five years later, in 2001 (Fig. 5-5). It was one of the first books in the growing body of literature on "comfort women." It's humbling and gratifying that even now, 17 years since its publication, it's still cited in subsequent literature on "comfort women." I would like to conclude this chapter on an optimistic note: the torch is being passed on to younger generations.

The clearest evidence of this is that Dr. Jung-Sil Lee, who is a quarter-century younger than either Mrs. Hahm or myself, is the primary editor of this volume. She has been the president of WCCW for the past five years and an art historian. Interest among young people within and outside of Korea on the subject remains strong. For example, on my family's recent trip to Korea, my grandchildren insisted on attending the noontime Wednesday Demonstration in front of the Japanese Embassy in Seoul. They sat on the curb of the street across from the Japanese Embassy holding signboards that they could not read (I had to make sure they held them right side up) but they chanted slogans together with nearly 100 students as young as eight or ten years old. It was one of the hottest days of the summer with the heat-index of 105°F, but the animated voices of young protesters echoed through the streets of Seoul and through the palace grounds of the last dynasty of Korea, which Japan terminated.

A truly enduring legacy, unthinkable at the time of our conference, is that an impressive number of students engage in graduate studies on the subject. The contribution in this publication by Frank Joseph Shulman, one of the best-known bibliographers in Asian Studies, is an annotated bibliography of forty-six doctoral

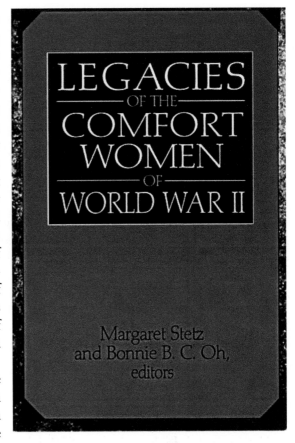

Fig. 5-5. The book cover of *Legacies of the Comfort Women of World War II* as the conference proceedings and additional contributions, East Gate Book, M.E. Sharpe, 2001.

dissertations on the subject from the years 1995–2004. Shulman also provides the ethnic origins of these dissertation writers: Seventeen Korean, eighteen Western, seven Japanese, and four Asian of ethnic origins of Chinese and of Thai.[4] Such a chapter will render this volume an indispensable source book for "comfort women" studies for years to come.

When convening the Georgetown conference, we could have hardly imagined the scope of its impact: on developing "comfort women" issues, in endowing legacies on "comfort women," and enriching and expanding educational fields. The timing might have been right and the planners of the conference can hardly take all the credit for its success. But the fact remains that the conveners having the daring to tackle as controversial an issue as "comfort women" yielded the lasting effect.

---

[1] Pierre Thomas, "War Crimes List Bars 16 Japanese from U.S," *The Washington Post*, December 4, 1996, https://www.washingtonpost.com/archive/politics/1996/12/04/war-crimes-list-bars-16-japanese-from-us/2dc9a6a0-a607-42b8-8f44-83d9c31a65cb/.

[2] Nicholas D. Kristof, "Japan Fund for War's 'Comfort Women' Is in Crisis," *The New York Times*, May 13, 1996, https://www.nytimes.com/1996/05/13/world/japan-fund-for-war-s-comfort-women-is-in-crisis.html?searchResultPosition=5.

[3] Iris Chang, *The Rape of Nanking, The Forgotten Holocaust of World War II* (New York: Penguin Books, 1997).

[4] Frank Joseph Shulman, Comfort Women Bibliography 12-27-18 (RTF). Rtf from Shulman email to Jung-Sil Lee and Bonnie Oh, 12/27/2018.

# 6. GIRLS AND MILITARY SEXUAL SLAVERY THROUGH A FEMINIST INTERSECTIONAL LENS

*Margaret D. Stetz*

**Abstract:** This chapter examines how and why the testimonies of Asian survivors of military sexual slavery within the "comfort system" achieved a sympathetic reception in the U.S. during the 1990s and the means by which these narratives circulated, especially throughout feminist communities. It also explores some ways in which the feminist understanding of these stories has altered, as American feminism itself has shifted toward intersectional perspectives that highlight oppression based on social categories such as ethnicity and age, rather than gender alone.

The belated entry of "comfort women's" stories into the histories of World War II that circulate in the West was never merely a consequence of the silence of those who had survived Japanese military sexual slavery. It was always a matter related to reception—to what listeners on the other side of the globe wanted to hear and were willing (or unwilling) to confront. In the U.S. in particular, widespread indifference on the part of non-Asian populations to the sufferings of Asian women lasted for many decades after 1945. Certainly, it was fueled, throughout the 1960s and 1970s, by the war in Vietnam, the coverage of which often deliberately ignored the realities of so-called "others" across the Pacific. For some Americans, the epiphany that Asian women's war experiences in general were complex, multi-faceted, and "had for too long been dismissed" in the West did not come until the 1990s, when historians such as Karen Gottschang Turner and Phan Thanh Hao, writing about North Vietnamese women, worked to explode the stereotype of "passive, inert female accessories to the American story."[1] A multitude of factors had to come together to create a different climate of response to Asian women's voices. Fortunately, many of these were in place by the early 1990s, when word reached the West of Kim Hak-soon's public testimony about her imprisonment and daily sexual assaults within the "comfort system."

## Building the U.S. Audience for "Comfort Women" Issues

Among the turning points in shaping a sympathetic U.S. reception for Kim Hak-soon's accounts of captivity and rape by Japanese soldiers in the 1940s were reports of related atrocities during the civil war in the former Yugoslavia—military sexual assaults that were occurring not in earlier decades, but at that very moment. Western journalists and human rights workers wrote graphically of the organized "war crimes" that were being committed by Serbian forces against Bosnian Muslim women held in rape camps, thus making it impossible to deny the reality of the phenomenon of wartime military sexual slavery, whether present or past.[2] It was the exposure of the systematic nature of these atrocities that helped to create a new public understanding of rape as a matter of wartime policy—a crime for which not merely individual soldiers should be held responsible, but ultimately the highest reaches of the military and political institutions that had determined and directed their illegal actions.

Equally crucial in ensuring a sympathetic hearing of the testimonies given not only by Kim Hak-soon, but by other elderly Asian survivors who soon began to come forward under the designation of former "comfort women," were the shifts in public consciousness achieved by members of the American feminist community. From the start of Second Wave feminism in the 1960s, they had been pressing with increasing success for the view that, as the popular slogan goes, "the personal is political" and, therefore, for recognition that what happens to individual women is more than merely of individual concern. By the 1990s, commentators such as Patricia L. N. Donat and John D'Emilio were able to write retrospectively about the advances of "the 1970s, [when] rape became an important issue within the feminist movement," and about the resulting widespread acknowledgment of rape "as an act of violence, *not* of sex as psychoanalytic theorists had previously held. Rape was a form of domination and control" [italics in original].[3] All of these developments affected not only the attitudes of the American public as a whole, but the readiness of U.S. feminist movements in particular to unite with their Asian counterparts in support of the demands of "comfort system" survivors for official Japanese governmental apologies and redress. At the same time, the intervention of Asian American women—some of whom identified themselves explicitly as feminists, as well as campaigners for human rights—proved of tremendous importance in forging coalitions across national and cultural borders in the mid-1990s, as well as in countering Japanese right-wing resistance to these new calls for justice.

Before this transnational work on behalf of "comfort women" began, another significant piece had fallen into place in the U.S.: the emergence of Asian American activism as a political force. This included the founding of numerous organizations dedicated to addressing issues that affected diverse Asian American communities—organizations that sponsored high-visibility events, cultural exhibitions, conferences, and even protests. So, too, the 1980s and early 1990s witnessed the concurrent growth of Asian American Studies programs and academic associations, along with scholarly journals and monograph series. All of this meant that, when the "comfort women" narratives reached the U.S., they could be disseminated widely and then studied and analyzed; they would not be allowed to vanish with the conclusion of a journalistic news cycle. Even as a variety of writers, researchers, and creative artists recognized the significance of the survivors' experiences and of their growing calls for justice, there were platforms available to promulgate efforts on their behalf, as well as audiences ready to respond.

Among the early proponents of investigation into and circulation of topics related to "comfort women" were two interdisciplinary journals focused on Asian American subject matter. In 1995, *Muae: A Journal of Transcultural Production* appeared in print, published in New York by Kaya Production, which announced its mission as a publishing firm devoted to Asian diasporic literature, art, and cultural criticism. The inaugural issue of *Muae* contained three diverse, yet significant, ways of increasing public knowledge about the formerly hidden experiences that were then coming to light. *Muae*'s section of contributions dedicated to exploring different approaches to these histories began with "To Live Without Shame," the eight-page-long testimony, translated into English, of a Korean survivor named Hwang Keum-ju, regarding her transportation to a "comfort station" in China and then captivity and repeated daily rapes by Japanese soldiers until the end of the war. Hwang's testimony emphasized the formal, regularized nature of life in a "comfort station," with its scheduled medical checkups for venereal disease, but also the fact that murder was a common occurrence as part of the system—that "comfort women" who displayed signs of severe or intractable infection were removed and never seen alive again. This personal account was followed by a scholarly analysis of the historical framework against which such atrocities had been organized and perpetrated: "An Overview of the Colonial and Socio-economic Background of Japanese Military Sex Slavery in Korea" by Chung Chin-sung. The last of the selections in this triad consisted of reproductions of two works of art by the Korean American painter, Miran Kim, including her 1993 *Chongshin-dae-#1*, in which the artist infused the question of the World War II-era "comfort system" with contemporaneity and immediacy by employing her own naked body as the basis for her portrait of a military sex slave from the past.

Going even further to raise awareness, the academic journal *Positions: East Asia Cultures Critique* (founded in 1993 and published by Duke University Press in Durham, North Carolina) titled its entire "special issue" of Spring 1997 "The Comfort Women: Colonialism, War, and Sex." It offered eight scholarly articles dedicated to the topic, along with a "Portfolio" reproducing works of art by two Korean "comfort system" survivors, two Japanese artists, and two Korean American artists, all taking up the challenge of using media ranging from photography to watercolor to sculpture to convey a history for which the visual record was scant.[4] In the Introduction to this issue, which was guest edited by Chungmoo Choi, there was no mistaking the fact that these many sorts of representations were being given to the public in hopes of inspiring a multi-faceted movement of support, rather than purely as a means to increase scholarly knowledge about this suppressed part of the World War II chronicles. *Positions* quite literally turned to its advantage multiple *positions* as a journal bringing together transnational audiences. It extended the reach of information about the "comfort system," while also allowing diverse readers to consider how to regard the human rights implications of it and how to move forward in lessening the psychic pain still endured by the survivors, to whom the Japanese government had refused to apologize either fully or officially. Such scholarship in *Positions*, as in *Muae*, encouraged the formation of multi-ethnic and multi-national coalitions beyond the printed page.

When, therefore, an NPO such as the Washington Coalition for Comfort Women Issues, Inc. (WCCW) was founded in 1992 to promote education and action on behalf of the victims of Japanese military sexual slavery, it soon discovered a wide base of alliances and partnerships on which to draw in linking Americans both of Asian and non-Asian descent with the elderly Asian survivors abroad. These networks of support were forming everywhere from university campuses, to art galleries, to the halls of Congress, as well as in public venues that screened relevant films. Some of the earliest information about the "comfort system" was, in fact, transmitted through film, especially via the widely viewed documentary *In the Name of the Emperor* (1995), directed by Christine Choy and Nancy Tong, which played in commercial cinemas in most major U.S. cities. Later, Dai Sil Kim-Gibson's documentary *Silence Broken: Korean Comfort Women* (2000), reached an even wider viewership, when it was shown nationally on television via the Public Broadcasting System (PBS).

Also important, moreover, in disseminating and interpreting the historical narratives of victimization by Imperial Japan were works of literary fiction by Asian American authors. These reached an increasingly interested public both through conventional means such as bookstores and through the new vehicle of online bookselling, which began in the mid-1990s and enabled readers to access more rapidly the productions of smaller presses (such as Spinsters Ink, publishers of work by Therese Park). Among the most influential novels were two that appeared almost simultaneously: Nora Okja Keller's *Comfort Woman: A Novel* (1997) and Therese Park's *A Gift of the Emperor* (1997). Both foregrounded the perspectives of the female survivors of the "comfort system," with the former relating these as flashbacks to situations from decades earlier and the latter using a linear chronological structure to create the illusion of carrying readers along through the first-person narrator's sufferings as they were happening. Even more prominently featured, however, in an array of literary journals and newspaper book reviews was Chang-rae Lee's well-regarded novel, *A Gesture Life* (1999), which told the story of a "comfort station" through the memories of a male fictional character who had been a participant in its atrocities, as the military physician assigned to oversee its captives' health. Both Keller and Lee made direct appeals to the concerns of American readers by setting their works in the U.S., many years after the time when these war crimes were committed in Asia, and by showing the lasting impact in the present of these unaddressed and unresolved histories. Thus, as the horrific details of the "comfort system" were being revealed throughout the 1990s, a broad swath of the public across the U.S. was exposed to them and urged to accept these reports as both reliable and important.

## U.S. Feminism and the "Comfort System"

Nonetheless, the ways in which "comfort women's" experiences initially were framed in U.S. discourse sometimes proved more limited than they might otherwise have been, due to political perspectives that were, by the early 1990s, in the process of changing, but had not yet fully done so. American feminism in particular was embroiled in a radical, yet still incomplete, process of evolution that affected how matters related to women were looked at. From the moment of its emergence in the 1960s, Second Wave feminists had emphasized the concept of a unitary "sisterhood," as enshrined in the titles of Robin Morgan's two major edited collections of essays, *Sisterhood Is Powerful* (1970) and *Sisterhood Is Global* (1984). While this notion was never as simplistic as it was later accused of being, it did often focus on finding commonalities, rather than on discovering and examining differences, and thus on talking about "women" as a group. Around 1992, however, as R. Claire Snyder reports, the African American feminist activist Rebecca Walker "kicked off the new movement" that would come to be known as the Third Wave.[5] Led by "feminists of color," it offered "major theoretical challenges" to "the idea of a shared women's experience or identity."[6] Even as it refuted "the universalist claim that all women share a set of common experiences," it did not reject the importance of personal narratives; on the contrary, the primacy of "the personal story" still stood as one of the "hallmarks" of this new wave.[7] In place of a monolithic "category of 'women,'" though, it affirmed the value of diverse "personal narratives that illustrate an intersectional and multiperspectival version" of reality.[8]

Gradually over the next two decades, the principle of intersectionality became the central tenet of American feminism—one that would begin to influence how testimonies by the "comfort women" survivors were read and which elements of their stories would move to the foreground. Writing in 2014 about intersectionality for a mass newspaper audience, Ava Vidal would underscore its aim of making everyone cognizant of and precise in crediting "all the multilayered facets in life" of "women of all backgrounds."[9] Although the term "intersectionality" did not come to prominence until after its use in 1989 by the African American legal scholar and critical race theorist Kimberlé Crenshaw, its roots as an idea and a practice lay in the long struggle of women of color in the U.S. to name and render visible the numerous, interlocking categories—not only gender, but race, ethnicity, sexuality, ability/disability, religion, age, socio-economic status, and others—that resulted in varying, unequal degrees of oppression and that underpinned "marginalization and subjugation."[10]

Once the personal narratives of "comfort system" survivors, along with their accusations that the Japanese government had never been held legally accountable for the war crimes committed against them, began to be disseminated in English translation, an array of volumes of testimonies appeared in the U.S. (and, of course, they continue to do so). Some of the best known have been individual memoirs, such as the Filipina survivor Maria Rosa Henson's *Comfort Woman* (1996) and the Dutch-Indonesian (later Australian) survivor Jan Ruff O'Herne's *Fifty Years of Silence* (1994), with the latter inspiring a documentary, directed by Ned Lander, that was shown on American network television by the Public Broadcasting System.[11] Collections of testimonies have also circulated widely. Until recently, the majority of these have come from Korean survivors, including accounts archived by The Korean Council for Women Drafted for Military Sexual Slavery by Japan as *True Stories of the Korean Comfort Women* (1993; translated in 1995); Dai Sil Kim-Gibson's *Silence Broken: Korean Comfort Women* (1999), which served, too, as the basis of a documentary film that she directed and that was broadcast on American television; the volume *Comfort Women Speak: Testimony by Sex Slaves of the Japanese Military* (2000) issued by the WCCW; and *Can You Hear Us? The Untold Narratives of Comfort Women* (2014).[12] That the preponderance of these collected oral histories of World War II-era sexual slavery reflected a Korean perspective alone may unwittingly have helped to shape a somewhat monolithic view of what it meant to be a "comfort woman" and thus discouraged more intersectional readings—ones that could highlight specific differences in the way that the Japanese military's atrocities were carried out and also experienced by diverse populations.

With the publication, for instance, of M. Evelina Galang's *Lolas' House: Filipino Women Living with War* (2017), it has become possible even for non-scholarly audiences to recognize unique patterns of criminal activity by the Japanese military against women in the Philippines—thus to see that military sexual slavery there involved a set of conditions that were not the same as for the Korean victims who had told their stories in the earlier volumes.

Ethnicity and nationality, along with particular political and historical circumstances—not gender alone—determined what it meant to be a so-called "comfort woman" across Asia. In *Lolas' House*, Galang presents the first-person narratives of sixteen named survivors, all of whose ordeals began after 1942, following the invasion of their country by the Japanese Army in late 1941. Their Korean counterparts had been raised in a nation occupied by Imperial Japan for many decades, following the annexation of Korea in 1910. As subjects of the Japanese Emperor, Koreans were forcibly recruited—through coercion in some instances and deception in others, as well as outright abduction—then trafficked in a systematic fashion, to be imprisoned in military brothels that were scattered across the Pacific, far from their homeland. Transported like supplies by train, truck, and ship, Korean victims often had no notion as to where the "comfort stations" to which they had been confined were located. Escape thus became impossible; they were cut off entirely from contact with their families; their situation was completely hopeless. The few who managed to live through the war and be liberated emerged from captivity with no resources and no easy way to travel home. Traumatized, brutalized, and dissociated from their former identities, many never did return or did so only after a long, arduous struggle that constituted further victimization.

What becomes clear from the testimonies in *Lolas' House* of the sixteen survivors is how similar a "comfort woman's" experience might be, in terms of the atrocities to which she was subjected, yet how different in terms of the circumstances. None of the Filipinas whom Galang interviewed was trafficked to another country. Some were imprisoned and raped repeatedly in surroundings that were near to home and even familiar to them. There was little evidence of the kind of bureaucratic organization and planning that went into the "comfort system" devised by Japanese government officials—a carefully thought-out system that deployed the bodies of Koreans as military supplies. Abductions of Filipinas by Japanese soldiers were carried out in seemingly random fashion. While Korean survivors described military brothels that placed "comfort women" in individually partitioned areas and distributed tickets for access to them, as well as having imposed regulations regarding separate times for officers and enlisted men, the Filipina survivors in *Lolas' House* spoke of a chaotic atmosphere of mass rapes.

Urduja Samonte, for example, tells Evelina Galang of a forced march alongside all the residents of her own and the neighboring towns, until thousands of them had reached the municipality of New Washington. At that point, the Japanese soldiers separated the families:

> And all the women, they put inside . . . in the basement of a . . . warehouse. They didn't speak to us—but threw us one by one into one of three rooms. I counted twenty-five women in my room. There were no chairs. No beds. No rugs to sleep on, only the cold floor. . . . The Japanese entered our room. Not caring where they were, they'd choose a girl and rape her right there on the floor in front of all of us. Two Japanese came at me at one time, each pulling on an arm. I could feel my skin slipping out of me. . . .[13]

In its use of Koreans, the "comfort system" devised by the Japanese government carefully and deliberately kept both the victims themselves and any knowledge of their fate away from the general populace of their home communities—a plan meant to lessen the likelihood of mass outrage and rebellion in Korea against the authority of the Japanese colonial administrators. A very different policy appears to have guided the practice of military sexual slavery in the Philippines, where little seems to have been done to maintain secrecy about it. Given the need to subdue a newly conquered nation, the Japanese army instead kept their Filipina captives in close proximity to the local population, evidently as an exercise in communal intimidation and humiliation, in order to demonstrate the absolute power and impunity that now was theirs.

Another survivor, Atanacia Cortez, describes to Galang how for "seven months the Japanese kept me in a room above the dungeon" in Fort Santiago, where "I was raped several times a day."[14] Her sufferings must have been known throughout the community, as eventually her mother-in-law arrived in the company of "her friend, a Japanese reverend," and was able to arrange her release.[15] Later, though, after Cortez had obtained a job in a restaurant by agreeing to work for food rather than wages, "one night a group of Japanese soldiers" came in. "I ran out the back . . . right into a Chinese cemetery," where they caught up with her: "I hid in that grave, covering myself up with fronds and soil, only my feet stuck out. The soldier pulled me out and into the open air. He raped me until I lost consciousness."[16] She was found in that state by the cemetery's caretaker and returned to the restaurant—where, presumably, every Filipino present would have been aware of what had been done to her and would have feared for their own safety. The sense of stigmatization and dishonor that haunted Korean survivors of military rape and prevented some from ever returning to their families and homes after the war, leaving them permanently displaced, had to be dealt with more immediately by Filipina survivors, many of whom were treated as outcasts. By focusing on additional categories of identity such as ethnicity and nationality, rather than on gender alone, an intersectional approach to the stories of "comfort women" can, therefore, illuminate the particular cruelties inflicted on the victims and the differing political rationales behind these physical and psychological abuses.

## Age as an Intersectional Category of Oppression

Perhaps more important, however, is what an intersectional perspective that examines additional categories of identity as sources of interlocking oppression reveals about one feature that was shared by "comfort system" victims in many nations—i.e., their very young age. Whether one looks at the narratives of Korean or Filipina survivors, at those of the Chinese survivors collected and analyzed by Peipei Qiu, Su Zhiliang, and Chen Lifei in *Chinese Comfort Women: Testimonies from Imperial Japan's Sex Slaves* (2013), or at the short accounts of Indonesian survivors that follow their photographic portraits in Jan Banning and Hilde Janssen's volume, *Comfort Women/Troost Meisjes* (2010), it is clear that very large numbers, if not the majority, of all the so-called "comfort women" could by no legal standard be classified as "women."[17] They were instead underage girls—far below the legal age of adulthood that was in place even in Japan during the 1930s and 1940s at the time of the Asia-Pacific War. Numerous survivors from a variety of Asian nations report having been held captive and raped by the Japanese military when they were as young as twelve to fourteen-years-old. Military brothels filled with girls under the age of nineteen were common. Despite the continuing false claims by right-wing Japanese nationalists that "comfort women" were paid sex workers who had volunteered to take on these roles, relatively few of the victims of this system actually were at or above the age when they could legally have given such consent. Many were children or adolescents and thus, even under Japanese statutes, mere juveniles. To use them for sex, let alone to traffic them for that purpose, was a violation of international laws (including those that went by the name of anti-white slavery legislation) to which Japan had agreed decades earlier.

If early feminist-informed responses in the U.S. to the revelations about the wartime "comfort system" sometimes erred in treating this subject monolithically, as though the experiences of those of different ethnicities and nationalities were identical, so they did not always highlight sufficiently the flaws in the very term "women," when applied to the victims and/or survivors. American Second Wave feminism began as a *women's* liberation movement, for and by adults; rarely did it focus specifically on girls. In the academic sphere, what became known as "Girls Studies" did not arise as an interdisciplinary field until the 1990s. At the moment when the testimonies of "comfort system" survivors first circulated, the question of how to think about girlhood as a separate and equally significant category of identity was still an open one, as was the issue of how to talk about the particular trauma endured by underage victims of organized sexual assault. Merely substituting the phrase "girls and women" for the word "women," when referring to those held in military sexual slavery, has proven an inadequate acknowledgment of this problem.

There is still much work to be done on this subject—in terms of research, critical analysis, and teaching—although the material for study is widely available in the U.S., thanks to such invaluable volumes as *Comfort Women Speak: Testimony by Sex Slaves of the Japanese Military*, compiled by Sangmie Choi Schellstede and produced by the WCCW. The testimony there, for instance, of Kim Soon-duk makes plain that the so-called recruitment of underage Korean girls was no accident or coincidence, but a planned Japanese governmental strategy: "When I was 16 years old, Japanese officials told us that girls 15 and older should not stay in Korea, but should instead go to Japan to work at military supply factories or become military nurses." She goes on to explain that "there was a commonly used term in Japanese, 'girl delivery,' just like the farmers' mandatory delivery of harvested rice to the government," to cover this specified roundup of those who were still adolescents.[18] Of course, Kim herself, though "promised a job as a military nurse," was instead shipped first to Japan to be raped initially by an officer and then sent to Shanghai "to a damaged house that was covered with a tent. Rooms were divided into tiny cubicles. Each of our 50 girls was assigned to one of these cubicles. Now this house became a brothel, and we were sex slaves in it."[19] Kim recounts her frequent thoughts of suicide, while a captive. What she does not discuss in detail, however, is the irreparable, lifelong psychological damage inflicted upon very young girls like herself who have not yet fashioned a mature sense of self, at a time when they have all sense of agency and human value stripped from them—when their own worthlessness has been violently impressed upon them at such an early stage of development. That is part of the ongoing mental trauma that she chooses not to explore, while also making plain that she remains unhealed from it. Decades later, as she recounts, "I still have nightmares. I then scream to wake myself up. Nowadays, people often come here to interview me about my life as a 'comfort woman.'

I cannot see them as often as I used to. My nightmares become worse after remembering the past at these interviews."[20]

Increasingly, representations in popular culture of Korean victims and survivors of the "comfort system" have started to look more intersectionally at these figures and to consider the importance of girlhood to their stories. This is especially true of several feature films by South Korean writers and directors that have also circulated in the U.S. with English subtitles, both in theatrical release and in DVD versions, as well as through screenings on campuses and at special events arranged by NPOs such as the WCCW. These fictionalized films treat the age of their protagonists not in a purely sensational way—that is, not primarily as an occasion for inspiring horror in the viewers at the systematic rapes of ones so young—but as an opportunity to show these girls as individuals, both before and after their forcible recruitment into military sexual slavery. By giving them distinct personalities, temperaments, interests, talents, and relationships with one another, the filmmakers invest the characters with dignity and worth *as girls*, the very thing that was deliberately denied their real-life counterparts when they were targeted for "girl delivery" and reduced to objects.

Among these recent films are *Snowy Road* (2015), written by Yoo Bo-ra and directed by Lee Na-jeong, and *Spirits' Homecoming* (2016), written and directed by Cho Jung-rae. Both present the stories not of an isolated teenaged protagonist, but of a pair of girls who bond with one another throughout their ordeal, although in each case only one member of the duo lives beyond the point of liberation from a "comfort station" and is left to bear witness to the past, sharing the joint histories with a later generation of girls. These films are indeed about "comfort," but not in the sense that viewers might expect. Each one refuses to explore that concept in terms of what the Japanese soldiers demanded of the trafficked and imprisoned teenagers; "comfort" is instead what girls provided for one another, under the most harrowing and appalling circumstances. In this sense, both films reclaim the older feminist notion of sisterhood, though from an intersectional perspective that takes into account how girls' emotions, understanding (or lack of comprehension) of their plights, as well as conflicts with and attachments to one another differ from those experienced by mature women. *Snowy Road* and *Spirits' Homecoming* alike, moreover, carefully integrate these fictionalized accounts of girls in wartime, which draw self-consciously on the filmmakers' research and conversations with aged survivors of military sexual slavery,[21] with the stories of adolescent girls in latter-day Korea who have been subjected to other kinds of criminal exploitation or abuse, thus emphasizing the social, political, and cultural importance of this population in itself.

## The Feminist Future: Calling Out Military Sex Slavery

If evolving feminist perspectives have had a noticeable impact on how scholars, activists, and the general public, especially in the U.S., have come to view this historical war crime, so the issue of Japan's "comfort system" has, in turn, influenced the ways in which Western feminist critics have been thinking and writing about questions of military sexual slavery. Certainly, the outcry raised by survivors—amplified by the voices of their supporters in organizations such as the WCCW, Inc.—has encouraged feminist theorists to put the subject of the "comfort system" front and center in any discussion of institutionalized sexual violence. It has, moreover, led American feminists to reject soundly the continued insistence by right-wing Japanese "deniers" that this was an instance of sex work performed by well-paid volunteers and to give credence, instead, to what survivors such as Hwang Keum-ju had insisted from the outset: "I was never paid during the time I was a 'comfort woman.' No money, not even coupons"; meanwhile, "The soldiers didn't treat 'comfort women' like humans. As a rule, we were beaten every day."[22] Such daily brutality was no mere accident, but was instead endemic to a system that was meant to give Japanese soldiers facing death themselves a sense of power and control over someone and something else—over a group defined as inferior by virtue of their gender, ethnicity/nationality, and age. General scholarly works, especially feminist-inflected ones, now regularly feature discussions of the "comfort system" any time the topic of wartime violence directed against girls and/or women arises, even if their focus is not specifically on Asia or solely on World War II.

This development is clear in studies such as Elizabeth D. Heineman's edited collection, *Sexual Violence in Conflict Zones: From the Ancient World to the Era of Human Rights* (2011), as well as Kerry F. Crawford's *Wartime Sexual Violence: From Silence to Condemnation of a Weapon of War* (2017). The latter, in particular, makes a point of locating the plight of those "enslaved as 'comfort women'" within a broader analysis of "atrocities" involving sex and of exploring the reasons behind a seeming lack of global outrage "during the first half of the twentieth century," after they were committed. As Crawford says,

> These atrocities were met with a profound silence from the international community because the social taboo assigned to sexual violence inhibited public discussion of such atrocities, because all sides of the war reportedly had some involvement in or knowledge of sexualized attacks and exploitation, and because there was no consensus that sexual violence was anything other than inevitable in war.[23]

At the same time, in her Introduction to *Sexual Violence in Conflict Zones*, Heineman reminds readers of the dangers of drawing conclusions about the "comfort system" and of the later responses to it that are too broad, for an awareness of "cross-cultural factors, culturally specific conventions . . . longer term historical developments, and shorter-term historical contingencies" is always necessary to "understand not simply the fact of sexual violence but its scale and the forms it took."[24]

In the first decade after Kim Hak-soon's public testimony, among the most important non-Asian or non-Asian American commentators in the U.S. on the "comfort system" was the feminist political scientist Cynthia Enloe who, in *Maneuvers: The International Politics of Militarizing Women's Lives* (2000), provided an astute and nuanced examination—one that led the way toward an intersectional analysis of the differing ethnic and cultural experiences involved, even if it did not make explicit the significance of age as a factor in the population targeted for exploitation. To be sure, Enloe's initial presentation of the topic in *Maneuvers* did not appear so promising. Rather than devote a separate chapter to it, Enloe subsumed the topic of "the Japanese imperial army's World War II forced mobilization of an estimated 200,000 Asian women . . . [as] what Asian feminists think are more accurately called 'military sexual slaves'"[25] under a heading labeled "The Prostitute, the Colonel, and the Nationalist." No one familiar at the time with the "comfort women" controversy would, of course, have thought to find any mention of it in a chapter with such a title. Supporters of the survivors, such as the members of The Korean Council for the Women Drafted for Military Sexual Slavery by Japan—no doubt some of the "Asian feminists" to whom Enloe had alluded—were vociferous in their objections to the use of the word "prostitute" in connection with the "comfort system's" victims. Even to consider the situation of the former "comfort women" within the larger ongoing problem of worldwide military prostitution, rather than to single it out as a unique war crime institutionalized by the Japanese government, was to risk being deeply offensive.

From a feminist standpoint, however, Enloe nonetheless redeemed herself by explicitly linking the "five decades of silence cloaking the stories of the 'comfort women'" not merely to "the women's fear of being shamed and the Japanese postwar officials' desire to avoid any accountability," but to the attitudes and actions of "the U.S. government," which tried desperately to shield its new ally.[26] Locating misogyny and the abuses inherent to patriarchy not only in an Asian world of Others, but in American military ideology at home and abroad, Enloe drew analogies between one institutionalized version of sexual violence and another, denouncing both. Simultaneously, she made plain the heroism and resolve both of the survivors and of those across Asia who had been supporting them: "It was women who first insisted that the experiences of the 'comfort women' be seen as a national political issue by the South Korean government"[27] (where, indeed, matters still stand today). At the same time, what she did not do, at least at this point in her study of the subject, was to distinguish the legal position of those who were of age when joining the postwar "prostitution industry servicing American soldiers in South Korea"[28] from those who were underage, when they were imprisoned in Japanese military brothels, and then to consider the degree to which these differing circumstances were indeed analogous. Girls, it seems, were not yet visible as girl *children* amidst Enloe's focus on "the politics of the actual recruitment and control of women to service male soldiers."[29]

Enloe's continuing influence can be seen in the more recent work of feminist scholars such as Laura Barberán Reinares. The latter's *Sex Trafficking in Post Colonial Literature: Transnational Narratives from Joyce to Bolaño* looks, as does Enloe's study, to the ties that bind Asian histories of war crimes and present-day U.S. realities of sexual exploitation and violence, as it "move[s] from focusing solely on third-world evil traffickers" to "addressing as well the predatory capitalism that generates trafficking in the first place."[30] She is forthright, moreover, about wishing, as does Enloe, not only to expose the ills of the past, but to dismantle current and future militarism, state-supported violence, and the patriarchal structures that undergird these phenomena: "War, in fact, perpetuates social inequalities for the benefit of a capitalist, imperialist military-industrial complex that directly profits from armed conflicts—and, as argued throughout, gendered social inequality breeds sex trafficking."[31] But precisely how this also breeds the trafficking of girl children, in particular—and why it often did so within the "comfort system"—remains largely unexplored.

## Coda

In an article titled "We Need White Women to Call to Their Sisters and Be the Influence They Need" for the December 2018 issue of the mass-market American fashion magazine, *Harper's Bazaar*, Tamika D. Mallory—a Black feminist activist who was among the lead organizers of the 2017 Women's March that followed the inauguration of Donald Trump as President—has warned that "mainstream feminism is at a crossroads," while also reminding readers that when "women come together to protect the rights of the most marginalized, we are powerful."[32] Of course, defending those rights begins with acknowledging that certain "marginalized" groups are in fact distinct populations, in need of respect, as well as protection. The term "comfort women" is today actively being disavowed in the U.S., not merely because it hides the reality of military sexual slavery, but also because it masks the systematic targeting of so many girl children and adolescents between the ages of twelve and nineteen, who were far from meeting the criteria for being identified as "women." To use this phrase without qualifying it is, therefore, to consign girls of the past to invisibility, which does nothing to advance the prospects of girls in either the present or future. As with education about the Holocaust, the movement in the U.S. to support justice for "comfort system" survivors is not solely a matter of righting historical wrongs—i.e., about requiring the Japanese government to accept full legal responsibility for its war crimes; it is and has always been about declaring "Never again." With the increasing spread of feminist intersectional principles and the recognition of the rights of girls, that commitment will only strengthen.

---

[1] Karen Gottschang Turner, "Introduction: Lucky Distance," in *Even the Women Must Fight: Memories of War from North Vietnam*, by Karen Gottschang Turner with Phan Thanh Hao (New York: John Wiley), 1998.

[2] Robert Fisk, "Bosnia War Crimes: 'The Rapes Went on Day and Night," *Independent* (UK), February 8, 1993, https://www.independent.co.uk/news/world/europe/bosnia-war-crimes-the-rapes-went-on-day-and-night-robert-fisk-in-mostar-gathers-detailed-evidence-of-1471656.html.

[3] Patricia L. N. Donat and John D'Emilio, "A Feminist Redefinition of Rape and Sexual Assault: Historical Foundations and Change," in *Gender Violence: Interdisciplinary Perspectives*, ed. Laura L. O'Toole and Jessica R. Schiffman (New York and London: New York University Press, 1997), 188.

[4] The contents of this Spring 1997 special issue of *Positions: East Asia Cultural Critique* related to military sexual slavery were as follows. Articles: Chungmoo Choi, "Guest Editor's Introduction"; Norma Field, "War and Apology: Japan, Asia, the Fiftieth, and After"; Hyunah Yang, "Revisiting the Issue of Korean 'Military Comfort Women': The Question of Truth and Positionality"; Hyun Sook Kim, "History and Memory: The 'Comfort Women' Controversy"; Won Soon Park, "Japanese Reparations Policies and the 'Comfort Women' Question"; Fujime Yuki, "The Licensed Prostitution System and the Prostitution Abolition Movement in Modern Japan"; Song Youn-ok, "Japanese Colonial Rule and State-Managed Prostitution: Korea's Licensed Prostitutes"; Chin Sung Chung, "The Origin and Development of the Military Sexual Slavery Problem in Imperial Japan"; Dai Sil Kim-Gibson, "They Are Our Grandmas." The section titled "Portfolio" contained the following: Kang Tok-kyong and Kim Sun-dok, "Artwork by Former Comfort Women"; Tomiyama Taeko and Shimada Yoshiko, "Artwork by Japanese Artists"; Yong Soon Min and Sasha Y. Lee, "Artwork by Korean American Artists."

[5] R. Claire Snyder, "What Is Third-Wave Feminism? A New Directions Essay," *Signs: Journal of Women in Culture and Society* 34, no. 1 (Autumn 2008): 176.

[6] Ibid., 183.

[7] Ibid., 184.

[8] Ibid., 175.

9 Ava Vidal, "'Intersectional Feminism': What the Hell Is It? (And Why You Should Care)," *Telegraph* (UK), January 15, 2014, https://www.telegraph.co.uk/women/womens-life/10572435/Intersectional-feminism.-What-the-hell-is-it-And-why-you-should-care.html.

10 G. L. A. Harris, R. Finn Sumner, and M. C. González-Prats, *Women Veterans: Lifting the Veil of Invisibility* (New York and London: Routledge, 2018), 11.

11 Maria Rosa Henson, *Comfort Woman: Slave of Destiny*, ed. Sheila S. Coronel (Manila: Philippine Center for Investigative Journalism, 1996); Jan Ruff O'Herne, *Fifty Years of Silence* (Sydney: Editions Tom Thompson/HarperCollins, 1994).

12 Keith Howard, ed., *True Stories of the Korean Comfort Women*, translated by Young Joo Lee. Cassell: New York and London, 1995; Dai Sil Kim-Gibson, *Silence Broken: Korean Comfort Women*. Parkersburg, IA: Mid-Prairie Books, 1999; Sangmie Choi Schellstede, ed. and the Washington Coalition for Comfort Women Issues, Inc. (WCCW), *Comfort Women Speak: Testimony by Sex Slaves of the Japanese Military*. New York: Holmes and Meier, 2000; The Commission on Verification and Support for the Victims of Forced Mobilization under Japanese Colonialism in Korea, *Can You Hear Us? The Untold Narratives of Comfort Women* (Seoul: Park In-Hwan [chairman], The Commission on Verification and Support for the Victims of Forced Mobilization under Japanese Colonialism in Korea), 2014 (2013 in Korean version).

13 M. Evelina Galang, *Lolas' House: Filipino Women Living with War* (Evanston, IL: Northwestern University Press, 2017), 206–07.

14 Ibid., 188.

15 Ibid., 189.

16 Ibid., 191.

17 *See* Peipei Qiu, Su Zhiliang, and Chen Lifei, *Chinese Comfort Women: Testimonies from Imperial Japan's Sex Slaves* (Oxford: Oxford University Press, 2013); Jan Banning and Hilde Janssen, *Comfort Women/Troost Meisjes* (Utrecht: Ipso Facto/Seltmann, 2010).

18 "Kim Soon-duk," in Schellstede, *Comfort Women Speak,* 37.

19 Ibid., 38.

20 Ibid., 40.

21 Si-soo Park and Da-hee Kim, "A Movie Made to Heal Tortured Souls of 'Comfort Women,'" *Korea Times*, March 3, 2016, https://www.koreatimes.co.kr/www/news/culture/2016/03/141_199491.html.

22 Kum-ju Hwang, "To Live Without Shame," *Muae: A Journal of Transcultural Production* 1 (1995), 199.

23 Kerry F. Crawford, *Wartime Sexual Violence: From Silence to Condemnation of a Weapon of War* (Washington, D.C.: Georgetown University Press, 2017), 13.

24 Elizabeth D. Heineman, *Sexual Violence in Conflict Zones: From the Ancient World to the Era of Human Rights* (Philadelphia: University of Pennsylvania Press, 2011), 13.

25 Cynthia Enloe, *Maneuvers: The International Politics of Militarizing Women's Lives* (Berkeley and Los Angeles: University of California Press, 2000), 80.

26 Ibid., 84.

27 Ibid., 86.

28 Ibid., 91.

29 Ibid., 85.

30 Laura Barberán Reinares, *Sex Trafficking in Postcolonial Literature: Transnational Narratives from Joyce to Bolaño* (New York and London: Routledge, 2015), 10.

31 Ibid., 67.

32 Tamika D. Mallory, "We Need White Women to Call to Their Sisters and Be the Influence They Need," *Harper's Bazaar*, December 2018, 244.

## RECOMMENDED RESOURCES

Banning, Jan and Hilde Janssen. *Comfort Women/Troost Meisjes*. Utrecht: Ipso Facto/Seltmann, 2010.

Chai, Alice Yun. "Asian-Pacific Feminist Coalition Politics; The Chongshindae/Jugunianfu ('Comfort Women') Movement," *Korean Studies* 17 (1993): 67–91.

Choi, Chung-Moo. ed. "Special Issue: The Comfort Women: Colonialism, War, and Sex." *Positions: East Asia Cultures Critique* 5:1 (Spring 1997).

Chung, Chin-sung. "An Overview of the Colonial and Socio-economic Background of Japanese Military Sex Slavery in Korea." *Muae: A Journal of Transcultural Production* 1 (1995): 204–15.

Crawford, Kerry F. *Wartime Sexual Violence: From Silence to Condemnation of a Weapon of War*. Washington, D.C.: Georgetown University Press, 2017.

Enloe, Cynthia. *Maneuvers: The International Politics of Militarizing Women's Lives*. Berkeley and Los Angeles: University of California Press, 2000.

Galang, M. Evelina. *Lolas' House: Filipino Women Living with War*. Evanston. IL: Northwestern University Press, 2017.

Heineman, Elizabeth D. ed. *Sexual Violence in Conflict Zones: From the Ancient World to the Era of Human Rights*. Philadelphia: University of Pennsylvania Press, 2011.

Henson, Maria Rosa. *Comfort Woman: Slave of Destiny*, edited by Sheila S. Coronel. Manila: Philippine Center for Investigative Journalism, 1996.

Howard, Keith. ed. *True Stories of the Korean Comfort Women*, translated by Young Joo Lee. Cassell: New York and London, 1995.

Hwang, Kum-ju. "To Live Without Shame." *Muae: A Journal of Transcultural Production* 1 (1995): 195–203.

Keller, Nora Okja. *Comfort Woman: A Novel*. New York: Viking, 1997.

Kim, Miran. "Paintings." *Muae: A Journal of Transcultural Production* 1 (1995): 216–18.

Kim-Gibson, Dai Sil. *Silence Broken: Korean Comfort Women*. Parkersburg, IA: Mid-Prairie Books, 1999.

Lee, Chang-rae. *A Gesture Life*. New York: Riverhead, 1999.

Park, Therese. *A Gift of the Emperor*. Duluth, MN: Spinsters Ink, 1997.

Qiu, Peipei, Su Zhiliang, and Chen Lifei. *Chinese Comfort Women: Testimonies from Imperial Japan's Sex Slaves*. Oxford: Oxford University Press, 2013.

Reinares, Laura Barberán. *Sex Trafficking in Post-Colonial Literature: Transnational Narratives from Joyce to Bolaño*. New York and London: Routledge, 2015.

Ruff O'Herne, Jan. *Fifty Years of Silence*. Sydney: Editions Tom Thompson/HarperCollins, 1994.

Schellstede, Sangmie Choi. ed. and the Washington Coalition for Comfort Women Issues, Inc. *Comfort Women Speak: Testimony by Sex Slaves of the Japanese Military*. New York: Holmes and Meier, 2000.

Son, Elizabeth W. *Embodied Reckonings: 'Comfort Women,' Performance, and Transpacific Redress*. Ann Arbor: University of Michigan Press, 2018.

Stetz, Margaret D. "Reframing the 'Comfort Women' Issue: New Representations of an Old War Crime." *Genocide and Mass Violence in Asia: An Introductory Reader*, edited by Frank Jacob. Berlin: De Gruyter, 2019. 61-77.

-----."Teaching about the 'Comfort System' of World War II: The Hidden Stories of Girls." In *War and Sexual Violence: New Perspectives in a New Era*, edited by Sarah K. Danielsson. "War (Hi)Stories" series. Leiden, Netherlands and Paderborn, Germany: Brill/ Ferdinand Schöningh, 2019. 35-49.

-----."What the West Failed to Learn about War from the 'Comfort Women.'" In *Gender Violence: Interdisciplinary Perspectives*, 2nd Ed., edited by Laura L. O'Toole, Jessica R. Schiffman, and Margie L. Kiter Edwards. New York and London: New York University Press, 2007. 223–39.

The Commission on Verification and Support for the Victims of Forced Mobilization under Japanese Colonialism in Korea. *Can You Hear Us? The Untold Narratives of Comfort Women*. Seoul: Park In-Hwan (Publisher), 2014.

# 7. CAN THE ARTS HEAL THE WARTIME TRAUMA OF SEX SLAVES? CASE STUDY OF VISUAL ART, FILM, AND PERFORMING ARTS

*Jung-Sil Lee*

**Abstract**: This chapter deals with the artistic representation of "comfort women" history either by the victims or artists. Artists who sympathized with the stories of victims performed interviews, conducted studies, and researched to appropriate archival documents and photos in an effort to recontextualize wartime sex crimes to current broader dialogues about women's rights and sexual violence. These artists sometimes assume various roles in their projects such as reporters, historians, or educators, with each role holding onto the responsibility in adapting factual and truthful information while making them more thriving. As Christian Boltanski succinctly says, "art making is not just telling the truth but making the truth felt." In this chapter, I include part of my presentation on this theme from an art history conference. The main focus of this chapter is to provide an overview of the subject of works and compile the scope of artistic endeavors in the U.S. while revealing the increasing artistic interests in extensive and diverse ways which have produced positive outcomes and impact to the audience. This chapter will focus on visual art: all genres of fine art, film, musical, and opera. The public art form, memorials, will be assessed in chapter 10 while literature and social media representation are left for further examination.

## Introduction

Many artists throughout history have drawn upon human calamity as their theme and subject matter. Specifically, contemporary artists, filmmakers, and memorial designers have turned their attention towards sexual crimes and atrocities against women during wartime. Women, children, elderly, and the infirmed suffered to a greater extent due to their vulnerability. The 2016 exhibition in New York, *Collateral Damage,* that I curated, dealt with how women have been victims of sexual assault and exploitation, some of which included discussions about "comfort women."[1] "Comfort women" is a euphemism branding women and girls who were forced into sexual slavery by the Imperial Japanese Army before and during World War II. Estimates regarding the number of victims vary from as few as 50,000 to as many as 400,000.[2] The women were taken from many occupied countries including Korea, China, Japan, Philippines, Malaysia, Dutch East Indies, Burma, East Timor, and Vietnam. Their bodies were violated as a war tactic and the plight of the suffering of women during times of conflict continues long afterwards, not only because of the lingering psychological and emotional trauma, but also due to the social and cultural stigma attached to their horrendous experience (Fig. 7-1).

This chapter will analyze the ways in which painters, sculptors, film makers, and other visual artists appropriate the history of "comfort women" atrocities and represent them anew in their media with their own interpretation. In accordance with the scope of this book, this study mainly examines the geographical occurrences of this form limited to the U.S. For the last 28 years, a tremendous number of cultural products have been created and this study is not able to cover all of them. Still, this attempt at cataloguing could pave the way to a more thorough examination and understanding of artistic representations of wartime trauma. Among many cultural products for "comfort women," this chapter assesses main art exhibitions and three major art genres that dealt with "comfort women": visual art, film, and performing arts (musical and opera). While putting forth effort to catalogue works by "comfort women" victims and exhibitions in the U.S. (A.7-1 and R.7), this chapter will mainly focus on artists or exhibitions curated by me or sponsored by the Washington Coalition for Comfort Women Issues (WCCW). Before highlighting professional artistic representations of "comfort women" history, I wish to emphasize the importance of the works created by the victims, who inspired and triggered many other art works and functioned as educational tools and historical evidence.

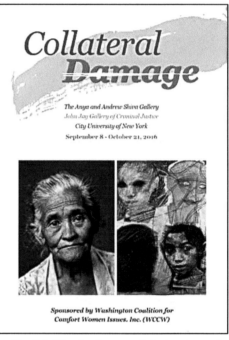

Fig. 7-1. The front cover of the brochure of *Collateral Damage,* The Anya and Andrew Shiva Gallery, John Jay College of Criminal Justice, CUNY: September 8–October 21, 2016.

## The Works of Art by Victims of the "Comfort Women" System

The original purpose of arts creation during the prehistoric era was for ritual use, mainly to wish for something important or to heal a distorted self and to cure physical illness. Today, although there are many other reasons to produce art, 'healing' or 'redress' is still one of the most important objectives of the arts. Although all different types of post-traumatic psychological symptoms, including post-traumatic stress disorder (PTSD), are difficult to approach because individuals must relive painful and traumatic events, the process of healing could remedy their helplessness, fear, and horror caused by flashbacks or nightmares. For South Korean former military sex slaves, called "comfort women," art therapy had been used to help them process their horrific experiences along with other therapies.[3]

Their undesired label as "comfort women" refers to the women and girls who were deceived and forcefully recruited as factory workers or trafficked as prostitutes by the Imperial Japanese Army. The labeling has been denied by those victims residing in the House of Sharing, Korea, criticizing it as a crude objectification forced upon them that focuses on how the women were used as tools more than as a statement of their will as human beings. As former

Secretary of State Hillary Clinton termed, "enforced military sex slaves" would be a more accurate term to describe the victims. The survivors preferred to simply be called "halmoni" which means grandmother in Korean and is simply the name given to all older ladies in Korea. The rejection of the title of "comfort women" and choice of their own label is an important statement because it denotes their positive process of building self-esteem and confidence in sharing their testimony about what happened (Fig. 7-2).

Fig. 7-2. Former "comfort woman" Bae Chun-hee during an art therapy session, House of Sharing, September 22, 2011.

*Halmonies* are normally storytellers who are respected as sources of wisdom and assume a matriarchal role alongside the grandfather in Korean familial structures. Unfortunately, most of these women never wed and thus did not have any children or grandchildren. Their rightful position as *halmoni* was unattainable for them and they had to be silent as their stories were too shameful for them to share in the context of a Confucian Korean society. After former victim Kim Hak-soon bravely stepped forward to testify about her experience to the public, one by one, other *halmonies* started to tell their stories. Based on extensive discussions with survivors, professionals working with post-trauma therapy generally conclude that in order to come to terms with the overwhelming impact of their trauma, it must be "narrativized."

These women's storytelling is the first, but very foundational step in an "imperative need to let people know . . . one's buried truth" so as to move on with their lives.[4] Margo Machida suggested that "merely reclaiming the memory fragments of a damaged life may only provide superficial closure" and "to extricate oneself from being possessed and defined by a trauma . . . with its perpetual state of insecurity, episodes of forgetfulness, and compulsion to endlessly repeat or re-enact a time of vulnerability, a person has to construct a narrative with another."[5] "Constructing narrative with another" is realized thanks to the communal living house, called the House of Sharing. The House of Sharing has enabled the women to have an organizational base where they have given testimonies to many experts in the hope of getting an official apology and reparation from the Japanese government. By providing the individual with the social means to re-externalize their extreme experience, in other words, literally shifting the trauma beyond the confines of the self and then retrieving it, traumatic events can be reintegrated and released.[6]

Telling their testimonies in writing is oftentimes difficult for the victims, not only because many of them are illiterate but also because it is so painful and difficult to do so.[7] In these cases, the medium of visual art serves to provide a forum through which these women can properly express their experiences and emotions. When they came back home after the war was over, these women struggled to cope with disease, debilitating injuries, sterility, and psychological trauma. The physical and mental scars of their trauma continue to persist to this day. Kang Duk-kyung, who was the first resident in the House of Sharing, had endometriosis, a fallopian tube disorder, as well as bladder infections only naming physical pain[8] (Fig. 7-3 – Fig. 7-9).

Before the formal art therapy sessions were held, the first president of the House of Sharing found an art teacher who could teach the halmonies the foundation of art making. Among the first residents of the House of Sharing, Kim Soon-duk, Kang Duk-kyung, Lee Yong-nyeo, and Lee Yong-soo started to take art lessons. Later, Kim Bok-dong and Bae Chun-hee joined the group. From 1993, the art class met for three years. Therapy was directed by artist Lee Kyung-shin and Dr. Kim Sunhyun, professor of Clinical Art Therapy of Cha Hospital, Seoul, Korea.[9] Dr. Kim treated seven victims to help them confront their past and develop their own narrative surrounding this unforgettable pain. When the victims tried to speak about themselves, they confessed it was hard for them to verbalize their pain, but through drawing and painting, they could find an outlet.[10] During a session, they would be asked to draw or paint about such topics as their lives before, during, and after the war, their hopes, and what they would do if they were not trafficked to the "comfort women" station. Many of them were hesitant about doing the art therapy at first, yet, by starting out with peaceful past scenes, they were eventually able to open up to drawing the darkest period of their lives. Kim Soon-duk said, "Once I expressed my past, which I had kept inside for a long time, my wounds seemed to heal. My heart became soothed without any distraction."[11] Art making for her functions as a healing process, another form of testimony, and important historical documentation.[12]

There are two main types of paintings: one showing their peaceful past before trafficking, hometown landscape, portraiture, and genre painting; the other type: fear, anger, sadness, and the aggressiveness experienced by a "comfort woman" in an abstract or figurative way. The latter type, in many cases, is accompanied by iconography of aggressive attributes such as swords, guns, soldiers, and trampled bodies showing the natural process of revisiting and narrating their experience. In the way that these paintings depict historical facts with criticism and intention to expose the hidden stories, they could be categorized as "Minjung art" (meaning "people's art"), a democratic art form that followed an increase in the rights of middle- to lower- class people starting in the 1980s in South Korea.[13]

These women's works also inspired many other artists, writers, and film makers. Cho Jung-rae produced and directed the inspiring film *Spirits' Homecoming* after encountering the work by former "comfort woman" Kang Il-chul. Kang was taken as a sex slave when she was sixteen during the War and later painted what she saw at the "comfort women" station— "burning bodies of girls" (Fig.7-9) after they had been abused, assaulted, and killed for various reasons.[14] Art therapy treatment seems to be an indirect and subtle way to redress their traumas and reconcile the conflict, at the same time, it provided the potential of a 'soft power' as an effective means of persuasion, as suggested by Joseph Nye of Harvard University.[15] Art, like other soft power tools, has an ability to attract and co-opt rather than coerce as a means of communication; proven by the fact that after the tour of art exhibitions of victims' works from 1997 to 1998 in 28 Japanese cities, the artwork inspired significant empathy from the Japanese and appreciation letters from them were compiled and published as *Confessed to Balsam* in which we can see the conscience of the Japanese and their repentance.[16]

In 2000, the U.S. traveling exhibition titled *Quest for Justice: The Story of Korean 'Comfort Women' as Told Through Their Art*, was organized. Among the 32 works on display were Kim Soon-duk's acrylic works such as *Unblossomed Flower, Stolen Away* (Fig. 7-3), and *In That Place, at That Time* (Fig. 7-4), which graphically retold the horrific moments in her life. From October 6 through October 12, 2000, at Barnard College, the exhibition was sponsored by the East Asian Institute, Barnard College, Young Koreans United, and the New York Alliance for Peace and Reunification of Korea. Featured artist Kim Soon-duk, gave a keynote talk at the opening of the exhibit on her experience as a "comfort woman." Rhonda Copelon, professor of law at the City University of New York, and Gabrielle Kirk McDonald, former president of the International War Crimes Tribunal in the former Yugoslavia, also spoke at the opening. A documentary film, *Silence Broken: Korean Comfort Women* directed by Dai-Sil Kim Gibson, was screened continuously during the exhibit. The exhibition continued at the Lotus Art Gallery in Los Angeles from October 19 to 25 before going on to Philadelphia and 28 more cities in the U.S.[17]

Fig. 7-3. Kim Soon-duk, *Stolen Away*, 1995, Acrylic on Canvas, 154 x 114.5 cm © *House of Sharing, Korea.*

Fig. 7-4. Kim Soon-duk, *In that Place, at the Moment 2*, 1995, Acrylic on Paper, 39 x 53 cm © *House of Sharing, Korea.*

Fig. 7-5. Kim Soon-duk, *Colonial Mushroom Taxation*, 1995, Acrylic on Paper, 39 x 53 cm © *House of Sharing, Korea.*

Fig. 7-6. Kang Duk-kyung, *Innocence Stolen*, 1995, Acrylic on Paper, 87 x 130 cm © *House of Sharing, Korea.*

Fig. 7-7. Kang Duk-kyung, *Punish the Guilty! – For the Sake of Peace*, 1995, 87 x 129 cm © *House of Sharing, Korea.*

Fig. 7-8. Kang Duk-kyung, *Apologize Before Us*, 1995, Acrylic on Paper, 48.5 x 37 cm © *House of Sharing, Korea.*

Fig. 7-9. Kang Il-chul, *The Burning of Virgins*, 2004, Acrylic on Paper, 39 x 53 cm © *House of Sharing, Korea*

## Visual Artists and Art Exhibitions

Inspired by the victims' artworks and testimonies, many contemporary artists responded to this horrific history through their own means of expression: painting, printing, sculpture, installation, photography, mixed media, media art, and performance art. This section covers works mostly created by American, Korean American, Japanese, Chinese, Dutch, and a few Korean artists. These are the names of just some of the artists - two dimensional works: Miran Kim, Hung Liu, Steven Cavallo, Tomiyama Taeko, Eileen Halpin, Su Kwak, Jin Powell, Lauren Chai, Christian Poirot, Heejun Song; photographers: Ahn Sehong, Jan Banning, Yunghi Kim, Sasha Yungju Lee, Arin Yoon, Kenji G. Taguma; mixed media artists: Yong Soon Min, Yoshiko Shimada, Rose Camastro Pritchett, Sooyoung Seo; sculptors: Kim Seo-kyung, Kim Un-Sung, Steven Whyte, Junghwa Kim Paik, and Yoosooja Han; installation artists: Christian Boltanski, Chang-Jin Lee, Andrew Ward, Mono Higuchi, Son Jungeun; performance artist: Shine Shin-Kim; media artists: Airan Kang, Jane Jin Kaisen, and Duckyoung Kim.

As a curator of "comfort women" themed art exhibitions in 2012, 2014, 2016, and 2017, I focus this chapter on the artists with whom I have collaborated. The first "art" exhibition of "comfort women" sponsored by WCCW was in December 2012. While WCCW organized and exhibited archival photos and documents for Congress and other public places as described in chapter one, as a curator, I wanted to search its artistic representation and organized the first visual artist participating exhibition. In 2012, in commemoration of the 20th anniversary of WCCW's foundation, as a vice president, I chaired and organized a conference and art exhibition. Christine Choi, WCCW president, Young Chan Ro, George Mason University professor and director of Korean Studies Center, and Walter Kravitz, director of the GMU Gallery, sponsored this project and made possible the venue for both projects.[18]

For the exhibition "Unveiling the Truth: The Sorrow and Hope of 'Comfort Women,'" I invited Korean American, Japanese, and American artists as well as filmmaker Dai Sil Kim-Gibson. The participating artists were Dai Sil Kim-Gibson, Steven Cavallo, Chang-Jin Lee, Sasha Yungju Lee, Yong Soon Min, Youngmi Song Organ, Yoshiko Shimada, In-Soon Shin, and Arin Yoon. Most of the artists learned these stories directly from the survivors, while some of them became activists and educators to raise public awareness on the issue. Each artistic translation is both a remembrance of the scars of war and a therapeutic outlet through which the audience can connect to the experiences of the women or identify their own sexual traumas. In the exhibition catalogue, I mentioned the direction and nature of the "comfort women" movement and artists' involvement beyond art making (A.7-2).

The issues surrounding former "comfort women" should not be politicized. They involve human rights, women's rights, universal justice, and the acknowledgment of human suffering and past wrongdoings. As the exhibition sub-title proposes, today's handful of survivors dwell in unsettled sorrow yet cultivate hopes that reach out to other victims of war, particularly of sexual violence. Sasha Lee, Youngmi Organ, Yoshiko Shimada, and In-Soon Shin, visualize the vulnerable female body and dream in a literal or symbolic way. Arin Yoon shows how these women live today, in a documentary style, which encourages the viewer to look deeper and engage in stories within the portraits. Steve Cavallo and Yong Soon Min are actively engaged in the "comfort women" movement through their artistic projects and activism, which recently resulted in a memorial dedicated to the former "comfort women." Dai Sil Kim-Gibson and Chang-Jin Lee produced a documentary film and videos on "comfort women" with minimal interference, providing a media outlet to unveil hidden stories that need to be shared with the world.

Before and during the exhibition, Yong Soon Min distributed T-shirts for us to wear as part of her performance and activism. By inscribing every year since the Japanese authorities established the first comfort station in 1931 on black T-shirts and wearing them, Min intensely commemorates the history of "comfort women." *When* urges other people to wear black T-shirts with a year of their birth on the front and the explanation on the back. That action of wearing the year and explanation on their own bodies encouraged them to deeply reflect upon and feel the painful history of "comfort women" and their long struggles to gain justice. Min has worked on histories of Korea using her body as a metaphor of colonized land (Fig. 7-10).[19]

When counts every year since Japan established the first comfort station in 1931. It is hoped that the Japanese government will accept unequivocal and official responsibility for the comfort women war crime. I wear a year of support for the Korean Council for the Women Drafted for Military Sex Slavery by Japan.

When은 일본이 1931년 처음 위안소를 설치한 이후의 한 해 한 해를 세어봅니다. 일본 정부가 위안부 여성에게 저지른 범죄에 대한 명백하고 공식적인 책임을 받아들이기를 기원합니다. 저는 한국정신대문제대책협의회의 활동을 위해 그 중 한 해의 의미를 담은 티셔츠를 입습니다.

© Yong Soon Min

Fig. 7-10. Yong Soon Min, *When*, 2012, Installation (T-shirt), 24 x 32 in. © *Yong Soon Min*

Japanese American artist Yoshiko Shimada was born in Tokyo in 1959 but worked in many places around the world including Germany. Shimada was deeply influenced by a group of German artists who were actively engaging issues of Germany's post-war responsibility.

Realizing that the mainstream accounts of Japan's wartime past have been marked by dishonest and nostalgic views, she began to explore the subject of her own country's war responsibility and the roles of Japanese women. Shimada's etching *Shooting Lesson* from the "Past Imperfect" series exemplifies her deep engagement in the issues of war and women. The work features images of Japanese housewives learning to shoot along with images of Korean "comfort women" at four corners. *Shooting Lesson* reveals a contradiction in the masculinist Japanese nationalism that espouses patriotic women while actively participating in the violation and abuse of women's bodies (Fig. 7-11).

Fig. 7-11. Yoshiko Shimada, *A House of Comfort Women*, 1992. Etching, 18 x 24 in. © *Yoshiko Shimada*

The exhibition was a very meaningful and valuable opportunity for the audience to get to know Steve Cavallo, Chang-Jin Lee, and Arin Yoon with whom I've worked on other occasions. In 2014, I had another opportunity to curate the exhibition *The Sorrow and Hope of Comfort Women*, a seminar and exhibition at Catholic University.[20] For this occasion, the House of Sharing generously allowed me to reprint the works of "comfort women" victims to exhibit, including the works by Kang Duk-kyung and Kim Soon-duk. Sunsook Shin (painting), Chang-Jin Lee (mixed media), Yoosooja Han (painting and sculpture), Junghwa Kim Paik (metal art), Eileen Halpin (digital painting), and Steve Cavallo (painting) were invited and some archival material and documentary photos taken by Han Won Sang, a YTN (Yonhap Television News) reporter, were included. Given that it was on the campus of a Catholic institution, I intentionally assimilated the pain and sacrifice of "comfort women" with that of Christian martyrs or even Jesus. This case was shown in the work of Junghwa Kim Paik's *Thorn I* which is reminiscent of the crown of thorns Jesus wore during his crucifixion. In his works *Hope and*

*Memory, In My Past,* and *Lamentation,* Steven Cavallo (Fig. 7-12) also incorporated his images of "comfort women" victims with themes surrounding the crucifixion and the crown of thorns of Jesus because both of them were sacrificed as innocents.

Fig. 7-12. Steve Cavallo, *Lamentation,* 2012, watercolor, 22 x 26 in. © *Steve Cavallo*

In 2015, I submitted the proposal of another "comfort women" exhibition to John Jay College of Criminal Justice, City University of New York. Although the initial proposal was not accepted due to its potential political undertones, the revised proposal was accepted with the re-title *Collateral Damage* that was co-curated with Thalia Vrachopoulos, an art history professor of the institution. The exhibition opened in the Anya and Andrew Shiva Gallery from September 8 to October 21, 2016 sponsored by WCCW. The invited artists were Jan Banning, Steve Cavallo, Mona Higuchi, Su Kwak, Chang-Jin Lee, Despo Magoni, Despina Meimaroglou, Yong Soon Min, Min Sun Oh, Frank van Osch, Junghwa Kim Paik, Jin Powell, and Lydia Venieri. Among the artists, Jin Powell, Junghwa Kim Paik, and Min Sun Oh were artist award recipients from the 2015 Art Competition on the theme of "comfort women" organized by WCCW. John Jay College of Criminal Justice strongly advocates human rights and is one of few locations with a center for international human rights. Along with the exhibit, the symposium *Collateral Damage: Wartime Atrocity and Trauma* was organized in the exhibit hall with sponsorship by the Northeast Asian History Foundation. I invited George Andreopoulos, professor of political science and the founding director of the Center for International Human Rights at John Jay College of Criminal Justice, Professor Bonnie Oh, Professor Laura Barberán Reinares, and Professor Tomomi Emoto[21] (A.7-3).

This exhibition and the symposium offered a discussion on how and why women and children, the more vulnerable, were sexually assaulted and violated in the course of war. The plight of women who suffered during times of conflict continued in the aftermath of war, not only due to enormous psychological and emotional trauma, but also as a result of the social and cultural stigma attached to their horrendous experiences. The "comfort women" case led to expanded discussion of rampant violence during WWII, the Vietnam War, the rise of the Khmer Rouge, and other conflicts where innocent non-combatants were afflicted. During the opening reception, artist Shine Shin-Kim led an interactive group performance *One Heart Project* consisting of a ritual dance, music, and audience participation with a colorful quilt fabric under the direction of the artist Kim (Fig. 7-13). The whole process was meaningful and touching as well as educational. Many students stayed late to pose serious questions that I later discovered were because of class assignments related to this exhibition. It was a huge advantage to have an exhibition on a college campus that could fulfill the curatorial intention to educate the next generation and a large audience.

Fig. 7-13. Shine Shin-Kim, *One Heart,* performance scene during the opening ceremony of the exhibition *Collateral Damage,* at John Jay College of Criminal Justice. New York. 2016. Duration 10 min. © *WCCWVRC*

In 2017, I was invited as a chief curator for the exhibition "Truth: Promise for Peace," co-organized by the Ministry of Gender Equality and Family, Korean Institute for Gender Equality Promotion and Education, and the National Women's History Exhibition Hall. This exhibition was significant as it was the first government funded "comfort women" exhibition in South Korea and travelled to four different cities.[22] The exhibition was designed to showcase the history of "comfort women" and promote a peaceful and better future without war or violence against women. It consisted of two dimensions: one was historical and the other was artistic, while the entire exhibition described the journey of "comfort women" victims; the historical background during the Japanese colonial period, lives in the comfort stations, their homecoming after the war ended, "comfort women" activism up to the present date, and their application as a global women's rights issue and current activism. Each phase was accessed by historical artifacts and resources as well as artistic interpretations of it.

Fig. 7-14. Junghwa Kim Paik, *In Memory of Her*, 2017, mixed media, 23 x 40 x 7 in. © *Junghwa Kim Paik*

The goal of this exhibition was to make the audience understand, remember, and sympathize with "comfort women" history and create a consensus of hope for peace and redress. For this reason, Paik's *In Memory of Her* was selected for the poster, invitation card, banner, and as the work of prologue of the story telling (Fig. 7-14). It is metal art with lots of butterflies and the empty chair reminiscent of the Statue of Peace, now the most striking metaphor of former "comfort women." For the historical document to prove its veracity, Kang Jeong-sook took charge of collecting historical sources, and I curated the artistic works; Hung Liu, Airan Kang, Tomiyama Taeko, Junghwa Kim Paik, Heejun Song, Jan Banning, Arin Yoon, Changjin Lee, Frank van Osch, and Siha Kim were invited, and their paintings, drawings, photography, print, media art, metal art, film, and installation art were exhibited. At the exit of the exhibition, visitors were invited to sit in the empty chair of Siha Kim's installation work and write a postcard to the survivors, closing the journey of the "comfort women" exhibition. In 2018, I further explored the meaning of three female artists' works from this exhibition in the academic conference CAA (College Art Association). I introduce here the excerpt from the paper that dealt with the artist's position as a reporter or historian (Fig. 7-15).[23]

Fig. 7-15. *Truth: Promise for Peace.* Exhibition organized by The Ministry of Gender Equality and Family, Jung-Sil Lee, chief curator explains the concept of the exhibition to grandma Lee Yong-soo and the audience. In front of the installation work, Seoul, July 3, 2017 - September 2, 2017.

**Case Study of Three Female Artists**

I examined the styles and significance of the works of three female artists: Hung Liu, Tomiyama Taeko, and Chang-Jin Lee, who have all appropriated archival photos or established documents to create their own artistic works. The art produced by these three women highlight the ways in which one can re-contextualize traumatic history. And, by doing so, they assume an approach akin to wartime journalism exposing the crimes and travesties resulting from warfare. Although these three artists avoid overshadowing these horrendous events through their own subjectivity, they nonetheless infuse their work with their own interpretations, thereby appropriating historical events for their narratives. Each artist brings a new perspective to the issues of "comfort women" history by layering content and symbol with formal arrangements. This allows them to balance objectivity with subjectivity to provide valid and impactful commentary on wartime atrocities. This dark period of Asian history is still hotly debated and contested between the Japanese right-wing government and sympathetic groups of activists and feminists.

The Chinese American painter Hung Liu was born in China in 1948. She grew up during the war, suffered from famine and the continual unrest during the Maoist era, before immigrating to America in 1984. Known primarily as a painter, she challenges the documentary authority and perceived infallible historicity of historical photographs by appropriating these through the more personal process of painting. Initially, Liu's freedom to paint was repressed by Chinese authorities, and she was able to only draw from live models rather than resort to historical photographs. But despite the risks, Liu covertly found ways to use such photos while in China and continued when she moved to the U.S.[24] Liu's obsession with history and photographs stems from the hardships of her youth. The Communist Party, after the Cultural Revolution (1966–1969), destroyed or confiscated her family photos when her father was imprisoned. Since that time, historic photographs have been the primary and most meaningful sources of inspiration throughout her career. Over time, her adaption of these images to her purposes have become more layered and complex.

Curator Heather Lineberry noted, "The history layering of content and formal approaches found in her paintings was what Liu has called 'pastiches of style and clashes of cultures. . . .' The paintings hover between realistic and abstract, narrative and symbolic, allowing for multiple interpretations by the viewer."[25] Liu's sources have been the archival photos from the National Archives and Records Administration (NARA) (Fig. 7-16) to which she has added her own responses and commentaries far beyond simple chronicling. Among many of her historical references, she created numerous "comfort women" series. The women of *Strange Fruit: Comfort Women,* painted in 2001, are based on photographs of Korean "comfort women" from NARA. To develop the imagery for her paintings, Liu manipulates each photograph, changes the scale, or edits the compositional arrangement. The vertical streaks throughout Liu's works invoke a somber quality and she notes that "these marks are a metaphor for an implied unconsciousness of girls."[26] With a painting style infused with this fluidity, Liu expresses her own sadness as well as theirs.

Fig. 7-16. Archival photograph of "comfort women," at a comfort station in Tengchong, China while being taken to a POW camp in September, 1944. Hung Liu (cover artist) saw this photo in a Chinese magazine (老照片) that inspired her work. *NARA.* (*See* book cover art *Comfort Women* by Hung Liu).

Liu painted the eight individual portraits and the women as a group based on archival photographs. Just as the water streaks across her paintings draw the viewers' eyes down to the plain garments of each woman—highlighting their uniformity symbolic of their loss of identity—lines also draw viewers' eyes upwards. Upon following this path, Liu departs from her source material as the background fades away into a deep red hue, taking the images of the women's captors with them. Now, those same garments that serve to strip away the women's identities also serve to put them in stark contrast to the background. In this, she departs from the source photograph and therefore, commemorates these anonymous "comfort women" as recognizable individuals, the crimson background referencing the Chinese understanding of red with celebration, revolution, and blood. The red releases energy and life into the painting like a ray of hope and dignity, a sharp contrast to the gray-tone of history encoded in the black and white photograph. Indeed, this sentiment is represented a final time as our eyes, having moved through a rollercoaster of despair and hope, fall on the image of the Japanese swords, now faded into the background and covered with the brilliant images of butterflies, symbols of the dignity of Chinese empresses. Adorned with these butterflies, their beauty and perseverance defy the deplorable system that promoted this abuse.[27] In the later version of *Comfort Women* (2006), a "cynical" fish in the background, taken from the 17th century Chinese painter Bada Shanren, as explained by Liu, rolls its critical eyes as a witness to the time of despair and hope.[28] Likewise, Liu might convey a similar complexity in her works with a critical commentary on this unresolved history as she pays a celebratory homage to the survivors (Fig. 7-16-1 cover image).

Tomiyama Taeko is a rare Japanese artist who has treated the theme of "comfort women" in her art in conjunction with consistent criticism of war and injustice at large. Few artists have dealt with that subject directly in Japan, not only because this history is uncomfortable to the Japanese people, but also because it is considered taboo.[29] Her outspoken rendering of Japanese guilt and Japan's colonial history made her unique, but also an outcast in the Japanese art world. Taeko was born in Kobe, Japan in 1921. At age twelve, she moved with her family to Dalien and Harbin in what was then Manchuria where she witnessed the beginning of the Sino-Japanese War. After being exposed to global political injustice including the Kwangju Uprising in the 1980s in Korea,[30] she produced work depicting coal and ore mines in Kyushu. Through the exploration of the hidden history of conscripted Korean mine workers in Kyushu, she produced the film, *Hajike Hosenka* (*Pop Out, Balsam Seed!* 1986). At showings of the film, she began to hear stories about Korean "comfort women." With sympathetic intent, Taeko produced a series of large oil paintings and prints of the subject, such as *Memories of the Sea* (1986) and *At the Bottom of the Pacific* (1985).[31] In the latter work, she portrays the symbol of colonial Japan as a metaphor for the death of the victims while including the *miko (mudang-shaman)* as a witness who is depicted as a crying eye in the center. The silhouette of the Japanese warship Yamato on the coast of Java is blurred; remains of those who died during WWII are scattered in the sea; symbols of Japanese imperialism, such as the standard and banner, envelop the victims of war. She spotlights the women who never returned to their homes and were left to drown in the Pacific Ocean[32] (Fig. 7-17).

A decade later, with more knowledge as a witness, reporter, and historian, Taeko combined printed text, fragments of journals, characters, religious symbols, and photos regarding the tragedy of "comfort women." The method she used was a collage of mixed media to invoke multiple layers of meaning and to criticize the cruelty of imperialism and its war crimes by superimposing diverse archival media sources. Her *Comfort Women* is part of a series of fifteen works titled, *The Sorrows of War and the Post-war Era: What a Woman Artist Saw*

(2015) in which a witness' gaze reflects a camera aperture or a reporter's eye. She emphasized the role of feminist artists in reporting and archiving these events during Imperial Japan's reign while not forgoing their equally important role in consoling the souls of the living and dead victims, like traditional Korean shamans. She frequently includes the shaman's altar, instrument, mask, or thread as a symbol of being a medium between the living and the dead; a bridge between the present and the past.

In the series of collages, the artist frequently quotes elements from her earlier works, employing collage techniques as an objective and non-authoritarian method that allows her to literally "place the present alongside the past" and create new meanings. As she "translates" or "transfers" images from her earlier works across time and space, the collage comes to not only speak of past sorrows that this female artist visualizes, but of experiences and memories that continue to be lived and contested in the present time.[33] She reports the past beyond temporal and physical barriers.

Tomiyama then took the subject of Asian women who were being trafficked to Japan, a staggeringly profitable business at the time, and still huge today. *Sold Off to the Continent* focused on the ongoing plight of Asian women in Japan who are forced into prostitution through imprisonment and debt peonage. In 1994, Tomiyama created a series of serigraphs modeled on traditional woodblock prints that depict young Japanese women sent to the continent in the late nineteenth century to earn foreign exchange for the nation in the brothels of Southeast Asia. Visually, the serigraphs refer to the long tradition of depicting women of the Japanese

Fig. 7-17. Tomiyama Taeko, *At the Bottom of the Pacific*, 1985, digital print from oil painting, 70 x 50 cm. © *Tomiyama Taeko*

demi-monde in Ukiyo-e prints as well as to the even longer tradition of selling daughters into prostitution.[34]

New York-based Korean American artist Chang-Jin Lee recreated a military comfort station as an example of installation art. For the multimedia installation, she used historical references in conjunction with video recordings of "comfort women" survivors and Japanese soldiers in seven different countries in Asia. Outside of the installation, banners with welcoming greetings and regulations hung from ceiling to floor, creating fabric walls. During the war, banners at the entrances of military "comfort stations" welcomed and attracted soldiers. The realistic banners, in multiple languages, display historical written texts such as "Official Military Hometown Comfort Station," "Japanese Girls Dedicating Their Hearts and Bodies in Service," and "Grand Welcome to Victorious, Courageous Soldiers." In one corner sits an empty washing bowl, evoking a sense of loss. On the walls, fake Japanese name plaques are hung, just as they were in the original "comfort stations." Girls were forced to wear kimonos and use Japanese names to obscure and erase their national identity. Lee turns her work into a blunt, vacuumed space filled with objects based on her careful research and field trips, perfectly preserving this painful past (Fig. 7-18).

Fig. 7-18. Chang-Jin Lee, *Re-creation of a Military Comfort Station*, 2017 Seoul, Korea, multimedia installation © *Chang-Jin Lee*

Inside, a black and white video of women survivors and a Japanese soldier is projected on a window. The video is based on the artist's interviews across Asia, with Korean, Chinese, Taiwanese, Indonesian, Filipino, and Dutch survivors, and a former Japanese soldier Yasuji Kaneko. Also, color video of the artist's recordings of former "comfort station" buildings are projected on a kimono belt upon a tatami bed. One video is of "Dai Salon" in Shanghai, China, established in 1932, as the first ever "comfort station." Another video is of two former Indonesian "comfort stations"—including one with Emah Kastima, an Indonesian woman survivor, who was held for 2 years during the war. In Chang-Jin Lee's duty as a journalistic artist, she presents the events while dispassionately restraining her own commentary. Still, this installation allows the viewer to get into the space of the "comfort station" filled with many references to the experiences of the women. With her versions of "comfort women" photography outlined with gold backgrounds, Lee pays homage to the women by balancing aesthetics with the horror through which they lived and equalizing the artistic supremacy and their existence.

Each of these artists have taken a different aspect of history, whether that be a physical object or firsthand account, and made that the basis of their art. By recapturing past events and objects, each artist aligns herself with the spirit of the "comfort women" of the past in order to convey a timeless message. By compiling and editing their art in unique ways, these artists capture and present historic events whose importance might have been lost or distorted by time founded only upon the photographs documenting their lives. In this regard, the three women artists have fulfilled their role not just as reporters of the past but also as narrators and editors by adding their own interpretations to these images of war found in archived materials. While neutral archival images wouldn't convey such empathy, the truth behind these stories, or the gratification of symbolism, these artists made the images meaningful, powerful, and truthful; paying their respects to the survivors and allowing the souls of those who have passed to find peace.

## Films and Performing Arts

"Seeing is believing." Indeed, sight is perhaps the most important sensory input that defines the human experience. One of the great mediums of sight-based experience, film, is well known for its extensive influence and popularity on popular culture since its inception. It is with this medium of cinematography that the public was introduced to the "comfort women" issue, sparking a movement. In July 2017, the Seoul National University Research Team came upon the first video footage of the "comfort women" in the National Archives II based in Maryland. The 18 second clip filmed by U.S. troops in the Chinese Yunnan province previously occupied by Japan depicts the only known visual footage of girls and women in "comfort stations." The footage shows a man who appears to be a Chinese officer along with other members of the U.S.-China combined forces speaking to seven Korean women. These seven, who would later become known as part of a group called "comfort women" appear lined up by a wall with demeanors of depression, hesitation, and guilt. They were freed in 1944[35] (A.7-4).

WCCW produced the very first documentary film ('video') "Comfort Women" with founding President Dongwoo Lee Hahm (director), her husband, Doochan Hahm (camera man), Simon Lee (editor), and vice president at the time Sangmie Choi Schellstede (narrator) in 1995.[36] It was screened at the United Methodist Building located near the U.S. Capitol Hill and the Supreme Court. The films on "comfort women" have increased tremendously throughout the world, a fact which WCCW and other activists have recognized (R.10).

For the last 28 years, WCCW has been dedicated to promoting public awareness and educating the next generation about the ordeal of "comfort women" through film screenings. Starting in 2012, I organized film screenings about "comfort women" and invited film directors; "Silence Broken" screened with Director Dai Sil Kim-Gibson at George Mason University in conjunction with an exhibition and conference. Director Kim-Gibson produced "Silence Broken" after her interactions with the "comfort women" as a translator for their testimonies since 1992. She produced the film in 2000 which screened in many venues and universities[37] (Fig. 7-19).

Fig. 7-19. Dai Sil Kim-Gibson, *Silence Broken*, film screening poster, designed by Tori Hinn, April 24, 2013, Chase Center Auditorium, Rhode Island School of Design.

Afterwards, numerous film screenings on "comfort women" were held: "Spirits' Homecoming" at Messiah Presbyterian Church with Director Cho Jung-rae (2016), "Apology" with Director Tiffany Hsiung (2017), and "Spirits' Homecoming II" with Director Cho Jung-rae at both the George Washington University and the University of Maryland Global Campus (2017). In 2018, WCCW organized an International Comfort Women film festival at American University. "Silence" with Director Park Maeui (2019) and "My Name is Kim Bok-dong" were screened at George Mason University (2019).

The 2018 film festival, "Sexual Violence in Warfare: The Films of Unhealed Wounds" was held October 11th to the 13th. WCCW and the American University School of Communication (SOC) co-hosted the film festival at the Malsi Doyle and Michael Forman Theater, SOC at American University in Washington, D.C. Myungho (Lucy) Nam chaired the film festival committee consisting of Jung-Sil Lee, Christopher Simpson, Jongsuk Thomas Nam (program director), Helen Won, Jackie Kim, Edward Jang, Aileen Chung, and JeeEun Chung. Nine international films highlighted the history and trauma of the "comfort women." Four of the films are from Korea, two from Australia, and one each from China, Canada, and the Netherlands. The lives of Dutch, Chinese, Korean, Filipino, and Indonesian former "comfort women" are portrayed either in fictional works or as documentaries (A.7-5) (Fig. 7-20).

Along with the film screening, either the film director or experts are invited to discuss the film shown; former Congressman Mike Honda, Ok Cha Soh, Myungho (Lucy), Christopher Simpson, Sami Lauri, Wing Chi Chan, Jung-Sil Lee, Chung Moo-sung, Yi Seung-hyeon,

Tiffany Hsiung, Professor Greg Metcalf (UMCP), and Mindy Kotler. Mindy Kotler organized a roundtable discussion on the last day of the film festival about *The Art of the Witness: Film in Persevering the History of the Comfort Women* where several of the directors discussed their work with scholars of the arts and gender. The film festival helped to expand awareness of the ways in which sexual violence has been weaponized throughout history during times of war and armed conflicts. By using the medium of the visual arts—film—the directors preserve and honor the voice of the "witness" in telling the "comfort women" history and suffering.

Fig. 7-20. International Film Festival "Sexual Violence in Warfare: The Films of Unhealed Wounds" poster, Malsi Doyle & Michael Forman Theater, American University, November 9-11, 2018. © *WCCWVRC*

WCCW will continue to organize and support the upcoming film screening events as well as produce a documentary film about the 28 years of the "comfort women movement" in the U.S. [38] Although "comfort women" film production began as a way to document the existing material and testimony of survivors, it has since diversified into fictional film or eclectic film dualities of fiction and documentary as seen in *A Long Way Around* (2017). Films like *For Her* (2017) with its effective animation and use of the victim's voices in their testimony makes these films and their telling of the "comfort women" history all the more powerful. *I Can Speak* (2017) by Kim Hyun-Suk, likewise, saw commercial success and provided a bright light with humor on an otherwise grim topic.

In 2019, two important films, *My Name is Kim Bok-dong* and *Shusenjo-The Main Battleground of the Comfort Women Issue* were released and screened. *My Name is Kim Bok-dong* is dedicated to the late Kim Bok-dong, champion of human rights and initiator of the Nabi Foundation. [39] The other documentary film, *Shusenjo*, directed by Japanese American Miki Dezaki,[40] traveled to several US universities in the fall of 2019 and posed fundamental questions about the current controversy as well as the Japanese government's denial of wartime responsibility to the "comfort women."

Artists express their sympathy towards the "comfort women" history not only in films but also in the form of musicals and operas. The play *Comfort Women* (1999, 2004)[41] by Chungmi Kim was first put on in Little Tokyo in Los Angeles (1999), then off Broadway, New York (2004), becoming popular in South Korea. The *Comfort Women: A New Musical* first premiered at the Theatre at St. Clement's on off-Broadway New York in 2015 and WCCW invited main figures of the musical, Meagan Lee Hodson and Garett T.K. Taketa along with Director Dimo Hyunjun Kim to the first anniversary of the Comfort Women Memorial Peace

Garden in 2015. As the first ever all-Asian off-Broadway cast led by an Asian director, the show sold out in 2015 and was nominated for Best Off-Broadway Musical by Broadway World. The 2018 revival ran at the Peter Jay Sharp Theater from July 20th (first preview) to September 2nd and continued in Los Angeles in 2019 (Fig. 7-21).[42]

In commemoration of the second anniversary of the Young Girl's Statue for Peace in Atlanta, Georgia, the Atlanta Comfort Women Memorial Task Force organized the ceremony, exhibition of artworks painted by former "comfort women," and an opera performance in the Korean Cultural Center of Greater Atlanta on June 28, 2019 (Fig. 7-22). The opera titled *A Stolen Girl's Story* was shown in collaboration with the Korean American Association of Greater Atlanta. In line with their pledge, the team prepared this event with the resolution that "We will never forget. We will teach the truth."[43] This opera is a collaborative work with composer Jaesin Lee, conductor Hyungrok Kim, stage director Sam Yoon, and singers Jee Yeun Kim, Hyunjee Yoon, and Un-Chong Christopher. The opera and art exhibition were supported by the dedicated efforts of the Atlanta Task Force under the leadership of Baik Kyu Kim and Kelly Ahn. The performance paved the way for diverse artistic expression of "comfort women" history for American advocates and I expect more works like this performance in the near future.

Fig. 7-21. *Comfort Women: A New Musical* poster, Dimo Kim (director), New York, July 31, 2015.

All artists appropriated and expressed the history of "comfort women" in their own interpretation through their artistic media. Although this chapter chronicles only a few of them in terms of scope and genre, diverse artistic responses should be produced more as one of the most persuasive and powerful tools to educate and to garner support regarding the issue. More "comfort women" museum building and curation of exhibitions are recommended. One such new presentation is the "Eternal Testimony Project" launched by the research team of Professor Kim Ju-Sub of Sogang University's School of Media, Arts and Science on October 26, 2019. Professor Kim was inspired and received advice from the New Dimensions in Testimony (NDT) of the University of Southern California Shoah Foundation, where the science team created an interactive software to memorialize the testimonies of Holocaust survivors ad infinitum online. USC Prof. Sin-Hwa Kang served as mediator to the science team, but the initial idead was sparked and suggested by Dr. Suejung Huh, founder of the venture Ohhh Inc.[44] Through interactive artificial intelligence (A.I.) technology, "comfort women" victims can share their stories and answer questions posed by the audience through holograms which appear like a real presence.

Fig. 7-22. Opera *A Stolen Girl's Story*, in the 2nd anniversary celebration of Atlanta Young Girl's Statue for Peace, Korean American Association of Greater Atlanta, Jee yeun Kim and Hyunjee Yoon on stage, June 28, 2019. © *Atlanta Comfort Women Memorial Task Force*

Fig. 7-23. Grandmother Lee Yong-soo watches her recorded testimony in the "Eternal Testimony Project." October 2019, Technical Director, Prof. Kim Ju-sub of Sogang University's School of Media, Arts and Science and CARE. © *Sogang University and CARE*

This project would be an ideal alternative at a time when no survivors are left (Fig. 7-23). The most important element was the testimony of the victims on over a thousand questions submitted by expert institutions. It was physically strenuous, but the elderly victim, Lee Yong-soo volunteered, making this project possible. When someone asks a question, A.I. will seek an appropriate answer making it possible for the person and the hologram to engage in a natural conversation. To make this process more vivid, Professor Kim's team made Chroma key videos of the elderly woman, a method used to synthesize the image with a separate background. They used holograms to allow people the experience of actually facing the elderly woman.[45]

The team still needs more funds and further collaboration from scholars and activists to completely anticipate potential questions currently devised by CARE. Such an effort will be exemplary in its convergence of artistic, scientific, and archival values for the future "comfort women" art production field.

# Bibliography

Banning, Jan and Hilde Janssen (text). *Comfort Women/Troost Meisjes*. Utrecht: Ipso Facto/Seltmann, 2015.

"Comfort Women: Researchers claim first Known Film." *BBC News*, July 10, 2017, https://www.bbc.com/news/world-asia-40552812.

Danto, Arthur C. "Beauty for Ashes." In *Regarding Beauty*, Neal Benezra and Ola M. Viso, editors and curators, Washington, D.C.: Hirshhorn Museum and Sculpture Garden, 1999-2000.

Ha, Yae-Jin. "Comfort Women Wanted: Uncovering Violent Past and Entering New Age of Activism through Visual Language." *Penn Humanities Forum* 2013-2014: *Violence, University of Pennsylvania* (May 2014).

Hein, Laura and Nobuko Tanaka. "Brushing with Authority: The Life and Art of Tomiyama Taeko." *The Asia Pacific Journal; Japan Focus* 8: 13 (March 29, 2010).

Horlyck, Charlotte. *Korean Art from the 19ᵗʰ Century to the Present*. London: Reaktion Books Ltd, 2017.

Jang, Yang-hee. "Comfort Women Exhibition in US University." *VOA*, Dec. 2, 2014, https://www.voakorea.com/korea/korea-social-issues/2542237.

Kim-Gibson, Dai Sil. *Silence Broken: Korean Comfort Women*. Iowa: Mid-Prairie Books Parkersburg, 1999.

Kim, Chan-ho. "Hologram Enables the 'Eternal Testimony' on the Tragedy of the Comfort Women in the Japanese Military." *Kyunghang Sinmun*, October 29, 2019. Accessed November 12, 2019, http://english.khan.co.kr/khan_art_view.html?artid=201910291815447&code=710100

Kim, Elaine H., Margo Machida, and Sharon Mizota. *Fresh Talk/ Daring Gazes: Conversations on Asian American Art*. Berkeley: University of California Press, 2003.

Kim, Sun-Hyun. *Art Therapy for Comfort Women: Art that Became History*. Paju, Korea: *Korean Studies Information* (2012); Seoul: Idam Books, 2012.

*Last Tear: A Photo Essay of our Discoveries and Experiences*. US-Korea Institute at SAIS, Fading Away. 2015.

150

Laub, Dori, "Truth and Testimony." In *Testimony: Crises of Witnessing in Literature, Psychoanalysis, and History*. Edited by Dori Laub and Soshana Felman, New York: Routledge, 1992.

Lee, Jeewon, Young-Sook Kwak, Yoon-Jung Kim, Eun-Ji Kim, E. Jin Park, Yunmi Shin, Bun-Hee Lee, So Hee Lee, Hee Yeon Jung, Inseon Lee, Jung Im Hwang, Dongsik Kim, and Soyoung Irene Lee. "Psychiatric Sequelae of Former 'Comfort Women,' Survivors of the Japanese Military Sexual Slavery during World War II." *Psychiatry Investigation*, vol. 15, no. 4 (April, 2018): 336-343.

Lee, Jung-Sil. "Artists Meet the Trauma and Hope of the 'Comfort Women.'" In *Truth: Promise for Peace*, exhibition catalog, 114-117, Seoul: The Ministry of Gender Equlity and Family, 2017.

Machida, Margo. "Trauma, Social Memory, and Art." In *Unsettled Visions*. Durham and London: Duke University Press, 2008.

Magee, Seana. "Former Sex Slaves Use Art to Tell Story: Paintings to be shown in the U.S. after successful run in Japan." *The Japan Times*, October 18, 2000, Accessed August 1, 2018, https://www.japantimes.co.jp/news/2000/10/18/national/former-sex-slaves-use-art-to-tell-story/#.XeRApuhKiUk

Nye, Joseph. *Soft Power: The Means to Success in World Politics*. New York: Public Affairs, 2004.

Qui, Peipei, Su Zhiliang, and Chen Lifei. *Chinese Comfort Women*. New York: Oxford University Press, 2013.

Stetz, Margaret and Bonnie Oh. "Tomiyama Taeko's a Memory of the Sea." In *Legacies of the Comfort Women of World War II*, 201 – 208, Armonk, New York and London: M. E. Sharpe, 2001.

*Unblossomed Flower: A Collection of Paintings by Former Military Comfort Women*. Kwangju: The Historical Museum of Sexual Slavery by the Japanese Military, 2000.

Yoon, Jungmo. *Touch-Me-Nots*. Kwangju: House of Sharing, 2015.

[1] *Collateral Damage*, The Anya and Andrew Shiva Gallery, John Jay College of Criminal Justice, City University of New York, September 8 – October 21, 2016, chief curator Jung-Sil Lee and sponsored by Washington Coalition for Comfort Women Issues, Inc.

[2] Peipei Qui, Su Zhiliang, and Chen Lifei, *Chinese Comfort Women* (New York: Oxford University Press, 2013), 37-42.

[3] Diverse types of therapy sessions are held such as art and music therapy, planting therapy, dance therapy. Ahn Shin-kwon, director of House of Sharing, interview by Jung-Sil Lee. Nov. 9, 2018.

[4] Dori Laub, "Truth and Testimony," in *Testimony: Crises of Witnessing in Literature, Psychoanalysis, and History*, ed. Dori Laub and Soshana Felman (New York: Routledge, 1992), 63.

[5] Margo Machida, "Trauma, Social Memory, and Art," in *Unsettled Visions* (Durham and London: Duke University Press, 2008), 128.

[6] Laub, ibid., 69.

[7] Hye-Jin (former president of the House of Sharing) mentioned that she realized that many victims had no chance to learn how to write. "Dialogue for the Preparation of Collected Paintings Book" in *Unblossomed Flower: A Collection of Paintings by Former Military Comfort Women* (Kwangju: The Historical Museum of Sexual Slavery by the Japanese Military, 2000).

[8] "The victims showed high current and lifetime prevalence of post-traumatic disorder, major depressive disorder, somatic symptom disorder, social anxiety disorder, panic disorder, and alcohol use disorder. Participants showed high suicidality and the majority of participants still reported being ashamed of being former 'comfort women' after all these years. This article highlights the fact that the trauma has affected the mental health and social functioning of former 'comfort women' throughout their lives, and even to the present day." Lee. J and others, "Psychiatric Sequelae of Former 'Comfort Women,' Survivors of the Japanese Military Sexual Slavery during World War II." *Psychiatry Investigation*. 15: 4 (Apr, 2018):336-343.

[9] Sun-Hyun Kim, *Art Therapy for Comfort Women: Art that Became History* (Paju, Korea: Korean Studies Information, 2012, Seoul: Idam Books, 2012), 179-196.

[10] Discussion of the meaning of works produced through art therapy by grandmothers can be found in "Comfort Women Wanted:  Uncovering Violent Past and Entering New Age of Activism through Visual Language" by Yae-Jin Ha, *Penn Humanities Forum* 2013-2014: *Violence, University of Pennsylvania* (May 2014).

[11] *The House of Sharing*, interview of Kim Sook-duk by Jung-Sil Lee.

[12] Ibid. 8.

[13] For themes and tendency of Minjung Art, *see Korean Art from the 19ᵗʰ Century to the Present*, by Charlotte Horlyck (London: Reaktion Books Ltd, 2017), chapter 5 Art and Politics of the 1980s and Mid-1990s.

[14] For further studies on their trauma and evaluation *see* "Post-traumatic Stress Disorder in former "comfort women" by Min SK, Lee CH, Kim JY, and Sim EJ, in *The Israel Journal of Psychiatry and Related Science*, 2011;48:3:161-9; "Psychiatric Sequelae of Former 'Comfort Women,' Survivors of the Japanese Military Sexual Slavery during World War II" by Lee J, Kwak YS, Kim YJ, Kim EJ, Park EJ, Shin Y, Lee BH, Lee SH, Jung HY, Lee I, Hwang JI, Kim D, Lee SI. In *Psychiatry Investigation* 15:4 (April 2018): 336-343.

[15] Joseph S. Nye, *Soft Power: The Means to Success in World Politics* (New York: Public Affairs, 2004).

[16] *See* "Dialogue for the Preparation of Collected Paintings Book," in *Unblossomed Flower: A Collection of Painting by Former Military Comfort Women*, ibid.

[17] Seana K. Magee, "Former Sex Slaves Use Art to Tell Story: Paintings to be shown in the U.S. after successful run in Japan," *The Japan Times*, October 18, 2000,
https://www.japantimes.co.jp/news/2000/10/18/national/former-sex-slaves-use-art-to-tell-story/#.XeRApuhKiUk.

[18] *Unveiling the Truth: The Sorrow and Hope of "Comfort Women,"* November 26 – December 14, 2012, Mason Hall Atrium Gallery, George Mason University, curated by Jung-Sil Lee, sponsored by WCCW, ArTrio, Korean Studies Center, George Mason University Gallery, and the Academy of Korean Studies, Korea.

[19] Elaine H. Kim, Margo Machida, and Sharon Mizota, *Fresh Talk/ Daring Gazes: Conversations on Asian American Art* (Berkeley: University of California Press, 2003); "Min positions her body as landscape or homeland, labeling her chest 'Heartland' and her arms as 'Occupied Territory,'" 125.

[20] *The Sorrow and Hope of Comfort Women: Seminar and Exhibition,* November 25, 2014 – Jan. 12, 2015, curated by Jung-Sil Lee, co-hosted by WCCW and the National Catholic School of Social Service's Center for International Social Development (CISD), cosponsored by WCCW, Kowin, and Northeast Asian History Foundation.

[21] The symposium *Collateral Damage: Wartime Atrocity and Trauma* was funded by WCCW and Northeast Asian History Foundation and co-moderated by Jung-Sil Lee and Thalia Vrachopoulos, drew huge student attendance.

[22] *Truth: Promise for Peace* opened on July 3, 2017 and travelled up to September 2nd to Seoul, Jeonjoo, Daejeon, Daegu. During the closing ceremony there was the seminar on "comfort women" in Daegu.

[23] Jung-Sil Lee, "Appropriating, Reporting, and Re-Contexualizing of Wartime Sex Crimes by Female Artists," *Has anyone ever seen an image of war? Reassessing the visual culture of war and related disasters, violence, and torture in the modern and contemporary moment* (Panel Title), College Art Association, 2019 Annual Conference, February 15, 2019.

[24] Kelley, Jeff (curator). *Hung Liu: Scales of History.* Fresno Art Museum, Walter Maciel Gallery, Sep 23, 2016 – April 28, 2017, https://www.fresnoartmuseum.org/exhibitions/past-exhibits/fall-winter-spring-2016-17/.

[25] Heather Lineberry (senior curator at ASU Art Museum) with Sandy Harthorn (curator at Boise Art Museum), Exhibition catalog essay on "Strange Fruit: New Painting by Hung Liu's" at The Laguna Art Museum (February, 2003).

[26] Sandy Harthorn, Curator of Art Boise Art Museum, "Living in the Layers: Hung Liu's New Paintings," in catalog essay, ibid. 7.

[27] Arthur C. Danto, "Beauty for Ashes," *Regarding Beauty,* Neal Benezra and Ola M. Viso, editors and curators (Washington, D.C.: Hirshhorn Museum and Sculpture Garden, 1999-2000), 196.

[28] Hung Liu, interview by Jung-Sil Lee, May 2017.

[29] Laura Hein and Nobuko Tanaka, "Brushing with Authority: The Life and Art of Tomiyama Taeko," *The Asia Pacific Journal; Japan Focus* 8: 13 (March 29, 2010).

[30] Her work has been exhibited at the Gwangju Biennale (1995, 2000), the Echigo Tsumari Art Triennial in Niigata, Japan (2009), and in Ruhr, Philadelphia and Evanston (2005-6), as well as in Berlin (2015).

[31] For a detailed analysis of the three works of Taeko *see* "Tomiyama Taeko's a Memory of the Sea" by Margaret Stetz and Bonnie Oh (co-edited) in *Legacies of the Comfort Women of World War II* (Armonk, New York and London: M. E. Sharpe, 2001), 201 – 208.

[32] Jung-Sil Lee, "Artists Meet the Trauma and Hope of the 'Comfort Women,'" catalogue entry in *Truth: Promise for Peace*, exhibition organized by National Women's History Museum in Seoul, Korea, 2017: 114-117.

[33] Rebecca Jennison, "The Military Comfort Women and Art in Japan-Remembrance and Reconciliation in Tomiyama Taeko's Art," in the catalogue *Truth: Promise for Peace*, ibid., 118-121.

[34] *See* Linda Gertner Zatlin "'Comfort Women' and the Cultural Tradition of Prostitution in Japanese Erotic Art" in *Legacies of the Comfort Women of World War II*, ibid., 26-41.

[35] "Comfort Women: Researchers claim first Known Film," *BBC News,* July 10, 2017, https://www.bbc.com/news/world-asia-40552812

[36] "Comfort Women" Video. 1995. The first important testimony of Korean "comfort women" who were in Korea or visited the U.S. and narrated by Sangmie Choi Shellstede.

[37] Dai Sil Kim-Gibson, *Silence Broken: Korean Comfort Women* (Iowa: Mid-Prairie Books Parkersburg, 1999).

[38] Task force team for the documentary film production of "Comfort Women Movement" are Jung-Sil Lee (Writer and Director), Edward Jang (Director of Photography), Jackie Kim (Translator), Jaeheup Kim (Camera Man), Wooyoung Kim (Editor) who are chroniclers of the "comfort women" activism in the U.S.

[39] https://www.hancinema.net/korean_movie_My_name_is_KIM_Bok-dong.php.

[40] The director, Miki Dezaki explains his film, "The 'comfort women' issue is perhaps Japan's most contentious present-day diplomatic quandary. Inside Japan, the issue is dividing the country across clear ideological lines. Supporters and detractors of 'comfort women' are caught in a relentless battle over empirical evidence, the validity of oral testimony, the number of victims, the meaning of sexual slavery, and the definition of coercive recruitment. Credibility, legitimacy and influence serve as the rallying cry for all those involved in the battle. This film delves deep into the most contentious debates and uncovers the hidden intentions of the supporters and detractors of 'comfort women.' Most importantly it finds answers to some of the biggest questions for Japanese and Koreans: Were 'comfort women' prostitutes or sex slaves? Were they coercively recruited? And,

does Japan have a legal responsibility to apologize to the former 'comfort women?'":
https://www.shusenjo.com/.

41 Chungmi Kim, *Comfort Women* [formerly called Hanako] (1999, 2004).

42 *Comfort Women: A New Musical* is about Korean "comfort women" sold as sex slaves for the Imperial Japanese Army during WWII. The story revolves around a young Korean woman, Goeun, who was promised a job in Japan, but is soon transported to Indonesia as one of the "comfort women." The audience witnesses how such a tragedy can permanently and painfully transform the life of a young woman, https://www.dimokimfactory.org.

43 The details will be discussed in chapter 10 on "comfort women" memorials.

44 Dr. Suejung Huh recalled her initial idea of applying the scientific method to "comfort women" history came after learning about the work done for holocaust victims of the Jewish community. Huh called on "comfort women" activists and supporters to help initiate this project in the early 2018. The initial group consisted of Suejung Huh, Sin-Hwa Kang, Phyllis Kim (KAFC), Grace Oh and Kilwon Cho (Kowin), Angela Oh (LA Nabi), and Jung-Sil Lee (WCCW).

45 Chan-ho Kim, "Hologram Enables the 'Eternal Testimony' on the Tragedy of the Comfort Women in the Japanese Military," *Kyunghang Sinmun*, Oct. 29, 2019, http://english.khan.co.kr/khan_art_view.html?artid=201910291815447&code=710100.

# 8. WESTERN-LANGUAGE DOCTORAL DISSERTATIONS ON THE KOREAN "COMFORT WOMEN" 1995–2004

## AN ANNOTATED BIBLIOGRAPHY WITH BRIEF INFORMATION ABOUT THE EDUCATIONAL BACKGROUNDS OF THE DISSERTATION AUTHORS

*Frank Joseph Shulman*

### Introduction

The earliest known doctoral dissertation about the Korean "comfort women" dates from 1995. This chronologically arranged bibliography identifies that title and provides an overview of all of the studies completed for the Ph.D., D.Min. and Th.D. degrees during the ensuing decade that deal either in their entirety or, in most cases, just in part with the issue of the Japanese military sexual enslavement of Korean women during World War II. The bibliographical entries for these forty-six dissertations—written at thirty-six universities in the United States, Canada, Germany, and the United Kingdom—are among the entries for nearly 15,000 Western-language dissertations that are being prepared for publication by the University of Michigan Press in my forthcoming reference work, "The First Century of Doctoral Dissertations on Korea, 1903-2004," a multidisciplinary, descriptively annotated, subject classified, and indexed bibliography of Western-language studies that deal in some way with Korea, with the Korean people, and with Korean international students and émigrés and were accepted by 950 accredited universities, theological seminaries, and other higher degree-awarding institutions in forty-one countries around the world. By offering the present entrée to the earliest dissertations written about the "comfort women"—works that by and large are not as well known as the larger body of books and articles on this subject that appeared in print between 1995 and 2004—and by increasing current awareness of them, this chapter seeks to expand the readership of these studies and to facilitate their greater use.

In addition to most standard bibliographical details, the present bibliography contains the table of contents of each dissertation, the name(s) of the senior faculty member(s) who directed each one, each author's academic major or academic department (e.g., Ph.D. in Anthropology), information about the availability of the dissertations, and citations to their published abstracts or summaries as well as to book-length monographs written by the authors that are related in one or more ways to their dissertations. The descriptive annotations generally include brief statements about or selected highlights of the authors' overall thesis research and the context within which the "comfort women" issue is covered. Most often this is expressed in the authors' own words. All of the entries are based on a personal examination of the dissertation typescripts rather than on secondary sources. The McCune-Reischauer

Romanization system is used throughout, but in all of the annotations, Korean names and terms are also provided according to the Revised Romanization system for Korean. Together with the authors' years of birth and, in the majority of cases, their earlier academic degrees and the titles of their master's theses, the inclusion of this information also enables the bibliography to serve as an English-language biographical source about the educational backgrounds and some of the research of seventeen Korean, eighteen Western, seven Japanese, and four other Asian scholars—thirty-eight of them women and eight of them men—who in one way or another expressed an early interest in Korea's wartime "comfort women."

**Keys**:

DAI = *Dissertation Abstracts International* volume, issue and page numbers (printed monthly between 1938 and 2012) for identifying the first appearance of the published abstract of a specific dissertation.

UMI = University Microfilms International number for identifying the publication number of a specific dissertation in the "ProQuest Dissertations and Theses Global (PQDT Global)" database and for ordering copies of it in electronic, microform and printed formats from ProQuest LLC in Ann Arbor, Michigan. For further information, contact: ProQuest, 789 East Eisenhower Parkway, Ann Arbor, MI 48108, U.S.A. Tel: 1-800-521-0600; e-mail disspub@proquest.com; or go to https://dissexpress.proquest.com. Copies of all UMI dissertations are also readily available in microform and/or electronic format at the Library of Congress in Washington, D.C. *Note*: ProQuest was known for many years as University Microfilms International, or UMI. This bibliography has opted to continue using "UMI" in all of its relevant entries.

Adviser(s) = Name(s) of the senior faculty member(s) who directed the author's doctoral dissertation or who chaired the author's dissertation committee.

*Contents* = Table of Contents—limited primarily to the titles of individual chapters—of the dissertation.

EThOS = Electronic Theses Online Service identification number for use when requesting a copy of a British doctoral dissertation that is available through the British Library at Boston Spa in West Yorkshire.

*Index to Theses* (London) = Citation to a published abstract in the *Index to Theses with Abstracts Accepted for Higher Degrees by the Universities of Great Britain and Ireland and the Council for National Academic Awards* (London)

**Note regarding diacritical marks**: In the Romanization of names, words and other terms, the circumflex is used as the accent mark in place of the breve in Korean and the macron in Japanese.

**Keywords:**

*A Gesture Life* (novel); academic scholarship; annotated bibliography; apologies; biographical information; Chang-rae Lee (1965- ); colonial Korea; *Comfort Woman* (novel); "comfort women"; compensation; controversies; dissertation abstracts; dissertation authors; doctoral dissertations; educational background; ethnography; European scholarship; female body; feminism; identity; gender; Japanese government; Japanese military; Japanese-Korean relations; Korean American literature; Korean government; Korean-Japanese relations; lawsuits; Nora Okja Keller (1965- ); Pacific War; postcolonialism; scholarly research; sexual slavery; soldiers; suffering; survivors; testimonies; trauma; women; World War II

## 1995

1.
PARK, You-me [BAK, Yu-mi / PAK, Yu-mi] (1960- ).
***From Comfort Women to Women Warriors: Domesticity, Motherhood, and Women's Labour in the Discourse of Imperialism.*** George Washington University [United States], 1995 (Ph.D. in English). Adviser: Tara Ghoshal Wallace. vii, 306p. DAI 56, no. 2 (August 1995): 560-A; UMI 9522072.

Park, the recipient of both a B.A. (1982) and an M.A. (1984) degree from Seoul National University, explored "the ways in which women's sexuality, body, work and space have been regulated, policed and violated in imperial and patriarchal formations." She began her dissertation by focusing on contemporary Korea. Through her analyses of two short stories— "Pit" (The Light) (1988) by Yun Chông-mo and "Kkûnnaji anhûn norae" (The Song That Hasn't Ended) (1993) by Kim Pyôr-a ("Bit" by Yun Jeong-mo and "Kkeunnaji anheun norae" by Gim Byeor-a)—Park looked at how "certain Korean narratives participated in, or tried to subvert, the objectification and commodification of women" and "raised questions about the metaphorization of women's bodies and labor in specific contexts of nationalist literature." For her coverage of the "comfort women," see chapter 1 (pages 1-47): "Bodies against Metaphors: Decolonization and the Discourse of Body in Korean Nationalist Literature."

*Contents*: 1. Bodies against Metaphors: Decolonization and the Discourse of Body in Korean Nationalist Literature. 2. "Hidden from History": Women, Language and Imperialism in Mary Wollstonecraft's Earlier Writings. 3. Refiguring Motherhood in the Imperialist Context: Female Body and Articulation in Mary Wollstonecraft's *The Wrongs of Woman, or Maria*. 4. "Fearless Intercourse with the Brother and Friend": Discourse and Influence in the Imperialist Britain of *Mansfield Park*. 5. "A Woman's Portion": Transportable Domesticity and Comfort in *Persuasion*. 6. Women Writing Revolutions: Anti-Imperialist Struggle and the Representation of Women Warriors. Bibliography: pp. 297-306.

## 1996

2.

WINTER, Sandra Lee  (1939- ).

**An Unsung Lament: The Suffering of Korean Women Taken for Military Sexual Slavery during World War II.**  San Francisco Theological Seminary [United States], 1996 (D.Min. in Advanced Pastoral Studies).  Adviser: Warren Wokyeng Lee.  4, iv, 177p.  No published abstract.  Winter's dissertation is housed at the Graduate Theological Union's branch library on the San Francisco Theological Seminary campus. Contact the Graduate Theological Union Library (2400 Ridge Road, Berkeley, Calif. 94709-1212, U.S.A.) for information regarding the availability of copies (call number D810.C698 W56 1996 SFTS).

Winter, an ordained minister since 1981 of the Presbyterian Church (USA) and a graduate of both Rhodes College in Memphis, Tennessee (B.A. in Christian Education, 1961) and the Pacific School of Religion at Berkeley (M.Div., 1980), addressed the church and people of faith in the United States with the intent of increasing their awareness of what she regarded as one of the worst cases of sexual violence in history: the sexual enslavement of Korean women by the Japanese military during World War II. She first traced the "history and rationale of the Japanese military's Comfort Women Program." described the ordeal of the women who survived as well as those who died, and discussed the "activities of the groups that were seeking reparations and justice." She then presented the testimonies (the "*Han*-stories") of thirteen elderly Korean women in which they described their abduction, their experiences as sexual slaves, and the "poverty, ill health, shame, loneliness, and pain" of their lives after the war. Winter's final chapter "moved from a theology of suffering to a theology of resurrection" in which she advocated the integration of "Korean shamanist traditions" with "Minjung Theology and resurrection theology."

*Contents*: 1. Introduction: Unsung Lament. 2. Unfolding Drama. 3. Echoes. 4. Theological Vision. Appendix: pp. 162-71. Bibliography: pp. 172-77.

## 1998

3.

KIM, Kyounghee  [GIM, Gyeong-hui / KIM, Kyông-hûi]  (1964- ).

**Gender Politics in South Korea: The Contemporary Women's Movement and Gender Policies, 1980-1996.**  University of Wisconsin at Madison [United States], 1998 (Ph.D. in Sociology).  Adviser: Pamela E. Oliver.  x, 293p.  DAI 59, no. 5 (November 1998): 1799-A; UMI 9814794.

Focusing on the Korean Women's Association United (Yôsông Tanch'e yônhap/Yeoseong Dancheyeonhap) and its activities, Kim, a graduate of Yonsei University in Seoul (B.A., 1987), tried to "explain the changes that took place in the progressive Korean women's movement in terms of structural factors (political opportunity structure and movement structure) and interpretive factors (movement frame and political discourse)." For much of her analysis, she divided her time frame into three periods that reflected the changes and characteristics of the political opportunity structure and the women's movement: "the emergence and development of the minjung women's movement, 1980-1986; the development of the united progressive women's movement in transition politics, 1987-1992; and the politics of engagement and of proposing alternatives, 1993-1996." National reunification, equal employment rights, the protection of motherhood, legislation on sexual violence and harassment, and the plight of the "comfort women" were among the specific issues addressed. For Kim's coverage of the latter, see especially the section "Women's Movement in Transition Politics: 1987-1992: Frames and Issues of the Women's Movement: Toward Gender-Specific Issues, 1990-1992: Reunification and the Chungshindae (Comfort Women) Movement" on pages 182-95.

*Contents*: 1. Introduction. 2. A Theoretical Framework. 3. Background for Understanding Gender Politics in Korea. 4. Emergence and Development of the Minjung Women's Movement: 1980-1986. 5. Women's Movement in Transition Politics: 1987-1992. 6. Promoting Policy Alternatives: 1993-1996. 7. Conclusion: Comparative Perspectives on Women's Movements Around the World. 3 figures. 25 tables. Bibliography: pp. 274-93.

## 1999

4.

AHN, Yonson [AN, Yeon-seon / AN, Yôn-sôn] (1963- ).

***Korean "Comfort Women" and Military Sexual Slavery in World War II***. University of Warwick [United Kingdom], 1999 (Ph.D. in Women and Gender Studies, Centre for the Study of Women and Gender). Advisers: Joanna Liddle and Terry Lovell. 279p. Abstract published in *Index to Theses* (London): entry no. 50-5234. Also DAI 36, no. 2: section C. EThOS Persistent ID: uk.bl.ethos.323148. A microfilm copy is available at the Center for Research Libraries in Chicago, Illinois (call number P-80000145) and may be borrowed through interlibrary loan.

Ahn's major aim was to indicate how "the masculinity of the Japanese soldiers during World War II, the femininity of the Korean 'comfort women,' and the national identities of both were re/constructed through the enforcement of the subject-positionings of gender, colonialism and nationalism" within the context of the "comfort station" system. Basing her study on personal narratives, testimonies and official documents obtained through in-depth interviews with thirteen former "comfort women" and seventeen military veterans, she "argued that the development of gender and national identities contributed to the construction of Japanese colonialism, and that the 'comfort women' system helped to produce and reproduce Japan as an imperial state with power over the lives and human resources of her colonies." In particular, Ahn stated, "the maintenance of the military system depended on the circulation of these concepts of masculinity and femininity" and the regulation of these identities was "a crucial means through which Japan expanded her colonies by military means." Chapters 4 and 5 (pages 99-160) respectively detail the recruitment, family background, sexual initiation, daily life, contestation and resistance of the women; the motivations, regulations, control, violence and "legitimation" of the soldiers; and the relationships that existed between them. *Note*: Ahn, a native of Seoul, also earned a B.A. in Chemistry (1985) at Soongsil University in Seoul and an M.A. in Women's Studies (1988) at Ewha Woman's University, where she wrote a master's thesis entitled "Han'guk singminji chabonjuûi kwajôngesô yôsông nodong ûi sôngyôge kwanhan yôn'gu" ("Hanguk singminji chabonjuui gwajeongeseo yeoseong nodong ui seongyeoge gwanhan yeongu") [A Study of the Characteristics of the Labor of Korean Women in the Progression to Capitalism under Japanese Colonialism with a Focus on the Textile Industry during the 1930s].

*Contents*: 1. Introduction. 2. Literature Review and Conceptual Framework. 3. Researching Military Sexual Slavery. 4. Stories of the "comfort women." 5. Stories of the Soldiers. 6. Military Masculinity. 7. Enslaved Sexualised Femininity. 8. National Identities. 9. Conclusion. Bibliography: pp. 257-74. Appendix: pp. 275-79.

Published as *Sông noye wa pyôngsa mandûlgi* (*Seong noye wa byeongsa mandeulgi*) [Sexual Slavery and the Making of Soldiers], by An Yôn-sôn (An Yeon-seon). Sôul-si: Samin, 2004. 340p. Related publication: *Whose Comfort? Body, Sexuality and Identities of Korean 'Comfort Women' and Japanese Soldiers during WWII*, by Yonson Ahn. Hackensack, N.J. and London: World Scientific, 2019.

5.

HOANG, Young-ju [HWANG, Yeong-ju / HWANG, Yông-ju] (1967- ).

**Soul, Body, and House: A Feminist Critique of Contemporary State Practices in Korea**. University of Hull [United Kingdom], 1999 (Ph.D. in Politics). Adviser: Costas M. Constantious. v, 215p. Abstract published in *Index to Theses* (London): entry no. 50-5453. Also DAI 36, no. 2: section C. EThOS Persistent ID: uk.bl.ethos.310317. A microfilm copy is available at the Center for Research Libraries in Chicago, Illinois (call number P-80000125) and may be borrowed through interlibrary loan.

Hoang, a graduate of both Pusan University of Foreign Studies (B.A. in International Relations) and Hankuk University of Foreign Studies in Seoul (M.A. in Comparative Politics), drew on feminist theory to analyze militarism in Korea with particular reference to the Japanese colonial period (1910-1945), the Korean War era (1950-1953), and "militaristic state practices" between 1962 and 1987; capitalism, especially during the "state-led economic development" of the 1960s-1990s; and democratization, particularly from 1987 through the 1990s. His studies endeavored "to rediscover the role of women in the formation of the Korean state, to redefine and criticize the masculinized modern, and to re-evaluate the traditional discussion of state theory." In addition, Hoang "examined how women's bodies were exploited by various state practices for the benefit of state security," "assessed the relation of the *kisaeng* (*gisaeng*) (professional female entertainers) tradition to the 'comfort women' during World War II and to prostitution in military camps" after the Korean War, and showed that North Korean women engaged in two tasks: "being 'wise mothers and good wives' and serving as revolutionary fighters."

*Contents*: Introduction. 1. A Feminist Critique of the Modern State. 2. Women in Early Korean History. 3. Beautiful Soul, State Redemption. 4. Colonised Body, State Exploitation. 5. Safe House, State Domestication. 6. The Indigenous Other: Revolutionary Women in North Korea. Conclusion. Bibliography: pp. 197-213.

6.

ISHIBASHI, Mari (1963- ).

**Japan's New Foreign Policy Style and Its Impact on the Policy toward the Korean Minority in Japan.** University of Notre Dame [United States], 1999 (Ph.D. in Government and International Studies). Adviser: Peter R. Moody, Jr. xvi, 377p. DAI 60, no. 3 (Sept. 1999): 868-A; UMI 9921853.

Ishibashi, a graduate of Jôchi Daigaku [Sophia University] in Tokyo (B.A. in Political Science, 1987) and the University of Notre Dame (M.A. in Peace Studies, 1990), "examined the interrelationship of Japan's domestic and foreign policy with a focus on how her rising economic status in the international system affected her domestic policy towards her Korean minority." Using Robert D. Putnam's 'two-level games' as her analytic framework for five longitudinal case studies (1950s-1990s) to test the hypothesis that Japan's treatment of Koreans depended in part on the extent to which Japanese foreign policy makers were concerned with their country's 'prestige' or reputation" abroad, she "elaborated on how the government reconciled domestic bureaucratic regulatory forces of 'assimilation' with international forces of 'accommodation.'" In short, Ishibashi argued, "the more Japan was concerned with issues of international prestige, the more accommodating she became towards Korean minority interests." In chapter 8 (pages 304-42), Ishibashi supplemented her first four case studies with an analysis of the government's establishment in 1994 of an "apology program for historical studies and exchanges with Asian nations." While this program did not include direct compensation to former "comfort women," she indicated that it was "the first significant step in acknowledging the scope of Japan's wartime brutality and responsibility" since it was "part of the policy-change that reflected the similar policy dynamics of her other studies and provided some theoretical insights into the nature of Japan's new foreign policy style." *Note*: Ishibashi did not write any master's thesis.

*Contents*: Introduction. 1. Prejudice and Discrimination: History and Current Predicament of the Korean Residents in the Japanese Society. 2. Contending Theoretical Models of Japanese Policy-Making and Intermestic Issue Area: Relevance to Korean Residents. 3. From "Old" to "New" Foreign Policy Style: Its Ideological and Popular Underpinning of the National *Taikoku* Debate. 4. The 1959 Korean Repatriation. 5. The 1965 Republic of Korea-Japanese Normalization Treaty. 6. The International Human Rights Covenants in 1979 and the Convention Relating to the Status of Refugees and the Protocol Relating to the Status of Refugees in 1981. 7. The 1992 Abolition of Finger-Printing. 8. The 1994 Establishment of Apology Program for Comfort Women. Conclusion: Contending Theoretical Models in Japanese Policy-Making and Intermestic Issue-Area. 3 tables. Bibliography: pp. 362-77.

7.

WENDER, Melissa Louise (1967- ).

**Lamentation as History: Literature of Koreans in Japan, 1965-1999.** University of Chicago [United States], 1999 (Ph.D. in East Asian Languages and Civilizations). Adviser: Norma M. Field. xi, 259p. DAI 60, no. 8 (February 2000): 2934-A; UMI 9943132. The abstract of this dissertation has also been published in the journal *Japanese Language and Literature* 35, no. 2 (October 2001): 246-47.

Written by a graduate of Harvard University (B.A. in East Asian Languages and Civilizations, 1988) and the University of Chicago (M.A.), this dissertation is a roughly chronological account and analysis of the postwar "literature and grassroots struggles" of the Korean minority of Japan. Wender's study includes analyses of the fiction of Ri Kaisei (1935- ) (Yi Hoe-sông/Lee Hoeseong/Lee Hoesung), the first non-Japanese writer to win the prestigious Akutagawa Prize; a pair of stories by Kin Kakuei (1938-1985) together with an account of a "battle against employment discrimination that is often called the first citizens' movement by Koreans in Japan"; the works of Chong Ch'u-wôl (Jong Chu-wol/Chon Chuworu) (1944- ) and Kim Ch'ang-saeng (Gim Chang-saeng) (1951- ), who fought for the repeal of the fingerprinting requirement stipulated in the Alien Registration Law; the fiction of Yi Yang-ji (1955-1992) (Yi Yang-ji/Lee Yangji) and her "literary appropriation of Korean shamanism"; the "fiction of Yû Miri (1968- ); and the debates surrounding the inclusion of the history of 'comfort women' in middle school Japanese textbooks." *Note*: Wender also earned the degree of M.Ed. in Secondary Education and Teaching (2010) at the University of Massachusetts at Boston.

*Contents*: 1. Introduction. 2. Mother Korea. 3. Uncircumcised Ethnicity. 4. Women Write Ikaino. 5. Words That Breathe. 6. Private Traumas, Public Therapies. 7. Afterword. Bibliography: pp. 244-59.

Published as *Lamentations as History: Narratives by Koreans in Japan, 1965-2000*, by Melissa L. Wender. Stanford, Calif.: Stanford University Press, 2005. xiii, 252p. Related publication: *Into the Light: An Anthology of Literature by Koreans in Japan*, edited by Melissa L. Wender. Honolulu: University of Hawaii Press, 2011. ix, 226p.

## 2000

8.
CHOY, Gregory Paul  (1960- ).
**Sites of Function in Asian American Literature: Tropics of Place, Agents of Space**. University of Washington [United States], 2000 (Ph.D. in English).  Adviser: Johnnella E. Butler. 2, ii, 168p. DAI 60, no. 11 (May 2000): 4008-A; UMI 9952813.

"Arguing for the significance of place and space as central organizing tropes of particular themes in Asian American literature." Choy attempted to "discern along thematic lines how selected Asian American texts relate to cultural, social and historical differences among ethnic backgrounds as they are incorporated along similar themes." For his treatment of the issue of the Korean "comfort women," see chapter 4 (pages 134-59)—"Voice and Memory Back to Korea"—which analyzes "transnational themes of home and memory" in two contemporary Korean American novels: Nora Okja Keller's *Comfort Woman* (1997) and Heinz Insu Fenkl's *Memories of My Ghost Brother* (1996). *Note*: In addition to his doctorate, Choy earned a B.A. in Liberal Studies (1984) at the University of California at Santa Barbara and an M.A. in English (1990) at California Polytechnical State University at San Luis Obispo. He indicated in his dissertation that his father was "one of the very first Korean Americans to have fought for America in the Korean War."

*Contents*: Introduction. 1. Yearning for Place: *No-No Boy*. 2. Marked on the Body: Frank Chin and Jeffrey Paul Chan. 3. Commonalities of the National and Transnational: *Homebase* and *Dictee*. 4. Voice and Memory Back to Korea: *Comfort Woman* and *Memories of My Ghost Brother*. Bibliography: pp.160-65.


9.
DUCKE, Isa Anna Klara (1969- ).
**Status as a Factor in Japanese Foreign Policy Making toward Korea** . University of London [United Kingdom], 2000 (Ph.D. in Political Science, School of Oriental and African Studies). Adviser: Lesley Connors. 243p. Abstract published in *Index to Theses* (London): entry no. 50-7985. Also DAI 70, no. 26 (2009): section C. EThOS Persistent ID: uk.bl.ethos.326232.

After presenting a framework in which "status, based either on prestige or on a positive reputation or moral authority, can be a power resource similar to military or economic strength." Ducke argued that "an imbalance in status existed between Japan and South Korea" due to Korea's historical relationship with and victimization by Japan. She discussed both the "mechanisms" of the "status power" derived from this special relationship which Seoul exploited to "pressure Tokyo on certain policies" and the "domestic Japanese differences over the appropriate ways to raise Japan's status" in a number of case studies. The latter ranged from such "issues as war apologies, Japanese history textbooks, and the 'comfort women'" to such economic and political matters as the 1981 South Korean loan request, the dispute over Tokto (Dokdo) in the East Sea/Sea of Japan, and issues related to North Korea and Korean reunification.

*Contents*: Introduction: The Concept of Status as a Factor in International Relations. 1. The Legacy of the Past. 2. Japanese-South Korean Economic Relations. 3. Japan's North Korea Policy. 4. Korean Unification. Conclusion. 13 figures. 1 table. Bibliography: pp. 227-43.

Published as *Status Power: Japanese Foreign Policy Making toward Korea*, by Isa Ducke. New York and London: Routledge, 2002. xiv, 243p. (East Asia: history, politics, sociology, culture). Related publication: *Japan und Korea auf dem Weg in eine gemeinsame Zukunft: Aufgaben und Perspektiven* [Japan and Korea on the Path to a Common Future: Tasks and Prospects], edited by Isa Ducke and Sven Saaler. München: Iudicium, 2003. 232p. (Monographien aus dem Deutschen Institut für Japanstudien, Bd.36).


10.
DUNCAN, Patricia Lee (1970- ).
**A History of Un/Saying: Silences, Memory, and Historiography in Asian American Women's Narratives** . Emory University [United States], 2000 (Ph.D. in Women's Studies, Institute for Women's Studies). Adviser: Julie L. Abraham. 4, 255p. DAI 61, no. 4 (October 2000): 1646-47-A; UMI 9968353.

Duncan explored "the meanings of silence and speech in the writings" of six Chinese, Japanese and Korean American authors including Theresa Hak Kyung Cha (1951-1982) and Nora Okja Keller (1965- ), and suggested that they "deployed silence as a means of resistance." "Juxtaposing their 'unofficial narratives'—*China Men* (1980), *The Woman Warrior* (1976), *Camp Notes* (1976), *Obasan* (1982), *Dictée* (1982) and *Comfort Woman* (1997)—against the histories that exclude them, these writers argued for the recognition of their cultural participation and offered analyses of the intersections among gender, race, nation, and sexuality." See especially chapter 4 (pages 142-90): "'Cartographies of Silence': Language and Nation in Theresa Hak Kyung Cha's *Dictée*." and chapter 5 (pages 191-237): "Silence and Public Discourse: Interventions into Dominant National and Sexual Narratives in Anchee Min's *Red Azalea* and Nora Okja Keller's *Comfort Woman*." *Note*: In addition to her doctorate, Duncan earned a B.A. in Psychology (1992) at Vassar College and an M.A. in Women's Studies (1996) at Emory University.

*Contents*: 1. The Uses of Silence and the "Will to Unsay." 2. What Makes an American? Histories of Immigration and Exclusion of Asians in the U.S. in Maxine Hong Kingston's *China Men*. 3. "White Sound" and Silences from Stone: Discursive Silences in the Internment Writings of Mitsuye Yamada and Joy Kogawa. 4. "Cartographies of Silence": Language and Nation in Theresa Hak Kyung Cha's *Dictée*. 5. Silence and Public Discourse: Interventions into Dominant National and Sexual Narratives in Anchee Min's *Red Azalea* and Nora Okja Keller's *Comfort Woman*. Conclusion: "Tell This Silence": Asian American Women's Narratives and Feminist Movement. Bibliography: pp. 248-55.

Published as *Tell This Silence: Asian American Women Writers and the Politics of Speech*, by Patti Duncan. Iowa City: University of Iowa Press, 2004. xvi, 274p.

11.
KATZOFF, Beth Sara (1968- ).
***For the Sake of the Nation for the Sake of Women: The Pragmatism of Japanese Feminisms in the Asia-Pacific War (1931-1945)***. Columbia University [United States], 2000 (Ph.D. in History). Adviser: Carol N. Gluck. vii, 311p. DAI 61, no. 9 (March 2001): 3717-A; UMI 9985911.

Katzoff examined the "consistent and pragmatic use by Japanese feminists of the rhetoric and institutions of nationalism to achieve social, political, and economic advancement for Japanese women" from the outbreak of the Manchurian Incident through the end of World War II, and studied their pursuit of such feminist goals as suffrage for women, greater opportunities for war work, the protection of motherhood, and the "increased participation of women in public institutions on both the national and local levels." She concluded "by tracing the wartime roots of trends in postwar Japanese feminism," and on pages 270-281 of chapter 5 discussed the debates among Japanese feminists over the issue of wartime military sexual slavery under the headings "Reconciling the Past: The *Jûgun ianfu* Issue" and "Military Sexual Slavery as a Feminist Issue." Katzoff indicated that it was only during the 1990s, as Korean victims began speaking out and as the "comfort women" issue gained international attention, that Japanese feminists became deeply concerned about the wartime victimization of other Asian women. Most feminists objected to their government's rejection of legal responsibility—it accepted only "moral responsibility"—for Japan's wartime crimes, and they came to view "military sexual slavery not merely as a discrete phenomenon of the past but as an ongoing, unresolved issue in the present." *Note*: In addition to her doctorate, Katzoff earned a B.A. in Government and Asian Studies (1990) at Cornell University and an M.A. in Regional Studies: East Asia (1992) at Harvard University, where she wrote a master's thesis entitled "Japanese Women in Reverse Course: A Study of the Magazine *Fujin kôron* and the Debates Concerning Women in Postwar Japan, 1946-1959."

*Contents*: 1. Interrogating Japanese Feminisms during the Asia-Pacific War. 2. The Pragmatics of Japanese Feminisms. 3. "We are Japanese Women": Nationalism, Feminism, and the Dai Nihon Fujinkai. 4. Neighborhood as Nation: Feminists' Discourse on the *Tonarigumi*. 5. The Wartime Roots of Postwar Japanese Feminisms. 2 figures. Bibliography: pp. 289-311.

12.

NOZAKI, Yoshiko (1956- ).

**Textbook Controversy and the Production of Public Truth: Japanese Education, Nationalism, and Saburo Ienaga's Court Challenges**. University of Wisconsin at Madison [United States], 2000 (Ph.D. in Educational Policy Studies). Adviser: Michael W. Apple. vi, 403p. DAI 61, no. 8 (February 2001): 3088-A; UMI 9982223.

Focusing on the three lawsuits filed by the prominent Japanese historian Ienaga Saburô (1913-2002) in 1965, 1966 and 1982 that "challenged the Japanese state's *de facto* censorship of school textbooks." Nozaki explored "Japan's postwar struggle over its 'official history'" as represented in elementary and secondary school history textbooks authorized by the Ministry of Education, and considered several related issues in the field of curriculum studies including the question: "Whose knowledge ought to be represented in the schools?" In chapter 8 (pages 314-75)—"The Politics of History"—she looked at "the processes through which the new meanings of 'comfort women' (*ianfu*) were developed, contested and circulated." More specifically, Nozaki asserted that "the issue of 'comfort women' exposed the gendered nature of 'nation' and 'national history' as they were constructed in Japan, and suggested that the struggle for oppositional and alternative national narratives might need to reflect on postmodernist views of history." *Note*: In addition to her doctorate, Nozaki earned a B.A. in Japanese History at Nagoya Daigaku [Nagoya University] and an M.A. in Educational Policy Studies at the University of Wisconsin at Madison. She apparently did not write a master's thesis.

*Contents*: 1. Introduction: Saburo Ienaga and the Struggle over Educational and Historical Truth. 2. Theory and Methods: Tensions, Dilemmas, and Struggles. 3. The Beginnings: The Struggle over the Japanese National Narrative and Identity in the Early Postwar Years, 1945-1965. 4. The Politics over Education: Oppositional Forces and Saburo Ienaga's First and Second Textbook Lawsuits, 1950s-1970s. 5. Counter-Memories of the Asia-Pacific War: The Struggle for Recognition, the History Controversy, and School Textbooks in the 1970s. 6. Saburo Ienaga's Third Lawsuit and Strategic Conjunctures: Changing Inter- and Intra-National Relations and the Textbook Controversy in the 1980s. 7. What Is Historical Fact? Differing

Views on History, Historical Narrative, and History Education in the Court Disputes. 8. The Politics of History: The Issue of "comfort women" and the Revival of Japan's Nationalist Movement in the 1990s. 9. Conclusion: The Supreme Court Decision on Saburo Ienaga's Third Textbook Lawsuit and the Continuation of the Struggle over "Truth in Textbooks." Bibliography: pp. 397-403.

Published as *War Memory, Nationalism and Education in Post-War Japan, 1945-2007: The Japanese History Textbook Controversy and Ienaga Saburo's Court Challenges*, by Yoshiko Nozaki. London and New York: Routledge, 2008. xx, 198p. (Routledge contemporary Japan series, 20).


13.
TWELBECK, Kirsten (1965- ).
**No Korean Is Whole, Wherever He or She May Be: Erfindungen von Korean America seit 1965**. [Text in German: No Korean Is Whole, Wherever He or She May Be: Fabrications of Korean America since 1965.] Freie Universität Berlin [Free University of Berlin] [Germany], 2000 (Dr. phil., John-F.-Kennedy-Institut für Nordamerikastudien: Abteilung Kultur). Adviser: Winfried Fluck. 310p. No published abstract.

Twelbeck explored the overall image of Korean Americans over several generations and in different media, beginning with an analysis of the television series M*A*S*H and a study of Pearl Buck's *The Living Reed* (1963). She read the novel's multi-generational representation of gender relations in Korea as an effort not only to further cross-cultural understanding but also to promote gender equality in the United States itself. Then, in part two, Twelbeck discussed "Korean America from five perspectives" by focusing on five contemporary Korean American writers—Peter Hyun (1906-1993), Ty Pak (1938- ), Theresa Hak Kyung Cha (1951-1982), Chang-rae Lee (1965- ) and Nora Okja Keller (1965- )—and by analyzing five of their works: Hyun's *In the New World: The Making of a Korean American* (1995), Pak's *Guilt Payment* (1983), Cha's *Dictée* (1982), Lee's *Native Speaker* (1995), and Keller's *Comfort Woman* (1997). Her study of *Comfort Woman* in conjunction with *Native Speaker* casts both books as exemplary writings by second generation Korean Americans and argues that Keller relied on the history of "comfort women" to create a specifically Korean American female identity, to draw attention to war crimes directed against women, and to bring direct charges against the Japanese government. *Note*: In addition to her doctorate, Twelbeck earned an intermediate university degree (Zwischenprüfung) at Universität Erlangen-Nürnberg (1988) and a master's degree at the John F. Kennedy Institute of Freie Universität Berlin (1992), where she wrote a 158 page master's thesis (Magisterarbeit) in American Studies and Theater & Drama entitled "Autobiographien von Immigrantinnen: Entwürfe für einen multikulturellen Pluralismus?" [Autobiographies of Female Immigrants: Designs for a Multicultural Pluralism?]. It deals with Maxine Hong Kingston's *The Woman Warrior* and Theresa Hak Chung Ha's *Dictée*.

*Contents*: Einleitung: Strangers from a Different Shore. Erster Teil: Das Eigene im Fremden. 1. Korean America: Im Schatten des Stereotyps. 2. Korea als ideales Amerika: Geschlechterdemokratie in Pearl S. Buck's The Living Reed. 3. Korea als Ursprungskatastrophe: Sa-i-ku. Zweiter Teil: Korean America aus fünf Perspektiven. 1. Die Maskulinisierung von Korean America: Peter Hyuns In the New World. 2. Die Koreanisierung einer psychischen Struktur: Ty Paks Guilt Payment. 3. Entführung in eine andere Wirklichkeit: Theresa Hak Kyung Chas DICTEE. 4. Versöhnung mit der Herkunft: Chang-rae Lees Native Speaker und Nora Okja Keller's *Comfort Woman*. Schlussbemerkungen. Bibliography: pp. 289-309.

*Contents Translated*: Introduction: Strangers from a Different Shore. Part One: Self and Other. 1. Korean America: In the Shadow of the Stereotype. 2. Korea as the Ideal America: Gender Democracy in Pearl S. Buck's *The Living Reed*. 3. Korean Trauma: *Sa-i-ku*. Part Two: Korean America from Five Perspectives. 1. The Masculinization of Korean America: Peter Hyun's *In the New World*. 2. The Koreanization of a Psychic Structure: Ty Pak's *Guilt Payment*. 3. Towards a Different Reality: Theresa Hak Kyung Cha's *Dictée*. 4. Reconciliation with the Origin: Chang-rae Lee's *Native Speaker* and Nora Okja Keller's *Comfort Woman*. Closing Remarks.

Revised version published as *No Korean Is Whole, Wherever He or She May Be: Erfindungen von Korean America seit 1965*, by Kirsten Twelbeck. Frankfurt and New York: Peter Lang, 2002. 310p. (Europäische Hochschulschriften: Reihe 14, Angelsächsische Sprache und Literatur, Bd. 393).

## 2001

14.

FUHRT, Volker (1962- ).

***Erzwungene Reue: Vergangenheitsbewältigung und Kriegsschulddiskussion in Japan 1952-1998.*** [Text in German: Enforced Remorse: Overcoming the Past and Discussing War Guilt in Japan, 1952-1998.] Martin-Luther-Universität Halle-Wittenberg [University of Halle] [Germany], 2001 (Dr. phil., Fachbereich Geschichte, Philosophie und Sozialwissenschaften: Seminar für Japanologie). Adviser: Gesine Foljanty-Jost. 243p. No published abstract.

Fuhrt discussed the ways in which questions of war guilt and the efforts to deal with the past characterized Japan's relationships with China and South Korea. He first focused on the controversy in the early 1980s surrounding Japanese textbooks and Japan's diplomatic conflicts with her neighbors over the depiction of the Sino-Japanese War (1937-1945) and Japanese colonialism in Korea. Fuhrt then analyzed the controversies during the 1990s regarding the Japanese military's use of "comfort women" in World War II, discussing, *inter alia*, some of the individual attempts at redress through both the media and international organizations, primarily from the standpoint of the reactions of the Japanese government. See especially chapter 3 (pages 47-79) in which he examined the normalization of Japan's relations with South Korea, and chapter 5 (pages 145-87), which focuses on the question of restitution to war victims as illustrated in the case of the military "comfort women." *Note*: In addition to his doctorate, Fuhrt earned a master's degree (1990) at the Seminar für Japanologie, Rheinische Friedrich-Wilhelms-Universität Bonn [Seminar for Japanese Studies of the University of Bonn], where he wrote a 178 page master's thesis (Magisterarbeit) in German entitled "Politische Vergangenheitsbewältigung in Japan der 1980er Jahre: Geschichtslehrbücher als Auslöser diplomatischer Konflikte" [Political Aspects of Overcoming the Past in Japan during the 1980s: History Textbooks as a Trigger of Diplomatic Conflicts].

*Contents*: 1. Einleitung. 2. Vergangenheitsbewältigung und Kriegsschulddiskussion im Überblick. 3. Im Zeichen reinen Gewissens: Die Normalisierung der Beziehungen zu Südkorea. 4. Der Schulbuchstreit von 1982: Wende zur breiten Thematisierung der Kriegsschuldfrage. 5. Die neue Dimension: Wiedergutmachung an Kriegsopfern in den 1990er Jahren am Beispiel der "Militärtrösterinnen" (*jûgun ianfu*). 6. Zusammenfassung und Ergebnis. Bibliography: pp. 200-43.

*Contents Translated*: 1. Introduction. 2. Overcoming the Past and Discussing War Guilt at a Glance. 3. Indication of a Clear Conscience: The Normalization of Relations with South Korea. 4. The Textbook Controversy of 1982: Turning to a Broad Discussion of the Question of War Guilt. 5. The New Dimension: Reparations to War Victims in the 1990s: The Example of the "Military Comfort Women" (*jûgun ianfu*). 6. Summary and Result.

Published as *Erzwungene Reue: Vergangenheitsbewältigung und Kriegsschulddiskussion in Japan 1952-1998*, by Volker Fuhrt. Hamburg: Kovac, 2002. 243p. (Schriftenreihe Studien zur Zeitgeschichte, Bd. 24).

15.
KIM, Jean Kyoung  (1960- ).

**Woman and Nation: An Intercontextual Reading of the Gospel of John**. Vanderbilt University [United States], 2001 (Ph.D. in Religion).  Adviser: Daniel M. Patte.  viii, 274p. DAI 63, no. 1 (July 2002): 228-A; UMI 3038817. "Thinking historically about existing social memories." Kim began her study of the religio-political dimension of the *Gospel of John* with a chapter (pages 1-39) that "addressed the conflict between male discourse (including colonialist/nationalist discourse) and feminist discourse" and sought to provide a "contesting site from which to read the hidden side of a history/text, which reflected the colonized women's sexuality in a colonial context or/and nationalist context." With respect to the "comfort women," see especially pages 7-12—"Reading the Female Body as History/Text: Women in a Decolonizing Text: Chong-sindae (Comfort Women)"—in which Kim "utilized the ruins of colonialism as a lens through which to view the Gospel as a nationalist narrative rather than as a Christian missionary document." and in which she "drew a parallel between Johannine female characters and contemporary women in a (de)colonizing context." In so doing, she criticized not only the Japanese government and military but also the "Korean gendered nationalism that was based on an 'honor-and-shame' culture." which "imposed the ideology of chastity on women's sexuality" and induced most Koreans as well as the Korean government to cover up the country's shameful past. *Note*: Kim indicated that during World War II, her mother (Park Bu-Shik) married her father "for no other reason than that her mother's family was afraid that she might otherwise be recruited as a 'comfort woman' under Japanese colonialism."

*Contents*: 1. Reading the Female Body as History/Text: Women in a (De)colonizing Text. 2. Intercultural Approach. 3. The Mother of Jesus at Cana (John 2:1-11). 4. The Samaritan Woman (John 4:1-42). 5. The Adulteress Woman (John 7:53-8:11). 6. Mary and Martha (John

11-12). 7. The Mother of Jesus (John 19:25-27). 8. Conclusion: An Ethical Reading of the Bible. Bibliography: pp. 239-74.

Published as *Woman and Nation: An Intercontextual Reading of the Gospel of John from a Postcolonial Perspective*, by Jean K. Kim. Leiden, The Netherlands and Boston, Mass.: Brill Academic Publishers, 2004. viii, 262p. (Biblical interpretation series, 69).

16.
KIM, Un Hey [GIM, Eun-hye / KIM, Ûn-hye] (1963- ).
**Subjectivity and Difference: Toward a Korean Christian Feminism**. Claremont Graduate University [United States], 2001 (Ph.D. in Religion). Adviser: Karen Baker-Fletcher. ix, 263p. DAI 63, no. 1 (July 2002): 238-A; UMI 3039104.

Kim asserted that feminist theologians have found it necessary "to rethink female subjectivity towards a new vision of feminist theology that stresses particularity and difference rather than universality and commonality." With that in mind, she dealt at length with the writings of Rosemary Radford Ruether (American feminist scholar and theologian, 1936- ), Luce Irigaray (Belgian feminist and philosopher, 1930- ) and Trinh T. Minh-ha (Vietnamese American filmmaker, writer and feminist, 1952- ) in an effort to study this new form of subjectivity. Furthermore, in order to "construct a new form of subjectivity towards a Korean Christian feminism," she chose Taoism (Daoism) "as the philosophical and cultural foundation on which to begin her own search about how one's subjectivity is formed and changed." Kim "concluded that we find the forming subjectivity as a flux of change informed by the passion and desire of Korean Christian women to let differences be." For her interest in the "comfort women," see pages 201-215—"Autobiographical Essay about the Formation of My Subjectivity as a Korean Christian Woman"—where she indicated how the impact of hearing the firsthand account of an old woman who had been forced to be a prostitute to Japanese soldiers led her to confront the "comfort women" issue more seriously and to "research and work for the 'comfort women' as an activist and researcher." *Note*: In addition to her doctorate, Kim earned the degrees of B.A. in Business Administration (1986) at Seoul Women's University, Master of Divinity [M.Div.] (1990) at the Presbyterian Theological College and Seminary in Seoul, and Master of Sacred Theology [S.T.M.] (1996) at Drew University, where she wrote a 42 page master's thesis entitled "Changing World View in the West and in the East Focused on Time and Space in I Ching."

*Contents*: Introduction and Presentation of the Problem. 1. Rosemary Redford Ruether's Notion of "Woman" and "Women's Experience": Subjectivity and the Notion of Difference. 2. Critique of Modern Subject and Feminist Theory of Subjectivity. 3. Theory of Subjectivities and the Notion of Difference. 4. Luce Irigaray's Deconstruction and Construction of Female Subjectivity. 5. Trinh T. Minh-ha's Subjectivity of Postcolonial Feminism and Third World Feminist Theology. 6. A New Form of Korean Christian Women's Subjectivity in Daoism: The Study of Zhuangzi and Laozi. Conclusion. Bibliography: pp. 258-63.

17.

KISHIMOTO, Kyoko.

***Race and History Wars in the 50th Anniversary of the End of World War II: A Comparative Analysis of the U.S. and Japanese Media***. Bowling Green State University [United States], 2001 (Ph.D. in American Culture Studies). Adviser: Rachel Buff. viii, 206p. DAI 62, no. 6 (December 2001): 2149-A; UMI 3016155.

Kishimoto analyzed the "process of the racialization of the 'other' and the conflict between history and memory in terms of the power politics" of the victor and the vanquished through a comparative analysis of the 1995 media coverage of the end of World War II. In the course of discussing the "continuing Japanese ethnocentric depictions of other Asians" and the "prevalence of the orthodox approach to the war in the Japanese government's failure to apologize and compensate for Japan's wartime aggression and colonization." she dealt at length in chapter 3 (pages 124-84) with the government's reluctance to formally acknowledge responsibility for Japan's wartime atrocities, with the demands for the state's payment of reparations to individuals who suffered under Japanese colonization, and with the coverage of the war—including the issue of the "comfort women"—in the elementary and high school textbooks that were approved by the Ministry of Education. Kishimoto concluded that the *Asahi shimbun* and other Japanese news media, Japanese scholars and Japanese citizens were far more concerned than government officials and conservative politicians about the "ramifications of the government's failure to assume its responsibility." *Note*: Kishimoto earned both a B.A. (1993) and an M.A. (1996) degree at Tôkyô Daigaku [University of Tokyo] as well as an M.A. in Popular Culture (1995) at Bowling Green State University, where she wrote a master's thesis entitled "'Going Where No One Has Gone Before': An Analysis of the Correspondence of Star Trek Fans" (vi, 103p.).

*Contents*: Introduction. 1. Literature Review. 2. Media Coverage of the 50th Anniversary in the U.S. 3. Media Coverage of the 50th Anniversary in Japan. 4. Conclusion. Appendix: pp. 199-201. Bibliography: pp. 202-06.


18.

LI, Huihui (1961- ).

***Representations of Code Switching in Asian American Women's Literature***. Texas A&M University [United States], 2001 (Ph.D. in English). Adviser: Pamela R. Matthews and J. Lawrence Mitchell. ix, 241p. DAI 62, no. 7 (Jan. 2002): 2425-A; UMI 3020079.

Li, a graduate of China's Hunan Normal University [Hunan shifan daxue] (B.A. in English, 1982) and Texas A&M University (M.A. in Literature and Linguistics, 1995), "applied discourse analysis to an investigation of the use of code switching" by some twelve Chinese, Japanese, Korean and South Asian American women writers. Placing their texts "within larger historical and social contexts." she argued that "its use can illuminate fundamental social and political issues including the formation of minority group identities and ethnic boundaries." Ronyoung Kim (the pen name of Gloria Hahn) (1926-1987) and Nora Okja Keller (1965- ) are the two Korean American authors whose works she analyzed. More specifically, Li indicated that Kim in *Clay Walls* (1987) and Keller in *Comfort Woman* (1997) tried to create a

170

discourse which conveys political and social meaning through personal histories and sought to depict the "unhomely" conditions of Korean immigrants in the United States in a vivid manner. She focused on how they used code switching to enrich the representation of Korean culture, community and nationality. See especially chapter 3 (pages 59-99): "Reasserting 'Home': Memory and Geography."

*Contents*: 1. Code Switching in Literary Discourse: An Introduction. 2. The "Unhomed" within the English Language. 3. Reasserting "Home": Memory and Geography. 4. Exploring a Silent Zone: The Untold Story. 5. Reclaiming Identity: Self-Narratives. 6. A Border Discourse: Novelty and Intertextuality. 7. Literary Code Switching and Asian American Literary Tradition: Conclusions. 12 figures. 11 tables. Bibliography: pp. 225-34. Appendices [A-B]: pp. 235-40.

19.

OH, Sandra Si Yun (1969- ).

***Martyrdom in Korean American Literature: Resistance and Paradox in East Goes West, Quiet Odyssey, Comfort Woman and Dictee.*** University of California at Berkeley [United States], 2001 (Ph.D. in Rhetoric). Adviser: Judith P. Butler. iii, 162p. DAI 63, no. 3 (Sept. 2002): 947-A; UMI 3044615.

Oh, a graduate of the University of California at Berkeley (B.A., 1992 and M.A., 1995), explored the "literary negotiation of identity" in *East Goes West* (1937), *Quiet Odyssey* (1990), and *Comfort Woman* (1997)—three works respectively by Younghill Kang (Kang Yong-hûl/Gang Yong-heul) (1903-1972), Mary Paik Lee (Paek Kwang-sôn/Baek Gwang Seon/Paik Kuang Sun) (1900-1995), and Nora Okja Keller (1965- ) that "celebrate the Korean national martyr of the colonial period." Her study "identified three interdependent but distinct elements that are fundamental to martyrdom: sacrifice, witness and spectacle." In chapter 3 (pages 91-143), she wrote that *Comfort Woman* reveals that "while the maimed body may serve to perpetuate oppressive, patriarchal regimes in an economy of spectacle and power, the way that the wounded body signifies within the spectacle is not fixed and can be appropriated for resistant purposes." Oh concluded her dissertation with an examination of martyrdom in Theresa Hak Kyung Cha's *Dictée* (1982) in which she "explored the limits and possibilities of the martyr figure as a resistant literary strategy and suggested that the martyr's predominance in Korean American literature could be attributed to its ability to reflect the paradoxical position of being a resistant colonized subject."

*Contents*: Introduction. 1. Sacrifice and the American Dream in Younghill Kang's *East Goes West*. 2. Strategic Witnessing in Mary Paik Lee's *Quiet Odyssey*. 3. Spectacle and the Body in Nora Okja Keller's *Comfort Woman*. Conclusion. Bibliography: pp. 160-62.

20.

SERAPHIM, Franziska (1965- ).

***Negotiating the Post-War: Politics and Memory in Japan, 1945-1995.*** Columbia University [United States], 2001 (Ph.D. in Japanese History). Adviser: Carol Gluck. xvii, 369p. DAI 61, no. 12 (June 2001): 4905-A; UMI 9998213.

Seraphim studied the "processes of appropriating selective memories of the past for specific political interests through the lens" of five national civic organizations that were established between 1946 and 1950 and that continued thereafter to participate actively in public life. Chapter 8 (pp. 270-317)—"Changing Geographies of Memory: War Responsibility for the Post-War"—includes her discussion of the lawsuits that former Korean "comfort women" filed in the early 1990s for formal recognition and compensation for their wartime suffering, the emergence of public attention to the compensation debate, the public pressure on the government from within and outside of Japan, and the "new type of organized memory—entered on the cross-national experience of individuals—that arose and summoned older special interests to a genuinely public contest." *Note*: A native of Germany, Seraphim also earned a B.A. in Asian Studies at the University of California at Berkeley (1991) and an M.A. in Japanese History (1992) at Columbia University, where she wrote a 68 page master's thesis entitled "The Debate about War Responsibility in Early Postwar Japan, 1945-1960."

*Contents*: Preface. Introduction: The Political Topography of Memory. Part One: Public Space for Private Memory. Introduction. 1. Politics of Essentialism: The Association of Shinto Shrines (Jinja honchô). 2. Fashioning National Heroes: The Japan Association of War-Bereaved Families (Nihon izokukai). 3. Forging Political Subjectivity: The Japan Teachers' Union (Nikkyôso). 4. People-to-People Diplomacy: The Japan-China Friendship Association (Nitchû yûkô kyôkai). 5. Commemorative Pacifism: The Japan Association for Memorializing Student-Soldiers Fallen in Battle (Wadatsumikai). Part Two: Memories of War in Public Contention. Introduction. 6. Relocating Okinawa: Shifting Dimensions of Memory in the Debate about Reversion. 7. Public Splits at Yasukuni Shrine: Organizing Memory vis-à-vis the State. 8. Changing Geographies of Memory: War Responsibility and the Post-War. Conclusion. Bibliography: pp. 333-69.

Published as *War Memory and Social Politics in Japan, 1945-2005*, by Franziska Seraphim. Cambridge, Mass.: Harvard University Asia Center, 2006. xv, 409p. (Harvard East Asian monographs, 278).

21.
TIEDEMANN, Heidi Janean (1971- ).
**After the Fact: Contemporary Feminist Fiction and Historical Trauma**. University of Toronto [Canada], 2001 (Ph.D. in English). Adviser: Jill L. Matus. 2, 3, 253p. DAI 62, no. 11 (May 2002): 3963-A; UMI NQ63656. Electronic (online) access: URL: http://www.nlc-bnc.ca/obj/s4/f2/dsk3/ftp04/NQ63656.pdf.

Tiedemann (also known as Heidi Tiedemann Darrach) examined the "connections between therapeutic discourses of psychic trauma, contemporary historical fiction, and feminist fiction and theory" by studying the efforts of five American and Canadian writers—Julia Alvarez (1950- ), Margaret Atwood (1939- ), Edwidge Danticat (1969- ), Nora Okja Keller (1965- ) and Joy Kogawa (1934- )—"to use historical fiction as a means of testifying to traumatic events of the past." See especially chapter 3 (pages 111-60)—"Transgenerational Trauma and Impossible Mourning in Joy Kogawa's *Obasan* and Nora Okja Keller's *Comfort Woman*"—in which she "analyzed theories of testimony and transgenerational trauma within the context of two novels that situate young daughters as the partial and inadequate witnesses to their mothers' suffering." Each of these novels "highlights the significance of rituals of mourning and commemoration in the wake of traumatic loss, and they suggest alternative modes of witnessing, notably an attentiveness to religious forms of witness" (through Korean shamanism in the case of *Comfort Woman*).

*Contents*: Introduction. 1. Contemporary Theories of Literary Testimony and Witnessing. 2. Hysteria and Traumatic Testimony in therapeutic Encounter: Margaret Atwood's *Alias Grace*. 3. Transgenerational Trauma and Impossible Mourning in Joy Kogawa's *Obasan* and Nora Okja Keller's *Comfort Woman*. 4. Surviving to Tell the Story: Julia Alvarez's *In the Time of the Butterflies* and Edwidge Danticat's *The Farming of Bones*. Conclusion. Bibliography: pp. 211-53.

## 2002

22.
BAE, Changmii [BAE, Chang-mi / PAE, Ch'ang-mi].
**The Symbolic Landscape of National Identity: Planning, Politics, and Culture in South Korea**. University of Southern California [United States], 2002 (Ph.D. in Urban and Regional Planning). Adviser: David C. Sloane. xiv, 288p. DAI 64, no. 6 (December 2003): 2282-A; UMI 3093734.

Bae, a student at the University of Southern California from 1991 to 2001, chronicled the history of the Government-General Building in Seoul (Chosôn Ch'ongdokpu Ch'ôngsa/Joseon Chongdokbu Cheongsa), a neo-classical, gray granite building that was constructed on the site of the Kyôngbok (Gyeongbok) Royal Palace, served as the headquarters of the Japanese colonial government, became the Capitol building housing the National Assembly under the first Republic of Korea, was transformed into the National Museum of Korea in 1983, and was demolished in 1995. "For many Koreans, it was the most important visible symbol of Japan's colonization of Korea." Bae "attempted to unravel the complex process of constructing national identity through the manipulation of this site." "The story of this building from its construction to its eventual destruction," she wrote, "is the articulation of the images of Korea from the pre-colonial to the post-colonial periods, reflecting Korea's changing political and economic context. The site's alteration is a projection of different and changing self-images." In the Prologue (pages x-xiv) to her dissertation, Bae discussed how she first read about the "comfort women" while in Seoul in 1995. She felt that their sad stories "alluded to the symbolic meaning" of the building and that Japan's colonial government house "bore some analogy to the brutal violation of Korean women by the Japanese military." Critical of the "collective apathy" to and the "long lapse in the public recognition" of the women's plight, Bae chose to explore the history of the building "from the critical perspective of women's issues in Korea"—issues that were not explicitly referred to but rather became "a silent subtext" to her dissertation.

*Contents*: Prologue. 1. Introduction. 2. National Identity and Post-Colonial. 3. Kyongbok Palace and Pre-Colonial Seoul. 4. The Japanese Government House and the Colonial Transformation of Seoul: 1910-1945. 5. Chungang Cheong as the Capital Hall of Post-Colonial

South Korea. 6. National Museum of Korea. 7. Identity, Politics and Space: The Demolition of the CCC [Chosôn Ch'ongdokpu Ch'ôngsa]. Conclusion. 32 figures and maps. Bibliography: pp. 274-88.


23.

DENNEHY, Kristine (1966- ).

***Memories of Colonial Korea in Postwar Japan.*** University of California at Los Angeles [United States], 2002 (Ph.D. in History). Adviser: Miriam R. Silverberg. viii, 227p. DAI 63, no. 10 (Apr. 2003): 3676-A; UMI 3066440.

Dennehy, a graduate of Georgetown University (B.S. in Japanese, 1988) and Jôchi Daigaku [Sophia University] in Tokyo (M.A. in Asian Studies, 1991), "traced the historical formation of competing evaluations of the colonial period (1910-1945) between 1945 and 1965 in order to show how different groups of Japanese intellectuals and political activists critiqued Japan's imperialist past in Korea and argued for the significance of their scholarship within the context of the efforts to fulfill the promise of a new postwar democratic order in Japan." Among them were Japanese historians, former colonial officials in Korea, and intellectuals of Korean descent in postwar Japan. One of Dennehy's contentions was that "a number of these intellectuals constructed new narratives of colonial Korean history as a way to condemn continuities from Japan's prewar and wartime past, such as the discriminatory Japanese policies and attitudes towards Koreans" (e.g., fingerprinting). Former colonial officials, on the other hand, exerted efforts from the late 1950s onwards "to establish archives of historical materials and a body of scholarship that would vindicate their record in colonial Korea." In chapter 6 (pages 182-206)—"Conclusion"—Dennehy briefly discussed the Korean "comfort women" issue, which she characterized as yet "another manifestation of the controversial nature of evaluations of Japan's imperialist past in Korea," the work of various groups to convene the Women's International War Crimes Tribunal on Japan's Military Sexual Slavery in Tokyo in December 2000, and the negative Japanese reactions to it. Dennehy based part of her dissertation research on the holdings of the Gordon W. Prange Collection at the University of Maryland, College Park Libraries.

*Contents*: 1. Introduction. 2. Marxist Responses to Colonialist Historiography. 3. Resident Korean Narratives of a Unified Korea. 4. "Accurate" Histories of Colonial Korea. 5. Korean History as a Form of Political Resistance. 6. Conclusion. Bibliography: pp. 207-27.


24.

DOOTSDEEMALACHANOK THONGTHIRAJ [THONGTHIRAJ, Dootsdeemalachanok] (1971- ).

***Words and Acts of Rage: Resisting the Sex Industry in Asian American Literature and Film.*** University of California at Los Angeles [United States], 2002 (Ph.D. in English). Advisers: King-Kok Cheung and Sonia Saldívar-Hull. xiii, 224p. DAI 64, no. 1 (July 2003): 146-A; UMI 3078116.

This dissertation by a Thai American student is a comparative study of Asian American fiction that "questions the stereotype of Asian prostitutes as passive victims." Chapter 4 (pages

155-209)—"'Rhythmic Rustlings' and Other Acts of Resistance in Nora Okja Keller's *Comfort Woman*" (1997)—"discusses how marginal spaces and discourses in the novel *Comfort Woman* express Keller's radical vision of defiant Korean 'comfort women.' She first imagines how nonverbal gestures and songs encoded with subversive messages circumvent enforced silence and isolation. Keller then creates a Korean shamanist world that defies a history of domination." *Note*: Dootsdeemalachanok, a native of Pasadena, California, also earned both a B.A. in Women's Studies (1994) and an M.A. in English (1997) at UCLA.

*Contents*: Introduction. 1. Memories, Mirrors, and Self-Discovery in Etsuko Kizawa's *NY Geisha*. 2. Self-Preservation and Asian Male Sex Workers in Russell Leong's *Phoenix Eyes*. 3. Rediscovering Selves, Reinscribing Lives: The Daily Writings of Evelyn Lau and Wanwadee Larsen. 4. "Rhythmic Rustlings" and Other Acts of Resistance in Nora Okja Keller's *Comfort Woman*. Epilogue. Bibliography: pp. 215-24.

25.

LEE, Myung-Sook [YI, Myeong-suk / YI, Myông-suk] (1950- ).

**From Silence to Speaking: A Pastoral Approach to Empowering Voices of Korean Female Survivors of Sexual Abuse.** Claremont School of Theology [formerly known as School of Theology at Claremont] [United States], 2002 (Ph.D. in Theology and Personality: Pastoral Care and Counseling). Adviser: William M. Clements. vii, 226p. DAI 65, no. 10 (Apr. 2005): 3849-A. Contact the Claremont School of Theology Library (1325 North College Ave., Claremont, Calif. 91711, U.S.A.) for information regarding the availability of copies (call number CST DISSERTATIONS A 2002 L4).

Lee "explored the subjective experiences of four female survivors of sexual abuse, one of the most widespread forms of violence against women, and developed a pastoral context for working with such individuals in the Korean Christian church community." Her primary objective was to "enable pastors to use their gifts in pastoral care both to minister personally to survivors of sexual abuse and to mobilize the laity to provide care to the wounded." Lee based part of her study on intensive personal interviews that covered the women's "family backgrounds, the nature of their abuse, its effect, their decision to break their silence, their religious concerns, their current status and their future life plans." She also developed "a model of survivor groups, with a focus on life stories, for the purpose of empowering the voices of sexual abuse survivors." Chapter 2 (pages 19-38)—"Female Survivors of Sexual Abuse in Korean Literature"—presents a review of the treatment of sexual abuse in feminist and sociological studies, studies in counseling, and studies in Christian religion in order to see the "cultural context of sexual abuse and to establish the present status of this study in relation to existing research of sexually abused women (i.e., 'comfort women') in Korea."

*Contents*: 1. Introduction. 2. Female Survivors of Sexual Abuse in Korean Literature. 3. A Profile: Stories of Sexual Abuse Survivors. 4. Sufferings of Korean Female Survivors of Sexual Abuse and Their Needs for Healing. 5. The Power of Telling the Truth and Its Implications for Survivors of Sexual Abuse. 6. Pastoral Theological and Care Issues Related to Survivors of Sexual Abuse. 7. Conclusion. Appendices [A-C]: pp. 210-13. Bibliography: pp. 214-26.

26.

PARK, Chong Kuk  [BAK, Jong-guk / PAK, Chong-guk]  (1960- ).

**Incorporating a Critical Theological Perspective into Korean Christian Broadcasting in California**.  San Francisco Theological Seminary [United States], 2002 (D.Min. in Advanced Pastoral Studies).  Adviser: Warren Wokyeng Lee.  107p.  No published abstract.  Park's dissertation is housed at the Graduate Theological Union's branch library on the San Francisco Theological Seminary campus. Contact the Graduate Theological Union Library (2400 Ridge Road, Berkeley, Calif. 94709-1212, U.S.A.) for information regarding the availability of copies (call number BV655.2.C35 P37 2002 SFTS).

Park sought to improve the quality of Christian broadcasting to the Korean American community in California—broadcasting that he criticized for being "by and large fundamentalistic and simplistic" in nature—by "incorporating a critical theological perspective in its programming" that would "address the deep and complex intellectual, emotional and spiritual needs of the Korean immigrants who were struggling to survive in their new host society." To that end, he produced five new radio programs in Korean that addressed the following key issues: "the relations between the African American and Korean American communities, the generation gap, youth identity problems, human sexuality, and the plight of the Korean 'comfort women.'"

*Contents*: 1. Social Analysis Step. 2. Theological Resources Step. 3. The Critical Theological Project of Korean Christian Broadcasting. 4. Conclusion. Figures. Bibliography: pp. 104-07.

27.

YAMAZAKI, Jane Welton  (1942- ).

**A Nation Apologizes: Japanese Apologies for World War II**.  Wayne State University [United States], 2002 (Ph.D. in Communication: Speech Communication).  Adviser: Mary M. Garrett.  vi, 331p.  DAI 63, no. 3 (Sept. 2002): 929-A; UMI 3047596. The abstract of this dissertation has also been published in the journal *Japanese Language and Literature* 36, no. 2 (October 2002): 281-82.

Yamazaki "examined the phenomenon of national apology for historical wrongdoing from a rhetorical perspective" with particular consideration of a number of Japanese government apologies that were made between 1984 and 1995. Her findings included three motives for such apologies, one of which—the restoration of a relationship—corresponded to "apologies to specific nation-states such as Korea." See especially chapter 3 (pages 90-136), which focuses on Emperor Hirohito's apologies to Presidents Chun Doo Hwan (1984) and Roh Tae Woo (1990) as well as on Prime Minister Kaifu Toshiki's apology to President Roh (1990); and chapter 4 (pages 137-90), which deals in part with the controversy over Japanese apologies, the extent to which they succeeded or failed, and the question of compensation to the wartime "comfort women," many of whom were Korean. *Note*: In addition to her doctorate, Yamazaki earned a B.A. in Mathematics (1964) at the College of Wooster in Wooster, Ohio; the degree of Master of Arts in Teaching [M.A.T.] (1965) at Northwestern University; and an M.A. in East Asian History (1976) at the University of Virginia, where she wrote a 73 page master's thesis entitled "Disaster, Rumor, and Prejudice: The Korean Massacre during the 1923 Kanto Earthquake."

*Contents*: Introduction. 1. Literature Review. 2. Accusations, Accusers and Audience. 3. The Early Apologies: Repairing Relationships. 4. The Crisis Apology: "comfort women." 5. Hosokawa Apologizes: Learning from the Past. 6. The Anti-Apologies: Conservative Apologia. 7. Murayama Apology on the 50th Anniversary of the War: The Transcendent Apology. 8. Conclusions. Appendices [A-B]: pp. 273-306. Bibliography: pp. 307-28.

Revised and updated version published as *Japanese Apologies for World War II: A Rhetorical Study*, by Jane W. Yamazaki. London and New York: Routledge, 2006. x, 196p. (Routledge contemporary Japan series, 3).

## 2003

28.

BERNER, Heike (1970- ).

***Home Is Where the Heart Is? Identity and Belonging in Asian American Literature***. Ruhr-Universität Bochum [Ruhr University of Bochum] [Germany], 2003 (Dr. phil., Fakultät für Philologie). Adviser: David D. Galloway. 229, 1p. No published abstract. Contact the library of the Ruhr University of Bochum (Universitätsbibliothek Bochum, Universitätsstrasse 150, 44801 Bochum, Germany) for information regarding the availability of copies (call number Universitätsbibliothek UB22487). Electronic (online) access: URL: http://www-brs.ub.ruhr-uni-bochum.de/netahtml/HSS/Diss/BernerHeike/diss.pdf. URN: urn:nbn:de:hbz:294-7426.

Berner "described and analyzed the major trends that occurred in theoretical discussion about the concepts of identity and belonging in Asian America, as well as their reflection in Asian American literature" since the 1960s in particular. In chapter 5 (pages 104-87)— "Korean America"—she examined Nora Okja Keller's *Comfort Woman* (1997), Chang-rae Lee's *Native Speaker* (1995), and three novels by Leonard Chang: *The Fruit 'n Food* (1996), *Dispatches from the Cold* (1998), and *Over the Shoulder* (2001). Berner also discussed "identity and the self" in the art of Jean Shin (1971- ), Young Chung (1972- ), Yong Soon Min (1953- ), and Kyungmi Shin (1963- ); and sketched the "role of Korean history in contemporary Korean American literature and the visual arts." In her discussion of *Comfort Woman*, she focused on Keller's "elaborate narrative strategies"—including "the interplay between content and narrative technique" and the "influence of the act of narration on the depiction of the mother-daughter relation and the questions of identity and belonging." *Note*: In addition to her doctorate, Berner earned both an M.A. in European Studies (1994) at Katholieke Universiteit Leuven [Catholic University of Leuven] in Belgium and an M.A. in American Studies (1998) at Ruhr-Universität Bochum, where she wrote a 109 page master's thesis entitled "How Charlie Chan Died and What Became of Him Afterwards: On Identity in Asian American Literature."

*Contents*: 1. Introduction. 2. Discourses on Identity in Asian America. 3. Identity and Belonging in Asian American Classics. 4. Contemporary Chinese and Japanese American Literature: A Few Examples. 5. Korean America. 6. Current Stereotypes. 7. Conclusion. 44 plates. Bibliography: pp. 215-29.

29.

CARROLL, Hamilton Ely Marsden (1969- ).

**Narrating the Postnational: Fictions of Citizenship at the Limits of the Nation**. Indiana University [United States], 2003 (Ph.D. in English and American Studies). Adviser: Eva Cherniavsky. viii, 194, 4p. DAI 65, no. 5 (November 2004): 1778-A; UMI 3133858.

This analysis of "a range of contemporary American films and fictional texts" dealing with "citizenship, subjectivity, and nation examines how shifting relations between the nation and the state are rendered in contemporary the U.S. cultural forms." Chapter 1 (pages 12-47)— "Traumatic Patriarchy"—argues that Chang-rae Lee's 1999 novel *A Gesture Life* "critically engages issues of gender and immigrant subject formation as it rewrites a paradigmatic immigration and assimilation narrative in a transnational frame." In so doing, it "pivots on the failed assimilation narrative" of Doc Hata, "a Japanese-American male protagonist, staked against his traumatization" of Kkutaeh, a Korean "comfort woman" and later on of his adopted Korean American daughter. *Note*: In addition to his doctorate, Carroll earned both a B.A. (1997) and an M.A. (1997) degree in English at Emory University, where he wrote a 73 page master's thesis entitled "Breaking the (Post) code: A Hypertext Exploration of Freud, Lacan, and Derrida."

*Contents*: Introduction. Section One: The Subject of Miscegenation: Constructing Citizenship and the Crisis of Interiority. 1. Traumatic Patriarchy: Reading Gendered Nationalisms in Chang-rae Lee's *A Gesture Life*. 2. The Glyph of the Father: Monstrous Reproduction, Race, and Nation in *Blade*. 3. "Forget the Alamo": National Historiography and Post-Oedipal Interventions in John Sayles' *Lone Star*. Section Two: Border Logics: Mapping the Nation at Its Limits. 4. Tourism and Territory: Constructing the Nation in John Sayles's *Men with Guns* (*Hombres Armados*). 5. "Against the Grain of Time": Mapping a Postnational Cartography in Leslie Marmon Silko's *Almanac of the Dead*. Epilogue: Romancing the Nation: Male Sentimentality and the National Domestic in Steven Soderbergh's *Traffic*. 14 figures. Bibliographical footnotes.

30.

CHO, Sungran [CHO, Sông-nan / JO, Seong-nan] (1957- ).

**Mourning Work: Historical Trauma and the Women on the Cross(road): Readings in Modern Women Writers of the Diaspora**. State University of New York at Buffalo [also officially known as University at Buffalo since 1962] [United States], 2003 (Ph.D. in English). Adviser: Roy Roussel. xi, 150p. DAI 63, no. 12 (June 2003): 4311-A; UMI 3076472.

In chapter 2 (pages 64-105)—an analysis of Nora Okja Keller's novel *Comfort Woman* (1997)—Cho "explored the effect of historical trauma through the next generation in the figure of the daughter, in the form of transgenerational haunting." She indicated that Keller "portrayed both the liberation of a 'comfort woman' from her closeted life" and the "material legacy of unwritten history that is discovered and excavated by the future generation in her rendering of the daughter's discovery of her dead mother's past, recorded in a cassette tape."

*Contents*: Introduction: Mourning, Burial, PostColonial *Unheimlich*. 1. Hysteria, a House, and the Measure of Dwelling in Toni Morrison's *Beloved*. 2. Mourning Work: Shame, Trauma, and Speech Acts in Nora Okja Keller's *Comfort Woman*. 3. Luci(fer)'s Tears: The Ambivalence of Post-Colonial Hospitality and Post-Exilic Eminence in Jamaica Kincaid's *Lucy*. Bibliography: pp. 148-50.

31.

HO, Jennifer Ann (1970- ).

**Consumption and Identity in Asian American Coming-of-Age Novels**. Boston University [United States], 2003 (Ph.D. in English). Adviser: Susan L. Mizruchi. x, 284p. DAI 63, no. 10 (Apr. 2003): 3553-A; UMI 3069263.

Ho, the recipient of degrees in English Literature from both the University of California at Santa Barbara (B.A., 1992) and Boston University (M.A., 1996), "examined theme of consumption in Asian American *Bildungsromane* with a focus on scenes of cooking and eating as representations of ethnic identity formation." Through the use of "four discrete modes of identification—historic pride, consumerism, mourning and fusion"—she examined "how Chinese, Japanese and Korean American adolescents challenged and revised their cultural legacies and experiment with alternative ethnic affiliations through their relationships to food." In chapter 3 (pages 104-42)—"Feeding the Spirit"—Ho "showed the relationship between food in rituals of mourning and the longing for an ethnic motherland in Lan Cao's *Monkey Bridge* (1997) and Nora Okja Keller's *Comfort Woman*" (1997).

*Contents:* Introduction: Feeding Identity, Subverting Stereotypes: Food and Consumption in Contemporary Asian American Bildungsromane. 1. Consuming Asian American History in Frank Chin's *Donald Duk*. 2. To Eat, To Buy, To Be: Consumption as Identity in Lois Ann Yamanaka's *Wild Meat and the Bully Burgers*. 3. Feeding the Spirit: Mourning for the Mother(land) in Lan Cao's *Monkey Bridge* and Nora Okja Keller's *Comfort Woman*. 4. Fusion Creations in Gus Lee's *China Boy* and Gish Jen's *Mona in the Promised Land*. Conclusion: Hungry for More? Bibliography: pp. 247-77.

Published as *Consumption and Identity in Asian American Coming-of-Age Novels*, by Jennifer Ann Ho. New York and London: Routledge, 2005. ix, 202p. (Studies in Asian Americans).

32.

JANG, Jennifer Leigh (1969- ).

**Redressing the Pained Body: The Politics of Sentimentality in Asian American Literature**. Brown University [United States], 2003 (Ph.D. in American Civilization). Advisers: Robert G. Lee and Daniel Y. Kim. viii, 190p. DAI 64, no. 4 (October 2003): 1255-A; UMI 3087280.

Jang, a graduate of Amherst College (B.A., 1991) and Brown University (M.A. in American Civilization, 1995), "claimed that Asian American literature has been and remains a deeply sentimental literature." In chapter 2 (pages 61-102), she compared three novels respectively by Lois-Ann Yamanaka (1961- ) (*Wild Meat and the Bully Burgers*), Patti Kim (1970- )

(*A Cab Called Reliable*) and Fae Myenne Ng (1956- ) (*Bone*). In chapter 3 (pages 103-47), in turn, Jang examined two Korean "comfort women" novels by Korean American writers—*Comfort Woman* (1997) by Nora Okja Keller (1965- ) and *A Gesture Life* (1997) by Chang-rae Lee (1965- )—to "show that while Asian American histories of exclusion and racism have resulted in an abundance of novels that spectacularize suffering, collective pain may be better represented through a focus upon the mundane and quotidian effects of violence."

*Contents*: Introduction. 1. Frank Chin and the Problem with Sympathy. 2. Not Their Mothers' Daughters: Reimagining the Gendered Logic of Origins. 3. Scenes of Subjection in Two "Korean 'Comfort Woman'" Novels. 4. So Someone Watching Can Cry Too: Violence and Sympathy in *Wild Meat and the Bully Burgers*. Bibliography: pp. 181-90.

33.
KIMURA, Maki (1969- ).

**Modernity, Testimonies, and Women's Agency: The Issue of "Comfort Women" of the Second World War.** University of London [United Kingdom], 2003 (Ph.D. in Gender Studies, London School of Economics and Political Science). Adviser: Anne Phillips. 336p. DAI 70/38: section C. EThOS Persistent ID: uk.bl.ethos.408539. Also DXN079813.

Kimura, the recipient of both a B.A. (1993) and an M.A. (1995) degree in Political Science from Waseda Daigaku [Waseda University] in Tokyo, approached the "comfort women" issue by "examining the relationship between modernity and the regulation of sexuality (including gender, race and the body)" and by "exploring the 'comfort women's' own testimonies." In chapter 4 (pages 128-80), she discussed the testimonies of a number of Korean women and Japanese soldiers, dealt with "some of the debates in Japan (from the 1990s onwards) concerning the reading of these testimonies." and argued that the women's testimonies should not be dealt with as "truth/fact" because their significance does not lie in their historical accuracy but rather in the way in which these women suffered through their ordeal. The testimonies covered the backgrounds of the "comfort women," how they were recruited and forced into having sex at the so-called "comfort stations," their living conditions and the violence that occurred there, and their lives afterwards. Chapter 5 (pages 181-216), in turn, focuses on the "methodological issues inherent in listening to testimonies and narratives including those raised in the feminist literature" in order to identify a better way for handling the "comfort women's" narratives, while chapter 6 (pages 217-61) addresses the question of how to "represent the voices of the women" as well as the "possibility of their true and transparent representations." *Note*: Kimura did not write any master's thesis.

*Contents*: 1. Introduction. 2. Modernity and Evil. 3. The Origin of Licensed Prostitution and Its Development in Japan. 4. Reading the Testimonies. 5. Listening to Women's Voices. 6. Representation and Its Limits. 7. Women's Agency. 8. Conclusion. Bibliography: pp. 297-336.

Revised and updated version published as *Unfolding the "Comfort Women" Debates: Modernity, Violence, Women's Voices*, by Maki Kimura. Houndmills, Basingstoke, Hampshire and New York: Palgrave Macmillan, 2016. vii, 283p. (Gender and sexualities in history).

34.

MORIOKA-STEFFENS, Tamayo Irene.

***Asian Pacific American Identities: An Historical Perspective through theatre Productions of the East West Players, 1965 to 2000.*** Claremont Graduate University [United States], 2003 (Ph.D. in History). Advisers: Elazar Barkan and Robert Dawidoff. x, 733p. DAI 64, no. 2 (August 2003): 626-A; UMI 3079312.

Through her analysis of the main stage production scripts—more precisely, the scripts, audiotapes, and videotapes—of the East West Players in Los Angeles as well as through her interviews of playwrights and company directors, Morioka-Steffens investigated the ways in which "particular aspects of Asian Pacific American identities were expressed over time through Asian Pacific American theater productions." Almost one-half of the company's 153 seasonal plays, revues and revivals were by and/or about Japanese Americans; twenty-five percent were by Chinese Americans; and nearly all of the remaining productions were by Filipino and Korean Americans—among them the playwrights Soon-Teck Oh (1943- ), Sung J. Rno (1967- ), and Chungmi Kim (1963- ). Premiered in 1999, Kim's *Hanako*, a full-length play about two elderly Korean women who were victimized as "comfort women" and who went to New York to protest and demonstrate for redress, expresses the domination and brutality that Korean women endured under Japanese colonial rule.

*Contents*: Preface. Introduction. 1. Contexts. 2. Origins. 3. Adaptations. 4. Obstacles. 5. Interactions. Conclusion. Photographs. Addendum [Content Listing of Plays, Chronology of Productions (and) Summary of Playwright Interviews]: pp. 691-715. Bibliography: pp. 716-33.

35.

NISHIMURA, Amy Natsue (1969- ).

***Talking in Pidgin and Silence: Local Writers of Hawai'i.*** University of Oregon [United States], 2003 (Ph.D. in Comparative Literature). Adviser: Linda Kintz. ix, 239p. DAI 64, no. 8 (February 2004): 2877-A; UMI 3102182.

Nishimura, a native of Honolulu, analyzed selected narratives and poems by Lee Tonouchi (1972- ), Lois-Ann Yamanaka (1961- ), Juliana Spahr (1966- ), Gary Pak (1952- ), R. Zamora Linmark (1968- ), Nora Okja Keller (1965- ) and Lisa Linn Kanae (1960- ) in order to "demonstrate how Pidgin, otherwise known as Hawaiian Creole English, has a diverse, working-class heritage" and "is representative of a polyvocal society." Focusing on two postwar local authors of Korean ancestry, chapter 3 (pages 115-74)—"Othered Voices of Local Literature"—discusses how Gary Pak and Nora Okja Keller respectively highlight fractures within the Local community in their novels *A Ricepaper Airplane* (1998) and *Comfort Woman* (1997) "at the same time as their texts attempt to define the desire for a cohesive Local community—a place that feels like their national homeland, a place that offers stability and comfort." In the course of writing about *Comfort Woman*, Nishimura pointed out that while the novel deals primarily with the issue of the Korean "comfort women," it "also acknowledges how Korean women in Hawaii had been objectified" and subjected to vicious stereotyping. *Note*: In addition to her doctorate, Nishimura earned a B.A. in English (1992) at the University of Hawaii at Manoa and an M.A. in English (1996) at California State Polytechnic at Pomona, where she wrote a 96 page master's thesis entitled "Examining the 'Restored' Editions of Richard Wright's Native Son and Black Boy."

*Contents*: Introduction: Negotiating the Local. 1. Imperialism and Hawaii's Dual Identities. 2. Local Writers: Pidgin Politics and Poetics. 3. Othered Voices of Local Literature: Gary Pak and Nora Okja Keller. 4. Lois-Ann Yamanaka's and Chris McKinney's Local Products of Hawai'i. Conclusion. Bibliography: pp. 223-39.

36.

VanRHEENEN, Beth  (1952- ).

***The Emergent Self: Identity, Trauma, and the Neo-Gothic in The Woman Warrior, Comfort Woman, Beloved, and Ceremony***. Wayne State University [United States], 2003 (Ph.D. in English). Adviser: Ross J. Pudaloff. iii, 231p. DAI 64, no. 12 (June 2004): 4469-A; UMI 3116545.

VanRheenen studied the "problems of identity formation—specifically, the social and psychological dimensions of establishing identity—in four ethnic American novels": Maxine Hong Kingston's *The Woman Warrior* (1976), Nora Okja Keller's *Comfort Woman* (1997), Toni Morrison's *Beloved* (1987), and Leslie Marmon *Silko's Ceremony* (1977). See especially chapter 3 (pages 64-121)—on Keller's *Comfort Woman*—in which she examined the disintegration of the protagonist's identity, due to the historical horrors of World War II, as well as her formation of a new identity through the spiritual forces that haunt and befriend her. *Note*: In addition to her doctorate, VanRheenen earned a B.A. in English (1974) at Harding University in Searcy, Arkansas, and an M.A. in English (1977) at the University of North Texas, where she wrote a 111 page master's thesis entitled "Edwin Shrake: An Introduction and Interpretation."

*Contents*: 1. Introduction. 2. *The Woman Warrior*. 3. *Comfort Woman*. 4. *Beloved*. 5. *Ceremony*. Bibliography: pp. 223-28.

## 2004

37.

CHUNG, Haeng-ja Sachiko  [CHÔNG, Haeng-ja / JEONG, Haeng-ja]  (1964- ).

***Performing Sex, Selling Heart: Korean Nightclub Hostesses in Japan***. University of California at Los Angeles [United States], 2004 (Ph.D. in Anthropology). Adviser: Mariko Tamanoi. xi, 464p. DAI 65, no. 9 (March 2005): 3436-A; UMI 3146620. Korean language abstract on pages 137-38 of *Han'guk yŏn'gu illyuhak paksa hagwi nonmun ch'orokchip (1949-2014)*, compiled and edited by O Myŏng-sŏk and the Department of Anthropology, Seoul National University. Sôul: Sôul Taehakkyo Illyu Hakkwa, 2016 = *Hanguk yeongu illyuhak baksa hagwi nonmun chorokjip (1949-2014)*, compiled and edited by O Myeong-seok, et al. Seoul: Seoul Daehakgyo Illyu Hakkwa, 2016 [A Collection of Abstracts of Doctoral Dissertations on Korea in the Field of Anthropology, 1949-2014].

Chung investigated the "emotional, sexual and ethnic work of Korean nightclub hostesses" in Japan, where they were "required to perform the contradictory roles of both displaying Korean ethnic characteristics and 'passing' as Japanese." She based her ethnographic study on several research methods including participant observation as a paid hostess, interviews, and library research at sites in Nagoya, Osaka and a few smaller cities, "using Arlie Russell Hochschild's model of emotional labor (emotion management of both others and oneself) and (post)colonial theories." In chapter 6 (pages 175-202), Chung introduced the voices of contemporary Korean hostesses in Japan and linked them with Korean sex slaves during the colonial period by highlighting "the continual sexual exploitation of Korean women." The "postcolonial reality" faced by Koreans in Japan, their continued treatment as second-class citizens, and the perpetuation of discriminatory practices against them are among the other themes that permeate her dissertation. *Note*: Chung, a native of Kyoto, earned both a B.A. in Korean Language (1987) and an M.A. in East Asian Studies (1989) at Ôsaka Gaikokugo Daigaku [Osaka University of Foreign Studies], where she wrote a master's thesis in Japanese entitled "Chôsengo no fukugo dôshi no keitaiteki imiteki bunrui ni yoru bunseki to sono ichi kôsatsu: '~komu' dôshi no taiô hyôgen o chûshin ni" [An Analysis of Korean Compound Verbs by Morphological and Semantic Classes and an Examination That Focuses on Corresponding Expressions with '-*komu*' Verbs].

*Contents*: Part One: My Story and Theories. 1. Introduction: Stories of Koreans in Japan. 2. Colonialism: Race/Ethnicity, Sexuality, Performance, and Psychology. 3. Theories of Emotional Labor. 4. The Ethnographer with Multiple Identities: From (Native) Anthropologist to Call Girl? Part Two: History of Sex Work. 5. Modern History of Sex Work in Japan. 6. From Sex Slaves to Nightclub Hostesses. 7. Sex Tourism and Transnational Migration. Part Three: Club Rose as Transnational Space and Postcolonial Reality. 8. Sex Tourism and Transnational Migration. 9. System of Desire, Kinds of Work. 10. Workers at Club Rose: Gender, Hierarchy, Visa, and Income. Part Four: Emotional Labor and Sex Work Without Sex. 11. Visa Rhapsody: Migrant Koreans. 12. Hostessing: Emotional Labor and Sex Without Sex. 13. Psychological Impacts of Colonialism and Emotional Labor. 14. Conclusion: The Korean Returned to the United States. 15 tables. Bibliography: pp. 416-64.


38.

EFIRD, Robert Arthur (1967- ).

***Japan's War Orphans and New Overseas Chinese: History, Identification and (Multi)ethnicity***. University of Washington [United States], 2004 (Ph.D. in Anthropology). Advisers: Ann Anagnost and Stevan Harrell. iii, 206p. DAI 65, no. 10 (Apr. 2005): 3884-A; UMI 3151601.

Efird, the recipient of a B.A. in Socio-Cultural Anthropology (1990) from Yale University, an M.A. in Regional Studies: East Asia (1994) from Harvard University, and an M.A. in Anthropology (1998) from the University of Washington, studied the historical circumstances, the "belated 'repatriation' to Japan." and the "difficulties of the post-settlement lives" of the children of Japanese parentage who were stranded in China at the end of World War II. In the course of discussing the claims for adequate financial compensation which these war orphans lodged against the Japanese government, Efird repeatedly referred to the government's legal responsibility for the establishment and management of military brothels and the recruitment and treatment of the "comfort women" because in both cases the "responsibility lay with the state that prosecuted the war." *Note*: Efird did not write any master's thesis.

*Contents*: 1. Introducing the War Orphans. 2. Japan's "War Orphans" and the Loss of the Past. 3. Japanese Volunteers and the War Orphans. 4. Re-presenting War Orphan Narratives. 5. Repatriate Youth and Multiethnic Japan(ese). 6. Repatriates and Patriots: War Orphans and Japan's "New Overseas Chinese." 7. Beyond Ethnicity to. . . Advocacy? Bibliography: pp. 195-205.

39.
KIM, Hyunjung  [GIM, Hyeon-jung / KIM, Hyôn-jung]  (1970- ).
**Choreographies of Gender and Nationalism in Contemporary South Korean Dance**.  University of California at Riverside [United States], 2004 (Ph.D. in Dance History and Theory).  Adviser: Jacqueline Shea Murphy.  xi, 221p.  DAI 65, no. 10 (Apr. 2005): 3607-A; UMI 3151712.

"Expanding the definition of 'Korean dance' within the context of cultural nationalism." Kim showed "how contemporary Korean dancers (re)claimed agency in creating contemporary Korean identity and how their choreography opened up the possibility for a bodily (re)writing of gendered and subaltern histories." In particular, she examined "four major trends of cultural nationalism"; indicated "how choreographers and dancers embodied, theorized, and in some ways redirected the complex, layered history of (post)colonialism"; and "addressed the gendered context of Korean nationalism in the concert form" of the traditional Korean dance known as *salp'uri (salpuri)*. Kim based part of her research on "careful readings" of *Gut-Play* (2001) by An Ae-sun (Ahn Ae-soon), *Willow: The Tree of Life* (1996) by Kang Mi-ri (Gang Mi-ri), and *Here Myself Alone* (1997) and *Où Vont-Ils Comme Ça* (1997) by Kim Yông-hûi (Gim Yeong-hui/Kim Young-hee). And in chapter 3 (pages 102-44), where she expanded on the "notion of shamanism and *salp'uri*" and "reinvigorated new forms of healing and exorcism." she drew upon shamanic elements to "reinvent a new form of healing for 'comfort women' in her performance." *Note*: In addition to her doctorate, Kim earned both a B.A. (1993) and an M.A. (1995) degree in Dance at Ewha Woman's University in Seoul.

*Contents*: Introduction. 1. Spirituality-Based Anticolonial Nationalism. 2. Institutionalized, Gendered Nationalism. 3. Redirected Gendered Nationalism. 4. Aggressive, Internationalized, Global Nationalism. 29 figures. Bibliography: pp. 201-21.

40.
KIM, Nami.
**Constructing "Asian Women": A Critical Examination of Cultural-Theological Rhetoric**.  Harvard University [United States], 2004 (Th.D. in Religion, Gender and Culture, Harvard Divinity School).  Adviser: Elisabeth Schussler Fiorenza.  ix, 247p.  DAI 66, no. 1 (July 2005): 219-A; UMI 3160341.

Kim, the recipient of both a B.A. (1991) and an M.A. (1993) degree in Christian Studies from Ewha Woman's University in Seoul and the degree of Master of Divinity [M.Div.] (1996) from the Candler School of Theology at Emory University, examined the "homogeneous category of 'Asian women' in various cultural and theological discourses" and called for a reassessment of its use in Christian feminist theology because it inadvertently treated Asian women as "an historical monolithic group" and "discursively constructed them as helpless victims of oppression." In chapter 2 (pages 59-117), a critical examination of Japan's military comfort system, she demonstrated the difficulty of using this category since "hierarchically structured differences" among "Asian women" existed along the axes of race/ethnicity, class, and nationality under Japanese colonial rule. Kim endeavored to show this by interweaving the testimonies of former "comfort women" with an analysis of various scripts that she called "scripts of denial, scripts of universalization and scripts of nationalism"—scripts which "discursively construct Japan's military comfort system differently by legitimizing it or denouncing it for various purposes." Unlike the stereotypical portrayal of Asian women, she noted, the "comfort women" were "speaking subjects who broke the 'collusion of silence.' "In addition, Kim discussed how a feminist analysis "exposed the interlocking structures of domination that produced the differences among Asian women along the lines of nationality, race/ethnicity and class." *Note*: Kim is also the author of a master's thesis at Ewha Woman's University (1993) entitled "Kot'onge taehan sinhakchôk ihae: maemannûn yôsông ûi kyônghôme kûn'gô haesô" ("Gotonge daehan sinhakjeok ihae: maemanneun yeoseong ui gyeongheome geungeo haeseo") [A Theological Understanding of Suffering: Based on the Experiences of "Battered Women"].

*Contents*: Introduction. 1. Problematizing the Category of "Asian Women." 2. Japan's Military Sexual Slavery ("comfort women"). 3. Oppression of "Asian/Eastern/Oriental Women" and "Ethnic Religion(s)" in the Missionary and the Contemporary Feminist Discourses. 4. A Genealogy of the Unifying Category of "Asian" in Asian Theology. Conclusion: Toward a Critical Global Feminist Theology. Bibliography: pp. 234-47.

41.
LIND, Jennifer Mary (1969- ).
***Sorry States: Apologies in International Politics***. Massachusetts Institute of Technology [United States], 2004 (Ph.D. in Political Science). Adviser: Barry R. Posen. 436p. DAI 65, no. 9 (March 2005): 3555-A. Electronic (online) access: URL: http://hdl.handle.net/1721.1/28500. Copies may also be ordered from the Microreproduction Laboratory, MIT Libraries, Room 14-0551, Cambridge, Mass. 02139-4307 (U.S.A.).

Lind "outlined an 'apology theory' of international politics" in which she "posited that a state's policies of remembrance affect the perception of its intentions in the eyes of other states and thereby influence the degree to which others see it as threatening." She tested this theory in two empirical case studies—the South Korean threat perception of Japan, and the French threat perception of Germany—and in two mini-cases involving Australia and China. See especially chapter 3 (pages 135-214)—"The Effects of Remembrance in Japan-ROK

Relations"—in which Lind examined the "negative effect that Japan's consistently unapologetic policies of remembrance (glorification and denial)" relating to the colonization of Korea and Japanese actions during World War II (notably in regard to the "comfort women" issue) had on "South Korean perceptions of Japanese intentions" and studied "the relative importance of remembrance, relative to other factors" such as "the reassuring presence of the U.S. offshore balancer" in the South Korean perception of Japan as a threat. *Note*: In addition to her doctorate, Lind earned a B.A. in English (1991) at the University of California at Berkeley and the degree of Master in Pacific International Affairs [M.P.I.A.] (1996) at the University of California at San Diego. She did not write any master's thesis.

*Contents*: Introduction. 1. The Apology Theory. [Part One:] Asia. 2. Japanese Remembrances since World War II. 3. The Effects of Remembrance in Japan-ROK Relations. 4. Japanese Remembrances and Perceptions in China and Australia. [Part Two:] Europe. 5. German Remembrance since World War II. 6. The Effects of German Apologies in Franco-German Relations. Conclusion. 6 figures. 11 tables. Bibliography: pp. 419-36.

Published as *Sorry States: Apologies in International Politics*, by Jennifer Lind. Ithaca, NY, and London: Cornell University Press, 2008. x, 242p. (Cornell studies in security affairs).


42.

MILLER, Christopher Hill (1965- ).

**Exile and Recuperation in the Postmodern Novel**. University of South Carolina [United States], 2004 (Ph.D. in English). Adviser: David G. Cowart. iii, 225p. DAI 65, no. 12 (June 2005): 4559-A; UMI 3157169.

Miller, a graduate of the University of North Carolina at Chapel Hill (B.A. in English, 1987) and North Carolina State University (M.A. in English, 1991), studied the plots of exile in the postmodern novels and autobiographies of Chang-rae Lee (1965- ) and eleven other authors. See especially chapter 10 (pages 158-83)—"Silently Articulating the Future of the Past in the Present: Chang-rae Lee's *A Gesture Life*"—in which Miller refers to Korean "comfort women" in the course of analyzing the "frequent paradigm of exile and recuperation in the isolation of the protagonist (a Japanese émigré named Franklin Hata), in his literal and figurative exile, and in the diminishing recuperations he attempts following World War II."

*Contents*: 1. Introduction. 2. Exiles and Imperialists: Don DeLillo's *The Names*. 3. The National Unconscious: Walter Abish's Palimpsest of Modern Germany. 4. Gynesic Sorties into the Archaeology of Exile: Kathy Acker's Parodic Quests and Questors. 5. Interpellation and Nostalgia: Michael Ondaatje's *The English Patient*. 6. White Mythologies and Memories of Memories: Richard Powers' *Galatea 2.2*. 7. Simulacra and Cyberspace: The Precession of Exile and Recuperation in William Gibson's *Neuromancer*. 8. The Present Like a Palimpsest, Written over the Past Imperfect: Jamaica Kincaid's *Lucy*. 9. Exiles and Returns in Divided Home and Mother Lands: Edwidge Danticat's *Breath, Eyes, Memory*. 10. Silently Articulating the Future of the Past in the Present: Chang-rae Lee's *A Gesture Life*. 11. Women's Exilic Autobiography: Judith Ortiz Cofer, Maxine Hong Kingston, and Le Ly Hayslip. 12. Conclusion. Bibliography: pp. 215-25.

43.

PARK, Jung Woo (Hugo)  [BAK, Jeong-u / PAK, Chông-u]  (1965- ).

**The Korean Catholic Church and Feminism: A Study of Four Korean Catholic Feminist Groups and Their Members**. Fordham University [United States], 2004 (Ph.D. in Sociology). Adviser: James R. Kelly. vi, 290, 3p. DAI 65, no. 3 (Sept. 2004): 1126-A; UMI 3125023.

Park, an ordained Catholic priest of the Archdiocese of Seoul, a 1987 graduate (B.Th.) of the Catholic University of Korea in Seoul, and a recipient of the degree of M.A. in Sociology (1998) from Fordham University, used both a survey questionnaire and in-depth interviews to "examine the feminist consciousness" of the members of four Catholic Korean feminist groups: The Korean Catholic Women's Community for a New World (Sesang ûl Yônûn Ch'ônjugyo Yôsông Tongch'e/Sesang eul Yeoneun Cheonjugyo Yeoseong Dongche), The Women's Community in the Sisters Association in Korea (Han'guk Yôja Sudohoe Changsang Yônhaphoe/Hanguk Yeoja Sudohoe Jangsang Yeonhaphoe), The Catholic Women's Research Institute of Korea (Kat'ollik Yôsông Yôn'guwôn/Gatollik Yeoseong Yeonguwon), and The Association of Catholic Feminist Theologians (Kat'ollik Yôsông Sinhakhoe/Gatollik Yeoseong Sinhakhoe). He "examined the sociocultural factors that contributed to the emergence of Korean Catholic feminism and to the formation" of these groups; studied the membership, "perspectives, goals and aspirations of each group" their activities and their problems, their interrelationships, and "their relationships with Church authority"; and investigated the "consciousness of the members of these groups in terms of their identity as Catholics and as feminists." Park addressed the issue of the "comfort women" on pages 93-95 of chapter 3—"The Origins and Backgrounds of the Korean Catholic Feminist Movement: The Modern Feminist Movement in Korea: The Chongsindae"—and in chapter 4 (pages 104-98) while discussing the involvement of these four groups in various social issues.

*Contents*: Introduction. 1. Literature Review and Theoretical Approaches. 2. Methodology. 3. The Origins and Backgrounds of the Korean Catholic Feminist Movement. 4. The Four Korean Catholic Feminist Groups. 5. Korean Catholic Feminist Women and Feminism. 6. Conclusions. Bibliography: pp. 258-69. Appendices [A-D]: pp. 270-90.

44.

PARK, Soyang  [BAK, So-yang / PAK, So-yang]  (1972- ).

**The Visual Culture of Haunting in Post Colonial Korea**. University of London [United Kingdom], 2004 (Ph.D. in Historical and Cultural Studies, Goldsmiths College). Adviser: Howard Caygill.  364p. DAI 74, no. 9: section C. EThOS Persistent ID: uk.bl.ethos.406551.

Originally submitted under the title "The Visual Culture of Haunting: The Ethics and Aesthetics of the Real in Modern South Korea." this dissertation explores "the history and psychology of the Minjung Realist Art and Culture Movement that emerged during the democratization period of the 1980s and early 1990s." Dealing with works by such artists and filmmakers as Im Ok-sang (Im Ok-sang/Lim Oksang) (1950- ), O Yun (O Yun/Oh Yoon) (1946-1986), Pyôn Yông-ju (Byeon Yeong-ju/Byun Youngjoo) (1966- ), and Yi Kyông-sin (Yi

Gyeong-sin/Lee Gyeong-sin/Lee Kyungsin) (1968- ), Park examined "how the emergent culture—a 'visual culture of haunting'—was instigated and formed by numerous haunted subjects and the return of repressed memories." Her study also explored "how repressed and silenced 'subaltern' groups, especially the former Korean comfort women, gradually came into historical light as they provided their testimonies in this emergent cultural and political milieu." Chapter 4 (pages 187-234) introduces the testimonies of Kim Haksun (Gim Hak-sun/Kim Hak-soon) (1924-1997) and Kim Yunsim (Gim Yun-sim) through which Park traced "the remarkable shift in the subjectivity of these 'comfort women' from a body of shame to a body of responsibility" and examined the role of the feminist intellectuals who worked with them. Chapter 5 (pages 235-305), in turn, introduces and analyzes the process whereby Pyŏn's documentary films *Najûn Moksori 1* and *2 (Najeun Moksori 1* and *2/Nazen Moksori 1* and *2*) (1995)—films which "witness the innermost voices and life performances of these women"— were produced, and discusses over one hundred paintings made by three "comfort women" survivors: Kang Tôk-kyông (Gang Deok-gyeong/Kang Duk-kyung) (1929-1997), Kim Sun-dôk (Gim Sun-deok/Kim Sun-duk) (1921-2004) and Yi Yong-nyô (Yi Yong-nyeo/Lee Yong-nyeo) (1926-2013). *Note*: Park earned a B.A. in Science of Art at Hongik University (Seoul) in 1995 and an M.A. in History of Art (Twentieth Century) at the University of London's Goldsmiths College in 1999. Her master's thesis dealt with minjung art and included a discussion of the works of Im Ok-sang and O Yun; however, a copy of it is not currently available.

*Contents*: 1. Theorizing the Visual Culture of Haunting: Ethics and Aesthetics in Postcolonial Korea in the 1980s and 1990s. 2. The Haunting of the "Real": The Works of Lim Oksang and Oh Yoon. 3. The Vision of Haunting: The Vision Machine of *Han*. 4. Silence, Subaltern Speech, and The Intellectual. 5. Trauma, Transference, and Representation: A Reading of Film, *Nazen Moksori* and Paintings of The Former Sexual Slave Women. 6. The Work of Memory and Progress. 81 figures Bibliography: pp. 331-45. Color Figures: pp. 353-64.


45.
WAHNG, Selena.
***The "Illogics" of Masculine Deterritorialization: Asian and Asian American Racial Performativities, Regendered Embodiments, and Collective Assemblages of Enunciation.*** New York University [United States], 2004 (Ph.D. in Performance Studies). Adviser: José Esteban Muñoz. iii, 582p. DAI 65, no. 3 (Sept. 2004): 1148-A; UMI 3127505.

Wahng "juxtaposed two sites—Korean sex slaves for the Japanese Imperial Army during World War II, and Asian American female-to-male transgendered masculinities in relation to visuality and sexual penetrability—in order to examine the specific performances of racializations within each site and how these racializations inform, and are informed by, embodied gendered experiences and acts of testimonies and discourses." Chapters 3 and 4 (pages 182-338) "organize and examine phenomenologically unique aspects of Korean wartime sex slaves as separate assemblages through an analysis of their testimonies and personal narratives" and an examination of such assemblages as the "provision of masculinized military clothing as the 'uniform' for military sex slaves" and the "feminization of Japanese military prostitutes in contrast to the defeminization and masculinization of Korean sex slaves."

*Contents*: 1. Introduction: Deterritorializations and Rhizomatic Configurations. 2. The Deterritorialization and Reterritorialization of Korea as a Sexualized Colony through the Licensed Prostitution and Military Sex Slavery Systems. 3. Rape and Diaspora, No. 606 Injections, and Nonreproductive Penetrabilities: The Coercive Regendering of Korean Sex Slaves for the Japanese Military during the Pacific War. 4. Bastards, Masculine Cross-Dressing, Liminalities, and Homogendered Alliances: The Coercive Regendering of Korean Sex Slaves during the Pacific War. 5. Deterritorialized Masculinities, FTM [Female-to-Male] Discourses, Homogenderal Alliances, and Sexual Penetrability. 6. Asian American Masculinity, Sexual Penetrability, and the Facialization of Racialization. 7. Conclusion: The Postural Schema, Castration, Deterritorialization, Performativities, and Nomadologies. Bibliography: pp. 561- 82.

46.

YAMAGUCHI, Tomomi (1967- ).

**Feminism Fractured: An Ethnography of the Dissolution and Textual Reinvention of a Japanese Feminist Group**. University of Michigan [United States], 2004 (Ph.D. in Anthropology). Adviser: Jennifer Robertson. xii, 517p. DAI 65, no. 2 (August 2004): 589-A; UMI 3122078.

Yamaguchi, a self-proclaimed "young feminist" and native of Tokyo who earned a B.A. in Language / Communication (1990) at Kokusai Kirisutokyô Daigaku [International Christian University] in Tokyo and an M.A. in Communication Studies (1992) at the University of Michigan, ethnographically chronicled the dissolution of the feminist group *Kôdô-suru Onna-tachi no Kai* in 1996 and the "emergence of new collective and conflicting meanings and interpretations about its twenty-year history and the history and current state of feminism in Japan." In chapter 5 (pages 285-351), she briefly wrote about the stream of feminist activism that arose around the issue of the wartime "comfort women" during the early 1990s, when Kim Haksun (Gim Hak-sun/Kim Hak-soon) (1924-1997) and others came forward to talk about their wartime experiences and filed a lawsuit in the Tokyo District Court against the Japanese government. As the plight of the "comfort women" (*ianfu*) became more widely known, Yamaguchi wrote, "Japanese feminists were forced to re-think the women's movement own history of supporting Japan's war efforts during World War II as well as the fact that they had kept forgetting about Japan's history as a colonizer, not only during wartime but also in the post-colonial context."

*Contents*: Introduction. 1. Dissolution. 2. *Kôdô-suru Kai* in the History of Post-War Feminism. 3. Fighting Words. 4. Failed Solidarity: Labor. 5. Feminist Networking, the Body Politicism, and Body Politics. 6. Writing up the Missing History. 7. Feminism as Chronology. Epilogue. Appendices [A-C]: pp. 476-96. 18 figures. Bibliography: pp. 497-517.

# Dissertation Author Index

All numbers refer to entry numbers

# 9. ASSESSING THE TRANSNATIONAL "COMFORT WOMEN" MOVEMENT, 1992–2019

*Yangmo Ku*

**Abstract**: Since the early 1990s, a variety of self-organized advocacy groups in South Korea, Japan, the United States, and other nations have undertaken an extensive transnational movement in order to deal with the rights of "comfort women" who suffered tremendously from Japanese soldiers' inhumane treatment during World War II. As a result of this transnational activism, the issue of "comfort women," which was largely forgotten until the late 1980s, has been widely publicized in the world community. Such a movement also prompted the Japanese government to change from its originally indifferent stance on its past misdeeds to somewhat apologetic attitudes and strong nationalistic reaction. Given these facts, this chapter first examines the historical background of the issue of "comfort women" and then explores how the transnational "comfort women" movement was originated. After looking into the main activities of the transnational movement, the chapter assesses its achievements and limitations considering to what extent and how such a movement has affected the Japanese government's stance on the issue of "comfort women."

## Introduction

Since the early 1990s, a variety of self-organized advocacy groups in South Korea, Japan, the United States, and other nations have undertaken an extensive transnational movement (or activism)[1] in order to deal with the rights of "comfort women" who suffered tremendously from Japanese soldiers' inhumane treatment during World War II. As detailed in later sections, The Korean Council for the Women Drafted for Military Sexual Slavery by Japan (hereafter The Korean Council)[2] has played a key role in launching and maintaining the transnational "comfort women" movement. Such a movement, however, would not have been very powerful without continual, strong support from many other civil society groups, such as the Washington Coalition for Comfort Women Issues (WCCW) and other advocacy groups all over the world (R.9).

This transnational movement has awakened the international community by widely publicizing the issue of "comfort women," which was largely concealed and forgotten until the late 1980s. The movement has also resonated well with the currently ongoing issues of wartime sexual violence and women's rights violations, which arose as a significant issue after the end of the Cold War. Moreover, as a result of such a vibrant movement, the Japanese government has changed from its originally indifferent stance on its past misdeeds to somewhat apologetic attitudes. However, the transnational "comfort women" movement has unintentionally sparked a strong backlash within Japanese society.[3]

Given these facts, this chapter begins with a brief historical background of the "comfort women" issue. The chapter then explores how the transnational "comfort women" movement originated and developed over the last three decades. It assesses both the achievements and the limitations that the transnational "comfort women" movement has shown considering to what extent and how such a movement has affected the Japanese government's stance on the issue. Finally, the chapter provides some suggestions for the future transnational "comfort women" movement.

## The Origin of the Transnational "Comfort Women" Movement[4]

*Historical Background*: During the Asia-Pacific War, imperial Japan forcibly drafted vast numbers of women from its colonized and occupied countries into military prostitution. It has been estimated that these "comfort women," ranging from 50,000 to 200,000, were forced into sexual slavery for Japanese troops between 1932 and 1945.[5] "Comfort Stations" were first established in Shanghai around 1932, yet the outbreak of the second Sino-Japanese War in 1937 prompted the Japanese military to adopt the general policy of establishing military brothels in various occupied locations.[6] Despite the lack of accurate information, unearthed documents and testimonies show that Koreans made up about 80 to 90 percent of "comfort women," and were mostly between their mid-teens and early twenties.[7] The most commonly used method of recruitment was to deceive women with false promises of employment in Japan. Among other methods were recruitment by more violent means such as abduction and human trafficking, and destitute families selling daughters into indentured prostitution.[8]

The Japanese imperial government and army decided to set up the military "comfort women" system mainly for the following three reasons.[9] The first was to prevent rapes of civilians by Japanese troops, which often provoked strong anti-Japanese sentiments in occupied countries. The second motive was to protect Japanese soldiers from sexually transmitted diseases (STDs) by enforcing them to exclusively use military comfort stations. The Japanese military authorities had already found the prevalence of STDs among Japanese soldiers during the Japanese advance into Siberia between 1918 and 1922 to be quite problematic. The third was to encourage the spirit of the soldiers. The military leadership believed that the extension of the war led to the weakening of their fighting spirit, thus causing many difficulties in managing occupied territories.

The conditions under which these "comfort women" were forced to serve as sex slaves were—unsurprisingly—harsh and traumatic. Under the surveillance of military authorities, a woman would have to serve twenty or thirty men in a single day, and in extreme cases the number increased to sixty.[10] In the process, the "comfort women" were subject to mental anguish, sexually transmitted diseases, and violence from soldiers. Even following the end of hostilities, the comfort women's plight did not necessarily improve, and in many cases, worsened.[11] Many were abandoned at their stations or were killed by retreating Japanese troops.[12] In some cases, they were forced to commit suicide along with the soldiers. While some survivors were sent back to their homelands by the Allied forces, others stayed abroad because of their deep pain and humiliation. Surviving victims continued to suffer physical afflictions and mental illnesses in addition to facing significant social discrimination.[13]

*The Emergence of the Transnational "Comfort Women" Movement*

It was not until the late 1980s that societal actors in South Korea and Japan began to seriously address the "comfort women" issue, although a number of books concerning the "comfort women" issue had been published in Japan. In 1988, the Korean Church Women United and Professor Yun Chung-ok conducted field research in Japan to examine the issue of military "comfort women" with the support of a Japanese organization—the Association to Challenge the Prostitution Issue.[14] Their research, presented at an international conference in April 1988, first raised the underlying connection between the "comfort women" issue in colonial Korea and Japanese men's sex tourism in contemporary Korea.

Following this event, the Korean Church Women United sought to publicize the "comfort women" issue while addressing the increase in Japanese men traveling to Korea for sex tourism following the 1988 Seoul Olympics.[15] As a result, a number of Korean women's organizations, the majority of which were associated with Christian churches, joined the nascent campaign calling for resolution of the "comfort women" issue. In January 1989, members of the women's groups staged a street demonstration in Seoul against the Korean government's plan to send an emissary to the funeral of Emperor Hirohito. Korean activists seized a similar opportunity to raise the question of reparations for "comfort women" when Korean President Roh Tae-woo announced his State Visit to Japan in May 1990. Prior to Roh's visit, they issued a list of demands to be made to the Japanese government, including an investigation of the "comfort women" issue and an apology for Japan's involvement.

Meanwhile, Japanese Socialist Party member Motooka Shoji raised the issue of "comfort women" in the upper house of the Diet in June 1990, requesting that the Japanese government investigate the historical matter.[16] A Japanese government representative replied, "After listening to elderly people and piecing together what they say, it appears that the wartime 'comfort women' were taken by private entrepreneurs to different places, going where the military went. Frankly, even if one were to conduct an inquiry into the circumstances, it would not yield any results."[17] As a result, Korean women's organizations sent an open letter to Japanese Prime Minister Kaifu Toshiki before his visit to Korea in October 1990, demanding Japan's admission of culpability, an apology, and compensation for the sufferings of the former "comfort women." South Korean women's leaders also formed two new NGOs to conduct a more systematic campaign for redressing the "comfort women" issue. The Korean Research Institute of Chongshindae (KRIC), which began as a small study group in July 1990, was formed to conduct scholarly research and circulate information on the issue. The second was The Korean Council, which was formed in November 1990 as an activist umbrella organization that consisted of thirty-seven women's groups.[18]

From its outset, The Korean Council sought to examine this issue with the support of the KRIC. In this process, a Korean victim first reported her suffering as a "comfort woman" during World War II. Subsequently, The Korean Council appealed to the former victim—Kim Hak-soon—to deliver public testimony on her ordeal in August 1991.[19] In a press conference, Kim stated through bitter tears that at age 17 she had been forced to serve Japanese troops as a sex worker and even now suffers from her terrible experiences. Kim's testimony attracted much attention from the Japanese public, notably promoting the cooperation of many

Japanese groups with The Korean Council. Among these groups were the Association of Japanese Women, the Young Women's Christian Association (YWCA), the National Council of Churches in Japan (NCCJ), and the Asian Women's Association.[20] In December 1991, Kim and two other victims also filed a class-action lawsuit against the Japanese government, requesting twenty million yen each for compensation.

Along with Kim's testimony and litigation, the uncovering of official documents in Japan significantly strengthened the transnational "comfort women" movement. In January 1992, historian Yoshimi Yoshiaki unearthed several documents regarding military "comfort women" at the National Institute of Defense Studies Library in Tokyo.[21] The national daily newspaper, *Asahi Shimbun*, reported Yoshimi's discovery of the official documents on January 11, 1992, notably increasing public interest in the "comfort women" issue.[22] These documents proved that the Japanese government had been involved in establishing and managing the military "comfort women" system. A key document entitled, "Matters concerning the recruitment of women to work in military comfort stations," issued on March 4, 1938, with the authorization of the War Minister Sugiyama Hajime, reads as follows:

> Notice from the Adjutant to the Chiefs of Staff of the North China Area Army and Central China Expeditionary Force. . . . There are many things [about the rounding up of comfort women] that require careful attention. In the future, armies in the field will control the recruiting of women and will use scrupulous care in selecting people to carry out this task. This task will be performed in close cooperation with the military police or local police force of the area. You are hereby notified of the order [of the Minister of War] to carry out this task with the utmost regard for preserving the honor of the army and for avoiding social problems.[23]

The appearance of documentary evidence and the subsequent media coverage motivated many lawyers, historians, and intellectuals to actively engage the issue and to view it as part of Japan's postwar responsibility. Facing the Japanese government's tepid reaction to the issue, concerned lawyers and historians created an executive committee in September 1992 to host the International Public Hearing Concerning Japan's Postwar Compensation in Tokyo in December 1992.[24] The executive committee invited surviving former "comfort women" from six countries (South/North Korea, the Philippines, China, Taiwan, and the Netherlands) to testify at the public hearing. A former Korean "comfort woman," Kang Soon-Ae said that she was forced to serve about 30 Japanese soldiers per day as a sex worker in various places, including China and Palau, in the South Pacific after she was kidnapped by Japanese military police at age 14. After she gave a detailed narrative of her appalling experiences at a comfort station in Indonesia, the only non-Asian woman, Jan Ruff O'Herne stated, "It was my deep faith in God that helped me survive all that I suffered at the brutal, savage hands of the Japanese. I have forgiven the Japanese for what they did to me, but I can never forget."[25]

Following this event, in April 1993, the executive committee established the first non-governmental organization committed to research on Japanese war crimes—the Center for Research and Documentation on Japan's War Responsibility (JWRC). The JWRC conducted fact-finding research and greatly supported the transnational movement for redress of wartime sexual slavery against women. [26] Responding to the demand from the International Commission of Jurists, the JWRC issued its first research report on the "comfort women" issue in June 1993. The JWRC published a quarterly journal, *Senso Sekinin Kenkyu* (*Report on Japan's War Responsibility*) starting in September 1993 and provided the UN special rapporteur with important information on the issue.[27] The JWRC also held joint seminars to address the "comfort women" issue in August and December 1993 and assisted The Korean Council in filing a lawsuit against the Japanese government in the Permanent Court of Arbitration (PCA).[28] As shown thus far, the "comfort women" movement largely remained in South Korean and Japanese societies at the initial stage, but the movement has rapidly extended to the world community as time progressed.

## Main Activities of the Transnational "Comfort Women" Movement

Over the last three decades, the transnational "comfort women" movement has concentrated on the subsequent four activities: (1) mobilizing the international community to push the Japanese government to fully come to terms with the issue of "comfort women"; (2) supporting surviving victims; (3) establishing the "comfort women" statues/monuments and museums within South Korea, Japan, the U.S., and other nations to honor former victims and educate next generations; and (4) engaging in international solidarity activities to support women and children suffering from sexual violence in conflict.

### International Pressure

The transnational activists' main endeavor has been to push the Japanese government to sincerely address the "comfort women" issue as follows: (1) admit the Japanese military sexual slavery system as a war crime; (2) disclose official documents; (3) deliver an official apology; (4) pay legal reparations to the victims; (5) punish those responsible; (6) record the sexual slavery system in history textbooks; and (7) erect a memorial monument and build an archive.[29] To achieve these goals, transnational activist groups have adopted various strategies.

Above all, since January 8, 1992 The Korean Council has played a central role in holding a weekly protest event, called the Wednesday Demonstration, to push for the Japanese government's settlement of the "comfort women" issue in front of the Japanese Embassy in Seoul. At the early stage, about 20-member organizations of The Korean Council were mainly in charge of hosting the weekly protests. As time went by, however, many other Korean civic groups dealing with the subjects of peace, labor, religion, and culture/arts have actively participated in the Wednesday Demonstrations held in Seoul and other local cities. This solidarity through the protest has continually extended to the international community. For example, on August 10, 2005, the Wednesday Demonstration simultaneously took place in 30 different cities of nine countries, including the U.S., Japan, Germany, the Netherlands, Canada, the Philippines, and Taiwan. These acts of solidarity happened at every 100th demonstration.

Many students at all levels have regularly taken part in the demonstrations, so the event has become a vital education platform on peace and human rights for next generations.[30] Thus, the Wednesday Demonstrations have become a symbolic icon of the transnational "comfort women" movement, marking the 1,400[th] on August 14, 2019.

Fig. 9-1. 1,395[th] Wednesday Demonstration in front of Japanese Embassy in Seoul, South Korea, July 10, 2019. *Photo by Yangmo Ku*

On top of these long-lasting, weekly demonstrations, The Korean Council has built solidarity among victims, support groups, and citizens from many Asian nations through the holding of the Asian Solidarity Conference (ASC).[31] Among the main support groups have been the Asian Center for Women's Human Rights in the Philippines, the Taipei Women's Rescue Foundation, and the Violence Against Women in War Network, Japan (VAWW-Net Japan). Starting with the first conference held in August 1992, the transnational activists have organized the ASC 15 times so far in Seoul, Tokyo, and Manila. At the ASCs, they keenly discussed how to resolve the "comfort women" issue and made numerous joint statements to request the Japanese government's genuine dealings with the matter, despite occasional divisions among the support groups due to the issues of punishing those responsible for the military "comfort women" system and the Asian Women's Fund.[32] One particularly important outcome of the Asian Solidarity Conference was the decision to hold the Women's International War Crimes Tribunal 2000 in Tokyo. This Tribunal's primary goals were "to establish that Japan's military sexual slavery constitutes a war crime against women, to identify those responsible for the crime, and to record the complete findings and proceedings of the tribunal for history."[33] Although having no legally binding force, the Tribunal declared Emperor Hirohito guilty of war crimes and reconfirmed the Japanese government's responsibility for establishing and managing the military "comfort women" system.[34] The 2000 Tribunal was possible due to the support from more than 150 NGOs in Asia and international law experts, who had participated in the International Criminal Tribunal for the former Yugoslavia and Rwanda.[35]

Another means of imposing pressure on the Japanese government has been for The Korean Council and other support groups to bring the issue of "comfort women" to international organizations, such as the United Nations and the International Labor Organization (ILO). As a result of this effort, Radhika Coomaraswamy, Special Rapporteur on Violence against Women at the UN Human Rights Commission, investigated the issue of "comfort women" in North/South Korea and Japan, issuing a report in 1996 that fully reflected the voices of the transnational activist groups. In 1998, Gay McDougall, Special Rapporteur at the UN Sub-Commission on the Promotion and Protection of the Human Rights, also submitted a final report titled "Systematic rape, sexual slavery and slavery-like practices during armed conflict." In this report, McDougall concluded, "the Japanese government remains liable for grave violations of human rights and humanitarian law, violations that amount in their totality to crimes against humanity."[36] The report also emphasized the need for mechanisms to provide legal compensation and to prosecute Japan's perpetrators who were responsible for establishing and maintaining the sex slave system.

Moreover, beginning in 1995, The Korean Council and labor unions in South Korea and Japan continued to raise the issue of "comfort women" at the ILO. As a consequence of this endeavor, the ILO often acknowledged the military "comfort women" system as a violation of the ILO's 1930 Forced Labor Convention and demanded the Japanese government's proper dealings with the issue in its annual experts' committee reports. However, the ILO failed to adopt the issue as an agenda item of its annual International Labor Conference due mainly to the Japanese government's strong opposition.[37]

Furthermore, transnational activist groups have striven to persuade many nations' congressional and parliamentary members to pass resolutions on the issue of "comfort women." Although such resolutions had no legally binding force, the transnational activists regarded them as an important instrument for publicizing the sex slave issue and pushing for changes in the Japanese government's attitude. This attempt first began in the U.S. in the mid-1990s.

In response to the demands and activism of The Korean Council, the Washington Coalition for Comfort Women Issues (WCCW) played a pivotal role in persuading the U.S. House of Representatives by various means, including demonstrations, lecturing tours, press conferences, archival exhibitions, hearings, and inviting former "comfort women" to the U.S. Congress.[38] The WCCW and other Korean American civic groups jointly launched a nationwide campaign to publicize the "comfort women" issue and garner support from American society. As a consequence of these efforts, a series of resolutions, which demand the Japanese government to release its official apology and pay legal reparations to former victims, were presented to the U.S. Congress from 1996 to 2006. Due mainly to the Japanese government's active lobbying, these resolutions were not adopted at the plenary sessions of Congress.

The transnational activists, however, did not give up their campaigning, and U.S. Congressman Mike Honda submitted House Resolution 121 on January 31, 2007. After that, a subcommittee of the House Committee on Foreign Affairs hosted a hearing on protecting human rights of "comfort women" on February 15, 2007. In the hearing, Korean and Dutch "comfort women" victims gave testimonies about their horrible experiences as sex slaves, thus creating a great sensation in the international community through extensive media coverage.[39] Despite the Japanese government's tremendous efforts of lobbying to prevent its passage, the U.S. Congress finally passed H.Res. 121 on July 30, 2007, which called upon the Japanese government to "acknowledge, apologize, and accept historical responsibility in a clear and unequivocal manner for its Imperial Armed Forces' coercion of young women into sexual slavery."[40] H.Res. 121 thus paved the way for the passage of a series of resolutions on the issue of "comfort women" in the EU, Dutch, Canadian, and South Korean parliaments.

*Support for Surviving Victims*

In addition to pushing the Japanese government to fully address the issue of "comfort women," civil society groups have paid great attention to taking care of surviving "comfort women." Since the "comfort women" issue came to the surface in the early 1990s, 239 Korean women have registered as victims of Japanese military sexual slavery with the South Korean government.[41] For these victims, civil society organizations such as the Korean Buddhist Commission on Human Rights raised funds from various groups and individuals, opening a communal home called the House of Sharing in Seoul in October 1992. After several moves to different districts within Seoul, the House of Sharing was finally settled in Gwangju City in December 1995. The newly-built complex for the victims consists of two buildings, one as living space and the other as an education center. This facility has provided surviving victims with residence, meals, and health care programs in addition to serving as a platform for social gatherings with external visitors. As of August 2019, six victims reside in the House of Sharing out of only 20 "comfort women" survivors in South Korea.

The Korean Council has also provided various forms of support and welfare programs to improve the survivors' lives. Among the supporting programs are regular phone calls and visits to the surviving victims, hosting birthday/holiday events, and providing a shelter for survivors called Peaceful Our Home.[42] In conjunction with these organizations within the Seoul metropolitan area, other civil groups have supported "comfort women" survivors who live in regional areas, including Daegu City, Changwon City, and Tongyoung City. Such groups have regularly visited the victims, provided meals and health care programs, hosted monthly meetings for hearing testimonies, and jointly participated in social events.[43] Those support groups have made every effort to help the victims overcome isolation from their families and society and restore sociality in their daily lives.

Moreover, Korean civil activists strongly persuaded the Kim Dae-jung government (1998–2002) to provide "comfort women" survivors with financial support. Facing internal and external pressure, in 1995 the Japanese government helped the establishment of the Asian Women's Fund (AWF), which was a non-governmental fund designed to express a sense of national atonement from the Japanese people to the surviving victims. To implement this atonement project, the AWF contained three major elements: (1) to provide "atonement money" (two million yen per person) donated by the Japanese people to former "comfort women"; (2) to send a letter from the Japanese Prime Minister to surviving victims; and (3) to disburse "about 830 million yen from government funds over a five-year period for victims' medical care and welfare."[44] As soon as this atonement project was launched, many civil society groups vehemently opposed the AWF because they perceived it as the Japanese government's means of avoiding direct, official, and national level compensation to the victims. As a result of Korean activists' intense lobbying, in 1998 the Kim Dae-jung administration paid an equivalent amount of atonement money (about $26,000), suggested by the AWF, to each survivor.[45] Such payments were made under the condition that the recipients would not accept AWF money.

*Establishment of "Comfort Women" Museums and Statues/Monuments*

As surviving victims grew older and many of them passed away, in the late 1990s "comfort women" activists began aspiring to build museums for commemorating and honoring former "comfort women" and educating next generations not to repeat similar crimes. In August 1998, the Museum of Sexual Slavery by Japanese Military, the world's first museum that solely focuses on the issue of "comfort women," was established at the House of Sharing in Gwangju City with support from many organizations and citizens.[46] As a result of eight years of planning and fund-raising campaigns, The Korean Council opened the War and Women's Human Rights Museum in Seoul in May 2012 despite harsh opposition from many Korean independence movement groups.[47] A number of groups and individuals, including Korean diasporas in the U.S., Germany, and Australia as well as Japanese churches, activists, and teachers, made donations for the opening of this museum. Two local support groups for former "comfort women," The Korean Council Busan and Daegu Citizen's Forum for Halmuni, also opened the National Women's Historical Hall in Busan City in September 2004 and the Heeum Museum of Sexual Slavery by Japanese Military in Daegu City in December 2015.[48] Moreover, in July 2005 Japanese civic groups, VAWW-NET Japan and the Women's Fund for Peace and Human Rights, founded the Women's Archive Museum of War and Peace in Tokyo, which was designed to preserve all records on the Women's International War Crimes Tribunal 2000 and materials related to the issue of "comfort women."[49] Furthermore, with support from the Shanghai Normal University, Su Zhiliang, a historian and director of the Research Center for Chinese Comfort Women, opened the Chinese Comfort Women History Museum in Shanghai in October 2016.[50]

The Korean Council has also made great efforts to spread the message of human rights and peace through supporting the establishment of the Statue of Peace, which symbolizes the victims' youth that was stolen and calls for an apology and remembrance. Thus, at the 1,000[th]

Wednesday Demonstration on December 14, 2011, the Statue of Peace, often called "*Sonyeosang*"in Korea or "Comfort Woman" Statue in Japan, was for the first time established in front of the Japanese Embassy in Seoul.[51] From then on, with support of many other civic groups about 102 Statues of Peace were erected within South Korea and about 24 outside of the nation, including in the United States, Canada, Australia, Germany, and China.[52]

Meanwhile, the erections of the Statue of Peace have been highly controversial in the international community as well as for Japan-South Korea relations. Many advocates for the "comfort women" movement agree that the Statue of Peace is primarily aimed not to fuel anti-Japanese sentiment but to educate the public about such a serious human rights violation and to prevent history from repeating itself.[53] On the other hand, the Japanese government has been extremely sensitive and resistant to the installations of Statues of Peace all around the world. For instance, when South Korean civil activists installed another "comfort women" statue outside the Japanese consulate in Busan in December 2016, the Japanese government recalled its Ambassador to South Korea and its Consul General in Busan and declared the suspension of high-level economic talks with the ROK government.[54] In addition, when the "comfort women" monument was first unveiled in San Francisco on September 22, 2017, Yamada Jun, the Consul General of Japan in the city, stated:

> The aim of current comfort women memorial movements seems to perpetuate and fixate on certain one-sided interpretations. This is unwarranted and hardly conducive to objective fact finding and mutual agreement, let alone a final reconciliation. Rather, they are rapidly alienating the entire Japanese public, who could otherwise be sympathetic to the wartime plight of these women, by unduly exacerbating emotional antagonism.[55]

Suga Yoshihide, Japan's chief cabinet secretary, also said at a news conference that "erecting comfort women statues in the United States and other countries is in conflict with our country's stance and extremely regrettable." As a result, in October 2018 the mayor of Osaka, Japan, terminated the city's long-term sister city relationship with San Francisco in protest of the monument statue.[56] Moreover, a bronze statue depicting a "comfort woman" was removed in the Philippines under the pressure of the Japanese government two days after it was unveiled to the public on December 28, 2018. Before the removal, the Japanese Embassy in Manila expressed the idea that "We believe that the establishment of a 'comfort woman' statue in other countries, including this case, is extremely disappointing, not compatible with the Japanese government."[57]

### International Solidarity Movement

Another significant project of the transnational "comfort women" movement was "to engage in international solidarity activities to support women and children suffering from sexual violence in conflict and aim to prevent and eradicate sexual violence in conflict."[58] To this end, on March 8, 2012 the two "comfort women" victims, Kim Bok-dong and Gil Won-ok, took the initiative in founding the so-called Butterfly Fund in solidarity with many citizens.

This fund has been used to support victims of sexual violence in Vietnam, Uganda, the Democratic Republic of Congo, and other regions. Receiving funds, civic groups in those nations, including the REMED, the Can Rewede Pee, and the Golden Women Vision in Uganda, have provided many victims with part of their housing fees, meals, health care, and scholarships for their children, thus helping them to be financially independent.

In addition, the Justice Foundation created the Kim Bok-dong Peace Prize in 2018 to commemorate the former "comfort woman" who courageously spoke out against military sexual slavery. Its first recipient was Acan Sylvia Obal, Director of the Golden Women Vision in Uganda, who has sought to raise awareness of wartime sexual violence and has supported victims of wartime sexual violence around the world.[59] And the 2019 Kim Bok-dong Peace Prize was awarded to Vasfije Krasniqi-Goodman, the first survivor of sexual violence during the Kosovo War (1998-1999) to publicly share her traumatic story, in honor of her bravery and commitment to human rights.[60] In 2020, furthermore, The Korean Council plans to open the Kim Bok-dong Center in Uganda, which aims to support many victims of sexual violence during the nation's longstanding civil war (early 1990s–2008).[61] In addition to a historical monument for Japanese military "comfort women" and Kim Bok-dong, the center consists of a history museum on Uganda's civil war, a shelter for victims, office space, an education room and a work studio for victims, and a playground for victims' children. This project is being conducted in solidarity with the Golden Women Vision in Uganda.

## Accomplishments and Limitations of the Transnational "Comfort Women" Movement

This long-standing transnational "comfort women" movement has made highly significant accomplishments. First of all, the transnational movement has contributed to converting many victims of sexual violence during conflict to human rights (women's rights) activists. With the durable support from civil society organizations, "comfort women" survivors came out of their long silence and have actively sought to publicize the issue of "comfort women" in the international community. Former victims have frequently done interviews with media outlets, filmmakers, and researchers. To give testimonies, they have participated in a number of international conferences and events, including the 1993 World Conference on Human Rights in Vienna, the 1995 World Conference on Women in Beijing, the 2000 Women's International War Crimes Tribunal in Tokyo, the 2007 hearing at the U.S. Congress, and the 1992–2018 Asian Solidarity Conferences. It is needless to say that their passionate activities have considerably heightened the vitality of the transnational "comfort women" movement in the world community over the long period of time. As noted before, furthermore, former victims and transnational activist groups established the Butterfly Fund and the Kim Bok-dong Peace Prize, supporting other victims of sexual violence in Uganda, the Democratic Republic of Congo, Kosovo, and Vietnam. Thus, they have extended the transnational "comfort women" movement to other regions that suffered from wartime sexual violence and helped those victims to raise their voices in the international community.

Second, the issue of "comfort women," which had been long concealed and forgotten until the late 1980s, has become a salient human rights issue in the world community through the vibrant transnational activism. As depicted in the previous sections, civic society groups in South Korea, Japan, the U.S., and other nations have jointly promoted issue resonance in the international community mainly through sharing information, pressuring the Japanese government, and working with media, international organizations, and many other nations. To a certain extent, the transnational activists were able to attract extensive attention because, in the early 1990s when the "comfort women" movement first started, the world community became extremely sensitive to the issue of sexual violence in conflict. After the demise of the Cold War, the Yugoslavian and Rwandan civil wars revealed the severity of wartime sexual violence and women's rights violations.[62]

Nevertheless, the biggest reason behind the powerful movement has been arguably the civil activists' enduring, strong commitment to the restoration of former victims' honor and rights on top of the surviving victims' strong will to address the issue. For instance, the current representative of The Korean Council, Yoon Mee-hyang, first joined the institution in the early 1990s and has consistently devoted herself to the transnational movement over the last 30 years. One example showing this commitment is that The Korean Council has been able to host the Wednesday Demonstrations since January 1992, serving as a platform for remembrance, solidarity, and education, regardless of participants' gender, age, or nationality. In addition, starting in 1992, WCCW's former presidents, Dongwoo Lee Hahm and Ok Cha Soh, fully dedicated their time and passion to organizing a series of protests, college tours, press conferences, hearings, and archival exhibitions in the United States.[63] Their activities laid the groundwork for the passage of H.Res. 121 in the U.S. Congress in July 2007 and attracted wide-ranging attention on the issue of "comfort women" from American society.

Third, the transnational movement played a critical role in turning the Japanese government's originally indifferent stance on the issue of "comfort women" to a slightly more apologetic direction, although a strong backlash has often erupted in Japanese society. Until the early 1990s when the movement was initially launched, the Japanese government largely denied its involvement in the establishment and management of the military "comfort women" system. In reaction to significant pressure imposed by the transnational movement, the Japanese government came to acknowledge its moral, not legal, responsibility for the suffering inflicted on the former "comfort women." For example, in August 1993 the Japanese government issued the Kono Statement that partially admitted its involvement in the forceful recruitment of "comfort women." Chief Cabinet Secretary Kono Yohei announced:

> Then Japanese military was, directly or indirectly, involved in the establishment and management of the comfort stations and the transfer of comfort women. The recruitment of the comfort women was conducted mainly by private recruiters who acted in response to the request of the military. The Government study has revealed that in many cases they were recruited against their own will, through coaxing, coercion, etc., and that, at times, administrative/military personnel directly took part in the recruitments. They lived in misery at comfort stations under a coercive atmosphere. . . .

Undeniably, this was an act, with the involvement of the military authorities of the day, that severely injured the honor and dignity of many women.[64]

Prime Minister Murayama Tomiichi also made a series of apologetic statements regarding the "comfort women" issue. Murayama commented in August 1994 that "on the issue of wartime 'comfort women,' which seriously stained the honor and dignity of many women, I would like to take this opportunity once again to express my profound and sincere remorse and apologies."[65] In July 1995, he also stated:

> The problem of the so-called wartime comfort women is one such scar, which, with the involvement of the Japanese military forces of the time, seriously stained the honor and dignity of many women. This is entirely inexcusable. I offer my profound apology to all those who, as wartime comfort women, suffered emotional and physical wounds that can never be closed.[66]

It is safe to say that the direct causes of the Japanese government's changed behavior were due to a former victim Kim Hak-soon's public testimony and historian Yoshimi Yoshiaki's finding of historical documents proving the Japanese government's involvement in the military "comfort women" system. However, the initial transnational "comfort women" movement motivated Kim to give testimony and provided a context for Yoshimi's historical findings. There is no denying that the transnational activism strongly pushed the Japanese government to act by promoting issue resonance in the world community.

Despite the above-mentioned achievements, the transnational "comfort women" movement is not free from some shortcomings and criticisms. This movement worked as a double-edged sword in resolving the issue of "comfort women" between South Korea and Japan. As noted above, such powerful transnational activism played a vital role in pushing the Japanese government to take a somewhat apologetic stance on the issue. On the other hand, it has been extremely difficult for the South Korean and Japanese governments to reach a successful political settlement over the issue due to the seven demands made by The Korean Council. In the normative sense, the Japanese government should accept all those requests based on its past horrible wrongdoings. In the practical sense, however, the Japanese government has not been ready to address the demands because it has been gradually moving in a more politically conservative direction. Rather than willingly coming to terms with the past wrongs, conservative Japanese political leaders have glossed over and even justified past misdeeds since the mid-1990s. Under the circumstance, there has been little room for the two governments to maneuver in resolving the issue of "comfort women." The 2015 "comfort women" agreement, which was made between the South Korean and Japanese governments under U.S. pressure, was a good example to show the difficulty of attaining a successful political settlement of the issue.[67]

Another shortcoming that the powerful transnational "comfort women" movement has unintentionally produced would be the lack of historical research on the issue of "comfort women" within South Korea.[68] A number of historical documents on "comfort women" have been mostly found by Japanese and Chinese historians, such as Yoshimi Yoshiaki at Chuo University in Tokyo and Su Zhiliang at Shanghai Normal University. Korean historians have not paid much attention to conducting historical research with respect to the origin and development of the military "comfort women" system in the context of the Japanese colonial rule over Korea from 1910 to 1945, as argued by a Korean researcher.[69] As the core power and opinion leader, The Korean Council has mostly dominated political discourse on the issue of "comfort women" in South Korean society. Recently, the research team of professor Chung Chin-sung of the Seoul National University Human Rights Center placed enormous effort to discover archiving documents and visual resources and has positively influenced the academic research of other institutions.[70]

## Concluding Remarks

The transnational "comfort women" movement has been greatly successful in awakening the international community about such an important human rights and women's rights violation and is likely to be a continual catalyst to prevent the violation of women's rights during the conflict all around the world, given the movement's enduring, far-reaching solidarity activities. However, this movement is confronted with a big challenge. Considering the nationalistic political inclination and continual historical revisionism driven by the current Abe Shinzo government, it would be extremely difficult to expect that the Japanese government would fully come to terms with the issue of "comfort women" in accordance with the requests incessantly made by activists. On top of this obstacle, the small numbers of surviving victims are quickly passing away over time. Nevertheless, the transnational "comfort women" movement should continue as an instrument for prompting many Japanese people who love peace to act and educate the next generations on the importance of human rights, justice, and reconciliation.

In this context, it would be urgently necessary for the South Korean and Japanese societies to make every effort to reduce the wide perception gap between the two nations on not only the issue of "comfort women" but also other historical matters, such as the (il)legality of the Japanese colonial rule over Korea, forced labor, and history textbooks. To achieve this goal, the two nations should consistently invest their resources in history dialogues among experts, educators, and students, large-scale youth exchanges, and cultural exchanges between sister cities in both countries. Political leaders in both nations should not use history disputes for their parochial political interests, and such activities should continue regardless of political conditions. Without the notable decrease of the history perception gap through these efforts, it would be very difficult to find any solution to get out of a vicious cycle of history disputes and deterioration of the relationship between South Korea and Japan. This phenomenon is evidently shown in the recently worsened South Korea-Japan relations. A history dispute caused by the forced labor issue is seriously damaging the two nations' economic and security relationships. More than ever, highly sophisticated and diversified discourses on the issues of "comfort women" are needed to expand the mutual understanding and eventual peacebuilding.

## Bibliography

Asian Women's Fund. *The Comfort Women Issue and AWF*. Tokyo: AWF, 2007.

Chung, Chin-Sung. "Korean Women Drafted for Military Sexual Slavery by Japan." In *True Stories of the Korean Comfort Women,* edited by Keith Howard, London: Cassell, 1995.

Chung, Chin-Sung. *Hyundae Ilbon ǔi Sahoe Undongron* [Social Movements in Modern Japan]. Seoul: Nanam Publishing House, 2001.

Chung, Chin-Sung. *Ilbonkun Sung Noyeje: Ilbonkun Yianbu Munje ǔi Silsang kwa keo Haekyeol ul uihan Undong* [Japanese Army's Sexual Slavery: The Reality of Japanese Army's Comfort Women Issue and the Movement for Its Resolution]. Seoul: Seoul National University Press, 2004.

Chung, Eunjeong. "Hanil Chogukjǒk Onghomang e kwanhan Yǒngu [The Study of Korea-Japan Transnational Advocacy Network]" M.A. Thesis. Seoul: Kyunghee University, 2004.

Hayashi, Hirofumi. "The Japanese Movement to Protest Wartime Sexual Violence: A Survey of Japanese and International Literature." *Critical Asian Studies*, Vol. 33, No. 4 (2001).

Kim, Changrok et al. "Research Report for the Establishment of National Japanese Military Comfort Women Research Institute and History Museum." South Korean Ministry of Gender Equality and Family, May 2018: 1-169.

Kim, Ji Young and Jeyong Sohn. "Settlement Without Consensus: International Pressure, Domestic Backlash, and the Comfort Women in Japan." *Pacific Affairs* 90: 1 (March 2017): 77-99.

Ku, Yangmo. "Comfort Women Controversy and Its Implications for Japan-ROK Reconciliation." In *Routledge Handbook of Memory and Reconciliation in East Asia*, edited by Mikyoung Kim, 261-76. New York: Routledge, 2016.

Lee, Won-deog et al. "Ilbongun Wianbu Pihaeja Munje e kwanhan Bogoseo [Report on the Japanese Military Comfort Women Issue]" South Korean Ministry of Gender Equality and Family, April 2017: 1-216.

McDougall, Gay J. *Systematic rape, sexual slavery and slavery-like practices during armed conflict: final report*. UN Sub-Commission on the Promotion and Protection of Human Rights, June 22, 1998, E/CN.4/Sub.2/1998/13: 121. https://www.refworld.org/docid/3b00f44114.html

Mitsui, Hideko. "The resignification of the comfort women through NGO trials." In *Rethinking Historical Injustice and Reconciliation in Northeast Asia*, edited by Gi-Wook Shin, Soon-Won Park, and Daqing Yang, New York: Routledge, 2007.

Piper, Nicola. "Transnational women's activism in Japan and Korea: the unresolved issue of military sexual slavery." *Global Networks*, vol. 1., no. 2 (2001).

Price, Richard. "Transnational Civil Society and Advocacy in World Politics." *World Politics* 55 (July 2003): 579-606.

Soh, Sarah. "Japan's National/Asian Women's Fund for Comfort Women." *Pacific Affairs* 76, No. 2 (2003): 209-33.

Soh, Sarah. *The Comfort Women: Sexual Violence and Postcolonial Memory in Korea and Japan.* Chicago: The University of Chicago Press, 2008.

The Korean Council. *Hanguk Jeongshindae Munje Daechaek Hyeopuihoi 20 Nyonsa* [20 Years of the Korean Council for the Women Drafted for Military Sexual Slavery by Japan]. Seoul: Hanul Academy, 2014.

The Korean Council for Justice and Remembrance for the Issues of Military Sexual Slavery by Japan. http://www.womenandwar.net/.

Yoshimi, Yoshiaki. *Comfort Women: Sexual Slavery in the Japanese Military during World War II*, translated by Suzanne O'Brien. New York: Columbia University Press, 2000.

---

[1] Richard Price, "Transnational Civil Society and Advocacy in World Politics," *World Politics* 55 (July 2003): 580: In this chapter, the transnational movement (or transnational activism) is defined as "voluntary collective action across state borders that self-organized advocacy groups undertake in pursuit of what they deem to be the wider public interest," as Richard Price notes.

[2] In July 2018, The Korean Council for the Women Drafted for Military Sexual Slavery by Japan and the Foundation for Justice and Remembrance merged as The Korean Council for Justice and Remembrance for the Issues of Military Sexual Slavery by Japan.

[3] Ji Young Kim and Jeyong Sohn, "Settlement Without Consensus: International Pressure, Domestic Backlash, and the Comfort Women in Japan," *Pacific Affairs* 90: 1 (March 2017): 77-99.

[4] This section is mainly derived from Yangmo Ku, "Comfort Women Controversy and Its Implications for Japan-ROK Reconciliation," *Routledge Handbook of Memory and Reconciliation in East Asia*, ed. Mikyoung Kim (New York: Routledge, 2016), 261-264.

[5] Asian Women's Fund, *The Comfort Women Issue and AWF* (Tokyo: AWF, 2007): 111-16; Nicola Piper, "Transnational women's activism in Japan and Korea: the unresolved issue of military sexual slavery," *Global Networks*, vol. 1., no. 2 (2001): 161: It is very difficult to determine the exact number of comfort women due to the absence of documents with comprehensive data.

[6] Yoshimi Yoshiaki, *Comfort Women: Sexual Slavery in the Japanese Military during World War II*, translated by Suzanne O'Brien (New York: Columbia University Press, 2000), 43-51; p. 91: "Japanese, American, and Dutch official documents have confirmed the existence of military comfort stations in the following areas: China, Hong Kong, French Indochina, the Philippines, Malaysia, Singapore, British Borneo, the Dutch East Indies, Burma, Thailand, New Guinea, the Japanese Okinawan archipelago, the Bonin Islands, Hokkaido, the Kurile Islands, and Sakhalin."

[7] Chin-Sung Chung, "Korean Women Drafted for Military Sexual Slavery by Japan," in *True Stories of the Korean Comfort Women*, ed. Keith Howard (London: Cassell, 1995), 16-19.

[8] Sarah Soh, *The Comfort Women: Sexual Violence and Postcolonial Memory in Korea and Japan* (Chicago: The University of Chicago Press, 2008): 107; 139-40.

[9] Chin-Sung Chung, *Ilbonkun Sung Noyeje: Ilbonkun Yianbu Munje ŭi Silsang kwa keo Haekyeol ul uihan Undong* [Japanese Army's Sexual Slavery: The Reality of Japanese Army's Comfort Women Issue and the Movement for Its Resolution], (Seoul: Seoul National University Press, 2004), 88-90; Yoshimi, *Comfort Women*, 47-75.

[10] Yoshimi, *Comfort Women*, 139-151.

[11] Radhika Coomaraswamy, *Report on the mission to the Democratic People's Republic of Korea, the Republic of Korea and Japan on the issue of military sexual slavery in wartime*, Commission on Human Rights, E/CN.4/1996/53/Add.1, 14-21; Chung, "Korean Women Drafted for Military Sexual Slavery by Japan": 23-24.

[12] Soh, *The Comfort Women*, 141.

[13] Yoshimi, *Comfort Women*, 196-97: Social discrimination was another serious pain that former "comfort women" endured after they returned to their homes. For instance, Korean former "comfort woman" "Kim Hak-soon married but was told by her husband that she was a filthy woman, who'd had sex with soldiers." Another Filipina comfort woman Gertrude Balisalisa testified that "her husband treated her like a person with a contagious disease, and her parents and relatives looked down on her as if she was something filthy."

[14] Chin-Sung Chung, *Hyundae Ilbon ŭi Sahoe Undongron* [Social Movements in Modern Japan] (Seoul: Nanam Publishing House, 2001), 165.

[15] Eunjeong Chung, "Hanil Chogukjŏk Onghomang e kwanhan Yŏngu [The Study of Korea-Japan Transnational Advocacy Network]" M.A. Thesis. (Seoul: Kyunghee University, 2004), 39.

[16] Chung, *Hyundae Ilbon ŭi Sahoe Undongron*, 166.

[17] Quoted in Asian Women's Fund, *The Comfort Women Issue and AWF*, 117.

[18] Soh, *The Comfort Women*, 57: Chŏngsindae Research Association later changed its name to Korean Research Institute for Chongshindae (KRIC).

[19] Piper, "Transnational women's activism in Japan and Korea," 162; Chung, "Hanil Chogukjŏk Onghomang e kwanhan Yŏngu," 40.

[20] Chung, *Hyundae Ilbon ŭi Sahoe Undongron*, 167-68: Korean activists also contributed to the creation of new civic groups like the Japanese Women's Network for Comfort Women by giving lectures and showing films related to the issues of comfort women.

[21] Hirofumi Hayashi, "The Japanese Movement to Protest Wartime Sexual Violence: A Survey of Japanese and International Literature" *Critical Asian Studies* 33, no. 4 (2001): 573; Chung, "Korean Women Drafted for Military Sexual Slavery by Japan," 26: Military documents concerning comfort women were also found in the United States. As Chung notes, "in November 1991 a record entitled, "Headquarters, the U.S. Naval Military Government" dated Okinawa, November 1945, was discovered. In December, the report of the United States Offices of War, Information Psychological Warfare Team dated August, September and October 1944 was released."

[22] Soh, *The Comfort Women*, 63; Philip Seaton, "Reporting the Comfort Women Issue, 1991-1992: Japan's Contested War Memories in the National Press, *Japanese Studies* 26, no. 1 (May 2006): 103-105.

[23] Quoted in Yoshimi, *Comfort Women*, 58-59.

[24] Soh, *The Comfort Women*, 63-64; Hideko Mitsui, "The resignification of the comfort women through NGO trials" in *Rethinking Historical Injustice and Reconciliation in Northeast Asia*, eds. Gi-Wook Shin, Soon-Won Park, and Daqing Yang (New York: Routledge, 2007), 39-41: With the act of "listening" to surviving victims' life stories, the public hearing placed much weight on legal analysis that established the survivors' rights to individual reparation for their traumatic experiences. To this end, the executive committee also called a delegation of legal experts from various countries (the Netherlands, Canada, the U.S., South Korea, and Japan) to the historic event.

[25] Quoted in Soh, *The Comfort Women*, 64.

[26] Hayashi, "The Japanese Movement to Protest Wartime Sexual Violence," 574.

[27] Soh, *The Comfort Women*, 65.

[28] Chung, *Hyundae Ilbon ŭi Sahoe Undongron*, 170-76: Their efforts to file a suit in the PCA became unsuccessful when the Japanese government finally refused to accept an agreement of the PCA lawsuit in January 1995.

[29] The Korean Council for Justice and Remembrance for the Issues of Military Sexual Slavery by Japan: http://www.womenandwar.net/

[30] Idem., *Hanguk Jeongshindae Munje Daechaek Hyeopuihoi 20 Nyonsa* [20 Years of The Korean Council for the Women Drafted for Military Sexual Slavery by Japan] (Seoul: Hanul Academy, 2014): 128-38.

[31] Ibid., 84-99.

[32] Chin-Sung Chung, *Hyundae Ilbon ŭi Sahoe Undongron* [Social Movements in Modern Japan] (Seoul: Nanam Publishing House, 2001): 179-80: Many transnational activist groups vehemently opposed the AWF, but some groups in Japan, particularly the Association of Japanese Women (*Nihon Bujing Kaigi*), the Association for Solidifying Japan's War Responsibility (*Nihon no Sengo Sekining o Shikiri Saseru Kai*) and the *Jichirou*, an influential local labor union, supported the AWF because they thought it was a best solution to the issue under Japan's political conditions, though not fully satisfactory.

[33] Nicola Piper, "Transnational women's activism in Japan and Korea: the unresolved issue of military sexual slavery," *Global Networks* vol 1, no. 2 (2001): 155-170.

[34] Hayashi, "The Japanese Movement to Protest Wartime Sexual Violence": 579.

[35] Hideko Mitsui, "The resignification of the comfort women through NGO trials," in *Rethinking Historical Injustice and Reconciliation in Northeast Asia*, eds. Gi-Wook Shin, Soon-Won Park, and Daqing Yang (New York: Routledge, 2007): 46.

[36] Gay J. McDougall, *Systematic rape, sexual slavery and slavery-like practices during armed conflict: final report,* UN Sub-Commission on the Promotion and Protection of Human Rights, June 22, 1998, E/CN.4/Sub.2/1998/13: 55, https://www.refworld.org/docid/3b00f44114.html.

[37] The Korean Council, *Hanguk Jeongshindae Munje Daechaek Hyeopuihoi 20 Nyonsa* [20 Years of The Korean Council], 106-14.

[38] Author interview with the President of WCCW, Jung-Sil Lee, Washington DC, May 15, 2019.

[39] *See* chapter 2 and 3 of this volume for details of House Hearing of 2007 for the House Resolution 121.

[40] H.Res. 121: https://www.congress.gov/bill/110th-congress/house-resolution/121.

[41] House of Sharing http://www.nanum.org/eng/sub1/sub1.php.

[42] The Korean Council for Justice and Remembrance for the Issues of Military Sexual Slavery by Japan: http://www.womenandwar.net/.

[43] Won-deog Lee et al., "Ilbongun Wianbu Pihaeja Munje e kwanhan Bogoseo [Report on the Japanese Military Comfort Women Issue]" Ministry of Gender Equality and Family, April 2017: 161-62.

[44] Asian Women's Fund, *The Comfort Women Issue and AWF*, 125.

[45] Sarah Soh, "Japan's National/Asian Women's Fund for Comfort Women," *Pacific Affairs* 76, no. 2 (2003): 228-30: In December 1997, the Taiwan government also paid about $17,000 to each survivor with the same condition as the Korean government requested.

[46] House of Sharing: http://www.nanum.org/eng/sub2/sub1.php.

[47] The Korean Council, *Hanguk Jeongshindae Munje Daechaek Hyeopuihoi 20 Nyonsa* [20 Years of The Korean Council], 248-58: Many independence movement groups vehemently opposed the establishment of the comfort women museum within the Seodaemun Independence Park in which many Korean independence activists had been imprisoned during the Japanese colonial rule over Korea (1910-1945). The two primary reasons behind their opposition were for the museum to damage the honor of such independence activists and to give next generations a distorted historical perception that the Korean people only experienced sufferings by imperial Japan.

[48] National Women's Historical Hall: https://www.facebook.com/pg/busanherhistory/reviews/?referrer=page_recommendations_see_all&ref=page_internal; The Heeum Museum of Sexual Slavery by Japanese Military: http://www.heeummuseum.com/

[49] Women's Archive Museum of War and Peace: https://wam-peace.org/en/about.

[50] Changrok Kim et al., "Research Report for the Establishment of National Japanese Military Comfort Women Research Institute and History Museum," South Korean Ministry of Gender Equality and Family, May 2018: 70-74.

[51] The Korean Council for Justice and Remembrance for the Issues of Military Sexual Slavery by Japan: http://www.womenandwar.net/.

[52] Kim et al., "Research Report," 35.

[53] Agnes Constante, "Who are the 'comfort women,' and why are the U.S.-based memorials for them controversial?" *NBC News*, March 7, 2019, https://www.nbcnews.com/news/asian-america/who-are-comfort-women-why-are-u-s-based-memorials-n997656.

[54] Reji Yoshida and Ayako Mie, "Japan recalls envoys over new 'comfort women' statue in Busan," *The Japan Times*, January 6, 2017, https://www.japantimes.co.jp/news/2017/01/06/national/politics-diplomacy/japan-pulls-envoy-south-korea-comfort-women-dispute/#.WfJAlzsftOo.

[55] Jacey Fortin, "Comfort Women Statue in San Francisco Leads a Japanese City to Cut Ties," *The New York Times*, November 25, 2017, https://www.nytimes.com/2017/11/25/world/asia/comfort-women-statue.html.

[56] Christine Hauser, "'It Is Not Coming Down': San Francisco Defends 'Comfort Women' Statue as Japan Protests," *The New York Times*, October 4, 2018, https://www.nytimes.com/2018/10/04/us/osaka-sf-comfort-women-statue.html.

[57] Elizabeth Shim, "Statue dedicated to 'comfort women' removed in the Philippines," *UPI World News*, January 3, 2019, https://www.upi.com/Top_News/World-News/2019/01/03/Statue-dedicated-to-comfort-women-removed-in-the-Philippines/4461546541049/.

[58] The Korean Council.

[59] *Hankyoreh*, "Acan Sylvia Obal of Uganda awarded first Kim Bok-dong Peace Prize," August 15, 2018, http://english.hani.co.kr/arti/english_edition/e_international/857723.html.

[60] Idem., "Kosovo War survivor of sexual violence awarded 2019 Kim Bok-dong Prize," June 19, 2019, http://english.hani.co.kr/arti/english_edition/e_international/898540.html.

[61] The Korean Council.

[62] Won-deog Lee et al., "Ilbongun Wianbu Pihaeja Munje e kwanhan Bogoseo [Report on the Japanese Military Comfort Women Issue]" Ministry of Gender Equality and Family, April 2017: 158.

[63] Author interview with the President of WCCW, Jung-Sil Lee, Washington, D.C., May 15, 2019.

[64] Ministry of Foreign Affairs of Japan: http:// www.mofa.go.jp/policy/women/fund/state9308.html.

[65] Idem., http://www.mofa.go.jp/policy/women/fund/state9507.html.

[66] Idem.

[67] Yangmo Ku, "What is it for? Assessing the South Korea-Japan Deal on the Comfort Women Issue" *E-International Relations*, February 18, 2016, https://www.e-ir.info/2016/02/18/what-is-it-for-assessing-the-south-korea-japan-deal-on-the-comfort-women-issue/.

[68] Yoonchan Cho, "Ilbongun Wianbu Yongu Center [Japanese Military Comfort Women Research Center]," *Kyunghyang Shinmun*, March 19, 2019, http://news.khan.co.kr/kh_news/khan_art_view.html?art_id=201903192036005.

[69] Author interview, Seoul, July 11, 2019.

[70] Nam Eun-ju, "Recently discovered historical records show presence of comfort women on Chuuk Islands," *Hankyoreh*, December 29, 2017, http://english.hani.co.kr/arti/english_edition/e_international/825576.html

# 10. THE ROLES OF "COMFORT WOMEN" MEMORIALS IN THE U.S.: CONTINUED ACTIVATION OF THE SPIRIT OF HOUSE RESOLUTION 121

*Jung-Sil Lee*

**Abstract:** "Comfort Women" Memorials have been built around the globe to commemorate the struggle and trauma of "comfort women." The Japanese government continues to concern itself mostly with the physical presence and existence of the memorials as pernicious reminders of their inaction regarding the wrongdoings of the past. Meanwhile, the memorials have become a driving force and impetus to the activists of the "comfort women" redress movement. The memorials were built to educate the public on the history of the issue, but also to provide a transformative "liminal" space for viewers who might have had their own traumatic experiences.[1] "Comfort women" victims who were ostracized from society and were vulnerable to the slightest negative judgment, found no recourse in the public space where they could be consoled, remembered, or justified. This is the same as other victims of sexual violence who are doubly victimized, first by their aggressor and second by society. This chapter chronicles the most well-known "comfort women" memorials in the U.S., specifically in how and why they were built, the process it took to construct them, the response and outcome of the unveiling, and the significance of their presence to create contemporary discourses of the issue.

## Introduction

Memorials in public venues often help traumatized people with wounded pasts grieve as a memorial can offer a way to externalize internalized suffering. Through the memorialization process, feelings of shame and guilt seated in victims of sexual violence can be healed into something manageable and in some cases, positively healthy, turning suffering into power.[2] I met a woman crying on the butterfly bench after the unveiling ceremony of the Comfort Women Peace Garden in Fairfax, Virginia in 2014, built by WCCW. She explained that she was a victim of sexual violence during her childhood and could identify with the repressed pain in the case of "comfort women." She was strongly sympathetic to the history of "comfort women" and found herself healing and recovering herself from the clutches of her own traumatic memories. This therapeutic function is one of the tangible benefits of "comfort women" memorials in the local community (*see* Fig. 1-15).

The "comfort women" memorials [hereafter "the memorial(s)"] built in the U.S. garnered different public reaction than those built in Asian cities and countries; the memorials in the U.S. created diverse and intense controversy and were defaced with vandalism.[3] It is also a difficult task to historicize past events and figures from Asia onto American soil. Sometimes, this task encountered opposition out of racism and sexism. The organizations that support "comfort women" activism and women's rights in more than 10 different cities of the U.S. commissioned the memorials which ranged from modest stone slabs to elaborate figurative, lifelike statues of girls that emphasize their young age when they were induced or abducted and consequently subjugated into the "comfort women" system. The memorials' supporters aim to honor and rebuild the victims' dignity, to educate viewers on the history of this wartime atrocity, to warn and ensure these atrocities may never happen again, and to promote contemporary women's rights against any sex crimes (R.8).

While activists demanded an official apology and legal reparations from Japan for their World War II-era war crimes, the memorials became a reminder and emblem of the victims' horrific memories and wartime wrongdoings which provoked harsh criticism from Japanese hardline nationalist and historical revisionist factions. One time, when I asked a Japanese official from the Japanese Embassy why the Japanese, or rather, a local Japanese American, are particularly uncomfortable with the Statue of Peace (Statue of Girl, *Sonyeosang*), his first answer was that it "undermines the dignity of Japan and symbolizes un-forgiveness vis-à-vis Japan."[4] Ironically, his comment exemplifies the Japanese government's position as being the pointing-out of Japan's shameful and yet-unreconciled past. Forgiveness is only possible with the genuine contrition of the perpetrator; "acknowledge, accept, and apologize" are the three demands victims seek from the Japanese government.

In 2018, I presented a paper at the College Art Association (CAA) that examined the underlying politics and controversies of "comfort women" memorials in the U.S., related court cases, an unplanned outburst of publicity, and the unique ways in which activists dealt with a plurality of opinions. In the paper, I examined how the points of view toward the memorials eventually generated new discourse that made the memorial even more educational and comprehensible to the public.[5] Therefore, for this chapter, I limit myself to introducing all the U.S. "comfort women" memorials chronologically, the context, procedure, significance, specific intention of their construction, and to recognize the activists who built them and the surrounding activism.

## The First "Comfort Women" Memorial in the U.S.

The initial goal of the first "comfort women" memorial was to celebrate the passage of House Resolution 121 and to commemorate its spirit and a milestone in a more tangible and stable way. Three years after the passage of H.Res. 121 (see part I of this book), the first memorial of its kind was built on October 23, 2010 in Palisades Park, Bergen County, New Jersey through the efforts of the Korean American Voters Council (KAVC, later known as Korean American Civic Empowerment - KACE) and painter Steven Cavallo. The purpose of the memorial was to remember the bravery and endurance of victims in achieving the outcome as the inspiration for the Resolution. Cavallo and other artists hosted a "comfort women" themed exhibition in 2010 at Palisades Park Multimedia Center and Public Library to raise money to donate to a Korean shelter for victims called "House of Sharing" (A.10-1).[6] This purpose was the first motivation to raise awareness of the issue, where Cavallo and KAVC spearheaded the memorial project. Cavallo recalls that he started to have meetings with KAVC lawyer, Che Jin Park, first and then with others.[7] This first building of a memorial was meaningful as it was the first step in igniting the latent spirit of House Resolution 121, passed three years earlier which had slowed down. The visual and physical presence is much more powerful than the words, documents, and events that could be immaterial, transient, and abstract.

The memorial committee decided to build the memorial near the public library in Palisades Park because they believed the centrality of the location will help educate the people of the town. Cavallo, as a library employee, believed that "he could maintain the area before and after work more easily."[8] Cavallo oversaw the erection of the memorial, signed on the contract plaque, and designed the memorial (A.10-2). The boulder was furnished by Bergen County and the venue was donated by the city government of Palisades Park, the plaque mounted in the boulder was funded by KAVC and the New York House Resolution 121 Coalition.[9]

The supporters inscribed on the plaque are "County of Bergen, County Executive, The Board of Chosen Freeholders, and The Borough of Palisades Park." During the dedication ceremony, among many in attendance were: Dongchan Kim - the director of KAVC, student interns Haemin Chung and Youngduck Kim, co-representatives of New York House Resolution 121 Coalition, David Ganz, freeholder of Bergen County, James Rotundo, mayor of Palisades Park, Jason Kim, deputy mayor of Palisades city council, and Jungcheol Lee, city council member.[10] During the fourth anniversary ceremony, the deputy mayor of Palisades Park, Jason Kim, explained that the memorial served two functions: fostering empathy toward "comfort women," and more importantly, educating the younger generations about atrocious crimes against humanity.[11] He asserted that the venue choice in front of the public library would be an ideal location in terms of historicizing the issue and to legitimize its relevance to American history.

Fig. 10-1-1. The First Comfort Women Memorial, Palisades Park Public Library, New Jersey. October 23, 2010.

Despite Cavallo's efforts, the monument lit a powder keg of controversy when several members of the Japanese Parliament (Diet) visiting the town requested the plaque be removed.[12] The site was also vandalized with a wooden stake. Cavallo recalled how some of the older Palisades Park residents expressed their dissatisfaction and disapproval of the memorial saying that it would not fit the neighborhood, criticism stemming from racism. Absence of coalition for the cause in the area meant further educational activities could not be held. KAVC turned to focus more on the immediate issues of Korean Americans' voting

rights. However, Jason Kim testified to the strong healing power of the memorial both for the victims and other visitors manifested in ritual gestures such as laying flowers, touching the stone slab, and mourning.[13] The Palisades memorial became the first pilgrimage site of the "comfort women" issue that paved the way for many more memorials in the U.S. and other nations - an entire year earlier than the Statue of Peace in Seoul (2011) hoping for "reconciliation and peace building."[14] The memorial also triggered the passage of another "Comfort Women Resolution," the Senate Concurrent Resolution 124 in the state of New Jersey, under the sponsorship of Senator Loretta Weinberg in September 2012 (A.10-3).[15] This resolution was the first civic response to H.Res. 121 five years after its passage (Fig. 10-1-2).

Fig. 10-1-2. The first "comfort women" memorial, grandma Lee Yong-soo, Steve Cavallo, Dongchan Kim, and Phyllis Kim.

## More Memorials Followed

After the first "comfort women" memorial was installed in Palisades Park, NJ, the second memorial was unveiled on June 18, 2012 at Veterans Memorial, Eisenhower Park, Westbury, NY in Nassau County. David Chulwoo Lee, the representative of the Korean American Public Affairs Committee explained, "The red granite monument symbolizes the hardship and blood of the comfort women."[16] Nassau County, which manages the Memorial Park, is also in charge of maintaining the monument. In the same fashion as the first memorial, the Japanese Consulate General in New York called for the removal of this New York monument and Japanese lawmakers blamed pro-North Korean organizations for orchestrating the memorial.[17] Yet, David Lee refused the request to remove the memorial.

Two years later, in 2014, the fifth memorial flanked the second one. The memorial consisted of two stone slabs inscribed with New York State Resolution J 304 which was signed by the State Assembly and the New York Senate in 2013 (A.10-4). It was sponsored by Senator

Elaine Phillips and was unveiled by New York Senator Tony Avella, Assemblyman Chuck Lavine, Assemblywoman Michelle Schimel, and leaders of Korean American and human rights groups. David Lee, president of the Korean American Public Affairs Committee, stated, "This issue is not about embarrassing Japan." Avella pointed out Japan's denial of the responsibility as "a shame on the country" and said "it has nothing to do with the present people of Japan or the present leadership, but I think it's important . . . to recognize what happened."[18] The park is also filled with all different types of memorials and is home to a September 11th Memorial (Fig. 10-2-1, Fig. 10-2-2).

Fig. 10-2-1. The second and fifth "comfort women" memorials, Eisenhower Park, NY, 2012 and 2014.

Fig. 10-2-2. The fifth memorial, Veterans Memorial, Eisenhower Park, NY, Jan. 24, 2014. Inscription of New York State Senate Resolution J 304.

The third memorial for "comfort women" was erected at the Bergen County Courthouse, in New Jersey on March 8, 2013 in celebration of International Women's Day, sponsored by the Comfort Women Memorial Committee (Fig. 10-3). Chejin Park, a committee member and a staff attorney of KAVC, recalled that the Bergen County Justice Center (Courthouse) was the initial intended location for the first memorial. He said that there were already four other preexisting memorials commemorating the history of human rights: the Holocaust, Armenian Genocide, the Irish Great Hunger, and African American Slavery. Especially, Park consulted the detailed procedure of erecting memorials from the members of the African American Association.[19] Yet, the sudden change in political climate made it difficult for the committee to pursue the memorial in front of the Justice Center.

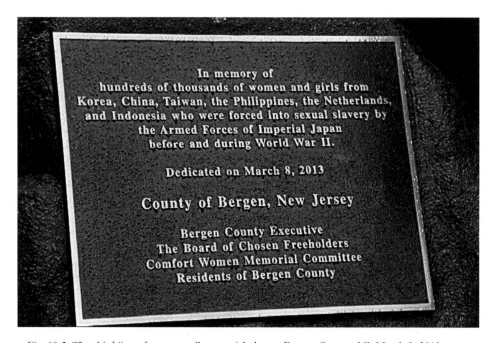

Fig. 10-3. The third "comfort women" memorial plaque, Bergen County, NJ. March 8, 2013.

According to Park, it was only possible after the new county executive Kathleen Donovan made a trip to South Korea, met former "comfort women" at the House of Sharing, and became sympathetic to the issue. She shared, "I cannot imagine the agony and the suffering that those women went through in the years of World War II, but the dignity and grace of them now would astonish all of us."[20] One of the attendees and cosponsors of House Resolution 121, Congressman Bill Pascrell, also met former "comfort women" when they visited Washington, D.C.[21] He told the attendees that the stories the women told of their ordeal "strengthen our commitment to the preservation of human rights." Dongchan Kim, president of KAVC, pointed out, "By having the memorial at this location, the Bergen County government is officially recognizing the 'comfort women' isssue as the same kind of international human rights violation as the other four human rights abuses remembered by the County in front of the Bergen County Courthouse."[22] Positive local responses extended to view "the memorial as an important bridge that solidifies the relationship between the American and Korean peoples."[23]

Notable achievements surrounding the memorial in Bergen County was to pass New Jersey State Comfort Women Resolution ACR 159, sponsored by Assemblyman Gordon M. Johnson (A.10-5).[24] This resolution is the third state resolution after California (1999) and New York (2013). The content of this resolution included the urgency of a Japanese apology but also revealed the strong support of the New Jersey State Assembly regarding the "comfort women" issue. This resolution, as stated in the website of KACE, "not only states that Japan must apologize for its crimes, but also represents the New Jersey State Assembly's stance on the "comfort women" issue."[25]

Despite the support of local politicians, in November 2012, a Japanese group bought a full-page ad in the *Star-Ledger* criticizing the erection of the memorial and created a Youtube video with a distorted view of "comfort women."[26] Instead of peaceful reconciliation, the Palisades and Bergen County memorials ignited a "History War," as termed by Japanese Prime Minister Shinzo Abe and *Sankei Shimbun,* which brought about "anti-comfort women discourse" during the building of the 2013 Glendale memorial. The major denial of war crimes by Japanese right-wing supporters rested in the argument that the women were not forcibly conscripted but rather were "well-paid and voluntary prostitutes." The phrase "History War" became widely known after the *Sankei* newspaper started to publish a series in a column titled "History War" in which Arimoto Dakashi insisted that the "comfort women" issue sparked the current "History War" taking place in the U.S. He posits that there were three major enemies of the Japanese state who instigated this war: China, Korea, and the *Asahi* newspaper, the first major institutional acknowledgment of "comfort women" history for the first time within Japan.[27] The rationale was that these three enemies were trying to degrade and taint the name of Japan, and Japan should fight back by disseminating protective counter-narratives.

The major groups and figureheads of the denial[28] are either mainland Japanese or Japanese who live in America but not Japanese Americans who were not even aware of the memorial or the historical facts. Japanese American activist and scholar Emi Koyama was surprised to see the newspaper article titled "Japanese Americans are against Comfort Women Memorial" which explained how the memorial caused hate crimes and shame against Japanese Americans. However, per her investigation, there are zero instances of hate crimes or discrimination against Japanese Americans because of this issue.[29] Rather, numerous Japanese American organizations actively joined and supported the building of the Glendale memorial such as the NCRR (the National Coalition for Redress/Reparations) and the JACL (Japanese American Citizens League).

## The Statue of Peace (Statue of Girl)

The Statue of Peace (Statue of Girl), the most well-known "comfort women" memorial, was first erected in Seoul, South Korea on December 14, 2011. The Statue of Peace was installed in front of the Japanese Embassy in Seoul to commemorate the 1000th Wednesday Demonstration by The Korean Council for the Women Drafted for Military Sexual Slavery by

Japan (in Korean: "Jungdaehyup" which recently changed its name to The Korean Council for Justice and Remembrance for the Issues of Military Sexual Slavery by Japan) and Korean victims of sexual slavery.[30] The surviving women and Korean activists unveiled the bronze lifelike statue charged with symbolism as an emblem of "comfort women" resistance. Afterwards, other statues have been installed all over Korea and the world, and have become the most famous emblem of "comfort women" redress movement.

The Statue of Peace was designed by the sculptor couple Kim Seo-kyung and Kim Eun-sung. The cast of the Statue of Peace was erected in Central Park, Glendale, California as the first of its kind outside of Korea on July 30, 2013 and the fourth "comfort women" memorial in the U.S. (Fig. 10-4). Statues of Peace are now erected in 102 locations in Korea to date and nine outside of Korea were unveiled afterwards; Canada (2015), Germany (2017), America (2013, 2014, 2017, 2019, 2020), China (2016), Australia (2016), and two more to come.

Fig. 10-4. The fourth memorial, Statue of Peace, Glendale, California. July 30, 2013 © *CARE (formerly KAFC)*.

The Statue of Peace in Glendale, CA was initiated by the Korean American civic group "121 Coalition of California" which was originally formed to support House Resolution 121 in 2007. In commemoration of the fifth anniversary of H.Res. 121 and in proclamation of "Comfort Women Day" in the city of Glendale in 2012, the Korean American Forum of California (KAFC, which changed its name to CARE in 2019) was formed and hosted two "comfort women" exhibits—one in Glendale and another in Los Angeles that, according to Phyllis Kim, the representative of KAFC, triggered the hope to have a memorial. "Comfort women" activists decided to erect a "comfort women" memorial to promote the spirit of H.Res. 121. KAFC searched for a venue and a design for the memorial. With much support from the Planning Commission of the City of Glendale and with guidance from Lee Changyeop, Glendale planning commissioner, KAFC was able to build the memorial in front of the Glendale Public Library.[31] The unveiling ceremony took place on July 30, 2013.

The Statue of Peace memorial features a life-sized bronze statue of a girl sitting in a chair accompanied by a second empty chair, as if inviting another person to sit. The total height is just 5 feet, and, without a high pedestal, the girl is easily accessible whether the viewer is sitting or standing right next to her. The empty chair alludes to the silent invitation to the victims who have already passed. The sculptor wanted to evoke the audience's sympathy and encourage physical proximity and contact with the statue; the girl's neck is often adorned with different props placed by visitors such as a flower wreath, scarf, necklace, hat, and so on, depending on the weather. The girl represents, presumably, a Korean girl as she is wearing a modified Korean traditional garment dated to the late 19th and early 20th centuries. According to the sculptor, her hair is unconventionally cut off implying her ostracism from her hometown.[32] Her facial expression is neutral and based on the preexisting girl figurines of Kim Seo-kyung. Although originally intending to showcase the older figure of the victims, they changed the sculpture to depict the image of a young girl in the past while still including a shadow of an aged victim near the bottom of the monument, connecting the past and the present, and alluding to the timelessness of their mental and emotional pain.

Every factor of the Statue of Peace denotes a certain meaning or message set by the sculptors; the young girl shows the average age of the sex slaves, who at the time ranged from 13 to 19 years old; her tight fists represent the girl's firm resolution for deliverance of justice; her bare and unsettled feet represent abandonment from a cold and unsympathetic world and by social norms rooted in Korean Confucianism, which kept them from going back to their hometowns; the bird on the girl's shoulder symbolizes a bond between the audience and the deceased victims—a symbol of life that tethers the living to the lost; the empty chair beside the girl symbolizes the survivors who are dying of old age without having yet witnessed the fulfillment of their call for justice and solidarity; the shadow of the girl is that of an old woman and the passage of time spent in silence; the butterfly[33] in the shadow represents hope that victims may resurrect one day to receive their apology.[34]

### "Comfort Women" Memorial Peace Garden in Fairfax, Virginia

While the controversy of the Statue of Peace in Glendale continued to unfold, other "comfort women" memorials were erected in several more cities in response to the heated issue of the "comfort women" redress movement. The Washington Coalition for Comfort Women Issues (WCCW) decided to erect the "comfort women" memorial by acquiring the unanimous support of the board of WCCW in December 2012. Unlike the Glendale memorial, the Comfort Women Memorial Peace Garden in the Fairfax County Government Center of Fairfax, Virginia did not encounter such controversy mainly due to its location on county government property, its non-figurative shape, and the universal nature of the description.

County Chairman Sharon Bulova, a major supporter of the memorial, saw that the horror of modern–day human trafficking issues shared commonality with the history of "comfort women." Thus, Bulova believed that the memorial could serve as a reminder of the suffering of all women who were denied their human rights and raise awareness of increased sex trafficking in Fairfax County.[35] Her role was critical as she supported this project with her executive power, sans a supervisors' vote, after hearing the WCCW presentation of the project. The WCCW memorial committee, looking for permission to erect the memorial in any park they could find in Fairfax County, was surprised when Bulova, so touched by the "comfort women" issue, recommended a site adjacent to a preexisting 9/11 memorial on the park of the County Government Center.[36] Throughout the design process, Bulova received a few email complaints and a visit from the Japanese Consul General, yet her adamant stance toward the issue remained steadfast.[37]

It took all of 2013 to design and raise funds for the memorial. The initial hope was to have the memorial designed by Baltimore-based David Gerlach, a metal sculptor with whom Jung-Sil Lee and Christine Choi met regularly, to create the semi-abstract design encoding "comfort women" history and to have a symbolic shape of the future globalized "comfort women" movement. The original nine feet high design did not correspond with the Fairfax County government's expectation. They suggested a

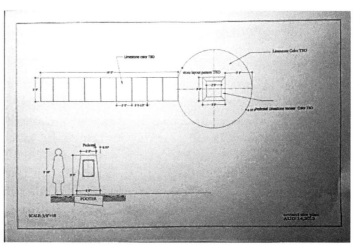

Fig. 10-5. Drawing plan for Comfort Women Memorial Peace Garden (CWMPG) in Fairfax County, VA suggested by WCCW, August 13, 2013.

simpler and smaller stone slab so as to not exceed the dimensions of the adjacent 9/11 memorial which is also a tombstone-like stone slab and not to protrude more than three feet from the ground. The committee redesigned it while proposing to still have a grander design

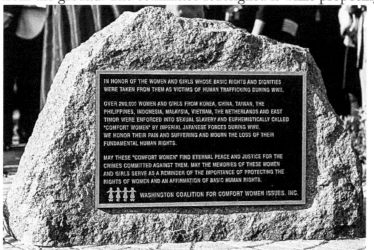

and dimension (Fig.10-5), but the final agreement was to have the stone slab with a maximum height of three feet and the surrounding plot to have a garden and benches.[38] The committee was rather disappointed not to have an artistic design or the larger dimensions that they wanted, but they found the right boulder and right benches, in the shape of a large butterfly that were welcomed by the county.[39]

Fig. 10-6. The sixth memorial, CWMPG Fairfax, VA plaque inscription, 2014.

On one side of the plaque is a summary of H.Res. 121 passed in 2007 in line with the spirit in which it was written, while the other side has the inscription of its multi-dimensional perspectives and potential new dimension of dialogue on "comfort women" issues (Fig. 10-6).[40] The unveiling ceremony was "respectful, moving, and beautiful," as described by Grace Wolf, honorary co-chair of the committee and Herndon Councilwoman, who described that "the memorial is not just for Korean Americans or Asian Americans but for all."[41] This memorial became a pilgrimage site to remember and honor "comfort women" victims, as well as an educational field trip site to discuss human rights by local and national visiting students and supporting groups.[42] The mood of the unveiling ceremony was uniquely respectful especially because of the live butterfly release performed by two high school students dedicated to the attending former "comfort woman" Kang Il-chul, as a part of the moving ritual to simulate and signify hope and freedom from discrimination (Fig. 10-7).[43]

Fig. 10-7. Butterfly release ritual during the unveiling ceremony of CWMPG in Fairfax County, Virginia by two high school students, Jonathan D. Kim (the first WCCW intern) and Easter Cho, May 30, 2014.

Afterwards, WCCW made a booklet explaining the "comfort women" issues and movement, then hosted academic conferences, internship programs, webinar lectures, forums, film screenings on–site or referring the site to envision the issue in multiple perspectives. To culminate the educational perspective of the memorials and the issue, WCCW published the book *Comfort Women: New Perspectives* written by WCCW interns on November 2019.[44]

That same year, 2014, the seventh "comfort women" memorial was built on August 4th in the Liberty Plaza at the intersection of 30th Street and Palisade Avenue, Union City, NJ. The monument is the first memorial that "the U.S. government has raised funds for and erected while all six previous monuments were funded by associations of Korean residents in the United States."[45] The shape of the memorial is similar to the Fairfax one, except it has a big butterfly sculpture. Former Korean "comfort women" Lee Ok-sun (87 years old at the time) and Kang Il-chul (86) attended the ceremony. A butterfly-shaped figure mounted on a stone slab conveys similar symbolism of the hope of escape, rejuvenation, and liberation that also alludes to the rite of passage from helpless victims to the fearless free.

During the unveiling ceremony, the Mayor of Union City, Brian Stack, emphasized the nature of the memorial as educational for human rights and giving lessons to the next generation. Lucio Fernandez, the commissioner of public affairs, explained the universal human rights issue and that he felt the memorial was a necessity in Union City (Fig. 10-8).[46] State Senator Sandra Bolden Cunningham mentioned, women's status as historically some form of slavery tying in the importance of these same issues in African American slavery. Dawn Zimmer, mayor of Hoboken, pointed out that sexual slavery is still happening globally.[47]

Councilman Zareh Sinanyan mentioned that "we're taking a meaningful step to show our moral support, sense of camaraderie, and our sharing of the pain that our Korean American brothers and sisters feel about this issue." Jersey City's Women Rising was also in attendance at the event, with member Margaret Abrams explaining that "the monument will empower victims to seek assistance and encourage others to report criminal activities and put an end to human trafficking."[48]

These two "comfort women" memorials in Fairfax

Fig. 10-8. The seventh "comfort women" memorial, Union City, NJ, 2014.

and Union City strive to convey a broader message of sex crimes overcoming the bilateral political conflict, believing that the abstract shape of the memorial without a detailed figure can be more instructive and accessible to the community. Due to the theme of the "comfort women" memorial, it stimulates discussion, response, and controversy anyway. As Laura Brandon asserts, "the inherent nature of war-related memorials is to provoke debate,"[49] whether it is positive or negative, to bring it into the forum of the public sphere. Two memorials were created, one organized by WCCW and erected on government property and the other with local government funds and efforts, both drawing broader attention to the issue.

## More Statues of Peace in Other Regions in the U.S.

Five more Statue of Peace memorials were erected in the U.S. after the one in Glendale, CA in 2013; Michigan, Atlanta, New York, Virginia, and Connecticut. The bronze replica of the Statue of Peace, originally installed in Seoul, Korea, and then Glendale, has been built more broadly throughout the world. The eighth memorial in the U.S. and the second Statue of Peace was erected in Southfield, Michigan on August 16, 2014, a year after the Glendale memorial. However, the behind-the-scenes story tells us the inception of the idea for the memorial was initiated as far earlier as 2011 and the intention was to erect it in a public venue, not in the current location of a private property in front of the Korean American Cultural Center.[50]

Through two phone interviews with Moonjae Park and David Shin, I was informed that it took more time to unveil the memorial and there were unwanted conflicts and misunderstandings among activists. David Shin, who served as the president of the Korean American Association in 2011, had the idea to have a "comfort women" memorial in Michigan. He contacted Chejin Park, the first executor of the Palisades memorial building, to ask questions and learn from their experience. Park shared every step and procedure along with legal advice. In the fall, Moonjae Park joined the Michigan team and proposed to switch the stone boulder to the Statue of Peace. The foundational committee of the "comfort women" memorial, David Shin, Deukyeol Kim, Jongdae Kim, and Moonjae Park, all agreed to have the Statue of Peace with excitement for its powerful efficacy to the community (Fig. 10-9).

In order to augment the funds, they expanded supporting groups to the Korean American Women's Association and Korean American Cultural Center. They, as the founding committee, processed necessary regulations to meet state law, IRS procedures, and customs processing until they were eventually excluded from the process by the newly formed committee. David Shin pointed out that "the memorial should have been erected in any public space not to be exclusively Korean issue, and should be associated with ongoing educational programs and events."[51] They put forth enormous effort to erect it at Southfield City Library but various hindrances led the committee to build the memorial in front of the Korean American Cultural Center.[52]

Lee Byung-joon, president of the Michigan Korean American Women's Association, played a pivotal role in raising funds for the statue. He said that the statue was to be installed in a public library in Detroit before protests arose from Denso Corporation, a Japanese auto parts manufacturer in the area, and the Japanese Consulate General, which said it would "encourage division in the area." [53] Approximately 150 people attended the ceremony, counting among them Southfield City Councilman Sidney Lantz, Korean War veterans, and representatives of Korean American associations in Detroit, Ann Arbor, and Southfield residents. Unfortunately, the educational program that was expected to follow

Fig. 10-9. The eighth memorial, Southfield, Michigan, Statue of Peace, August 16, 2014.

could not be implemented because the committee couldn't continue to be as successful and active of a supporting civic group as in the past.

In Atlanta, Georgia, the chairman of the Atlanta Comfort Women Memorial Task Force (TF), Baik Kyu Kim, told me that the Atlanta TF is comprised of Americans of Anglo-European, Australian, Chinese, Filipino, Indian, Indonesian, Japanese, Korean, Nepali, Taiwanese, Thai, Malaysian and Vietnamese descent. He also recalled that the TF faced objection right away once the project was submitted in 2017; the TF originally planned to keep the statue closer to the Atlanta downtown area but because of pushback caused by the Japanese government and colluding Atlanta corporations, it was not realized. When they tried to have an official agreement with the Center for Civil Rights and Human Rights regarding building the ninth "comfort women" statue on its grounds, the Japanese Consul General and the Chamber of Commerce of Metro Atlanta pressured the board of the Center with the withdrawal of local Japanese businesses.[54] Also, a Tokyo based man named Ken Kato, sent out emails to business donors of the Center for Civil and Human Rights, as well as to Invest Atlanta with the subject line: "Vicious Defamation Campaign against Japanese." He made the case that details of the history of "comfort women" are in dispute, and that efforts to memorialize these women are South Korean propaganda. Kato pointed to what he believes is evidence that "comfort women" were "well-paid" prostitutes, some of whom even fell in love with and married their clients (Fig. 10-10).[55]

In this threatening and unfavorable situation, the Center had to cancel the project that outraged the supporting residents and TF committee. Coca-Cola Japan even contacted the main American offices who then sent representatives of the Coca-Cola headquarters in Atlanta to pressure the Chamber of Commerce to influence the local government.[56] John Park, a City Council member in the nearby city of Brookhaven, took up the mission and worked with Helen Ho to persuade the City Council of Brookhaven and Mayor John Arthur Ernst to adopt

the memorial to raise awareness of the ongoing problems of sex and human trafficking taking place in Atlanta and the world today.[57] The city resolution of acceptance for donation of the Young Girl's Statue for Peace was passed and the planned location was moved to Brookhaven Park (A.10-6-1 and A.10-6-2).

Councilmember Bates Mattison praised the TF for its work and said he hopes installing "comfort women" statues will help bring peace

Fig. 10-10. The first anniversary ceremony of the Young Girl's Statue for Peace, Brookhaven, Atlanta, Georgia, June 28, 2018.

in the community. "We must shine a light on that history . . . so we are aware of it and learn from it," he said. "This is not about a nationality feeling they should be ashamed." The council received a standing ovation after the vote.[58]  Tim Echolas, a Georgia Public Service Commissioner who is the Statewide Advisor to the TF, said that Brookhaven has led the state in the fight against sex trafficking. Kelly Ahn, a leader of the TF, said that despite intense counter lobbying, the city council reached a unanimous decision to build the memorial in a Brookhaven Park in June 28, 2017.  In 2019, during the second anniversary of the memorial, the TF organized a creative opera, *A Stolen Girl's Story,* to continue to commemorate the history and keep it alive.[59]

The tenth "comfort women" memorial was built in Cliffside Park, New Jersey on July 19, 2017. It was built in the front garden of Trinity Episcopal Church near Cliffside Park, New Jersey, by the local Korean community, the Bergen County Korean American Association led by Kim Jin-sook.[60] It was funded by Han Chang-Yeon, former president of the Korean American Association of Greater New York, and took three years to gain approval by the city of Fort Lee for installation. The stone tablet is engraved with a picture of a girl, reminiscent of a "comfort woman" crouching with her face in her hands, as well as a description of the atrocity that took place. The design was created by lawyer Robert Kovik who also drafted the inscription of the memorial. Yet, due to the conflict with the Korean American Association of Fort Lee, which was dissatisfied in terms of the design and wording of the memorial, the final location was shifted to Cliffside Park. The memorial was widely supported by American veterans of the Korean War and local officials (Fig. 10-11).[61]

Fig. 10-11. The tenth "comfort women" memorial, Cliffside Park, NJ, 2017.

## Globalized Nature of the "Comfort Women" Memorial in San Francisco

The eleventh "comfort women" memorial was unveiled in San Francisco on September 22, 2017 at St. Mary's Square Annex, San Francisco, California. The memorial co-chairs, retired Chinese San Francisco Superior Court judges Lillian Sing and Julie Tang were activists surrounding the Nanjing massacre and were part of the group RNRC (Rape of Nanjing Redress Coalition) influenced by Iris Chang's book, *The Rape of Nanking.* When they turned to the "comfort women" memorial project, it was supported by many advocate groups, including CWJC (Comfort Women Justice Coalition) and KAFC, and they received permission from the San Francisco city council to erect the memorial. As they proclaimed in their statement on the unveiling ceremony, "Through our memorial, we remember all our grandmothers who are alive, and all those who have passed on but are still with us in both spirit and memory. Through our transnational, multiethnic solidarity, we are also resolved to restore justice to those whose lives and suffering have been erased by nationalist politics or expediency." For them, "comfort women" survivors represent a significant portion of women's wartime history marked by sexual victimization and trauma, and from its inception, the memorial has been marked with a global message due to the multiethnic group coalition.

The memorial represents "comfort women" survivors of three nationalities: Korean, Chinese, and Filipino, along with Kim Hak-soon, who was the first to come forth and give testimony about her past story in 1991. The set of statues was designed by sculptor Steven Whyte, the winner of the competition. He put these girls' statues on top of a 5-foot tall pedestal and in the shadow of these girls stands a statue of Kim Hak-soon. The girls stand amidst the busy San Francisco downtown traffic in their respective traditional gowns looking over the world, holding hands in silent, but staunch defiance (Fig. 10-12). The column represents their catch phrase, "Column of Strength." The organizers clearly stated the global character of the movement and memorial: "following their footsteps, we stand in solidarity with all those who have suffered from sexual violence. We are thinking of those in our communities who have been forced into sex trafficking, of the Yazidi women, the women in Syria, in Congo, and in Juarez, Mexico, and all those living near military bases. We are also thinking of those who suffered from sexual violence in the past, during the trans-Atlantic slave trade and the genocide of indigenous people."[62]

Once the San Francisco memorial was unveiled, it gained worldwide attention due to its global nature and visible downtown location, which led to the most heated controversy surrounding the "comfort women" memorial. Jan Yamada, the Japanese consul general in San Francisco, told *World Views* that the installation was "destined to be yet another addition to the existing quagmire surrounding the 'controversial statue.'" A spokesman for Japan's Foreign Ministry said the statue was "regrettable and incompatible with the position and efforts of the government of Japan"[63] Osaka Mayor Yoshimura Hirofumi, finally ended the

60-year-old sister city relationship after the mayor of San Francisco accepted the memorial as the city's property (Fig. 10-13).

Fig. 10-12. The eleventh "comfort women" memorial: "Column of Strength," San Francisco, CA, September 22, 2017 © *Comfort Women Justice Coalition (CWJC)*

226

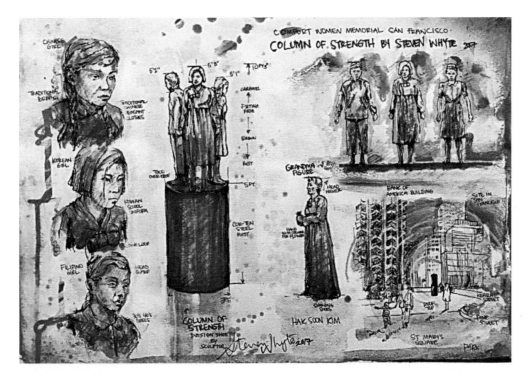

Fig. 10-13. San Francisco "comfort women" memorial: "Column of Strength" unveiling ceremony brochure © *Comfort Women Justice Coalition (CWJC)*

The president of Comfort Women Justice Coalition (CWJC), Judith Mirkinson stated, "the statue was unveiled at a time when many women were feeling emboldened to talk about sexual assault due to the current 'Me Too movement' and when statues in general had become lightning rods for political debate."[64] When California's State Board of Education approved a new Historical-Social Framework for California Public Schools that included a section on "comfort women" in World War II, they had a clear legitimacy of inclusion. In San Francisco Board of Education "comfort women" History Resolution No. 158-25A1, the board found that there is strong connection between commercially sexually exploited children (CSEC), victims of trafficking in the area of San Francisco and the education of prevention, awareness, and trauma treatment. The resolution ends (A.10-7):

> The superintendent and district staff create a task force with community experts to work in consultation to incorporate an educational component of the history of "comfort women" of WWII under the Japanese military in its curriculum to educate the community about the harmful effects of sex trafficking in its historical and modern day context for the purpose of preventing and protecting the youth community from sexual exploitation and trafficking.[65]

Another organization, the Education for Social Justice Foundation (ESJF), was founded in 2017 in response to the educational need of a San Francisco memorial. Co-founders of

ESJF, Russ Lowe and Nancy M. Lee, created another *Teacher's Resource Guide* for "comfort women" history and issues, which included historical background of "comfort women," primary source documents, lesson plans, worksheets, and activity sheets. It is intended for students to determine critical elements of a memorial; to determine its purpose and effectiveness; see the memorial, read major articles, then complete the worksheet with questions of purpose, symbolism, meaning, and controversies of the memorial (A.10-8).

The twelfth "comfort women" memorial is another Statue of Peace installed on October 13, 2017 at the Museum of Korean American Heritage in Manhattan by the New York Korean American Association of Greater New York. Unlike other memorials of its kind, the Manhattan Statue of Peace did not provoke any conflict as it is located inside a Korean Museum on private property. Dr. Pyong Gap Min, a sociology professor and director of the Research Center for Korean Community at Queens College who hosted the conference *Redress movement for the Victims of Japanese Military Sexual Slavery: Looking Back at the 27 year Movement* around the time of its unveiling, said that the statue's influence is "minimal" because of its location—indoors on the sixth floor of a complex where it will likely attract less attention than it would in a prominent space in New York City.[66] The statue is not the same structure as other Statue of Peace memorials. It is designed with less weight and is moveable to exhibit in other locations (Fig. 10-14).

Fig. 10-14. The twelfth Statue of Peace, New York, NY, October 2017 © *KAAGNY*

Fig. 10-15. The thirteenth "comfort women" memorial Fort Lee, NJ. May 23, 2018

The thirteenth "comfort women" memorial was built by a Fort Lee (NJ) high school student organization in May 23, 2018. Per an interview with Eunjoo Hong, President of the Korean American Association in Fort Lee and advisor of the group, the students formed the organization Youth Council of Fort Lee (YCFL) on the occasion of the film screening of "Spirit's Homecoming" in New Jersey Theater with shock and passion for justice and redress of "comfort women."[67] The students carried out the entire process of memorial building, such as presenting at civic council meetings, fundraising, designing, and construction (A.10-9-1, 10-9-2). In December 2017, the Fort Lee Mayor and Council unanimously approved of the "comfort women" memorial. The team says that "their goal was not to assess blame but to honor the memory of these strong women. . . . It is the YCFL's hope that this monument can serve as a beacon of hope for a better future avoiding these types of crimes against humanity on all fronts." The memorial building project in Fort Lee will be remembered and valued as an outcome of students' endeavor to pave the way to carry on the movement to the next generation (Fig. 10-15).

The fourteenth memorial was unveiled on October 27, 2019 in Annandale, Virginia. Annandale is the largest Korean town in the Washington metropolitan area. The statue was initially donated by The Korean Council and TwoSol cosmetics to the Korean American community in the D.C. area. The Washington Butterfly for Hope (D.C. Nabi) held a welcoming ceremony for the arrival of the statue on December 10, 2016 at Sylvan Theater near the Washington Monument in D.C., but it was not easy to find a permanent home.[68] Almost three years later, a new committee was formed by the Washington Coalition for Comfort Women, Washington Butterfly for Hope, and the National Unification Advisory Council D.C. chapter. This is the fifth Statue of Peace in the U.S. (Fig. 10-16) (A.10-10).

Fig. 10-16. The fourteenth memorial: Statue of Peace, Annandale, VA. Committee members at the unveiling ceremony with grandmother Gil Won-ok, October 27, 2019.

The co-chair of the Committee of Statue of Peace, Jung-Sil Lee, proclaimed the significance of the presence of the Annandale statue during the unveiling ceremony:

1.  The Statue is intended to honor and commemorate the grandmothers' bravery and endurance, it is also for longing for justice and a peaceful world without sexual violence and war.

2. It is a physical and ongoing reminder of the past wrongdoing and inaction of the Japanese government, to the demands of victims, which is an official apology and legal reparation, once suggested by House Resolution 121, championed by former congressman Mike Honda and 167 cosponsors in 2007.

3. The Statue will provide the educational cornerstone for women's rights and dignity; justice for humanity; a peaceful world against war and injustice. It will be a teachable memorial for the public and the next generation.

4. The Statue will also function as the most salient entity to fueling the coalition of 28 years of the "comfort women" redress movement, in the U.S. It will become a place of pilgrimage for any activists, educators, scholars, and artists for the issue.

5. The Statue is not only for the grandmothers but for all victims of sexual assault and it will be the space for empathy with the pain of victims, and healing from their own trauma.[69]

For the ceremony, former victim and survivor, grandmother Gil Won-ok (92), and Yoon Mee-hyang, the chair of The Korean Council, visited from Korea and participated in the ceremony, poetry reading, and other cultural performances. "The Space for Remembrance" was set up right next to the Statue in an office space donated by Eric Shin, owner of the printing company. The Committee exhibits "comfort women" related brochures, books, postcards, and other relevant products to the visitors of the Statue of Peace. Karen Keys-Gamarra, Fairfax County School Board member, spoke about its relevance for the county's educational mission in terms of advocating for human rights during the ceremony. The Committee aims to proceed to instill educational curriculum for both Fairfax County, Virginia and Montgomery County, MD. Around the same time, WCCW published a book written exclusively by WCCW youth interns who were trained and conducted research for almost two years.

Fig. 10-17. Gil Won-ok, former "comfort woman" sitting next to the Statue of Peace. Unveiling ceremony, Annandale, Virginia, October 27, 2019.

Joey D. Kim was dedicated to the "comfort women" memorials and its relation to political statements, resolutions, and new discourses[70] (Fig. 10-17) (A.10-11).

There will be more "comfort women" memorials built to serve as a constant physical impetus for memorialization, discourse, and public education regarding "comfort women."[71] The Statue of Peace, especially, has become one of the emblems of victims and has been created in diverse shapes and materials. The portable statue was exhibited in Japan's Aichi

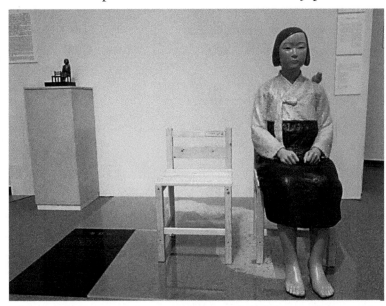

Triennale on August 15, 2019 in the section "After 'Freedom of Expression?'" that "drew hundreds of complaints; one person even threatened to burn down the museum. As a result, organizers decided to close the section just three days later."[72] Right after the incident, however, Spanish art collector Tatxo Benet purchased the Statue along with other censored artworks to be permanently preserved in his upcoming "Freedom Museum" in Barcelona, Spain (Fig. 10-18).

Fig. 10-18. Artists Kim Seo-kyung's and Kim Eun-sung's Statue of Peace (2011) in Aichi Triennale, 2019 © *Kim Seo-kyung and Kim Eun-sung*

All this action to deny and eliminate history at any cost by Japanese right-wing revisionists has instead served to bring more attention to the issue, making these works even more famous and promoting awareness of the past and present of these trafficked girls, unwantedly named as "comfort women."[73] The Butterfly Fund, launched by Kim Bok-dong and Gil Won-ok. joins a growing movement around the world to support victims of human trafficking and sexual abuse and exploitation; whether that be in Vietnam, Uganda, the DRC, or ISIS territories. Indeed, in lock step with the empowerment of women's voices in the "Me Too movement" in the States, the Butterfly Fund and other organizations and movements are seeing the fruits of their labor in the changing discourse around these issues. Whether intentional or not, the duality of the image of the butterfly—as a symbol of transformation for the "comfort women" through the healing power of art, or as a declaration of their desire to have their actions make larger impacts on society as a whole in the future (the butterfly effect)—it is clear that in both cases, the work of these butterflies are not yet finished and will continue to impact our hearts, minds, and societies for generations to come.

# Bibliography

"Comfort Women Memorial erected near NMYC." *The Korea Times*, August 5, 2014.

"Comfort Women Memorial Set Up in New York City." *The Chosun Ilbo*, June 18, 2012.

"New York Lawmakers unveil second 'comfort women' memorial." *The Japan Times News*, Jan 26, 2014.

Bemma, Adam. "South Korea: World's Longest Protest over Comfort Women." *Aljazeera*, September 7, 2017. https://www.aljazeera.com/news/2017/09/south-korea-world-longest-protest-comfort-women-170908024721239.html; *see* Yoon Mihyang, *Wednesday for Twenty Years*, Seoul: Woongjin Junior, 2010.

Blair, Annabelle. "New York City's first 'comfort women' statue remembers sex victims." *QNS*, October 31, 2017.

Brandon, Laure. *Art & War*. New York: I.B. Tauris & Co Ltd, 2007.

Burrow, Megan. "Westwood artists work to keep history alive." *Pascack Valley Community Life*, Oct 14, 2010.

Chung, Catherine. "Comfort Women' Monument unveiled in New Jersey." *The Korea Herald*, July 20, 2017.

Eliade, Mircea. *The Encyclopedia of Religion* 12: 405. New York: Macmillan Publishing Company, 1987.

Fortin, Jacey. "'Comfort Women' Statue in San Francisco Leads a Japanese City to Cut Ties." *Asia Pacific*, November 25, 2017.

Hagen, Lisa. "Atlanta Debates How to Recognize History of 'Comfort Women.'" *WABE (Where Atlanta Meets NPR)*, March 9, 2017. https://www.wabe.org/atlanta-debates-how-recognize-history-comfort-women/

Harlow, Kristance. "Let Us Heal: On Surviving and the Controversial 'Comfort Women.'" *Rewire.News*, April 4, 2017. https://rewire.news/article/2017/04/04/let-us-heal-on-surviving-comfort-woman/

Heinis, John. "Comfort Women Monument Unveiled in Union City." *Hudson County View*, August 5, 2014.

Ikuhito, Hata. "History Wars Japan-False Indictment of the Century." *Sankei newspaper publisher*, 2014-2015.

Kayzerman, Julie. "Comfort Women Visit Union City for Unveiling of Liberty Plaza Monument." *Jersey Journal*, August 5, 2014.

Kim, Joey. "Positive Interaction between Comfort Women Memorials and House Resolutions it the U.S." In *Comfort Women: New Perspectives,* edited by Jonathan D. Kim, Christopher Sung, and Min Suh Lee, 44-58. San Francisco: Blurb Publisher, 2019.

Kim, Jonathan, ed. "Introduction: comfort Women Movement Matters in the U.S. Education System." In *Comfort Women: New Perspectives,* San Francisco: Blurb Publisher, 2019.

Kim, Seo-kyung and Eun-sung Kim. *The Promise imprinted in the Empty Chair*. Seoul: Mal Publisher, 2016.

Koyama, Emi. "The U.S. as 'Major Battleground' for 'Comfort Woman' Revisionism: The Screening of Scottsboro Girls at Central Washington University." *Asia Pacific Journal* 13: 22 (June 3, 2015): 1-7. https://apjjf.org/Emi-Koyama/4324.html.

Lee, Jung-Sil. "Unforeseen Controversy: Reconciliation and Re-contextualization of Wartime Atrocities through *Comfort Women Memorials* in the U.S." In *Teachable Monument: Using Public Art to Spark Dialogue & Confront Controversies,* edited by Sierra Rooney and Jennifer Wingate, with Harriet Senie. New York: Bloomsbury Publishing Inc, forthcoming 2020.

McCarthy, Mary M. "How the Japan-Korea 'Comfort Women' Debate Plays out in the U.S." *The Diplomat,* August 4, 2017. https://thediplomat.com/2017/08/how-the-japan-korea-comfort-women-debate-plays-out-in-the-us/.

McCarthy, Mary M. "the U.S. Comfort Women Memorials: Vehicles for Understanding and Change." *Asia Pacific Bulletin* no. 275 (Aug 12, 2014). https://www.eastwestcenter.org/publications/us-comfort-women-memorials-vehicles-understanding-and-change.

Nguyen, Andy. "Glendale's Comfort Women Statue vandalized with unknown brown substance." *Glendale News Press,* July 25, 2019. https://www.latimes.com/socal/glendale-news-press/news/story/2019-07-25/glendale-comfort-women-statue-vandalized

Pes, Javier. "A Sculpture That Was Censored from Japans's Aichi Triennale Will Become a Centerpiece of a New Museum for Banned Art." *Artnet News,* August 15, 2019.

Piccirillo, Ann and Patch Staff. "Bergen County dedicates Memorial to Comfort Women." *Patch,* March 8, 2013.

Schirch, Lisa. *Ritual and Symbol in Peacebuilding.* Bloomfield: Kumarian Press, 2005.

Semple, Kirk. "In New Jersey, Memorial for 'Comfort Women' Deepens Old Animosity." *The New York Times,* May 18, 2012.

Song, Euyong. "Unveiling Ceremony of the First Comfort Women Memorial." *The Korean New York Daily,* Oct 25, 2010.

Sullivan, S.P. "Bergen County marks International Women's Day with Korean 'comfort women' memorial." *N J Advance Media for NJ.com,* March 8, 2013.

Taylor, Adam. "Why Japan is losing its battle against statues of colonial-era 'comfort women.'" *The Washington Post,* September 21, 2017.

The Korea Times New York staff. "Conflict between Korean orgs stalls Fort Lee comfort women memorial." *The Korea Times,* July 8, 2015.

Treichel, Tamara. "Fairfax County's New Comfort Women Memorial Courts Controversy." *Asian Fortune,* July 15, 2014.

Turnbull, Colin. "Liminality: a synthesis of subjective and objective experience." In *By Means of Performance: Intercultural Studies of Theatre and Ritual,* edited by Richard Schechner and Willa Appel, Cambridge: Cambridge University Press, 1989.

[1] Colin Turnbull, "Liminality: a synthesis of subjective and objective experience," in *By Means of Performance: Intercultural Studies of Theatre and Ritual,* ed. Richard Schechner and Willa Appel (Cambridge: Cambridge University Press, 1989), 73–74: "disorder is ordered, doubts and problems removed, the 'right' course of action made clear with a rightness that is both moral and structural since the inevitable discrepancies between belief and practice in the external world are among the many problems ordered and removed in the liminal state."

[2] Kristance Harlow, "Let Us Heal: On Surviving and the Controversial 'Comfort Women,'" *Rewire.News,* April 4, 2017, https://rewire.news/article/2017/04/04/let-us-heal-on-surviving-comfort-woman/.

[3] A few days before the KAFC's 7th anniversary, the Statue of Peace in Glendale was vandalized: Andy Nguyen, "Glendale's Comfort Women Statue vandalized with unknown brown substance," *Glendale News Press,* July 25, 2019, https://www.latimes.com/socal/glendale-news-press/news/story/2019-07-25/glendale-comfort-women-statue-vandalized.

[4] Japanese officer, K. H. from Japanese Embassy in Washington, D.C., interview by Jung-Sil Lee, November 1, 2017.

[5] Jung-Sil Lee, "Unforeseen Controversy: Reconciliation and Re-contextualization of Wartime Atrocities through *Comfort Women Memorials* in the U.S.," in *Teachable Monument: Using Public Art to Spark Dialogue & Confront Controversies,* ed. Sierra Rooney and Jennifer Wingate, with Harriet Senie. (New York: Bloomsbury Publishing Inc, forthcoming 2020).

[6] Steve Cavallo, interview by Jung-Sil Lee, June 25, 2019. Cavallo organized fundraising silent auction for 65 artists' works along with Kyung Hwa Cavallo, Dai Sil Kim-Gibson (filmmaker). Dongsuk Kim (director of KAVC now KACE), mayor James Rotundo supported the event and Mr. and Mrs. Cavallo made a trip to the House of Sharing in Seoul to deliver the raised fund $1,200 to the victims.

[7] Cavallo recalls that more direct motivation for him to focus on the memorial was grassroots activism by high school students who were leading the plea for support for the issue as summer interns led by KAVC in 2009.

[8] Megan Burrow, "Westwood artists work to keep history alive," *Pascack Valley Community Life*, October 14, 2010.

[9] Che Jin Park, interview by Jung-Sil Lee, July 30, 2019.

[10] Euyong Song, "Unveiling Ceremony of the First Comfort Women Memorial," *The Korean New York Daily,* October 25, 2010.

[11] Office of Deputy Mayor, Jason Kim, "Come from the Shadows: Art and Writings," in the Fourth Anniversary Ceremony Catalog, Palisades Park Public Library, October 23, 2014.

[12] Kirk Semple, "In New Jersey, Memorial for 'Comfort Women' Deepens Old Animosity," *The New York Times,* May 18, 2012.

[13] Ritual is conscious and voluntary, repetitious and stylized symbolic bodily actions that are centered on cosmic structures and /or sacred presence: Mircea Eliade, ed., *The Encyclopedia of Religion* 12 (New York: Macmillan Publishing company, 1987): 405.

[14] Lisa Schirch, *Ritual and Symbol in Peacebuilding* (Bloomfield: Kumarian Press, 2005), 16–17; She defines ritual as a symbolic and physical act that communicates through symbols, myths, and metaphors, allowing for multiple interpretations; ritual aims to form or transform people's worldviews, identities, and relationships.

[15] Bill Title: Commemorates suffering endured by "comfort women" during forced internment in Japanese military camps. Sponsored by Senator Loretta Weinberg, District 37 (Bergen), Senator Kevin J. O'Toole, District 40 (Bergen, Essex, Morris and Passaic), Cosponsored by Senators Allen and Gordon.

[16] "Comfort Women Memorial Set Up in New York City," *The Chosun Ilbo,* June 18, 2012.

[17] Ibid., "Petitions were posted on the White House's 'We the People' petition website on May 10, calling for removing the [comfort women] monument and not supporting 'any international harassment related to this issue against the people of Japan.' A total of 32,075 signatures had been gathered on as of last Saturday. The White House must give an official response to any petition with more than 25,000 signatures."

[18] "New York Lawmakers unveil second 'comfort women' memorial," *The Japan Times News,* Jan. 26, 2014.

[19] Chejin Park, interview by Jung-Sil Lee, July 30, 2019.

[20] Ann Piccirillo and Patch Staff, "Bergen County dedicates Memorial to Comfort Women," *Patch,* March 8, 2013.

[21] S.P. Sullivan, "Bergen County marks International Women's Women's Day with Korean 'comfort women' memorial," *N J Advance Media for NJ.com,* March 8, 2013.

[22] Piccirillo and Patch Staff, *op. cit.*

[23] Sullivan, "Bergen County," 2.

[24] New Jersey State Resolution ACR 159 Comfort Women Resolution was proposed by Gordon Johnson and Connie Wagner on September 24, 2012 and was passed in the Assembly Committee on Women and Children by 6 votes and 1 abstaining. https://www.njleg.state.nj.us/2012/Bills/ACR/159_R1.PDF.

[25] KACE: https://us.kace.org/2013/new-jersey-state-comfort-women-resolution-acr-159-about-to-be-passed/.

[26] The advertisement was created by the "Committee for Historical Facts" who consist of Japanese extreme rightist, journalist, composer, and a professor. The YouTube video titled "Sex, Lies, and Comfort Women" was fabricated on 2012 and 2013 with a little extended version. On the website of KACE: https://us.kace.org/2012/comfort-women-historical-distortion-advertisement-on-a-new-jersey-newspaper/.

[27] Hata Ikuhito, "History Wars Japan-False Indictment of the Century," *Sankei newspaper publisher,* 2014-2015.

[28] Mera Koichi is a major figure who established The Institute of Japan Revival in 2006. Emi Koyama studies broadly examined their activities in detail in her booklet "Against Japanese 'comfort women' Denialism in the U.S." and her recent book chapter "Attack on comfort women memorial in the U.S." in *Comfort Women Overseas* (Seoul: Eomoonhak sa, 2017), 63–111.

[29] Emi Koyama, "The U.S. as 'Major Battleground' for 'Comfort Woman' Revisionism: The Screening of Scottsboro Girls at Central Washington University," *Asia Pacific Journal* 13: 22 (June 3, 2015).

[30] On the base of the Statue of Peace, the inscription says "December 14, 2011 marks the 1000th Wednesday Demonstration for the resolution of the Japanese Military Sexual Slavery issue after its first rally on January 8, 1992 in front of the Japanese Embassy. This peace monument stands to commemorate the spirit and the deep history of the Wednesday Demonstration." The Wednesday Demonstration was listed in March 2002 in the Guinness Book of Records as the world's oldest rally on a single theme. Adam Bemma, "South Korea: World's Longest Protest over Comfort Women," *Aljazeera,* September 7, 2017, https://www.aljazeera.com/news/2017/09/south-korea-world-longest-protest-comfort-women-170908024721239.html; *see* Yoon Mihyang, *Wednesday for Twenty Years* (Seoul: Woongjin Junior, 2010).

[31] Phyllis Kim, Yoon Sukwon, Joachim Youn, Kean Hwang, Roy Hong, Jung-ran Shin, and Yooha Song are among many. Phyllis Kim, interview by Jung-Sil Lee, September 23, 2017.

[32] Kim Seo-kyung and Kim Eun-sung, *The Promise Imprinted in the Empty Chair* (Seoul: Mal Publisher, 2016), 64–97.

[33] The butterfly has become the long-term symbol of victims as newly transformed activists, especially after the donation by one of the victims, Kim Bok-dong, who donated all the funds she received to help the women in Congo and Bosnia to build a shelter for the women who were raped and had children. Recently, Pope Francis offered condolences to these women during his visit to Korea, at a Mass for peace and reconciliation in Seoul, Korea on August 18, 2014. Pope Francis received a butterfly pin, symbolizing the victims' plight and their resolution to be arbiters of peace. The way in which a butterfly takes flight serves as a metaphor of the "rite of passage" of the victimized women who desire to regain their dignity and freedom from discrimination, violence, and oppression by bettering themselves to overcome their past trauma and conflicts.

[34] Kim Seo-kyung and Kim Eun-sung, *The Promise Imprinted in the Empty Chair*, 64–97.

[35] Sharon Bulova, Chairman of Fairfax Supervisors, interview by Jung-Sil Lee on May 1, 2019 in her office of Fairfax Government Center.

[36] The WCCW Memorial Committee was formed with William Hwang (chair), Grace H. Wolf (honorary co-chair), Christine Choi (president), Jung-Sil Lee (VP), Sami Lauri (VP), Helen Won (secretary).

[37] Mary M. McCarthy, "The U.S. Comfort Women Memorials: Vehicles for Understanding and Change," *Asia Pacific Bulletin* (Aug 12, 2014): 2.

[38] WCCW Committee had to amend the height of the memorial a few times from 9 feet, 6 feet, 5 feet, and finally 3 feet along with giving up the artistic half abstract sculpture on top of the high pedestal.

[39] David Gerlach was asked by WCCW to design butterfly benches instead, but he recommended that we buy ready-made chairs due to the high cost, and introduced us to the site where we purchased the two of them.

[40] The inscription says: "May these 'Comfort Women' find eternal peace and justice for the crimes committed against them. May the memories of these women and girls serve as a reminder of the importance of protecting the rights of women and an affirmation of basic human rights." Washington Coalition for Comfort Women Issues, Inc. May 30, 2014.

[41] Mary M. McCarthy, "How the Japan-Korea 'Comfort Women' Debate Plays out in the U.S.," *The Diplomat* (August 4, 2017).

[42] The butterfly metal benches surround the stone memorials symbolizing how the grandmothers who, in the fight for their justice, metamorphosed from being treated as the lowest of creatures that crawl unseen to their current state of empowerment, beauty, and confidence as butterflies, flying away from a painful past; Tamara Treichel, "Fairfax County's New Comfort Women Memorial Courts Controversy," *Asian Fortune*, July 15, 2014.

[43] For detailed experience of the ritual, *see* Jonathan Kim, "Introduction: Comfort Women Movement Matters in the U.S. Education System," in *Comfort Women: New Perspectives* (San Francisco: Blurb Publisher, 2019), 12.

[44] Jonathan D. Kim, Christopher Sung, and Min Suh Lee, eds., *Comfort Women: New Perspective* (San Francisco: Blurb Publisher, 2019).

[45] "Comfort Women Memorial erected near NMYC," *The Korea Times,* August 5, 2014.

[46] John Heinis, "Comfort Women Monument Unveiled in Union City," *Hudson County View,* August 5, 2014.

[47] https://www.youtube.com/watch?v=aiEMophelac.

[48] Julie Kayzerman, "Comfort Women Visit Union City for Unveiling of Liberty Plaza Monument," *Jersey Journal,* August 5, 2014.

[49] Laure Brandon, *Art & War* (New York: I.B. Tauris & Co Ltd, 2007), 129.

[50] One of the initiators, Moonjae Park, recalls that his opposition to the private venue for the memorial and his involvement in KANCC caused him to be excluded from the process of the memorial building. He spearheaded the one-page public announcement "Open Letter to Shinzo Abe," *New York Times*, 2011: Moonjae Park, interview by Jung-Sil Lee, July 1, 2019.

[51] David Shin, interview by Jung-Sil Lee, July 23, 2019.

[52] Sidney Ranch, city council member helped them a lot trying to link the Holocaust Museum and library director. David Ewick library director were approached by Japan Business Society of Detroit and Japanese Embassy with the promise of the donation to the library. David Shin interview by Jung-sil Lee, also *see* the details "In the 1 year Anniversary of Statue of Girl," editorial column, *Michigan Korean Times*, July 25, 2015, https://www.youtube.com/watch?time_continue=128&v=87CftAa6y6M

[53] *See* the interview with Lee Byung-joon, *The Korea Times,* August 18, 2014.

[54] "The Government of Japan is seriously concerned that the memorial in Atlanta may cause discrimination, humiliation or bullying against members of the Japanese community in Atlanta who wish to live in peace," Deputy Consul General Yasukata Fukahori said in an emailed statement, Lisa Hagen, "Atlanta Debates How to Recognize History of 'Comfort Women,'" *WABE (Where Atlanta Meets NPR),* March 9, 2017, https://www.wabe.org/atlanta-debates-how-recognize-history-comfort-women/

[55] Ibid.

[56] John Park, Brookhaven City Councilmember, interview by Jung-Sil Lee, June 29, 2019.

[57] The city of Brookhaven decided to adopt the memorial and proclaimed the Resolution to accept donation of artwork: State of Georgia, Dekalb County, City of Brookhaven, "Res. 2017-05-03," approved by John Arthur Ernst, Jr., Mayor.

[58] http://ygpm.org/news_en_view.php?no=17.

[59] Kelly Ahn, Atlanta Comfort Women Memorial Task Force member; for the second anniversary, the Task Force team organized an art exhibition, poem reading, and creative opera in the center of Korean American Association of Greater Atlanta on June 28, 2019, interview by Jung-Sil Lee, June 29, 2019.

[60] Jin-sook Kim, president of Bergen County Korean American Association, interview by Jung-Sil Lee on November 13, 2019. She recalls that it took four years to build the current location after failure to build on Abbott Boulevard, Fort Lee where large Japanese and Korean populations reside and is a much busier public quarter. The reason for the failure was a disaccord with the Fort Lee Korean American Association: *The Korea Times,* New York staff, "Conflict between Korean orgs stalls Fort Lee comfort women memorial," *The Korea Times*, July 8, 2015.

[61] Catherine Chung, "'Comfort Women' Monument unveiled in New Jersey," *The Korea Herald*, July 20, 2017.

[62] Judith Mirkinson, president of CWJC, press release during the unveiling ceremony, September 22, 2017.

[63] Adam Taylor, "Why Japan is losing its battle against statues of colonial-era 'comfort women,'" *The Washington Post*, September 21, 2017.

[64] Jacey Fortin, "'Comfort Women' Statue in San Francisco Leads a Japanese City to Cut Ties," *Asia Pacific*, November 25, 2017.

[65] Resolution No. 158-25A1: https://archive.sfusd.edu/en/assets/sfusd-staff/about-SFUSD/files/resolutions/158-25A1.pdf.

[66] Annabelle Blair, "New York City's first 'comfort women' statue remembers sex victims," *QNS*, October 31, 2017.

[67] YCFL started by 9 youths and now includes 35 members from all over Bergen County, https://youthcouncilfortlee.org/.

[68] In March 2017, Salisbury University almost placed the statue on their campus with the advocacy of Professor Taehyun Nam, but the University cancelled the plan only a few days before the scheduled unveiling ceremony without clear explanation, Hyunsook Cho, representative of *Washington Butterfly for Hope*, interview by Jung-Sil Lee, https://www.facebook.com/groups/1687517071499196/?ref=bookmarks.

[69] Jung-Sil Lee, co-chair of the Committee of Statue of Peace, during the welcoming remarks at the unveiling ceremony of the Statue of Peace. October 27, 2019 at Annandale, Virginia.

[70] Joey Kim, "Positive Interaction between Comfort Women Memorials and House Resolutions it the U.S.," *Comfort Women: New Perspectives* (San Francisco: Blurb Publisher, 2019), 44–58.

[71] The two more Statues of Peace were built: one in Hamden, CT on December 7, 2019 (unveiling ceremony on March 1, 2020), and the other in Houston, Texas on December 11, 2019.

[72] Javier Pes, "A Sculpture That Was Censored from Japan's Aichi Triennale Will Become a Centerpiece of a New Museum for Banned Art," *Artnet News*, 15 August, 2019, www.news.artnet.com.

# Appendices

# A.1-1. WCCW MISSION STATEMENT DECEMBER 1992 TO DECEMBER 2019

### 1. Mission Statement of 2018

The Washington Coalition for Comfort women Issues, Inc (WCCW) was founded in December 1992 in Washington D.C. to advocate rights of wartime victims and their lawful reparation. Our mission is to being the voice for "comfort women," and to contribute to eradication and prevention of sex crimes against women by promoting public awareness.

WCCW dedicates to "Comfort Women," victims who were euphemistically called by Japanese military to refer to women who were imprisoned and forced into sexual slavery during World War II. WCCW believes that the Japanese government must clearly acknowledge its responsibility in perpetrating the atrocity against these Comfort Women, give official apology, provide redress from government sources, and open all government records regarding its involvement. Until these steps are taken, WCCW asserts that Japan should not be permitted a permanent seat on the United Nations Security Council.

WCCW is an independent, non-profit, non-partisan, research and educational organization and welcomes persons of all gender, race, and nationality.

### 2. Mission Statement of 2015

The Washington Coalition for Comfort women Issues, Inc (WCCW) was founded on December 1992 in Washington DC advocating rights for wartime victims and their lawful reparation. WCCW dedicates itself to being the voice for "comfort women," victims who were euphemistically called by Japanese military to refer to women who were imprisoned and forced into sexual slavery during World War II.

WCCW believes that the Japanese government must clearly acknowledge its responsibility in perpetrating the atrocity against these comfort women, give official apology, provide redress from government sources, and open all government records regarding its involvement. Until these steps are taken, WCCW asserts that Japan should not be permitted a permanent seat on the United Nations Security Council. WCCW is an independent, non-profit, non-partisan, research and educational organization under IRC 501(c)(3). WCCW welcomes persons of all gender, race, and nationality

### 3. WCCW Mission Statement of 2000

The Washington Coalition for Comfort Women Issues (WCCW) was founded in December 1992 to promote research and education pertaining to crimes against Comfort Women during World War II. It is an independent, non-profit, non-partisan educational organization that welcomes persons of every nationality.

The WCCW believes that the Japanese government must clearly acknowledge its responsibility for crimes against Comfort Women. The Japanese government should officially apologize to these victims, provide redress from government sources, not from the so-called Privat Fund, and open all government records regarding its involvement in these heinous crimes. Until these steps are taken, the WCCW believes that Japan should not be permitted a permanent seat on the United Nations Security Council.

### 4. Mission Statement of 1992

WCCW believes that the Japanese government must clearly acknowledge its responsibility for crimes against committed against "Comfort Women." The Japanese government should officially apologize to these victims; provide redress from government resources; correct false statements concerning the issue that have appeared in government-issued textbooks; and open all government records regarding its involvement in these heinous crimes. Until these steps are taken, WCCW believes that Japan should be denied a permanent seat on the United Nations Security Council.

WCCW is a non-profit, non-partisan, 501© (3) organization.

www.comfort-women.org

# A.1-2. WCCW PRESS RELEASE FOR JUSTICE AND PEACE TO STEVE REISS AT *THE WASHINGTON POST*, MARCH 1, 1993

*ATTN: Steve REISS*

*METRO Desk*
*The WASHINGTON POST*

DEMONSTRATION FOR JUSTICE AND PEACE
Massachusetts Ave. & California Street, N.W.
Washington, D.C.

March 1, 1993    11:00 AM - 12:30 PM

We are outraged over the recent discovery that the Japanese government forcibly recruited several hundred thousand women, including Korean, Chinese, Philippine, and European women, into sexual enslavement as "the Emperor's gift to the Japanese Imperial Forces" during World War II. We are incensed over the Japanese government's continuation of orchestrated cover-up efforts to conceal their sanction of this gross and brutal violation of human rights. We are indignant over the Japanese government's persistent refusal to make full disclosure on this issue and to accept complete responsibility and accountability for their role in this inhumane and shocking treatment of women.

WE DEMAND:

1. APOLOGIES: That the Japanese government and its Emperor make full apologies to the surviving women who were used as sexual slaves by the Japanese government.

2. JAPAN'S LEGAL RESPONSIBILITY: That the Japanese government:
   i)   establish an independent Fact-Finding Committee and Damage Report Center;
   ii)  encourage and assist individual witnesses to testify on this issue without threat or reprisal; and
   iii) take measures to provide reparation for the individual survivors and their families as clear acknowledgment of their responsibility for these crimes.

3. UNITED NATIONS INVESTIGATIONS: That the U.N. Commission on Human Rights and its Sub-Committees on Women and Minorities:
   i)   conduct a thorough investigation of this Japanese government sanctioned systematic recruitment by force of women at a near global level to serve as sexual slaves;
   ii)  conduct a thorough investigation of the continuing efforts by the Japanese government to cover up this gross injustice and violation of international principles of justice, reciprocity and equality of human rights; and
   iii) adopt a resolution that identifies and defines government sanctioned sexual violation of women and recruitment of women as sexual slaves as a violation of human rights and as a crime against humanity.

4. GLOBAL SOLIDARITY FOR HUMAN RIGHTS MOVEMENTS: That the governments of Japan, the Republic of Korea, the Democratic People's Republic of Korea, People's Republic of China, Netherlands, Philippines, Taiwan and other countries as well as international human rights organizations work to uncover and release all pertinent information on every aspect of this issue in order to accomplish three tasks:
   i)   to redress and make amends for these incredibly violent acts of injustice that were forced upon these women;
   ii)  to make these events known to the world community in order to prevent such crimes against humanity from ever being perpetrated again; and
   iii) to educate future generations to respect the dignity and human rights of all human beings.

WASHINGTON COALITION FOR "COMFORT WOMEN" ISSUES

For further information, please contact:  (Tel/Fax) (703) 560-7718

(*D. HAHM*)

# A.1-3. WCCW LETTER TO JAPANESE PRIME MINISTER HOSOKAWA, SEPTEMBER 24, 1993

## WCCW

Washington Coalition for Comfort Women Issues
2179 Wolftrap Court, Vienna, Virginia 22182
Tel/Fax (703) 560-7718

SEPTEMBER 24, 1993

His Excellency, Morihiro Hosokawa
Prime Minister of Japan
c/o Embassy of Japan
Washington, D.C. 20008

Excellency:

We, the Washington Coalition for Comfort Women Issues (WCCW), congratulate you on your election to the Office of Prime Minister and warmly welcome you to Washington, D.C. WCCW represents the collective interests of parties who seek redress for injuries inflicted upon those several hundred thousands of women, commonly referred to as "Comfort Women", who were forcibly recruited into sexual enslavement by the Japanese military during World War II. In April 1993, WCCW presented your office with a petition which addressed our concerns and contained more than 8,000 signatures of United States residents and citizens.

We commend your courage in acknowledging the serious violations of human rights of the Comfort Women committed by the Japanese military in occupied Asia territories before and during World War II. However, there still remain several important issues to be addressed regarding the Comfort Women, and we invite you to meet with us to discuss these matters briefly outlined as follows:

First, we would like to know what plans you have for fair and equitable reparation for the injuries suffered by these women and their families.

Second, we request that the Japanese government disclose all records and data in its possession and/or control regarding the Comfort Women. These records should include, but not be limited to, the exact number of the Comfort Women, their geographical locations of assignment, and complete details regarding the outcome of each individual case.

Third, we propose that a memorial be established to commemorate the lives of the Comfort Women similar to the Holocaust Museum in Washington, D.C. A memorial will serve to ensure that such violations of international human rights will never be repeated.

We believe that complete resolution of the Comfort Women issues must address all of the above points. Equitable resolution of these issues will go far in reaffirming the honor of Japan in the international community.

We would very much appreciate your meeting with us, and look forward to hearing from you.

Yours Sincerely,

Dongwoo Lee Hahm
Chairperson

# A.1-4. CONGRESSMEN'S LETTER TO JAPANESE PRIME MINISTER HOSOKAWA, NOVEMBER 3, 1993

**Congress of the United States**
**House of Representatives**
**Washington, DC 20515**

November 3, 1993

His Excellency Morihiro Hosokawa
Prime Minister of Japan
6-1 Nagata-cho 1-Chome
Chiyoda-ku, Tokyo 100
Japan

Dear Prime Minister Hosokawa:

As members of the U.S. Congress, we welcome the Japanese Government's recent acknowledgement that the Japanese military was directly involved in establishing and managing military brothels (comfort stations) throughout Asia between 1932 and 1945. We consider it particularly important that the Japanese Government also admitted the use of "coaxing, coercion and other measures" to recruit many of the "comfort women." These are essential steps toward clarifying accountability for human rights abuses committed during World War II.

We respectfully urge the Japanese Government to take additional steps to ensure justice for women who were compelled to work as prostitutes in the military brothels. Many of these women have alleged that recruiters used force or deception to deliver them to military brothels. Numerous reportedly suffered long after they escaped or were released from the brothels because the social stigma attached to sexual abuse turned them into social outcasts in their home countries.

A number of former "comfort women" have filed lawsuits seeking official apologies and monetary compensation. We urge you to ensure that the allegations in these cases are investigated promptly and impartially. ' ' " ' "ur government to cooperate fully with the rec...ly appo..... .nited Nations special rapporteur on sexual slavery in order to provide a complete account of the "comfort women" policy. Additionally, just . it was important for the ... .overnment to decide in 19. .xtend long-overdue offic.... apologies and to pay co ...tion to surviving American citizens of Japanese descent wh. .e wrongfully forced into internment camps during World War II, we strongly urge your government to do the same for women su. .ors of forced service .n military brothels.

244

His Excellency Morihiro Hosokawa
November 3, 1993
Page Two


These steps cannot undo regrettable chapters of history, but will
hopefully ease the continuing agony of the women survivors, pave
the way for improved relations between Japan and its neighbors,
and enhance Japan's credibility as a major advocate of human
rights world wide.

Thank you for your consideration.  We look forward to hearing
from you and working with your new Administration.

Sincerely,


PATSY T. MINK

CONSTANCE A. MORELLA

ROBERT A. UNDERWOOD

LESLIE L. BYRNE

ROBERT MATSUI

NEIL ABERCROMBIE

WILLIAM J. JEFFERSON

NANCY PELOSI

NORMAN Y. MINETA

DON EDWARDS

245

His Excellency Morihiro Hosokawa
November 3, 1993
Page Three

DAVID E. BONIOR

RONALD V. DELLUMS

RONALD K. MACHTLEY

JOSE E. SERRANO

WILLIAM J. HUGHES

BENJAMIN A. GILMAN

MICHAEL J. KOPETSKI

GARY L. ACKERMAN

EDWARD J. MARKEY

TOM LANTOS

SUSAN MOLINARI

MEYERS

PETER T. KING

KAREN L. THURMAN

246

FOR ATTN: Mr. R.W. APPLE, The New York Times

# Demonstration Rally For Full Redress
# For Japan's War Crimes

(Japanese Emperor Akihito's Visit to Washington D.C. on June 11-15)

## Sunday, June 12, 1994

## Lafayette Park, Washington D.C.
(Across from the White House, on Pennsylvania Ave. side)

### Japan Must Compensate the War Victims!

### Japan Guilty of Military Sex Slavery!

### No Permanent Seat for Japan at UN Security Council!

### Japan - War Criminal - Repent!

Testimony by Hwang, Kum-ju, sex slavery victim
Lee, Hyo Jae, Representative of Korean Council for Women Drafted for
    Sexual Slavery By Japan
(Both from Seoul, Korea)

| | | |
|---|---|---|
| 1:00 p.m. | - | Rally organized by United Against Japan for Justice And True History |
| 4:00 p.m. | - | Rally organized by Asians and Americans United to Redress Japanese War Crimes |

Sponsored by: - Asians and Americans United to Redress Japanese War Crimes
        (703) 356-5151
      - United Against Japan For Justice And True History  (301) 622-3053

247

## *Asians and Americans United to Redress Japanese War Crimes*
*10900 Sutton Dr., Upper Marlboro, Md. 20772 and 1155 Old Gate Ct., McLean, Va. 22012*

```
Media Contact and Interviews:
    Mrs. Dongwoo Lee Hahm  (703)356-5151
    Dr. Shu-Chin Yang      (301)656-0109
```

# More than 100 Asian-American Business, Church and Social Groups Protest Japanese Emperor's Visit

# Press Conference 9:00 am, Friday June 3, National Press Building
Zenger Room -- Continental breakfast served at 8:30 am, Press conference at 9:00 am

More than one hundred Asian-American organizations have united to jointly demand that Japan not be permitted to join the United Nations Security Council until the serious, unresolved issues of World War II Japanese war crimes are fairly settled.

At present, Japan's government refuses to recognize or redress its role in the sexual slavery and institutionalized rape of some 200,000 "Comfort Women," most of them Korean, who were held as prisoners in field brothels for Japanese soldiers.

Japan's government also refuses to recognize or redress its role in biological warfare in China, or in thousands of incidents of mass killings and group executions of resistance fighters in China, the Philippines, Indonesia, and other Asian countries. The myth that Japan was not responsible for the rape of Nanking and similar atrocities remains widespread among senior Japanese government, military and security officials, notwithstanding the recent forced resignation of Justice Minister Nagano.

We say, the Japanese Emperor must use his moral authority to force Japan's government and armed forces to recognize and redress these crimes. That act will both aid the individual victims,

(more)

# A.1-6. WCCW LETTER TO PRESIDENT CLINTON AND EMPEROR AKIHITO, JUNE 6, 1994

**WCCW** 워싱톤지역 정신대문제 대책위원회
**Washington Coalition for Comfort Women Issues**
1155 Old Gate Court, McLean, VA 22102 • Tel (703) 356-5151 • Fax (703) 356-1525

June 6, 1994

The President
The White House
1600 Pennsylvania Avenue, N.W.
Washington, DC 20500

Dear Mr. President:

I am writing in regard to your scheduled meeting with Japanese Emperor Akihito on June 13, 1994.

I respectfully urge you to express to the Japanese Emperor your concern over Japan's failure to redress the gross violation of human rights of the thousands of Korean and other Asian girls, who were forced into military sexual slavery as "Comfort Women" for the Japanese military during World War II.

As you may know, Japan has admitted its direct involvement in this crime against humanity (8/5/93 NYT). However, the Japanese government has not prosecuted any officials responsible for these very serious crimes nor has it paid any reparations to the surviving victims. The Japanese Emperor has not formally apologized on this issue.

How can we allow such an irresponsible, duplicitous country to become a permanent member of the United Nations Security Council? Before that happens, Japan must fulfill its moral and legal obligations to the "Comfort Women" and other victims of Japan's aggression in Asia.

There are hundreds of surviving "Comfort Women" who are now in their 60's and 70's. These elderly women are still seeking justice. We need your help and attention in this matter. Please address this human rights issue with the Japanese Emperor.

Thank you for your attention.

Respectfully yours,

Dongwoo Lee Hahm,
Chairperson

# WCCW 워싱톤지역 정신대문제 대책위원회

## Washington Coalition for Comfort Women Issues

1155 Old Gate Court, McLean, VA 22102 • Tel (703) 356-5151 • Fax (703) 356-1525

### WCCW Message
### to
### President Clinton and Emperor Akihito

We are demonstrating today to send a message to President Clinton and to Japanese Emperor Akihito, who will meet tomorrow morning at the White House. We protest the Japanese government's failure to atone for the heinous war crimes it committed during World War II and we call on Emperor Akihito to use his moral authority to force Japan to pay redress to its victims, particularly to the hundreds of thousands of women enslaved as sexual "comfort women" for Japanese troops during the war.

Millions of Asians suffered during Japan's war of aggression. China alone suffered more than ten million dead, with some casualty estimates running twice that high. In Korea, Japanese military police forcibly recruited approximately 200,000 young women as sexual slaves, then held them prisoner in military brothels throughout the war. Similar crimes occurred in the Philippines, Southeast Asia, and throughout the territories occupied by Japan.

But for the past half century, senior Japanese leaders have denied Japan's responsibility for these crimes and have sought to distort history. As recently as May 4, Japanese justice minister Nagano openly declared that "It's wrong to call this war 'Japan's invasion of Asia' (or) 'a war of aggression' and that the "Nanjing massacre and the rest is a fabrication" (N.Y.Times, May 5, 1994).

When we celebrated the 50th anniversary of D-Day, we celebrated not only the Allies' military victory but also the destruction of Nazism. In the case of Japan, the Allies won a military victory but they have not defeated the ideology of Japanese imperialism, which remains deeply rooted today in the minds of many Japanese leaders.

Recently, for example, "Japan's government has evidently decided to cancel the Emperor's planned visit to Pearl Harbor... on the grounds that an imperial visit might be construed as an official apology for the sneak attack in 1941," as the Washington Post reported from Tokyo (5/20/94). Later, "Emperor Akihito

250

said... that he feels grief for the millions who died or suffered during World War II, but he declined to say anything about

Japan's role in starting the Pacific war or about the responsibility of his father, the late Emperor Hirohito, the Post reported (June 4, 1994).

Unlike Germany, Japan has refused to pay reparations to individual victims of Japanese war crimes, nor has it prosecuted any war criminals on its own accord. Japan's rejection of responsibility for its war crimes demonstrates that the present Japan's government is not serious about repenting for its past.

Japan's victims in Asia are crying for justice. Japan must sincerely apologize and pay reparations for what it did to Koreans, Chinese, and other Asians during the war. The United Nations and the world must reject Japan's drive for a permanent seat on the United Nations Security Council until that country has fulfilled its moral and legal obligations to the victims of its military aggression in Asia, particularly to the "comfort women" whose lives and dignity Japan attempted to destroy.

Therefore, we today insist that President Clinton raise these important human rights issues during his meeting with Emperor Akihito. He should advise Akihito to use his moral authority to lead Japan to honor the rights of others and to become a genuinely peace-loving nation. Unless Akihito leads Japan to end its present practice of ignoring the just claims of "comfort women" and other Asian victims, the Emperor's claim that he desires "friendly relations based on mutual understanding" cannot be taken seriously and should not be accepted.

# A.1-7. METHODIST BISHOP YOUNG JIN CHO, DECLARATION AT RALLY (KOREAN AND ENGLISH), JUNE 12, 1994

**WCCW** 워싱톤지역 정신대문제 대책위원회

**Washington Coalition for Comfort Women Issues**

1155 Old Gate Court, McLean, VA 22102 • Tel (703) 356-5151 • Fax (703) 356-1525

## 선 언 문

오늘 우리는 인류의 영원한 평화와 진정한 정의의 실현을 염원하며 여기 모였다. 이 땅위에 다시는 가슴 아픈 역사의 참극이 재현되지 않기를 기원하며 이렇게 우리의 뜻을 모았다.

제2차 세계대전이 종식된 지 어언 반세기에 접어든 오늘 우리는 아직도 매듭지어 지지 않은 전쟁범죄의 참상을 소리 높여 호소한다. 일본 군국주의 발길 아래 짓밟힌 수많은 생명들의 한에 찬 탄식과 아픔을 여기 토로한다.

대동아의 공존공영 이란 미명아래 징발되어 낯선 땅의 탄광 속에서, 군수공장에서 땀을 쏟은 우리의 젊은이들, 특별히 종군위안부로 끌려가 일본군의 성폭행 앞에 꽃다운 젊음을 유린당한 조국땅의 여인들이 뿌린 눈물과 한에 찬 탄식은 아직도 우리의 가슴 속에 저려오는 아픔으로 남아있다.

역사상 유례없는 엄청난 인권유린의 범죄 앞에서 일본국은 아직도 세계의 도처에서 들려오는 양심의 소리에 귀를 가리우고 용기있는 수습의 길을 외면하고 있다. 탄식과 원망의 세월을 딛고 일어서서 외치는 생존자들의 용기있는 증언 앞에 체면치레의 언사만을 되풀이 하고 있다. 한걸음 나아가 이제는 막대한 경제력을 앞세우고 유엔 안전보장이사회의 상임 이사국 진출을 획책하고 있다. 부끄러운 역사의 청산없이 정의와 평화를 논하는 유엔의 무대에서 영향력의 행사를 서두르고 있다.

여기에 가까운 이웃나라 일본 국왕의 미국 방문을 따뜻이 맞이할 수 없는 우리의 안타까움이 있다. 우리는 어두운 전쟁범죄의 부끄러움 없는 청산이 새역사 창조의 지름길이며 이 땅위에 다시는 이같은 범죄의 재현을 막는 길임을 믿는다. 일본국의 용기있고 과감한 과거 역사의 청산이 새로운 세계의 평화와 정의 구현에 공헌하는 길임을 확신한다.

이에 역사의 아픔을 넘어서서 새날을 대망하는 워싱톤의 재미 한국인은 일본 국왕의 워싱톤 방문을 맞아 아래와 같이 우리의 결의를 천명한다.

1. 일본국은 은폐되고 있는 종군위안부 문제를 비롯한 전쟁범죄의 진상을 하늘을 우러러 부끄러움이 없는 성실함으로 공개하여 왜곡된 역사를 바로 잡으라.

2. 일본국은 그들이 저지른 엄청난 전쟁범죄를 역사 앞에 사과하고 생존하는 종군위안부를 비롯한 피해자들의 눈물과 상처를 가슴으로 껴안는 선의의 대책을 강구하라.

3. 미국 행정부는 제2차 세계대전 기간 동안 일본국이 저지른 수많은 인권 유린의 범죄가 성실히 청산될 때까지 일본의 유엔 안전보장이사회 상임이사국 진출에 대한 지원을 유보하라.

4. 워싱톤의 재미 한국인은 일본국의 왜곡된 역사가 바로 잡히고 전쟁범죄로 짓밟힌 피해자들의 눈물과 탄식이 씨매임을 받아 이 땅위에 정의가 강같이 흐르는 그날이 올 때까지 우리의 뜻과 의지를 모아 이 일을 계속 추진해 갈 것을 다짐한다.

1994년 6월 12일

일본의 전쟁범죄를 규탄하는 워싱톤지역 재미한국인 대회

Washington Coalition for Comfort Women Issues

## Declaration

We are gathered here today with hope for the realization of eternal peace and true justice for humankind. We come together in purpose to request that the heart-breaking tragedies of history not be repeated.

Today, with half a century passed since the end of World War II, we raise our voices in appeal against the horrors of war crimes that remain unresolved. We express a sigh of deep sorrow and pain over the countless lives that were trampled under the trails of Japanese militarism.

Requisitioned in the pits of a strange land under the ideology of the Greater East Asia Co-Prosperity Sphere, the sweat shed by our young people in munition factories—and in particular the tears spilled in our motherland by our women whose blossoming youths were devastated by the capture and sexual abuse they faced as wartime sex slaves under the Japanese military—leave pain in our hearts today.

Amid this unprecedented abuse of human rights in history and the cries of conscience heard from all over the world today, Japan still covers its ears and turns away from the path of courage. In response to the survivors of an era of suffering and contempt who have stood up to proclaim their courageous testimonies, Japan repeatedly offers mere words for the sake of appearances. Furthermore, now with considerable economic power, Japan aims to advance its seat in the United Nations Security Council to permanent status. Without settling its own shameful history, Japan is rushing to gain influence on the stage of the UN, which stands for justice and peace.

It is unfortunate that we cannot wholeheartedly welcome the Emperor of our neighboring nation Japan's visit to the U.S. We believe that the settlement of these dark war crimes will pave the path to a new era in history and prevent the repetition of the same crimes in the future. We are certain that Japan's bold and courageous settlement of its history will implement a new world of peace and justice.

As the Emperor of Japan's visit to Washington, D.C. approaches, we the Korean-Americans of the greater D.C. area, who aspire to go beyond the pains of the past and begin a new era, hereby make clear our resolutions as follows:

1. Japan should make public the covered-up issue of comfort women, as well as the reality of its war crimes, and correct distorted records of history.

2. Japan should apologize for its enormous war crimes and take good measures to ease the wounds and tears of comfort women survivors and victims.

3. The U.S. should hold back its support of Japan's advancement to a permanent seat in the United Nations Security Council until Japan sincerely settles its violation of human rights and war crimes committed during World War II.

4. We the Korean-Americans of the greater D.C. area pledge to come together in will and purpose and continue this work until the day arrives when Japan corrects its distorted history, the tears and groans of the innocent victims are resolved, and justice flows like a river through this land.

June 12, 1994
Conference for Washington Korean-Americans in Denunciation of Japanese War Crimes

253

# A.1-8. WCCW LETTER TO CONGRESS FOR ABE'S VISIT TO THE U.S., MARCH 18, 2015

## Washington Coalition for Comfort Women Issues, Inc.
### 워싱턴지역 정신대문제 대책위원회
www.comfort-women.org / email: wccwcontact@gmail.com

March 18, 2015
**The Honorable Congressmen**
**Re: Japanese Prime Minister Shinzo Abe's Address to a Joint Session of Congress**

Dear Congressmen and Congresswomen,

The Second World War saw countless women taken from their homes to be trafficked as prostitutes for the Imperial Japanese Army. The transgressions taken upon these victims mark the largest case of human trafficking in the 20th century. After the outbreak of the Sino-Japanese War in July 1937, the Japanese army established the official brothels called "comfort stations" throughout the war zone and controlled their operation until Japan's defeat in August 1945. The trade of comfort women is a massive violation of human rights that has been left out of history until former comfort woman, Kim Hak-Sun, bravely stepped forward to testify about her experience to the public.

The Japanese government, which endorsed such egregious violations of human liberties and dignity, is now demanding the American textbook manufacturer McGraw Hill, to delete any reference to these World War II victims of human trafficking along with the attack on Pearl Harbor. In honor of the memory and the courage of the women who have died or survived only to forever be crippled and traumatized, for the women at large who have also known the forceful hand of sexual slavery, I implore congressmen of the U.S. to support the rights and dignity of wartime victims and stop this blatant censoring of history and those that survived to tell their stories. On behalf of the Washington Coalition for Comfort Women Issues (WCCW), we ask that congressmen to stand up against those that may silence their voices.

Japanese Prime Minister Abe's revisionism that seeks to ignore and challenge the US House Resolution 121, which calls on the Japanese government to formally apologize, and acknowledge historical responsibility in a clear, unequivocal manner, goes against everything the American people stand for. Regardless of nationality or gender, the very fundamental idea of human rights remains true, and we must not let one man sway the moral standard of the civilized world. It is said that although we may strive to forgive, we must never forget. As it was for the Jewish victims in the Nazi work camps, or the victims of the 9/11 attacks, we have stood strong in our beliefs, and I now ask the congressmen to stand again for what is right, and take actions that will serve as an example for future generations about the importance of human rights and to acknowledge the bravery and endurance of these women. I urge you to solve the issue of the past before forwarding and write the new history.

Sincerely,

Dr. Jungsil Lee, President of WCCW

## A.1-8-1. WCCW PRESS CONFERENCE AT RAYBURN HOUSE OFFICE BUILDING, APRIL 23, 2015

WASHINGTON COALITION for COMFORT WOMEN ISSUES

Thursday, April 23, 2015 @ 12:15pm, 2456 Rayburn Building

**WCCW holds Press Conference to demand Prime Minister Abe to officially apologize for its Imperial Armed Forces' coercion of young women into sexual slavery during World War II**

**(Washington, DC)** – The Washington Coalition for Comfort Women Issues (WCCW) will hold a press conference to demand Japanese Prime Minister Abe to officially acknowledge and accept historical responsibility in a clear and unequivocal manner for its Imperial Armed Forces' coercion of young women into sexual slavery, known to the world as *comfort women* during World War II in his address to the joint session of the United States Congress.

WCCW was founded in December 1992 in Washington D.C. to advocate rights of wartime victims and their lawful reparation. Our mission is to contribute to eradication and prevention of sex crimes against women by promoting public awareness.

1. Introduction, Soohyun Koo, Chair of Public Relations Committee, WCCW
2. Washington Coalition for Comfort Women Issues, Dr. Jungsil Lee, President
3. Testimonial of Comfort Women Victim, Ms.Yong Soo Lee
4. US-Korea Institute, Johns Hopkins Univ., Mr. Dennis P. Halpin
5. Korea American Association of Washington Area, Ms. Sojung Lim, President
6. Amnesty International USA, Mr. T Kumar, International Advocacy Director
7. ROC Veteran Association of Greater Washington, Mr. Stan Tsai, Vice President
8. Asian Pacific WWII Atrocities Memorial, Mr. Jeffery Chen, President
9. Q & A

For more information, please contact Soohyun Koo, the Chair of Public Relations Committee at (571) 235-1180 or Jungsil Lee, the President at (301) 755-7067, wccwcontact@gmail.com.

http://www.comfort-women.org/

255

## A.1-9. FULL PAGE "OPEN LETTER" OF WCCW, *THE WASHINGTON POST*, APRIL 27, 2015

# A.1-10. JUNG-SIL LEE, "THE FUTURE OF THE 'COMFORT WOMEN' MOVEMENT," *THE WASHINGTON TIMES*, OCTOBER 15, 2015

## APPENDIX C

# LOOKING FORWARD
### The essential alliance of Korea and America on the world stage

# The Future of the 'Comfort Women' Movement

**By Jungsil Lee**

Artwork by Kim Sun-deok and Kang Duck-young. All image rights belong to the Sharing House, the shelter for the victims, built and run by the Buddhist temple located in Kyungido, Korea. Used with permission.

THURSDAY • OCTOBER 15 • 2015 | A SPECIAL REPORT PREPARED BY THE WASHINGTON TIMES ADVOCACY DEPARTMENT

To this day, religious and some Korean political leaders have withheld their support for comfort women, choosing not to take a stance on this issue. Although disappointed, I remain resolute in our mission. Now it has fallen upon me and our organization to outline the direction that the Washington Coalition for Comfort Women Issues should take.

The issue of "comfort women" has been the epicenter of heated debates for the past two decades. These women were coerced by the Japanese imperial military into sexual slavery during World War II. During his last visit to the United States, Japanese Prime Minister Shinzo Abe produced an official statement that clearly fell short of a sincere apology, disappointing both the victims and their supporters.

Of course, it is hard to avoid the issue's political ramifications, but we should remain cognizant of and keep fresh the horrific atrocities that these women, most of them barely into their teens, endured. If this were not enough, the silence and inaction of the Japanese government have only added to their suffering.

There are several dimensions that add depth to this issue: the human rights grass-roots movement, the feminist perspective, anti-war sentiment, healing rituals, artistic expressions, educational possibilities and many more.

In spite of these many approaches, the comfort women issue has generally been viewed through a pinhole, creating a moral dichotomy, an all-or-nothing, black-or-white outlook. The impression that it is only a Korean-Japanese issue has prevented the movement from achieving global attention. Despite its worldwide implications, having the two countries at the root has kept others from seeing the larger picture.

Although the experiences of the comfort women led to some of the most appalling wartime atrocities, the inaction of world powers and the general ambivalence regarding these human rights violations are baffling and unacceptable. Such is the frustration of the supporters of the movement. Although we have protested and continue to protest the Japanese government's wartime injustices, our demands for an official apology and reparations have been met with silence. Despite passage in 2007 of House Resolution 121, sponsored by Rep. Mike Honda, there has not been much progress in shifting the mindset of the Japanese government.

As Japan continues to sidestep the issue, the fight for justice has slowly become one of attrition. One by one, the victims are passing away, and soon none will be left to tell the tale. Yet those of us in this fight refuse to keep silent, not allowing the Japanese government to sweep the matter under the rug. The Washington Coalition for Comfort Women Issues will make sure that these women occupy a prominent place in the annals of history. What are we doing to make this happen?

I first encountered the issue back in 2009. At the time, while I was organizing art exhibitions and seminars, I saw that this could be used as a powerful tool to highlight the matter. I also learned that a traveling exhibition in Japan depicting artwork created by the surviving comfort women had moved many Japanese. Letters poured in from them, apologizing on behalf of their government. Japanese children wrote letters to the sufferers, which were later compiled into a book, creating one strand between Korea and Japan. Even these small gestures have contributed to the healing that these women desperately need.

This summer, I attended a concert dedicated to comfort women where three distinguished Japanese musicians performed. It was another gesture toward healing. Before that, I watched the musical "Comfort Women" at an off-Broadway theater in New York. These events have unlocked the gates of artistic expression, and more continue to pour in. Last year, we celebrated the publication of a book about comfort women, "Daughters of the Dragon" by William Andrews. And this summer I saw the "Last Tear," a documentary film on this issue directed by Christopher Lee. The Washington Coalition for Comfort Women Issues was active in promoting all these events.

I was even asked to teach a graduate course on comfort women as part of a curriculum on feminist narratives and women's rights. While this course couldn't be organized, the Washington Coalition for Comfort Women Issues has launched a Web seminar for people around the world who want to learn more about this unfortunate time. Among other things, the students research and archive the stories of victims and connect their experiences to atrocities committed against women today. These include women trafficked by the Islamic State group and children kidnapped and used as sex slaves. We will even turn our sights inward, to our own borders, and link this issue to sex trafficking in the United States.

The Washington Coalition for Comfort Women Issues will take a leading role in teaching others and working toward a just and equitable resolution to this problem. Each little gesture, each letter written, each song sung, and each book written in honor of these victims is like a drop of water. As more drops come together, they create ponds, which grow into lakes, which grow into roaring oceans. Our movement will become like the waves of a tsunami — unstoppable.

The rainwaters are calm yet rapid, incessant in their descent. These waters will one day cut through mountains. We at the Washington Coalition for Comfort Women Issues continue to urge President Obama and Congress to pressure the Japanese government to issue a long-overdue apology to these women, who have suffered enough. We also welcome support from anybody who would like to help us in this pursuit, especially by expressions in artistic or academic forms.

*Jungsil Lee, PhD, is an art historian and professor and director at the Washington University of Virginia. She is also president of Washington Coalition for Comfort Women Issues (Comfort-Women.org).*

# A.1-11. WCCW LETTER TO JAPANESE EMPEROR JULY 1, 2015

**Washington Coalition for Comfort Women Issues, Inc.**

**위싱턴지역 정신대문제 대책위원회**

www.comfort-women.org / email: wccwcontact@gmail.com

2520 Massachusetts Ave NW
Washington DC 20008
July 1, 2015

Emperor and Empress of Japan,

You are recognized around the world as moral and spiritual leaders of the Japanese people, as well as for your efforts to advance world peace and reconciliation. This letter is a heartfelt appeal to you to exercise your leadership to speak clearly to your people and Mr. Abe's administration the rationality to resolve the issues and move forward to the better world.

We write to you on behalf of the Asian American groups of the Washington Metropolitan Area as well as many other human right organizations to express our concern about Japanese Prime Minister Shinzo Abe's past address to Congress on April 29, 2015. This concern is shared by the 250,000 Korean Americans living in the Washington metropolitan area and also by the 1.7 million Korean Americans living throughout the USA, let alone Koreans in the Korea peninsula.

As you are aware, during the World War II, euphemistically 'comfort women' a very large number of women and girls in Asian were forced into the government sanctioned system of sexual slavery operated for the Imperial Army and Navy. The survivors were for decades treated with shame and contempt in Japan and in their home countries. With very recent demise, there are only 49 survivors in South Korea, and very old and ill with physical and mental suffering and trauma. there are many more survivors like them throughout Asia and the world.

This is because Japanese government leaders continue today to use tricks of language to refuse to frankly acknowledge the wartime government's direct, central role in this terrible war crime. For example, Japanese Prime Minister Abe had stated that he is deeply saddened but it was not an unequivocal acknowledgement the wartime government's central responsibility for the wrongdoing committed against these women.

Mr. Abe's revisionism ignores and challenges the U.S. House Resolution 121 passed by the House in 2007, which calls on the Japanese government to formally acknowledge and apologize historical responsibility in a clear, unequivocal manner. Instead, Mr. Abe honors the class A war criminals who were convicted by the Tokyo Tribunal for the Pearl harbor attack, as national heroes by his frequent visits to Yasukuni Shrine.

Mr. Abe's speech to the joint session of Congress was disappointing. The House Chamber is a sacred ground in American history, where President Roosevelt passionately delivered his "Infamy Speech." There was no place better than the US Capitol for Mr. Abe to accept the Japanese Imperial government's

## Washington Coalition for Comfort Women Issues, Inc.
### 위싱턴지역 정신대문제 대책위원회
www.comfort-women.org / email: wccwcontact@gmail.com

role in crimes against humanity during the World War II, and offer a direct and sincere apology from the modern government to all victims of the war crimes.

Japan's own national interest, as well as that of its neighbors and the United States, is best served by the Japanese government's clear acknowledgement of the responsibility. Through the humble acceptance of the past history, Mr. Abe will be a sincere and brave leader who faced the truth and wrote a bright future of Japan and other countries On behalf of the Washington Coalition for Comfort Women Issues (WCCW), we hope that Japan would overcome its shameful past by facing the historical facts, not by hiding or covering up, and become a genuine model in the global community that others want to emulate.

As next month of August 2015 will mark the 70th anniversary of the end of World War II and Korean Independence from Japan, Prime Minister Abe's upcoming statement can help both Korea and Japan to move forward. Clear and definitive statements acknowledging and accepting Imperial Japan's responsibility for past crimes in the form of a public apology by the Prime Minister will help us to turn this page from the dark past and the victims could be relieved out of their burden.

We, Korean Americans, are asking for your support in conveying the critical need to resolve these concerns to Prime Minister Abe. It would be greatly appreciated if you act the role to encourage the Japanese government to resolve this long-standing issue for good and redress the pain and suffering of those Comfort Women who are still alive.

Sincerely,

Julie Jungsil Lee, Ph.D.
President of WCCW
P.O.Box 60961
Potomac, MD 20859 USA

wccwcontact@gmail.com
www.comfort-women.org

# A.1-12. WCCW OFFICIAL STATEMENT ON 2015 KOREA-JAPAN AGREEMENT AT THE UN PRESS CONFERENCE, MARCH 8, 2016

## Special Report

### 1. Foreign Minister Kishida

The Government of Japan and the Government of the Republic of Korea (ROK) have intensively discussed the issue of comfort women between Japan and the ROK at bilateral meetings including the Director-General consultations. Based on the result of such discussions, I, on behalf of the Government of Japan, state the following:

(1)   The issue of comfort women, with an involvement of the Japanese military authorities at that time, was a grave affront to the honor and dignity of large numbers of women, and the Government of Japan is painfully aware of responsibilities from this perspective. As Prime Minister of Japan, Prime Minister Abe expresses anew his most sincere apologies and remorse to all the women who underwent immeasurable and painful experiences and suffered incurable physical and psychological wounds as comfort women.

(2)   The Government of Japan has been sincerely dealing with this issue. Building on such experience, the Government of Japan will now take measures to heal psychological wounds of all former comfort women through its budget. To be more specific, it has been decided that the Government of the ROK establish a foundation for the purpose of providing support for the former comfort women, that its funds be contributed by the Government of Japan as a one-time contribution through its budget, and that projects for recovering the honor and dignity and healing the psychological wounds of all former comfort women be carried out under the cooperation between the Government of Japan and the Government of the ROK.

(3)   While stating the above, the Government of Japan confirms that this issue is resolved finally and irreversibly with this announcement, on the premise that the Government will steadily implement the measures specified in (2) above. In addition, together with the Government of the ROK, the Government of Japan will refrain from accusing or criticizing each other regarding this issue in the international community, including at the United Nations.

## 2. Foreign Minister Yun

The Government of the Republic of Korea (ROK) and the Government of Japan have intensively discussed the issue of comfort women between the ROK and Japan at bilateral meetings including the Director-General consultations. Based on the result of such discussions, I, on behalf of the Government of the ROK, state the following:

(1) The Government of the ROK values the GOJ's announcement and efforts made by the Government of Japan in the lead-up to the issuance of the announcement and confirms, together with the GOJ, that the issue is resolved finally and irreversibly with this announcement, on the premise that the Government of Japan will steadily implement the measures specified in 1. (2) above. The Government of the ROK will cooperate in the implementation of the Government of Japan's measures.

(2) The Government of the ROK acknowledges the fact that the Government of Japan is concerned about the statue built in front of the Embassy of Japan in Seoul from the viewpoint of preventing any disturbance of the peace of the mission or impairment of its dignity, and will strive to solve this issue in an appropriate manner through taking measures such as consulting with related organizations about possible ways of addressing this issue.

(3) The Government of the ROK, together with the Government of Japan, will refrain from accusing or criticizing each other regarding this issue in the international community, including at the United Nations, on the premise that the Government of Japan will steadily implement the measures it announced.

## WCCW Statement

**Official Statement of WCCW, Inc. (Washington Coalition for Comfort Women Issues) on 2015 Korea-Japan Bilateral Agreement on Comfort Women**

March 8th of 2016, Press Conference at UN Headquarters, New York (written by Jungsil Lee, President of WCCW)

After last year's joint agreement issued by the Republic of Korea and Japan on the issues of the "comfort women," WCCW members have been appalled by the Japanese government's continued denial and whitewashing of the historical facts that had already been acknowledged by their previous officials. Their recent statement proves that the agreement was not sincere and genuine. True reconciliation would not be possible without real and perpetual efforts in a clear and unequivocal manner.

WCCW, an organization whose mission is to advocate for the rights of wartime victims-military sex slaves- and their lawful reparation, expected and hoped for progress in terms of the lawful reparation and official treatment followed by the agreement of two countries, but the recent activities of the Japanese government failed to reveal this hope is headed for the right direction. We support the recent recommendation by CEDAW (Committee on the Elimination of Discrimination against Women).

1. WCCW envisions 'comfort women' issues as a global human rights issue and women's rights movement that stretch over 11 nations who had experienced similar atrocities as well as today's violations of women's rights around the globe. Therefore, we do not narrow down the issue to solely a Korean-Japanese political agenda. Rather, we will continue to advocate, research, and educate the importance of human rights through this history.

2. The agreement made no provisions whatsoever for comfort women survivors from North Korea, China, Taiwan, Philippines, Indonesia, Dutch-Indi, Malaysia, Thailand, Burma, East Timor, Guam, India, and Vietnam. The agreement must include restitution and sincere apology from the Japanese government for all comfort women of all nationalities.

3. WCCW will make sure that these women occupy a prominent place in the annals of history and are provided with legal reparations not only to honor their bravery and endurance but also to commemorate the importance of human dignity. If the agreement is sincere and unequivocal, the world will see that the Japanese government will open their archival records concerning wartime and postwar treatment, create policies to reconcile with the comfort women, and cease to rewrite the past history; the Japanese government will contribute to writing of accurate accounts of the history and will promote educating its own people and the future generation about the war crimes against humanity.

4. WCCW hopes to watch the issue be resolved by a series of gradual, ongoing, and sincere accomplishments toward all victimized nations, not through a single political deal with the expression "finally and irreversibly." Although WCCW promotes a peaceful reconciliation and is eager to see the final and completed resolution, we do not believe that one bilateral agreement cannot and must not cease or delete the whole history of the war or stop activities by human rights advocates and NGO's.

5. WCCW expresses deep regrets to see that the agreement includes the possible removal or relocation of the Girl statue in front of the Embassy of Japan in Seoul that has a huge symbolic value for Koreans, the victims, and importance of civil rights.

6. WCCW would like to see the end of the Japanese government's diplomatic and publicity efforts to humiliate comfort women survivors and to revise the past, or to interfere with people's right to study, research, and speak out about their experiences and opinions. That is precisely the reason that WCCW launched the "Webinar Project" through which we research, archive, and publish the unarguable historical material about comfort women.

WCCW has been so honored to fight for and be the voice for these voiceless women for the last 23 years since 1992. We cannot possibly imagine their sufferings, but we have learned from and been inspired by the survivors. We sincerely hope that these women will finally find what they have been seeking: peace and dignity.

WCCW Members and WCCW Board of
Directors wccwcontact@gmail.com
www.comfort-women.org

**THE DOCTORS ARE IN**

Physicians take to the Hill to try to prevent cuts to their Medicare fees, **P 20**

**THE GREENHOUSE EFFECT**

Members urge EPA to allow Calif. to impose new emissions standards, **P 22**

# BUSINESS & LOBBYING

PAGE 18 WWW.THEHILL.COM       WEDNESDAY, SEPTEMBER 27, 2006

## LOBBYING WORLD

• **Mildred Webber** will become the National Association of Broadcasters' (NAB) new senior vice president of government relations next month, leaving the office of House Majority Whip Roy Blunt (R-Mo.), where she served as deputy chief of staff. Webber is also a veteran of the George H.W. Bush and Reagan administrations.

• **Mary-Lacey Reuther** is the newest vice president at Barbour Griffith & Rogers, specializing in healthcare policy. She recently left the Centers for Medicare and Medicaid Services (CMS), where she helped departing Director Mark McClellan implement the Medicare Part D benefit. She is also a veteran of the Food and Drug Administration and the Medical Device Manufacturers Association.

• **Allen "Beau" Greenwood**, a former staff member on both House and Senate Agriculture Committees, has arrived at CropLife America, where he will serve as executive vice president of government and public affairs, taking responsibility for advocacy and communications. Greenwood previously lobbied for the New York Stock Exchange and held a senior post at the Commodity Futures Trading Commission.

### Who's moved where on K Street

• **Patrick O'Brien** has joined America's Community Bankers as director of government relations and COMPAC, the group's political committee. O'Brien is a former assistant vice president at Baker & Daniels and spent three years as director of federal government relations for Independent Insurance Agents & Brokers of America after leaving the office of Sen. Ted Kennedy (D-Mass.). Jennifer Shaw has also been promoted to COMPAC administrator.

• **Tom Amis and Nik Patel** have joined Alston & Bird as partners in the Leveraged Capital Group, while Amis will also co-chair the firm's renewable energy division and work alongside former Senate Minority Leader Tom Daschle (D-S.D.). Both Amis and Patel come from Baker Botts. Amis is a veteran counsel to the Overseas Private Investment Corporation.

• **William Longbrake** has been named senior policy advisor to the Financial Services Roundtable, and he will continue to serve as vice chair of Washington Mutual while taking on the job. Longbrake is a former official at the Office of the Comptroller of the Currency and the Federal Deposit Insurance Corporation.

# Korean-Americans seek resolution on sex slavery

*By Roxana Tiron*

Rep. Lane Evans (D-Ill.)

FILE PHOTO

The Korean-American community is mounting an intense grassroots lobbying campaign in support of a House resolution calling for Japan to formally acknowledge and accept responsibility for sexually enslaving women during World War II.

The controversial resolution, even though it does not have the force of law, is putting the Japanese government on the defensive. Japan argues that it has already apologized and atoned for the treatment of the so-called "comfort women."

Critics of the resolution argue that it is misguided and would send mixed signals to Japan.

During its occupation of Asia and the Pacific Islands from the 1930s through the duration of WWII, Japan used as many as 200,000 young women from Korea, China, the Philippines, and in some cases Western Europe, for sexual servitude, a program designed to increase the efficiency and morale of the Japanese soldiers.

The women were subject to beatings, extreme sexual violence and torture. Often women serviced up to 36 men a day. Many women were killed if they became ill or too tired. Some survivors committed suicide from shame and physical pain.

Rep. Lane Evans (D-Ill.) has sponsored a bill calling on Japan to accept responsibility for operating such a program and has been trying to bring the measure to the House floor for about four years. The legislation is the Korean-American community's top issue this election year.

And now Evans and the Korean community are the closest they have ever been to seeing congressional action on it.

The International Relations Committee marked up the resolution in mid-September. Rep. Chris Smith (R-N.J.), the

> FROM THE 1930s THROUGH THE DURATION OF WWII, JAPAN USED AS MANY AS 200,000 YOUNG WOMEN FOR SEXUAL SERVITUDE.

panel's chairman of the Africa, Global Human Rights and International Operations subcommittee, co-authored the resolution with Evans.

Evans has a close relationship with Ok Cha Soh, the president of the Washington Coalition for Comfort Women who has championed the survivors' cause.

Several congressional sources have said that the panel's chairman, Rep. Henry Hyde (R-Ill.), made a commitment to move the bill to Evans, who suffers from Parkinson's disease and is retiring at the end of this Congress. Fellow-Illinoisan Hyde also is retiring this year.

But despite the bond between the two

departing lawmakers, another Illinoisan could be standing in the way.

It is up to House Speaker Dennis Hastert (R-Ill.) and Majority Leader John Boehner (R-Ohio) to decide whether to put the resolution on the suspensions calendar this week.

Hyde already has formally asked the Speaker to place the resolution on the suspension calendar and already about half of the resolution's co-sponsors have signed a letter to the Speaker to ask for the same thing, according to a House source.

"I do not think Hastert was too pleased with the resolution, wondering about the relationship with Japan," said a GOP aide familiar with the issue.

Hastert spent time in Japan in his first year of graduate school and travels to the nation often. Some GOP sources have said he is interested in following in former Speaker Tom Foley's (D-Wash.) footsteps and becoming the country's ambassador one day.

But at the same time, the Speaker's office is hearing a lot from the Korean-Americans, said the GOP aide. Among the co-sponsors of the resolution are Rep. Mike Honda (D-Calif.), a Japanese-American and Reps. Neil Abercrombie (D-Hawaii) and Ed Case (D-Hawaii), whose states have a large population of Japanese-Americans.

The American Korean Coalition held

his annual convention in Chicago and one of its top issues was Resolution 759, according to the GOP aide.

Meanwhile, the Korean American Association in Washington, which represents about 200,000 Korean-American in the area, is leading a national campaign for the bill and has started a letter-writing campaign to Congress.

The Korean-American community, acting on behalf of the South-Asian nations that had some of its female citizens suffer under the sexual enslavement program, is pressing for the adoption of the resolution because very few comfort women are still alive.

The resolution is meant to encourage Japan to be honest about past mistakes and to educate its next generations about crimes against humanity, according to supporters of the resolution.

Supporters of the resolution also argue that none of the actions that Japan has taken on this issue are official and that the government refuses to provide direct compensation to victims.

In response, Japan has quietly lobbied against the resolution, arguing that it already has done its part in settling the issue. The Japanese Embassy has been working with Hogan & Hartson as well as Hecht, Spencer and Associates to raise awareness about what it has already done to address the issue.

Former Minority Leader Bob Michel (R-Ill.) and Bill Hecht, both lobbyists, have pressed Japan's case on the Hill ear-

SEE WOMEN PAGE 20

# A.1-14. WCCW NEWSLETTER WITH THE OP-ED BY REP. LANE EVANS, FEBRUARY 2007

**NEWS** From **Washington Coalition for Comfort Women Issues, Inc.**

2750 Gallows Road #303, Vienna, VA 22180-7133

Vol. XI, February 2007

# A Salute to Congressman Evans
# A Man of Action

*The Washington Coalition for Comfort Women Issues, Inc. (WCCW) and our many esteemed friends wish to pay tribute to the remarkable accomplishments over a productive and inspirational career of the Honorable Congressman Lane Evans.*

Over the course of his career in public service, Congressman Evans indefatigable fight in the pursuit of justice for the women otherwise forgotten by history known simply as "Comfort Women" has deeply touched all of us. These victims of Japanese imperialism had been all but erased from the public memory and most politicians, concentrating on the daily demands of voters, paid them little attention.

But Congressman Evans strongly believed that, "We (as members of Congress) have a duty to fight for those who have been exploited and abused, and to speak up for the victims who can no longer speak for themselves. We must act and we must speak out, because in the end, people will not remember the words of their enemies, but the silence of their friends. We must not remain silent." (Press Conference on the Capitol Hill, March, 24, 2005). His words gave new hope to these women, now in their seventies and eighties, that justice could at last be found. And thanks to Congressman Evans' efforts, those women were able to visit the United States and bravely present their case to the American people.

Such men as Congressman Evans are rare indeed. He has served as a voice for those who were silenced. He has held up and supported those who demanded in the face of public apathy that the government of Japan extend an official apology for the sexual servitudes imposed on women during WWII. Congressman Evans has offered hope to those who had been told they were not worthy and in doing so inspired all of us.

*His Personal Care for the visiting Grand Ma & Chaparone, March 2006*

*Farewell Evening for Congress Evans with the Korean Ambassador, Lee, Tae Sik, Mr. Kim, Young Keun, the President of Korean Asso. of Greater Washington, and Dr. Ok Cha Soh, September 2006*

**—— WCCW**

265

# A.1-15. STATEMENT BY DR. OK CHA SOH, DURING HOUSE HEARING, FEBRUARY 2007

## *Summary of the House Hearing Statement*

Ok Cha Soh, Ph.D.
*President*
*Washington Coalition for Comfort Women Issues, Inc.*
*e-mail : okchasoh@bible.edu*

Over the six decades have passed since the end of World War II, yet the atrocities of the Japanese Imperial Army still remains as grief and sorrow in the heart of each individual; the wounds of the victims are yet to be healed, It has been almost 15 years since we began to pay attention to the long-concealed history of sex slavery by the Japanese Imperial Army. Stripped of their dignity and robbed of their honor even in their home lands, surviving Comfort Women were forced for many years to live their lives under the veil of shame, silently shouldering the burden of their horrific experience. They waited a very long time. We believe they should wait no longer.

It should be noted that there was also a racial discrimination of the Comfort Women by the Allied forces, primarily meaning the United States. At the end of World War II, Japanese were defeated. Naturally, the power of dealing with the war crimes was in the hands of Allied forces, the United States. If those 200,000 girls and women who were subject to this brutal sexual slavery had been primarily European or American Whites, do you think that the issue of the solving Comfort women would have keep ignored as it has been for all these years?

The example of the Batavia Trial speaks eloquently for this. In 1946, an Allied Military Tribunal took place in Jakarta, Indonesia. That was the only military tribunal concerning the sexual victims of Comfort Women system and the Batavia Trial convicted Washio Awochi and other Japanese war criminals for kidnapping Dutch nurses and forcing them into sexual slavery. That trial is often cited today as a key legal precedent in prosecution of suspects who organize mass rapes in war time, tortures, and corporations complicit in crimes against humanity. Nevertheless, the fact remains that no Japanese government official, military officer or corporation was ever prosecuted for the far larger, longer-running, and even more deadly organized crimes committed against hundreds of thousands of Asian women during WW II. In particular, our country, the United States, had clear evidence at the time of the criminal nature and operation of Japan's systematic sexual slavery of these women and girls yet did not bring charges against those who had persecuted and murdered them.

The Asian Women's Fund requires any surviving Comfort Women to sign legal papers that would end any legal rights she has to seek redress in the courts of any country for the suffering she has faced at the hands of the Japanese government or Japanese corporations. Similarly, the supposed 'atonement' fund refuses to pay damages to the families of Comfort Women who were murdered during World War II or died during the 50-plus years between 1945 and when the fund was created. This practice raises questions. If the fund is truly intended to express remorse and atonement for crimes committed, through what sort of logic does it now require the surviving Comfort Women to abandon their rights?

Current Japanese government claims that the apology had been made already by their former Prime Misters. The most basic problem is that the comments express remorse that 'bad things happened' to Comfort Women, yet refuse Japanese Imperial government's responsibility for doing bad things. They are carefully worded and evasive. Nevertheless, it is perfectly clear to both Japanese government and other Asian countries that the Japanese government is not actually accepting responsibility. That is also why they use the charade of a 'private' fund. If they paid the money from the government, it would be a clear admission that the government is responsible for its crime. If they refuse to pay from the government and instead give it to a private 'front' organization, then the government can say the payments are 'charity' and not an admission of responsibility. That is precisely the argument that the Japanese government makes today.

There is also an easier way to understand why the statements are inadequate. They are full of euphemisms that have the effects of concealing the truth. None of the statements mention the word, 'rape.' None of them mention 'slavery.' None mention 'kidnapping' and 'imprisonment, or 'the summary execution of women and girls." Equally important, none of the statements say frankly that this treatment of tens of thousands of women was authorized and organized at the highest level of the Japanese government and military --- a fact that has now been clearly established. When a government uses a form like this, the thing that we must do is to look at the actual actions and deeds of the government. There, the record of Japan's actions is, if anything, even less convincing that the statements of Kono and others. The examples are the refusal of cooperation with the U.S. Department of Justice, textbook censorship, repeated visits of Yasukuni Shrine, etc.

The Japanese government and their western sympathizers argue that nothing more than these euphemisms and the form of false charity of the Asian Women's Fund can be expected, because of Asians' concerns about face. Concerns about face have no standing when it comes to the issue of responsibility for mass enslavement and rape of women and girls, especially considering the current day Japanese government's ongoing effort to hide the information about the crimes. Japan's present-day leaders need to come to understand that frank admission and restitution is the way to gain more face, and to gain more respect and confidence from others. Whether they now understand it or not, they continue to lose face in the international society, and especially among women worldwide, by attempting to hide and deny the responsibility of the wartime Japanese Imperial government and military. These activities are damaging to U.S.-Japanese relations, whether they are intended to be or not. Japan's refusal to acknowledge responsibility for the war crimes is not only an injustice for surviving Comfort Women. As equally important as that is, it undermines international law as such on the issue of rape during war. The issue is not simply redress for a historical wrong, it is also essential to the success of future prosecutions of criminals who use rape as a weapon of war.

The Japanese government today refuses to assist the U.S. Department of Justice in identifying WWII-era criminals responsible for crimes against Comfort Women. Japanese government refuses to cooperate. To date, the Japanese government's effort to carry out the U.N. recommendations has been clearly inadequate. It is in Japan's own interest, as well as in the best interests of the U.S. and Japanese relations, for the present Japanese government to squarely face its obligations under international law.

Permit to recall former Cong. Lane Evans who used to say regarding Comfort Women, "I believe we have a duty; we have a duty to help those who need our help. We have a duty to stand up for those who cannot stand up for themselves.....Because in the end, people will remember not the words of their enemies, but the silence of their friends. We must not remain silent."

It is our duty that we give those women the dignity and the respect they deserve.

# A.1-16. WCCW SUPPORTING STATEMENT AT THE HEARING FOR MARYLAND COMFORT WOMEN RESOLUTION SJ3, MARCH 6, 2015.

**Washington Coalition for Comfort Women Issues, Inc.**
위싱턴지역 정신대문제 대책위원회
www.comfort-women.org / email: wccwcontact@gmail.com

Senate Judicial Proceedings Committee
11 Bladen Street
2 East Miller Senate Office Building
Annapolis, MD 21401

March 6, 2015

To: Senate Education, Health and Environmental Affairs Committee,

On behalf of Washington Coalition for Comfort Women Issues (WCCW), Inc. we strongly support **the passage of SJ 3** which recognizes the sexual slaves so called "Comfort Women" who were forcefully recruited as factory workers or trafficked as prostitutes by the Imperial Japanese Army during the World War II. It highlights the plight of victims of human trafficking at large, and these victims became historical examples of the largest case of human trafficking in the 20th century. Young women from Korean, Taiwanese, Chinese, Indonesian, East Timorese, Filipinos, and Dutch were died or survived with lingering trauma and injured or crippled by excessive sexual labor, and they are not appropriately recognized.

The need for the passage of the resolution is becoming even more important as the Japanese government recently demanded American textbook manufacturer McGraw Hill, to delete any reference to victims of World War II human trafficking in addition to the attack on Pearl Harbor, the Bataan death March, the Nanking Massacre, as reported by the major news reporters such as the New York Times and Washington Post January 2015.

After a sacred ground of America, U.S. House of Representatives passed House Resolution 121 calling on the Japanese government to formally acknowledge, apologize, and accept historical responsibility in a clear and unequivocal manner for the sexual enslavement of "comfort women." However, Mr. Abe's revisionism ignores and challenges to the United States, the country of champion of human rights. To educate the next generation the importance of women's right, to acknowledge the victims bravery and endurance, to keep the justice and dignity of human being I urge that the Senate Joint Resolution 3 should be passed.

Sincerely yours,

Jungsil Lee, Ph.D.
President, WCCW

267

# A.1-17. MARYLAND COMFORT WOMEN RESOLUTION SJ3, MARCH 6, 2015

## SENATE JOINT RESOLUTION 3

P5                                                                                    5lr2479

By: **Senators Lee, Bates, Montgomery, Nathan–Pulliam, ~~and Ready~~ Ready,**
**Conway, Pinsky, Kagan, Rosapepe, Salling, Simonaire, Waugh, and Young**
Introduced and read first time: February 6, 2015
Assigned to: Education, Health, and Environmental Affairs

Committee Report: Favorable with amendments
Senate action: Adopted
Read second time: March 13, 2015

RESOLUTION NO. _____

1   A Senate Joint Resolution concerning

2   **Honoring the Surviving Human Trafficking Victims of Asia and the Pacific**
3   **Islands During World War II**

4   FOR the purpose of extending the profound hope of the General Assembly of Maryland that
5       the historical record of the crimes against the "ianfu" or "comfort women" of World
6       War II will serve as a lasting reminder to the world that crimes against humanity
7       will not be condoned or tolerated; providing that a copy of this resolution be
8       forwarded by the Department of Legislative Services to certain individuals; and
9       generally relating to honoring the surviving victims of human trafficking in Asia and
10      the Pacific Islands during World War II.

11      WHEREAS, The government of Japan, during its colonial and wartime occupation
12  of Asia and the Pacific Islands from the 1930s through the duration of World War II,
13  commissioned the acquisition of young women, estimated to number more than 200,000,
14  for the sole purpose of sexual slavery to the Imperial Armed Forces, who became known to
15  the world as "ianfu" or "comfort women"; and

16      WHEREAS, Many of the survivors have testified that they were kidnapped by
17  Imperial Japanese soldiers and forced to serve as prostitutes, often enduring cruelty such
18  as gang rape, forced abortions, humiliation, and sexual violence, resulting in mutilation,
19  permanent health damage, death, or suicide; and

20      WHEREAS, The people of Maryland honor the surviving victims who are now at the
21  end of their lives, but were victimized at the beginning of their lives when they were too
22  young to consent to prostitution and were ostracized even though they were clearly victims;
23  and

EXPLANATION:
  Underlining indicates amendments to bill.
  ~~Strike out~~ indicates matter stricken by amendment.

1        WHEREAS, The Maryland General Assembly is determined to combat human
2 trafficking in modern times through all appropriate legislative action, education initiatives,
3 and commemorations to the victims of this horrible injustice and crime that has been
4 perpetrated against so many people throughout history; now, therefore, be it

5        RESOLVED BY THE GENERAL ASSEMBLY OF MARYLAND, That the General
6 Assembly of Maryland hereby extends its profound hope that the historical record of the
7 crimes against the "ianfu" or "comfort women" of World War II will serve as a lasting
8 reminder to the world that crimes against humanity will not be condoned or tolerated; and
9 be it further

10        RESOLVED, That a copy of this Resolution be forwarded by the Department of
11 Legislative Services to the Honorable Lawrence J. Hogan, Jr., Governor of Maryland; the
12 Honorable Thomas V. Mike Miller, Jr., President of the Senate of Maryland; and the
13 Honorable Michael E. Busch, Speaker of the House of Delegates.

Approved:

_____

                                                 President of the Senate.

_____

                                      Speaker of the House of Delegates.

# A.1-18. DEPARTMENT OF JUSTICE PRESS RELEASE FOR *THE WASHINGTON POST*, DECEMBER 3, 1996

 **Department of Justice**

FOR IMMEDIATE RELEASE                                    CRM
TUESDAY, DECEMBER 3, 1996                        (202) 514-2008
                                            TDD (202) 514-1888

### SUSPECTED JAPANESE WAR CRIMINALS PLACED ON "WATCH LIST" OF EXCLUDABLE ALIENS

**First Time Japanese War Crime Suspects Have Been Placed on List**

The Justice Department announced today that 16 Japanese citizens have been placed on the U.S. Government's "watchlist" of aliens who are ineligible to enter the United States. Those placed on the watchlist either were members of Japanese Imperial Army units that conducted inhumane and frequently fatal experiments on humans or were involved in the operation of the so-called "comfort woman stations," where hundreds of thousands of women were forced to have sexual relations with Imperial Army officers and enlisted men.

Eli M. Rosenbaum, the Director of the Office of Special Investigations, said that the men whose names have been added to the watchlist are now prohibited from entering the United States by 8 U.S.C. Section 1182(a)(3)(E), known as the "Holtzman Amendment". That law bars individuals who, in association with or under the direction of Nazi Germany or any government that was an ally of Nazi Germany, participated in acts of persecution during World War II.

Some of the men being barred from entering the United States were members of "Unit 731," an infamous Japanese army detachment in Manchuria that conducted inhumane and frequently lethal pseudo-medical experiments -- including vivisection -- on thousands of non-volunteer prisoners of war and civilians. These acts have been documented and described in U.S. and Japanese publications.

The other men ineligible to enter the United States are suspected of involvement in the Imperial Army's establishment, maintenance and utilization of forced sex centers. Women and girls were taken principally from Korea, China, Taiwan, the Philippines, Malaysia, Burma and what is now Indonesia. They were held captive in the "comfort stations" and, as noted in the 1994 report, Comfort Women, issued by the Geneva-based International Commission of Jurists, "were beaten and tortured in addition to being repeatedly raped day after day by officers and soldiers."

Only a few of the perpetrators were tried, all by the Dutch government, for victimizing Dutch women in Indonesia. In response to demands made by international women's and human rights groups, the Japanese Government undertook an investigation, and in 1992 released numerous documents that confirm the official involvement of the Japanese army in the operation of the Comfort Women stations.

This is first time that individuals not involved in European atrocities were placed on the watchlist under a 1979 law barring individuals implicated in acts of persecution committed under the auspices of Nazi Germany or its wartime allies from travel to the

United States.  Mr. Rosenbaum, whose office enforces the law,
said it was expected that additional former members of the
Japanese armed forces would be added to the watchlist as the
investigation continues.

More than one hundred suspected participants in Nazi-
sponsored persecution in wartime Europe have been prevented from
entering the United States since 1989, when the Office of Special
Investigations began compiling statistics on this aspect of its
work.  More that 60,000 individuals associated with Nazi
persecution have been placed on the watchlist since OSI's 1979
creation.

Today's action became possible as increased documentation
and witness testimony about Japanese war crimes became available
to researchers in recent years.  The Office of Special
Investigations hired a Japanese-speaking staff member to work on
these cases.

Said Director Rosenbaum, "A veritable explosion in interest
in these crimes on the part of scholars and the international
human rights community made it possible to conclusively identify
suspects."  Rosenbaum expressed gratitude for the "outstanding
assistance" his office received from contacts in the academic
world and human rights organizations in the United States, Japan
and elsewhere.

"By barring from the United States those suspected of acts
of persecution in Unit 731 or in the forced sex centers, the U.S.
Government is demonstrating that it remembers the victims and

their suffering, and that it wants to deter others form committing such heinous acts," said Rosenbaum.

# # #

**WASHINGTON ED**

**Southern California's Newspaper**

# Los Angele

**Los Angele**

CIRCULATION:
1,021,121 DAILY / 1,391,076 SUNDAY

12/13/96

COPYRIGHT 1996
THE TIMES MIRROR CO

**WASHINGTON ED**

## COLUMN ONE

# Justice Delayed 50 Years

■ Addition of 16 Japanese names to U.S. list of suspected WWII war criminals heartens victim who was abducted as child 'sex slave.' But others believe the action is too little, too late.

**By SONNI EFRON**
TIMES STAFF WRITER

TOKYO—Kim Yoon Sim was playing outside her home in the Korean mountains in 1943 when a truck drove up and two Japanese, a soldier and a police officer, invited her to come for a ride.

Trucks being a rarity at the time, the 14-year-old girl climbed aboard—and spent the rest of World War II enslaved by the Japanese Imperial Army in China, where she was forced to provide sex for several thousand soldiers. Kim said she was beaten, starved and tortured, her hands smashed by the secret police after a failed escape.

Against all odds, Kim made it back to Korea alive—then spent five decades hiding her past from her mother, from the husband who rejected her because her broken body could not conceive a child, even from her sympathetic sister.

"From the time I was 14, I have had this life. I have lived all this time like a fallen leaf that has been stamped on many times," Kim said. "I am a person who has been thrown away."

This September, however, the 67-year-old journeyed to Wash-

## Disney Divorce

Creative Artists Agency founder Michael Ovitz, one of Hollywood's best-known figures, resigned Thursday as president of the Walt Disney Co.

### WHY IT DIDN'T WORK

Critics say Ovitz's skills as an agent never translated to the duties of a corporate executive. Others say Disney Chairman Michael Eisner was unwilling to carve out clear turf for Ovitz.

### THE CONTRACT SETTLEMENT

Sources say Ovitz will walk away from his 14 months at Disney with a severance valued at $90 million.

### WHAT NEXT

Some believe he may be a candidate to run Sony's entertainment operations or will set up a new business venture. But other entertainment industry executives believe Ovitz is unlikely to return as head of a large entertainment company—unless he owns it.

Ovitz, left, with Michael Eisner at No

# State Embraces Phonics in Approving New Texts

■ **Reading:** 'Whole language' books, which have come under increasing criticism, are excluded from list.

**By RICHARD LEE COLVIN**
TIMES EDUCATION WRITER

not be left to chance.

Critics had complained that the whole language approach, which

# LAX to Ur Expa

**By DEBOR and JAMES**
SPECIAL TO THI

Officials plan to inc

...ington, along with five other Korean women, and bared details of their abduction and ordeal to investigators from a special unit of the U.S. Justice Department charged with identifying World War II war criminals.

Last week, Kim's careworn face beamed at the news that the Justice Department had placed the names of 16 Japanese on a "watch list" of suspected war criminals barred from entering the United States.

The U.S. move has been seen by some Japanese as hypocritical, 50 years overdue and possibly counterproductive now that some geriatric culprits have begun clearing their consciences before they die.

But Kim feels vindicated.

"Please tell them in America how grateful I am," said Kim, who has never received official acknowledgment from Japan that what was done to her was a crime.

"Before I die, I want this issue resolved," she said, wiping away tears with her crabbed and thickened fingers. "Japan should punish the people who did this. They should prosecute them. . . . The Japanese government knows

**Please see JUSTICE, A4**

### Clinton to Keep Reno, Sources Say

In a move that would end one of the White House's major personnel dramas, sources say that President Clinton appears to have decided to keep Atty. Gen. Janet Reno in her post. **A5**

---

SACRAMENTO—With hundreds of millions of dollars for publishing companies at stake—along with how a generation of California children will learn to read—the State Board of Education on Thursday adopted a new list of approved textbooks, leaving off two widely used programs that embrace the "whole language" teaching method that has come to dominate California schools over the last eight years.

The decision is a milestone in a nearly two-year campaign by state officials to improve students' reading performance, which tests have found to be among the worst in the nation. And it demonstrates the state's willingness to throw its financial weight behind the call for restoring "systematic, explicit"

> **■ BABY TALK**
> Infants are able to distinguish words far earlier than believed, researchers contend. A5

phonics lessons to classrooms.

After hearing two dozen speakers, most endorsing such an approach, the board voted unanimously—with one abstention—to approve 16 instructional programs for use through eighth grade.

From the Bible to McGuffey's readers to Dick and Jane, the books used to teach reading have always had a profound influence on reading instruction. Those adopted Thursday reintroduce the idea that children's grasp of phonics should

---

became the rage in recent years, failed to teach not only the sounds within words but such basics as spelling.

The whole language approach gained ascendancy in California the last time the state approved a list of textbooks, in 1988. Districts were urged then to purchase those

**Please see TEXTS, A9**

---

## Cuts Said No Major Risk to Space Shuttle

**By RALPH VARTABEDIAN**
TIMES STAFF WRITER

WASHINGTON—A White House-commissioned safety study of the nation's space shuttles, due for release next week, has concluded that budget cuts, workforce reductions and the fleet's advancing age have not demonstrably increased the risk of accidents.

Nonetheless, the report cautions the National Aeronautics and Space Administration that it faces a range of potential safety problems and urges it to exercise greater caution in maintaining oversight of the private contractors that are taking over shuttle operations.

The report offers as clean a bill of
**Please see SHUTTLE, A6**

---

# Iran Boosts Arms Supplies to Hezbollah, Reports Say

**■ Mideast:** Military capability of extremists in Lebanon aided by monthly jet shipments, U.S. sources contend.

**By ROBIN WRIGHT**
TIMES STAFF WRITER

WASHINGTON—Iran is now flying at least three 747 jumbo cargo jets of supplies monthly to Syria for shipment to Lebanon's Hezbollah forces in an effort to upgrade the arms capabilities of Tehran's allies, according to Pentagon and U.S. intelligence sources.

The shipments are primarily weapons, though they contain some humanitarian supplies. The weapons include the Russian-made Sagger antitank missile that

United States that the shipments also contain modified long-range Katyusha rockets with a reach of 25 miles that could be launched from Lebanon as far south as Haifa, Israel's third-largest city—a claim that U.S. officials have been unable to confirm.

Any heightening of Iran's role in Lebanon raises grave concern in Washington, where experts are anxious not only about Tehran's intent but that of Syria. Unlike some other nations in the region, Iran has not joined U.S.-led efforts to bring peace to the Mideast by resolving its conflicts with Israel.

**WORLD**

# JUSTICE: Victim Remembers

Continued from A1

everything; how long are they going to keep hiding it?"

According to Eli Rosenbaum, chief of the Justice Department unit responsible for identifying World War II war criminals, some of the 16 Japanese added to the "watch list" were members of the Imperial Army's notorious Unit 731, which conducted biological warfare and gruesome medical experiments on thousands of prisoners.

The rest of those on the list were members of the units that ran the front-line sex stations, at which anywhere from 20,000 to 200,000 women from Korea, Taiwan, China, the Philippines, the Netherlands East Indies, now know as Indonesia, were forced to serve as what the Japanese call "comfort women" and the Koreans "military sex slaves."

None of the men who ordered these systematic horrors were punished by the United States or Japan, although some captured members of Unit 731 were convicted of war crimes in China and the Soviet Union.

Last weekend, Kim came to Tokyo on a lecture tour sponsored by Japanese activists to educate the public about Japan's wartime activities and to pressure their government to buck the nation's powerful and unrepentant apologists for militarism by offering an unfettered acknowledgment of wrongdoing to its still-suspicious Asian neighbors.

Sitting on a bare stage with an interpreter at her side, Kim explained to about 300 Japanese in the audience how she was rounded up with dozens of other young women and shipped in a filthy train to a harbor where they were loaded on a boat to China.

"On the ship, I cried and cried and begged them to let me go home," Kim said. "They tied up my hands and feet and said, 'If you really want to go home, we'll send you.'" Her captors dangled her over the side of the ship and told her that if she opened her mouth again, they would throw her overboard.

The women wound up in army barracks in Harbin, China. During the day, they were hidden underground and heard bombers streaking overhead. At night, soldiers stood in line for them; Kim said she was forced to have sex with five or six men each night.

"Since I was so young, my uterus was displaced," she said. "I hurt so badly I couldn't stand. I had to crawl. All they did was give me a shot. I lay on the bed for three days. Then they made me take men again. There was nothing to do but give up, so I just let them do it.

"I cannot tell you the details," Kim told the audience as she stared at the table before her. "All I can say is that when the men would come in, if I was wearing underwear they would tell me to take it off, and if I didn't do it fast enough they would hit me. So after awhile, I stopped wearing underwear."

The women were given numbers and made to stand at roll call. They were forbidden to speak Korean. Any infraction brought beatings.

"They said in Japanese, 'Even if one of us soldiers kills 10 of you Koreans, nothing will happen to us,'" Kim said.

One woman became pregnant, but was made to continue to have sex with the soldiers until her labor began. A nurse arrived for the delivery, and carried the newborn, believed to be dead, away in a sack. Three days later, the mother was forced to resume servicing soldiers.

One day, the women were walking down to a stream to do laundry when they noticed an indentation in the earth and saw a human hand. Terrified, they dug up the corpse. It was one of the "comfort women" who had fallen ill and been taken away wrapped in her blanket. The soldiers had said she was taken to a hospital. Her body was still wrapped in the blanket.

"I realized that all the women that had been taken away to the hospital had probably been killed," Kim said.

Soon after, Kim fled the camp and walked all night. When she knocked on a door of a house, it turned out to be occupied by Japanese soldiers. The secret police were called, and Kim was accused of spying.

The police poured water over her, jabbed her chest with pens, and put sticks between her fingers and stamped on her hands to make her talk. She was returned to the barracks and beaten again.

After a year, the women were moved to a different area, where the Japanese soldiers seemed weaker and more discouraged, no barbed wire surrounded the camp and security was lax. As the Japanese position weakened, one man warned Kim that if the women stayed there, they would all be killed. Indeed, some Imperial Army units did slaughter prisoners as they retreated, according to historians.

Kim decided to make another escape attempt.

This time, she ran all night and at dawn came to a harbor. She stowed away on a Chinese civilian ship; eventually she was passed to another ship that left her on an island off the coast of Korea. It was a leper colony. Kindly inhabitants wrote to Kim's mother, who came to fetch the daughter who had disappeared two years earlier and was believed dead.

"Korean society was so strict that once a woman left home, she was not allowed to come back; even if she had a fight with her husband, she could not return to her parents' home. And I had been gone a long time," Kim said. "My mother said I could not come home."

Ashamed to admit what had happened, Kim told her mother that she had been kidnapped by the Japanese and forced to work in a factory.

She was sent to live with relatives, and a husband was found for her. He demanded to know why her sexual organs seemed abnormal. She told him she was deformed from birth. But when she did not have a child, he began to beat her and then sent her away.

Kim left her village and worked as a laborer and a maid. She remarried at 26, again hiding her past. To her surprise, she bore a child. But her daughter was mute, and her second marriage failed. She raised the child alone, and now cares for two grandchildren.

After the former "sex slaves" began to tell their stories in 1991, the Korean government put out a call for those who had been forced to labor for the Japanese.

Kim kept her silence, but her sister registered Kim's name. Eventually an official came to interview Kim and elicited the truth.

Across the Sea of Japan, coming to terms with the past has been almost as difficult a process.

After evading the issue of "comfort women" for years, the Japanese government acknowledged their existence in 1993.

Two years later, then-Prime Minister Tomiichi Murayama of the Socialist Democratic Party apologized to the women.

However, hemmed in by conservative Liberal Democratic Party coalition partners, Murayama did not comply with demands that Japan acknowledge that the forced sex system was a systematic and official policy, and so the apology has been rejected as inadequate by the South Korean and Taiwanese governments.

The Japanese government has set up a private committee to raise money from the public to compensate the women. Since last summer, six Filipinas have accepted $18,000 each and a letter of apology from Prime Minister Ryutaro Hashimoto. One South Korean also reportedly is ready to accept the payment. Japan has also promised to allocate about $27,000 from the national budget to each woman who accepts the compensation

KAZUKUNI YAMAMOTO, For The Times
On tour to educate Japanese on wartime activities, Kim Yoon Sim tells of how she was enslaved by the Imperial Army during WWII.

package, to pay for housing and medical care.

The Japanese government has maintained that wartime guilt and reparations issues were settled by treaties and a treaty after the war, and the vaguely defined payments to the women are not government reparations.

Korean activists complain that payments in lieu of official reparations imply that the "comfort women" were paid prostitutes who worked in private brothels, as Japanese conservatives have argued, rather than abductees dragooned by the invading army.

"I will not accept compensation," Kim said angrily. "This is not a question of money, and we are not doing this because we need money. I feel insulted. If the Japanese government really feels sorry, then they would prosecute the criminals."

Far from being prepared to prosecute, Japan is still racked by debate over its wartime responsibility. Many Japanese are outraged that the Ministry of Education has added descriptions of the "comfort women" to all high school textbooks and will add a mention in junior high textbooks next year.

Members of the far right call this historical "masochism" and say Japan is being hounded to make payoffs for wartime misdeeds of which other nations are equally guilty.

Thirty-eight members of parliament have organized a campaign to lobby the government to delete references to "comfort women" from textbooks.

Despite survivors' testimony and hundreds of books, articles and films documenting the episode, revisionists are fighting for the historical conscience of the next generation of Japanese.

One leading revisionist is a Tokyo University professor, Nobukatsu Fujioka. He was quoted this month criticizing the Ministry of Education stance in Sankei Shimbun, Japan's fourth largest newspaper—in an article that did not include any rebuttal of his views.

"There is no evidence that the Japanese Imperial Army forcefully abducted comfort women," Fujioka said. "But the government is going to put this in the textbooks and teach our children lies."

*Chieki Kitada of The Times' Tokyo Bureau contributed to this story.*

# WWII War Crimes List in 1996 Puzzles Japan

**By SONNI EFRON**
TIMES STAFF WRITER

TOKYO—Why has the United States decided to crack down on suspected Japanese war criminals 50 years after granting them immunity from prosecution?

Japanese scratched their heads last week at the unexpected announcement that the U.S. Justice Department had

Eli Rosenbaum, chief of the U.S. Justice Department unit charged with identifying Axis war criminals.

It was apparently the first public admission by a U.S. official that the U.S. erred when it granted immunity to Ishii, who has been compared to Nazi doctor Josef Mengele.

"They should have been prosecuted," Rosenbaum said. His unit had given priority to investigating Nazi war criminals, he said.

deference to Justice Department policy, which aims to keep the guilty guessing by never revealing who is—and is not—blacklisted from entering the United States.

A Foreign Ministry spokesman had no comment Tuesday on citizens' demands for an investigation of the 16 people listed.

Several Japanese intellectuals expressed concern that the legal move against the alleged war criminals could have a chilling effect on retrogressive cultists who have begun to

# WWII War Crimes List in 1996 Puzzles Japan

TIMES STAFF WRITER

TOKYO—Why has the United States decided to crack down on suspected Japanese war criminals 50 years after granting them immunity from prosecution?

Japanese scratched their heads last week at the unexpected announcement that the U.S. Justice Department had included former members of an infamous bacterial warfare research unit on a "watch list" of 16 suspected Japanese World War II war criminals prohibited from entering the United States.

"I don't understand why it's happening now; they're all in their 80s," Japan Women's University professor Ikuo Takagi said.

The United States has been aware of the identities of the Unit 731 leaders and of their gruesome experiments on human subjects since the end of the war. Details of Unit 731 atrocities have appeared in the Western and Japanese media for more than a decade.

In secret laboratories in occupied China, Unit 731 researchers tested poison gas and biological weapons on prisoners; injected human guinea pigs with toxins and bacteria and monitored how they died; froze and defrosted victims' limbs to study frostbite; and vivisected humans without anesthetic.

After the war, the United States concluded that the results of these experiments were "of the highest intelligence value."

Fearful that those results would fall into Soviet hands, the U.S. occupation authorities gave the head of Japan's bacterial warfare program, Dr. Shiro Ishii, and his colleagues immunity from prosecution at the Tokyo War Crimes Trials in exchange for their secret data.

"I can't defend the decision not to prosecute them," said Eli Rosenbaum, chief of the U.S. Justice Department unit charged with identifying Axis war criminals.

It was apparently the first public admission by a U.S. official that the U.S. erred when it granted immunity to Ishii, who has been compared to Nazi doctor Josef Mengele.

"They should have been prosecuted," Rosenbaum said. His unit had given priority to investigating Nazi war criminals, he said.

Many of Ishii's intimates went on to distinguished careers in postwar Japan, holding posts in the National Institute of Health, serving as medical school deans and laboratory heads. One key Ishii disciple, Ryoichi Naito, founded Green Cross, a leading pharmaceutical company, bought a Los Angeles company as a subsidiary and traveled to the United States often until his death in 1982.

Takagi and other Japanese intellectuals said they agree in principle with the Justice Department action.

But many consider it pointless to target offenders now—particularly since Japan, unlike Germany, never adopted a war crimes law with which to prosecute them. The Tokyo War Crimes Trials were held under U.S. auspices.

But activists said they hope that the U.S. move will increase pressure on the Japanese government, which has yet to offer an apology for its World War II crimes that Asian neighbors find convincing. They are also demanding that Japan launch a thorough investigation of the 16 alleged war criminals and set the historical record straight.

The Justice Department announcement was reported in the Japanese media but seems to have attracted little attention. A senior Japanese official said Japan would not protest the existence of the watch list, since decisions about entry visas are the sovereign prerogative of each country.

Washington has given Tokyo the 16 names, but the Japanese Foreign Ministry said it will not release them in deference to Justice Department policy, which aims to keep the guilty guessing by never revealing who is—and is not—blacklisted from entering the United States.

A Foreign Ministry spokesman had no comment Tuesday on citizens' demands for an investigation of the 16 people listed.

Several Japanese intellectuals expressed concern that the legal move against the alleged war criminals could have a chilling effect on octogenarian culprits who have begun to unburden themselves about their wartime activities before they die.

Some, such as former army surgeon Ken Yuasa, who once drilled holes into prisoners' brains to take tissue samples, have hit the lecture circuit to publicize and atone for their sins. Others helped mount a traveling exhibit to inform the Japanese public about Unit 731.

"I'm upset because the top guys, who should be treated as war criminals, have already died," said Yuasa's wife, Keiko. "Why do the Americans have to treat the underlings who are still alive like this?"

But Yuasa said he understands and would accept a U.S. decision to bar him—if his name is on the list.

Yoshio Shinozuka, who as a 16-year-old conscript cultured lethal bacteria in Ishii's lab in Harbin, China, agreed.

"The American announcement shows that these were crimes against humanity," said Shinozuka, 73. "I wish the U.S. government had done it much earlier, although the Japanese government hasn't done it yet. It's too late now to punish those who had the heaviest responsibility. But it's appropriate that my name be on the list....

"As a person who carried out orders, I must bear responsibility."

*Times staff writer Norman Kempster in Washington and Chiaki Kitada of The Times' Tokyo Bureau contributed to this story.*

# Pressure Mounts on France in Selection of New U.N. Leader

TIMES STAFF WRITER

UNITED NATIONS—The complex process of picking the next leader of the United Nations reached a critical juncture Thursday when France emerged as the lone holdout blocking the selection

lopsided margin is not enough for Annan's appointment.

Pressure immediately mounted on France to change its vote when balloting resumes today, in part because the three African members of the council all moved into Annan's column on Thursday. The French have cast themselves as a

although the American delegation has refrained from public comment on any candidates.

Last month, the U.S. vetoed the reelection of Secretary-General Boutros Boutros-Ghali, a favorite of the French, saying he has not been supportive enough of U.N. reform.

French officials here and in Paris on Thursday discounted reports that their opposition to Annan stems from linguistic concerns.

English is the official language of Ghana. Annan speaks English and French, but Paris is said to oppose him in part because French is not his first language.

"If you want continuity, you with Boutros. If you want someo new and different, you go outsid said the source, who called Annar U.N. bureaucrat.

Annan's defenders said he h compiled an impressive record administrator of the U.N. peac keeping department. They no

# Los Angeles Times

DATE: 6-25-98
PAGE: A-4

# U.S. Bars Visit by 2 Repentant Japanese Soldiers

■ **History:** They were to be part of tour chronicling WWII-era atrocities in which they participated. Law forbids entry to suspected war criminals.

By RONALD J. OSTROW
TIMES STAFF WRITER

WASHINGTON—Shiro Azuma and Yoshio Shinozuka, two aging Japanese veterans who repeatedly have admitted participating in World War II-era atrocities, wanted to bring their quest for redemption to the United States.

The Justice Department, however, is blocking them from entering the country.

The men, one of whom participated in the 1937 Rape of Nanking and the other in the Japanese army's infamous medical experimentation Unit 731, were scheduled to take part in a historical tour called "The Forgotten Holocaust of World War II in Asia."

Tour organizers said that the former soldiers are essential to telling the full stories of the atrocities. Their lawyer said that their testimony in the tour would help Americans learn from the past.

But Eli M. Rosenbaum, director of the Justice Department's office of special investigations, best known as for its Nazi-hunting activity, said that permitting the two Japanese veterans into the United States would mark an "unprecedented departure" from his office's enforcement of the law that prohibits suspected war criminals from entering the United States.

Rosenbaum, in a letter dated Monday to Keiichiro Ichinose, the Tokyo lawyer for the men, noted that the United States has "a reasonable basis to suspect [that they] assisted or otherwise participated in acts of Axis-sponsored persecution between 1933 and 1945," the legal standard for keeping them out.

Ichinose acknowledged both men had "admitted that they commit atrocious action" during World War II.

As an Imperial Army soldier in China in 1937, Azuma, now 86, joined his comrades in unleashing six weeks of breathtaking brutality during what has come to be known as the Rape of Nanking—murdering and raping as many as 350,000 civilians.

In a 1995 interview with The Times at his home in rural Japan, Azuma said: "When we raped the women, we thought of them as humans but when we killed them we thought of them as pigs. This was the Japanese army at the time." Shinozuka, 75, was an army conscript in 1939 when he was assigned to Unit 731's headquarters in Japanese-occupied Manchuria. He helped develop lethal bacteria. Unit 731 researchers used thousands of prisoners of war as human guinea pigs, testing poison gas and biological weapons, injecting them with bacteria and freezing and defrosting their limbs to study frostbite, and vivisecting them without anesthetic.

In December, 1996, when Rosenbaum's office first added 16 Japanese citizens to the U.S. government's "watch list" of suspected war criminals ineligible to enter the United States, Shinozuka told The Times: "It's appropriate that my name be on the list."

Ichinose has appealed the decision to Atty. Gen. Janet Reno.

The tour is scheduled to move Saturday from Toronto through New York, Washington and Vancouver, Canada, winding up in San Francisco on the July 4 weekend.

Justice officials said Wednesday that Reno has the appeal under consideration, leaving the door open to an eleventh-hour decision to use her authority to temporarily "parole" the men into the country "for reasons deemed strictly in the public interest."

Canadian authorities also have barred the two men. In a letter to Ichinose, Canada's immigration control officer said that Azuma and Shinozuka would not be allowed to enter his country because they had "perpetrated or were complicit in atrocities during the Second World War."

On Wednesday, Japanese lawyers for the men were considering challenging the prohibition by putting Shinozuka on a plane bound from Tokyo to Chicago. If Shinozuka did make it onto the plane, under normal procedures U.S. immigration authorities could be expected to hold him at Chicago's O'Hare Airport.

The atrocities are especially controversial in Japan. Azuma's adversaries now include Japanese citizens who deny that the atrocities occurred, have threatened him with death and condemn him for dishonoring those who died in the name of the emperor.

Azuma is appealing a court ruling against him in a case brought by his former army captain, who contends that Azuma lied in his diary describing the captain's alleged role in burning alive a Chinese person wrapped in a postal bag, according to Ichinose.

Iris Chang's best-selling book, "The Rape of Nanking," has focused renewed attention on what some consider one of the most brutal massacres in history.

Allowing the two repentant Japanese into the United States to give their testimony would contrast sharply with how Rosenbaum's office has dealt with the more than 60,000 individuals linked to Nazi persecution in Europe who have been on the watch list since his office's creation 20 years ago.

Rosenbaum noted that last year 45 suspects in Nazi persecutions were stopped at U.S. ports of entry and 23 of them were found to be excludable and were barred from entering the country.

"Where does one draw the line and for

70

Cont'd

whom?" Rosenbaum asked in an interview. If the two Japanese are permitted in, "are we then going to have an open market for Nazi war criminals to go on a lecture tour of the U.S.?" While the testimony of the two aging ex-soldiers "would strengthen the case of those who are drawing long-overdue attention to these crimes," Rosenbaum said, they could do so by videotape or "live by satellite."

The original 16 Japanese citizens put on the Justice Department watch list—the number has since doubled—were cited because they were members of Japanese Imperial Army units that conducted inhumane and frequently fatal experiments on humans or because they were involved in operating so-called "comfort women stations," where hundreds of thousands of women were forced to have sexual relations with Imperial Army officers and enlisted men.

The women and girls were taken principally from Korea, China, Taiwan, the Philippines, Malaysia, Burma and what is now Indonesia. In a 1994 report, the Geneva-based International Commission of Jurists said that the captives "were beaten and tortured in addition to being repeatedly raped day after day by officers and soldiers."

In urging Reno to open the door to Azuma and Shinozuka, Ichinose noted that the United States earlier had granted immunity from prosecution to Unit 731 veterans much higher up than Shinozuka.

After the war ended in 1945, the United States concluded that the results of the experiments conducted by Unit 731 were "of the highest intelligence value." Fearing that the data would fall into Soviet hands, U.S. occupation authorities granted immunity from prosecution at the Tokyo War Crimes Trials to Dr. Shiro Ishii, head of the program, and his colleagues in exchange for their data.

*NYTimes 27 June 98*

# U.S. Bars Japanese Who Admits War Crime

**By JAMES DAO**

WASHINGTON, June 26 — Two years ago, when the Department of Justice created a list of suspected Japanese war criminals who would be prohibited from entering the United States, veterans and Asian-American groups were delighted. Finally, they said, people who had raped, butchered or experimented on civilians and prisoners during World War II would be treated like the ex-Nazis who faced similar prohibitions.

But this week, when American officials used that watch list for the first time to bar a Japanese man from entering the country, those same groups were enraged. The reason was simple: The man, Yoshio Shinozuka, was their guest.

Mr. Shinozuka had been a member of a Japanese military unit that conducted biological experiments on war prisoners in Manchuria. He was to lecture about Japanese war crimes as part of an entourage of Japanese lawyers and former soldiers scheduled to visit New York, Washington and other cities in the coming weeks.

Their aim, which some State Department officials share, is to build pressure on the Japanese Government to make formal apologies to its war victims and pay them reparations.

"This is a miscarriage of law," said Tzu Ping Shao, a founder of a New York group called the Alliance in Memory of Victims of the Nanjing Massacre, which sponsored Mr. Shinozuka. "They are not touring for pleasure, they are not doing business or trying to sell books. They are here just to repent, to apologize, to explain, to expose, to do everything just."

Immigration officials blocked Mr. Shinozuka from entering the country at O'Hare International Airport in Chicago on Wednesday and then put him on the next flight to Tokyo. On Thursday, Attorney General Janet Reno rejected an appeal by Mr. Shinozuka's lawyer.

A second man who planned to join the American lecture tour, Shiro Azuma, was also recently notified by the Department of Justice that he was on the watch list and could not enter the country. Mr. Azuma has confessed to raping women during the Rape of Nanking. Historians estimate that as many as 300,000 Chinese were killed in Nanking in seven weeks in 1937 and 1938.

There is another twist to the story. Mr. Shinozuka, 75, and Mr. Azuma, 86, are on the watch list because they publicly recanted their crimes. Those forceful apologies, which earned them the enmity of many Japanese, also brought them to the attention of the American officials who added their names to the watch list.

"In these two cases, it is the fact that they spoke publicly that brought them to our attention," said Eli M. Rosenbaum, director of the Office of Special Investigations, which handles World War II-era war crimes for the Justice Department. "I appreciate the irony of that, but the law must be applied in all cases."

"I think what these men have to say is important and it deserves a

## Victim groups protest the exclusion of those who apologize.

wide audience," he added, "but that audience can be reached without having them physically enter the United States."

Mr. Rosenbaum's office was set up in 1979 when Congress passed a law requiring the United States to denaturalize, deport or block the entry of anyone suspected of committing war crimes for the Nazis or their allies. Since then, the office has stripped American citizenship from 59 people, all European immigrants, and barred several hundred others from entering the country. There are now 60,000 people on the watch list, of whom only 33 are Japanese.

The most famous of the office's targets was Kurt Waldheim, the former United Nations Secretary General. In 1987, when he was President of Austria, he was prohibited from visiting the United States after documents were released implicating him in the deportation of Greek Jews to death camps while he served in the German Army during the war.

Mr. Rosenbaum said Justice Department officials felt that they could not make an exception for Mr. Azuma and Mr. Shinozuka because that would encourage a flood of waiver applications from unsavory characters wanting to apologize in America for their crimes.

"Is the Government supposed to evaluate their sincerity?" he asked. "What happens if they come here and refuse to leave, or fall ill and we can't remove them? And I wonder whether people are prepared for the spectacle on their evening news of Nazi and Japanese war criminals dining at the best restaurants in Manhattan and Los Angeles. I doubt it."

Asian-Americans and human rights advocates have been united in demanding that Japan take greater responsibility for its war crimes. But they are divided over the decision to deny Mr. Shinozuka and Mr. Azuma entry into the United States. The Simon Wiesenthal Center in Los Angeles and a Washington group representing Korean women who were forced to provide sex to Japanese soldiers have supported the Justice Department's position.

"A week doesn't go by that one of these people doesn't try to have a vacation in the United States," said Rabbi Abraham Cooper, associate dean of the Simon Wiesenthal Center, which has offered to let Mr. Azuma and Mr. Shinozuka speak to Americans from Japan through its video-conferencing center. "This is an important symbolic punishment. Once you breach it, it all will go."

But the rights groups sponsoring the two men say the United States should encourage their speaking out, not punish it, since both have faced severe ostracism, including death threats, in Japan. Many conservatives in Japan contend that events like the Rape of Nanking never occurred. And mainstream politicians often portray the nation as a victim, not the aggressor, in World War II, emphasizing the point that the United States dropped atom bombs on Hiroshima and Nagasaki.

"All rules should have exceptions for the right reasons," said Gilbert M. Hair, executive director of the Center for Internee Rights in Miami Beach, whose father died while a prisoner of the Japanese.

# Japan Blocking Probe of War Criminals, U.S. Says

■ **Diplomacy:** Justice Department criticizes 'only country in the world' that doesn't provide assistance.

By TERESA WATANABE
TIMES RELIGION WRITER

Japan is stymieing American efforts to identify suspected war criminals by failing to cooperate with requests for information, U.S. officials have publicly charged—a statement that is certain to reignite questions over the sincerity of Japanese apologies for past war misdeeds.

"Japan is the only country in the world from whom we seek assistance that does not provide it," Eli M. Rosenbaum, director of the Justice Department's office of special investigations, said this week in the government's first public criticism of Japan.

"It is wrong. For a friendly government to know there are people we're trying to keep out of our country and be unwilling even to give you birth dates is wrong."

Although the government in the past has deliberately not commented about the issue, "there just comes a time when it's obvious they are not going to assist and there is no point in refraining from disclosing this any longer," Rosenbaum said.

The government statement came about in part from efforts by the Simon Wiesenthal Center, which has been widening its human rights mission beyond issues of Nazi war crimes to include the bitterly divisive subject of Japan's war misdeeds.

The center's involvement in the war crimes issue began last year, when Los Angeles writer Kinue Tokudome invited Rabbi Abraham Cooper, the center's associate dean, to meet with six repentant Japanese war veterans in Tokyo.

Moved by the gripping confessions—one man tearfully recalled how he cut down a 12-year-old boy begging for his life to teach other soldiers how to kill—Cooper sought to publicize their stories in a video conference in August.

He also stepped up efforts to obtain a public statement from the U.S. government about Japan's record.

Unlike Germany and other European nations that have cooperated extensively with U.S. efforts, Japan, despite years of requests, has not granted access to archival records or even confirmed the birth dates of suspected war criminals independently identified by U.S. investigators, Rosenbaum said.

The Justice Department office was charged in 1978 with deporting, or barring from entry into the United States, perpetrators of World War II crimes against humanity from Germany and its former Axis allies.

Japanese officials in Washington declined to comment.

Within Japan, intense domestic opposition to cooperation, along with concerns over legal liability if privacy rights are violated, are known to be factors hobbling the government.

The issue of wartime atrocities, such as the 1937 slaughter of Chinese in the city of Nanjing, germ warfare research by the Japanese army and forced sexual servitude to Japanese troops of women, primarily Koreans and Chinese, has dogged the Japanese for more than half a century.

Last week, Japanese Ambassador Kunihiko Saito went on television in the United States to debate Iris Chang, author of the best-selling book, "The Rape of Nanking," and argue—again—that Japan has apologized numerous times for its war misdeeds.

"I don't really understand why some people in [Asia] refuse somehow to admit that Japan has recognized its responsibility and offered apologies," Saito said in the debate, which took place on Public Broadcasting System's NewsHour with Jim Lehrer.

Despite Japan's efforts to rectify its past—including a string of apologies, a privately funded compensation program and textbook revisions to more fully reflect the wartime record—its lack of cooperation on the war criminal issue is certain to raise fresh accusations of insincerity.

CONT.

281

# A.1-18-2. NPR TRANSCRIPT OF ELI ROSENBAUM, DECEMBER 7, 1996

1ST STORY of Level 1 printed in FULL format.

NPR

SHOW: WEEKEND SATURDAY (NPR 12:00 am ET)

DECEMBER 7, 1996, SATURDAY

Transcript # 96120703-214

TYPE: INTERVIEW

SECTION: News; Domestic

LENGTH: 1414 words

HEADLINE: Japan War Crimes

GUESTS: Eli Rosenbaum

BYLINE: Scott Simon, Washington, DC

HIGHLIGHT:
Scott talks with Eli Rosenbaum of the Justice Department. abou announcement this
week that Japanese citizens suspected of crimes during World War II will be
banned from entering the U.S.

BODY:

SCOTT SIMON, HOST: The U.S. Justice Department this week announced that 16
Japanese citizens, suspected of committing crimes against humanity during World
War II, will be banned from entering the United States.

The department, which has identified more than 100 Nazi war criminals since
1979, has never before singled out Japanese persecutors. The names of those
people were not disclosed, but some reportedly were veterans of Japanese army
unit in Manchuria that conducted brutal pseudo-medical experiments.

Still others on the list are believed to have forced hundreds of thousands of
women in Japan's occupied territories into brothels run for the military.

Eli Rosenbaum heads the Department's Office of Special Investigations which
compiled that list and joins us in our studio. Thanks very much for being with
us.

ELI ROSENBAUM, DEPARTMENT OF JUSTICE, OFFICE OF SPECIAL INVESTIGATIONS: Good to
be here Scott.

SIMON: And why has the Office of Special Investigations chosen not to disclose

WEEKEND SATURDAY (NPR), DECEMBER 7, 1996

the names of the people?

ROSENBAUM: The purpose of putting these names on the watch list is not only to keep these 16 individuals from entering the United States, but it is to serve as a deterrent to others who were involved in those same crimes, a deterrent to keep them from even seeking entry to the United States.

SIMON: Mm-hmm.  So you don't want people to see that their name is not only list and then try and get in?

ROSENBAUM: Precisely.

SIMON: Why did it take all these years for this office to become interested in Japanese war criminals?

ROSENBAUM: Our office was established rather late in the game, decades after it should have been created.

SIMON: Mm-hmm.

ROSENBAUM: We were not created until 1979.  We became interested in the Japanese cases, not long after we were established in the 1980s.  The researched proved daunting.  It's much more difficult research than is research in the European cases.

SIMON: Mm-hmm.

In, in the European situation, we have archives here in Washington and elsewhere in the United States, archives all over Europe practically bursting at the seams with captured Nazi records and trial records from post-war prosecutions and the like.  There is comparatively little documentation in the Japanese cases.

It is frankly, only fairly recently, that victims started coming forward and it was the, the courage of the victims in doing so that caused people in many spheres, including the media, to begin finally to focus on these crimes.

SIMON: There are some Japanese historians, who are not necessarily apologists for Japan's rule during World War II, who have had a antithetical response and have said essentially, that the U.S.  is now trying to track down people that it originally let off 50 years ago.

ROSENBAUM: Clearly, there are prosecutions that did not take place, that ought to have taken place.  We can't undo that shortcoming.  However, it is one thing to discuss prosecution in Japan and it is another to discuss entry into the United States.

SIMON: These guys we're talking about must be pretty old now, into their 70s.  And I guess some people would ask "if we're talking about a group of people who are in their 70s, of course it was a terrible, tragic mistake, maybe worse, not to bring them to justice 50 years ago.  But what does it harm the world or the United States now if a 75 year old man, who was once a monster of a human being, wants to come to Southern California and see his grand kids and go to Disney World?"

ROSENBAUM: The simple answer is, we enforce the law. The passage of time has in no way lessened the gravity of the offenses. I think for the United States to look the other way, would send the worst possible message to a world that is still suffering through the ravages of, of ethnic strife of the, the perpetration of large scale atrocities in places like Bosnia and Rwanda and elsewhere.

I think therefore, that doing what we do sends an important symbolic message and is the kind of moral leadership, if you will, that the world expects from the United States.

SIMON: Mr. Rosenbaum, thank you very much for being with us.

ROSENBAUM: Thank you.

SIMON: Eli Rosenbaum is the Director of the Justice Department's Office of Special Investigations.

# A.1-18-3. TRANSCRIPT OF ELI ROSENBAUM AT WCCW 25<sup>TH</sup> ANNIVERSARY CEREMONY, DECEMBER 16, 2017

**Remarks by Eli Rosenbaum, United States Department of Justice**
**25th Anniversary Banquet of the Washington Coalition for Comfort Women Issues**
**University of Maryland, Rockville, MD, December 16, 2017**

Good evening.

It is a joy and a privilege to join everyone here tonight to celebrate 25 years of extraordinary work and great accomplishment by WCCW in the cause of pursuing historical and compensatory justice on behalf of the so-called "comfort women" – really women *and children . . . girls* – victimized by forces of the Imperial Japanese Army during the Second World War. I deeply admire the tenacity and courage with which the leaders and members of this organization have waged these exceedingly difficult battles.

As some of you know, I have been a prosecutor and investigator of suspected human rights violators for more than 30 years. My former office at the U.S. Department of Justice was created in 1979 in order to identify, investigate and take legal action against participants in World War II-era crimes of persecution perpetrated on behalf of Nazi Germany and its allies.

At the time that I became Director of my Justice Department unit, back in 1994, virtually all of our cases had involved European Nazi perpetrators. I was determined to change that – Japan was, after all, an ally of Nazi Germany – and we quickly began attempting to develop cases involving Japanese perpetrators, particularly offenders who were involved in the crimes committed against the comfort women and also offenders who participated in the criminal "experiments" committed by the infamous "Unit 731" of the Japanese Army.

Our inability to gain access to the records we most wanted to see in Japan hampered our investigative efforts. Japan, alone among the countries from which we sought investigative assistance in our World War II matters, did not provide meaningful help. But ultimately, even without that access that we sought, my office was able to identify a number of perpetrators who were still alive – living in Japan, though, not in America – and we promptly took action to place them on the U.S. immigration "watchlist" so that they could never, ever enter this great country.

My small office had to fight to get officials in our government to agree to let us make this landmark action public. And then we had to fight to obtain authorization to mention in the Justice Department's public announcement the fact that the crimes perpetrated against the victims in the comfort women cases included rape. Can you imagine that there was resistance to *that*? Well, my friends, *there was*. It was "explained" to us by one U.S. official that some in Japan would be offended if our government used the "R-word." We won that battle too, and our "explicit" press release was issued by the Justice Department on December 3, 1996. That announcement of the U.S. move to bar Japanese perpetrators made headlines all over the world, and it put the U.S. government firmly and publicly where Congressman Honda has always said we should be – on the side of the victims.

I must tell you that all of us at the Department of Justice who worked on these cases found enormous inspiration in the remarkable courage of the women survivors from Korea and other countries who joined hands to call for an end to silence, an end to denial, and an end to injustice. WCCW was, and remains, at the forefront of those who support the victims and fight with great passion and energy on their behalf. In fact, I can say that WCCW was responsible for the single most inspiring and moving experience I have had in all my years at the Department of Justice. It occurred when Mrs. Dongwoo Hahm and John Lee of WCCW brought survivor Kim Yoon-shim to our offices in Washington, on October 2, 1996 – two months before we made our public announcement. A paragon of dignity and bravery, she summoned the courage to relate to us her horrific experiences of victimization, which had begun when she was abducted off the streets of her village by Japanese soldiers. She was just 13 years old at the time she was kidnapped. *Thirteen years old*. There were some case-hardened prosecutors in the meeting – and also our Korean-American college intern – but by the time Kim Yoon Shim finished, there was, I can assure, not a single dry eye in the room. I thought of her valor and gentleness often in the following months, as my colleagues and I had to defend our government's actions in barring the perpetrators against legal and other attacks. To this day, I think often of that 1996 meeting.

Four years later, again thanks to WCCW, I had the unforgettable privilege of meeting another heroic survivor, Grandma Yong-soo Lee, whom I last saw at this organization's 2007 annual banquet. I am so sorry that she could not make the trip from Korea to join us this evening, but at least we were able to see her recorded video message just now. I know that she is in our thoughts – and always in our hearts.

Finally, let me be sure to thank WCCW for this wonderful recognition, which I would like to think acknowledges the dedication and skill that my Justice Department colleagues past and present – especially Susan Siegal, Ronnie Edelman, Elizabeth White, and Steven Rogers – brought to their stellar work in the comfort women and Unit 731 cases. In that work, all of us were inspired by the moral leadership of this great organization and the plight of the victims whose rights WCCW continues to fight for, every day. I am sure that this organization will go on to many additional successes in the years to come.

God bless you all, and thank you again, so very much.

# A.1-19. LETTER TO PRESIDENT OBAMA, JULY 27, 2010 AND LETTER FROM THE WHITE HOUSE, AUGUST 17, 2010

## Washington Coalition for Comfort Women Issues, Inc.

### 워 싱 턴 지 역 정 신 대 문 제 대 책 위 원 회

12401 Rivers Edge Drive Potomac, Maryland 20854
www.comfort-women.org  E-mail: chrisychoi@verizon.net Tel: 202 746 2186

July 27, 2010

Mr. Barack Obama
The President of the United States of America
The White House
1600 Pennsylvania Avenue N.W.
Washington D.C. 20500

Dear Mr. President,

As you are aware, the U.S. House of Representatives unanimously passed in July, 2007 Resolution 121 in which the House resolved that the Government of Japan should officially apologize to the women drafted for military sexual slavery during the Second World War commonly known as "comfort women." Three years have passed without any such official apology by the Japanese Government and any reparation for the comfort women.

Recently a group of 78 surviving comfort women in Korea had the honor and privilege to write to you personally with an appeal for your help in resolving this painful and long-lasting issue with Japan. The appeal was made in the context of the clear will of the American people as expressed in H.R. 121. A copy of this letter dated May 31, 2010 is attached for your reference.

Washington Coalition for Comfort Women Issues, Inc. (WCCW), an NGO of U.S. citizens and residents dedicated solely to supporting the comfort women all over the world in seeking rightful redress from the Japanese Government, joins these women and we ask you and your Administration to help in securing the Japanese Government's official apology and reparation for the comfort women in accordance with H.R. 121.

Respectfully yours,

Christine Choi
President, WCCW

287

THE WHITE HOUSE

August 17, 2010

Dear Friend:

Thank you for sharing your thoughts with me. Many Americans have written to me about human rights around the world, and I appreciate your perspective.

The United States was founded on the principles of freedom and equality, and our history is marked with triumphs and struggles in fulfilling these timeless ideals. Our task is never finished, and protecting these core values is a shared obligation. No region is free from violations of human rights, and no nation should be silent in the fight against them. When innocents in places like Bosnia and Darfur are slaughtered, that is a stain on our collective conscience. I am committed to reinvigorating America's leadership on a range of international human rights issues.

As you may know, the United States has rejoined the United Nations Human Rights Council and is working to make this body as effective as possible. My Administration intends to advocate for human rights in other international settings as well. In our relations with other countries, the issue of human rights will be raised as clearly, persistently, and effectively as possible. Among other things, we will promote respect for the rights of minorities and women, the equal administration of justice, and the freedom for people to live as they choose.

Our commitment to human rights is an essential element of American foreign policy and one of our best national security assets. Through it, we will help to shut down torture chambers, replace tyranny with good governance, and enlist free nations in the common cause of liberty.

To learn more about my Administration's human rights agenda, please visit: www.WhiteHouse.gov. Thank you again for writing.

Sincerely,

288

# A.1-20. GEORGE MASON CONFERENCE "KOREAN/ASIAN COMFORT WOMEN ISSUES THEN AND NOW" DECEMBER 1, 2012 IN COMMEMORATION OF WCCW 20TH ANNIVERSARY

WCCW 2012 Symposium Outline:

Theme: *Korean/Asian Comfort Women Issues Then and Now: Tracing its Historical, Political, and Cultural Aspects of the Comfort Women Movement in U.S. and Korea*

Venue: Atrium next to Edwin Meese III Conference Room, Mason Hall, The George Mason University, Fairfax, Virginia

Time: December 1, 2012 (Saturday) 3:00 - 6:00 pm. (three hours) (Panel discussion followed by questions and discussions)

Keynote Speaker: Rep. Mike Honda

Chair and Moderator of the Symposium: Jungsil Lee, Ph.D. Adjunct Professor at Towson University and Corcoran College of Art & Design, CEO/President of ArTrio, VP of WCCW

Participants and The Title of Paper

1. Yong Soon Min, Professor of University of California, Irvine, and department chair of Studio Art: "Two Hard Won Successes for Comfort Women."

2. Louise I. Shelley, Ph.D. Director of Terrorism, Transnational Crime, and Corruption Center and Professor of Public Policy of George Mason University: "Comfort Women in the context of Human Trafficking Issues during the World War II."

3. Margaret Stetz, Ph.D. Mae and Robert Carter Professor of Women's Studies and Professor of Humanities, University of Delaware, Dept. of Women and Gender Studies: "Teaching 'Comfort Women' Issues in the U. S. from Feminist Perspective."

4. Bonnie B.C. Oh, Ph.D. Distinguished Emeritus Professor of Korean Studies, Georgetown University: "Looking Back to the First Academic Conference 'The Comfort Women of World War II: Legacy & Lessons' in Georgetown University."

5. Chris Simpson, Professor of American University: "Jung Shin Dae: Co-Evolution of Gender Iniquity, Imperialism, and Resistance."

6. Dongwoo Lee Hahm, Chair of Board of WCCW: "History of Twenty Years of WCCW."

7. Ok Cha Soh, Ph.D. Professor of Washington Bible College: "Comfort Women, the Past and the Future."

8. Mindy Kotler, Ph.D. Director of Asia Policy Point: "Suggested Solutions to the Comfort Women Issue."

# A.1-21. WCCW PROPOSAL FOR BERKSHIRE CONFERENCE JUNE 3, 2017

https://berks.confex.com/berks/berks17/convo/sessions/proof.cgi

## Your session submission has been received

Click [ here ] to print this page.

You have submitted the following Session to 2017 Berkshire Conference on the History of Women, Genders and Sexualities. Receipt of this notice does not guarantee that your submission was complete, free of errors, or accepted for presentation.

## Narrative, Appropriation, and Styles of Objectivity when Confronting Sex Crimes Against Humanity

**Topic:** Slavery and Other Forms of Unfree Labor
**Session Title:** Narrative, Appropriation, and Styles of Objectivity when Confronting Sex Crimes Against Humanity
**Submitter Email:** juliee77@gmail.com
**Keywords:** Crime and Violence, East Asia, Military, Slavery and World War II

**Session Abstract:**

'Narrative, Appropriation, and Styles of Objectivity when Confronting Crimes Against Humanity'

The struggle for dignity and justice for 'Comfort Women' and other victims of military sexual slavery has risen from obscurity to become a major international issue during the past 25 years. This evolving shift in the perceptions of the public, academics, media, and some international leaders provides a framework for discussion of the complex interactions and rivalries among activists and historians.

Many agree that *any* narrative or historical synthesis is at least in part an appropriation due to authors', and sponsors' choices of whose voices are important or worthy of representation. In most cases, though not all, these appropriations reinforce the general contours of power in the political-economic and cultural settings in which they take place.

Claims of 'objectivity' of one type or another have long served to make these appropriations appear to be natural, inevitable or even desirable. Said another way, claims of objectivity legitimize the authority of academics, historians, mass media, pundits, courts, and other structures of power to synthesize and narrate the lived experience of millions of otherwise largely disenfranchised people. Meanwhile, survivors and 'activists' – themselves often disenfranchised – have long attempted to break, redefine, or in some instances exploit the same systems of appropriation and representation of human experience.

Navigating these complexities becomes especially urgent when confronting mass crimes that by their nature have are deeply embedded in the political-economic and cultural context that gave birth to the mass crime in the first place.

Organizer

Jungsil Lee
**Email:** juliee77@gmail.com -- Will not be published

WCCW

2/5/2016 7:23 PM

## A.1-22. FAIRFAX COUNTY HUMAN RIGHTS AWARD GIVEN TO WCCW, JUNE 8, 2015

# A.1-23. MARYLAND GENERAL ASSEMBLY OFFICIAL CITATION AND MARYLAND LEGISLATIVE ASIAN AMERICAN AND PACIFIC ISLANDER CAUCUS OFFICIAL CITATION GIVEN TO WCCW, DECEMBER 16, 2017

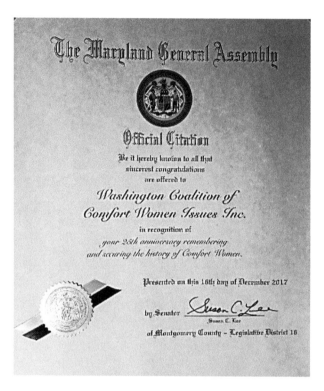

# A.4-1. LETTER FROM HENRY J. HYDE TO JAPANESE AMBASSADOR RYOZO KATO, OCTOBER 20, 2005

HENRY J. HYDE, ILLINOIS
Chairman

JAMES A. LEACH, IOWA
CHRISTOPHER H. SMITH, New Jersey, Vice Chairman
DAN BURTON, Indiana
ELTON GALLEGLY, California
ILEANA ROS-LEHTINEN, Florida
DANA ROHRABACHER, California
EDWARD R. ROYCE, California
PETER T. KING, New York
STEVE CHABOT, Ohio
THOMAS G. TANCREDO, Colorado
RON PAUL, Texas
DARRELL ISSA, California
JEFF FLAKE, Arizona
JO ANN DAVIS, Virginia
MARK GREEN, Wisconsin
JERRY WELLER, Illinois
MIKE PENCE, Indiana
THADDEUS G. McCOTTER, Michigan
KATHERINE HARRIS, Florida
JOE WILSON, South Carolina
JOHN BOOZMAN, Arkansas
J. GRESHAM BARRETT, South Carolina
CONNIE MACK, Florida
JEFF FORTENBERRY, Nebraska
MICHAEL McCAUL, Texas
TED POE, Texas

THOMAS E. MOONEY
Staff Director/General Counsel

JOHN WALKER ROBERTS
Deputy Staff Director

TOM LANTOS, California
Ranking Democratic Member

HOWARD L. BERMAN, California
GARY L. ACKERMAN, New York
ENI F.H. FALEOMAVAEGA, American Samoa
DONALD M. PAYNE, New Jersey
ROBERT MENENDEZ, New Jersey
SHERROD BROWN, Ohio
BRAD SHERMAN, California
ROBERT WEXLER, Florida
ELIOT L. ENGEL, New York
WILLIAM D. DELAHUNT, Massachusetts
GREGORY W. MEEKS, New York
BARBARA LEE, California
JOSEPH CROWLEY, New York
EARL BLUMENAUER, Oregon
SHELLEY BERKLEY, Nevada
GRACE F. NAPOLITANO, California
ADAM B. SCHIFF, California
DIANE E. WATSON, California
ADAM SMITH, Washington
BETTY McCOLLUM, Minnesota
BEN CHANDLER, Kentucky
DENNIS A. CARDOZA, California

ROBERT R. KING
Democratic Staff Director

PETER M. YEO
Democratic Deputy Staff Director

DAVID S. ABRAMOWITZ
Democratic Chief Counsel

## One Hundred Ninth Congress

## Congress of the United States
### Committee on International Relations
#### House of Representatives
#### Washington, DC 20515

(202) 225-5021

http://www.house.gov/international_relations/

October 20, 2005

His Excellency Ryozo Kato
Ambassador Extraordinary and Plenipotentiary
Embassy of Japan
2520 Massachusetts Avenue, N.W.
Washington, D.C. 20008

Dear Mr. Ambassador:

I am writing to express my gratitude to you and your hard-working Embassy staff for arranging a briefing last week, given by officials from Tokyo, for International Relations Committee staff on certain issues involving the current state of Japanese-Chinese relations. It is the hope of all Washington observers of Asia that outstanding concerns between Tokyo and Beijing can be resolved in a constructive and harmonious manner.

In this regard, I feel some regret over the continued visits of Japanese Government officials to the Yasukuni Shrine in Tokyo. As a World War II veteran of the Pacific, I deeply sympathize with the desire to honor the memory of the soldiers and civilians of all nations who died in the greatest conflagration of the Twentieth Century. I also understand the pain felt by those who lost loved ones in that horrific war.

The Yasukuni Shrine, however, honors more than these persons. It pays tribute to the memory of Hideki Tojo and other convicted war criminals who gave the orders for the unprovoked attack on the U.S. Pacific Fleet at Pearl Harbor on December 7, 1941. This attack then plunged the nations of the Asia-Pacific region into four years of total warfare. The Shrine, thus, has become a symbol throughout Asia and the rest of the world of unresolved history from the Second World War and of those militaristic attitudes which spawned the War in the Pacific.

The judgment of history, both at Nuremberg and at Tokyo, is clear: the Axis Powers of Nazi Germany, Fascist Italy and the militarist Japanese Empire waged a war of aggression which threatened the basic democratic institutions and human rights of peoples throughout the world. General Douglas MacArthur, using his authority as Supreme Commander of the Allied Forces,

293

authorized the establishment in Tokyo of the International Military Tribunal for the Far East (IMFTE), comprised of a panel of judges from the Allied nations. Charges were brought against individuals for "crimes against peace, conventional war crimes, and crimes against humanity." The defendants were found guilty. This was no more "victor's justice" than was the judgment at Nuremberg.

Together our two nations, as close allies, face a number of compelling issues. Security issues, including the North Korean nuclear threat, will continue to be discussed when the next round of the Six-Party Talks is convened in Beijing. Trade and economic issues, as well as broader regional matters, will be topics when the Asia-Pacific Economic Cooperation (APEC) Summit is held next month in Pusan, Republic of Korea. While the truth of what occurred in the Second World War must and will prevail, I am concerned that a renewed discussion of history at this critical juncture will distract nations in the region from carrying out a constructive dialogue on the issues at hand. Such a result will not serve the national interests of either of our nations.

Best wishes for continued cooperation based on the friendly ties which bind our two governments and peoples.

Sincerely,

HENRY J. HYDE
Chairman

HJH:dph/mco

294

# A.4-2. LETTER FROM HENRY J. HYDE TO J. DENNIS HASTERT, SPEAKER OF HOUSE REPRESENTATIVES, APRIL 26, 2006

HENRY J. HYDE, Illinois
CHAIRMAN

JAMES A. LEACH, Iowa
CHRISTOPHER H. SMITH, New Jersey, Vice Chairman
DAN BURTON, Indiana
ELTON GALLEGLY, California
ILEANA ROS-LEHTINEN, Florida
DANA ROHRABACHER, California
EDWARD R. ROYCE, California
PETER T. KING, New York
STEVE CHABOT, Ohio
THOMAS G. TANCREDO, Colorado
RON PAUL, Texas
DARRELL ISSA, California
JEFF FLAKE, Arizona
JO ANN DAVIS, Virginia
MARK GREEN, Wisconsin
JERRY WELLER, Illinois
MIKE PENCE, Indiana
THADDEUS G. McCOTTER, Michigan
KATHERINE HARRIS, Florida
JOE WILSON, South Carolina
JOHN BOOZMAN, Arkansas
J. GRESHAM BARRETT, South Carolina
CONNIE MACK, Florida
JEFF FORTENBERRY, Nebraska
MICHAEL McCAUL, Texas
TED POE, Texas

THOMAS E. MOONEY
Staff Director/General Counsel

JONATHAN B. SCHARFEN
Deputy Staff Director/Chief Counsel

TOM LANTOS, California
Ranking Democratic Member

HOWARD L. BERMAN, California
GARY L. ACKERMAN, New York
ENI F.H. FALEOMAVAEGA, American Samoa
DONALD M. PAYNE, New Jersey
SHERROD BROWN, Ohio
BRAD SHERMAN, California
ROBERT WEXLER, Florida
ELIOT L. ENGEL, New York
WILLIAM D. DELAHUNT, Massachusetts
GREGORY W. MEEKS, New York
BARBARA LEE, California
JOSEPH CROWLEY, New York
EARL BLUMENAUER, Oregon
SHELLEY BERKLEY, Nevada
GRACE F. NAPOLITANO, California
ADAM B. SCHIFF, California
DIANE E. WATSON, California
ADAM SMITH, Washington
BETTY McCOLLUM, Minnesota
BEN CHANDLER, Kentucky
DENNIS A. CARDOZA, California
RUSS CARNAHAN, Missouri

ROBERT R. KING
Democratic Staff Director

PETER M YEO
Democratic Deputy Staff Director

DAVID S. ABRAMOWITZ
Democratic Chief Counsel

One Hundred Ninth Congress

## Congress of the United States
### Committee on International Relations
#### House of Representatives
#### Washington, DC 20515

(202) 225-5021

http://www.house.gov/international_relations/

April 26, 2006

The Honorable J. Dennis Hastert
Speaker of the House of Representatives
U.S. House of Representatives
H-232, The Capitol
Washington, D.C. 20515

Dear Mr. Speaker:

      I am writing to you in response to news reports that His Excellency Junichiro Koizumi, the Prime Minister of Japan, will pay an official visit to Washington in June. We in the Congress certainly welcome the visit of the leader of the staunch ally that has stood with us in addressing such critical issues as the North Korean nuclear threat, the reconstruction of Afghanistan, the stabilization of the situation in Iraq, and the maintenance of peace in the Taiwan Straits. A summit meeting with President Bush, including a constructive dialogue on the unresolved beef issue and the realignment of U.S. forces within the Asia/Pacific region, would also be well received.

      There has been some press speculation that the expected visit by Prime Minister Koizumi might include the suggestion that he address a Joint Session of the Congress. That would also be most welcome with one important qualification: Prime Minister Koizumi, who will retire in September, has made a public pledge that he will visit the Yasukuni Shrine in Tokyo during every year of his Prime Ministership. He has not yet made such a visit in 2006. There is some suggestion that he will do so on or around August 15, the sixty-first anniversary of the end of hostilities in the Pacific War.

      This visit could give rise to potential embarrassment for the Congress, since President Franklin Roosevelt addressed his "date which will live in infamy" speech to this very same body on December 8, 1941. It would be an awkward juxtaposition of events if the Japanese Prime Minister were to visit a shrine that pays homage to Hideki Tojo and other leaders of Imperial Japan, who gave the orders for the unprovoked attack on the U.S. Pacific Fleet at Pearl Harbor, a mere few weeks after his appearance before the United States Congress. I am concerned that the

The Honorable J. Dennis Hastert
April 26, 2006
Page Two

dwindling number of living World War II veterans, who still remember Pearl Harbor as a younger generation of Americans remembers September 11th, would be concerned and even offended by such an occurrence.

It would be optimal if some prior assurance could be given to the Congress and to America's World War II generation that such a sequence of events will not take place.

With best wishes,

Sincerely,

HENRY J. HYDE
Chairman

HJH:dph/mco

296

## A.4-3. LISA WILLIAMS' OP-ED IN *THE KYUNGHYANG SHINMUN*, JULY 31, 2017

**Of Grandmothers, Sunflowers, and H.Res. 121**

By: Dr. Lisa Williams

In 2007, two Members of Congress colluded – and changed the outcome for surviving victims, euphemistically known as "Comfort Women," who had been forced into sexual slavery by Imperial Armed Forces during Japan's colonial and wartime occupation of Asia and the Pacific Islands from the 1930s through the duration of World War II.

The late Congressman Eni F.H. Faleomavaega of American Samoa and the gentleman from California, former Congressman Mike Honda, like brothers, were born to advocate for and on behalf of these women who had been brutalized in Japan's military brothels.

First and foremost, Eni and Mike revered these precious women, and lovingly referred to them as "grandmothers" – their grandmothers – yours and mine. Arm in arm, they worked together to bring about justice – or whatever justice can be brought about until His Kingdom comes.

Congressman Honda, a Japanese-American, courageously bucked tradition, introducing House Resolution (H.Res.) 121 – calling upon the government of Japan to formally acknowledge, apologize, and accept historical responsibility for its egregious actions. While others had dared to introduce a Resolution in the past on behalf of our "grandmothers," no Japanese American had ever done so.

The gentleman from American Samoa agreed to hold a hearing on the Resolution. Congressman Faleomavaega was the first Asian-Pacific American in U.S. history to serve as Chairman of the influential U.S. House of Representatives' Foreign Affairs Subcommittee on Asia, the Pacific, and the Global Environment – also known as the Asia Pacific Subcommittee – and he determined that his first hearing would be on H. Res. 121. No hearing had ever been held in the U.S. Congress – House or Senate – for our "grandmothers" until Faleomavaega gaveled the hearing to order. The hearing was historic. It lit the world on fire.

Mr. Honda testified at the hearing. Three surviving "grandmothers" – Ms. Jan Ruff O'Herne, Ms. Kun-ja Kim, Ms. Yong-soo Lee – also testified. Their testimony was riveting, powerful, heart wrenching, moving and necessary. Transcripts from the hearing may be accessed at http://www.alpha-canada.org/wp-content/themes/bcalphatheme/Testimonies/Protecting%20the%20Human%20Rights%20of%20Comfort%20Women%20Hearing%20Transcript%20in%20US%20Congress%2015Feb2007.pdf. To this day, as Faleomavaega said, "their testimony stands as a matter of record, immovable and unalterable, and I would encourage all to read it."

Regrettably, in 2014, the White House allowed a petition to be posted on the President's "We the People" website in support of taking down a "Comfort Women" memorial in Glendale, California. But thanks be to the Korean-American community for keeping this issue alive. Or, as Elie Wiesel so beautifully stated about Holocaust Remembrance Day – "For the dead and the living, we must bear witness" – and so the Korean-American community did.

I commend Mr. Dong Suk Kim and the Korean American Civic Empowerment for Community (KACE) for their hard work, which led to the passage of H.Res. 121. I also applaud the work of Mr. Dennis Halpin, former professional staff member of the U.S. House of Representatives' Foreign Affairs' Committee, an unsung hero in advancing this journey, as was the late Chairman Henry Hyde who marked up H.Res. 759 in September 2016, becoming the first Committee Chairman to mark-up in Committee a "Comfort Women" Resolution. H.Res. 759 was introduced by Congressman Lane Evans of Illinois.

Regarding H.Res. 121, I also commend Mr. Peter Yeo, who served as Deputy Staff Director for the Foreign Affairs Committee, which was chaired by Congressman Tom Lantos (D-CA), the first and only Holocaust survivor to serve in the U.S. Congress. Without the support of Mr. Yeo and Chairman Lantos, and Ranking Member Ileana Ros-Lehtinen, H.Res. 121 would never have been passed.

Now, as we celebrate the ten-year anniversary of the passage of H.Res. 121, I assure you that if he could be, Mr. Faleomavaega would be here to pay tribute to each and every one of you, and to thank you for your service. But, Faleomavaega passed away in February of this year. Ms. Kim Kun-ja passed away only days ago.

Due to these circumstances, I offer this statement on Faleomavaega's behalf. As Chairman Faleomavaega's former Chief of Staff and former and first woman to have served as staff director of the Asia Pacific Subcommittee, I bear witness, too. Faleomavaega cared deeply for our "grandmothers." He loved them. Every time he was in South Korea, he visited and danced with them at the House of Sharing on the outskirts of Seoul. It was my privilege to accompany Faleomavaega and witness the special bond they shared. Mike Honda also had that privilege and those bonds.

Simply put, Congressman Faleomavaega considered the passage of H.Res. 121 as one of the most important Resolutions ever passed by the U.S. House of Representatives during his service from 1989-2015 – because it led to an apology from Japan. But Chairman Faleomavaega left this world believing Japan's apology was not good enough, and that Japan should do so much more. However, in my own simple way, I choose to believe that Congressman Faleomavaega and Ms. Kim are at peace – dancing away on the outskirts and "in-skirts" of heaven – probably to the tune of his own CD – Faleomavaega Sings Samoan Songs.

As one pioneer put it, the journey home ain't always easy. We'll have a "hard time" getting there. But along the way, "we'll see things we've never before seen – great herds of buffalo and big cedar trees on the hills, and maybe even vast expanses of sunflowers in bloom."

Of H.Res. 121, of Chairman Faleomavaega, Congressman Honda, and Ms. Kim, of President Moon who reverentially sent flowers to the hospital where Ms. Kim's body was kept, of Ms. O'Herne and Ms. Lee, of our "grandmothers" here and before – of each one of you, including the Washington Coalition for Comfort Women Issues (WCCW) – to me, you are like vast expanses of sunflowers in bloom.

I pay special tribute to you – and also to President Moon Jae-in for his courage in taking up the cause of remembering.  For the living and the dead, may we keep bearing witness until the day comes, as promised in Revelation 21:4, when "God shall wipe away all tears from their eyes; and there shall be no more death, neither sorrow, nor crying, neither shall there be any more pain."

*Dr. Lisa Williams is the former Staff Director for the U.S. House of Representatives' Foreign Affairs' Subcommittee on Asia, the Pacific, and the Global Environment, and the first woman to have served in the position.*

# A.4-4. AMENITIES IN THE JAPANESE ARMED FORCES, G-2 LIBRARY, NOVEMBER 15, 1945

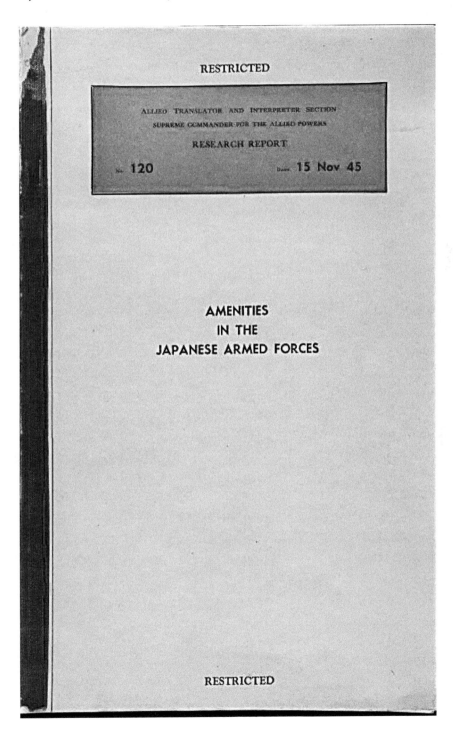

RESTRICTED

ALLIED TRANSLATOR AND INTERPRETER SECTION
SUPREME COMMANDER FOR THE ALLIED POWERS

RESEARCH REPORT

No. 120                    Date. 15 Nov 45

AMENITIES
IN THE
JAPANESE ARMED FORCES

RESTRICTED

ALLIED TRANSLATOR AND INTERPRETER SECTION

SUPREME COMMANDER FOR THE ALLIED POWERS

# RESEARCH REPORT

---

**SUBJECT:** AMENITIES IN THE JAPANESE ARMED FORCES

I. G. No. 6310
B. I. D. No. 1228

---

**DATE OF ISSUE** 15 November 1945

**No.** 120

**SUMMARY:**

1. This report covers information available at ATIS up to 31 March 1945 on amenities furnished by the Japanese to their armed forces.

2. There has been no attempt to establish the existence of rules regarding the availability for purchase or gratuitous issue of canteen stores, since there is a great variation, depending upon the type of troops and the area, in the handling of amenities.

3. Information has also been given as to the availability to the troops of such amusements as shows, movies, geisha entertainment, and brothels.

4. References are quoted regarding the amount of war news passed on to troops by field newspapers, bulletins, and radios.

HNB/SRE/CHR.vb

Distribution H

SIDNEY F. MASHBIR
COLONEL, S.C.
COORDINATOR

---

**SOURCES:** Captured Documents.
Statements of Prisoners of War.

(INFORMATION SHOULD BE ASSESSED ACCORDINGLY)

i

## A.4-5. FORMER REP. ENI FALEOMAVAEGA'S OP-ED IN *THE HILL*, JANUARY 8, 2016

https://thehill.com/blogs/congress-blog/foreign-policy/265124-japans-comfort-women-apology-not-good-enough

# Japan's 'comfort women' apology not good enough

BY FORMER REP. ENI F.H. FALEOMAVAEGA (D-A.S.) — 01/08/16 04:00 PM EST
THE VIEWS EXPRESSED BY CONTRIBUTORS ARE THEIR OWN AND NOT THE VIEW OF THE HILL

**122** SHARES

The Foreign Ministries of the Republic of Korea and Japan recently announced that a deal has been reached to "finally and irreversibly" resolve the historically sensitive issue of "comfort women" – the euphemism used to refer to the innocent girls who were abducted and forced into sexual servitude by Japanese Imperial Forces during World War II.

U.S. Secretary of State John Kerry heralded the "resolution of the comfort women issue" and applauded Japanese Prime Minister Abe for having the "courage" to reach this agreement, although no survivors, now affectionately known as "grandmothers," were consulted before, during or after the announcement of the agreement or the posting of Kerry's press statement. Until they are, it is my sincere hope that those speaking on behalf of the United States will choose their words more responsibly when referring to human suffering because, in this case, proclaiming that the issue is "resolved" or that it takes "courage" to apologize for wrongdoing is an affront to all "grandmothers" past and present.

While I understand the necessity for trilateral economic ties and security cooperation, the word "courage" is only rightly applied to the victims who were brutalized by Japanese Imperial Forces – not to the perpetrators and perpetuators of the crime. On many occasions, I have met with "comfort women" survivors – my "grandmothers" – at the House of Sharing in Gyeonngi Province in South Korea. In my official capacity as chairman of the U.S. House of Representatives Foreign Affairs Subcommittee on Asia, the Pacific, and the Global Environment, I also held a hearing in 2007 in which three "grandmothers" – two Korean and one Dutch – courageously spoke for many, recollecting the humiliation and torture they endured. To this day and always, there testimony stands as a matter of record, immovable and unalterable, and I would encourage any and all to read it.

President Park Geun-hye, who was then a National Assembly Member, attended that historic hearing – the first and only hearing of its kind held in the U.S. Congress. Her commitment to this issue is and always has been genuine and profound, and I urge the United States to learn from her example by being kinder to those whose hearts have been pierced with deep wounds.

In 2014, the White House allowed a petition to be posted on the president's "We the People" website in support of taking down a "comfort women" memorial in Glendale, California. Despite calls for the petition to be removed from the White House website, neither the U.S. Department of State nor the White House obliged. Why does any of this matter? It matters because civilized governments do not condone the targeting of civilians during war. In an unconscionable manner, the government of Japan – much like Boko Haram – condoned the targeting of civilians, stripping young girls from their homes and of their future. Out of respect and reverence for the young girls who once had hopes and dreams like your daughters and mine, the United States government should have removed the offensive petition from its government operated, taxpayer funded website, just like the United States should review Abe's apology before applauding.

By omitting any and all references to the daughters of China, the Philippines, Australia, South Pacific Island nations, Myanmar, Indonesia, the Netherlands, Taiwan and many others who were also used as sex slaves by Japan's Imperial Forces, or to stipulate that the $8.3 million promised by the government of Japan for the daughters of Korea is not compensation and may be contingent on the removal of a "comfort women" statue located in front of the Japanese Embassy in Seoul, Abe missed the mark of his apology on all points. In so doing, he managed to both regionalize the scope of suffering and marginalize Japan's war crimes.

This issue will never be finally and irreversibly resolved until the true and living Judge says so. Until then, I commend President Park for doing all she can to hold Japan accountable, and I applaud my "grandmothers" for their courage.

*Faleomavaega served as American Samoa's delegate in the House of Representatives from 1989 to 2015.*

**TAGS** JOHN KERRY

# A.5-1. KEYNOTE SPEECH BY MME. MUTSUKO MIKI IN GEORGETOWN UNIVERSITY CONFERENCE, SEPTEMBER 30, 1996. IN *MID ATLANTIC BULLETIN OF KOREAN STUDIES*, N. 35 (WINTER 1996): 1-3, 11-13

# MID ATLANTIC BULLETIN OF KOREAN STUDIES

Number 35    Georgetown University    Washington, D.C.    Winter 1996

### CONFERENCE ON COMFORT WOMEN OF WORLD WAR II
### WITH FILM SCREENINGS AND EXHIBITS HELD ON SEPTEMBER 30 - OCTOBER 4
### CLOSED WITH CRITICAL ACCLAIM

"Moving, informative, and well-balanced," were the comments overheard at the reception immediately following a half-day conference on the afternoon of September 30. When Ms. **Kim Yoon-sim**, a surviving victim of the Japanese military prostitution system, recounted her story, there hardly was a dry eye in the audience. Earlier in the afternoon, the atmosphere was equally charged, and not a sound was heard except the soft but firm and dignified voice of the 80-year-old keynote speaker, **Mrs. Mutsuko Miki**, widow of former Japanese Prime Minister **Takeo Miki**. Mme Miki spoke candidly and forcefully about the Japanese government's need to acknowledge the crime, formally apologize to, and compensate the victims out of official funds,

The conference entitled, "Comfort Women of World War II: Legacy and Lessons," was co-chaired by **Bonnie Oh**, the current Distinguished Research Professor of Korean Studies, and **Margaret D. Stetz**, Associate Professor of the Department of English and Women's Studies Program. And it was sponsored jointly by Georgetown University, the Washington Coalition for Comfort Women Issues (WCCW), and the Korea Society.* It consisted of four parts: a half-day international symposium held at the Bunn Intercultural Center Auditorium of Georgetown University main campus, film screenings on three consecutive evenings, enlarged photo exhibits on ten panels (6x4') in the Galleria (atrium) of the Intercultural Center for five days, and a two week - exhibit

*Ms. Kim Yoon-sim recounting her story as a "Comfort Woman."*

*Mme. Mutsuko Miki delivering the keynote address.*

of books, catalogues, and art work in a glass case. The opening session moderated by **Bonnie Oh** featured Dean **Robert L. Gallucci** of the School of Foreign Service, who welcomed the guests with a remark about the importance of an open dialog on sensitive and ethical issues in international relations, of which the Comfort Women issue was a part. A keynote address by Mutsuko Miki was

(continued p.2)

305

# GEORGETOWN KOREA LECTURE SERIES

Two to four public lectures (or conferences) are held annually at Georgetown University. The series, which replaced the former Washington Seminar on Korean Studies, is supported by the Georgetown Korean Studies Program, the Korea Society, and the Korean Information Center.

## 1996 LECTURE SERIES

The 1996 series is a mixture of big and small events: a public lecture and a seminar in the Spring and a conference and a seminar in the Fall.

### APRIL 29, 1996 (Lecture)

The 1996 lecture series sponsored a public lecture and a seminar in the Spring and an international symposium and a seminar in the Fall. The public lecture on April 29 was delivered by Rev. Dennis L. McNamara, S.J., Professor and Chair of the Department of Sociology and the first Y.H. Park Professor of Korean Studies at Georgetown University. Dr. McNamara's talk was entitled "Association and Adjustment: Restructuring Industry and Society in South Korea."

### MARCH 26, 1996 (Seminar)

In late March, Hyug Baeg Im, visiting professor in the Spring semester, from Ewha Women's University in Seoul, presented a paper, "Determinants of East Asian Miracle: Market, The State, or Institutions?"

### SEPTEMBER 30, 1996 (Conference)

On September 30, an afternoon conference, "Comfort Women of World War II: Legacy and Lessons," kicked off a series of events related to Comfort Women, three movie screenings, photo, artwork and book and exhibits. (See, p. 1 for more details.)

### NOVEMBER 6, 1996 (Seminar)

On the day after the national election, Charles Kartman, Principal Deputy Assistant Secretary of East Asian and Pacific Affairs of the U.S. Department of State, shared "An Insider's View of Korean-American Relations" at a seminar. This is part of Occasional Korea Seminars, sponsored by Korean Studies Program of the University.

## 1997 LECTURE SERIES

### FEBRUARY 19, 1997

Professor Ezra Vogel, Director of Fairbank Center for East Asian Research and Henry Ford II Professor of Social Science at Harvard University, will deliver the first lecture of 1997. He will speak on "A Shrimp Among Whales: Challenges for Korea." The lecture will be held at 5:30 p.m. in the Bunn Intercultural Center auditorium and is free of charge and open to the public.

---

followed by a question-and-answer session, eagerly participated by audience.

The academic panel was moderated by **Anne Cubilie** of English Department of Georgetown University. Three papers were presented in the panel. **Margaret D. Stetz** started with a paper entitled, "Wartime Sexual Violence Against Women: a Feminist Perspective," setting a general framework. **Dai Sil Kim-Gibson**, Washington, DC-area freelance author and filmmaker, read an abstract of a chapter, "Slaves of Sex: Comfort Women in World War II," from her forth-coming book on Comfort Women. **Yuki Tanaka** of Melbourne, Australia, presented a paper entitled, "'Why Comfort Women'?" He is also the author of a recently released book, "Hidden Horrors: the Japanese War Crimes of World War II." **Robin Levy** of the Human Rights Watch Washington Office discussed the first two papers, providing a human rights activist's perspective on the Comfort Women issues. **Chris Simpson** of American University com-

2

306

(continued from p.2)

mented on Tanaka's paper from the viewpoint of an academic volunteering in the WCCW.

The third and final part of the conference, "Testimony from the Frontline," was moderated by **David L. Kim**, Executive Director of the Korea Society Washington Office. The session started with the screening of a fifteen-minute film on Korean Comfort Women, produced by the WCCW. Mrs. **Dongwoo Lee Hahm**, President and founder of The WCCW, provided an update of the effort of her and various other organizations, including the United Nations, to bring about satisfactory conclusion to the Comfort Women issues. The highlight of the meeting was the testimony of Ms. Kim Yoon-sim of Seoul, Korea, who recalled her ordeal as a comfort woman from the time she was abducted when she, a curious 14-year old, was given a joy-ride in a Japanese military automobile. **James Reardon-Anderson**, Director of Asian Studies Program, who seemed riveted to the victim's testimony, closed the conference with a brief comment on the importance of ethics in the international relations curriculum.

*Additional support was provided by the Center for Women Policy Studies, Maryknoll Fathers and Brothers Justice and Peace Office of Washington, DC, Asia Pacific Center for Justice and Peace, Jhoon Rhee Taekwondo Foundation, and the following programs and organizations from Georgetown University: American Studies, Center for Australian and New Zealand Studies, Center for Minority Student Affairs, Communication, Culture and Technology Program, Department of East Asian Languages and Literatures, Department of English, Department of Government, Department of History, Department of Theology, Justice and Peace Certificate Program, Korean American Law Students Alliance, Korean Studies, Office of the Dean of Interdisciplinary Studies, Office of the Dean of Summer and Continuing Education, Office of the Dean of Students, Office of the Executive Vice-President for the Main Campus, Women's Center, and Women's Studies Program.*

## EDITOR'S NOTE

The editor gratefully acknowledges the financial support of Georgetown University's Asian Studies Program, the Mid-Atlantic Region of the Association for Asian Studies (MAR/AAS), and the Information Office of the Embassy of Korea. The editor would like to welcome new editorial assistant, **David Park**, in the School of Foreign Service and a new editorial board member, **Kathleen Burns**, Program Administrator for the Center for Australian and New Zealand Studies.

Special thanks goes to **Kay Won Lee**, Lauinger Library, Georgetown University, for her help with the bibliography, information, and reading of the entire draft. The editor gratefully acknowledges **Kathleen Burns'** willingness to read and edit the whole manuscript. Special words of gratitude go to **Dr. Dennis L. McNamara** and **Mme. Mutsuko Miki** of Tokyo, Japan, for allowing us to abridge and print their talks delivered as part of the Georgetown Series as the "feature" articles I and II for this issue of the Bulletin.

We welcome all comments, suggestions, and news items, including information about awards received, new publications, new projects, new sources of grants, fellowships and scholarships for both faculty and students interested in Korean studies. They should be addressed to:

EDITOR
MABKS
ASIAN STUDIES PROGRAM, ICC 512
GEORGETOWN UNIVERSITY
WASHINGTON, DC 20057

Any person in the Mid-Atlantic region who is interested in Korea may receive copies of the Bulletin free of charge upon request to the Editor. Persons outside the Mid-Atlantic Region are asked to subscribe at $5 per year, plus airmail postage if desired for those outside the United States.

3

307

## SPEECH BY MME. MUTSUKO MIKI

*[The following is an excerpt of the keynote speech delivered by Mme. Mutsuko Miki at the conference on "Comfort Women of World War II: Legacy and Lessons" on September 30, 1996.]*

It is a great pleasure for me to make a keynote speech at Georgetown University, a university which is well known in the world for its excellence in learning, particularly in the field of international affairs. This will be an unforgettable occasion for me. Furthermore I feel very strongly the importance of the subject matter of this conference, pertaining as it does to fundamental issues of human rights, war, and peace.

My husband, Takeo Miki, was elected as a member of the Japanese house of Representatives at age 31. He subsequently was reelected 19 times, serving in the House until he passed away at the age of 81. Despite his efforts before the war to steer Japan away from conflict with the United States [he was not successful in his effort and], my husband felt after the war a sense of unease concerning his inability to atone for Japan's failures, as well as his own, and it served as the motive force for his long political career. As I reflect back on his career and the concerns that guided him, it is clear to me that he recognized the tremendous abuse of basic human rights that were associated with the war. Recognizing the fundamental facts of the war, he then devoted himself to attempting to atone for them. And he was clear in his own mind that he, and Japan as a nation, had the responsibilities to seek to establish an enduring peace.

Initially, with the conclusion of the war, my husband said that he would resign his seat and run a grocery shop. I argued with him, however, telling him that he had responsibilities to help lead Japan toward a democratic future. As a young man who had enjoyed education in the United States before the war, he was well placed to help guide Japan away from its militarist past. I am happy to say that he agreed with me and continued his political career, including service as Prime Minister from 1974-1975. Like my husband, I, too, worked for peace, together with women of other Asian countries. I now serve as the chair of the Asian Women Friendship Association as well as the UN Women Association. In addition, I am a member of Peace in Asia, as well as Women's Role, a nongovernmental organization working for the unification of Korea. I have had the opportunity to visit both the Democratic People's Republic of Korea and the Republic of Korea.

In the course of candid discussions during those visits, I gained fresh impressions of the lasting scars left by the Pacific War. I firmly believe that the human contact and understanding gained through such interchanges, and the chance to gain insights of the human sufferings associated with the war, can provide meaningful basis for establishing international peace. In particular, if more people of all countries could learn from one another in these ways, I believe the prospects for peace would be stronger.

The plight of the so-called comfort women during the Pacific War raises a number of fundamental human rights issues. The women who suffered during the war present to us human suffering of tragic proportions. And these human stories are intertwined with national struggles for global prestige, and national security issues engaging life and death conflicts. Out of the conflict of these enormous historical forces comes the human tragedy of the comfort women. In 1991, these comfort women asked the Japanese government both for apologies for their war time suffering and for direct monetary compensation. The women worked through the Japanese courts and, in the process, brought to light previously hidden facts. The Japanese Ministry of Foreign Affairs insisted again and again that the issue had been settled with the signing of the peace treaties in San Francisco in 1951 as well as subsequent treaties, such as that with South Korea in 1965.

In 1991, twelve Korean victims of the Japanese military's wartime policies visited Japan and

(Miki...continued on p.12)

11

308

instituted a suit against the Japanese government. Their action rallied the sympathy of the Japanese people. In 1992, researchers unearthed records at Japan's Self-Defense Agency archives detailing the Imperial Japanese Army's involvement in the sexual enslavement and supervision of these women. These records clearly show the army's involvement in the establishment, management, and supervision of brothels, and the issuance of identity cards to the women involved. In short, these records make perfectly plain the Japanese government's direct participation in these schemes.

In August 1993, then Chief Cabinet Secretary Yohei Kono commented on the results of these records in the following terms: "the government of Japan would like to take this opportunity once again to extend its sincere apologies and remorse to all those, irrespective of place of origin, who suffered immeasurable pain and incurable physical and psychological wounds as 'comfort women'." In August 1994, anticipating the 50th anniversary of the end of the war, then Prime Minister Tomiichi Murayama declared: "On the issue of the treatment of the many 'comfort women,' and the damage done to their honor and dignity, I would like to take this opportunity once again to express my profound and sincere remorse and apologies."

Prime Minister Murayama expressed his highest remorse and apologies to those people who were injured under Japanese colonial domination and imperial Japan's war of aggression. His comments were widely reported in the international press, and many observers anticipated a settlement of the 'comfort women' issue on the 50th anniversary of the ending of the war. These expectations, however, ran headlong into the government's determination not to take on any additional commitments to compensate the victims of war. Instead, the government sought to organize private Japanese contributions and on several occasions requested me to endorse those efforts. In each case, I declined. I thought then and continue to believe that given the clear responsibility of the Japanese Imperial Army in the ill-treatment of these women, the Japanese government today bears a direct responsibility to pay compensation to the comfort women. I did not reach my decision without mixed feelings, however. By declining to endorse these government-encouraged private initiatives, I was simply delaying the day when these women, already well advanced in years, could enjoy the fruits of monetary compensation from Japan. In standing by principle, I was helping to delay delivery of justice to these women. As I worked on behalf of these women, seeking to reach those who today are indifferent to the suffering these women first endured over half a century ago, I wondered whether I might not be better able to help them by accepting the government's invitation to endorse one of the private fund raising initiatives. In this way, I thought, I might be able to influence their policies and secure Japanese government contributions to these women. Indeed, Prime Minister Murayama assured me that I would be free to continue to express my views on this issue and to try to influence government policies.

For these reasons, I agreed to play a role in raising funds for these women and endorsed the work of the Asian Women's fund. In traveling about and meeting a variety of people, I often was moved by the contributions made by Japanese people in a variety of walks of life. On the whole, however, I found that most people were rather indifferent about the efforts to raise funds for these women. My misgivings about these private efforts increased when Prime Minister Murayama of the Democratic Socialist Party resigned early this year, and was replaced by Liberal Democratic party leader Ryutaro Hashimoto. The new government showed no indications that it was prepared to catalyze support for the comfort women of Asia or other parts of the world. In short, the Asian Women Fund was not serving its stated purpose.

Let me repeat my conviction that given the Imperial Army's involvement in these outrages, the Japanese government should play a direct role in compensating these women. On August 14, 1996, the government released the text of "a letter expressing the country's remorse" to the victims and the damage done to "the honor and dignity of large numbers of women." These phrases appear twice in the letter. Hashimoto also expresses his "painful awareness" of Japan's "moral responsibility."

While this letter appears to express Japan's remorse with sincerity, it in fact employs carefully crafted language with the express intent of guarding against the acknowledgment of any financial responsibilities on the part of the Japanese government. What is really important about the letter is the implicit

12

message that the Japanese government refuses to accept any legal responsibility for the compensating the women victimized by the Japanese Imperial Army. The letter, in short, was written not out of sincere atonement for the undeniable tragedy of the historical facts, but rather with an eye on the probable treatment of lawsuits pending in Japan's legal system. The Prime Minister could speak of Japan's moral responsibility, but not the government's legal responsibility.

Why is the government behaving in this fashion? Officials fear that acceptance of responsibility for the compensation payments will simply encourage the lodging of further claims from other victims. These could include thousands of forced laborers and prisoners of war. The letter also skirts a variety of other issues. While it talks of the "honor and dignity of women," it does not address Japan's broader responsibilities for its colonial policies or its aggressiveness in launching war in the Pacific. Neither does the letter discuss the fates of the Chinese and Koreans who served in the Japanese army. Hashimoto's letter was in fact a step back from the earlier August 1993 letter by Kono. For example, while Kono's letter acknowledged that force was used in recruiting the comfort women, Hashimoto's letter ignores this point. Instead, this point is expressed in the letter by Hara, chair of the Asian Women's Fund. By using both letters, Hashimoto is able to minimize his expressions of the Japanese government's direct responsibility to these women. The government continues to proclaim that it has a practical scheme for compensating these women. At the same time, however, Hashimoto's letter avoids recognizing any direct responsibility on the part of the Japanese government.

Indeed, the general tone of Hashimoto's letter is not acceptable. There are two roughly synonymous Japanese words for "apology," *owabi* and *shazai*. This government avoided the latter, stronger term as it feared its use would weaken the government's legal position in a lawsuit filed by former comfort women. This general pattern of behavior on the part of the Japanese government is not acceptable. We cannot build constructive and friendly relations by repeating self-righteous slogans, criticisms and apologies, and a continuous cycle of arrogance-inducing distrust leading to misunderstandings. It is time for Japan's relations with her neighbors to move beyond this depressing pattern. A first step in breaking the cycle is the clear and unambiguous recognition of historical facts.

Constructive international relations and successful diplomacy rest on curbing hate and building on affinities between different peoples. The Japanese government should work to curb long festering hatreds and distrust, and try to promote cooperation and trust. Such steps, I believe, would be helped immeasurably through the forthright recognition of Japan's historical crimes and the payment of compensation to the victims of those crimes. Some Japanese people would rather hide from the issue of comfort women, feeling it brings disgrace upon the Japanese state. Those of us who want to address this issue forthrightly and put it behind us, however, are not content with simply hiding from this issue. It is precisely in order to rehabilitate the reputation of the Japanese state that we advocate direct payments of compensation to the victims of past policies of the state. It is natural for the Japanese people, as with those of other Asian nations, to have both a sense of national responsibility as well as one of pride. Peoples of all Asian nations can nurture their respective national prides while fostering cooperative international relationships. It is our duty and our hope that we can build such relations among the states and peoples of East Asia.

In closing, let me thank you very sincerely for inviting me to speak at this conference. And allow me to express my heartfelt wishes for a stimulating and instructive conference leading to fruitful results.

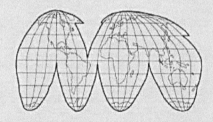

## A.5-2. "UNDERLYING SPIRIT" PHOTO EXHIBITION AND FORUM AT FREE MUSEUM OF PHILADELPHIA PROGRAM BROCHURE, THE FREE LIBRARY OF PHILADELPHIA: MARCH 19, 1999–MAY 31, 1999

# A.7-1. CATALOG OF WORKS CREATED BY FORMER "COMFORT WOMEN" RESIDING IN HOUSE OF SHARING

## List of painting

| NUMBER | NAME | TITLE | SIZE(cm) | MEDIUM | YEAR |
|---|---|---|---|---|---|
| 1-1. | Soon-Duk Kim | A Country House (Poongsangun DukchunMyun) | 53 × 38.8 | Acrylic on Paper | 1995 |
| 1-2. | Bok-Dong Kim | Country House | 39 × 53 | Wood-print | 1998 |
| 1-3. | Soon-Duk Kim | Bellflowers | 39 × 53 | Acrylic on Páper | 1994 |
| 1-4. | Duk-Kyung Kang | Hometown-Chinju Nam River | 52 × 37 | Acrylic on Paper | 1994 |
| 1-5. | Soon-Duk Kim | Bamboo Trees near Chinju Nam River | 53 × 39 | Acrylic on Paper | 1995 |
| 1-6. | Soon-Duk Kim | Our Old Home | 53 × 39 | Acrylic on Paper | 1993 |
| 1-7. | Bok-Dong Kim | Our Home in Yangsan 1 | 34 × 24 | Pencil on Paper | 1997 |
| 1-8. | Bok-Dong Kim | Childhood Memory (Design for Woodcut Print) | 43 × 32 | Pencil on Paper | 1998 |
| 1-9 | Soon-Duk Kim | Colonial Mushroom Taxation | 39 × 53 | Acrylic on Paper | 1995 |
| 1-10. | Bok-Dong Kim | Long Ago | 43 × 32 | Color Pencil on Paper | 1998 |
| 1-11. | Duk-Kyung Kang | Milieu of Snow Falling | 53 × 39 | Acrylic on Paper | 1994 |
| 1-12. | Soon-Duk Kim | Weaving Hemp Cloth | 53 × 36 | Acrylic on Canvas | 1998 |
| 1-13. | Soon-Duk Kim | Two Dogs in the Field- | 39 × 53 | Acrylic on Paper | 1993 |
| 1-14. | Soon-Duk Kim | Ox | 53 × 46 | Acrylic on Canvas | 1996 |
| 1-15. | Soon-Duk Kim | Colonial Seed Taxation | 140 × 93 | Acrylic on Canvas | 1995 |
| 1-16. | Soon-Duk Kim | Fear (Hiding in Older Sister's House) | 38.8 × 53 | Acrylic on Paper | 1995 |
| 2-1. | Bok-Dong Kim | The Day a 14 Year Old Girl is Stolen Away | 42 × 32 | Acrylic on Canvas | 1998 |
| 2-2. | Yong-Nyeo Lee | Chosun Maidens Stolen Away | 53 × 38.3 | Acrylic on Paper | 1995 |
| 2-3. | Soon-Duk Kim | Stolen Away | 154 × 114.5 | Acrylic on Canvas | 1995 |
| 2-4. | Soon-Duk Kim | Stolen Away in a Ship | 38.8 × 53 | Acrylic on Paper | 1995 |
| 2-5. | Soon-Duk Kim | In Shanghai | 39 × 53 | Acrylic on Paper | 1995 |
| 2-6. | Bok-Dong Kim | In Java | 34 × 24 | Color Pencil on Paper | 1997 |
| 2-7. | Bok-Dong Kim | Comfort Station in Singapore | 34 × 24 | Pencil on Paper | 1997 |
| 2-8. | Bok-Dong Kim | Old life as a Comfort Woman | 34 × 24 | Pencil on Paper | 1997 |
| 2-9. | Bok-Dong Kim | In Sumatra | 34 × 24 | Pencil on Paper | 1997 |
| 2-10. | Soon-Duk Kim | In that Place at that Moment in Time 2 | 39 × 53 | Acrylic on Paper | 1995 |
| 2-11. | Duk-Kyung Kang | Comfort Station in Matsushiro | 46 × 53 | Acrylic on Canvas | 1996 |
| 2-12. | Duk-Kyung Kang | Comfort Station in Labaul | 63 × 47 | Acrylic on Paper | 1995 |
| 2-13. | Soon-Duk Kim | Wretch Balsaml You Will Bloom Again When the Time Comes | 53 × 41 | Acrylic on Canvas | 1997 |
| 2-14. | Choon-Hee Bae | In China | 73 × 66 | Acrylic on Canvas | 1998 |
| 2-15. | Yong-Nyeo Lee | Girls Bathing | 38.8 × 53 | Acrylic on Paper | 1995 |
| 2-16. | Yong-Soo Lee | My Heart Like the Stars | 39 × 53 | Acrylic on Paper | 1993 |
| 2-17. | Choon-Hee Bae | Homesickness | 41 × 32 | Acrylic on Canvas | 1998 |
| 2-18. | Bok-Dong Kim | Remembering the Past | 43 × 32 | Color Pencil on Paper | 1998 |
| 2-19. | Bok-Dong Kim | Our Country-Yearning for Mother | 43 × 32 | Color Pencil on Paper | 1998 |
| 2-20. | Soon-Duk Kim | Liberation | 53 × 38.8 | Acrylic on Paper | 1994 |
| 3-1. | Duk-Kyung Kang | Innocence Stolen | 87 × 130 | Acrylic on Canvas | 1995 |
| 3-2. | Duk-Kyung Kang | Japanese Soldier Picking Pears | 80 × 131 | Acrylic on Canvas | 1995 |
| 3-3. | Yong-Soo Lee | My Lips Red as the Rainbow | 39 × 53 | Acrylic on Paper | 1993 |
| 3-4. | Duk-Kyung Kang | Untitled | 45 × 53 | Acrylic on Paper | 1996 |
| 3-5. | Bok-Dong Kim | A Glass of Wine Full of Emptiness | 34 × 24 | Color Pencil on Paper | 1997 |
| 3-6. | Bok-Dong Kim | As Youth Slips Away and Suddenly I am Old Grey | 34 × 24 | Color Pencil on Paper | 1998 |

| NUMBER | NAME | TITLE | SIZE(cm) | MEDIUM | YEAR |
|--------|------|-------|----------|--------|------|
| 3-7. | Duk-Kyung Kang | Bitterness of Comfort Women's Ghosts | 64×47 | Acrylic on Paper | 1995 |
| 3-8. | Yong-Soo Lee | Youth | 39×53 | Acrylic on Paper | 1993 |
| 3-9. | Duk-Kyung Kang | I Can't Take It Anymore | 39 x 63 | Acrylic on Paper | 1993 |
| 3-10. | Soon-Duk Kim | Unblossomed Flower | 29.8×58 | Acrylic on Embroidered Silk | 1995 |
| 3-11. | Yong-Nyeo Lee | Woman of Chosun | 39×53 | Color Pencil on Paper | 1995 |
| 3-12. | Soon-Duk Kim | Self-Portrait -Upside Down | 36×26 | Pencil on Paper | 1993 |
| 3-13. | Yong-Nyeo Lee | Self-portrait | 35.5×24.5 | Color Pencil on Paper | 1993 |
| 3-14. | Duk-Kyung Kang | Duk-Kyung (Composition) | 39×53 | Acrylic on Paper | 1994 |
| 3-15. | Duk-Kyung Kang | Complicated Life | 39×53 | Acrylic on Paper | 1993 |
| 3-16. | Yong-Soo Lee | Complicated Feeling | 39×53 | Acrylic on Paper | 1993 |
| 3-17. | Duk-Kyung Kang | Nightmare | 53×39 | Acrylic on Paper | 1995 |
| 3-18. | Duk-Kyung Kang | Yearning | 31.5×42 | Acrylic on Paper | 1995 |
| 3-19. | Duk-Kyung Kang | Because of Loneliness | 39×53 | Acrylic on Paper | 1994 |
| 3-20. | Soon-Duk Kim | Sincerity 1 | 39×53 | Acrylic on Paper | 1993 |
| 4-1. | Duk-Kyung Kang | Becoming a Bird | 53×39 | Acrylic on Paper | 1995 |
| 4-2. | Duk-Kyung Kang | Punish the Guilty!-For the Sake of Peace | 87×129 | Acrylic on Canvas | 1995 |
| 4-3. | Duk-Kyung Kang | Butterfly | 53×39 | Acrylic on Paper | 1995 |
| 4-4. | Duk-Kyung Kang | Apologize Before Us! | 48.5×37 | Acrylic on Paper | 1995 |
| 4-5. | Bok-Dong Kim | Japan Do Not Trespass-Dok Island Is Our Land | 60×50 | Acrylic on Canvas | 1998 |
| 4-6. | Duk-Kyung Kang | Apology | 53×39 | Acrylic on Paper | 1995 |
| 4-7. | Soon-Duk Kim | Meeting | 39×53 | Acrylic on Paper | 1995 |
| 4-8. | Soon-Duk Kim | Memorial Ceremony | 39×53 | Acrylic on Paper | 1994 |
| 4-9. | Bok-Dong Kim | The Leaves of that Gaunt Tree Will Blossom Someday | 34×24 | Color Pencil on Paper | 1998 |
| 4-10. | Duk-Kyung Kang | Floral Tribute for the Departed | 64×47 | Acrylic on Paper | 1995 |
| 4-11. | Duk-Kyung Kang | Sublimation of Han(Bitterness) | 53×39 | Acrylic on Paper | 1994 |
| 4-12. | Duk-Kyung Kang | Flock of Wild Geese in Deep Mountain | 39×53 | Acrylic on Paper | 1993 |
| 5-1. | Bok-Dong Kim | The Sun Sets Once Again Today | 43×32 | Watercolor on Paper | 1998 |
| 5-2. | Duk-Kyung Kang | Our Bad-tempered Teacher | 39×53 | Acrylic on Paper | 1993 |
| 5-3. | Soon-Duk Kim | April 8th (Buddha's Birthday) | 53×39 | Acrylic on Paper | 1994 |
| 5-4. | Bok-Dong Kim | Chicken Coop at the House of Sharing | 34×24 | Pencil on Paper | 1998 |
| 5-5. | Bok-Dong Kim | Pusan | 43×32 | Color Pencil on Paper | 1998 |
| 5-6. | Bok-Dong Kim | Woman Full of Han(Bitterness) Pray to Buddha! | 43×32 | Acrylic on Canvas | 1998 |
| 5-7. | Bok-Dong Kim | After Winter, Spring Will Come again | 43×32 | Color Pencil on Paper | 1998 |
| 5-8. | Bok-Dong Kim | A Buddhist Temple in Yangsan | 43×32 | Color Pencil on Paper | 1998 |
| 5-9. | Duk-Kyung Kang | Road Laminated by the Eye of Tiger | 64×47 | Acrylic on Paper | 1995 |
| 5-10. | Bok-Dong Kim | Old Diseased and Lonely Life | 43×32 | Color Pencil on Paper | 1998 |
| 5-11. | Yong-Nyeo Lee | A Place of Loneliness, Teochon (Current House of Sharing) | 39×53 | Acrylic on Paper | 1995 |
| 5-12. | Soon-Duk Kim | Road to the Temple (Spring Begins Good Fortune Awaits) | 39×53 | Acrylic on Paper | 1994 |
| 5-13. | Duk-Kyung Kang | Two People | 32×22 | Color Pencil on Paper | 1993 |

# A.7-2. FRONT PAGE AND "CURATORIAL INTENTION" FROM EXHIBITION BROCHURE "UNVEILING THE TRUTH: THE SORROW AND HOPE OF 'COMFORT WOMEN'" NOVEMBER 26–DECEMBER 14, 2012

*Unveiling the Truth:*
*The Sorrow and Hope of "Comfort Women"*

**Exhibition: November 26 – December 14, 2012**
Opening Reception: November 30, Friday, 6-8 pm
(7 pm Artist Talk and Film Screening)
**Mason Hall Artrium Gallery, George Mason University**
4400 University Drive, Fairfax, VA 22030
Gallery Hours: Monday to Friday, 9 am – 5 pm

*Presented by ArTrio & Washington Coalition for Comfort Women Issues*

**Sponsored by WCCW, ArTrio, Korean Studies Center, George Mason University Gallery,
and The Academy of Korean Studies, Korea** (한국학 중앙 연구원)

# Unveiling the Truth: The Sorrow and Hope of "Comfort Women"

The exhibition "Unveiling the Truth" brings together works created by distinguished Korean, Japanese, and American artists who have expressed their concerns with "comfort women" issues through their works. "Comfort women" is a euphemistic term used by the Japanese military to refer to women they imprisoned and forced into sexual slavery during World War II. This exhibition explores sexual violence, historical truths, the physical pain, and the mental trauma those women suffered. The artists interpret the women's experience in hopes of preventing future war crimes and to affirm basic human rights. The participating artists are Steve Cavallo, Dai Sil Kim-Gibson, Chang-Jin Lee, Sasha Yungju Lee, Yong Soon Min, Youngmi Song Organ, Yoshiko Shimada, In-Soon Shin, and Arin Yoon.

"Truth" is often defined as an unknowable yet indisputable reality that is ultimately revealed. "Comfort women" were often kidnapped and trafficked by the imperial military, then finally killed or abandoned when the war ended. They were humiliated, physically wounded, sexually assaulted, and repeatedly raped and tortured. Yet they remained silent for most of their lives, feeling ashamed to share their memories. Their stories rarely have been fully heard. Most of the artists featured in this exhibition learned these stories directly from surviving "comfort women" now gathered in the House of Sharing in Korea. Others have become activist speakers who educate others on the horrors of wartime sexual crimes. They have interacted with survivors as listeners, reporters, and companions. They are also artists who are able to express these women's genuine and sublime stories. Each artistic translation found here is both a remembrance of the scars of war and a therapeutic outlet through which the audience can connect to the experiences of the women or identify their own sexual traumas.

The issues surrounding former "comfort women" should not to be politicized. They involve human rights, women's rights, universal justice, and the acknowledgement of human suffering and past wrongdoings. As the exhibition sub-title proposes, today's handful of survivors dwell in unsettled sorrow yet cultivate hopes that reach out to other victims of war, particularly of sexual violence. Sasha Lee, Youngmi Organ, Yoshiko Shimada, and In-Soon Shin, visualize the vulnerable female body and dream in a literal or symbolic way. Arin Yoon shows how these women live today, in a documentary style, which encourages the viewer to look deeper and engage in stories within the portraits. Steve Cavallo and Yong Soon Min are actively engaged in the "comfort women" movement through their artistic projects and activism, which recently resulted in a memorial dedicated to the former "comfort women." Dai Sil Kim-Gibson and Chang-Jin Lee produced a documentary film and videos on "comfort women" with minimal interference, providing a media outlet to unveil hidden stories that need to be shared with the world.

I would like to express sincere thanks to Christine Choi, President of WCCW and its executive committee members; Professor Young-chan Ro, Director of Korean Studies Center; Professor Walter Kravitz, George Mason University Gallery Director; The Academy of Korean Studies, Korea; and ArTrio assistant curators, Moonjung Choi and Yookyoung Choi for their tireless efforts to make this exhibition possible.

Curator Jungsil Lee, Ph.D.

01

# A.7-3. "COLLATERAL DAMAGE: WARTIME ATROCITY AND TRAUMA" SYMPOSIUM BROCHURE OCTOBER 17, 2016

John Jay College of Criminal Justice, CUNY, New York (Cover Page and Curatorial Writing)

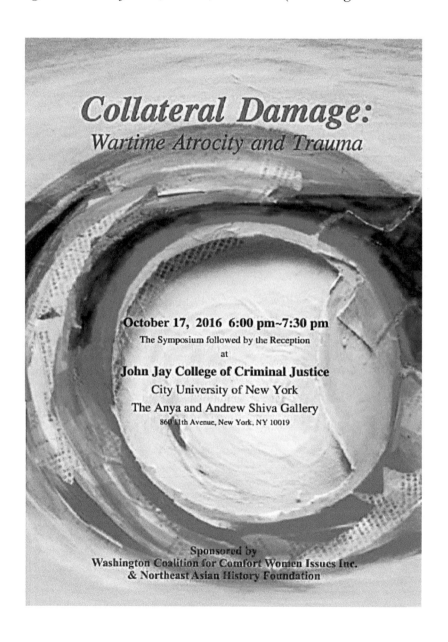

# Collateral Damage: *Wartime Atrocity and Trauma*

The Washington Coalition for Comfort Women Issues(WCCW) and John Jay College of Criminal Justice is co-organizing the symposium in conjunction with the exhibition *Collateral Damage* (Sep. 8th – Oct. 21st, 2016) at Anya and Andrew Shiva Gallery of John Jay College of Criminal Justice. This exhibition examines issues of rampant violence during WWII, the Vietnam War, the rise of the Khmer Rouge, and other conflicts where innocent non-combatants were affected. The exhibit especially focuses on "comfort women" who were abused during WWII by Japanese military. The symposium will discuss diverse approaches and interpretations of wartime atrocities as recurrent human rights violations, literary narratives of sexual violence, postcolonial discourses, and historical readings of geopolitics.

This panel presents how and why women and children, the more vulnerable, were sexually assaulted and violated in the course of war. The plight of women who suffered during times of conflict continued in the aftermath of war, not only because of the enormous psychological and emotional trauma, but also the social and cultural stigma attached to their horrendous experiences. On the panel, four speakers will share their expertise on human rights, sex crimes, human trafficking, wartime trauma and healing, and also its representation in literature and arts. The goal of symposium is to discuss of the importance of human rights issues and to find possible answers to commemorate and heal the trauma of wartime victims.

### Co-Moderator and Organizer: Dr. Jungsil Lee

Jungsil Lee is an art historian, curator, Professor at Washington University of Virginia, and the president of the Washington Coalition for Comfort Women Issues (WCCW) where she educates and promotes public awareness regarding wartime sex slaves during World War II, especially, "comfort women." She has organized numerous academic conferences and art exhibitions and played a central role in the building of the "Comfort Women Memorial Peace Garden" in Fairfax County, VA in 2014 to reclaim and rebuild the dignity of "comfort women". WCCW has developed a related educational program to let the world know the historical facts and speak about the comfort women's legacy. Her Ph.D. in Art History from University of Maryland is focused on the meaning of public memorial as a healing process. She has been devoted in fundraising, design, commissioning, and manufacturing of the memorial. She also has developed a webinar project in which students, scholars, and activists do research and archive historical material of comfort women.

### Co-Moderator: Dr. Thalia Vrachopoulos

Thalia Vrachopoulos holds a doctorate in the Philosophy of Art History from the City University of New York Graduate School. She has served as a curator for over one hundred national and international exhibitions accompanied by scholarly catalogues. Dr. Vrachopoulos is a full-time professor of the visual arts at John Jay College of Criminal Justice of the City University of New York. She has written scholarly essays and reviews for NYArts Magazine, Visual Culture AD, Part, +-0 , Public Art, Art in Culture, Art in Asia and Sculpture and has been included in many international panels. Dr. Vrachopoulos recently co-authored a book on Hilla Rebay, the founder of the Guggenheim Museum, which was  released in December 2005 by the Edwin Mellen Research Press. Dr. Vrachopoulos' contributions have been recorded and have become a permanent part of the Yale Library collection of Accomplished Women in the Arts. She is co-curator of Collateral Damage at John Jay College of Criminal Justice.

317

# A.7-4. WALTER RUNDLE "JAP 'COMFORT GIRLS'" C.B.I. ROUNDUP (NOVEMBER 30, 1944), 9

http://www.cbi-theater.com/roundup/roundup113044.html



## JAP 'COMFORT GIRLS'

By WALTER RUNDLE
United Press Correspondent

SALWEEN FRONT—(Delayed)—Chinese troops mopping up among the Japanese fortifications on the Salween Front, recently captured 10 Japanese and Korean women who had lived with the enemy troops throughout three months of shattering artillery bombardment and desperate close in fighting that fully reduced Sungshan Mountain.

The Japanese had shipped a supply of women to the forward fortresses at Sungshan and other large garrisons on the Salween Front. American liaison officers in action with the Chinese troops were inclined to doubt their own eyes when they first encountered this evidence of Japanese ruthlessness, at Tengchung where they found one Korean girl buried alive in a Japanese ammunition dump as a result of a nearby bomb burst.

With the help of a Japanese-speaking Chinese student who had escaped from Manchuria and now is serving with the Americans, the personal story of five of the pathetic women of Sungshan was obtained. Four of them were Korean peasant girls, 24 to 27 years old. They wore Western-type cotton dresses they said they'd purchased in Singapore.

### NOT WACs

They sat on low stools and eagerly puffed American cigarettes as they gradually relaxed from the shock of months of bomb and shell explosions. They said that early in the spring of 1942 Japanese political officers arrived in their home village, Pingyang, Korea. With propaganda posters and speeches the Japs began a recruitment campaign for "WAC" organizations which they said were to be sent to Singapore to do noncombatant work in rear areas—running rest camps for Japanese troops, entertaining and helping in hospitals. All four said they needed money desperately. One said her father, a farmer, had injured his knee and that for the $1,500 puppet currency (about $12 U.S.), given her when she enlisted, his doctor bills were paid.

A party of 18 such girls sailed from Korea in June, 1942. En-route, they said, they were told stories of Japanese victories and of a new empire being created in Southeast Asia. They said they first became worried when they were shipped direct through Singapore and that when they were placed on a train headed north from Rangoon they became certain of their fate.

[illegible]

When the party reached Sungshan, on the Salween front, the four were placed under the charge of a fifth woman—a 35-year-old regular Japanese prostitute who also was captured in the mopping up action.

There was a total of 24 girls at Sungshan. Among other duties, they had to wash Japanese soldiers clothing, cook their food and clean out the caves in which they lived. They said they were paid nothing and received no mail from home.

When Chinese troops attacked Sungshan, the girls lived below ground in caves. Fourteen of the original 24 were killed by shellfire. They said they all had been told they would be tortured if captured by the Chinese and all admitted they had believed such stories. They declined to give their correct names to protect their families but all said what they had lived through for the past two years had completely reversed their former naive trust of their Japanese overlords.

## SINATRALIA

BUFFALO—(UP)—It ain't safe even to look like Frank Sinatra!

During intermission period at a movie, 18-year-old Bernie Burns took a quick break for a drink of water. As he walked up the aisle, 8,000 squealing, squealing bobby-soxers swarmed upon him.

Drooled one sweet, young thing: "We thought he was was Frankie!"

## Educated Food; Cook And Baker School Opened

New vocational horizons have opened for ambitious young men in the India-Burma Theater with the establishment at Base Section No. 1, SOS, early this month of a Cooks and Bakers School, first in the theater.

Henceforth theater-wide kitchens will be plastered with smoke-smudged diplomas stating that Pvt. Spatula is qualified to open C-ration cans or whip up a little fricassee of water [illegible]. During the four-week [illegible] at the new culinary college, students of the skillet will spend their mornings in the classroom and afternoons on the range, learning about such dangers as soggy pie crust and sandy spinach.

In the final week, says our informant, "students will be assigned to the various [illegible] in Base Section No. 1 where they will prepare the meals and be given an opportunity to show their newly-learned cooking skill." Lucky lads in old Base No. 1 will thus head the list of guinea pigs for the theater's first educated slumburner... cooks with a conscience.

Brig. Gen. John A. Warden, CG of Base Section No. 1, welcomed the school's first students at the opening session. Maj. James K. [illegible] of the [illegible] is officer in charge, assisted by a staff of instructors which includes three lieutenants, a warrant officer and two enlisted men.

## Parent Expert Wrings Hands At Baby Leave

NEW YORK—(UP)—Dr. Kenneth Rose, director of the Planned Parenthood Federation, is all for bigger and better babies, but he doesn't believe that the British idea of giving overseas men furloughs for the purpose of producing progeny is foolproof.

Rose believes that if the war lasts another year, American wives will join their British sisters in asking that their better halves be given leave home so an addition may be made to the family.

But Rose says the idea is impractical both militarily and sociologically. Militarily because, as the British Government has told its anxious potential mothers, it is impossible to shift a "large body" of men in war time, and sociologically because "one can't expect to send G.I. Joe home and expect the wife to be pregnant just like that."

Rose declared it was known that a husband's battle experience "temporarily decreases the fertility of a married couple."

He admitted that the desire of British wives to have their husbands available to raise a family, was a natural outgrowth of the desire for parenthood, but said the only sane solution was a fast end to the war and speedy demobilization.

PS: Rose had no idea how to make a quick end of the war.

## RAF Secret Weapon Plague To U-Boats

WASHINGTON— (ANS) —For the past year, the RAF has effectively employed a lethal, secret weapon against U-boats—a Mosquito fighter plane equipped with a rapid-firing, six-pound gun slung beneath the fuselage, the British Information Services disclosed this week.

Firing shells that "look like red balls of fire," these "flying guns" have already disposed of at least one enemy sub, damaged several others and destroyed a JU-88 in flight at one-mile range.

It is said that use of the new weapon has forced the Nazis to adopt new convoy tactics in returning submarines to their home bases.

## PIN-POINT 'CHUTING

BY 10TH AIR FORCE SUPPLY WALLAHS

10TH AIR FORCE HQ, BURMA—You generally associate pin-point bombing with fighter and bomber planes.

But then you're not giving a fair shake to the gang who fly the 10th Air Force's Troop Carrier and Combat Cargo planes, who have a remarkable record for accuracy in supply dropping.

Battle lines in Burma have been so fluid at times that the pilots' instructions were out of date an hour after take-off. In many cases, they had to be briefed on new targets while in the air. But so fine has been their marksmanship, that seldom, if ever, have they 'chuted a package to the wrong team in the jungle warfare.

Less than two hours before the above picture was taken, the territory was in Jap hands. While the pilot was in the air, he was ordered to this point. Advance Allied patrols, left center, wait to pick up the packages.

## 'Mairzy Doats' DISCOVERED?

FRANCE — (ANS) — An American flight leader of a [illegible] squadron, on his way to attack a Nazi target recently in another of the fighter-bomber attacks which have wrought so much havoc with the enemy, received a radio message: "Return to base, Williams, headquarters has cancelled the mission."

"Okay," he replied suspiciously, "But first do me a favor, sing Mairzy Doats, will you?"

After a prolonged, embarrassed silence from the ground station, Williams called them: "Yeah, you Heinie so-and-so you don't know Mairzy Doats in Berlin, do you?" And the flight continued on its way.

## Hartford Accepts Blame For Tragedy

HARTFORD — (ANS) — This city, through municipal headquarters, "must bear some of the responsibility for the disastrous circus fire here last July," declared the Municipal Board of Inquiry in a report handed to Mayor William H. Mortensen.

The board, set up by the aldermen in July, said it found no city official or department [illegible] for major blame but that the city took few precautions to prevent such a disaster. The Big Top blaze took 168 lives.

## FRENCH ARREST P.G. WODEHOUSE

PARIS—(ANS)—British author and journalist P. G. Wodehouse has been arrested on charges of aiding the Germans by his five radio broadcasts during 1941, French police disclosed this week.

The 63-year-old humorist, the first British subject to be nabbed by the French roundup of alleged collaborationists, has been given a conditional release, forced to live three miles from Paris under police surveillance.

## HOSPITABLE LIEUTENANT'S GUESTS WERE 'WRONG UNS'

By ALBERT RAVENHOLT,
United Press Correspondent

SOUTHWEST CHINA—The remote southwestern corner of Yunnan province, where China borders on Burma and Indo-China, has long been noted for its intrigue, but Lt. William W. Guth, commanding a small American detachment in that area, was more than surprised when two well-dressed gentlemen were shot and dragged through the street past his headquarters less than an hour after they had been his honored guests.

Guth, his Chinese interpreter and three American enlisted men were sitting around in their bamboo bashas after dinner one evening listening to the radio when two men dressed in what these isolated areas, invited the strangers in to visit awhile. As Guth explains it, "They bowed politely and sat down. We talked about the weather and speculated on how soon the monsoon rains would be finished.

"My interpreter told me he judged by their Chinese accent that our visitors came originally from Peiping. I asked my visitors where they had served before, taking for granted from their uniforms that they were officers in one of the numerous guerrilla detachments in our area. They both said they had served for some time in Shanghai and later on in Nanking.

"When the American news came over the radio from Chungking at nine o'clock my interpreter gave the visitors a running translation. When the announcer [illegible] their heads in enthusiastic agreement, saying 'Mei kuo fei chi hen hao,' meaning in Chinese, 'American planes exceptionally good.'

"After the news broadcast we talked about various sections of America. Sgt. Paul J. Kinder explained his home was in Wapella, Ill., and Sgt. Russell J. Langlois explained he came from Long Island, N.Y., and therefore spoke English in a slightly different manner. Our visitors smoked some American cigarettes and I told them about my athletic career. They were particularly interested in swimming. After a little more pleasant chatting, the two visitors got up and excused themselves and said they were sorry to leave but they had an appointment to [illegible]

"They hadn't been gone more than 15 minutes when one of the local magistrate's guards rushed in and inquired if two strangers had visited us. We answered yes and added they had walked out towards the road, and the guard dashed out. About half an hour later we heard five shots. We grabbed our guns and took up our prearranged positions in case of trouble. Ten or 15 minutes later Chinese guards with torches and lots of commotion dragged two bodies up the street past our bashas. To our surprise, they were our two visitors.

"We examined their clothing and found their credentials as Japanese majors in their inside pockets. Chinese officials soon confirmed the identity of the visitors and said they probably had been members of special [illegible]

## Jackpot Fails, Court Pays Off

CHATTANOOGA— (UP) —A short, short story.

A man stepped up to a slot machine, inserted a coin and pulled the handle. He hit the jackpot. The machine refused to pay off. The man pitched it through a window.

He was hauled into court on a charge of malicious mischief. The [illegible]

# A.7-5. WCCW INTERNATIONAL FILM FESTIVAL "SEXUAL VIOLENCE IN WARFARE: THE FILMS OF UNHEALED WOUNDS" NOVEMBER 9-11, 2018, AMERICAN UNIVERSITY, BROCHURE COVER

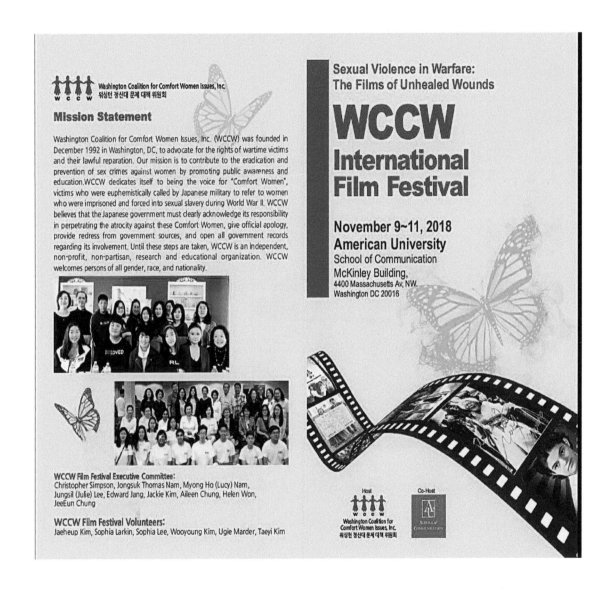

# A.10-1. MEGAN BURROW, "WESTWOOD ARTISTS WORK TO KEEP HISTORY ALIVE" PASCACK VALLEY COMMUNITY LIFE, OCTOBER 14, 2010

## ARTS & LEISURE
## COMMUNITY LIVING

**ART EXHIBIT**

# Westwood artists work to keep history alive

**BY MEGAN BURROW**
Of Community Life

Every Wednesday they gather outside the Japanese Embassy in Seoul, Korea to ask for acknowledgement, and an apology for the crimes committed against them more than half a century ago.

There are only about 80 of them still alive today, and many are too feeble to make the trip, but some still go every week – at over 900 weeks, it is the longest continuous protest in the world.

These women, were former "comfort women," a euphemism for the young women and girls taken from their homes either by force or coercion, many from Korea, and forced into sexual slavery by the Japanese military during World War II.

It is estimated that there were about 200,000 of these women during the war, most of whom did not survive, being repeatedly beaten and raped, and eventually killed. Most of the survivors were unable to have children as a result of their experience at these "comfort stations."

To this day, the government of Japan has not made an apology for these crimes.

Two Westwood artists, Steve Cavallo and Sei Ryun Chun, are hoping to bring light to this little known piece of history, through a plaque designed by Cavallo that will be on permanent display in front of the Palisades Park Library, and an exhibit, "Come From the Shadows," that will feature works inspired by the stories of these women.

PHOTOS COURTESY OF STEVE CAVALLO AND SEI RYUN CHUN

Westwood residents Steve Cavallo and Sei Ryun Chun are among a group of artists who will display their work as part of "Come From the Shadows," an exhibit at the Palisades Park Library designed to bring awareness to a little known piece of history, the suffering of "comfort women" — women and girls who were enslaved by the Japanese Imperial military during the 1930s through 1945.

Cavallo, the art director for the library, said he first became interested in the subject in 1991, when many of these women first stepped forward and told their stories.

Chun, a Korean native who moved to the United States about 30 years ago, said the women's storied touched her deeply. She hopes that through her art more people will become aware of the suffering of these women.

"It's a very, very sad history," she said. "But artistic expression brings it more close to the heart."

About a year and a half ago, Cavallo arranged for a film to be shown at the library about the comfort women called "Silence Broken." Afterwards many peo-ple, including James Rotundo, the mayor of Palisades Park, told Cavallo that this was the first time they had heard about the comfort women. The Korean American Voters Council said they would like place a memorial plaque at the Hackensack Courthouse in recognition of the crimes that took place against comfort women during World War II. When someone from Hackensack said there was no room for another memorial in front of the courthouse (there are already four on display) Rotundo lobbied to place one in front of the Palisades Park Library.

The memorial, the first of its kind in the United States, will be unveiled on the grounds of the library on Oct. 23. Cavallo, who

SEE ART, PAGE 47

# A.10-2. CONTRACT OF COMFORT WOMEN MEMORIAL PALISADES PARK AND WORDING, PROVIDED BY STEVE CAVALLO, AUGUST 20, 2010

# A.10-3. THE SENATE CONCURRENT RESOLUTION 124 IN THE STATE OF NEW JERSEY, UNDER THE SPONSORSHIP OF SENATOR LORETTA WEINBERG ON SEPTEMBER 2012

[First Reprint]
## SENATE CONCURRENT RESOLUTION No.
## 124
# STATE OF NEW JERSEY
## 215th LEGISLATURE

INTRODUCED SEPTEMBER 20, 2012

Sponsored by:
Senator  LORETTA WEINBERG
District 37 (Bergen)
Senator  KEVIN J. O'TOOLE
District 40 (Bergen, Essex, Morris and Passaic)

Co-Sponsored by:
Senators Allen and Gordon

SYNOPSIS
   Commemorates suffering endured by comfort women during forced internment in Japanese military camps.

CURRENT VERSION OF TEXT
   As reported by the Senate Health, Human Services and Senior Citizens Committee on June 3, 2013, with amendments.

A CONCURRENT RESOLUTION commemorating the suffering endured by comfort women during their forced internment in Japanese military camps.

WHEREAS, The term "comfort women" is a euphemism used by the Japanese government to describe women forced into sexual slavery by the [1]Imperial[1] Japanese [1][army] military[1] between 1932 and 1945; and

WHEREAS, The majority of [1]["comfort women"] comfort women[1] were of Korean or Chinese descent but women from Thailand, Vietnam, Indonesia, Malaysia, the Philippines, Australia, and the Netherlands were also interned in military comfort stations run directly by the [1]Imperial[1] Japanese [1][army] military[1] or by private agents working for the [1][army] military[1]; and

WHEREAS, Some of the women were sold to the comfort stations as minors, others were deceptively recruited by middlemen with the promise of employment and financial security, and still others were forcibly kidnapped and sent to "work" for soldiers stationed throughout the Japanese occupied territories; and

**WHEREAS,** Lack of official documentation, most destroyed on the orders of the Japanese government after World War II, has made it difficult to estimate the total number of comfort women; most historians and media sources approximate that about 200,000 young women were recruited or kidnapped by soldiers to serve in Japanese military brothels; and

**WHEREAS,** Approximately three-quarters of the comfort women have died as a direct result of the brutality inflicted on them during their internment. Those who survived were left infertile due to sexual violence or sexually transmitted diseases and many are now dying without proper acknowledgment by the Japanese government of the suffering they endured during their forced internment in military comfort stations; and

**WHEREAS,** It is fitting for this House to commemorate the fifth anniversary of the passage by the United States House of Representatives of [1][H.R.121] H.Res.121 (110th)[1] that called upon the Japanese government to accept historical responsibility for the sexual enslavement of comfort women by the [1]Imperial[1] Japanese [1][army] military[1] and educate future generations about these crimes; now, therefore,

**BE IT RESOLVED** *by the Senate of the State of New Jersey (the General Assembly concurring):*

1. The General Assembly commemorates and supports comfort women in their fight for proper acknowledgement by the Japanese government of the suffering they endured during their forced internment in military comfort stations and calls upon the Japanese government to accept historical responsibility for the sexual enslavement of comfort women by the [1]Imperial[1] Japanese [1][army] military[1] and educate future generations about these crimes.

2. Duly authenticated copies of this resolution, signed by the Speaker of the General Assembly and attested by the Clerk of the General Assembly and signed by the President of the Senate and attested by the Secretary of the Senate, shall be transmitted to the Embassy of the Republic of Korea in the United States[1][,] and[1] the Mayor and Council President of Palisades Park, New Jersey[1][, and the Korean American Voters' Council][1].

# A.10-4. NEW YORK STATE SENATE RESOLUTION J 304 ON JANUARY 2013

LEGISLATIVE RESOLUTION memorializing a Memorial Monument in the State of New York that pays tribute to those who have become known to the world as 'Comfort Women'

WHEREAS, During the Japanese colonial and wartime occupation of Asia and the Pacific Islands from the 1930s through the duration of World War II, approximately 200,000 young women were coerced into the Comfort Women system of forced military prostitution; and

WHEREAS, On June 16, 2012, the Comfort Women Memorial Monument was established in the Veterans Memorial at Eisenhower Park in Westbury, New York, to honor and commemorate the victims of the Comfort Women system; and

WHEREAS, The Memorial Monument, being the second memorial of its kind in the United States, symbolizes suffering endured by comfort women and serves as a reminder of the crime against humanity committed through the Comfort Women system; and

WHEREAS, It is the custom of this Legislative Body to recognize historical monuments within the State of New York that are established to increase awareness of serious events that have taken place in history; and

WHEREAS, The United Nations reports that 2.4 million people across the globe are victims of human trafficking at any one time, and 80 percent of them are being exploited as sexual slaves; now, therefore, be it

RESOLVED, That this Legislative Body pause in its deliberations to memorialize a Memorial Monument in the State of New York that pays tribute to those who have become known to the world as 'Comfort Women'; and be it further

RESOLVED, That copies of this Resolution, suitably engrossed, be transmitted to the Korean American Public Affairs Committee, the Kupferberg Holocaust Resource Center and Korean American Civic Empowerment.

# A.10-5. NEW JERSEY STATE ASSEMBLY CONCURRENT RESOLUTION 159, SEPTEMBER 2012

[First Reprint]

## ASSEMBLY CONCURRENT RESOLUTION
## No. 159

# STATE OF NEW JERSEY
## 215th LEGISLATURE

INTRODUCED SEPTEMBER 24, 2012

**Sponsored by:**
Assemblyman  GORDON M. JOHNSON
District 37 (Bergen)
Assemblywoman  CONNIE WAGNER
District 38 (Bergen and Passaic)

**Co-Sponsored by:**
Assemblywomen Mosquera, Vainieri Huttle, Assemblyman Chivukula, Senators Weinberg, O'Toole, Allen, Gordon, Addiego, Beck and Gill

**SYNOPSIS**
Commemorates suffering endured by comfort women during forced internment in Japanese military camps.

**CURRENT VERSION OF TEXT**
As reported by the Assembly Women and Children Committee on January 17, 2013, with amendments.

A CONCURRENT RESOLUTION commemorating the suffering endured by comfort women during their forced internment in Japanese military camps.

WHEREAS, The term "comfort women" is a euphemism used by the Japanese government to describe women forced into sexual slavery by the [1]Imperial[1] Japanese [1][army] military[1] between 1932 and 1945; and

WHEREAS, The majority of [1]["comfort women"] comfort women[1] were of Korean or Chinese descent but women from Thailand, Vietnam, Indonesia, Malaysia, the Philippines, Australia, and the Netherlands were also interned in military comfort stations run directly by the [1]Imperial[1] Japanese [1][army] military[1] or by private agents working for the [1][army] military[1]; and

WHEREAS, Some of the women were sold to the comfort stations as minors, others were deceptively recruited by middlemen with the promise of employment and financial security, and still others were forcibly

# A.10-6-1. MEETING FOR THE RESOLUTION OF THE CITY OF BROOKHAVEN ON MAY 3, 2017

**City of Brookhaven
Georgia**

**Resolution
RES-2017-05-03**

Approved
May 23, 2017 7:00 PM

**Consideration and Approval for Resolution to Approve Acceptance of Donation
for Art Work**

## Information

| | | |
|---|---|---|
| **Department:** | City Council | **Sponsors:** |
| **Category:** | Resolution | |

## Attachments

Printout
Resolution Human Trafficking (This file has not yet been converted to a viewable format)
RES2017-05-03ResolutionArtDonation (This file has not yet been converted to a viewable format)

## Meeting History

| | | |
|---|---|---|
| **May 23, 2017 7:00 PM** Video | **City Council** | **Regular Meeting** |

Mr. Sigman expressed this was an exciting time for the City of Brookhaven. The City had not accepted art work before. In many cases, a City was defined by its art work. The Resolution was an administrative matter, but overlaid with much bigger policy and social implementation for the community. The resolution was not only for accepting the gift but also a reflection of the culture and values of City and Council. He recommended approval.

Mayor spoke about Council Member John Park of District 2 had already planned a trip for that evening. He had texted multiple times that day to make sure all was o.k. He was supportive of this. He knew how he would vote. Mayor Ernst explained how this acceptance was important. He noted how he was a history major, and had studied history all of the time, and knowing history to lead the future. The history of comfort women started education process for sexual trafficking today. He asked Council to support acceptance of the art.

Council Member Jones made motion to accept the Resolution to approve the donation of art work. Council Member Gebbia seconded the motion.

Council Member Jones expressed how her breath had been taken away concerning the issue. She was grateful and humbled to have the privilege of having our government to recognize the suffering of the Korean Comfort Women, their loved ones, Korean people. She would cast her vote in honor of the 38 surviving Comfort Women and in loving honor of her beautiful Korean American nieces, Hannah Ho and Lillie Ho. She continued to express how she was grateful for Comfort Women Memorial Task Force. She looked forward to seeing this memorial in place and look forward to enjoying and sharing and honoring the story.

Council Member Mattison asked staff to provide information about the memorial art work. Mr. Sigman stated there would be a photo later that evening and the art work was attractive. It would be located in a City park. They were working with the Comfort Women organization about the landscape to accompany the art. It was not only art work that was historic, but also an opportunity to bring awareness to human trafficking issue of the Country today.

Council Member Mattison expressed he felt honored to have Brookhaven accept the art work. He explained how he hoped it would be a step to bring harmony, step of recognizing history had done horrible things in past, but hoped to be aware, discuss, and learn from history. It was not about any nationality. He was glad the Task Force had chosen Brookhaven and looked forward to the art work being located in Brookhaven.

Council Member Gebbia expressed he was honored that the Atlanta Comfort Women Task Force had considered Brookhaven. He spoke about how Brookhaven had a history of taking a stand on the sex trafficking issue. This was not country bashing this was making an expressive statement about events that happened in the past. He gave an example of incident that occurred in Germany in the past. The Comfort Women art work was making a statement. He spoke about having to be cognizant of the past, learning from history, and keeping reminders of past issues front and center in the present. He spoke about what was the right thing to do. This was a project to get behind. He expressed how they would like for the art work to be placed at the Peachtree Creek Greenway when it was completed. He thanked the Task Force for bringing the art work to Brookhaven.

# A.10-6-2. RESOLUTION OF THE CITY OF BROOKHAVEN, MAY 3, 2017

STATE OF GEORGIA
DEKALB COUNTY
CITY OF BROOKHAVEN

RES 2017-05-03

## A RESOLUTION OF THE CITY OF BROOKHAVEN TO ACCEPT DONATION OF ART WORK

**WHEREAS,** section 1.03 of the Charter of the City of Brookhaven authorizes the City Council to regulate the general health, safety and welfare, planning and zoning, public hazards, etc.; and

**WHEREAS,** section 2.11 of the Charter of the City of Brookhaven confers authority and power to the City Council to do such as it deems necessary or helpful to the peace, good order, protection of life and property, comfort, prosperity or well-being of the inhabitants of the City, and;

**WHEREAS,** since its inception in December 2012, the City of Brookhaven has remained committed to fighting the heinous crimes of human trafficking in all its forms and educating the public on the City's continuing efforts and overtures; and

**WHEREAS,** in 2014, the City of Brookhaven became first city in Georgia to be train its top managers and all city employees on how to recognize signs of child sex trafficking; and

**WHEREAS,** Comfort Women were women and girls forced into sexual slavery from Korea, China, the Philippines and other occupied countries or territories of the Pacific Theater during World War II, ultimately numbering hundreds of thousands by the end of the War; and

**WHEREAS,** the City of Brookhaven recognizes the danger and injustice of human trafficking in all of its forms, the historic plight of human trafficking victims like the Comfort Women of WWII, and the importance of the city to preserve history while educating and informing its citizens.

**NOW, THEREFORE BE IT RESOLVED** that the City of Brookhaven remains united in its commitment to eradicate human trafficking.

**BE IT FURTHER RESOLVED** that the City of Brookhaven officially recognizes the Comfort Women of WWII as one of the largest human trafficking events in history, dedicates a public space for the purposes of a memorial for Comfort Women to serve as a historic and educational reminder of the tragedy of human trafficking worldwide, accepts the donation of art work for public display, and makes all administrative arrangements for its installation in an appropriate location.

**PASSED AND ADOPTED** by the City Council of the City of Brookhaven, Georgia this 23rd day of May, 2017.

APPROVED:

John Arthur Ernst, Jr., Mayor

APPROVED AS TO FORM:

Christopher D. Balch
City Attorney

ATTEST:

Susan D. Hiott, City Clerk

# A.10-7. RESOLUTION 158-25A1, ADOPTED BY THE SAN FRANCISCO BOARD OF EDUCATION, OCTOBER 13, 2015

*Adopted by the Board of Education, as amended, at its Regular Meeting of October 13, 2015*

Subject: Resolution No. 158-25A1
### In Support of Countering Human Trafficking and Commercial Sexual Exploitation of Children
- Commissioner Emily M. Murase, Ph.D. and Student Delegates Teresia Chen and Miguel Tantiado

**WHEREAS:** According to both the federal Trafficking Victims Protection Act of 2000 (reauthorized in 2013) and the 2012 Californians Against Slavery and Exploitation Act, all commercial sex involving a minor is defined as human trafficking; and

**WHEREAS:** The Federal Bureau of Investigation has identified San Francisco as 1 of 13 "High Intensity Child Exploitation Areas" in the country; and

**WHEREAS:** The National Center for Missing and Exploited Children testified before Congress that the average age of commercially sexually exploited children (CSEC) survivors is 11 to 13 for boys and 12 to 14 for girls, many of whom are recruited from middle and high schools; particularly vulnerable students are homeless, LGBTQ, unaccompanied minors, undocumented, in the foster youth system, and/or possess special education needs, and

**WHEREAS:** In 2014, President Barack Obama signed into law the Preventing Sex Trafficking and Strengthening Families Act that calls for states to adopt an interagency protocol to address commercial sex involving minors, emphasizing consultation and collaboration with schools and educational agencies as part of the formation of the protocol; and

**WHEREAS:** The same year, the California Welfare and Institutions Code Section 300 was amended to recognize child sex trafficking as a form of child abuse and that, therefore, sexually trafficked children fell within the jurisdiction of the child welfare system; the California Department of Social Services' program for Commercially Sexually Exploited Children (CSEC) was established to provide funding to participating counties for training, prevention, and implementation of a CSEC protocol; and

**WHEREAS:** The City and County of San Francisco opted into the California Department of Social Service's CSEC Program and the Human Services Agency Family and Children's Services Division began to develop the city's interagency protocol for responding to sexually trafficked youth that is expected to be completed by October 2015; and

**WHEREAS:** In January 2015, the US Department of Education issued the *Human Trafficking in America's Schools Report,* which calls on school districts to 1) train staff to understand and identify human trafficking; 2) increase awareness about the issue among parents and students; and 3) develop a clear and comprehensive policy on responding to trafficking and CSEC; and

**WHEREAS:** Trafficked youth often do not recognize that they are human trafficking victims due a lack of understanding or denial of exploitation; and studies have indicated that 68% of CSEC survivors suffer from Post-Traumatic Stress Disorder with a documented increased risk of suicide and depression; and

Resolution No. 158-25A1
In Support of Countering Human Trafficking and Commercial Sexual Exploitation of Children -
Commissioner Emily M. Murase, Ph.D. and Student Delegates Teresia Chen and Miguel Tantiado
Page 2

**WHEREAS:** The US Department of Education reports that trauma from sexual exploitation impacts learning environment for CSEC survivors, often manifesting as behavioral problems due to low self-esteem, aggression, and truancy; and

**WHEREAS:** CSEC survivors often reject law enforcement and social services and require support and assistance from adults they trust, such as school administrators, teachers, counselors, social workers, nurses, other wellness and support staff who should therefore be trained in how to respond in a trauma-informed manner; and

**WHEREAS:** The California CSEC Model Interagency Protocol Framework urges educational agencies in each county to develop a mechanism for tracking CSEC as well as responding to exploited youth's educational needs, such as enrollment, truancy, and credit completion; and schools should have a clear procedure for coordinating CSEC response with other public agencies, such as the Police Department, District Attorney's Office, and Child Welfare Services; and

**WHEREAS:** In 2004, the Board of Education previously passed Resolution No. 45-25A16 to request that training be made available to school district staff on harassment, assault, abuse identification, and mandatory reporting; and

**WHEREAS:** The San Francisco Unified School District has already initiated training to staff at each of the high school Wellness Centers and student support staff pre-K – 8 on signs of and resources to address child sex trafficking and is a standing member of the Mayor's Task Force on Anti-Human Trafficking as well as the Human Services Agency Interagency CSEC Program Steering Committee; and

**WHEREAS:** Building on existing SFUSD initiatives to counter teen dating violence and bullying, students can play an important role in helping to identify CSEC among their peers; already, the SFUSD Student Advisory Council, composed of representatives from each of the high schools; Peer Resources; and the Wellness Center Youth Outreach Workers have demonstrated their effectiveness in reaching various groups of students.

**THEREFORE BE IT RESOLVED:** That the Board of Education of the San Francisco Unified School District requests that the Superintendent and district staff work with community partners to add language to the existing Child Abuse Reporting Board Policy to address human trafficking and commercial sexual exploitation of children and enforce a mandatory reporting protocol; and

**FURTHER BE IT RESOLVED:** That the Superintendent and district staff, in consultation with community experts, develop and adopt a comprehensive training for all school administrators, teachers, counselors, social workers, nurses, and other wellness and support staff regarding the identification and mandatory reporting of human trafficking; and

Resolution No. 158-25A1
In Support of Countering Human Trafficking and Commercial Sexual Exploitation of Children -
Commissioner Emily M. Murase, Ph.D. and Student Delegates Teresia Chen and Miguel Tantiado
Page 3

**BE IT FURTHER RESOLVED:** That the Superintendent and district staff, in consultation with community experts, develop and adopt an age appropriate unit to address healthy relationships and signs of human trafficking for inclusion in existing health curriculum; and

**FURTHER BE IT RESOLVED:** That the Superintendent and district staff create a task force with community experts to work in consultation to incorporate an educational component of the history of "Comfort Women" of WWII under the Japanese military in its curriculum to educate the community about the harmful effects of sex trafficking in its historical and modern day context for the purpose of preventing and protecting the youth community from sexual exploitation and trafficking; and.

**BE IT FURTHER RESOLVED:** That the Superintendent and district staff engage student leaders to communicate the signs of and resources for human trafficking among their peers.

Please Note:

> Referred by order of the Chair on 8/25/15 to the Curriculum and Program Committee.

> Taken up by the Curriculum and Program Committee on 10/5/15. Forwarded to the Board with a positive recommendation, as amended and with further amendments to be added by Dr. Murase, by general consent of the Committee.

> Adopted, as amended, 10/13/2015.

**8/25/15**

**10/13/15**

# A.10-8. "REMEMBERING AND HONORING MEMORIALS" BY FAYE KWAN, TEACHERS' RESOURCE GUIDE 2ND EDITION, EDUCATION FOR SOCIAL JUSTICE FOUNDATION (ESJF), FEBRUARY 2019, P.109

## Remembering And Honoring: Memorials
FAYE KWAN

**Purpose:** Students will determine critical elements of a memorial to determine its purpose and effectiveness.

**Objective:** Students will analyze a 'Comfort Woman' memorial, read multiple articles, and have a discussion.
CA H-SS Framework Standard: 10.11 Economic Integration and Contemporary Revolutions in Information, Technology, and Communications - Has the world become more peaceful? Is the nature of conflict changing? How do ideas about universal human rights relate to other value and identity systems in the contemporary world?
11.11 Contemporary American Society - How did the Cold War end and what foreign policy developments came out of it? In what ways have issues such as education; civil rights for people of color, immigrants, and lesbian, gay, bisexual, and transgender Americans, and disabled Americans; economic policy; the environment; and the status of women remained unchanged over time? In what ways have they changed?

**Suggested Time:** 1-2 class days

**Procedure:**

- Project images of 'comfort woman' statue -Sullivan, Justin. Allow students time to observe and respond to initial observation questions.

- Reading activity suggestions: Jigsaw, paired reading, Close reading, Close Collaboration. 3 articles of different length and difficulty are listed in materials.

- Students respond to questions.

- Class discussion.

**Materials:**

- Overhead projector

- Sullivan, Justin. "'Comfort Women' Statue In San Francisco Draws Ire From SF's Sister City in Japan." Zimbio, Getty Images North America, 31 Oct. 2017, www.zimbio.com/pictures/xXlE7ww5hXA/Comfort+Women+Statue+San+Francisco+Draws+Ire/5R928lE8_v0.

- "San Francisco Accepts 'Comfort Women' Statue." BBC News, BBC, 23 Nov. 2017, www.bbc.com/news/world-asia-42092477. (mild)

- Fortin, Jacey. "'Comfort Women' Statue in San Francisco Leads a Japanese City to Cut Ties."The New York Times, The New York Times, 25 Nov. 2017, www.nytimes.com/2017/11/25/world/asia/comfort-women-statue.html. (medium)

- McGrane, Sally. "An Important Statue for 'Comfort Women' in San Francisco." The New Yorker, The New Yorker, 12 Oct. 2017, www.newyorker.com/culture/culture-desk/an-important-statue-for-comfort-women-in-san-francisco. (spicy)

**Worksheet**

- Chronology: Formation of the 'Comfort Women' Justice Coalition, Eric Mar (optional)

# A.10-9-1. FORT LEE "COMFORT WOMEN" MEMORIAL DESIGN, 2018

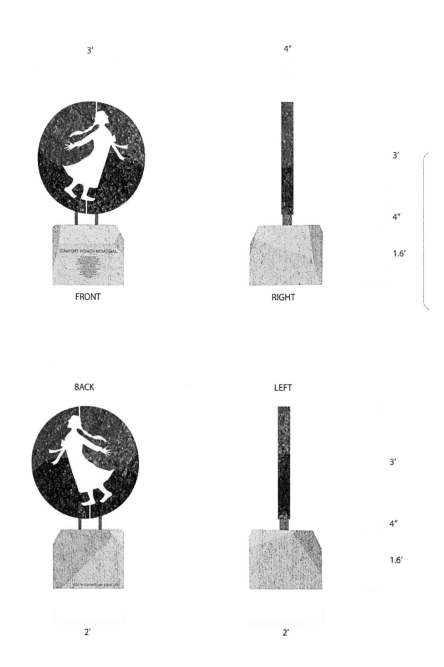

332

# A.10-9-2. FORT LEE MEMORIAL ARTIST STATEMENT, 2018

Fort Lee Comfort Women Memorial Design - Artist Statement
Euwan Kim

There is only one history. The past can't be anything other than what it was, yet it's presented in more than one way. History can be perversely molded, distorted, or even forgotten. When we ignore a part of history, we're ignoring people, people who were traumatized and then forgotten amongst years of oppression. The purpose of this comfort women memorial is to remind us of how history is a single entity, how we cannot simply ignore the scars in our society. We must heal them. That is what I wanted to do.

My inspiration, Kara Walker, is an African American artist who uses human silhouettes to illustrate our nation's violent history of racism. In her theater, paper silhouettes brutally attack, rape, whip, and murder each other, but the most disturbing effect lies in the contrast of colors; the silhouettes are black, but the background is white, referencing the racism embedded in the United States.

I was inspired by Kara Walker's contrast of colors, the sadness and injustice represented in the black against the pure white. In the memorial, I incorporated the same contrast but to send a different message. The comfort woman figure is cut into the stone to create a negative space in the circle. The gap in the stone is the gap in history that we're finally acknowledging. History with gaps creates a divided society, and conflict is inevitable when people feel empty. Comfort women had their own identities ripped away; their existence was denied and pushed out of history textbooks just so that society can feel a little happier for a little bit of time. If we don't recognize the comfort woman figure in this memorial, the stone has the outward appearance of a perfect circle but a deformed hole inside. When we fill in the gap, when we fill in our society with the history we have forgotten, only then can we create a unified circle, a unified society. The yin-yang symbol of the South Korean flag is the backdrop for this unified society; when the circle is complete, the comfort women are no longer victims. They are heroines... in Korea and in our Fort Lee community. I won't say that this memorial does complete justice for the crimes of the past. Kara Walker wasn't trying to dissolve the entire institution of racism. But the Comfort Women memorial is Fort Lee's time capsule. It brings back a piece of the past we lost and mends the fabric of our history. This isn't an end nor a start. It is a bridge that leads us to a more comprehensive community.

# A.10-10. SYMBOLIC MEANING OF THE STATUE OF PEACE, ASIA POLICY POINT WEBSITE

## 'Comfort women' statue explained

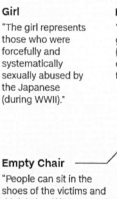

**Girl**

"The girl represents those who were forcefully and systematically sexually abused by the Japanese (during WWII)."

**Hair**

"We showed how these girls had their relationships (with family and friends) cut off against their will through the statue's cropped hair."

**Face**

"The face is of one who is angry about their treatment, but unafraid and with the will to resolve this issue."

**Bird**

"The bird is a symbol of peace, freedom and liberation. It connects those victims who 'returned to the sky' and the ones who are still left on the ground."

**Empty Chair**

"People can sit in the shoes of the victims and think 'what if it was me?', 'what if it was my family, my sister?'."

**Fists**

"The clenched fists represent how the victims will no longer stay silent about Japan's war crimes and want to tell the truth."

**Shadow**

"Despite the statue being a girl, its shadow is that of an old woman. It represents the hardship the victims had to suffer all this time."

**Heels**

"The heels are unattached to the ground, this represents the unstable lives of the victims, regarded as 'sluts' or 'prostitutes' and treated coldly by society."

### COMMONWEALTH of VIRGINIA
#### Office of the Governor

Ralph S. Northam
Governor

October 27, 2019

Dear Friends:

On behalf of the Commonwealth of Virginia, it is my honor to address and extend my best wishes to everyone attending the Statue of Peace unveiling ceremony. Thank you to the Washington Butterfly for Hope, the Washington Coalition for Comfort Women, and the National Unification Advisory Council, D.C. Chapter, for making this event possible today. The Statue of Peace, also called SoYeoSang, was designed by Kim Seo-Kyun and Kim Un-Sang.

The Statue of Peace serves as an important commemoration and will be the 5th Statue of Peace and the 14th "comfort women" memorial in the United States. To the survivors who are here with us today, we honor you and commend your bravery for speaking up, sharing your story, and advocating for human trafficking victims everywhere.

Human trafficking is a threat to public safety here in Virginia and across the United States, which is why I was proud to sign legislation last year to help us prevent these crimes by making it more difficult for human traffickers to post bail and leave jail to intimidate witnesses or continue their criminal activity. I am grateful to know that your organizations are working hard to advocate on behalf of the victims of trafficking and to prevent it.

Again, thank you for attending the Statue of Peace unveiling ceremony. It is an honor to serve as your Governor, and I send my best wishes for a successful evening.

Sincerely,

Ralph S. Northam

# Resources

# R.1. WASHINGTON COALITION FOR COMFORT WOMEN ISSUES (WCCW) ACTIVITIES FROM 1992 TO 2020

(WCCW Presidents, Dongwoo Lee Hahm, Ok Cha Soh, Christine Choi, edited by Jung-Sil Lee)

**1992**

November: Grandma Hwang Keum-ju, a former "comfort woman" of Japanese military sexual slavery during WWII testified at the United Methodist Church in Greater Washington that is covered by WTTG-TV (Fox 5).

December: Washington Coalition for Comfort Women Issues Inc. was founded with the founding president Dongwoo Lee Hahm.

**1993**

September: *Washington Post* publishes (October 1, 1993) a letter by the WCCW to Japanese Prime Minister Morihiro Hosokawa.

November: 24 U.S. Members of Congress send a petition to Japanese Prime Minister Morihiro Hosokawa urging his government to investigate the wartime sexual slavery regime known as the "comfort women."

**1994**

February: *Forum on Comfort Women* co-sponsored with Georgetown University Law Center Student Association, Washington, D.C.

March: Presentation on "comfort women" at the *International Women's Day Symposium on Women's Human Rights around the World* sponsored by the University of Richmond, Richmond, Virginia.

May: Sponsors a forum on "Comfort Women" in Washington, D.C. with Mr. Kenichi Takagi, Attorney-at-Law, Tokyo, Japan.

June: Organizes the *Asian and American United to Redress Japanese War Crimes rally* in front of the White House during Japanese Emperor Akihito's visit. WCCW demands President Bill Clinton raise the "comfort women" issue with Emperor Akihito.

October: Videotapes interviews with 15 surviving "comfort women" in Seoul in order to preserve their testimonies and to produce the documentary *Comfort Women*.

**1995**

April/May: First exhibition and the film screening of *Comfort Women* held at the United Methodist Building, near the U.S. Capitol and the Supreme Court.

| September: | WCCW representatives attend the *Fourth World Conference on Women: Action for Equality, Development and Peace* convened by the United Nations 4-15 September 1995 in Beijing, China. Exhibition and screening of the *Comfort Women* documentary. |
|---|---|
| November: | Exhibition and screening of *Comfort Women* at the Korean American Women UN Seminar held in New York City. |

## 1996

| March/April: | Attends the 52nd session of the UN Commission on Human Rights in Geneva, Switzerland. Submits petition on behalf of the "comfort women" to the 53 States members of the Commission on Human Rights. |
|---|---|
| April: | Invited to discuss the "comfort women" on *The Women Connection*, a television talk show in New York City. |
| June: | Provides historical pictures of "comfort women" to *Time* magazine. Time later featured a six-page article entitled "Japan: The Furor Over Making Apologies to the Comfort Women." |
| September: | International conference, *The Comfort Women of World War II: Legacy and Lessons*, held at Georgetown University sponsored by WCCW, Georgetown University, and The Korea Society, Washington, D.C. |
| October: | Arranges meeting with a Korean "comfort woman" and Mr. Eli Rosenbaum, Director of the Office of Special Investigations, U.S. Department of Justice. |
| December: | Justice Department announces (December 2, 1996) that 16 Japanese citizens have been placed on the U.S. Government's "watchlist" of aliens who are ineligible to enter the United States. Those placed on the watchlist either were members of Japanese Imperial Army units that conducted inhumane and frequently fatal experiments on humans or were involved in the operation of the so-called "comfort woman stations," where hundreds of thousands of women were forced to have sexual relations with Imperial Army officers and enlisted men. |

## 1997

| February: | Presents *WCCW Activities in U.S.* at an international symposium in Seoul, South Korea. |
|---|---|
| May: | WCCW President Dongwoo Lee Hahm requests at a press conference on Capitol Hill that "comfort women" issues be included among the war crimes to be listed in upcoming Congressional legislation. |
| July: | Congressman William O. Lipinski (D-IL) introduces H. Con. Res.126 into the U.S. House of Representatives. The resolution: *Calls upon the Government of Japan to: (1)* |

340

*formally issue an apology for the war crimes committed by the Japanese military during World War II; and (2) pay reparations to the victims.*

December:      Organizes a book signing for Therese Park, author of *A Gift of the Emperor.*

**1998**
June:          Organizes the exhibition *Comfort Women of World War II: An Indisputable Tragedy* held in the Rotunda of the Cannon House Office Building on Capitol Hill (June 1-4). Materials from the U.S. National Archives used.

**1999**
March/May:     Exhibition *Comfort Women of World War II* held at the Free Library of Philadelphia, Philadelphia, Pennsylvania.

March:         Presents WCCW documentary *Comfort Women* at KASCON XIII (Korean American Students Conference) held at Stanford University. The conference theme was *Empowering the Han* and was co-sponsored by University of California, Berkeley. Grandma Kim Yoon Sim, a former "comfort woman" is the keynote speaker.

**2000**
June:          Congressman Lane Evans (D-IL) introduces H. Con. Res. 357 (106th Congress) into the U.S. House of Representatives.

September:     Fifteen former "comfort women" from South Korea, China, the Philippines, and Taiwan file a lawsuit on September 18, 2000 against Japan in the United States District Court for the District of Columbia. In Hwang Keum-ju v. Japan, the plaintiffs allege that the Japanese military tortured and forced them into sexual slavery. [Citation: 172 F. Supp. 52 (D.D.C. 2001), aff'd, 332 F.3d 679 (D.C. Cir. 2003), vacated and remanded, 542 U.S. 901 (2004), aff'd on remand, 413 F.3d 45 (D.C. Cir. 2005), cert. denied, 546 U.S. 1208 (2006).]

September:     Organizes *Human Rights Awareness Year 2000 Remembrance: Women of Dignity and Honor* event at the Rayburn House Office Building on Capitol Hill. Ten surviving "comfort women" from Korea, Taiwan, Philippines, and Indonesia are honored as "Women of Dignity and Honor."

September:     Arranges public interviews with *Comfort Women of World War II* at the U.S. Holocaust Museum in Washington, D.C.

**2001**
April:         U.S. State Department issues (April 27) a Statement of Interest advising the U.S. District Court for the District of Columbia to dismiss the case, Hwang Keum-Ju v. Japan, arguing that it involved a political question that rendered the plaintiffs' claims nonjusticiable. The United States stated that, in this case, past treaties, namely the San

Francisco Peace Treaty and the 1965 treaty between Japan and Korea, addressed and were aimed at settling all war claims against Japan.

July: WCCW and Congressman Lane Evans (D-IL) hold a press conference at the U.S. Congress on "comfort women" issues with former "comfort woman" Grandma Kim Soon-duk.

Evans introduces H.Con.Res. 195 (107th Congress).

August: U.S. District Court for the District of Columbia holds a hearing on the class action lawsuit, Hwang Keum-ju v. Japan, filed by surviving "comfort women."

June-October: WCCW conducts a signature campaign to petition the U.S. Department of State and Department of Justice to allow "comfort women" their day in court by supporting the plaintiffs' in Hwang Keum-ju v. Japan.

September: United Nations Human Rights Committee recommends that Japan should: ensure school textbooks and other teaching materials present history in "a fair balanced manner;" compensate its wartime victims; and submit a report implementing said recommendations by June 30, 2006.

October: U.S. District Court for the District of Columbia grants Japan's motion to dismiss Hwang Keum-ju v. Japan on October 4, 2001, holding that Japan is entitled to sovereign immunity under the Foreign Sovereign Immunities Act (FSIA) and that the plaintiffs' claims presented a nonjusticiable political question.

November: Co-sponsors a forum/exhibit on "comfort women" with Cornell University, Harvard University, Yale University, New York University, Princeton University, and Georgetown University.
U.S. college tour *Lessons of Courage: Restoring Honor* at Georgetown University with Hwang Keum-ju, a former "comfort women," attending from Korea.

December: Launches a nationwide petition campaign supporting the appeal of the "comfort women" lawsuit, Hwang Keum-ju v. Japan, that is mailed to the U.S. Departments of State and Justice.
Participates in the 7th International Conference on Sino-Japanese Relations of WWII, in Crystal city, VA organized by the Global Alliance for Preserving the Truth of WWII.

## 2002

February: Ok Cha Soh presents on "comfort women" at the Regional Study Week, Gettysburg College, Gettysburg, Pennsylvania.

March: Dongwoo Lee Hahm attends *The Asian Regional Symposium Demanding Liquidation on Japan's Past* in Pyongyang, North Korea.
Midwest "Comfort Women Tour." Seminar and exhibition held at the University of Wisconsin, Northwestern University, Ohio State University, and University of Michigan with former "comfort woman" Grandma Choi Kap Sun.

| April: | *Sino-Japanese War Memorial* exhibition and panel discussion on *Comfort Women and Labor* hosted by American University and co-sponsored by WCCW. |
|---|---|
| May: | Co-sponsored with the Asia/Pacific American Awareness Foundation a symposium in Tampa, Florida on "comfort women.' *Comfort Women Speak* book talk held with former "comfort woman" Grandma Lee Ok-sun. |
| September: | Japanese Prime Minister Koizumi visits North Korea for a summit meeting with Kim Jong-Il, leader of North Korea. An urgent appeal is sent to "The Japan-North Korea Summit Meeting" to urge the two leaders to address reparations and an apology for Japan's colonial rule and war crimes. |
| October: | Ok Cha Soh participates in the Asian American study program at University of Maryland, College Park as a panel presenter on "Representation and Reparation of Justice"<br>Rally held in front of Japanese Embassy for the "comfort women" joined by the National Asian Pacific American Women's Forum (NAPAWF). |
| November: | Film Screening of Dai Sil Kim-Gibson's *Silence Broken* at George Washington University, Washington, D.C.<br>WCCW co-sponsors the Asian Studies Symposium on "comfort women" at Brown University with a former "comfort woman" Grandma Hwang Keum-ju in attendance. |
| December: | Appeal from district court decision in Hwang Keum-ju v. Japan filed in the United States Court of Appeals for the District of Columbia Circuit. Protest rally held in front of the court in Washington, D.C. |

**2003**

| February: | WCCW co-sponsors Boston Campus Tour on "comfort women": seminar and exhibit held at Boston College, Northeastern University, Boston University, MIT, Wellesley College, and Tufts University. Former "comfort woman" Grandma Kim Hwa Sun participates. |
|---|---|
| March: | WCCW participates in the Korean American Student Council (KASCON) conference at Cornell University. |
| June: | United States Court of Appeals for the D.C. Circuit affirms the U.S. District Court for the District of Columbia's dismissal of Hwang Keum-ju v. Japan on June 27, 2003. |
| June: | Congressman Lane Evans (D-IL) introduces H.Con.Res. 226 (108th Congress):<br>*Expresses the sense of Congress that the Government of Japan should: (1) issue an apology for the sexual enslavement of young women (known as "comfort women") during the colonial occupation of Asia and the Pacific Islands during World War II; (2) pay reparations to the victims; (3) educate future generations about this crime against humanity; and (4) publicly refute claims that the subjugation and enslavement of such women never occurred.* |

**2004**

| June: | U.S. Supreme Court vacates on June 14th the U.S. Court of Appeals for the D.C. Circuit decision in Hwang Keum-ju v. Japan because the Supreme Court had recently |
|---|---|

decided another case, Republic of Austria v. Altmann, that reached a different result under FISA. The Supreme Court remands the case back to the D.C. Circuit for further review.

September:   Georgetown University hosts an art exhibition *Line of Violence* by Andrew Ward and screening the film *Silence Broken* by Dai Sil Kim-Gibson, both focused on the "comfort women."

## 2004 -2005

November:   Worldwide signature campaign launched to oppose Japan securing a permanent seat on the UN Security Council: "No Apology, No Seat!"

## 2005

February:   Rep. Lane Evans (D-IL) introduces H.Con.Res. 68 (109th Congress).

March:   U.S. Court of Appeals for the D.C. Circuit holds a second argument in Hwang Keum-ju v. Japan.
Demonstration conducted in front of the U.S. Federal Court House, Washington, D.C. with former "comfort woman" Grandma Kang Il-chul participating.

March:   Press Conference at the U.S. Congress with Congressman Lane Evans (D-IL), former "comfort woman" Grandma Kang Il-chul, and a Chinese NGO representative.

May:   Ok Cha Soh attends an international conference demanding redress from Japan for the "comfort women" held in Tokyo, Japan.

June:   U.S. Court of Appeals for the D.C. Circuit on June 28th reaffirms the district court's 2001 dismissal of the complaint in Hwang Keum-ju v. Japan.

September:   Protest rally and press conference at the United Nations in New York City supporting the worldwide signature campaign against Japan holding a permanent seat on the UN Security Council: "No Apology, No Seat!

October:   Petition for a writ of certiorari for review of D.C. Circuit June 28th decision in Hwang Keum-ju v. Japan filed in the Supreme Court.

## 2006

February:   U.S. Supreme Court on February 21st denies Hwang Keum-ju's petition for a writ of certiorari.

February:   Congressman Lane Evans (D-IL) introduces a revised H. Con.Res. 68 as H. Res. 759.
V-Day 2006 Spotlight: *Justice to "Comfort Women*. Symposium and press conference held on Capitol Hill with Grandma Lee Yong-soo, a former "comfort woman" from Korea.

September:   H. Res. 759 passes by unanimous consent through the House Committee on International Relations chaired by Congressman Henry Hyde (R-IL). This is the first time a "comfort women" bill is reported out of committee.

344

December: H. Res. 759 not reported out to House floor for a vote during the Lame Duck session.

**2007**
January: Congressman Mike Honda (D-CA) introduces H.Res. 121 House floor urging the Japanese government to acknowledge, apologize and accept the historical responsibility in a clear and unambiguous manner for its Imperial Army's coercion of young women into sexual slavery.

February: House Committee on Foreign Affairs Subcommittee on Asia, the Pacific, and the Global Environment chaired by Congressman Eni Faleomavaega (D-AS) holds a hearing on *Protecting the Human Rights of Comfort Women*. Surviving victims Lee Yong-soo, Kim Kun-ja, and Jan Ruff O'Herne testify as well as experts Ms. Mindy Kotler and Dr. Ok Cha Soh.

June: Right-wing Japanese politicians, academics, and public intellectuals place a full-page an advertisement in the *Washington Post* entitled *The Facts* in an effort to discredit the "comfort women" and comparing U.S. occupation practices in Japan to "comfort stations." This angers many in Congress and raises the number of H.Res. 121 co-sponsors.

June: House Foreign Affairs Committee Chairman Tom Lantos (D-CA) holds a markup of H.Res. 121; it was ordered favorably out of Committee by a vote of 39-2.

July: H.Res. 121 passed by unanimous consent on the floor of the U.S. House of Representatives.

**2009**
July: Symposium, *War & Women's Human Rights*, held on the second anniversary of the passage of the H.Res. 121 at the Marvin Center, George Washington University, Washington, D.C. Co-sponsored by WCCW and The Korean Council for the Women Drafted for Military Sexual Slavery by Japan (The Korean Council).

**2010**
July: Letter sent to President Barack Obama asking his help in securing the Japanese Government's official apology and reparation for the "comfort women" during WWII in accordance with the U.S. Congress.

August: Protest rally held on the 100th Commemoration of the Japanese Annexation of Korea in front of the Japanese Embassy in Washington, D.C. Letter delivered to the Embassy for the Emperor and Empress of Japan to bring to their attention the urgent need to encourage the Japanese Government to resolve the "comfort women" issue.

**2012**
July 2012: Secretary of State Hillary Clinton corrects a State Department official who references the "comfort women" by stating that these women should be called what they are: "enforced sex slaves."

| November: | Symposium and art exhibition *Unveiling the Truth: The Sorrow and Hope of "Comfort Women"* to celebrate the 20th anniversary of WCCW, promote public awareness and to educate future generation co-hosted by WCCW and George Mason University, Fairfax, Virginia. |
| --- | --- |
| December: | Global Solidarity Action Day for the 1,000th Wednesday Demonstration. Rally held in front of the Japanese Embassy in Washington, D.C. |

## 2014

| May: | Unveiling ceremony for the Comfort Women Memorial Peace Garden at Fairfax County Government Center in partnership with the Fairfax County Government. The Peace Garden seeks to educate future generations with hope that the atrocities committed against "comfort women" will serve as a reminder and affirmation to the world that such crimes against humanity will not be condoned, tolerated, or forgotten. |
| --- | --- |
| August: | "Comfort Women Memorial Day" held on August 14. "Annual International day of solidarity and remembrance for the "comfort women." WCCW and Southeast Asian leaders prepare a letter to Japanese Prime Minister Abe Shinzo that is hand delivered to Ambassador Kenichiro Sasae in Washington, D.C. |
| November: | Seminar and exhibition *The Sorrow and Hope of "Comfort Women"* held at Catholic University of America in Washington, D.C., co-hosted with the WCCW. |

## 2015

| February: | WCCW forum held in Vienna, Virginia. Former WCCW co-chair Moon H. Rhee gives a presentation on how the public learned about the "comfort women" and how the WCCW was founded. |
| --- | --- |
| February: | Maryland State Senator Susan C. Lee (D) sponsors Senate Joint Resolution SJR0003 *Honoring the Surviving Human Trafficking Victims of Asia and the Pacific Islands During World War II*. WCCW President Jung-Sil Lee testifies for the "comfort women" at the February 11th State Senate Education, Health, and Environmental Affairs Committee hearing on SJR0003. |
| April: | Sponsors full-page "Open Letter to the Peoples of United States and Japan" in *The Washington Post* about the "comfort women" on the day Japanese Prime Minister Abe Shinzo speaks to a joint meeting of Congress. |
| April: | Organizes a protest rally with 30 other civic organizations of over 700 people on the U.S. Capitol grounds as Japanese Prime Minister Abe Shinzo spoke at the joint meeting of Congress. |
| May: | Organizes a panel discussion on *Wartime Atrocity against Women: The Comfort Women Case* for the Annual Kowinner World Convention. Jung-Sil Lee is organizer and moderator. |
| May: | First Anniversary of the *Comfort Women Memorial Peace Garden* at the Fairfax County Government Center. Showcases *Comfort Women: New Musical*. |

346

| June: | Joint protest with a surviving former "comfort woman" Grandma Kim Bok-dong and The Korean Council for the Women Drafted for Military Sexual Slavery by Japan (The Korean Council) in front of the Japanese Embassy in Washington, D.C. |
|---|---|
| August: | WCCW co-sponsors a concert dedicated to the "comfort women" by three distinguished Japanese American classical musicians at Segero Church, Olney, Maryland. |
| September: | Jung-Sil Lee is a guest panelist on the CCTV program *The Heat* to comment on Prime Minister Abe's visit and the "comfort women" issues. |
| October 15: | Jung-Sil Lee contributes to a special edition of *The Washington Times* an op-ed on "The Future of the 'Comfort Women' Movement." |
| October 30: | First WCCW "comfort women" essay, art, and research paper competition for junior and adult. |
| November: | One-year memorial ceremony of former U.S. Representative Lane Evans's passing, who spearheaded the "comfort women" issues at the U.S. Congress. |
| December: | Seminar on *The Accurate History Writing* with Mr. Dennis Halpin and Ms. Mindy Kotler at the WCCW's annual meeting. |
| | WCCW issues a Statement in response to a Korea-Japan bilateral agreement on the "comfort women" that is formally known as the "Announcement by Foreign Ministers of Japan and the Republic of Korea at the Joint Press Occasion." |

**2016**

| January: | Film Screening of *Spirits' Homecoming* at Messiah Presbyterian Church of Washington in Annandale, Virginia with Director Cho Jung-rae. |
|---|---|
| February: | Launches Webinar Pilot Program and crowd funding. |
| March: | WCCW holds a press conference at the UN against the December 2015 Korea-Japan bilateral agreement with former "comfort woman" Grandma Lee Yong-soo, Coalition Against Trafficking in Women (CATW), Korean American Civic Empowerment, and Korean American Forum of California in support of the March 11th statement by a group of United Nations human rights experts who urge the Japanese Government to implement without delay the recommendations made earlier that week on resolving the "comfort women" issues by the UN Committee on the Elimination of all Forms of Discrimination against Women (CEDAW). |
| April: | Southern Methodist University Human Rights Program in Dallas, Texas invites former "comfort woman" Grandma Lee Ok-sun, Director of House of Sharing Ahn Shin-kwon and WCCW President Jung-Sil Lee coordinates the event. |
| May: | George Washington University Capstone Conference of the Webinar Project, *History Writing: for Justice and Reconciliation of Comfort Women*. Co-sponsored by WCCW, George Washington University's Sigur Center for Asian Studies, and the University's History Department. |

| July: | Lecture by Jung-Sil Lee on *How to Teach Comfort Women Issues in a Korean Class* at the National Association for Korean Schools annual conference in Denver, Colorado. |
| --- | --- |
| September: | WCCW organizes the art exhibition *Collateral Damage* at The Anya and Andrew Shiva Gallery at John Jay College of Criminal Justice, City University of New York. Performance artist Shine Shin Kim and choreographer Chanmee Chung performed. |
| October: | WCCW organizes *Collateral Damage: Wartime Atrocity and Trauma* Conference at the John Jay College of Criminal Justice, City University of New York. |
| November: | WCCW participates in the Human Rights Film Festival in Calgary, Canada. President Jung-Sil Lee showcases "comfort women" history in the NGO/NPO exhibit at the conference. Jung-Sil Lee is a guest speaker at the film screening of *Apology* to discuss the "comfort women" issue and the activism of WCCW. Jin-joo Hwang, granddaughter of survivor Grandma Gil Won-ok also speaks. |
| December: | On International Human Rights Day, the Taipei Women's Rescue Foundation (TWRF) opens the first "comfort women" museum in Taipei, Taiwan. Chen Lien-hua, 92, a Taiwanese former "comfort woman" sent to the Philippines and Lee Yong-soo, 88, a Korean "comfort woman" survivor, who was sent to a Japanese military base in Hsinchu in northern Taiwan, attend the opening. Former Taiwan President Ma Ying-jeou, Taiwan's Culture Minister Cheng Li-chun and the Taipei Women's Rescue Foundation Executive Director Kang Shu-hua also attend. The American delegation to the museum opening includes Dennis Halpin and Phyllis Kim. |

## 2017

| July-<br>September: | WCCW President Jung-Sil Lee curates the exhibition *Truth: Promises for Peace*, Seoul that is installed in Seoul, Jeonjoo, Daejeon, and Daegu, South Korea that is organized and sponsored by the South Korean Ministry of Gender Equality and Family. WCCW contributes historical materials and photographs. |
| --- | --- |
| July: | WCCW hosts an award ceremony on the *10th Anniversary of the Passage of House Resolution 121* at the Rayburn House Office Building, Washington, D.C. |
| October: | WCCW founding President Dongwoo Lee Hahm and the 5th President Jung-Sil Lee present a co-authored paper *Tracing the Twenty-five Years of the Comfort Women Movement in the U.S.* at the 8th Annual Conference of The Research Center for Korean Community at Queens College, Queens, New York: *The Redress Movement for the Victims of Japanese Military Sexual Slavery: Looking Back at the 27 year Movement*. |
| October: | Hosts a screening of *Apology* and a panel discussion with its director Ms. Tiffany Hsiung. |
| November: | Forum and seminar with WCCW interns, Korean students, and young professionals at the *Global Network for Next Generation for Peace and Human Rights* meeting held at Fairfax County Government Center, Fairfax, Virginia. |

| December: | Hosts the WCCW 25th Anniversary Ceremony and Banquet at The Universities at Shady Grove, University of Maryland, Rockville, Maryland. Screening of *Spirits' Homecoming, II Unfinished Story* with its director Cho Jung-rae. |

**2018**

| January: | WCCW Visual Resource Center (VRC) launched. Its main goal is to archive interviews, videos, photos of the past WCCW activities, and the ephemera of the "comfort women" movement in the U.S. The team began filming a documentary on the history of the WCCW. |
| February: | President Jung-Sil Lee presents a paper "Unforeseen Controversy: Reconciliation and Re-contextualization through Comfort Women Memorials in the U.S." at the College Art Association (CAA) annual conference under the overarching theme *Teachable Monuments: Using Public Art to Spark Dialogue and Address Controversies* held at the Los Angeles Convention Center. |
| April: | WCCW hosts a lecture and an interview with Ms. Sunim Kang who helped to initiate "comfort women" activism before forming WCCW in 1992. |
| June-August: | Fifteen high school interns launch an archiving project. Interns learned about the history and current issues on "comfort women" in a series of lectures and field trips to the National Archives and Records Administration to learn how to research and locate textual and visual primary sources. |
| September: | Launched fellow team of George Washington University to compile materials related to resolutions of the U.S. House of Representative and other legislatures. |
| November: | WCCW co-hosts the International Film Festival *Sexual Violence in Warfare: The Films of Unhealed Wounds* on "comfort women" with the American University School of Communication at the school's Malsi Doyle and Michael Forman Theater. Showcased nine films from five countries and organized a director's panel discussion co-sponsored with Asia Policy Point. |
| December: | High school internship program/archiving project for the 2019 spring term launched. |

**2019**

| January: | Youth Intern Bookmaking Project launched with three co-editors and 21 students. |
| February: | WCCW President Jung-Sil Lee discusses "Appropriating, Reporting, and Re-Contexualizing of Wartime Sex Crimes by Female Artists" on the panel *Has Anyone Ever Seen an Image of War? Reassessing the Visual Culture of War and Related Disasters, Violence, and Torture in The Modern and Contemporary Moment* at the College Art Association (CAA) annual conference in New York City. |
| March: | WCCW annual board meeting. Votes for the installation of a *Statue of Peace* in the Washington, D.C. metropolitan area. |

| March: | Film Screening of *Silence* directed by Park Soo Nam at George Washington University and the Fairfax County Government Center. Includes panel discussion with Park Maeui, Professor Eunah Lee, and Professor Jungah Kim moderated by WCCW President Jung-Sil Lee. |
|---|---|
| June: | Film Screening of *Silence* and WCCW President Jung-Sil Lee was invited as the speaker on Win-TV, Chicago MBC, Chicago. |
| June: | Attends second anniversary ceremony of the Atlanta, Georgia Statue of Peace. |
| September: | Film Screening of *My Name is Kim Bok-dong* at George Washington University and George Mason University in collaboration with the Korean Studies at George Mason University, Washington Butterfly for Hope, and The Korean Council. |
| October: | Inaugural meeting of the six organizations that comprise the Committee for the Statue of Peace. |
| October: | Unveiling ceremony of *the Statue of Peace* in Annandale, Virginia in collaboration with the Washington Butterfly for Hope and the National Unification Advisory Council. |
| November: | Interns-authored book *Comfort Women: New Perspectives* publication ceremony held at Tysons Corners, Virginia. |
| December: | Archiving book project completed and WCCW E-Archive Project launched. |

**2020**

| February: | WCCW President Jung-Sil Lee and Professor Mike Mochizuki discuss the *Memorialization of Comfort Women* on a panel hosted by George Washington University's Organization of Asian Studies (OAS). |
|---|---|
| March: | WCCW attends the unveiling ceremony for the Connecticut Statue of Peace, which is the 15th "comfort women" memorial in the U.S. |
| July: | Publication ceremony for the archiving book *Comfort Women: A Movement for Justice and Women's Rights* co-edited by Jung-Sil Lee and Dennis Halpin on the WCCW's 28th Annual Meeting and the 6th Anniversary of Comfort Women Memorial Peace Garden in Fairfax, Virginia. |

# R.2. "COMFORT WOMEN" LEGISLATIVE HISTORY IN THE U.S. CONGRESS 1991–2016 (101ST TO 115TH CONGRESSES)

(Asia Policy Point)

## PRECURSORS

*No direct mention of "comfort women" but implied as part of a growing awareness of sexual violence as a crime and war crime.*

### ▶101st Congress (1989–1990)

**Violence Against Women Act of 1990 [S.2754]**
https://www.congress.gov/bill/101st-congress/senate-bill/2754
Sen. Biden, Joseph R., Jr. [D-DE] (Introduced 6/19/1990)
Cosponsors: 26
Committees: Judiciary
Latest Action: Senate - 10/19/1990 Placed on Senate Legislative Calendar under General Orders. Calendar No. 1007

### ▶102nd Congress (1991–1992)

**Women and Children First Act of 1992** (Introduced in House) [H.R.5218.IH]
https://www.congress.gov/bill/102nd-congress/house-bill/5218
Rep. Dannemeyer, William E. [R-CA-39] (Introduced 5/20/1992)
Cosponsors: None
Committees: House - Agriculture; Banking, Finance, and Urban Affairs; Education and Labor; Energy and Commerce; Judiciary; Post Office and Civil Service; Ways and Means

Latest Action: House - 07/20/1992 Referred to the Subcommittee on Human Resources

### ▶103rd Congress (1993–1994)

**Selective Legislation Focused on Rape During the Yugoslav Civil War**
**Expressing the sense of the Congress concerning rape and forced pregnancy of women and girls in the former Yugoslavia.** (Introduced in House) [H.Con.Res.45]
https://www.congress.gov/bill/103rd-congress/house-concurrent-resolution/45
Sponsor: Rep. Molinari, Susan [R-NY-13] (Introduced 2/18/1993)
Committees: House - Foreign Affairs
Cosponsors: 86
Latest Action: House - 3/9/1993 Referred to the Subcommittee on International Security, International Organizations and Human Rights.

**A resolution expressing the sense of the Senate concerning systematic rape in the conflict in the former Socialist Federal Republic of Yugoslavia.** (Introduced in Senate) [S.Res.35]
https://www.congress.gov/bill/103rd-congress/senate-resolution/35
Sen. Lautenberg, Frank R. [D-NJ] (Introduced 1/26/1993)
Committees: Senate - Foreign Relations
Cosponsors: 46
Latest Action: 10/21/1993 Sponsor introductory remarks on measure. (CR S14217-14229)

**To authorize the provision of assistance for the victims of torture, including rape and other war crimes, in the former Yugoslavia, and for the families of such victims.** (Introduced in House) [H.R.1377]
https://www.congress.gov/bill/103rd-congress/house-bill/1377
Rep. Hoyer, Steny H. [D-MD-5] (Introduced 3/16/1993)
Committees: House - Foreign Affairs
Cosponsors: 33
Latest Action:    House - 3/30/1993 Referred to the Subcommittee on Europe and the Middle East.

**A bill to authorize the provision of assistance to the victims of war in the former Yugoslavia, including the victims of torture, rape, and other war crimes and their families.** (Introduced in Senate) [S.416]
https://www.congress.gov/bill/103rd-congress/senate-bill/416
Sen. DeConcini, Dennis [D-AZ] (Introduced 2/24/1993)
Committees: Senate - Foreign Relations
Cosponsors: 16
Latest Action: 05/12/1993 Sponsor introductory remarks on measure. (CR S5781-5783)

**Expressing the sense of the House of Representatives concerning systematic rape in the conflict in Bosnia-Herzegovina.** (Introduced in House) [H.Res.32]
https://www.congress.gov/bill/103rd-congress/house-resolution/32
Rep. Miller, George [D-CA-7] (Introduced 1/6/1993)
Cosponsors: 127
Committees: House-Foreign Affairs
Latest Action: 3/18/1993 Executive Comment Received from State.

**Concerning the crisis in the former Yugoslavia.** (Introduced in House) [H.Con.Res.24]
https://www.congress.gov/bill/103rd-congress/house-concurrent-resolution/24
*(9) the United States Government, in conjunction with the United Nations and the European Community, should support and encourage the formation and development of an international war crimes commission to assist in the prosecuting of war crimes, including crimes against women, and other human rights violations in Bosnia-Herzegovina.*
Rep. Moran, James P. [D-VA-8] (Introduced 1/26/1993)
Cosponsors: 66
Latest Action: House - 2/11/1993 Referred to the Subcommittee on Europe and the Middle East.
Committees: House - Foreign Affairs; Judiciary
**Concerning the need for immediate investigation into violations of international law in the former Yugoslavia and prosecution of persons responsible for those violations.** (Introduced in House) [H.Con.Res.154]

https://www.congress.gov/bill/103rd-congress/house-concurrent-resolution/154
Sponsor: Rep. Molinari, Susan [R-NY-13] (Introduced 9/23/1993)
Committees: House - Foreign Affairs
Cosponsors: 39
Latest Action: House - 10/5/1993 Referred to the Subcommittee on Europe and the Middle East.

**Calling on the President to work to convene an international tribunal for war crimes committed in the former Yugoslavia.** (Introduced in House) [H.Con.Res.16]
https://www.congress.gov/bill/103rd-congress/house-concurrent-resolution/16
*Whereas horrible atrocities continue to be committed against civilian population of Bosnia-Hercegovina, including--(5) systematic sexual abuse, including the crime of rape, against women and girls as a method of torture.*

Rep. Wolf, Frank R. [R-VA-10] (Introduced 1/6/1993)
Cosponsors: 55
Committees: House-Foreign Affairs
Latest Action: 3/22/1993 Executive Comment Received from State.

**A resolution urging the criminal prosecution of persons committing crimes against humanity, including participation in mass rapes, in Bosnia-Herzegovina.** (Introduced in Senate) [S.Res.24]
https://www.congress.gov/bill/103rd-congress/senate-resolution/24
Sen. Danforth, John C. [R-MO] (Introduced 1/21/1993)
Cosponsors: 12
Committees: Senate - Foreign Relations
Latest Action: Senate - 1/21/1993 Referred to the Senate Foreign Relations

**A resolution expressing the sense of the Senate concerning the United Nation's arms embargo against Bosnia-Herzegovina, a nation's right to self-defense, and peace negotiations.** (Introduced in Senate) [S.Res.79]
https://www.congress.gov/bill/103rd-congress/senate-resolution/79
Sen. Feingold, Russell D. [D-WI] (Introduced 3/11/1993)
Committees: Senate - Foreign Relations
Cosponsors: 10
Latest Action: 6/24/1993 Sponsor introductory remarks on measure.

▶ **103rd Congress (1993–1994)**

*Committee Report:* **"The Response to Rape: Detours on the Road to Equal Justice." A Majority Staff Report Prepared for the use of the Committee on the Judiciary, United States Senate, 103rd Congress, First Session. U.S. Government Printing Office. May 1993. 67 pages.**
http://library.niwap.org/wp-content/uploads/2015/VAWA-Lghist-SenateJudiciary-6.93.pdf

**Violent Crime Control and Law Enforcement Act of 1994** (P.L. 103-322)
Violence Against Women Act (VAWA) is Title IV.
https://www.congress.gov/bill/103rd-congress/house-bill/3355
Sponsor: Rep. Brooks, Jack B. [D-TX-9] (Introduced 10/26/1993)

Committees: House - Judiciary
Committee Reports: H.Rept 103-324; H.Rept 103-694; H.Rept 103-711
Latest Action: 09/13/1994 Became Public Law No: 103-322.
**Reauthorized and strengthened 2000, 2006, 2013, Violence Against Women Act expired on December 21, 2018 and has not been reauthorized as of March 2020.**

## BILLS CONTAINING THE PHRASE "COMFORT WOMEN"

### ▶104th Congress (1995–1996)

**1. Expressing the sense of the Congress concerning the maltreatment of United States military and civilian prisoners by the Japanese during World War II.** (Introduced in House) [H.CON.RES.176.IH]
https://www.congress.gov/bill/104th-congress/house-concurrent-resolution/176
Sponsor: Rep Dornan, Robert K. [CA-46] (introduced 5/10/1996)
**Relevant section**
*Whereas in 1993 international jurists in Geneva, Switzerland, ruled that*
*"comfort women"—sex slaves of the Japanese military during World War II—deserve compensation of at least $40,000 for each individual for "extreme pain and suffering" suffered by such individuals;*
Committees: House - International Relations, Government Reform and Oversight
Cosponsors: 13

Latest Action: House - 5/14/1996 Referred to the Subcommittee on Asia and the Pacific.

### ▶105th Congress (1997–1998)

**2. Expressing the sense of Congress concerning the war crimes committed by the Japanese military during World War II.** (Introduced in House)[H.CON.RES.126.IH ]
https://www.congress.gov/bill/105th-congress/house-concurrent-resolution/126
Sponsor: Rep. Lipinski, William O. [D-IL-3] (Introduced 7/25/1997)
Committees: House - International Relations
Cosponsors: 78
Latest Action: House - 8/21/1997 Referred to the Subcommittee on International Operations and Human Rights.

### ▶106th Congress (1999–2000)

**3a. Petitions and Memorials (POM)—362. A joint resolution adopted by the Legislature of State of California relative to war crimes committed by the Japanese military during World War II; to the Committee on Foreign Relations**.
October 6, 1999, Congressional Record Issue: Vol. 145, No. 134 — Daily Edition, [Pages S12099–S12100]
https://www.congress.gov/crec/1999/10/06/modified/CREC-1999-10-06-pt1-PgS12099-4.htm
**California Assembly Joint Resolution No. 27**
Adopted August 26, 1999; Introduced June 22, 1999
http://leginfo.legislature.ca.gov/faces/billNavClient.xhtml?bill_id=199920000AJR27

**3b. [106th] Expressing the sense of Congress concerning the war crimes committed by the Japanese military during World War II.** (Introduced in the House) [H.CON.RES.357.IH]
https://www.congress.gov/bill/106th-congress/house-concurrent-resolution/357
Sponsor: Rep. Evans, Lane [D-IL-17] (Introduced 6/19/2000)
Committees: House - International Relations
Cosponsors: 46
Latest Action: House - 7/17/2000 Referred to the Subcommittee on Asia and the Pacific.

## ▶107th Congress (2001–2002)

**4. Expressing the sense of Congress that the Government of Japan should formally issue a clear and unambiguous apology for the sexual enslavement of young women during colonial occupation of Asia and World War II, known to the world as "comfort women," and for other purposes.** (Introduced in House)[H.CON.RES.195.IH]
https://www.congress.gov/bill/107th-congress/house-concurrent-resolution/195
Sponsor: Rep. Evans, Lane [D-IL-17] (Introduced 7/24/2001)
Committees: House - International Relations
Cosponsors: 27
Latest Action: House - 8/13/2001 Referred to the Subcommittee on East Asia and the Pacific.

## ▶108th Congress (2003–2004)

**5. Expressing the sense of Congress that the Government of Japan should formally issue a clear and unambiguous apology for the sexual enslavement of young women during colonial occupation of Asia and World War II, known to the world as "comfort women," and for other purposes.** (Introduced in House)[H.CON.RES.226.IH]
https://www.congress.gov/bill/108th-congress/house-concurrent-resolution/226
Sponsor: Rep. Evans, Lane [D-IL-17] (Introduced 6/23/2003)
Committees: House - International Relations
Cosponsors: 32
Latest Action: House - 6/23/2003 Referred to the House Committee on International Relations.

## ▶109th Congress (2005–2006)

**6. Expressing the sense of Congress that the Government of Japan should formally issue a clear and unambiguous apology for the sexual enslavement of young women during colonial occupation of Asia and World War II, known to the world as "comfort women," and for other purposes.** (Introduced in House) [H.CON.RES.68.IH]
https://www.congress.gov/bill/109th-congress/house-concurrent-resolution/68
Sponsor: Rep. Evans, Lane [D-IL-17] (Introduced 2/16/2005)
Committees: House - International Relations
Cosponsors: 15
Latest Action: House - 3/17/2005 Referred to the Subcommittee on Asia and the Pacific.

**7. [109ᵗʰ] Expressing the sense of the House of Representatives that the Government of Japan should formally acknowledge and accept responsibility for its sexual enslavement of young women, known to the world as "comfort women," during its colonial occupation of Asia and the Pacific Islands from the 1930s through the duration of World War II, and for other purposes.** (Introduced in House) [H.RES.759.IH]
https://www.congress.gov/bill/109th-congress/house-resolution/759
Sponsor: Rep. Evans, Lane [D-IL-17] (Introduced 4/4/2006)
Committees: House - International Relations
Cosponsors: 58
Latest Action: House - 9/13/2006 Committee Agreed to Seek Consideration Under Suspension of the Rules, (Amended) by Unanimous Consent.

## ►110ᵗʰ Congress (2007–2008)

**8. Whereas the Government of Japan, during its colonial and wartime occupation of Asia and the Pacific Islands from the 1930s through the duration of World War II, officially commissioned. . . (Engrossed as Agreed to or Passed by the House)** [H.RES.121.EH]
https://www.congress.gov/bill/110th-congress/house-resolution/121
Sponsor: Rep. Honda, Michael M. [D-CA-15] (Introduced 1/31/2007)
Committees: House - Foreign Affairs
Cosponsors: 167
Latest Action: House - 7/30/2007 The title of the measure was amended. Agreed to without objection. *Note that the final resolution differs from introduced resolution.*

## ►113ᵗʰ Congress (2013–2014)

**9. State, Foreign Operations, and Related Programs Appropriations Bill, 2014. July 30, 2013— Committed to the Committee of the Whole House on the State of the Union and ordered to be printed**

113ᵀᴴ CONGRESS 1ˢᵗ Session REPORT 113–185, HOUSE OF REPRESENTATIVES

Ms. Granger, from the Committee on Appropriations, submitted the following REPORT together with MINORITY VIEWS  [To accompany H.R. 2855] The Committee on Appropriations submits the following report in explanation of the accompanying bill making appropriations for the Department of State, foreign operations, and related programs, for the fiscal year ending September 30, 2014, and for other purposes.

**Department of State: Diplomatic and Consular Programs P 11**
https://www.congress.gov/113/crpt/hrpt185/CRPT-113hrpt185.pdf

*Asia-Pacific region—the Committee notes the passage of H.Res. 121 in the House of Representatives on July 30, 2007 and urges the Secretary of State to encourage the Government of Japan to address the issues raised in the resolution.*

**10. Recognizing the immense contributions of Congressman Michael M. Honda throughout his tenure in Congress.** (Introduced in House) [H.Res.952]
https://www.congress.gov/bill/114th-congress/house-resolution/952

*Whereas Congressman Michael M. Honda has been a leader for the Asian American and Pacific Islander community and helped to pass legislation to award Japanese American World War II veterans and Filipino American World War II veterans with the Congressional Gold Medal; Whereas Congressman Michael M. Honda has fought to bring justice and global attention to the plight and continued suffering of "comfort women" who were forced into sexual slavery during World War II;*

Rep. Chu, Judy [D-CA-27] (Introduced 12/8/2016)
Committees: House - House Administration
Cosponsors: 52
Latest Action: House - 12/8/2016 Referred to the House Committee on House Administration.
[Never reported out of Committee, Mike Honda lost his reelection bid in 2016]

*No further mention of "comfort women" in subsequent Congresses*

# R.3. OTHER "COMFORT WOMEN" RESOLUTIONS IN THE U.S.

(George Washington University Fellow Team: Jaeyop Kang, Kyong Sik Kang, Ju Han Kim, Nancy Welch, and Kyungchae Jang)

1. **Assembly Joint Resolution (AJR 27: August 26, 1999).** Introduced by Assembly Members Honda, Cardenas, Cunneen, Firebaugh, Granlund, Strom-Martin, and Wildman (coauthors: Senators Johnston and Speier); Relative to the war crimes committed by the Japanese military during World War II. http://www.leginfo.ca.gov/pub/99-00/bill/asm/ab_0001-0050/ajr_27_bill_19990826_chaptered.html

2. **Senate Concurrent Resolution (SCR 124: September 20, 2012).** Sponsored by Senator Loretta Weinberg (District 37, Bergen) and Senator Kevin J. O'Toole (District 40, Bergen, Essex, Morris, and Passaic) (cosponsored by Senators Allen and Gordon); Commemorates suffering endured by comfort women during forced internment in Japanese military camps. https://www.njleg.state.nj.us/2012/Bills/SCR/124_I1.HTM

3. **New Jersey Assembly Concurrent Resolution (ACR 159: September 24, 2012)**. Sponsored by Assemblyman Gordon M. Johnson (District 37 (Bergen) and Assemblywoman Connie Wagner (District 38 (Bergen and Passaic) (cosponsored by Assemblywomen Mosquera, Vainieri Huttle, Assemblyman Chivukula, Senators Weinberg, O'Toole, Allen, Gordon, Addiego, Beck and Gill); Commemorates suffering endured by comfort women during forced internment in Japanese military camps. https://www.njleg.state.nj.us/2012/Bills/ACR/159_R1.PDF

4. **New York State Senate Resolution (J 304: January 25, 2013).** Sponsored by Tony Avella, co-sponsored by Eric Adams, Joseph Addabbo, Greg Ball, and John Bonacic; Legislative Resolution memorializing a Memorial Monument in the State of New York that pays tribute to those who have become known to the world as "Comfort Women." https://legislation.nysenate.gov/pdf/bills/2013/J304

5. **Maryland Senate Joint Resolution (SJR 2, January 16, 2014).** Introduced by Senator Manno; Acknowledgment of the Sufferings of Sexually Enslaved Women ("Comfort Women") During World War II. https://legiscan.com/MD/text/SJ2/id/923194/Maryland-2014-SJ2-Introduced.pdf

6. **Maryland State Joint Resolution (SJR 3: February 6, 2015).** Introduced by Senators Lee, Bates, Montgomery, Nathan–Pulliam, and Ready; Assigned to: Education, Health, and Environmental Affairs; Honoring the Surviving Human Trafficking Victims of Asia and the Pacific Islands During World War II. http://mgaleg.maryland.gov/2015RS/bills/sj/sj0003f.pdf

7. **RES 158-25A1 (August 25, 2015, approved on October 13, 2015).** San Francisco Public School Board; In Support of Countering Human Trafficking and Commercial Sexual Exploitation of Children. https://archive.sfusd.edu/en/assets/sfusd-staff/about-SFUSD/files/resolutions/158-25A1.pdf

8. **RES 2017-05-03 (approved on May 23, 2017).** A Resolution of the City of Brookhaven to Accept Donation of Artwork. http://brookhavencityga.iqm2.com/Citizens/Detail_LegiFile.aspx?Frame=&MeetingID=1667&MediaPosition=9957.123&ID=2739&CssClass=

9. **Senate Resolution J 2648 (June 6, 2017).** Introduced by Senator Elaine Phillips; Commemorating the 5th Anniversary of the New York State Memorial Monument that pays tribute to "comfort women." https://legislation.nysenate.gov/pdf/bills/2017/J2648

# R.4. REPORTS ON "COMFORT WOMEN" ISSUES TO THE UNITED NATIONS

(GWU Fellow Team, Jaeyop Kang, Kyungchae Jang, Sungjun Kim, Sumi Lee, edited by Jung-Sil Lee)

**1993** **August**
Letter submitted by the Permanent Representative of the Democratic People's Republic of Korea to the United Nations addressed to the Secretary-General, 8/09/1993; Transmits letter concerning the issue of the "comfort women" for the Japanese army during the Second World War, and also transmits an interim fact-finding report on the issue. https://digitallibrary.un.org/record/171914?ln=en.

**1994** **December**
Comfort Women: an Unfinished Ordeal, by Ustinia Dolgopol and Snehal Paranjape, 12/01/1994; The mission inquired into the circumstances concerning sexual services obtained from Korean and Filipino women by the Japanese military during World War II. https://www.icj.org/comfort-women-an-unfinished-ordeal-report-of-a-mission/

**1996** **January**
Report of the Special Rapporteur on violence against women, its causes and consequences, Radhika Coomaraswamy, in accordance with Commission on Human Rights resolution 1994/45, 01/04/1996; Report on the mission to the Democratic People's Republic of Korea, the Republic of Korea and Japan on the issue of military sexual slavery in wartime. https://digitallibrary.un.org/record/228137?ln=en: https://www.un.org/en/ga/search/view_doc.asp?symbol=E/CN.4/1996/53/Add.1

**April**
Written Statement, "Further promotion and encouragement of human rights and fundamental freedoms, including the question of the programme and methods of work of the Commission on Human Rights by Liberation (Organization: London), 04/11/1996; Concerns Japan's response to the issue of forced recruitment of "comfort women" during the Second World War. https://digitallibrary.un.org/record/235473?ln=en

**1998** **June**
Systematic rape, sexual slavery and slavery-like practices during armed conflict: final report, submitted by Gay J. McDougall, UN. Special Rapporteur about Systematic Rape, Sexual Slavery and Slavery-like Practices during Wartime, 06/22/1998; "Appendix: An analysis of the legal liability of the Government of Japan for 'comfort women stations' established during the Second World War." p. 38-62. Includes bibliographical references. https://digitallibrary.un.org/record/257682?ln=en

**2000   June**

Systematic rape, sexual slavery and slavery-like practices during armed conflict: update to the final report, submitted by Gay J. McDougall, 06/06/2000; UN. Special Rapporteur on the Situation of Systematic Rape, Sexual Slavery and Slavery-like Practices during Wartime. https://digitallibrary.un.org/record/419092?ln=en

**2001   February**

Written Statement, "Integration of the human rights of women and the gender perspective: violence against women" submitted by the International Centre for Human Rights and Democratic Development (Canada), 02/13/2001; Concerns judgement of the Women's International War Crimes Tribunal on Japan's Military Sexual Slavery held in Tokyo, Dec. 8-12 2000.  https://digitallibrary.un.org/record/434094?ln=en

**2003   July**

Written Statement, "Specific human rights issues" submitted by Asian-Japan Women's Resource Centre, 07/31/2003; Concerns the issue of Japan's military sexual slavery ("comfort women") and transmits extract from draft Principles and Guidelines concerning Remedy and Reparations for Victims of Grave Sexual Violence in Armed Conflicts. https://digitallibrary.un.org/record/499965?ln=en

**2004   August**

Written Statement, "Specific human rights issues" submitted by Asia-Japan Women's Resource Center (AJWRC), 08/09/2004; Concerns the issue of Japan's military sexual slavery during the Second World War (the so-called "comfort women" issue). https://digitallibrary.un.org/record/527564?ln=en

**2005   August**

Written Statement, "Specific human rights issues : women and human rights : contemporary forms of slavery" submitted by Japan Fellowship of Reconciliation, 08/02/2005; Draws attention to judgements on a case of trafficking in 15 Japanese women in Nagasaki to a Japanese naval "comfort station" in Shanghai, China, in 1932. https://digitallibrary.un.org/record/554247?ln=en

**2006   June**

Letter from the Permanent Representative of the Democratic People's Republic of Korea to the United Nations, 06/21/2006; Transmits statement of the Ministry for Foreign Affairs concerning Japan's alleged internationalization of the "abduction issue," an issue of the 200,000 Korean women forced to serve a "comfort women" for the Japanese Imperial Army 50 years ago, already resolved by both Democratic People's Republic of Korea and Japan. https://digitallibrary.un.org/record/577625?ln=en

**2008   December**

Concluding Observations of the Human Rights Committee: Japan, UN Human Rights Committee (94th session: Geneva), 12/19/2008; The concern that the State party has still not accepted its responsibility for the "comfort women" system during the Second World War.  https://digitallibrary.un.org/record/646529?ln=en

2013 **June**
Concluding observations on the 3rd periodic report of Japan, adopted by the Committee (50th session), 29 April-17 May 2013; Committee on Economic, Social, and Cultural Rights, U.N. 06/10/2013; The Committee is concerned about the lasting negative effects of the exploitation to which "comfort women" were subjected on their enjoyment of economic, social, and cultural rights and their entitlement to reparation.
https://digitallibrary.un.org/record/751981?ln=en

2016 **March**
Recommendation, "Japan/ S. Korea: The long awaited apology to 'comfort women' victims is yet to come" by UN Committee on the Elimination of all Forms of Discrimination against Women (CEDAW), The experts are Ms. Eleonora Zielinska, Mr. Pablo de Greiff, Mr. Juan E. Mendez, March 4, 2016; "We urge Japan to implement CEDAW's new recommendations. This will grant effective access to justice, truth and adequate reparation to these women whose inalienable human rights were brutally violated by the State," the experts concluded.
https://www.ohchr.org/EN/NewsEvents/Pages/DisplayNews.aspx?NewsID=17209&LangID=E

2017 **May**
Convention against Torture and Other Cruel, Inhuman or Degrading Treatment or Punishment, Concluding observations on the combined third to fifth periodic reports of the Republic of Korea, Committee against Torture, 05/30/2017; The Committee appreciates having had the opportunity to engage in a constructive dialogue with the State party's delegation and the oral and written responses provided to the questions and concerns raised during its consideration of the report.
https://tbinternet.ohchr.org/_layouts/treatybodyexternal/Download.aspx?symbolno=CAT%2fC%2fKOR%2fCO%2f3-5&Lang=en

2018 **August**
U.N. Committee on the Elimination of Racial Discrimination (CERD) urged Japan to adopt a victim-centered approach toward "comfort women," 96th session, Aug 6-30, 2018; U.N. body urges Japan to take victim-centric approach to 'comfort women' issue and ensure safety of Okinawa residents.
https://tbinternet.ohchr.org/_layouts/treatybodyexternal/Download.aspx?symbolno=CERD%2fC%2fJPN%2fCO%2f10-11&Lang=en

# R.5. RECOMMENDED READINGS ON "COMFORT WOMEN"

(Compiled by Jung-Sil Lee)

## Books and Book Chapters

Ahn, Yonson. *Whose Comfort?: Body, Sexuality and Identities of Korean "Comfort Women" and Japanese Soldiers during WWII*. Hackensack, NJ and Singapore: World Scientific, 2019.

Buruma, Ian. *The Wages of Guilt: Memories of War in Germany and Japan*. New York: Meridian Books, 1995.

Choi, Chungmoo, ed. *The Comfort Women: Colonialism, War, and Sex. Positions: East Asia Cultures Critique* 5, no.1 (Spring 1997). Durham, NC: Duke University Press, 1997.

Dower, John W. *War Without Mercy*. New York: Pantheon Books, 1986.

Drinck, Barbara and Chung-noh Gross, eds. *Forced Prostitution in Times of War and Peace: Sexual Violence against Women and Girls*. Bielefeld, Germany: Kleine Verlag, 2007.

Gendry-Kim, Keum-suk. *Grass*. Translated by Janet Hong. Quebec: Drawn and Quarterly, 2019.

Galang, Evelina. *Lolas' House*. Evanston, Illinois: Curbstone Books, Northwestern University Press, 2017.

Henson, Maria Rosa. *Comfort Women: A Filipina's Story of Prostitution and Slavery Under the Japanese Military*. London, Boulder, New York, & Oxford, Rowman a Littlefield Publishers, Inc., 1999.

Hicks, George. *The Comfort Women: Japan's Brutal Regime of Enforced Prostitution in the Second World War*. New York: Norton & Company, 1994.

Hong, Yunshin. *"Comfort Stations" as Remembered by Okinawans during World War II*. Translated by Robert Ricketts. Leiden: Brill Publisher, 2020.

Keller, Nora Okja. *Comfort Woman*. London: Penguin, 1998.

Kim, Jonathan, Christopher Sung and Min Suh Lee, co-eds. *Comfort Women: New Perspectives*. San Francisco: Blurb Publisher, 2019.

Kim-Gibson, Dai Sil. *Silence Broken: Korean Comfort Women*. Parkersburg, Iowa: Mid-Prairie books, 1999.

Howard, Keith, ed. *True Stories of the Korean Comfort Women: Testimonies*. NY: Cassell, 1995.

Lee, Na-Young. "The Korean Women's Movement of Japanese Military 'Comfort Women': Navigating Between Nationalism and Feminism" in *Feminist Theory Reader: Local and Global Perspectives,* edited by Carole R. McCann and Seung-Kyung Kim, 576-585. New York: Routledge, 2017.

Min, Pyong Gap, Thomas Chung, and Sejung Sage Yim, ed. *Japanese Military Sexual Slavery: The Transnational Redress Movement for The Victims.* Berlin, Boston: De Gruyter, 2020.

Norma, Carolina. *The Japanese Comfort Women and Sexual Slavery During the China and Pacific Wars.* New York: Bloomsbury, 2016.

Pilzer, Joshua. *Hearts of Pine: Songs in the Lives of Three Korean Survivors of the Japanese Comfort Women.* Oxford: Oxford University Press, 2012.

Qui, Peipei, Su Zhiliang, and Chen Lifei. *Chinese Comfort Women.* New York: Oxford University Press, 2013.

Ruff O'Herne, Jan. *50 Years of Silence.* Sydney: Editions Tom Thompson, 1994.

Rumiko, Nishino, Kim Puja, and Onozawa Akane, co-eds. *Denying the Comfort Women: The Japanese State's Assault on Historical Truth.* Abingdon, Oxon, England: Routledge, 2018.

Savage, Kirk. *Monument Wars.* Berkeley, Los Angeles and London: University of California Press, 2009.

Schellstede, Sangmie Choi, ed. *Comfort Women Speak: Testimony by Sex Slaves of the Japanese Military.* New York: Holmes and Meier, 2000.

Shin, Gi-Wook and Daniel Sneider, *Divergent Memories: Opinion Leaders and the Asia-Pacific War.* Stanford, California: Stanford University Press, 2016.

Soh, Ok Cha and Lane Evans, "Legislation on 'Comfort Women' in the US Congress." *Forced Prostitution in Times of War and Peace: Sexual Violence against Women and Girls,* edited by Barbara Drinck and Chung-noh Gross, 288–292. Bielefeld: Kleine Verlag, 2007.

Soh, Sarah. *The Comfort Women: Sexual Violence and Postcolonial Memory in Korea and Japan.* Chicago: University of Chicago Press, 2008.

Son, Elizabeth W. *Embodied Reckonings: "Comfort Women," Performance, and Transpacific Redress.* Ann Arbor: University of Michigan Press, 2018.

Stetz, Margaret and Bonnie Oh, ed. *Legacies of the Comfort Women of World War II.* Armonk, New York: M.E. Sharpe, 2001.

Stetz, Margaret. "Reframing the 'Comfort Women' Issue: New Representations of an Old War Crime." In *Genocide and Mass Violence in Asia: An Introductory Reader,* series of Genocide and Mass

Violence in the Age of Extremes. Vol.1, edited by Frank Jacob, 61–77. Munich: De Gruyter Oldenbourg, 2019.

Stetz, Margaret. "Teaching about the 'Comfort System' of World War II: The Hidden Stories of Girls." *War and Sexual Violence: New Perspectives in a New Era*, edited by Sarah K. Danielsson, 35–50. Ferdinand Schoningh: 2019.

Tanaka, Yuki. *Japan's Comfort Women: The Military and Involuntary Prostitution During War and Occupation: Asia's Transformations.* NY: Routledge, 2002.

Ward, Thomas J and William D. Lay. *Park Statue Politics: World War II Comfort Women Memorials in the United States.* Bristol, England: E-International Relations Publishing, 2019.

Yamazaki, Tomoko. *Sandakan Brothel No. 8: An episode of the history of the lower-class Japanese Women.* Translated by Karen Colligan-Taylor. Armonk, NY: M. E. Sharpe, 1999.

Yang, Hyunah. "Re-membering the Korean Military Comfort Women: Nationalism, Sexuality, and Silencing." In *Dangerous Women: Gender and Korean Nationalism*, edited by Elaine H. Kim and Chungmoo Choi. New York: Routledge, 1998.

Yoon, Mee-Hyang. *25 Years of Wednesdays.* Translated by Lee, Koeun. Seoul: The Korean Council for Justice and Remembrance for the Issues of Military Sexual Slavery by Japan, 2019.

Yoshimi, Yoshiaki. *Sexual Slavery in the Japanese Military During World War II.* Translated by Suzanne O'Brien. New York: Columbia University Press, 1995.

## Articles in Journals

Akane, Onozawa "The Comfort Women and State Prostitution." *The Asia-Pacific Journal Japan Focus* 16: 10, no. 1 (May 2018). https://apjjf.org/2018/10/Onozawa.html

Argibay, Carmen M. "Sexual Slavery and the Comfort Women of World War II." *Berkeley Journal of International Law* 21: 2 (2003). https://lawcat.berkeley.edu/record/1118669

Arudou, Debito. "U.S. author recounts 'lecture' he got about 'comfort women' from uninvited Japanese guests." *Chinese American Forum* 30, no. 4 (April-June 2015), Except from Japan Times (March 2015): 35–37. http://caforumonline.net/CAFHandlerPDF.ashx?ID=409

Bisland, Beverly Milner (Lee), Jimin Kim, and Sunghee Shin. "Teaching about the Comfort Women during World War II and the Use of Personal Stories of the Victims." *Asian Literature in the Humanities and the Social Science* 24, no.3 (Winter 2019): 58–63. https://www.asianstudies.org/publications/eaa/archives/teaching-about-the-comfort-women-during-world-war-ii-and-the-use-of-personal-stories-of-the-victims/

Choi, Chungmoo, ed. "The Comfort Women: Colonialism, War, and Sex." Special Issue of *Positions: East Asia Cultures Critique* 5. No. 1 (Spring 1997).

Chuh, Kandice. "Discomforting Knowledge: Or, Korean 'Comfort Women' and Asian Americanist Critical Practice." *Journal of Asian American Studies* 6, no. 1 (February 2003): 5–23. https://muse.jhu.edu/article/49215

Dudden, Alexis. "We Came to Tell the Truth: Reflection on the Tokyo Women's Tribunal." *Critical Asian Studies* 33, no. 4 (December 2001): 591–602. https://www.tandfonline.com/doi/pdf/10.1080/146727101760107451?needAccess=true

Dudden, Alexis and K. Mizoguchi. "Abe's Violent Denial: Japan's Prime Minister and the 'Comfort Women.'" *The Asia-Pacific Journal Japan Focus* 5:3 (March 2007). https://apjjf.org/-Alexis-Dudden/2368/article.html

Harlow, Kristance. "Let Us Heal: On Surviving and the Controversial 'Comfort Woman.'" *Rewire. News* (April 2017). https://rewire.news/article/2017/04/04/let-us-heal-on-surviving-comfort-woman/

Hasunuma, Linda and Mary M McCarthy. "Creating a Collective Memory of the Comfort Women in the USA." *International Journal of Politics, Culture, and Society* 32, no. 2 (June 2019): 145 -162. https://www.researchgate.net/publication/329103095_Creating_a_Collective_Memory_of_the_Comfort_Women_in_the_USA

Hwang, Wonjae, Cho Wonbin, and Krista Wiegand. "Do Korean-Japanese historical disputes generate rally effects?" *Journal of Asian Studies* 77, no.3 (August 2018): 693–711.

Kang, Hyun Yi. "Conjuring 'Comfort Women': Mediated Affiliations and Disciplined Subjects in Korean/American Transnationality." *Journal of Asian American Studies* 6, no.1 (February 2003): 25–55. https://muse.jhu.edu/article/49217/pdf

Kang, Sung Hyun. "The U.S. Army Photography and the 'Seen Side' and 'Blind Side' of the Japanese Military Comfort Women: The Still Pictures and Motion Pictures of the Korean Comfort Girls in Myitkyina, Sungshan, and Tengchung." *Korea Journal* 59, no. 2 (Summer 2019): 144–176.

Kim, Mikyoung. "Memorializing Comfort Women: Memory and Human Rights in Korea-Japan Relations." *Asian Politics and Policy* 6, Issue 1 (November 2014): 83–96.
Memorializing Comfort Women: Memory and Human Rights in Korea-Japan Relations

Koyama, Emi. "The U.S. as 'Major Battleground' for 'Comfort Women' Revisionism: The Screening of Scottsboro Girls at Central Washington University." *The Asia-Pacific Journal Japan Focus* 13: 22, no.2 (June 2015). https://apjjf.org/Emi-Koyama/4324.html

Knop, Karen and Annelise Riles. "Space, Time, and Historical Injustice: A Feminist Conflict-of-laws Approach to the 'Comfort Women' Agreement." *Cornell Law Review* 102: 4 (May 2017): 853–927. https://scholarship.law.cornell.edu/cgi/viewcontent.cgi?article=4726&context=clr

Ku, Yangmo. "National Interest or Transnational Alliances? Japanese Policy on the Comfort Women Issue." *Journal of East Asian Studies* 15, no. 2 (May-August 2015): 243–69. https://www.cambridge.org/core/journals/journal-of-east-asian-studies/article/national-interest-or-transnational-alliances-japanese-policy-on-the-comfort-women-issue/FF362B60B3F74DF2480875E2A6DE02C3

Ku, Yangmo. "Privatized foreign policy? Explaining the Park Geun-hye administration's decision-making process." *Korea Journal* 59, no.1 (Spring 2019):106–134.

Lee, Na-young. "War and Women's Human Rights Museum: narrative museum, emotional space." *Public History & Museum* [Seoul] 1 (Dec 2018): 90–97.

Madsen, Deborah. "Nora Okja Keller's Comfort Woman and the Ethics of Literary Trauma." *Concentric: Literary and Cultural Studies* 33, no. 2 (September 2007): 81–97. http://www.concentric-literature.url.tw/issues/Ethics%20and%20Ethnicity/5.pdf

McCarthy, Mary M. "US Comfort Women Memorials: Vehicles for Understanding and Change." *Asia Pacific Bulletin at East-West Center*, no. 275 (August 2014). https://www.eastwestcenter.org/publications/us-comfort-women-memorials-vehicles-understanding-and-change

McCarthy, Mary M. "How the Japan-Korea Comfort Women Debate Plays out in the US." *The Diplomat* (August 2017). https://thediplomat.com/2017/08/how-the-japan-korea-comfort-women-debate-plays-out-in-the-us/

McDougall, Gay. "Addressing State Responsibility for the Crime of Military Sexual Slavery During the Second World War: Further Attempts for Justice for the 'Comfort Women.'" *The Korean Journal of International and Comparative Law* 1 (2013): 137–165.

Min, Pyong Gap. "Korean 'Comfort Women': The Intersection of Colonial Power, Gender, and Class." *Gender and Society* 17, no. 6 (December 2003): 938–957.

Min, Pyong Gap. "Controversies over Park Yu-ha's book." *Georgetown Journal of Asian Affairs* 3, no.2 (Spring 2017): 58–66.

Morris-Suzuki, Tessa. "Abe's WWII Statement Fails History 101." *East Asia Form* (August 2015). https://www.eastasiaforum.org/2015/08/18/abes-wwii-statement-fails-history-101/

Rooney, Sierra. "The Politics of Shame: The Glendale Comfort Women Memorial and the Complications of Transnational Commemorations." *de arte* 53: 2-3 (December 2018): 86–102. https://www.tandfonline.com/doi/abs/10.1080/00043389.2018.1481914

Son, Elizabeth W. "Transpacific Acts of Memory: The Afterlives of Hanako." *Theatre Survey* 57: 2 (May 2016): 264-274. https://www.cambridge.org/core/journals/theatre-survey/article/transpacific-acts-of-memory-the-afterlives-of-hanako/DCD2592012F324509B2FB0F3BC35FB07

Tokudome, Kinue. "Passage of H.Res. 121 on 'Comfort Women', the US Congress and Historical Memory in Japan." *The Asia-Pacific Journal Japan Focus* 5: 8 (August 2007). https://apjjf.org/-Kinue-TOKUDOME/2510/article.html

Wang, Edward, ed. "The Study of 'Comfort Women': Revealing a hidden Past – introduction." *Chinese Studies in History* 53, no. 1 (winter 2020): 1–5. The volume published by Philadelphia: Routledge (Taylor & Francis Group).

Watanabe, Kazuko. "Trafficking in Women's Bodies, Then and Now: The Issue of Military 'Comfort Women.'" *Women's Studies Quarterly* 27, no. 1/2 (Spring/Summer 1999): 19–31.

Yamaguchi Tomomi. "Revisionism, Utlranationalism, Sexism: Relations Between the Far Right and the Establishment over the 'CW Issue.'" *Social Science Japan Journal* 21, no.2 (Summer 2018): 193–212. https://academic.oup.com/ssjj/article-abstract/21/2/193/5054706?redirectedFrom=fulltext

Yamaguchi Tomomi. "The 'History Wars' and the 'Comfort Women' Issue: Revisionism and the Right-wing in Contemporary Japan and the U.S." Translated by Miho Matsugu. Introduction by Alexis Dudden. *The Asia-Pacific Journal Japan Focus* 18: 6, No. 3 (March 15, 2020). https://apjjf.org/2020/6/Yamaguchi.html

Yang, Ching Ja. "Are You Listening to the Voices of the Victims? My Critique of Park Yuha's Comfort Women of the Empire." *The Asia-Pacific Journal Japan Focus* 14: 17, no.1 (Sep 2016): 1–11.

## Media Articles

Constable, Pamela. "70 Years later, a Korean 'Comfort Women' demands apology from Japan." *The Washington Post*, April 22, 2015. https://www.washingtonpost.com/local/70-years-later-a-korean-comfort-woman-demands-apology-from-japan/2015/04/22/d1cf8794-e7ab-11e4-9767-6276fc9b0ada_story.html

Constante, Agnes. "New teacher's guide on 'comfort women' to be distributed across California schools." *NBC News, Asian America*, January 15, 2019. https://www.nbcnews.com/news/asian-america/new-teacher-s-guide-comfort-women-be-distributed-across-california-n959021

Faleomavaega, Eni F.H. "Time for Japan to apologize." *The Hill*, March 10, 2015. https://thehill.com/blogs/congress-blog/foreign-policy/235134-time-for-japan-to-apologize

Han, Sol and James Griffiths. "Why this statue of a young girl caused a diplomatic incident." *CNN World*, February 5, 2017. https://www.cnn.com/2017/02/05/asia/south-korea-comfort-women-statue/index.html

Japanese Lobby on "Comfort Women." *Newstapa*, July 18, 2019. https://newstapa.org/44187

Kotler, Mindy. "The Comfort Women and Japan's War on Truth." *The New York Times,* November 11, 2014. https://www.nytimes.com/2014/11/15/opinion/comfort-women-and-japans-war-on-truth.html

Lee, Jung-Sil. "The Future of the 'Comfort Women' Movement." *Washington Times,* October 14, 2015. https://www.washingtontimes.com/news/ 2015/oct/14/jungsil-lee-the-future-of-the-comfort-women-movement/

Lee, Woo-young. "Comfort Women Statues Magnet for Koreans." *The Korea Herald,* March 3, 2016. http://kpopherald.koreaherald.com/view.php?ud=201603031719352657027_2

Levine, Brittany and Jason Wells. "Glendale Unveils Comfort Women Statue, Honors Innocent Victims." *LA Times,* July 30, 2013. https://www.latimes.com/local/lanow/la-me-ln-glendale-comfort-women-20130730-story.html

Levine, Brittany. "Lawsuit seeks removal of Glendale Comfort Women statue." *LA Times,* February 22, 2014. https://www.latimes.com/local/lanow/la-xpm-2014-feb-22-la-me-ln-glendale-comfort-women-statue-sparks-lawsuit-20140222-story.html

Nikkei Asian Review Staff Writers. "Japan's New US Envoy Eyes Removal of 'Comfort Women' Statues," *Nikkei Asian Review,* February 16, 2018. https://asia.nikkei.com/Politics/International-relations/Japan-s-new-US-envoy-eyes-removal-of-comfort-women-statues

Olivo, Antonio. "Memorial to WWII Comfort Women Dedicated in Fairfax County amid Protests." *The Washington Post,* May 30, 2014. https://www.washingtonpost.com/local/memorial-to-wwii-comfort-women-dedicated-in-fairfax-county/2014/05/30/730a1248-e684-11e3-a86b-362fd5443d19_story.html

Seidman, Lila. "Down the Street from Vandalized Comfort Women Statue Is an Exhibit Honoring the Women." *LA Times,* August 1, 2019. https://www.latimes.com/socal/glendale-news-press/news/story/2019-08-01/comfort-women-memorial

Tiron, Roxana. "Korean-American Seek Resolution on Sex Slavery." *The Hill,* September 27, 2006.

Yanghee Jang. "25th Anniversary of Washington Coalition for Comfort Women Issues." *Voice of America,* December 21, 2017. https://www.voakorea.com/a/4175404.html

# R.6. LIST OF ACADEMIC CONFERENCES ON "COMFORT WOMEN" ISSUES IN THE U.S.

(Jung-Sil Lee, Jaeyop Kang, Yujin Jeong, Seunghyun Min, Taeeun Uhm)

**1996**    **September 30:** "Comfort Women of WWII, Lessons and Legacies," keynote speaker Mutsuko Miki, Bunn Intercultural Center, Georgetown University, film screening of *In the Name of the Emperor* by Christine Choy and Nancy Tong (Sept. 30); *The Murmuring* by Byun Young-ju (Oct. 1); *Camp Arirang* by Diana Lee (Oct.2); *The Women Outside* by Hye Jung Park and J. T. Takagi (Oct. 2), co-sponsored by Georgetown University, the Washington Coalition for Comfort Women Issues (WCCW), and the Korea Society.

**1999**    **May 26:** "The International Comfort Women Movement for Redress: Korean American Students Conference XIII," keynote speaker Chunghee Sarah Soh, A3C Couchroom at Stanford University, co-sponsored by Stanford Women's Coalition, KASCON XIII, AASA, PASU, SUN, TCS.
http://klamath.stanford.edu/~molinero/calendus/AASA/read/event_4714_AASA_read.html

**2002**    **November:** Symposium on "Comfort Women" at Brown University. A former "comfort women," Hwang Keum-ju joined from Korea. Co-sponsored the Asian Studies of Brown University and WCCW.
https://www.brown.edu/Student_Services/Asian_American_Student_Services/docs/visions vol4iss1.pdf

**2007**    **February 15**: "Interdisciplinary Conference on Human Trafficking and Protecting the Human Rights of Comfort Women," University of Nebraska.
https://digitalcommons.unl.edu/humantrafficking/

**2009**    **July 30:** "War & Women's Human Rights," International Conference for the second anniversary of the passage of House Resolution 121, George Washington University Marvin Center, co-sponsored by WCCW and The Korean Council.

**2012**    **December 1:** Symposium "Korean/Asian Comfort Women Issues Then and Now: Tracing the Historical, Political, and Cultural Aspects of the Comfort Women Movement in the U.S. and South Korea" along with art exhibition *Unveiling the Truth: The Sorrow and Hope of "Comfort Women"* and film screening of *Silence Broken* by Dai Sil Kim-Gibson to celebrate the 20th anniversary of WCCW, Atrium and Edwin Messe III Conference Room, Mason Hall, GMU, co-sponsored by WCCW and George Mason University.

**2014**    **September 18:** "Asia Transforming: Old Values and New Presences," "Remembering War Atrocities and Sex Trafficking in East Asia," "Breaking the Silence on Wartime Sexual Violence in the Asia-Pacific War," Hofstra University, Film Screening: Song of the Reed. Rochelle and Irwin A. Lowenfeld Conference and Exhibition Hall Joan and Donald E. Axinn Library:

https://news.hofstra.edu/2014/09/17/asia-transforming-tackles-the-tragic-history-of-comfort-women-sept-18/ Full conference information. https://www.hofstra.edu/pdf/community/culctr/culctr-asia-conference-schedule.pdf

**November 25:** "The Sorrow and Hope of 'Comfort Women'" Seminar and Exhibition, keynote speaker Rep. Mike Honda, The May Gallery of Mullen Library, Catholic University of America, co-sponsored by WCCW and Center for International Social Development (CISD) of National Catholic School of social Service.

2015   **January 17:** "Experiences of Korean Sex Slavery in the Japanese Comfort Women System during World War II, La Galeries 4, Second Floor, New Orleans Marriott, sponsored by Society for Social Work and Research (SSWR). https://sswr.confex.com/sswr/2015/webprogram/Paper24206.html

**March 31:** "The Uncomfortable Facts About Korean Comfort Women," Brigham Young University, Department of History, The Annual Mary Lou Fulton Mentored Research Conference. https://scholarsarchive.byu.edu/cgi/viewcontent.cgi?referer=https://www.google.com/&httpsredir=1&article=1265&context=fhssconference_studentpub

**May 1:** "Integrity of Memory: 'Comfort Women' in Focus," organized by Dr. Eunah Lee, one day workshop combined with art exhibition, panels, and breakout sessions. A keynote address by Uemura Takashi, Marquette University, Milwaukee, sponsored by the Center for Transnational Justice workshop and the Helen Way Klingler College of Arts & Sciences. https://www.marquette.edu/transnational-justice/workshops-and-conferences.php

**December 29:** Seminar *"Accurate History Writing"* in the WCCW annual meeting, speakers Dennis Halpin and Mindy Kotler. Korea-U.S. Science Cooperation Center, Vienna, VA.

2016   **May 2:** "History Writing: For Justice and Reconciliation of Comfort Women," The Sigur Center for Asian Studies at the George Washington University, Lindner Commons, co-organized and co-sponsored by WCCW, The Sigur Center for Asian Studies, and the Department of History of George Washington University.

**October 17:** "Collateral Damage: Wartime Atrocity and Trauma Conference," The Anya and Andrew Shiva Gallery, John Jay College of Criminal Justice, organized by WCCW and co-sponsored by WCCW, John Jay College of Criminal Justice, City University of New York, and Northeast Asian History Foundation. http://shivagallery.org/portfolio/symposium-collateral-damage-wartime-atrocity-and-trauma/

2017   **March 23–25:** "The National Association of Ethnic Studies Conference," Asian American Studies, San Francisco State University. https://aas.sfsu.edu/content/aas-faculty-and-students-present-national-association-ethnic-studies-conference

**June 1–4:** "Difficult Conversations: Thinking and Talking about Women, Genders, and Sexualities Inside and Outside the Academy," The Seventeenth Berkshire Conference on the History of Women, Genders, and Sexuality, Hofstra University; June 1, "Exploring Issues of Documenting and Preserving Survivors' Testimonies of Wartime Sexual Violence," chaired by Yuki Terazawa; June 2, "Comfort Women: Two Systems of Sexual Slavery and Historical Revisionism," chaired by Yukiko Hanawa; June 3, "Narrative, Appropriation, and Styles of Objectivity When Confronting Sex Crimes Against Humanity," chaired by Jung-Sil Lee. https://news.hofstra.edu/2017/04/05/worldwide-womens-history-event-comes-to-hofstra/

**October 13–14:** "The Redress Movement for the Victims of Japanese Military Sexual Slavery: Looking Back at the 27-year Movement," WCCW presents "Tracing the Twenty-five Years of Comfort Women Movement in the U.S.," The 8th Annual Conference of Research Center for Korean Community, Queens College, Rosenthal Library Auditorium. Organized by the Research Center for Korean community at Queens College. Co-sponsored by Research Foundation for Korean Community, The Academy of Korean Studies, and Queens College of CUNY. https://www.qc.cuny.edu/communications/news_services/releases/Pages/NewsArchive.aspx?ItemID=1900; https://www.koreanamericandatabank.org/images/PDF/Conference-Schedule_10-08-17.pdf

**2018**    **February 23:** "Unforeseen Controversy: Reconciliation and Re-contextualization through Comfort Women Memorials in the U.S." Jung-Sil Lee presented in the session *Teachable Monuments: Using Public Art to Spark Dialogue and Address Controversies* (PAD: Public Art Dialogue) at "College Art Association (CAA) conference," Los Angeles, LA Convention Center. https://conference2018.collegeart.org/programs/teachable-monuments-using-public-art-to-spark-dialogue-and-address-controversies/

**March 25:** *Representing the Unrepresentable: "Comfort Women" in Literature, Film, and Art* in the panel for "Association of Asian Studies (AAS) annual conference," "Artist as a Reporter: Appropriation the Past in the archival materials" presented by Jung-Sil Lee, Washington DC. https://www.asianstudies.org/wp-content/uploads/AAS-AC-2018-Program.pdf

**October 19–20:** "Comfort Women: The Legacy of Sexual Slavery in Asia," University of Pittsburgh, Asian Studies Center. https://www.ucis.pitt.edu/asc/events/legacy-of-comfort-women

**November 9–10:** "Weaponizing People: Militarization and Armed Conflict in Asia," Binghamton University downtown center. https://www.binghamton.edu/iaad/conference/schedule_acon.pdf

**2019**    **February 15:** "Appropriating, Reporting, and Re-Contexualizing of Wartime Sex Crimes by Female Artists" in *Has anyone ever seen an image of war? Reassessing the visual culture of war and related disasters, violence, and torture in the modern and contemporary moment* (panel title), "College Art Association (CAA) Conference." https://caa.confex.com/caa/2019/meetingapp.cgi/Session/1730

# R.7. THE LIST OF ARCHIVAL / VISUAL ART EXHIBITIONS OF "COMFORT WOMEN" ISSUES IN THE U.S.

(Jung-Sil Lee)

| | |
|---|---|
| **1995** | **April/May**: First WCCW archival document exhibition and the film screening of "Comfort Women" video at the United Methodist Building, near the U.S. Capitol and the Supreme Court. |
| | **August**: WCCW attended the "Fourth UN World Conference on Women in Beijing," Organized archival exhibition and the film screening of "Comfort Women" video. |
| | **November**: WCCW archival exhibition and screening of "Comfort Women" video at the Korean American Women U.N. Seminar, New York. |
| **1998** | **June 1–June 4:** WCCW organized archival exhibition "Comfort Women of World War II: An Indisputable Tragedy," Cannon House Office Building Rotunda on Capitol Hill. |
| **1999** | **March 3–May 3**: WCCW archival exhibition "Comfort Women of World War II" at the Free Library of Philadelphia. |
| **2000** | **October 6–October 12**: *Comfort Women Share Experiences*, art works created by "comfort women" during art therapy sessions, Barnard College, James Room, New York, co-sponsored by Barnard college, the East Asian Institute at the School of International and Public Affairs, Young Koreans United, and the New York Alliance for Peace and Reunification of Korea. |
| **2001** | **November:** WCCW co-sponsored forum/archival exhibition on "Comfort Women" joined by Cornell University, Harvard University, Yale, New York University, Princeton University, and Georgetown University. |
| **2002** | **January 26–April 28:** *Strange Fruit: New Paintings by Hung Liu* (cover image of this volume) Arizona State University Art Museum, Tempe, Arizona. Curator: Heather Lineberry, senior curator of ASU Art Museum, ASU Art Museum. |
| | **March**: WCCW organized mid-west "Comfort Women" tour of seminars/ archival exhibitions held at University of Wisconsin, Northwestern University, Ohio State University and University of Michigan. |
| | **April:** Sino-Japanese War Memorial Exhibit & Panel Discussion, "Comfort Women and Labor" co-hosted by American University and WCCW. |
| | **June 1–August 4:** *Strange Fruit: New Paintings by Hung Liu*, Boise Art Museum, Boise, Idaho. Curator: Heather Lineberry, senior curator of ASU Art Museum, ASU Art Museum. http://www.hungliu.com/comfort-women.html |

**2002–2003**  **October 27, 2002–October 23, 2003**: *Strange Fruit: New Paintings by Hung Liu*, Laguna Art Museum, Laguna Beach, CA. Curator: Heather Lineberry, senior curator of ASU Art Museum, ASU Art Museum.

**2003**  **March 8–May 4:** *Strange Fruit: New Paintings by Hung Liu*, Croker Art Museum, Sacramento. CA, Curator: Heather Lineberry, senior curator of ASU Art Museum, ASU Art Museum.

**2004**  **September:** *Comfort Women: Line of Violence* Art Exhibit at Georgetown University, installation by Andrew Ward and film *Silence Broken* by Dai Sil Kim-Gibson screened.

**2008**  *Comfort Women Wanted*, Installation of Public Art by Chang-Jin Lee in New York City, New York.

**2009**  **July 31–August 31**: *Ad-like Billboard*, installation work by Chang-Jin Lee, The Incheon Women Artists' Biennale, South Korea.  https://www.changjinlee.net/comfort-women-wanted/incheon-women-artists-biennale-korea/

**2010**  **October 14**: *Come From the Shadows: Comfort Women*, Steve Cavallo and Sei Ryun Chun and other artists, the Palisades Park Library.

**2011–2012**  **November 18, 2011–January 20, 2012**: *Comfort Women Wanted*, Installation work by Chang-Jin Lee, Spaces Gallery, Cleveland, Ohio.

**2012**  **November 26–December 14**: Art exhibition *Unveiling the Truth: The Sorrow and Hope of "Comfort Women"* Mason Hall Atrium Gallery, George Mason University, Curator: Jung-Sil Lee, co-organized by WCCW and George Mason University.

**2013**  **March 27–August 2**: Ahn Sehong, Photography of Comfort Women, Korea Press Center, Palisades Park, NJ. https://lens.blogs.nytimes.com/2013/03/27/a-wars-cold-comfort-in-china/

**May 6–October 2013**: *Comfort Women Wanted*, Installed Public Art by Chang-Jin Lee in New York City, New York, sponsored by New York City Department of Transportation.

**May 29**: *Comfort Women Wanted (video)*, by Chang-Jin Lee, Hauser & Wirth Gallery, New York, New York, sponsored by Hudson Valley MOCA.

**September 25**: *Comfort Women Wanted (video)*, by Chang-Jin Lee, Columbia University, New York, New York, Sponsor: Columbia University Center for Korean Research (CKR).

**November 1–December 1**: *Comfort Women Wanted*, by Chang-Jin Lee, Wood Street Galleries, Pittsburgh, PA.

| 2014 | **July 10–Sepember 14**: *Seowoon Jung (1924-2004) Life of Comfort Women,* Artpace San Antonio, San Antonio, TX. Curator: N'Gone Fall. Organized by Artpace San Antonio. https://artpace.org/works/iair/iair_summer_2014/seowoon-jung-1924-2004 |
|---|---|

**September 18, 2014–January 10, 2015**: *Comfort Women Wanted,* by Chang-Jin Lee, Charles D. Wang Center, Stony Brook University, Stony Brook, New York.

**November 25**: Art exhibition *The Sorrow and Hope of "Comfort Women."* The May Gallery of Mullen Library, Catholic University of America. Curator: Jung-Sil Lee, co-sponsored by WCCW and Center for International Social Development (CISD) of National Catholic School of social Service.

| 2015 | **February 17–April 3**: *Of Human Bondage,* works on Comfort Women of Steve Cavallo, Anya & Andrew Shiva Gallery, John Jay College of Criminal Justice. Curator: Thalia Vrachopoulos. |
|---|---|

**September 5–November 1**: *Forgotten Faces: the Comfort Women of World War II,* Fullerton Museum Center, Fullerton, CA. https://www.cityoffullerton.com/gov/departments/museum/exhibits/details/forgotten_faces_the_comfort_women_of_world_war_ii.asp

| 2016 | **September 8–October 21**: WCCW organized art exhibition *Collateral Damage* at The Anya and Andrew Shiva Gallery at John Jay College of Criminal Justice, City University of New York, New York. Performance by Shine Shin Kim and choreographer Chanmee Chung. Curators: Jung-Sil Lee and Thalia Vrachopoulos, co-sponsored by WCCW, John Jay College of Criminal Justice, City University of New York. http://shivagallery.org/portfolio/collateral-damage/ |
|---|---|

| 2017 | **July–September**: WCCW president Jung-Sil Lee curated the exhibition *Truth: Promises for Peace,* Seoul, a travelling exhibition in Seoul, Jeonjoo, Daejeon, and Daegu in Korea. WCCW collaborated in gathering historical materials and photography. Sponsored by Ministry of Gender Equality and Family. http://www.mogef.go.kr/nw/enw/nw_enw_s001d.do?mid=mda700&bbtSn=705216 |
|---|---|

**July 20–September 3**: *Do the Right Thing: (dis)comfort women,* ReflectSpace Gallery, Downtown Central Library, Glendale, CA.

| 2018 | **July 28–September 11**: *Do the Right Thing: Comfort Women Resist,* ReflectSpace Gallery, Downtown Central Library, Glendale, CA, Curator: Ara & Anahid Oshagan and Monica Hye Yeon Jun. |
|---|---|

**September 7–September 20**: *"Comfort Women"* Photo Exhibition of Kenji G.Taguma, San Francisco State Building.

**September 22–October 19**: City College of San Francisco Chinatown Campus, sponsored by California State Assemblyman Phil Ting (D-San Francisco) & Assemblyman David Chiu (D-San Francisco).

**September 16–September 22**: *Truth & Justice: Remembering "Comfort Women,"* Manilatown Heritage Foundation, co-organized by The Korean Council and Education for Social Justice Foundation (ESJF). http://www.e4sjf.org/blog/archives/09-2018

**October 19–November 15**: *The Comfort Women Project*, Menlo College Administration Building, Menlo College, Curator/Artist: Rose Camastro-Pritchett. https://www.menlo.edu/news/the-comfort-women-project-art-exhibition/

2019     **May 28–December 1**: *Korean Comfort Women and the U.S. Discoveries*, University of California, Irvine, Science Library, CA, Curator: Dr. Ying Zhang, Research Librarian Asian Studies, and UCI Libraries' Korea Foundation Library Intern Sukim Bae, Sponsor: UCI Libraries. https://news.uci.edu/2019/06/18/uci-libraries-host-exhibit-on-korean-comfort-women/

        **July 12–August 29**: *1 in 3: Sexual Violence Pandemic*, ReflectSpace Gallery, Downtown Central Library, Glendale, CA, Curator: Ara & Anahid Oshagan, with guest curator Monica Hye Yoen Jun from S. Korea, and in collaboration with Glenn Ruga of Social Documentary Network, sponsored by City of Glendale Library, Arts & Culture Department, the 8th Annual Commemoration of "COMFORT WOMAN DAY" in Glendale Organizing Committee, and the Korea-Glendale Sister City Association. https://www.glendaleca.gov/government/departments/library-arts-culture/reflectspace.

2020     **February 27–March 26**: *Historical Trauma*, Maya's Gallery, Silliman College, Yale University, Curator: Margaret Sun. organized by STAND with "Comfort Women," Yale student organization. https://yaledailynews.com/blog/2020/02/25/exhibition-surveys-historical-trauma-through-art/

# R.8. LIST OF "COMFORT WOMEN" MEMORIALS IN THE U.S.

(Jung-Sil Lee)

| Memorial (Statue of Peace) | Details | |
|---|---|---|
| Memorial #1 | Unveiling | October 23, 2010 (3rd anniversary of the passage H.Res. 121) |
| | Location | Palisades Park, Bergen County Library |
| | Address | 257 2nd Street, Palisades Park, New Jersey 09650 |
| | Organizer | KAVC (KACE), Steve Cavallo, Jason Kim |
| | Resolution | **Senate Concurrent Resolution (SCR 124)** |
| | Contact | Steve Cavallo |
| Memorial #2 | Unveiling | June 18, 2012 |
| | Location | Veterans Memorial, Eisenhower Park, Nassau County |
| | Address | 1899 Hempstead Turnpike, Westbury, New Jersey 11590 |
| | Organizer | Korean American Public Affairs Committee |
| | Contact | David Chulwoo Lee |
| Memorial #3 | Unveiling | March 8, 2013 |
| | Location | Courthouse, Bergen County |
| | Address | 12 Main Street, Hackensack, New Jersey 07601 |
| | Organizer | KAVC (Chejin Park) |
| | | Kathleen Donovan (County Executive) |
| | Resolution | **New Jersey State Resolution 159** |
| | Contact | Comfort Women Memorial Committee |
| Memorial #4 (Statue of Peace #1) | Unveiling | July 30, 2013 |
| | Location | Glendale, Public Library |
| | Address | 291 S. Louise Street, Glendale, California 91205 |
| | Organizer | CARE (former KAFC), Changyeop Lee |
| | Contact | *https://comfortwomenaction.org/about-us/* |

| | | |
|---|---|---|
| Memorial #5 | Unveiling | January 24, 2014 |
| | Location | Veterans Memorial, Eisenhower Park, Nassau County |
| | Address | 1899 Hempstead Turnpike, Westbury, New York 11590 |
| | Organizer | Senator Elaine Phillips (Sponsor) |
| | | Korean American Public Affairs Committee |
| | Resolution | **New York Resolution (J 304)** |
| | Contact | Comfort Women Memorial Committee |
| Memorial #6 | Unveiling | May 30, 2014 |
| | Location | Fairfax County Government Center, Fairfax County |
| | Address | 12000 Government Center Parkway, Fairfax, Virginia 22035 |
| | Organizer | Washington Coalition for Comfort Women Issues, Inc. (WCCW) |
| | Contact | www.comfort-women.org / wccwcontact@gmail.com |
| Memorial #7 | Unveiling | August 4, 2014 |
| | Location | Liberty Plaza, Union City, New Jersey |
| | Address | At the intersection of 30th St. and Palisade Avenue |
| | Organizer | The Commissioner of Public Affairs at Union City, Mayor |
| | | Brian Stack, and State Senator Sandra Cunningham |
| Memorial #8 (Statue of Peace #2) | Unveiling | August 16, 2014 |
| | Location | Southfield, Korean American Cultural Center |
| | Address | 24666 Northwestern HWY, Southfield, Michigan 48075 |
| | Organizer | David Shin, Moonjae Park, Deukyeol Kim (initiators) |
| | Contact | Michigan Korean American Women's Association |
| Memorial #9 (Statue of Peace #3) | Unveiling | June 28, 2017 |
| | Location | Blackburn Park, Brookhaven |
| | Address | 3493 Ashford Dunwoody Road, Atlanta, Georgia 30319 |
| | Organizer | Atlanta Comfort Women Memorial Task Force |
| | Resolution | **Resolution of the City of Brookhaven (RES 2017-05-03)** |
| | Contact | Baik Kyu Kim, Chairman of the Committee Task Force |

| Memorial #10 | Unveiling | July 19, 2017 |
|---|---|---|
| | Location | Cliffside Park, New Jersey |
| | Address | Trinity Episcopal Church, Cliffside Park, New Jersey |
| | Organizer | Bergen County Korean American Association |
| | Contact | Vivian Kim (*jin.viviana@gmail.com*) |
| Memorial #11 | Unveiling | September 22, 2017 |
| | Location | St. Mary's Square Annex, San Francisco |
| | Address | 651 California St., San Francisco, California 94108 |
| | Organizer | Comfort Women Justice Coalition (CWJC) |
| | Resolution | **Resolution No. 158-25A1** |
| | Contact | *https://remembercomfortwomen.org/* |
| Memorial #12 (Statue of Peace #4) | Unveiling | October 13, 2017 |
| | Location | The Museum of Korean American Heritage, New York |
| | Address | 149 West 24th St. 6th fl., New York, New York 10011 |
| | Organizer | Korean American Association of Greater New York |
| | Contact | *office@nykorean.org* |
| Memorial #13 | Unveiling | May 23, 2018 |
| | Location | Constitutional Park, New Jersey |
| | Address | Fletcher Ave & Lewis Street, Fort Lee, New Jersey 07024 |
| | Organizer | Fort Lee High School, Youth Council of Fort Lee |
| | Contact | *youthcouncilfortlee.org / youthcouncilfl@gmail.com* |
| Memorial #14 (Statue of Peace #5) | Unveiling | October 27, 2019 |
| | Location | In front of the The Korea Times Building |
| | Address | 7601 Little River Turnpike, Annandale, Virginia 22003 |
| | Organizer | The DC Committee of Statue of Peace |
| | Contact | *www.comfort-women.org / wccwcontact@gmail.com* |

| | | |
|---|---|---|
| Memorial #15 | Unveiling | March 1, 2020 Unveiling Ceremony (erected on December 7, 2019) |
| (Statue of Peace #6) | Location | Connecticut Korean American Society Building |
| | Address | 2073 State Street, Hamden, Connecticut 06517 |
| | Organizer | Stand with "Comfort Women" at Yale, The Korean American Society of Connecticut |
| | Contact | Minseung Yoo (*minseung.yoo@yale.edu*) |

# R.9. LIST OF SUPPORTING ORGANIZATIONS ON "COMFORT WOMEN" ISSUES

(Jaeheup Kim)

| Country/City | Organizations or Individuals | Website |
|---|---|---|
| **Australia** | | |
| Sydney | Friends of "Comfort Women" | *https://www.facebook.com/sysochu/* |
| Melbourne | Melbourne Comfort Women Memorial Task Force | *https://www.mcwm.org.au/* |
| **Canada** | | |
| Vancouver | ΛLPHA - BC | *http://www.global-alliance.net/* |
| | ALPHA - Canada (Association for Learning & Preserving the History of WWII in Asia) | *https://www.alpha-canada.org/* |
| Edmonton | ALPHA - Edmonton | *https://www.alpha-canada.org/* |
| Toronto | ALPHA - Toronto | *https://www.alpha-canada.org/* |
| Toronto | Hope 21 Korean Progressive Network in Canada | *https://www.apc.org/en/member/korean-progressive-network-jinbonet* |
| Toronto | Nabi Toronto | *https://www.facebook.com/NabiToronto/about* |
| Toronto | Women's Human Rights Education Institute | *https://www.channelfoundation.org/grants/whri/* |
| **China** | | |
| Shanghai | Chinese "Comfort Woman" History Museum | *http://www.warinasia.com/shanghai-normal-university-chinese-comfort-women-museum* |
| Nanjing | Nanjing Liji Lane Comfort Station Site Exhibition Hall | |
| Shanghai | Shanghai Anti-Japanese War Research Association | |
| Shanghai | Shanghai Historical Society | *https://www.historic-shanghai.com/* |
| Shanghai | The Chinese "Comfort Women" Research Center at Shanghai Normal University" | *http://www.warinasia.com/shanghai-normal-university-chinese-comfort-women-museum* |
| Yunnan | Yunnan Longling Donjiagou Comfort Station Site Exhibition Hall" | |

## Germany

| Berlin | Amnesty International Korea Co-Group | *https://www.amnesty.org/en/countries/* |
|---|---|---|
| Berlin | Courage Kim Hak-Soon Action on Reconciliation in the Asia-Pacific Region in Germany | |
| Berlin | Gunhan Coaltion for Peace and Justice | *https://www.cpwj.org/* |
| Berlin | Korea Verband | *https://www.koreaverband.de/* |
| Berlin | Soldaritaet Korean People in Europe | |

## Japan

| Tokyo | Women's Active Museum on War and Peace | *http://museu.ms/museum/details/17567/womens-active-museum-on-war-and-peace-wam* |
|---|---|---|
| Tokyo | Japan Nationwide Action for Resolution of the Japan's Military "Comfort Women" Issue | *https://www.opendemocracy.net/en/5050/japans-military-sexual-slavery-whose-agreement/* |
| Tokyo | Fight for Justice | *http://fightforjustice.info/?lang=en* |

## Korea

| Kwangju | House of Sharing | *http://www.nanum.org/eng/main/index.php* |
|---|---|---|
| Seoul | The Korean Council for Justice and Remembrance for the Issues of Military Sexual Slavery by Japan | *http://womenandwar.net/kr/about-us/* |
| Daegu | Heeum Museum | *http://museum.1945815.or.kr/* |

## Taiwan

| Taipei | AMA Museum | *http://www.twrf.org.tw/amamuseum/* |
|---|---|---|
| Taipei | Taipei Women's Rescue Foundation | *https://www.twrf.org.tw/eng/index.php* |

## USA

| Los Angeles, CA | 3.1 Women's Association, USA | *http://marchfirstusa.org/* |
|---|---|---|
| Cupertino, CA | Alliance for Preserving the Truth of Sino-Japanese War | *http://www.cnd.org/njmassacre/* |
| Los Angeles, CA | ALPHA - LA | *https://www.alpha-canada.org/* |

| | | |
|---|---|---|
| New York, NY | ALPHA - NJ | *https://www.alpha-canada.org/* |
| San Francisco, CA | The Association of Preserving History of WWII in Asia (AOHWA) | *http://www.global-alliance.net/* |
| Atlanta, GA | Atlanta Comfort Women Memorial Task Force | *http://www.ygpm.org/about_en.php* |
| Berkeley, CA | Bataan Legacy Historical Society | *http://bataanlegacy.org/index.html* |
| Monterey Park, CA | C.A.C.A. (Chinese American Citizens Alliance - Greater San Gabriel Valley Lodge | *http://www.cacagreatersangabrielvalley.org/* |
| New York, NY | Coalition Against Trafficking in Women (CATW-International) | *http://www.catwinternational.org/* |
| San Francisco, CA | Comfort Women Justice Coalition (CWJC) | *https://remembercomfortwomen.org/* |
| San Francisco, CA | Eclipse Rising | *http://eclipserising.blogspot.com/* |
| San Francisco, CA | Education for Social Justice Foundation (ESJF) | *http://www.e4sjf.org/* |
| San Diego, CA | Global Alliance for Preserving Historical Accuracy of Foreign Invasions in China (APHAFIC.ORG) | *http://www.aphafic.org/* |
| San Carlos, CA | Global Alliance for Preserving The History of WWII in Asia | *http://www.global-alliance.net/* |
| San Jose, CA | A Heart for Justice | *https://aheartforjustice.com/* |
| Oakland, CA | Japan Multicultural Relief Fund | *http://relief.jprn.org/* |
| New York, NY | Korean American Civic Empowerment (KACE) | *https://us.kace.org/* |
| Los Angeles, CA | Comfort Women Action for Redress & Education (former KAFC) | *https://comfortwomenaction.org/about-us/* |
| Los Angeles, CA | KOWIN - LA | *https://kowinla.org/en/post-797/* |
| Los Angeles, CA | Nabi Fund (LA Nabi) | *https://www.facebook.com/groups/LAnabi* |
| Los Angeles, CA | Nikkei for Civil Rights and Redress (NCRR) | *https://www.ncrr-la.org/index.php* |

| | | |
|---|---|---|
| Atlanta, GA | People in Solidarity with the Families of Sewol Ferry Victims | *https://www.facebook.com/solidarityforsewol* |
| Los Angeles, CA | Progressive Asian Network for Action | *https://b-m.facebook.com/progressiveasians/* |
| San Francisco, CA | Rape of Nanking Redress Coalition (RNRC) | *http://rnrc-us.org/history.htm* |
| Houston, TX | Still Small Voice Houston | *stillsmallvoicehouston@gmail.com* |
| New Haven, CT | Stand with "Comfort Women" | *https://www.yalestatueofpeace.org/* |
| Boston, MA | The Indo Project | *https://theindoproject.org/about/* |
| Dallas, TX | Unforgotten Butterflies | *https://www.facebook.com/unforgottenbutterflies/* |
| Washington, D.C. | Washington Coalition for Comfort Women Issues, Inc. (WCCW) | *http://www.comfort-women.org* |
| Oakland, CA | Women for Genuine Security | *http://www.genuinesecurity.org/* |
| Washington, D.C. | Washington, D.C. Butterfly for Hope | *https://www.facebook.com/groups/1687517071499196/* |
| Fort Lee, NJ | Youth Council of Fort Lee | *https://youthcouncilfortlee.org/* |

# R.10. LIST OF "COMFORT WOMEN" THEMED FILMS

(Edward Jang and Jung-Sil Lee)

**1944 September**: Director: Anonymous American Soldier
Title: ***Comfort Women*** / Category: Film footage / Nation: America
Running time: 0:17 min
Description: "Comfort women" standing in line in Yunnan Province, China. This is the only known footage of "comfort women" in existence.

**1974**: Director: Takamori Ryuichi
Title: ***Military Comfort Women*** / Nation: Japan
Running time: 86 min
Description: "Comfort women" was the euphemism used by the Japanese Imperial Army to refer to sexual slaves during World War II.

**1992**: Director: Wong Gang / Bruce Lee
Title: ***Military Comfort Women*** / Category: Documentary / Nation: China
Running time: 87 min
Description: Tomi Akiyama and her boyfriend Nakamura are troubled about allegations about a Comfort House in China. Tomi gets into the camp, first as a journalist, but is then captured and sent in as a participant.

**1994**: Director: Ned Lander
Title: ***50 Years of Silence*** / Category: Documentary / Nation: Australia
Running time: 57 min
Description: 50 Years of Silence is Jan Ruff-O-Herne's story. It spans five generations from a colonial life in Java, recorded on old home movies, through the war to a new start in England as a young bride and her migration, with her family, to Australia. It shows her extraordinary courage and dignity as she travels to Tokyo to give evidence at an international public hearing. After making headline news throughout the world, Jan continued to Holland to meet with other Dutch women who were similarly enslaved. Inspired by her example they too decided to make their stories public.

**1995**: Director: Christine Choy
Title: ***In the Name of the Emperor*** / Category: Documentary /Nation: American
Running time: 50 min
Description: A matter-of-fact documentary of the massacre of over 300,000 Chinese civilians by the Japanese in the so-called 'Rape of Nanjing' in 1937. In the name of the Japanese Emperor Hirohito, the desperate soldiers, enraged by intense Chinese resistance, stormed the then capital of China and over a six-week period systematically raped, tortured, and killed many of the inhabitants of that city. This is a matter of fact although polemical documentary, with many of the horrifyingly intense images taken from home movies made by an American missionary who was there.

**1995**: Director: Young-Joo Byun
Title: ***The Murmuring*** / Category: Documentary / Nation: Korea
Running time: 98 min

Description: The first installment in Byun Young-joo's trilogy documenting the past and present lives of Korean women and girls who were raped by the Japanese military during World War II.

**1997**: Director: Young-Joo Byun
Title: ***Habitual Sadness*** / Category: Documentary / Nation: Korean
Running time: 56 min

**1999:** Director: Young-Joo Byun
Title: ***My Own Breathing*** / Category: Documentary / Nation: Korea
Running time: 77 min
Description: Some Korean women were forced into sexual slavery by Japan during World War II. Decades later, the survivors attempt to lead normal lives, and gain recognition.

**2000**: Director: Dai Sil Kim-Gibson
Title: ***Silence Broken: Korean Comfort Women*** / Category: Documentary / Nation: American
Running time: 88 min
Description: A powerful and emotional documentary about Korean women forced into sexual servitude by the Japanese Imperial Army during World War II.

**2007**: Director: Zhongyi Ban
Title: ***Gai Shanxi and Her sisters*** / Category: Documentary / Nation: China
Running time: 80 min
Description: Gai Shanxi and Her Sisters (Gai Shan Xi He Ta De Jie Mei Men) tells the story of one woman's brutal ordeal as a "comfort woman" for the Japanese Army during World War II. Hou Dong-E, known as "Gai Shanxi," the fairest woman in China's Shanxi province, was one of the many women abducted from their villages to be sexually enslaved by Japanese soldiers stationed nearby. Fifty years later, she joined other women throughout Asia to seek justice and reparations, but she died before her demands were answered.

**2010:** Director: Frank van Osch / Hilde Janssen
Title: ***Because We Were Beautiful*** /Category: Documentary / Nation: Netherlands, Indonesia
Running time: 60min
Description: "Comfort women" they were called, the young girls who were systematically raped by the Japanese in the Second World War. These women, now in their eighties, have lived their entire life in humiliation and fear of what happened to them. They deserve to be heard, while it's still possible.

**2011**: Director: Tiffany Hsiung
Title: ***Within Every Woman*** / Category: Documentary / Nation: Canada
Running time: 34 min
Description: This documentary film depicts war crimes committed by the Japanese Imperial Army during World War II in Asia. It documents the systematic rape of over 200,000 young girls between the ages of nine and twenty-years-old during World War II in Asia. These atrocities and war crimes occurred between 1931 and 1945; however, to this day, the Japanese Government has not offered an official apology and many survivors still hide their shame.

**2013**: Director: Sylvia Yu Friedman
Title: ***Healing River*** / Category: Documentary / Nation: China
Running time: 20 min
Description: documenting the healing and reconciliation efforts by a Japanese team of Christians as they visited a group of "comfort women" survivors in Qinxian and Wuxiang areas in Shanxi province from 2008 to 2012.

**2013**: Director: Kim Joong-shik
Title: ***"Comfort Women" One Last Cry*** / Category: Documentary / Nation: Korea
Running time: 20 min
Description: This documentary begins in South Korea and moves on to meet victims in Wuhan, China, Shanghai, the Philippines, and Australia.

**2013**: Director: Shupu-den Film
Title: ***Story of Comfort Women*** / Category: Film / Nation: Japan
Running time: 10 min
Description: A sad story of Japanese and Korean women who had to choose to work as sex slaves during the WWII. These women came from poor regions of the Japanese Empire such as the north east region of the Japanese archipelago and southern part of Korean peninsula. Often sold to brothel owners by their parents.

**2013**: Director: Ke Guo
Title: ***Thirty-Two*** / Category: Documentary / Nation: China
Running time: 44 min
Description: December 1944, 24-year-old Wei Shaolan and her one-year-old daughter were seized and sent to a Japanese camp, where Wei was forced to work as a "comfort woman." Despite being physically and mentally abused, Wei unbelievably escaped the heavily guarded 'Comfort Station,' being pregnant, shamed, and unsure of what fate awaited her return home. This documentary presents the true legendary story of Wei Shaolan and follows her traumatic and courageous journey from forced prostitution to life today. 'Real Heroes' are people who can face life bravely even after a tormented life, and Wei's story offers inspiration to those faced with seemingly hopeless adversity.

**2014**: Director: Ki-jun Kim
Title: ***Never Ending Story*** / Category: Animation / Nation: Korea
Running time: 16 min
Description: An animation about the stories of Japanese sex slavery victims. This work stimulates the critical perspectives of the audiences in order to ensure a history-based approach based on facts. Unlike general character animation works which pursue immersion and empathy through the illusion of life that is created by the characters, this work demands the audiences to contemplate historical facts described in the work and make their own judgements. In order to serve these purposes, this work is characterized by its aesthetic properties and elements such as "sympathy," "typification," and "alienation effect." Furthermore, these elements effectively deliver the reality of historical facts that cannot be denied in a chronological narrative. Therefore, this study would sufficiently be of a value in reviewing the diversity in expression and the methodologies used in them, let alone the significance of the theme itself.

**2014**: Director: Sang-Rok Choo
Title: ***Tuning Fork*** / Category: Drama / Nation: Korea
Running time: 105 min
Description: The girl who was taken to China by a lie that she would get a job at a Japanese textile factory. After the end of World War II, they were liberated. However, the girl who could not return to her homeland, became a Korean Chinese grandmother. The only hope for the grandmother is her granddaughter "Hyang-ok (Joan)." Although "Hyang-ok" went to Korea for the first time with her grandma's dream of returning to her hometown, her grandmother is still alone in China and is waiting for her granddaughter's news.

**2015**: Director: Ke Guo
Title: ***Twenty-Two*** / Category: Documentary / Nation: China
Running time: 112 min
Description: An estimated 200,000 Chinese women were forced into prostitution by the Japanese Army during WWII. Only 22 of them remain today to speak out publicly. This documentary is not a film for political gains or narrow nationalistic purposes.

**2016**: Director: Soo-Nam Park
Title: ***Silence*** / Category: Documentary / Nation: Korea
Running time: 90 min
Description: In May 1994, 15 grandmothers came to Japan to ask for their own negotiations with rice and kimchi. This film is a record of the struggle of the victims of "comfort women" who broke away from the silence of half a century and recovered dignity and honor.

**2016**: Director: Tiffany Hsiung
Title: ***The Apology*** / Category: Documentary / Nation: China
Running time: 104 min
Description: This documentary won the 2016 Busan Cinephile Award at the Busan International Film Festival's Vision Awards. *The Apology* follows the personal journeys of three former "comfort women." Grandma Gil in South Korea, Grandma Cao in China, and Grandma Adela in the Philippines are facing their twilight years. In *The Apology* they speak intimately with Hsiung and give their first-hand accounts of the truth for the record, seeking apology.

**2016:** Director: Jo Jung-rae
Title: ***Spirits' Homecoming*** / Category: Film / Nation: Korea
Running time: 127 min
Description: Two Korean girls, Jung-Min (14) and Young-hee (15) are kidnapped by the Japanese Imperial Army and taken to a "Comfort Station" in China. There, they join other kidnapped girls in serving Japanese soldiers as sexual slaves known as "Comfort Women." By the end of the war, only one of the girls survives. Decades later, an elderly lady attempts to reunite with the spirit of her lost friend. Inspired by the testimony and painting by former "comfort woman" Kang Il-chul.

**2017:** Director: Na Jung Lee
Title: ***Snowy Road*** / Category: Drama / Nation: Korea
Running time: 121 min

Description: Two girls "Young Ae" and "Jongbun" faced the same fate, a hellish war and "Young Ae" makes a dangerous decision to end the terrible reality.

**2017**: Director: Jun-ki Kim
Title: *For Her* / Category: Animation / Nation: Korea
Running time: 14 min
Description: A Japanese Army grandfather who fought in World War II testifies about the massacre in China and about the Japanese military sexual slavery. The voice was a true recording of the testimony, and the animation film was created based on the true story.

**2017**: Director: Hyun-seok Kim
Title: *I Can Speak* / Category: Comedy, Drama / Nation: Korea
Running time: 119 min
Description: The film tells the story of an elderly woman (played by Na Moon Hee) who constantly files complaints with the local office about the wrongs that she sees around her daily life. Along the way, she forms an unlikely friendship with a junior civil service officer (played by Lee Je Hoon) who begins to teach her English. Though the film is a comedy, the genre serves as a vehicle to discuss the deeper topic of Korean "comfort women" during World War II.

**2017**: Director: Jo Jung-rae
Title: *Spirits' Homecoming Unfinished Stories* / Category: Documentary, Drama / Nation: Korea
Running time: 96 min
Description: "Ji Hee" encounters the trails of girls' stories along with the actual voices of the victims of Japanese Military Sexual Slavery. To remember the girls from the past, "Spirits' Homecoming Arirang" is sung and recorded.

**2017**: Director: Zhang Yueping
Title: *Great Cold* / Category: Documentary / Nation: China
Running time:  min
Description: The film *Great Cold*, or "Dahan" in Mandarin, tells the suffering and torture of the fictitious protagonist Cui Dani and her fellow villagers caused by Japanese invaders during WWII. "Dahan" is the first Chinese movie to focus on the stories of "comfort women" in north China's Shanxi, a province which was ransacked by the Japanese.

**2018**: Director: Yi Seung-hyeon
Title: *A Long Way Around* / Category: Documentary / Nation: Korea
Running time: 76 min
Description: A profound resonance through a grandmother's 20-year-old special routine. The film is a documentary based on the records of 20 years from the early 2000s in the House of Sharing. After working on the scenarios based on the images of the grandmothers' lives and "testimonies," Yi Seung-hyeon completed his first editions in March 2018, after several previews and numerous revisions, and finally in March 2019, he completed "A Long Way Around."

**2018**: Director: Ruby Challenger
Title: *Daily Bread* / Category: Biography / Nation: Australia
Running time: 15 min

Description: In a WWII internment camp in Indonesia, Jan Ruff O'Herne and a group of Dutch women and children face a daily struggle against abuse, disease, and starvation. The Japanese Camp Commandant and his beloved, fluffy white cat oversee the grueling camp regime. What is the price for a meal when women and children are starving? *Daily Bread* is based on an excerpt from the autobiography *Fifty Years of Silence* by Jan Ruff O'Herne, which was published by Random House and has been translated into five languages.

**2018**: Director: Kyu-dong Min
Title: ***Her Story*** / Category: Drama / Nation: Korea
Running time: 121 min
Description: 10 plaintiffs who suffered as "comfort women" during World War II and their 13 lawyers stand in a courtroom in Japan. They have gone through 23 difficult trials from 1992 to 1998.

**2018**: Director: Sung Hyun Lee
Title: ***Ae Eum Gil*** / Category: Documentary / Nation: Korea
Running time: 100 min
Description: Lee Ok-seon, who was dragged away to China by the Japanese army at the age of 16, finally comes back to her home country 58 years later. There, Lee became a family with all the other ladies who experienced similar sufferings, and walk together along the path for regaining the victims' honor and for solving the conundrum of sexual slavery, now a path to tread together. Even to this day, Ms. Lee takes her own "long way around" with her each step.

**2018**: Director: Miki Dezaki
Title: ***Shusenjo: The Main Battleground of the Comfort Women*** / Category: Documentary / Nation: Japan, USA, Korea / Running time: 120 min
Description: A Japanese American director digs deep into the controversial "comfort women" issue to settle the debate on whether the women were paid prostitutes or sex slaves, and reveals the motivations and intentions of the main actors pushing to revise history in Japan.

**2018**: Director: Sophie Emma Wells
Title: ***Ianfu*** / Category: Film / Nation: America
Running time: 10 min
Description: Based on accounts from "comfort woman" Hwang Keum-ju. This beautiful short film tells the story of 15-year-old Jade Goodwill who finds herself in the situation of being a "comfort woman" for the Japanese Military in World War II. This film was made to educate the public about the struggles of these women and to bring awareness to the topic.

**2019**: Director: Won Keun Song
Title: ***Kim Bok-dong*** / Category: Documentary / Nation: Korea
Running time: 107 min
Description: The story of "comfort woman" victim, Kim Bok-dong, who was a human rights and peace activist. It was a 27-year long journey that Kim Bok-dong struggled for Japan's apology until 1992, when she first declared herself a victim of the Japanese military "comfort women," until she passed away in 2019.

# R.11. "COMFORT STATIONS" OF JAPANESE MILITARY

© Women's Active Museum on War and Peace (WAM)

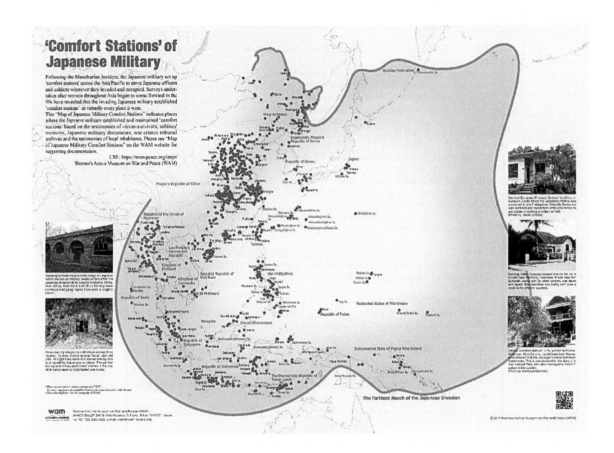

# R.12.1 RECORDS OF FORCED MOBILIZATION OF "COMFORT WOMEN"

© The Korean Council for Justice and Remembrance for the Issues of Military Sexual Slavery by Japan

---

**Records of "forced mobilization" of the Japanese military "comfort women"**

**Dutch Government Report[21]**

– In March 1942 in Blora, 20 European women were detained in 2 buildings by a Japanese troop during the Japanese invasion into Java. At least 14 women were raped by soldiers for three weeks.

– In January 1944 in Muntilan detention camp, Japanese soldiers and policemen drafted women and suppressed the riots among detainees with force… 13 of the women were sent to Magelang and were forced into prostitution.

– In April 1944 in Semerang, the Japanese military and civilian policemen arrested hundreds of women… 17 of them were sent to a 'comfort station' in Flores Island and were forced into prostitution.

**The Submitted Written Evidence and the Judgment in the International Military Tribunal for the Far East (Tokyo Trials)**

In Pontianak, the Japanese Naval Special Police Squad captured women on the street in order to supply women to comfort stations. They were forced to undergo a medical checkup and then sent to comfort stations.

– "Report on Enforced Prostitution in Western Borneo, N.E.I., during Japanese Naval Occupation," July 5, 1946

When the Japanese military slaughtered the residents of Sermata and Roean Islands in Moa Island, they drafted five daughters of the victims to comfort stations.

– Affidavit of Lt. Ohara Seidai, January 13, 1946

**Recognition in Japanese Courts**

Japanese military force abducted and raped Chinese women (including girls) living nearby the camp. They detained the women and raped them repeatedly, thus putting them virtually into the state of 'comfort women.'

– Judgment on the case of Chinese "comfort women" claiming compensation by Tokyo High Court

In 1942, Japanese soldiers and cooperating Chinese militants assaulted a village in Shanxi, and they abducted, detained, and raped women.

– Judgment on the case of Chinese "comfort women" claiming compensation by Tokyo District Court and High Court

All of the "Comfort Women" Plaintiffs were brought to the comfort stations through deception and forcefully turned into "Comfort Women" by rape. The comfort stations had deep relations with the Imperial Japanese Forces.

– Shimonoseki Prefectural Court Judgment[22]

---

[21] Excerpt taken and modified from Bart van Poelgeest, *Report of a Study of Dutch Government Documents on the Forced Prostitution of Dutch Women in the Dutch East Indies during the Japanese Occupation*, Unofficial Translation (January 24, 1994)

[22] Translated excerpt from Taihei Okada, Translation, "The 'Comfort Women' Case: Judgment of April 27, 1998, Shimonoseki Branch, Yamaguchi Prefectural Court, Japan," *Pacific Rim Law & Policy Journal* 8 (1999), available from https://digitalcommons.law.uw.edu/wilj/vol8/iss1/13

392

# R.12.2. OFFICIAL APOLOGY AND REPARATIONS

© The Korean Council for Justice and Remembrance for the Issues of Military Sexual Slavery by Japan

Question. Why do victims and activists call for official apology and reparations? How can this issue be resolved?

The Japanese government's crimes of organizing the "comfort women" system was not addressed during the International Military Tribunal for the Far East, and thus their crimes in systematically operating a forced sexual slavery system had not properly prosecuted in the aftermath of World War II. Positioning Japan as an important anti-communist ally in the Asia-Pacific region, the United States pressured Asian allies not to raise issues of reparations for war crimes committed by Japan.[26]

The Japanese Government claims that it already offered apologies and compensations on several occasions, from the 1965 Treaty between Republic of Korea and Japan, Asian Women's Fund, and 2015 Korea-Japan "Comfort Women" Agreement.

| List of Japanese Government's Attempts | | | |
|---|---|---|---|
| Attempts | Background | Measures | NOT an apology because... |
| 1965 Treaty on Basic Relations between Japan and the ROK | | Japanese Government gives "economic cooperation fund" to South Korea | The Japanese military sexual slavery issue was not discussed, as official documents released by the Korean Government in 2005 show. |
| 1993 Kono Statement | Chief Cabinet Secretary Yohei Kono after the government study on the Japanese military "comfort women" | -Acknowledged the Japanese military's involvement in forced mobilization of the victims -Led to creation of Asian Women's Fund | -The Kono Statement did not clarify the Japanese Military's planning, establishment, and management of the comfort stations and forced mobilization of victims. -The statement was not an official state apology approved by the Diet |
| Asian Women's Fund | Established in 1995 and dissolved in 2007 | Provided "consolation fund" from private donations | Asian Women's Fund was primarily financed through private funding and was not a formal apology and legal reparation from the Japanese Government, as noted in international human rights recommendations including the 2001 UN Committee on Economic, Social and Cultural Rights (E/C.12/1/Add.67, C.26.). |
| 1995 Murayama Statement | Prime Minister Tomiichi Murayama on the 50th anniversary of the end of | | -The Murayama Statement did not clarify the Japanese Military's planning, establishment, and management of the comfort |

---

[26] Keita Takayama, "Globalizing Critical Studies of 'official' Knowledge: Lessons from the Japanese History Textbook Controversy over 'Comfort Women,'" *British Journal of Sociology of Education* 30, no. 5 (2009): 579-580.

| | WWII | | stations and forced mobilization of victims.<br>-The statement was not an official state apology approved by the Diet |
|---|---|---|---|
| 2015 South Korea-Japan Agreement on the "Comfort Women" | South Korean and Japanese Government announced the treaty on December 28th, 2015. | -Japanese Government gives 1 billion JPY to ROK Government, as "consolation fund" to silence the issue "finally and irreversibly" and to "deal with" Statue of Peace<br>-Led to creation of Reconciliation and Healing Foundation, which was dissolved by the Korean Government on June 17, 2019 | -The 2015 Agreement failed to follow the principles of victim- centered approach, or 4 measures of principles to provide redress to the victims: victims were not included in the process, as noted in numerous United Nations human rights committees and experts (see Chronology)<br>-Victims and activists organized one-person protest, press interviews, international campaigns to annul the 2015 Agreement<br>-South Korean Ministry of Foreign Affairs taskforce (2017), Supreme Court (2019) confirms that the 2015 Agreement cannot serve as a resolution and was a political act |

However, the Japanese Government's attempts failed to meet the international human rights principles on redressing the victims of gross violations of human rights, recommendations from the United Nations human rights committees and other international organizations, and call for justice made by victims and activists since the 1990s.

According to international law, states that have committed crimes against humanity of rape and sexual slavery and war crimes have legal obligation to provide reparations.[27] However, Japan has not taken legal responsibility for the crimes they committed. For just resolution of the Japanese military "comfort women" issue, the Japanese Government should follow the international human rights principles to make official apology and legal reparations on premise of acknowledgement of its war crime.

Therefore, the Japanese Government should: 1) investigate the truth, 2) disclose historical records, 3) fulfill legal responsibilities (irrevocable apology, reparation, compensation, etc.), and 4) educate the issue to prevent recurrence.

---

[27] Amnesty International, "Still Waiting After 60 Years: Justice for Survivors of Japan's Military Sexual Slavery System," October 27, 2005, available from https://www.amnesty.org/en/documents/ASA22/012/2005/ja/

394

# INDEX

*Note: For Asian countries such as Korea, China and Japan where the family name precedes the given name, no comma is used. Persons of Asian ancestry or origin who have adopted the Western practice of giving the family name last are indexed with inversion and a comma. Where Asian names have been romanized with different spelling but refer to the same person, the dominant spelling is used first, with variants following.*

## A

*A Gesture Life*, 114, 178, 180, 186

Abe Shinzo, 9, 20, 36, 37, 43–46, 48, 62, 64, 67–72, 90, 204, 217

Aichi Triennale, 231

Amnesty International, 61, 62, 70

apology(-ies), 53, 69, 91, 92, 112, 163, 176, 177, 185, 186, 203

Armenian Genocide, 93, 216
    Resolution, 94

art therapy, 126, 128

Asia-Pacific War. *See* Pacific War

Asian American activist(s), 61, 67
    activism, 112

Asian Women's Fund (AWF), 14, 17, 64, 69, 103, 196, 199

Assembly Joint Resolution 27 (CA), 34, 53, 55

## B

Bae Chun-hee, 125, 126

Banning, Jan, 117, 133, 136, 138

Boltanski, Christian, 125, 133

Brookhaven, 224, 225

Bulova, Sharon, 219, 220

Bosnia, 14, 63, 84
    Bosnian Muslim women, 111

Burma, 14, 54, 63, 80, 84, 94, 125

Bush, George W., 48, 70, 78
    Administration, 49, 53, 58, 60, 63, 68, 80

butterfly, 221
    bench, 211, 220

Butterfly Fund, 200, 201, 231

## C

CARE (Comfort Women Action for Redress and Education), *see* KAFC (Korean American Forum of California)

Cavallo, Steven, 133–136, 212–214

Cho Jung-rae, 119, 128, 145

Choi, Christine, 8, 18, 19, 133, 220

Choy, Christine, 114

Civil Liberties Act of 1988, 38

civil society groups, 191, 198, 199

Clinton, Hillary Rodham, 45, 75, 127

395